# ERRATA

Catalogue no. 81-582-XPE occasional

**Education Indicators in Canada**
Report of the Pan-Canadian Education Indicators Program 1999

February 2000

---

## Appendix 2

A more complete list of universities, and community colleges and related institutions by jurisdiction and size of enrolment is available in Catalogue no. 81-582-XIE, and can be downloaded at the following Web sites:

<u>www.statcan.ca</u>
<u>www.cmec.ca</u>

Canadian Cataloguing in Publication Data

Education indicators in Canada: report of the
Pan-Canadian Education Indicators Program, 1999

Co-published by: Council of Ministers of Education, Canada.
Issued also in French under title: Indicateurs de l'éducation au Canada :
rapport du Programme d'indicateurs pancanadiens de l'éducation, 1999.
ISBN 0-660-17921-0
CS81-582-XPE

1. Educational indicators – Canada. 2. Education – Canada – Statistics.
I. Statistics Canada. Culture, Tourism and the Centre for Education Statistics.
II. Council of Ministers of Education (Canada). III. Pan-Canadian Education
Indicators Program. IV. Title.

LA412 E38 2000                                    370'.0971'021
C00-988000-3

This publication was prepared jointly by Statistics Canada and the Council of Ministers of Education, Canada (CMEC), in collaboration with the departments and ministries of the provinces and territories with responsibility for education and training. The funding contributed to the Pan-Canadian Education Indicators Program by Human Resources Development Canada is also gratefully acknowledged.

Data included here were taken from the sources indicated and were accurate at the time they were reported to Statistics Canada. They may, however, differ from the data made public by individual jurisdictions because Statistics Canada made adjustments to the data to enhance data comparability because of differences in the institutions reporting, and in the definitions and snapshot dates used. The definitions of the terms used are consistent with those found in other Statistics Canada and Canadian Education Statistics Council (CESC) publications. This publication includes the most recent data available. The Centre for Education Statistics will work with the provinces and territories to report more current data in future publications.

## Symbols

The following standard symbols are used in this publication

..  figures not available

... figures not appropriate or not applicable

-   nil or zero

--  amount too small to be expressed

p   preliminary figures

e   estimate

r   revised figures

x   confidential to meet secrecy requirements of the Statistics Act

# Table of Contents

**Chapter 1** ............................................................................................................. 1

Introduction and Overview .................................................................................... 1
The Pan-Canadian Education Indicators Program ................................................. 1
The development of the indicator set ..................................................................... 2
Future plans ........................................................................................................... 2
Overview of this publication .................................................................................. 2
Highlights and overall trends in education systems ............................................... 3
Context ................................................................................................................... 3
Features of education systems ................................................................................ 3
Education outcomes ............................................................................................... 4
Labour market outcomes ........................................................................................ 7
Endnotes ................................................................................................................. 8

**Chapter 2** ............................................................................................................. 9

The Context of Education ...................................................................................... 9
Highlights ............................................................................................................... 9

    2.1    Population characteristics and trends ........................................................ 10
            A.   Population distribution and projections ............................................. 10
            B.   Mobility of the population under age 24 .......................................... 14

    2.2    Children living in low-income situations ................................................. 17

    2.3    Educational attainment of the adult population ....................................... 20

**Chapter 3** ........................................................................................................... 25

Characteristics and Features of Education Systems ............................................ 25
Highlights ............................................................................................................. 25

    3.1    Schools and postsecondary institutions ................................................... 27

    3.2    Educators ................................................................................................. 28
            A.   Gender distribution ............................................................................ 29
            B.   Age distribution ................................................................................. 32
            C.   Employment status of elementary–secondary educators ................... 34
            D.   Salaries .............................................................................................. 35
            E.   Pupil–educator ratio in elementary–secondary schools .................... 35

    3.3    Participation in formal education ............................................................. 36
            A.   Participation in education by young children ................................... 36
            B.   Elementary–secondary enrolment ..................................................... 37
            C.   Trade–vocational enrolment ............................................................. 39
            D.   College enrolment ............................................................................ 41
            E.   University enrolment ........................................................................ 45
            F.   Adult participation in education ....................................................... 50

# Table of Contents

| | | | |
|---|---|---|---|
| 3.4 | Job-related adult education | | 51 |
| 3.5 | Education finances | | 53 |
| | A. | Expenditures by level of education | 54 |
| | B. | Educational expenditure per student | 56 |
| | C. | Education expenditure as a proportion of GDP | 58 |
| | D. | Public expenditure on education | 60 |
| | E. | Educational expenditure by resource category | 64 |
| | F. | Student debt | 67 |
| 3.6 | Information and communications technologies in schools | | 69 |
| | A. | Pupil-computer ratio | 70 |
| | B. | Internet connectivity | 71 |
| | C. | Internet activities of students | 71 |
| | D. | Obstacles to fuller use of information and communications technologies | 72 |
| References | | | 74 |

## Chapter 4 .............. 75

**Education Outcomes** .............. 75
**Highlights** .............. 75

| | | | |
|---|---|---|---|
| 4.1 | Student Achievement in Pan-Canadian and International Assessments | | 77 |
| | A. | School Achievement Indicators Program | 77 |
| | | SAIP mathematics assessments | 80 |
| | | SAIP reading and writing assessments | 81 |
| | | SAIP science assessment | 81 |
| | B. | Third International Mathematics and Science Study (TIMSS) | 82 |
| | C. | International Adult Literacy Survey (IALS) | 86 |
| 4.2 | Output rates | | 89 |
| | A. | High school completions | 89 |
| | B. | Postsecondary completions | 93 |
| 4.3 | Equity | | 96 |
| | A. | Educational attainment of the Aboriginal population | 96 |
| | B. | Educational attainment among linguistic groups | 101 |
| | C. | Participation in education by socio-economic status | 105 |
| Endnotes | | | 108 |

## Chapter 5 .............. 109

**Labour Market Outcomes** .............. 109
**Highlights** .............. 109

| | | | |
|---|---|---|---|
| 5.1 | Labour force participation | | 110 |
| | A. | Employment and unemployment rates | 111 |
| | B. | Underemployment rate | 116 |
| 5.2 | Flows between formal education and work | | 119 |
| 5.3 | Mobility of postsecondary students and graduates | | 126 |

# Table of Contents

**Appendices** ........................................................................................................................ 131

**Appendix 1** ........................................................................................................................ 133

Structure of Education and Training in Canada .................................................................. 133

**Appendix 2** ........................................................................................................................ 137

Universities by jurisdiction and size of full-time enrolment ................................................. 137
Community colleges and related institutions by jurisdiction and size of full-time enrolment ............................................. 141

**Appendix 3** ........................................................................................................................ 147

Data Sources Used in this Publication ................................................................................. 147

**Appendix 4** ........................................................................................................................ 159

Glossary of Terms Used in this Publication ......................................................................... 159

**Appendix 5** ........................................................................................................................ 171

The PCEIP Indicators Set ..................................................................................................... 171

EDUCATION INDICATORS IN CANADA

# TABLE OF CONTENTS

## FIGURES

| | | |
|---|---|---|
| FIGURE 2.1 | ESTIMATES AND PROJECTIONS OF THE POPULATION AGED 5 TO 14, 15 TO 19, AND 20 TO 24, CANADA AND JURISIDICTIONS, 1986 TO 2016 | 12 |
| FIGURE 2.2 | IMMIGRANT ARRIVALS AS A PERCENTAGE OF THE POPULATION, BY SELECTED AGE GROUPS, CANADA, 1976 TO 1997 | 16 |
| FIGURE 2.3 | NET INTERJURISDICTIONAL MIGRATION, BY JURISDICTION, AVERAGE PER YEAR FOR THE PERIODS 1971-79, 1980-89, AND 1990-97 | 16 |
| FIGURE 2.4 | NET INTERJURISDICTIONAL MIGRATION AS A PERCENTAGE OF THE POPULATION, BY JURISDICTION, AVERAGE PER YEAR FOR THE PERIODS 1971-79, 1980-89, 1990-97 | 17 |
| FIGURE 2.5 | PERCENTAGE OF CHILDREN 15 YEARS OF AGE AND YOUNGER IN LOW INCOME FAMILIES, CANADA, 1980 TO 1996 | 19 |
| FIGURE 2.6 | PERCENTAGE OF CHILDREN 15 YEARS OF AGE AND YOUNGER IN LOW INCOME FAMILIES, CANADA AND PROVINCES, 1996 | 19 |
| FIGURE 2.7 | PERCENTAGE OF CHILDREN AND YOUTH IN LOW INCOME FAMILIES, BY AGE, CANADA, 1996 | 20 |
| FIGURE 2.8 | DISTRIBUTION OF THE MALE POPULATION AGED 25 TO 54, BY HIGHEST COMPLETED LEVEL OF EDUCATION, CANADA AND PROVINCES, 1990 AND 1998 | 22 |
| FIGURE 2.9 | DISTRIBUTION OF THE FEMALE POPULATION AGED 25 TO 54, BY HIGHEST COMPLETED LEVEL OF EDUCATION, CANADA AND PROVINCES, 1990 AND 1998 | 22 |
| FIGURE 2.10 | DISTRIBUTION OF THE MALE POPULATION AGED 25 TO 29, BY HIGHEST COMPLETED LEVEL OF EDUCATION, CANADA AND PROVINCES, 1990 AND 1998 | 23 |
| FIGURE 2.11 | DISTRIBUTION OF THE FEMALE POPULATION AGED 25 TO 29, BY HIGHEST COMPLETED LEVEL OF EDUCATION, CANADA AND PROVINCES, 1990 AND 1998 | 23 |
| FIGURE 2.12 | PERCENTAGE OF THE POPULATION AGED 25 TO 64 THAT HAS COMPLETED POSTSECONDARY EDUCATION, OECD COUNTRIES, 1996 | 24 |
| FIGURE 3.1 | NUMBER OF FULL-TIME EDUCATORS IN PUBLIC ELEMENTARY–SECONDARY SCHOOLS IN CANADA, 1986-87 TO 1996-97 | 30 |
| FIGURE 3.2 | PERCENTAGE OF WOMEN AMONG FULL-TIME COMMUNITY COLLEGE EDUCATORS, CANADA AND JURISDICTIONS, 1986-87 AND 1996-97 | 30 |
| FIGURE 3.3 | PERCENTAGE OF WOMEN AMONG FULL-TIME UNIVERSITY FACULTY BY RANK, CANADA AND PROVINCES, 1987-88 AND 1997-98 | 31 |
| FIGURE 3.4 | AGE DISTRIBUTION OF EDUCATORS BY LEVEL OF EDUCATION VERSUS THAT OF THE OVERALL LABOUR FORCE, CANADA, 1996 | 33 |
| FIGURE 3.5 | PERCENTAGE OF EDUCATORS WORKING PART TIME IN PUBLIC ELEMENTARY–SECONDARY SCHOOLS, BY GENDER, CANADA, 1986-87 TO 1996-97 | 34 |
| FIGURE 3.6 | PUPIL–EDUCATOR RATIO IN PUBLIC ELEMENTARY–SECONDARY SCHOOLS, CANADA AND JURISDICTIONS, 1986-87 TO 1996-97 | 36 |
| FIGURE 3.7 | ELEMENTARY-SECONDARY ENROLMENT INDEX, CANADA AND JURISDICTIONS, 1986-87 TO 1996-97 | 38 |
| FIGURE 3.8 | INDEX OF ENROLMENT IN TRADE-VOCATIONAL PROGRAMS BY REGISTRATION STATUS, CANADA, 1987-88 TO 1995-96 | 40 |
| FIGURE 3.9 | PERCENTAGE CHANGE IN ENROLMENT IN TRADE-VOCATIONAL PROGRAMS, BY REGISTRATION STATUS, CANADA AND PROVINCES, 1987-88 TO 1995-96 | 40 |
| FIGURE 3.10 | PERCENTAGE OF WOMEN AMONG FULL-TIME ENROLMENTS IN TRADE-VOCATIONAL PROGRAMS, CANADA AND PROVINCES, 1987-88 AND 1995-96 | 41 |
| FIGURE 3.11 | COLLEGE ENROLMENT INDEX BY REGISTRATION STATUS, AND INDEX OF THE POPULATION AGED 18-21, CANADA, 1987-88 TO 1997-98 | 43 |
| FIGURE 3.12 | PERCENTAGE CHANGE IN FULL-TIME COLLEGE CAREER TECHNICAL ENROLMENT, CANADA AND JURISDICTIONS, 1987-88 TO 1997-98 | 43 |
| FIGURE 3.13 | FULL-TIME COLLEGE ENROLMENT AS A PERCENTAGE OF THE POPULATION AGED 18 TO 21, CANADA AND JURISDICTIONS, 1987-88 AND 1997-98 | 44 |
| FIGURE 3.14 | PERCENTAGE OF WOMEN AMONG FULL-TIME COLLEGE CAREER TECHNICAL ENROLMENTS, CANADA AND JURISDICTIONS, 1987-88 AND 1997-98 | 44 |
| FIGURE 3.15 | INDICES OF UNIVERSITY ENROLMENT BY REGISTRATION STATUS, AND INDICES OF POPULATION FOR SELECTED AGE GROUPS, CANADA, 1987-88 TO 1997-982 | 47 |
| FIGURE 3.16 | INDICES OF PARTICIPATION RATES IN UNDERGRADUATE PROGRAMS, CANADA, 1987-88 TO 1997-98 | 47 |
| FIGURE 3.17 | PERCENTAGE CHANGE IN UNIVERSITY ENROLMENT BY REGISTRATION STATUS, CANADA AND PROVINCES, 1987-88 TO 1997-98 | 48 |
| FIGURE 3.18 | FULL-TIME UNIVERSITY ENROLMENT AS A PERCENTAGE OF THE POPULATION AGED 18 TO 24, CANADA AND PROVINCES, 1987-88 AND 1997-98 | 48 |

# Table of Contents

| | | |
|---|---|---|
| Figure 3.19 | Percentage of women among full-time undergraduate enrolments, Canada and provinces, 1987-88 and 1997-98 | 49 |
| Figure 3.20 | Percentage of women among full-time graduate enrolments, Canada and provinces, 1987-88 and 1997-98 | 49 |
| Figure 3.21 | Participation in job-related training for adults in the 25 to 64 age group, by employment status, Canada and selected countries, 1994-95 | 51 |
| Figure 3.22 | Average duration of job-related training undertaken by employed adults in the 25 to 64 age group, Canada and selected countries, 1994-95 | 52 |
| Figure 3.23 | Per capita expenditures on education in constant 1998 dollars (thousands), Canada and jurisdictions, 1988-89 to 1998-99 | 55 |
| Figure 3.24 | Expenditure per student on public and private institutions, by level of education, Canada and jurisdictions, 1995, in Canadian dollars | 57 |
| Figure 3.25 | Expenditure per student on public and private institutions, by level of education, Canada and G-7 countries, 1995, in U.S. dollars converted using PPPs | 57 |
| Figure 3.26 | Educational expenditure from public and private sources for educational institutions as a percentage of GDP by level of education, Canada and jurisdictions, 1995 | 59 |
| Figure 3.27 | Educational expenditure from public and private sources for educational institutions as a percentage of GDP by level of education, Canada and G-7 countries, 1995 | 60 |
| Figure 3.28 | Public expenditure on education as a percentage of total public expenditure, by level of education, Canada and jurisdictions, 1995 | 61 |
| Figure 3.29 | Tuition fees and government contributions as a percentage of operating revenue of universities, Canada, 1982-83 to 1998-99 | 63 |
| Figure 3.30 | Average tuition fees in undergraduate arts programs and percentage change from 1988-89 to 1998-99, Canada and provinces | 63 |
| Figure 3.31 | Percent distribution of current educational expenditure by resource category for public and private institutions (1995), Canada and jurisdictions | 66 |
| Figure 3.32 | Average amount owed to student loan programs, by college and university graduates who borrowed from student loan programs, Canada, 1986, 1990, and 1995, in constant 1995 dollars | 68 |
| Figure 3.33 | Indices of median family income and average tuition fees in undergraduate arts programs, Canada, 1988 to 1999, in constant 1999 dollars | 69 |
| Figure 3.34 | Pupil-computer ratio in elementary-secondary schools, Canada and provinces, 1999 | 70 |
| Figure 3.35 | Percentage of students in elementary-secondary schools connected to the Internet, Canada and provinces, 1999 | 71 |
| Figure 4.1 | Performance of jurisdictions relative to Canada in SAIP assessments, showing percentage of 13-year-olds at level 2 or above | 78 |
| Figure 4.2 | Performance of jurisdictions relative to Canada in SAIP assessments, showing percentage of 16-year-olds at level 3 or above | 79 |
| Figure 4.3 | TIMSS International, Canadian, and provincial achievement scores in mathematics, 1994-95 | 84 |
| Figure 4.4 | TIMSS International, Canadian, and provincial achievement scores in science, 1994-95 | 85 |
| Figure 4.5 | Percentage of the population aged 16 to 25 and 26 to 65 at level 3 or above in the IALS document, prose, quantitative scales, Canada and other IALS participating countries, 1994-95 | 88 |
| Figure 4.6 | Percentage of the population aged 16 to 25 and 26 to 65 at level 3 or above in the IALS document, prose, quantitative scales, Canada and regions, 1994-95 | 89 |
| Figure 4.7 | Ratio of secondary graduates to the population at age 18 by gender, Canada and jurisdictions, 1997 | 92 |
| Figure 4.8 | High school completion rates of the population aged 19 to 20, by gender, Canada and provinces, 1991 to 1994 and 1995 to 1998 | 92 |
| Figure 4.9 | Index of diplomas and degrees granted, by level of education, Canada, 1976 to 1997 | 95 |
| Figure 4.10 | Distribution of the Aboriginal population aged 25 to 29 and 25 to 54, by highest level of education attained, Canada, 1996 | 98 |
| Figure 4.11 | Distribution of the non-Aboriginal population aged 25 to 29 and 25 to 54, by highest level of education attained, Canada, 1996 | 99 |
| Figure 4.12 | Distribution of the population aged 20 to 29, by highest level of education attained, Aboriginal and non-Aboriginal populations, Canada, 1986 and 1996 | 99 |
| Figure 4.13 | Distribution of the Aboriginal population aged 25 to 54, by highest level of education attained, Canada and jurisdictions, 1996 | 100 |
| Figure 4.14 | Distribution of the population aged 25 to 29, by highest level of education attained and by mother tongue, Canada, 1996 | 102 |
| Figure 4.15 | Percentage of the population aged 25 to 29 with less than high school education by mother tongue, Canada and jurisdictions, 1996 | 103 |

## TABLE OF CONTENTS

| | | |
|---|---|---|
| FIGURE 4.16 | PERCENTAGE OF THE POPULATION AGED 25 TO 29 WITH HIGH SCHOOL EDUCATION BY MOTHER TONGUE, CANADA AND JURISDICTIONS, 1996 | 103 |
| FIGURE 4.17 | PERCENTAGE OF THE POPULATION AGED 25 TO 29 WITH A COLLEGE/TRADE EDUCATION BY MOTHER TONGUE, CANADA AND JURISDICTIONS, 1996 | 104 |
| FIGURE 4.18 | PERCENTAGE OF THE POPULATION AGED 25 TO 29 WITH A UNIVERSITY EDUCATION BY MOTHER TONGUE, CANADA AND JURISDICTIONS, 1996 | 104 |
| FIGURE 4.19 | PERCENTAGE OF THE POPULATION AGED 18 TO 21 ATTENDING UNIVERSITY, BY FAMILY SOCIO-ECONOMIC STATUS, CANADA, 1986 AND 1994 | 107 |
| FIGURE 4.20 | PERCENTAGE OF THE POPULATION AGED 18 TO 21 WITH LESS THAN HIGH SCHOOL COMPLETION, BY FAMILY SOCIO-ECONOMIC STATUS, CANADA, 1994 | 107 |
| FIGURE 5.1 | EMPLOYMENT RATE OF MALES IN THE 25 TO 54 AGE GROUP BY EDUCATIONAL ATTAINMENT, CANADA AND PROVINCES, 1990 AND 1998 | 111 |
| FIGURE 5.2 | EMPLOYMENT RATE OF FEMALES IN THE 25 TO 54 AGE GROUP BY EDUCATIONAL ATTAINMENT, CANADA AND PROVINCES, 1990 AND 1998 | 112 |
| FIGURE 5.3 | EMPLOYMENT RATE OF MALES IN THE 25 TO 29 AGE GROUP BY EDUCATIONAL ATTAINMENT, CANADA AND PROVINCES, 1990 AND 1998 | 112 |
| FIGURE 5.4 | EMPLOYMENT RATE OF FEMALES IN THE 25 TO 29 AGE GROUP BY EDUCATIONAL ATTAINMENT, CANADA AND PROVINCES, 1990 AND 1998 | 113 |
| FIGURE 5.5 | UNEMPLOYMENT RATE OF MALES IN THE 25 TO 54 AGE GROUP BY EDUCATIONAL ATTAINMENT, CANADA AND PROVINCES, 1990 AND 1998 | 114 |
| FIGURE 5.6 | UNEMPLOYMENT RATE OF FEMALES IN THE 25 TO 54 AGE GROUP BY EDUCATIONAL ATTAINMENT, CANADA AND PROVINCES, 1990 AND 1998 | 114 |
| FIGURE 5.7 | UNEMPLOYMENT RATE OF MALES IN THE 25 TO 29 AGE GROUP BY EDUCATIONAL ATTAINMENT, CANADA AND PROVINCES, 1990 AND 1998 | 115 |
| FIGURE 5.8 | UNEMPLOYMENT RATE OF FEMALES IN THE 25 TO 29 AGE GROUP BY EDUCATIONAL ATTAINMENT, CANADA AND PROVINCES, 1990 AND 1998 | 115 |
| FIGURE 5.9 | INVOLUNTARY PART-TIME EMPLOYMENT RATE AND UNEMPLOYMENT RATE FOR PERSONS WITH HIGH SCHOOL COMPLETION OR LESS, 15 TO 24 AGE GROUP, CANADA, 1976 TO 1996 | 117 |
| FIGURE 5.10 | INVOLUNTARY PART-TIME EMPLOYMENT RATE AND UNEMPLOYMENT RATE FOR PERSONS WITH HIGH SCHOOL COMPLETION OR LESS, 25 TO 34 AGE GROUP, CANADA, 1976 TO 1996 | 117 |
| FIGURE 5.11 | INVOLUNTARY PART-TIME EMPLOYMENT RATE AND UNEMPLOYMENT RATE FOR PERSONS WITH HIGH SCHOOL COMPLETION OR LESS, 35 TO 54 AGE GROUP, CANADA, 1976 TO 1996 | 118 |
| FIGURE 5.12 | EDUCATION AND EMPLOYMENT ACTIVITIES OF YOUTH AGED 15 TO 19 YEARS, CANADA, 1976, 1986, AND 1996 | 119 |
| FIGURE 5.13 | EDUCATION AND EMPLOYMENT ACTIVITIES OF YOUTH AGED 20 TO 24 YEARS, CANADA, 1976, 1986, AND 1996 | 120 |
| FIGURE 5.14 | PERCENTAGE OF 1986 AND 1995 UNIVERSITY GRADUATES WORKING FULL TIME, TWO YEARS AFTER GRADUATION, BY GENDER AND FIELD OF STUDY, CANADA | 121 |
| FIGURE 5.15 | PERCENTAGE OF 1986 AND 1995 GRADUATES WORKING FULL TIME, TWO YEARS AFTER GRADUATION, BY LEVEL OF EDUCATION AND PROVINCE OF STUDY | 121 |
| FIGURE 5.16 | UNEMPLOYMENT RATE OF 1986 AND 1995 GRADUATES, TWO YEARS AFTER GRADUATION, BY LEVEL OF EDUCATION AND PROVINCE OF STUDY | 122 |
| FIGURE 5.17 | MEDIAN EARNINGS OF 1986 AND 1995 GRADUATES WORKING FULL TIME, TWO YEARS AFTER GRADUATION, BY LEVEL OF EDUCATION AND PROVINCE OF STUDY, (IN CONSTANT 1997 $000'S) | 123 |
| FIGURE 5.18 | MEDIAN EARNINGS OF 1986 AND 1995 UNIVERSITY GRADUATES WORKING FULL TIME, TWO YEARS AFTER GRADUATION, BY GENDER AND FIELD OF STUDY, CANADA (IN CONSTANT 1997 $000'S) | 124 |
| FIGURE 5.19 | PERCENTAGE OF 1986 AND 1995 GRADUATES WORKING FULL TIME TWO YEARS AFTER GRADUATION WHO ARE IN A JOB CLOSELY RELATED TO THEIR EDUCATION, BY PROVINCE OF STUDY AND LEVEL OF EDUCATION | 124 |
| FIGURE 5.20 | PERCENTAGE OF 1986 AND 1995 UNIVERSITY GRADUATES WORKING FULL TIME TWO YEARS AFTER GRADUATION WHO ARE IN A JOB CLOSELY RELATED TO THEIR EDUCATION, BY GENDER AND FIELD OF STUDY, CANADA | 125 |
| FIGURE 5.21 | MOBILITY CHARACTERISTICS OF THE CLASS OF 1995, UNIVERSITY GRADUATES, CANADA AND PROVINCES | 127 |
| FIGURE 5.22 | NET MIGRATION OF THE CLASS OF 1986, UNIVERSITY GRADUATES, BY PROVINCE OF STUDY | 128 |
| FIGURE 5.23 | NET MIGRATION OF THE CLASS OF 1995, UNIVERSITY GRADUATES, BY PROVINCE OF STUDY | 129 |

# TABLE OF CONTENTS

| | |
|---|---|
| **TABLES** | 175 |
| **CHAPTER 2 TABLES** | 177 |
| TABLE 2.1 | ESTIMATES AND PROJECTIONS OF THE POPULATION BY SELECTED AGE GROUPS, AND THE RATIOS OF YOUTH AND SENIORS TO THE WORKING-AGE POPULATION, CANADA AND JURISDICTIONS, 1986 TO 2016 ... 179 |
| TABLE 2.2 | NUMBER OF IMMIGRANT ARRIVALS AND IMMIGRANT ARRIVALS AS A PERCENTAGE OF THE POPULATION, SELECTED AGE GROUPS, CANADA, 1976 TO 1997 ... 181 |
| TABLE 2.3 | NUMBER OF IMMIGRANT ARRIVALS AND IMMIGRANT ARRIVALS AS A PERCENTAGE OF THE POPULATION, SELECTED AGE GROUPS, CANADA AND JURISDICTIONS, 1996 ... 181 |
| TABLE 2.4 | NET NUMBER OF INTERJURISDICTIONAL MIGRANTS AND INTERJURISDICTIONAL MIGRANTS AS A PERCENTAGE OF THE POPULATION, JURISDICTIONS, 1971 TO 1997 ... 182 |
| TABLE 2.5 | NUMBER AND PERCENTAGE OF THE POPULATION WHO MIGRATED WITHIN AND BETWEEN JURISDICTIONS, BY AGE GROUP, CANADA AND JURISDICTIONS, 1995 TO 1996 ... 183 |
| TABLE 2.6 | CHILDREN 15 YEARS OF AGE AND YOUNGER LIVING IN LOW INCOME FAMILIES, CANADA AND PROVINCES, 1980 TO 1996 ... 184 |
| TABLE 2.7 | PERCENTAGE DISTRIBUTION OF THE POPULATION AGED 25 TO 54, BY HIGHEST COMPLETED LEVEL OF EDUCATION AND GENDER, CANADA AND PROVINCES, 1990 AND 1998 ... 185 |
| TABLE 2.8 | PERCENTAGE DISTRIBUTION OF THE POPULATION AGED 25 TO 29, BY HIGHEST COMPLETED LEVEL OF EDUCATION AND GENDER, CANADA AND PROVINCES, 1990 AND 1998 ... 186 |
| **CHAPTER 3 TABLES** | 187 |
| TABLE 3.1 | INSTITUTIONS, BY LEVEL AND SIZE OF FULL-TIME ENROLMENT, CANADA AND JURISDICTIONS, 1996-97 ... 189 |
| TABLE 3.2 | PERCENTAGE DISTRIBUTION OF INSTITUTIONS, BY LEVEL AND SIZE OF FULL-TIME ENROLMENT, CANADA AND JURISDICTIONS, 1996-97 ... 190 |
| TABLE 3.3 | NUMBER OF FULL-TIME EDUCATORS IN PUBLIC ELEMENTARY–SECONDARY SCHOOLS BY GENDER, CANADA AND JURISDICTIONS, 1986-87 TO 1996-97 ... 191 |
| TABLE 3.4 | GENDER DISTRIBUTION OF FULL-TIME EDUCATORS IN PUBLIC ELEMENTARY–SECONDARY SCHOOLS, CANADA AND JURISDICTIONS, 1986-87 TO 1996-97 ... 192 |
| TABLE 3.5 | FULL-TIME COMMUNITY COLLEGE EDUCATORS BY GENDER, CANADA AND JURISDICTIONS, 1986-871 AND 1996-97 ... 192 |
| TABLE 3.6 | FULL-TIME UNIVERSITY FACULTY BY GENDER, CANADA AND JURISDICTIONS, 1987-88 AND 1997-98 ... 193 |
| TABLE 3.7 | FULL-TIME EDUCATORS IN ELEMENTARY–SECONDARY SCHOOLS, NUMBER AND DISTRIBUTION (%) BY AGE AND GENDER, AND MEDIAN AGE, CANADA AND JURISDICTIONS, 1996-97 ... 194 |
| TABLE 3.8 | FULL-TIME EDUCATORS IN COMMUNITY COLLEGES, NUMBER AND DISTRIBUTION (%) BY AGE AND GENDER, AND MEDIAN AGE, CANADA AND JURISDICTIONS, 1996-97 ... 195 |
| TABLE 3.9 | FULL-TIME EDUCATORS IN UNIVERSITIES, NUMBER AND DISTRIBUTION (%) BY AGE AND GENDER, AND MEDIAN AGE, CANADA AND JURISDICTIONS, 1996-97 ... 196 |
| TABLE 3.10 | NUMBER OF EDUCATORS WORKING PART TIME IN PUBLIC ELEMENTARY–SECONDARY SCHOOLS, BY GENDER, CANADA AND JURISDICTIONS, 1986-87 TO 1996-97 ... 197 |
| TABLE 3.11 | PERCENTAGE OF EDUCATORS WORKING PART TIME IN PUBLIC ELEMENTARY–SECONDARY SCHOOLS, BY GENDER, CANADA AND JURISDICTIONS, 1986-87 TO 1996-97 ... 198 |
| TABLE 3.12 | NUMBER AND AVERAGE SALARY OF FULL-TIME UNIVERSITY FACULTY, BY RANK AND GENDER, CANADA AND PROVINCES, 1987-88 AND 1997-98, IN CONSTANT 1997 DOLLARS ... 199 |
| TABLE 3.13 | PUPIL–EDUCATOR RATIO IN PUBLIC ELEMENTARY–SECONDARY SCHOOLS, CANADA AND JURISDICTIONS, 1986-87 TO 1996-97 ... 201 |
| TABLE 3.14 | PRE-ELEMENTARY ENROLMENT AND ENROLMENT RATE, CANADA AND JURISDICTIONS, 1986-87 TO 1996-97 ... 201 |
| TABLE 3.15 | ELEMENTARY-SECONDARY ENROLMENT AND PERCENTAGE ANNUAL CHANGE IN ENROLMENT, CANADA AND JURISDICTIONS, 1986-87 TO 1996-97 ... 202 |
| TABLE 3.16 | TRADE-VOCATIONAL ENROLMENT BY REGISTRATION STATUS AND GENDER, CANADA AND JURISDICTIONS, 1987-88 AND 1995-96 ... 203 |
| TABLE 3.17 | COLLEGE ENROLMENT BY REGISTRATION STATUS AND GENDER, CANADA AND JURISDICTIONS, 1987-88 AND 1997-98 ... 203 |
| TABLE 3.18 | UNIVERSITY ENROLMENT BY REGISTRATION STATUS AND GENDER, CANADA AND PROVINCES, 1987-88, 1991-92 AND 1997-98 ... 205 |
| TABLE 3.19 | PARTICIPATION OF ADULTS IN FORMAL EDUCATION AT ELEMENTARY-SECONDARY AND POSTSECONDARY LEVELS, BY AGE GROUP, CANADA AND PROVINCES, 1991 AND 1997 ... 207 |
| TABLE 3.20 | PERCENTAGE OF THE POPULATION AGED 25-54 PARTICIPATING IN JOB-RELATED ADULT EDUCATION AND TRAINING, BY GENDER AND EDUCATIONAL ATTAINMENT, CANADA AND JURISDICTIONS, 1991 AND 1997 ... 208 |

# TABLE OF CONTENTS

| | | |
|---|---|---|
| TABLE 3.21 | Participation rate and duration of job-related training undertaken by adults aged 25 to 64, Canada and selected countries, 1994-95 | 209 |
| TABLE 3.22 | Expenditures on education and index of expenditures by level of education (constant $1998 in millions), population (in thousands), and per capita expenditures on education (in constant $ 1998), and indices, Canada and jurisdictions, 1988-89 to 1998-99 | 209 |
| TABLE 3.23 | Expenditure per student (U.S. dollars converted using PPPs and Canadian dollars) on public and private institutions by level of education (based on full-time equivalents), Canada, jurisdictions and G-7 countries, 1995 | 212 |
| TABLE 3.24 | Educational expenditure from public and private sources for educational institutions as a percentage of GDP by level of education, Canada, jurisdictions, and G-7 countries, 1995 | 213 |
| TABLE 3.25 | Public expenditure on education as a percentage of total public expenditure by level of education, Canada, jurisdictions and G-7 countries, 1995 | 213 |
| TABLE 3.26 | Distribution of public and private sources of funds for educational institutions before (initial funds) and after (final funds) transfers from public sources, by level of education, Canada, jurisdictions and G-7 countries, 1995 | 214 |
| TABLE 3.27 | Average tuition fees in undergraduate arts programs, Canada and provinces, 1988-89 to 1998-99, in constant 1998 dollars | 214 |
| TABLE 3.28 | Educational expenditure on pre-elementary and elementary–secondary education by resource category for public and private institutions, Canada, jurisdictions and G-7 countries, 1995 | 215 |
| TABLE 3.29 | Educational expenditure on postsecondary education by resource category for public and private institutions Canada, jurisdictions and G-7 countries, 1995 | 216 |
| TABLE 3.30 | Percentage of college and unviversity graduates who borrowed from student loan programs, and average amount owing among borrowers at graduation and two years after graduation (in constant $ 1995), by level of education, Canada and provinces, graduating classes of 1986, 1990 and 1995 | 216 |
| TABLE 3.31 | Percentage of students in elementary-secondary schools using the Internet, by type of activity, Canada and provinces, 1999 | 218 |
| TABLE 3.32 | Percentage of students attending elementary-secondary schools affected by selected obstacles to fuller use of information and communications technologies in schools, by level of school, Canada and provinces, 1999 | 219 |

## Chapter 4 Tables ............ 221

| | | |
|---|---|---|
| TABLE 4.1 | Percentage of 13-year-olds at performance level 2 or above in SAIP assessments, Canada and jurisdictions | 223 |
| TABLE 4.2 | Percentage of 16 year olds at performance level 3 or above in SAIP assessments, Canada and jurisdictions | 224 |
| TABLE 4.3 | Percentage of 13-year-olds at performance level 2 or above in SAIP assessments, by gender, Canada | 225 |
| TABLE 4.4 | Percentage of 16-year-olds at performance level 3 or above in SAIP assessments, by gender, Canada | 225 |
| TABLE 4.5 | Percentage of the population aged 16 to 25 and 26 to 65 at each literacy level in the IALS document, prose, and quantitative scales, Canada, regions, and other IALS participating countries | 226 |
| TABLE 4.6 | Ratio (times 100) of upper secondary graduates to population at a typical age of graduation (from first educational program), G-7 countries, 1996 | 227 |
| TABLE 4.7 | Ratio of secondary graduates to population at age 18, by gender, Canada and jurisdictions, 1995 to 1997 | 227 |
| TABLE 4.8 | High school completion rates of the population aged 19 to 20, by gender, Canada and provinces, 1991 to 1994 and 1995 to 1998 | 228 |
| TABLE 4.9 | Number of diplomas and degrees granted, by level of education, Canada, 1976 to 1997 | 228 |
| TABLE 4.10 | Ratio of university graduates to the population at the typical age of graduation (times 100), by level of education and by jurisdiction of study, Canada and jurisdictions, 1991 to1997 | 229 |
| TABLE 4.11 | Ratio of university graduates to the population at the typical age of graduation (times 100), by level of education and by jurisdictions of residence, Canada and jurisdictions, 1991 to 1997 | 230 |
| TABLE 4.12 | Ratio of university graduates to the population at the typical age of graduation (times 100), by gender, field of study and level of education, Canada, 1987 and 1997 | 231 |
| TABLE 4.13 | Number of diplomas and degrees granted, by level of education, Canada and jurisdictions, 1991 to 1997 | 232 |
| TABLE 4.14 | Number of university degrees granted, by gender and field of study, Canada and provinces, 1987 | 233 |
| TABLE 4.15 | Number of university degrees granted, by gender and field of study, Canada and provinces, 1997 | 234 |

# TABLE OF CONTENTS

| | | |
|---|---|---|
| TABLE 4.16 | Distribution of the Aboriginal and non-Aboriginal populations aged 20 to 29, by highest level of education attained, 1986 and 1996 | 235 |
| TABLE 4.17 | Distribution of the Aboriginal population aged 25 to 29, by highest level of education attained, Canada and jurisdictions, 1996 | 235 |
| TABLE 4.18 | Distribution of the Aboriginal population aged 25 to 54, by highest level of education attained, Canada and jurisdictions, 1996 | 236 |
| TABLE 4.19 | Distribution the non-Aboriginal population aged 25 to 29, by highest level of education attained, Canada and jurisdictions, 1996 | 236 |
| TABLE 4.20 | Distribution of the non-Aboriginal population aged 25 to 54, by highest level of education attained, Canada and jurisdictions, 1996 | 237 |
| TABLE 4.21 | Distribution of the population aged 15 years and older, by mother tongue, Canada and jurisdictions, 1996 | 237 |

## CHAPTER 5 TABLES ................................................................................................. 239

| | | |
|---|---|---|
| TABLE 5.1 | Employment rate of the 25 to 54 age group by educational attainment and gender, Canada and provinces, 1990 and 1998 | 241 |
| TABLE 5.2 | Employment rates of the 25 to 29 age group by educational attainment and gender, Canada and provinces, 1990 and 1998 | 241 |
| TABLE 5.3 | Unemployment rates of the 25 to 54 age group by educational attainment and gender, Canada and provinces, 1990 and 1998 | 242 |
| TABLE 5.4 | Unemployment rates of the 25 to 29 age group by educational attainment and gender, Canada and provinces, 1990 and 1998 | 242 |
| TABLE 5.5 | Involuntary part-time workers as a percentage of the labour force, by educational attainment and selected age groups, Canada, 1976 to 1996 | 243 |
| TABLE 5.6 | Unemployment rate, by educational attainment and selected age groups, Canada, 1976 to 1996 | 243 |
| TABLE 5.7 | Level and change in part-time employment and involuntary part-time employment as a percentage of the labour force, Canada, 1976, 1986, and 1996 | 244 |
| TABLE 5.8 | Percentage of 1986 and 1995 university graduates working full time, two years after graduation, by gender and field of study, Canada | 244 |
| TABLE 5.9 | Percentage of 1986 and 1995 graduates working full time, two years after graduation, by level of education and province of study | 245 |
| TABLE 5.10 | Labour force participation rates of 1986 and 1995 graduates, two years after graduation, by level of education and province of study | 245 |
| TABLE 5.11 | Unemployment rate of 1986 and 1995 graduates, two years after graduation, by level of education and province of study | 245 |
| TABLE 5.12 | Median earnings of 1986 and 1995 graduates working full time, two years after graduation, by level of education and province of study (in constant 1997 $000's) | 246 |
| TABLE 5.13 | Median earnings of 1986 and 1995 university graduates working full time, by gender and field of study, two years after graduation, Canada (in constant 1997 $000's) | 246 |
| TABLE 5.14 | Percentage of 1986 and 1995 graduates working full time two years after graduation who are in a job closely related to their education, by province of study and level of education | 247 |
| TABLE 5.15 | Percentage of 1986 and 1995 university graduates working full time two years after graduation who are in a job closely related to their education, by gender and field of study, Canada | 247 |
| TABLE 5.16 | Migration characteristics of 1986 graduates in the period before enrolling and two years after graduation, Canada and jurisdictions | 248 |
| TABLE 5.17 | Migration characteristics of 1995 graduates in the period before enrolling and two years after graduation, Canada and jurisdictions | 249 |

| | |
|---|---|
| Committees and Organisations | 251 |
| Comments and Suggestions | 256 |

xiii

# CHAPTER 1

## INTRODUCTION AND OVERVIEW

Education, at all levels, from pre-primary to postsecondary through to adult education and training, plays a crucial role in the development of individuals and society. An educated work force, capable of using knowledge to generate innovation, is vital to a strong and prosperous economy. Education empowers people to be involved in the issues and debates affecting them and society. Indeed, in the Joint Ministerial Declaration of 1999, provincial and territorial ministers responsible for education and training affirmed that the future of our society depends on informed and educated citizens. The Organisation for Economic Co-operation and Development (OECD) has adopted the principle of lifelong learning to reflect the diversity of education and training that individuals will engage in over their lifetimes.

### THE PAN-CANADIAN EDUCATION INDICATORS PROGRAM

In the Victoria Declaration of 1993, the provincial and territorial ministers responsible for education and training agreed to create the Pan-Canadian Education Indicators Program (PCEIP) in order to develop a set of statistical measures that would provide information on education systems in Canada. Policy makers, practitioners and the general public can use these indicators to evaluate the performance of education systems and to inform decisions about education priorities and directions.[1] The PCEIP is a joint effort of Statistics Canada and the Council of Ministers of Education, Canada (CMEC).

The PCEIP indicator set is organized around a model of education systems that encompasses the context of education, the characteristics and features of education systems, and the outcomes they produce.

By combining discrete education statistics and giving them a context, indicators permit comparisons—between jurisdictions, over time, and with commonly accepted standards. More than one indicator is needed to capture the diverse aspects of education systems and to evaluate their performance. Although indicators can show trends and uncover interesting questions, they cannot by themselves provide explanations or permit conclusions to be drawn. Additional research will always be required to diagnose the causes of problems and suggest solutions. The aim of this report is to stimulate thinking and promote debate on education issues.

Using indicators to evaluate education systems is not unique to the PCEIP. Within Canada, many jurisdictions have developed education indicator systems, or are in the process of developing them. The diversity of education systems in Canada and the various methods used to define, collect and calculate data often restricts meaningful inter-jurisdictional comparisons of education indicators. As far as possible, the PCEIP presents data that are consistent across jurisdictions. Indeed, the goal of the PCEIP is to provide consistent and high-quality information on education for all of Canada to support informed decision-making, policy formulation and program development.

Internationally, the Indicators of Education Systems (INES) project, conducted by the Organisation for Economic Co-operation and Development (OECD), statistically measures and compares the education systems of its member countries and publishes the results annually in *Education at a Glance: OECD Indicators*. Canada has participated in this project since its inception in 1988. The biennial *World Education Report*, published by the United Nations Educational, Scientific and Cultural Organization (UNESCO), also uses education indicators to identify global trends in education. In a number of instances, the PCEIP incorporates INES indicators to provide an international framework for pan-Canadian and jurisdictional indicators.

## THE DEVELOPMENT OF THE INDICATOR SET

The first indicators under the PCEIP were published in 1996.[2] In 1997, consultations with provincial and territorial governments and other education stakeholders identified key policy issues that led to the definition of a new set of indicators. *"The 1999 PCEIP report"* is the first publication based on the new indicator set and includes results for about half of the indicators. The data included in this report were chosen on the basis of two criteria: the type of education information needed for policy development, and the practical availability of data. The data presented are the most recent available for the selected indicators.

## FUTURE PLANS

The next PCEIP report is scheduled for the fall of 2001. Program priorities include:

- monitoring the indicators presented here to ensure that up-to-date information is available in 2001 and making the needed adjustments to reflect emerging policy concerns
- continuing research to refine and select data for the remaining indicators
- improving data collection and reporting and cross-jurisdictional comparability
- consulting with the provincial and territorial governments and education stakeholders to increase the relevance and usefulness of the PCEIP.

## OVERVIEW OF THIS PUBLICATION

The indicators are grouped into four chapters. Chapter 2 sets the context for assessing the state of education in Canada by providing population trends, estimates of children living in low-income situations, and information on the educational attainment of the population. Chapter 3 profiles the characteristics and features of the education system, which includes educators, education finances, and the use of information and communications technologies in schools. Chapter 4 focuses on education outcomes, examining results of pan-Canadian and international achievement and assessment tests, and graduation rates at both the secondary and postsecondary levels. The chapter also includes an examination of equity issues. Chapter 5 explores the labour market outcomes experienced by individuals with different levels of education, focusing on the transition of recent postsecondary graduates from education to work.

INTRODUCTION AND OVERVIEW

## HIGHLIGHTS AND OVERALL TRENDS IN EDUCATION SYSTEMS

This report examines many facets of education in Canada. The selected indicators are divided among the chapters, and although some links between indicators are made, the analysis focuses primarily on the indicator under consideration. The rest of Chapter 1 provides an overview of some of the broad trends shown by the data, which often involve more than one indicator.

## CONTEXT

The demand for education services, through schools, colleges, universities, and other training programs, is affected by a number of factors. One major consideration is the size of the population, especially for elementary–secondary programs, where enrolment rates are close to 100% of the population between the age of five and the age at the end of compulsory schooling. Population projections show that in the Atlantic provinces, Quebec, Manitoba and Saskatchewan, the population 19 years of age and under is expected to decline over the next 15 years, lessening demand for elementary–secondary education services. In Ontario, Alberta, British Columbia, and the territories, the same age group is expected to increase, which will likely lead to the expansion of elementary–secondary systems in these jurisdictions. In addition to population factors, any increase in secondary school enrolment beyond the age of compulsory education would tend to increase demand.

*Canada's population aged 19 and under is projected to increase slightly over the next 15 years, although declines are projected in some jurisdictions.*

The demand for postsecondary education is dependent on a number of factors. The size of the youth population, for example, is expected to increase slightly on a pan-Canadian basis, albeit with increases in some jurisdictions and decreases in others. The demand for postsecondary education, however, is driven by the participation rate—the percentage of the population participating in postsecondary education. Historically, postsecondary education participation rates at the trade–vocational, college and university levels have been on the increase. However, university participation and enrolment rates have levelled off in the 1990s. The reasons for this are not understood. During this period, labour market conditions have generally improved, potentially resulting in a greater pull from the labour market. As well, tuition fees have risen and there has been little movement in family income. In addition to continued monitoring of trends in university participation, research to better understand the factors involved would be helpful.

In 1996, nearly 1.4 million children 15 years of age and younger in Canada were living in low-income households. These students were more likely to have lower levels of educational attainment than were students from families with higher socio-economic status. In 1994, students from the lowest income quartile were more likely not to have completed a high school education (34%) compared with those students whose parents were in the highest socio-economic quartile (23%).

*One child in five 15 years of age and younger in Canada comes from a lower income family, and is likely to face greater difficulties in education.*

Although Canadian education levels are already high by international standards, they have continued to improve in recent years. More Canadians are graduating from high school and more graduates are going on to higher education. Between 1990 and 1998, the percentage of 25- to 29-year-olds with less than high school education fell from 20% to 13%, while the percentage of university graduates increased—from 17% to 26%. Many adults are also upgrading and updating their education. In 1998, approximately 1.4 million Canadians adults aged 25 and over were enrolled in formal education programs.

*The educational attainment of Canadians has increased during the 1990s.*

## FEATURES OF EDUCATION SYSTEMS

The replacement of retiring postsecondary faculty is likely to become a pressing concern in the next decade. Close to half of full-time university faculty and almost 40% of college educators are 50 years of age or older. Today, there is a pool of Canadian graduates to draw from in hiring new faculty, given the growth in the number of

*Close to one-half of full-time university faculty and close to 40% of college staff will be eligible for retirement in the next decade.*

graduate degrees awarded at the master's level and especially at the doctorate level. This contrasts with the situation in the 1960s and early 1970s, when many faculty members were hired from outside Canada to fill the expanding need for university educators.

At the elementary–secondary level, where teachers tend to retire before age 60, if the average retirement age stays the same, about one-third of the current teaching force will retire over the next 10 years. At the pan-Canadian level, given the projected rate of increase in the population 19 years of age and under, there appears to be a reasonably good balance between the supply of new education graduates and the future demand for teachers, assuming current graduation rates are maintained. In jurisdictions where a reduced population size is expected to lead to declining enrolments, the number of retirees may allow education systems to adjust to new enrolment levels with minimal disruption. In rural areas, however, the desire to avoid long bus rides for students, and the corresponding need to keep schools open, may affect the number of teachers required. The pace at which current educators retire will also be affected by early retirement programs already in place, and by decisions on issues such as the pupil–educator ratio. In jurisdictions where enrolments are expected to increase, the recruitment of teachers is likely to become an important issue, reversing the trends of the past decade.

**Canada's investment in education is among the highest in the world.**

Canada's investment in education is among the highest in the world, as measured by OECD indicators of education expenditure. In 1995, the most recent year for which internationally comparable data are available, Canada had the highest expenditure on education as a proportion of GDP among G-7 countries, and the second highest per student expenditure.[3] Per student expenditures in Canada at all levels of education were $7,907 (Canadian dollars), with spending of $6,677 per student at the elementary–secondary level, and $14,182 per student at the postsecondary level.

**At a pan-Canadian level, per capita spending on education in constant dollars has dropped 7% over the last five years.**

As governments in Canada have moved to reduce deficits in recent years, there has been a decline in constant dollar per capita expenditures on education. Between 1994-95 and 1998-99, per capita spending on education dropped 7%, to just under $2,000. The decreases over the past five years have offset increases earlier in the decade, leaving the amount spent on education per capita in 1998-99 little changed from a decade ago.

Pan-Canadian expenditures at all levels of education fell $1.9 billion (in constant dollars) between 1994-95 and 1998-99, to an estimated $60.5 billion. Some reasons for the variations in expenditure patterns across jurisdictions include differences in population change and fiscal policy.

**University tuition fees more than doubled (in constant dollars) in the 1990s.**

As public funding for postsecondary education fell during the 1990s, educational institutions increased tuition fees. For example, average tuition fees for undergraduate arts programs more than doubled from $1,568 in 1988-89 to $3,199 in 1998-99. Community college tuition remains lower than university tuition in most programs.

**The debt levels of postsecondary graduates have more than doubled (in constant dollars) between the classes of 1986 and 1995.**

Graduates of postsecondary institutions in 1995 who borrowed to finance their education had accumulated larger debt loads, and were paying them off over a longer period, than graduates of the class of 1986. Among 1995 graduates with loans, the average amount owing two years after graduation was $8,300, over twice the amount owed by 1986 postsecondary graduates two years after graduation.

## EDUCATION OUTCOMES

**Pan-Canadian education outcomes compare favourably on an international level.**

Canadian students perform well in international science and mathematics assessments, and the Canadian population has comparable literacy skills to those of other nations. Results of the Third International Mathematics and Science Study (TIMSS), which assessed students from grades 4 and 8, placed Canadian Grade 8 students above the international mean in both subjects. Grade 4 students were above the international mean in science, and no different from the international mean in mathematics. The

International Adult Literacy Survey (IALS) placed the literacy of the Canadian adult population at about the middle of the countries studied, but ahead of the United States.

Since the late 1980s when the Organisation for Economic Co-operation and Development (OECD) began producing comparative education indicators, Canada has had the highest educational attainment of all OECD countries. In 1995, 48% of the Canadian population aged 25-64 had a postsecondary education, compared with the OECD mean of 23%. Over this period Canada has consistently placed among the top countries in terms of the percentage of university graduates, and has had the highest percentage with college qualifications.

**Among OECD countries, Canada has the highest percentage of the population with postsecondary qualifications.**

For the past two decades, the participation and performance of female students within educational systems has been an area of concern. Many of the indicators, however, show significant improvements in this area. Results from the School Achievement Indicators Program (SAIP), which tests 13- and 16-year-olds across Canada in mathematics and science, and in reading and writing, showed little gender differences in mathematics or science, and stronger reading and writing skills among female students.

**Significant improvements have occurred in the educational outcomes of females . . .**

Women now comprise more than half of all college and university enrolments and graduates. In 1997, females received 58% of university diplomas and degrees, up from 53% a decade earlier. Women accounted for more than 80% of the increase in the number of university graduates over the 10-year period. As well, the percentage of female graduates has increased in traditionally male-dominated fields. In engineering, for example, 21% of graduates were women in 1997; almost double the percentage in 1987, while almost half of commerce graduates were women in 1997 (48%), up from 43% a decade earlier.

A number of the indicators now suggest that there is a need to monitor the progress of male students in some areas. Not only did male secondary students have weaker reading and writing scores on SAIP than their female counterparts, but data on high school completion also show that male students are less likely to graduate. Between 1995 and 1998, among those aged 19 and 20, 84% of females had graduated from high school, compared with 78% of males. Males are also less likely to both participate in and complete postsecondary education.

**. . . now, in some areas, there is a need to monitor the progress of male students.**

As technology becomes an increasingly important part of everyday life, there is a greater need for graduates capable of innovative scientific work to develop and extend technological innovations. The labour market demand for science graduates is reflected in the high earnings and high rates of full-time employment of physical and applied science graduates, relative to graduates in other fields of study. Two years after graduation, 1995 graduates of physical and applied science had earnings that, while below those in the health professions, were above those of graduates in commerce and social sciences. Full-time employment rates for this group, while below those of graduates in commerce, were similar to those in health professions. Nevertheless, physical and applied science graduates accounted for a slightly smaller percentage of graduates in 1997 (20%) than 10 years earlier (21%). While Canadian elementary–secondary students have performed at or above the international mean on international assessments of science and mathematics achievement in recent years, it remains to be seen whether these results will translate into an increased number of students pursuing studies in the physical and applied sciences.

**There has been little change in the percentage of university graduates in physical and applied sciences.**

In 1997, 59% of university graduates were in the humanities and social sciences, representing close to one-half of male graduates and two-thirds of female graduates, up slightly from 58% of graduates in 1987. Labour market considerations are only one of a number of factors that influences an individual's decision about whether to pursue postsecondary education and which field of study to choose. Graduates of the humanities and social sciences, with the exception of graduates in education, have had weaker outcomes than graduates in other fields of study. For example, among 1995 graduates two years after graduation, humanities and social science graduates had lower rates of full-time employment (61% compared with 67% for all fields of

**The largest percentage of university graduates continues to be in the humanities, despite the weaker labour market outcomes of this field relative to others.**

study), and those working full time had lower median earnings ($32,000 compared with $34,000 for all fields).

Like all economically advanced countries, Canada has experienced major changes since the early 1980s. For example, the new information and communications technologies are now in widespread use and are being applied increasingly in the workplace and in everyday life. Adult education, whether general or job-related, helps people keep abreast of such changes by giving them the chance to complete secondary school, pursue higher education, and engage in employment training. Other opportunities afforded individuals by adult education include pursuing a special interest, developing literacy skills, and taking courses in English or French as a Second Language. These educational opportunities can enhance an individual's participation in society and in the workplace. In addition to enriching individual participants, adult education and training also enhances Canada's international competitiveness by contributing to the development and maintenance of an educated, skilled and flexible work force.

*Canada's rate of participation in adult education and training is similar to that of other developed countries.*

In 1997, approximately 27% of the population between the ages of 25 and 54 participated in specifically job-related adult education and training. Results from the 1994-95 International Adult Literacy Survey showed that, in Canada, the percentage of individuals aged 25 to 64 participating in job-related adult education and training, and the duration of training, were similar to the average for the seven countries taking part in the survey.

*Among 25- to 29-year-olds across jurisdictions, the educational attainment of anglophone and francophone minorities is generally similar to or better than that of the linguistic majorities.*

Generally, an individual's mother tongue (the first language spoken in the home, which is not necessarily the language of education) does not appear to be a barrier to educational attainment. Individuals aged 25 to 29 are representative of a cohort that has recently gone through the education system. In this age group, francophone minorities within most jurisdictions have a similar or lower percentage with less than high school education, and a similar or higher percentage with university education, than the corresponding anglophone majorities. In Quebec, in the anglophone minority, there is a lower percentage of people who have less than high school education and a higher percentage of people who have a university education than in the francophone majority.

Across jurisdictions, in the population whose mother tongue is neither English nor French, there is generally a higher percentage with university education as well as a higher percentage with less than high school education when compared with the linguistic majority.

The educational outcomes of Aboriginal Canadians have improved, but remain well below those of the non-Aboriginal population. In 1996, only 6% of the Aboriginal population aged 25 to 54 were university graduates, compared with 21% of the non-Aboriginal population. Of that same age group, 42% of the Aboriginal population had not graduated from high school, compared with 22% in the non-Aboriginal population.

In 1986, the rate of university participation was similar for individuals whose parents had a low or middle socio-economic status (SES), but well below that of individuals who came from high SES backgrounds. Between 1986 and 1994, the percentage attending university increased among all SES groups, but the rate of growth was fastest among those from middle SES backgrounds. This has resulted in a gap in university participation rates between those from low and middle SES backgrounds. Given that tuition fees and student debt levels have increased since 1994, there is a need for more recent data to monitor participation rates by SES.

## LABOUR MARKET OUTCOMES

With each level of education attained, employment rates rise and unemployment rates and the incidence of involuntary part-time employment falls. Information on recent postsecondary graduates shows progressively higher earnings with more advanced postsecondary qualifications. Regional differences in labour market outcomes are less evident among persons with higher levels of education than among those with lower levels of education.

Individuals who do not finish high school have significantly higher rates of unemployment, and those who are employed are more likely to be working part time when they would prefer to be working full time. Moreover, these differences in labour market outcomes have become more pronounced in the 1990s. In view of the importance of a high school education to securing employment, the increase in the high school completion rate in all jurisdictions in the 1990s is encouraging.

Two years after graduation, 1986 and 1995 graduates had similar unemployment rates. However, 1995 college and university graduates had lower rates of full-time employment and lower earnings (in constant dollars) when compared with 1986 graduates. Those who graduated from college and trade–vocational institutions in 1995 were generally less likely than 1986 graduates to be working in a job related to their field of study, although the education–job fit improved between 1986 and 1995 among university graduates.

Among the 1995 class of postsecondary graduates, college graduates experienced higher rates of full-time employment two years after graduation than either trade–vocational or university graduates. The same pattern existed and was even stronger among the class of 1986 two years after graduation.

Among 1995 graduates working full time two years after graduation, the median annual earnings of university graduates, at $34,000, were significantly higher than the median earnings of college graduates ($26,000) and trade–vocational graduates ($23,000). At all levels, earnings were about 4% to 6% less (in constant dollars) than those of 1986 graduates two years after graduation.

**Level of education plays a more consistent role in determining whether an individual is employed or unemployed than do regional factors.**

**The largest difference in labour market outcomes is between those who have completed high school and those who have not.**

**Postsecondary graduates in the 1990s have had slightly more difficulty than their predecessors in making the transition from school to work.**

**Among 1995 postsecondary graduates, college graduates were more likely to be employed full time . . .**

**. . . while university graduates working full time had higher earnings.**

## ENDNOTES

1 This report includes information from the 10 provinces, Yukon, and the Northwest Territories (including Nunavut for which separate statistical information was not yet available).

2 *Education Indicators in Canada*, Pan-Canadian Education Indicators Program, Canadian Education Statistics Council, 1996.

3 International expenditure comparisons are in terms of purchasing power parity exchange rates (PPPs) or the amount of a national currency that will buy the same basket of goods and services in a country as U.S. dollars in the United States.

# CHAPTER 2

## THE CONTEXT OF EDUCATION

- Population characteristics and trends
- Children living in low-income situations
- Educational attainment of the adult population

## HIGHLIGHTS

- The Canadian population aged 5 to 24 is projected to increase slightly through 2016, but the ratio of the population aged 5 to 24 to the working-age population is declining. The highest percentage population increase will be in the Northwest Territories and in British Columbia. The greatest decrease is projected for Newfoundland and Labrador.
- The number of children living in low-income families has risen since the 1980s. By 1996, nearly 1.4 million children 15 years of age or younger lived in a low-income family.
- The educational attainment of the population aged 25 to 54 has risen from 1990 to 1998. Young women (aged 25 to 29) are now achieving higher overall levels of educational attainment than are young men.

## 2.1 POPULATION CHARACTERISTICS AND TRENDS

**Population projections to 2016 provide a perspective on future demographic trends.**

Information on the distribution of the population, combined with projections of future changes in the population, help policy makers to foresee adjustments that may be needed in Canada's education systems, in order to meet the needs of changing student populations. Changes in the composition of the population may also have an impact on the capacity to fund the education systems, in that they may affect the size of the tax base from which public funds for education are drawn.

To make informed decisions on the distribution of resources in the education system—from decisions on teacher hiring, to investment in the construction and maintenance of buildings, to program planning that meets the educational needs of particular sectors of the population—policy makers must examine demographic trends over time. The way funding is allocated among the various levels of education is affected by enrolment expectations (see section 3.3), which are based on projections of the distribution of the population between age groups. The availability of funding may also be affected by changes in the size of the working-age population, which provides a substantial portion of the public funds used for education.

### A. POPULATION DISTRIBUTION AND PROJECTIONS

#### POLICY CONTEXT

**The data in this indicator show the population projected until 2016.**

The data here help to highlight the pressures anticipated on the education and training systems through the year 2016. Population estimates and projections are given for the population aged 5 to 24 and for more detailed breakdowns of this age group (Table and Figure 2.1). The same information is given for the working-age population (25 to 64) and the senior population (65 years and older) to provide a perspective on change in other population groups.

**The population projections are based on a medium growth model. For more details, see Appendix 3.**

In some jurisdictions, the population aged 5 to 24 is projected to decline. These jurisdictions are likely to experience less pressure over the long term on both current and capital expenditures, although the need to maintain an effective and accessible level of service may mean that this effect is not seen in the shorter term. Conversely, jurisdictions where the population aged 5 to 24 is projected to increase may face higher expenses related to the construction or expansion of buildings, or the accommodation of increasing numbers of students.

The data here do not provide insights into changes expected within jurisdictions, where pressures may differ from area to area. For example, the population growth in a jurisdiction might be concentrated in the cities, while institutions in rural areas might face the effects of a declining population.

Over the period 1996 to 2016, the growth in the populations aged 15-19 and 20-24 in Canada as a whole, and in some jurisdictions, will likely translate into postsecondary enrolment pressure. Because some students move away from their home jurisdiction for postsecondary education, the enrolment pressure may affect all jurisdictions, although the impact will depend on the relative strengths and availability of a jurisdiction's postsecondary programs (see section 5.3).

## FINDINGS

### CANADA

The pre-school population is expected to decline slightly from the 1996 level by 2001. It is expected to remain steady until 2006 and then to increase.

## THE CONTEXT OF EDUCATION

The population aged 5 to 24 is expected to continue to increase slightly. However, the ratio of this population to the working-age population (aged 25 to 64) has been declining since 1986 and will likely continue to decline until 2016. The declining ratio results from a shift in the distribution of the population. Since 1991, there has been only minimal growth in the population aged 5 to 24, while both the working-age population and senior population have experienced significant increases. Nevertheless, the population aged 5 to 24 is larger than the senior population; this is expected to continue until 2016.

*A slight increase is projected for the population aged 5 to 24.*

The growth of the working-age population relative to the combined populations of those aged 5 to 24 and over age 65 is expected to remain relatively stable through 2016. The working-age population will continue to represent the largest proportion of the population as a whole.

### JURISDICTIONS

The pre-school population is projected to decline from 1996 levels in the Atlantic Provinces and Saskatchewan, while remaining relatively stable in Quebec, Manitoba, and Yukon. In the other jurisdictions it will increase, with the highest increases projected for British Columbia and the Northwest Territories.

As can be seen in Table 2.1 and Figure 2.1, the patterns of increase and decrease for the population aged 5 to 24 vary considerably. In British Columbia and the Northwest Territories, a significant percentage increase in the population aged 5 to 24 is projected until 2016. Ontario and Alberta also show increases, while Quebec is expected to remain relatively stable. The population aged 5 to 24 in the Yukon is expected to increase slightly until 2006, and then to decline slightly. Manitoba, Saskatchewan and the Atlantic Provinces show projected declines. Significant declines are projected for Newfoundland and Labrador, New Brunswick, and Nova Scotia. Most jurisdictions will experience some fluctuations within the overall trend, except Newfoundland and Labrador and New Brunswick, which show consistent declines in all cohorts over time.

*Patterns of increase or decline among the population aged 5 to 24 vary across the jurisdictions.*

By 2006, in all jurisdictions, the 15 to 24 age group will be larger than the 5 to 14 age group. In Quebec, Ontario, Alberta, British Columbia, Yukon, and the Northwest Territories, an increase is projected for the 15 to 24 age group, which will likely translate into pressure on the postsecondary education systems to handle increased enrolments.

When interpreting the data, it is important to consider both the actual numbers and the percentage increase or decrease in the population. For example, Ontario is projected to experience a large increase of more than 700,000 people in the 5 to 24 age group between 1986 and 2016. This represents an increase of approximately 25%. In the Northwest Territories, the same group is projected to increase by just over 7,000 people. While this may appear negligible by comparison, it represents a higher percentage increase—33%. It is likely, therefore, to have as significant an impact on planning and resource allocation as the larger numbers in Ontario. The expected population increases in the Northwest Territories are likely to be concentrated in the eastern portion, now the territory of Nunavut.

In all jurisdictions, the ratio of the population aged 5 to 24 to the working-age population is projected to decline through to 2016, while the ratio of seniors to the working-age population is projected to increase—the outcome of an ageing population. These ratios of the population aged 5 to 24 and senior populations have been converging since 1986, and will continue to do so until 2016 (see Table 2.1).

*The ratio of the population aged 5 to 24 to the working-age population is expected to decline in all jurisdictions, while the ratio of seniors to the working-age population is expected to increase.*

# Education Indicators in Canada

FIGURE 2.1    ESTIMATES AND PROJECTIONS OF THE POPULATION AGED 5 TO 14, 15 TO 19, AND 20 TO 24, CANADA AND JURISIDICTIONS, 1986 TO 2016

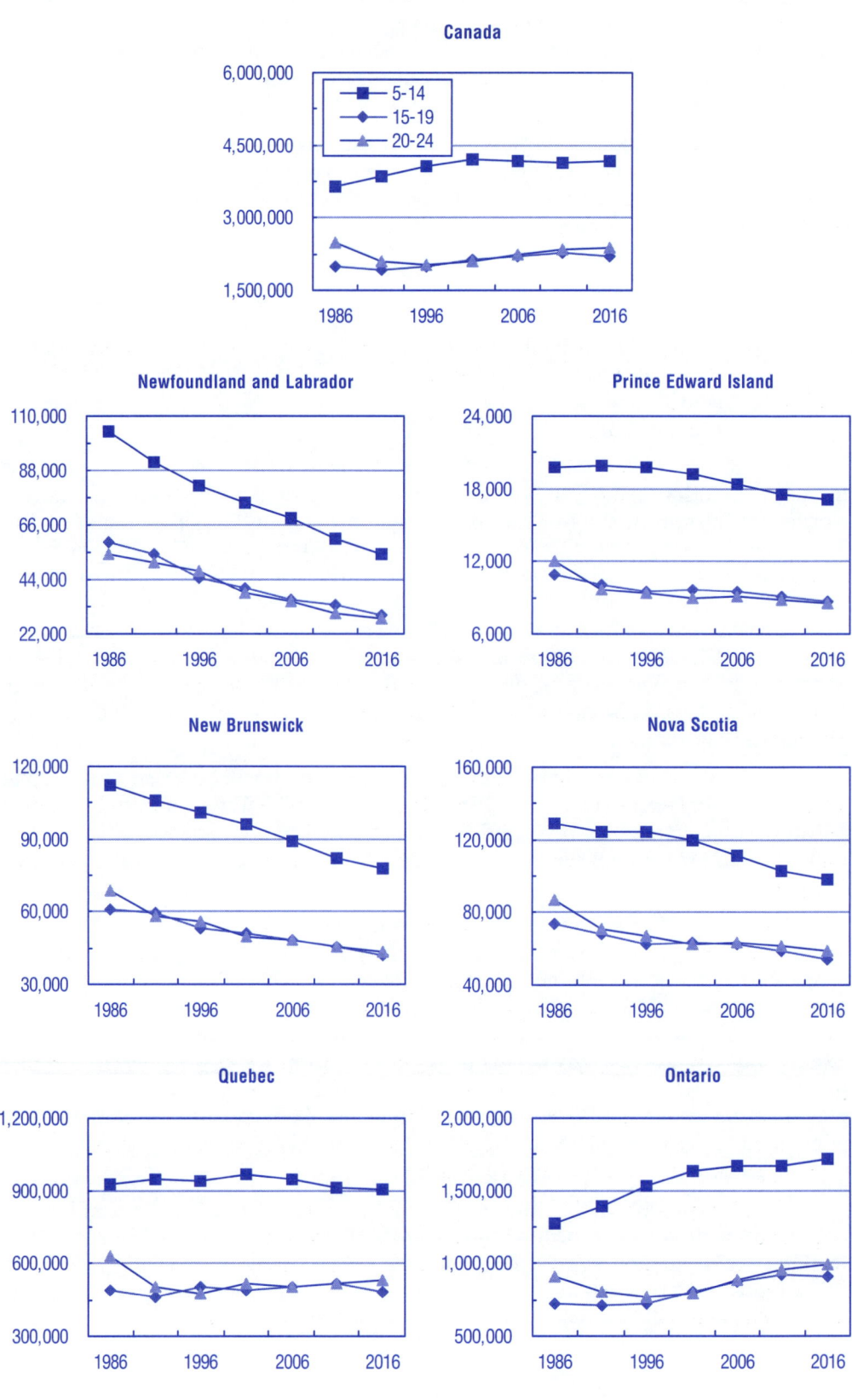

THE CONTEXT OF EDUCATION

FIGURE 2.1   ESTIMATES AND PROJECTIONS OF THE POPULATION AGED 5 TO 14, 15 TO 19, AND 20 TO 24, CANADA AND JURISIDICTIONS, 1986 TO 2016 (concluded)

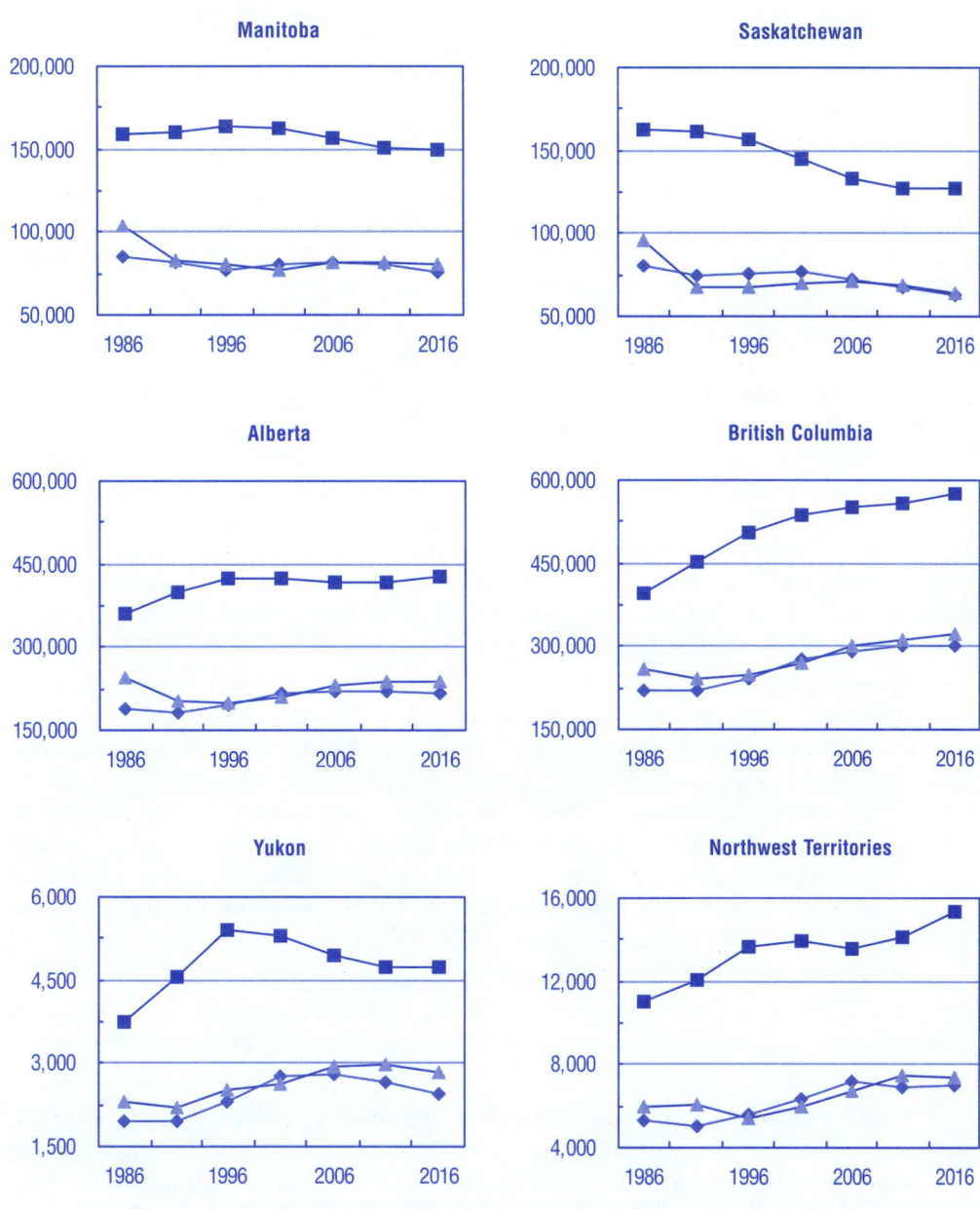

Note: The y-axis has been standardized to represent a four-fold (4x) range in the population with the exception of Newfoundland and Labrador. This jurisdiction is represented by a five-fold range in the population.

The data represent population projections based on a medium growth model. The assumptions underlying this model are outlined in Appendix 3.

Source: *Demography Division, Statistics Canada. 1994.* Population Projections for Canada, Provinces and Territories, 1993-2016, Statistics Canada Catalogue No. 91-520 (Occasional), *December 1994.*

# B. MOBILITY OF THE POPULATION UNDER AGE 24

## POLICY CONTEXT

*This indicator shows patterns of migration of the population under age 24 through data on immigration to Canada, and through data on movement within Canada, both from one jurisdiction to another and within jurisdictions.*

Immigration to Canada and migration between and within Canadian jurisdictions affect the education systems through their impact on enrolments. Immigration may also affect the system by creating a need for programs such as English or French as a Second Language. Net in- or out-migration of the population has implications for the tax base from which jurisdictions draw education funding. This effect is reinforced by the tendency of migration to reflect economic strengths and weaknesses. Migration affects the students themselves, since disruptions in home and school surroundings may influence performance. The introduction of new students, possibly from very different cultural or linguistic backgrounds, may also have an effect on existing students as they adjust to the needs of the newcomers.

The impact of immigration on individual jurisdictions will differ according to the proportion of immigrants moving to that jurisdiction. There is also regional variation in immigration within jurisdictions. For example, a large percentage of immigration to British Columbia and Ontario is concentrated in Vancouver and Toronto respectively. For jurisdictions that experience relatively high intra-jurisdictional migration, changes to enrolments in individual school districts may have as significant an impact on resource allocation as inter-jurisdictional migration. The effects of intra-jurisdictional migration are difficult to assess precisely because in some cases a relatively short-distance move could cross a census subdivision boundary and be classified as intra-jurisdictional. These short moves would likely have little impact on the education system.

*Inter-jurisdictional migration is often related to economic conditions in the jurisdictions.*

Inter-jurisdictional migration reflects, at least in part, the relative economic strengths and weaknesses of the jurisdictions. For example, the net in-migration experienced by Ontario and Alberta in 1997-98, and the net in-migration to British Columbia before that, coincided with economic resurgence in those jurisdictions. Based on the historical data, jurisdictions that experience economic growth, as Ontario, Alberta and British Columbia did in the 1990s, can expect an influx of students from other jurisdictions or other countries. Because migration patterns can change in response to shifts in economic conditions, policy makers cannot rely on past patterns to continue. As a result, these population shifts and their implications for policy and programs require regular monitoring.

The effects of out-migration are likely to be particularly pronounced in Newfoundland and Labrador, which has experienced consistent out-migration and a declining population.

In-migration of students may create a need for more teachers and more resources, including perhaps new school buildings, as well as pressure to use existing resources more efficiently. In some instances, institutions may need to consider the availability of language programs to accommodate students who do not speak an official language of their new jurisdiction.

Jurisdictions such as Prince Edward Island, Ontario, and Yukon, which have experienced considerable fluctuations between net in- and out-migration over a relatively short period, face particular challenges. Teachers hired and schools built in times of growth may no longer be needed in a period of out-migration. Conversely, sufficient resources may not have been allocated to support a shift to in-migration.

# FINDINGS

## CANADA

Immigration has fluctuated a good deal over the years. Immigration fell during the late 1970s and 1980s, but has reached higher levels in the 1990s, peaking in 1992 at 0.9% of the total population. New immigrants in the 4 to 24 age group consistently form a higher percentage of their age cohort than the percentage of new immigrants as a proportion of the total population. This means that proportionally more young immigrants are entering Canada.

The 1996 census data on inter- and intra-jurisdictional migration in Table 2.5 show that from 1995 to 1996, 1.0% of Canada's population moved from one jurisdiction to another and 4.6% of the population moved to a different census subdivision within their resident jurisdiction. Just over 40% of those moving between jurisdictions were aged 24 or less, while this group comprised only one-third of the overall population. This means that, as with immigration, inter-jurisdictional migrants include proportionally more young persons.

*Approximately 40% of inter-jurisdictional migrants were under age 24.*

In both categories of migrants in Table 2.5, more people aged 15 to 24 years moved than those aged 1 to 14 years. Migration, both within Canada and from outside Canada, is common at the postsecondary level, and institutions encourage migration by competing for students who meet entrance requirements (section 5.3). Not all people in these age groups are moving to attend school, however. The economic conditions of a jurisdiction are also likely to have an impact on this age group, many of whom may be seeking to enter the work force following completion of studies.

*Both immigration and migration are more common among the 15 to 24 age group than among younger people.*

## JURISDICTIONS

By far the largest number of new immigrants in 1996 went to Ontario. Ontario received more than twice as many new immigrants in all age cohorts as did British Columbia, the second most popular destination. Quebec and Alberta received the next largest influx of new immigrants. This pattern probably reflects the fact that the most popular destination points for immigrants (Toronto, Vancouver, and Montreal) are found in these jurisdictions (Table 2.3).

*Ontario, British Columbia, Quebec, and Alberta were the most common destination choices for immigrants.*

Table 2.4 shows that, with respect to inter-jurisdictional migration, only Prince Edward Island, Alberta and British Columbia experienced net in-migration between 1990 and 1997. In 1996 and 1997, Quebec experienced the largest net out-migration of any jurisdiction in the 1990s, losing more than 17,000 people. However, as a percentage of the population, Quebec's out-migration in 1997 was relatively small (-0.2%), compared with other jurisdictions, such as Yukon (-2.9%), Northwest Territories (-2.5%), and Newfoundland and Labrador (-2.1%).

British Columbia showed the most consistent net in-migration in the 1990s, and the highest in-migration as a percentage of the population (Figures 2.3 and 2.4). In 1997, however, all jurisdictions except Alberta and Ontario experienced net out-migration. In 1997, Alberta had a net in-migration of more than 46,000 people, the largest net migration of any jurisdiction in the 1990s.

*In 1997, only Alberta and Ontario experienced net gain from inter-jurisdictional migration.*

In all jurisdictions except the Territories, the percentage of the population who moved within the jurisdiction was higher than that of those who moved between jurisdictions. As with immigrants and inter-jurisdictional migrants, the percentage of intra-jurisdictional migrants aged 15 to 24 was higher than that of those aged 14 or less. In Quebec, Saskatchewan, and British Columbia, internal migration of persons aged 15-24 was more than 8%.

*The percentage of intra-jurisdictional migrants in the 15 to 24 age group was higher than in the 1 to 14 age group in all jurisdictions.*

EDUCATION INDICATORS IN CANADA

FIGURE 2.2   IMMIGRANT ARRIVALS AS A PERCENTAGE OF THE POPULATION, BY SELECTED AGE GROUPS, CANADA, **1976** TO **1997**

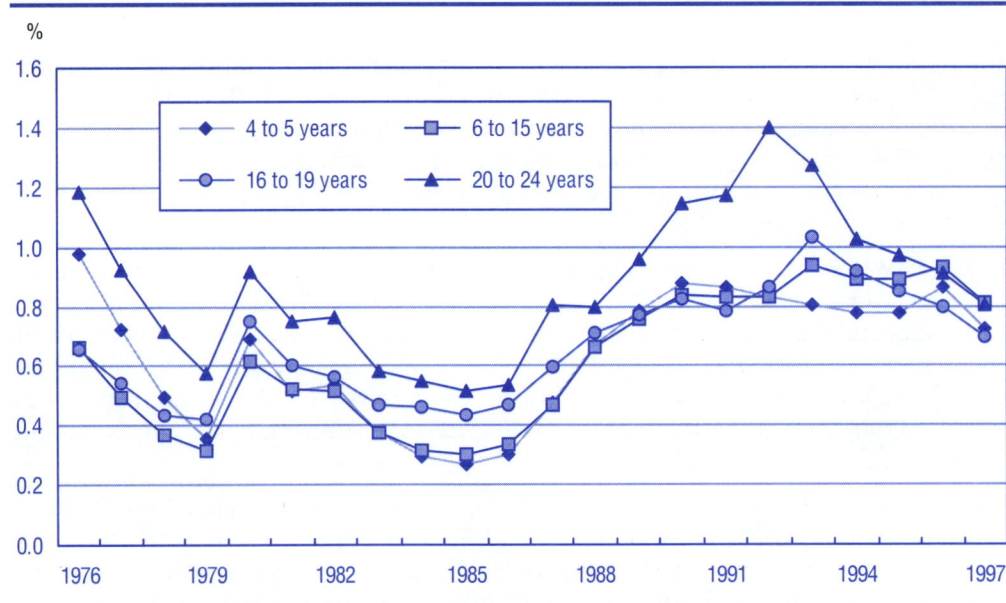

Source: Citizenship and Immigration Canada, and Demography Division, Statistics Canada.

FIGURE 2.3   NET INTERJURISDICTIONAL MIGRATION, BY JURISDICTION, AVERAGE PER YEAR FOR THE PERIODS **1971-79**, **1980-89**, AND **1990-97**

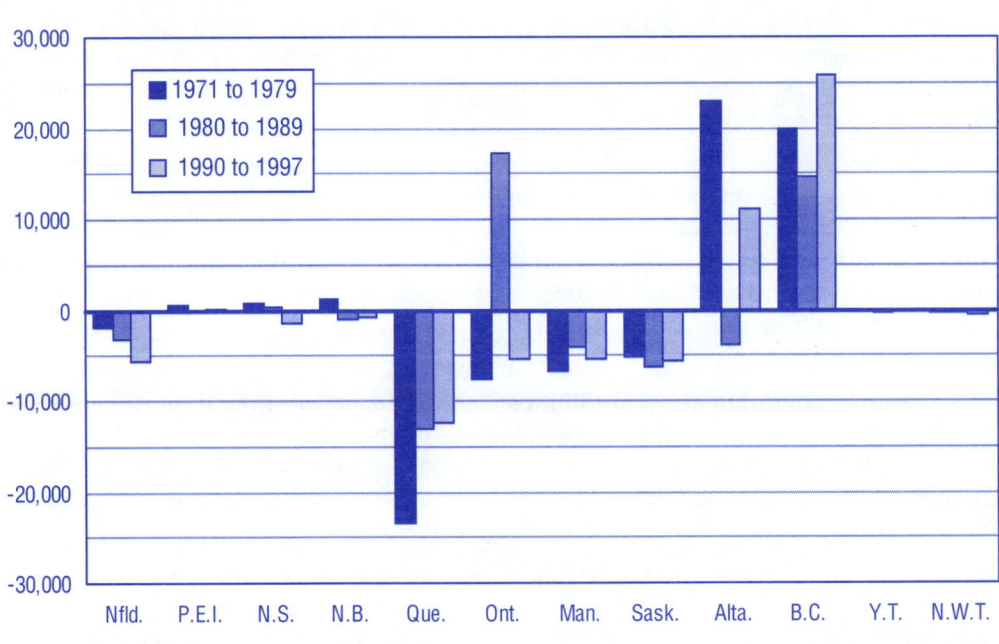

Source: Demography Division, Statistics Canada.

THE CONTEXT OF EDUCATION

FIGURE 2.4  NET INTERJURISDICTIONAL MIGRATION AS A PERCENTAGE OF THE POPULATION, BY JURISDICTION, AVERAGE PER YEAR FOR THE PERIODS **1971-79, 1980-89, 1990-97**

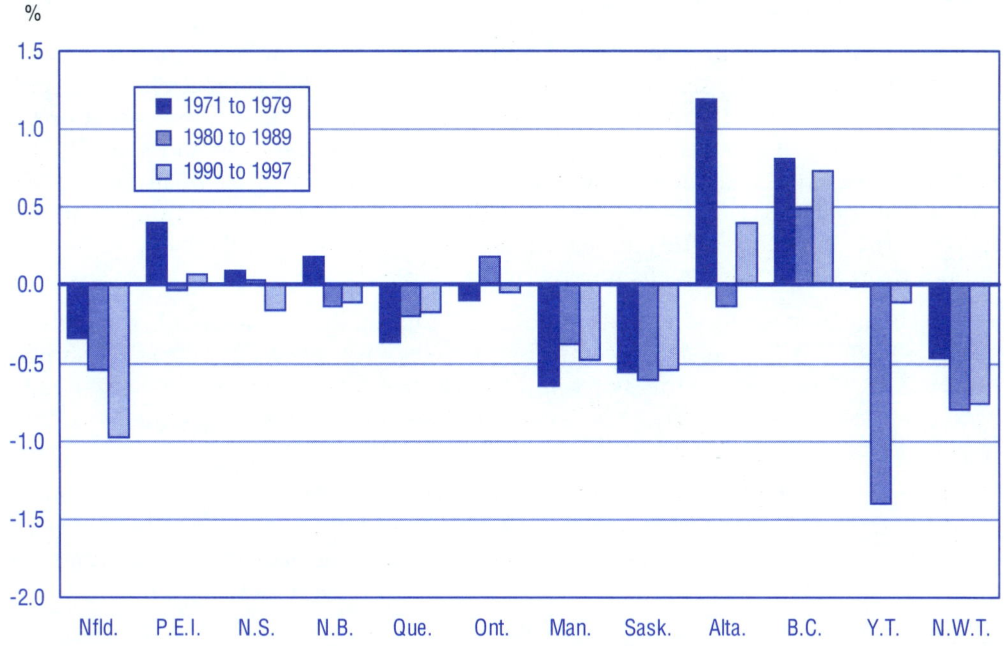

*Source: Demography Division, Statistics Canada.*

## 2.2 Children living in low-income situations

### Policy context

Many children in Canada live in low-income families. These children have higher rates of emotional and behavioural disorders, are less likely to perform well in school, and may experience a lower level of social acceptance by others. Information on the number of children in low-income situations, and the characteristics of those in such situations can help policy makers develop appropriate education policies and programs and better target them toward the children most in need.

**Children in low-income families face a range of disadvantages, which can affect their performance at school.**

The proportion of children in low-income families began to increase in the early 1990s, coinciding with a period of economic recession, and has continued to increase since then. The recovery that began in the mid-1990s was not accompanied by as high a rate of job growth as the recovery of the 1980s. In addition, changes in the availability of social programs (such as Employment Insurance and Social Assistance) may have contributed to higher percentages of children living in low-income families.

**The percentage of children living in low-income families rose between 1990 and 1996.**

Children in single-parent families, most of which are headed by women, are far more likely to be in low-income situations than are children in two-parent families. The fact that women generally earn less than men is a significant problem when the mother is a family's only income earner. Single-parent families are also more likely to depend on government transfer payments as their main source of income and are, therefore, more likely to be directly affected by changes to government policies.

Families with younger children have a higher incidence of low income. This is often because the parents, who tend to be younger, are earning lower wages since they have less experience than older workers.

# FINDINGS

## CANADA

**Nearly 1.4 million children in Canada were living in low-income families in 1996.**

In 1996, nearly 1.4 million children 15 years of age and younger were living in low-income families, representing about 22% (or one in five) children in Canada (Figures 2.5 and 2.6). The proportion of children living in low-income situations in the 1980s closely followed the business cycle. It increased during and just after the recession of 1981-82, and fell in the period of economic growth in the last half of the 1980s. The 1990s have shown a different pattern, however; the proportion of children living in low-income families increased during the recession of the early 1990s, but did not decrease during the ensuing recovery (Table 2.6).

The incidence of individuals under age 24 living in situations of low income is given in Figure 2.7 for several age groups. The data for those aged 18 to 24 should, however, be examined separately from those for the younger groups because people aged 18 to 24 are more likely to be living on their own, either as students with little income or as less experienced workers earning low wages.

Figure 2.7 also shows that a high proportion of children in low-income families is under the age of 9, and hence would be attending elementary school or pre-elementary programs. As mentioned above, this may be because their parents are younger, and have lower incomes.

## JURISDICTIONS

From Table 2.6, we can see that since 1980 there has been an overall increase in the percentage of children 15 years of age and under in low-income families in most jurisdictions. The variation among the jurisdictions has also decreased. In 1980, the percentage ranged from a high of 30% in Newfoundland and Labrador to a low of 11% in British Columbia, a range of 19 percentage points. In 1996, the percentage was lowest in Prince Edward Island (20%) and highest in Manitoba (28%)—a spread of only 8 percentage points.

In 1996, the percentage of children 15 years of age and under living in a low-income family situation was above the pan-Canadian rate of 22% in four jurisdictions: Nova Scotia, Quebec, Manitoba, and Saskatchewan. The only jurisdiction in which the percentage of children living in low-income families declined between 1980 and 1996 was Newfoundland and Labrador, which went from 30% to 21%. New Brunswick's rate remained stable over the same period. Both provinces experienced fluctuations within this overall pattern, however.

THE CONTEXT OF EDUCATION

FIGURE 2.5   PERCENTAGE OF CHILDREN 15 YEARS OF AGE AND YOUNGER IN LOW INCOME FAMILIES[1],
CANADA, 1980 TO 1996

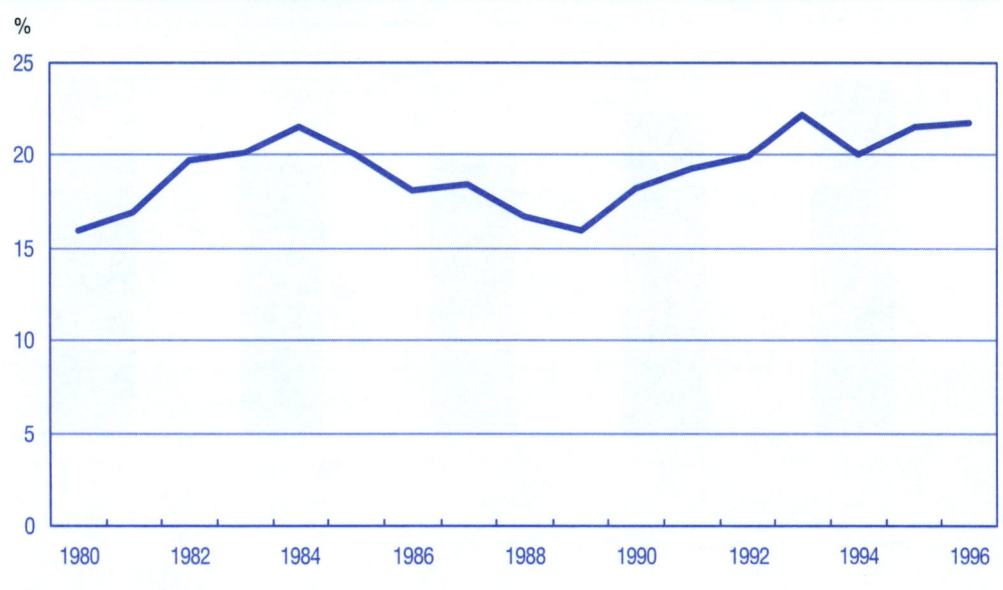

1   Estimates based on Low Income Cut-offs, 1992 base; See Appendix 4.
*Source: Survey of Consumer Finances, Statistics Canada.*

FIGURE 2.6   PERCENTAGE OF CHILDREN 15 YEARS OF AGE AND YOUNGER IN LOW INCOME FAMILIES[1],
CANADA AND PROVINCES, 1996

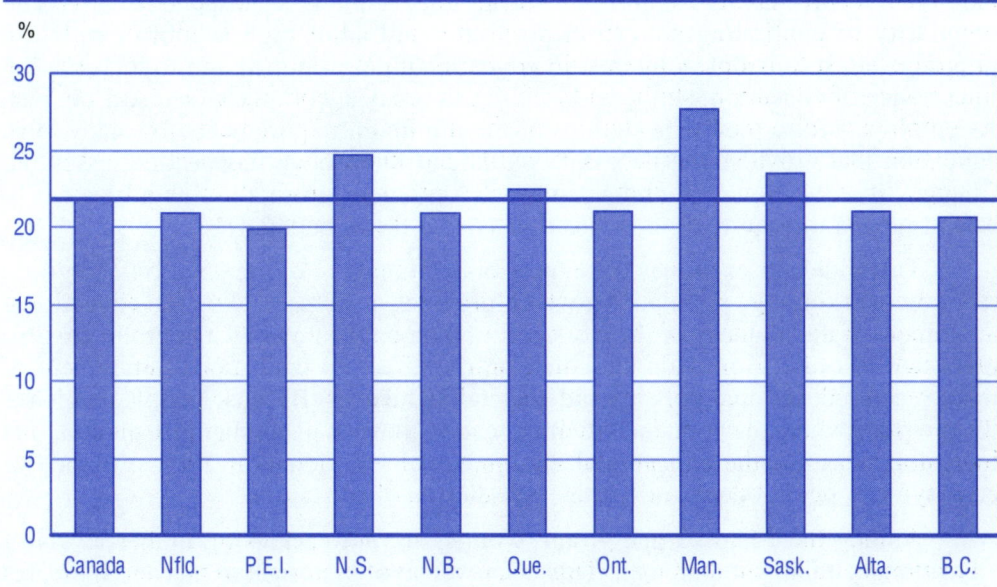

1   Estimates based on Low Income Cut-offs, 1992 base; See Appendix 4.
*Source: Survey of Consumer Finances, Statistics Canada.*

FIGURE 2.7    PERCENTAGE OF CHILDREN AND YOUTH IN LOW INCOME FAMILIES[1], BY AGE, CANADA, 1996

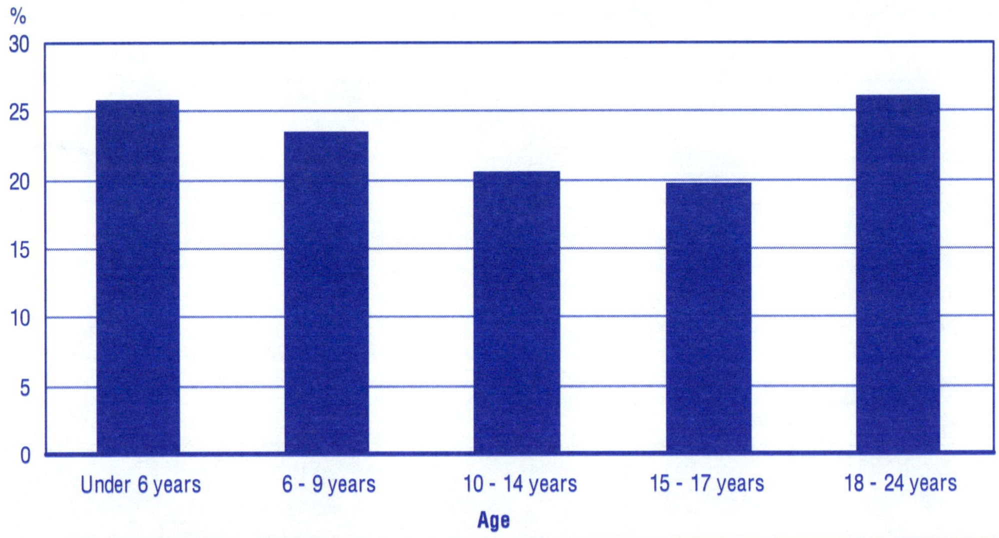

[Bar chart showing percentages by age group: Under 6 years ~26%, 6-9 years ~23.5%, 10-14 years ~21%, 15-17 years ~20%, 18-24 years ~26%]

1   Estimates based on Low Income Cut-offs, 1992 base; See Appendix 4
*Source: 1996 Census, Statistics Canada.*

## 2.3 EDUCATIONAL ATTAINMENT OF THE ADULT POPULATION

### POLICY CONTEXT

A high level of educational attainment—measured here by the level of education an individual reports having completed—carries both economic and social benefits. The popularity of continuing education programs and adult high school completion programs attest to people's interest in educational development and to the growing importance of education, skills, and training in today's workplace (see section 5.2). As employers raise their expectations of the minimum requirements for many jobs, education that provides the necessary skills and knowledge has become essential. Changes in educational attainment may also provide information about access to education and the equity of the education system (see Chapter 4).

**This indicator considers the educational attainment of the population aged 25 to 54, as well as the 25 to 29 age group, based on the level of schooling completed.**

This indicator examines the educational attainment of the 25 to 54 age group (the core working-age population), which provides a perspective on the educational attainment of the majority of the work force. Data on the 25 to 29 age group are also presented in order to provide a reading on the effect on educational attainment of more recent educational policies and societal influences. Because people can leave the province where they obtained their education to work in another jurisdiction, this indicator measures the educational attainment of individuals in their province of employment, but not necessarily their jurisdiction of education.

**Women, aged 25 to 29, have higher levels of educational attainment as a group than men in the same age group.**

Among the 25 to 29 age group, women are now achieving higher levels of educational attainment than men. This is a reversal of historical trends and indicates that policies aimed at improving women's educational outcomes have achieved a degree of success. It appears that policies in the future may be needed to address the lower educational attainment of men, especially in the younger age groups. Similar concerns about male achievement rates have been raised in the secondary school system, following the release of the recent School Achievement Indicators Program (SAIP) reading and writing results (see section 4.1), where the overall performance of boys was significantly lower than that of girls.

# FINDINGS

## CANADA

In general, the educational attainment of those aged 25 to 54 increased between 1990 and 1998 in Canada. The proportion of people with less than a high school education has decreased for both males and females, while the proportion of males and females who are college or university graduates has increased (see Figures 2.8 and 2.9).

By 1998, 12% of young Canadian women (aged 25 to 29) had less than a high school education and 61% were postsecondary graduates. Young men have not fared quite as well: 14% had not completed high school, while 55% were postsecondary graduates. Nevertheless, both men and women had higher levels of educational attainment than in 1990 (Figures 2.10 and 2.11 and Table 2.8).

Figure 2.12 reveals that, in 1996, 48% of Canadians between the ages of 25 and 64 had completed postsecondary education. This was 14% higher than in the United States, the country with the next highest percentage. Canada had a higher percentage of postsecondary college and trade–vocational (non-university) graduates than any other country shown, and the second highest percentage of university graduates, behind the United States. Although international comparisons need to be made with care, because of the effect differences in definitions can have on the results reported, Canada's results show the relatively high importance placed on postsecondary education in our society.

## JURISDICTIONS

The pan-Canadian trend toward higher levels of attainment is evident in all provinces for both the 25 to 54 and 25 to 29 age groups (Tables 2.7 and 2.8). In most jurisdictions, there were substantial increases in the percentages of people with postsecondary qualifications, especially at the college level.

For the 25 to 29 age group, the percentage increase among female university graduates was higher than for males in all jurisdictions. Among college graduates, the jurisdictions showed more varied results. Male graduates in Prince Edward Island had the highest percentage increase, followed by female graduates in Alberta. In general, for the 25 to 29 age group, greater increases were shown at the university level than at the college level. For the 25 to 54 age group, the gender trends were similar, but percentage increases tended to be higher for college graduates than for university graduates.

*Educational attainment increased between 1990 and 1998.*

*By 1998, 61% of women aged 25 to 29 and 55% of men the same age were postsecondary graduates.*

*The percentage of the Canadian population aged 25 to 64 with postsecondary education is the highest of the OECD countries.*

EDUCATION INDICATORS IN CANADA

FIGURE 2.8   DISTRIBUTION OF THE MALE POPULATION AGED 25 TO 54, BY HIGHEST COMPLETED LEVEL OF EDUCATION, CANADA AND PROVINCES, 1990 AND 1998

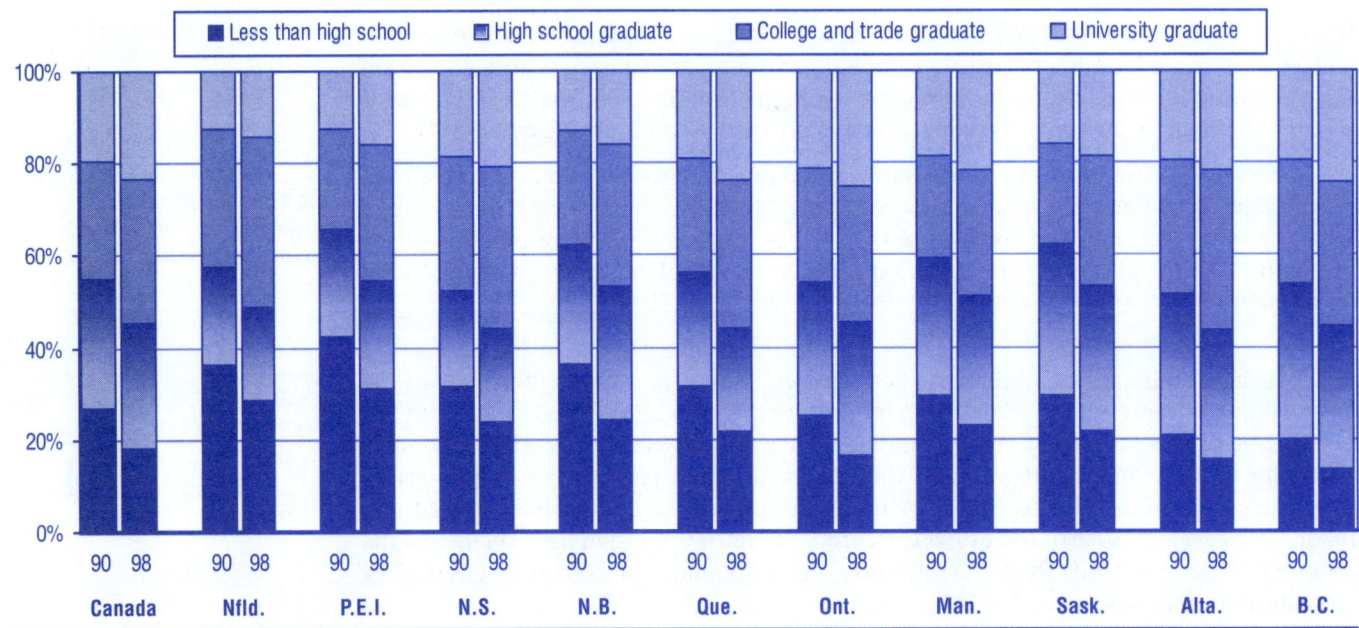

Note: 1 High school graduate includes individuals that have some postsecondary education (not completed).
*Source: Labour Force Survey, Statistics Canada.*

FIGURE 2.9   DISTRIBUTION OF THE FEMALE POPULATION AGED 25 TO 54, BY HIGHEST COMPLETED LEVEL OF EDUCATION, CANADA AND PROVINCES, 1990 AND 1998

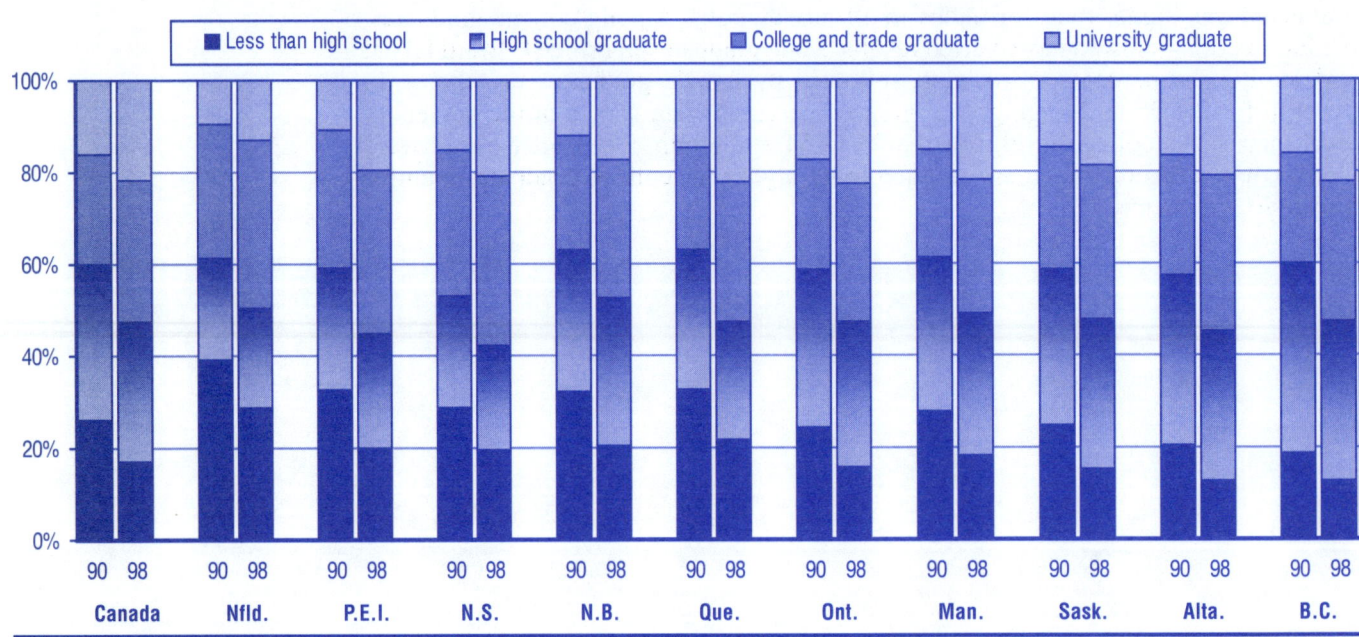

Note: 1 High school graduate includes individuals that have some postsecondary education (not completed).
*Source: Labour Force Survey, Statistics Canada.*

THE CONTEXT OF EDUCATION

FIGURE 2.10   DISTRIBUTION OF THE MALE POPULATION AGED 25 TO 29, BY HIGHEST COMPLETED LEVEL OF EDUCATION, CANADA AND PROVINCES, 1990 AND 1998

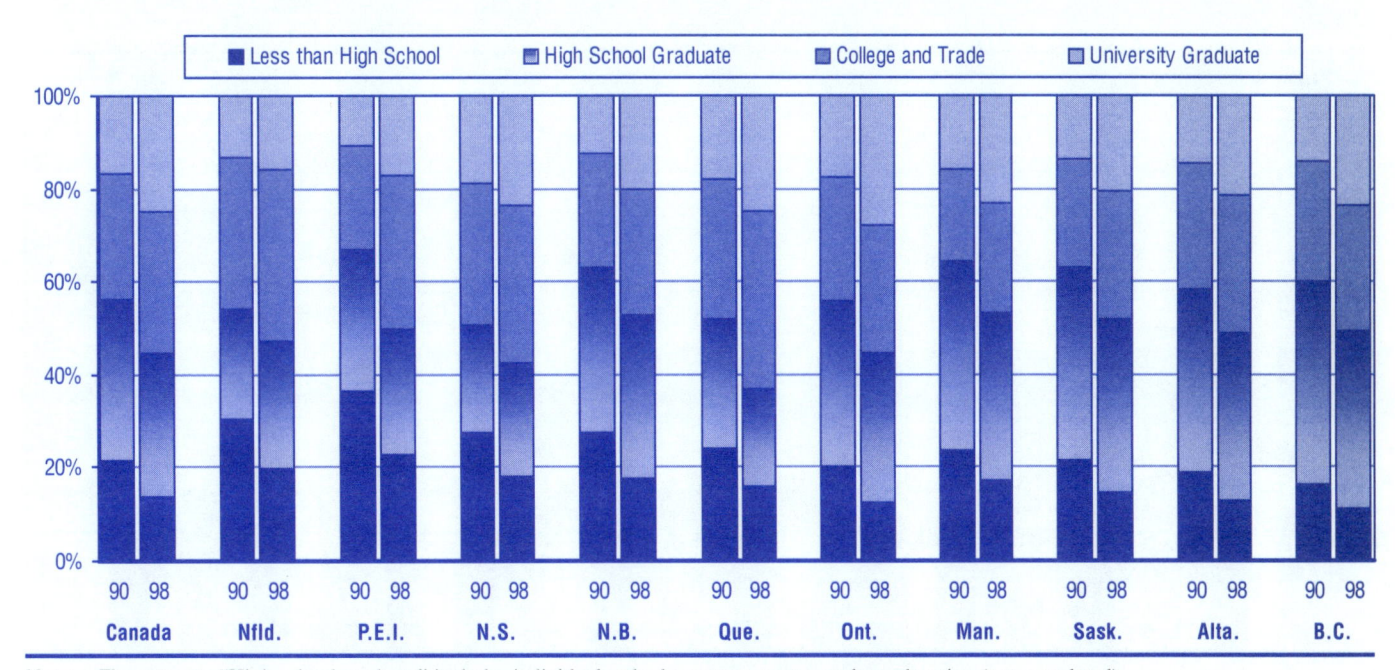

■ Less than High School    ▣ High School Graduate    ▣ College and Trade    ▣ University Graduate

Note:  The category "High school graduate" includes individuals who have some postsecondary education (not completed).
*Source:* Labour Force Survey, Statistics Canada.

FIGURE 2.11   DISTRIBUTION OF THE FEMALE POPULATION AGED 25 TO 29, BY HIGHEST COMPLETED LEVEL OF EDUCATION, CANADA AND PROVINCES, 1990 AND 1998

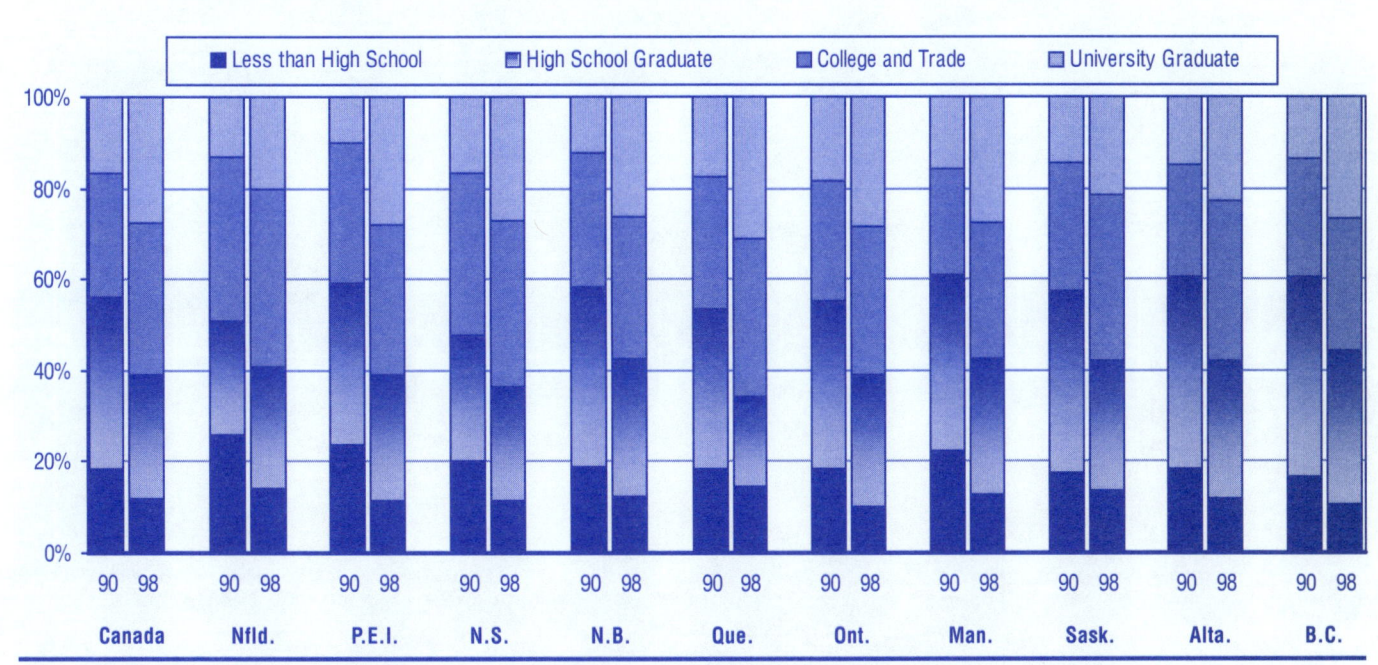

■ Less than High School    ▣ High School Graduate    ▣ College and Trade    ▣ University Graduate

Note:  The category "High school graduate" includes individuals who have some postsecondary education (not completed).
*Source:* Labour Force Survey, Statistics Canada.

Education Indicators in Canada

FIGURE 2.12  PERCENTAGE OF THE POPULATION AGED 25 TO 64 THAT HAS COMPLETED POSTSECONDARY EDUCATION, OECD COUNTRIES, 1996

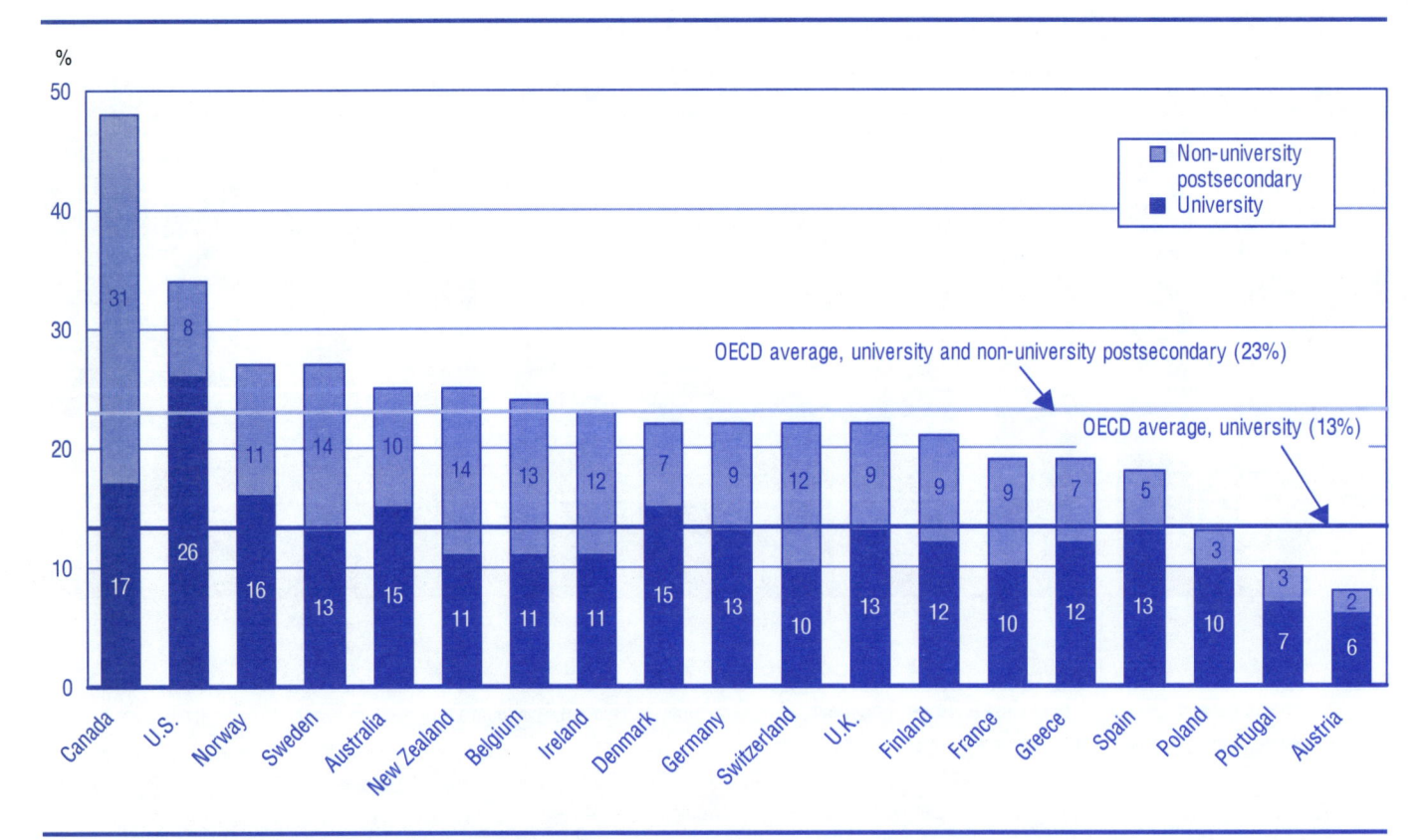

| Country | University | Non-university postsecondary |
|---|---|---|
| Canada | 17 | 31 |
| U.S. | 26 | 8 |
| Norway | 16 | 11 |
| Sweden | 13 | 14 |
| Australia | 15 | 10 |
| New Zealand | 11 | 14 |
| Belgium | 11 | 13 |
| Ireland | 11 | 12 |
| Denmark | 15 | 7 |
| Germany | 13 | 9 |
| Switzerland | 10 | 12 |
| U.K. | 13 | 9 |
| Finland | 12 | 9 |
| France | 10 | 9 |
| Greece | 12 | 7 |
| Spain | 13 | 5 |
| Poland | 10 | 3 |
| Portugal | 7 | 3 |
| Austria | 6 | 2 |

OECD average, university and non-university postsecondary (23%)
OECD average, university (13%)

Notes: The following OECD countries did not provide data for non-university postsecondary completions and are therefore not included in this figure: Czech Republic, Hungary, Italy, Korea, Luxembourg, Netherlands, and Turkey.

International comparisons need to be made with care because of the effect differences in definitions can have on the results reported.

Source: Education at a Glance: OECD Indicators *1998*, Table A1.1.

# CHAPTER 3

## CHARACTERISTICS AND FEATURES OF EDUCATION SYSTEMS

- Schools and postsecondary institutions
- Educators
- Participation in formal education
- Job-related adult education
- Education finances
- Information and communications technologies in schools

## HIGHLIGHTS

- In 1996-97, there were approximately 16,000 elementary and secondary schools in Canada. More than 95% of these had less than 1,000 students. Of Canada's 204 colleges, 90% had a full-time enrolment of 5,000 or less. Of its 76 universities, one-third had enrolments of 10,000 or more.

- As a group, educators tend to be older than the rest of the work force. Over each of the next two decades, a larger number of educators will be retiring than entered the occupation in the last decade. This will create an increased demand for educators to replace those leaving the profession. Replacing retiring faculty may become a particularly important issue for universities, where a sizeable percentage of teaching staff is nearing retirement age.

- The pupil–educator ratio in elementary–secondary education in Canada and most of its jurisdictions decreased from 1986-87 until 1991-92 and then began to climb again, returning to 1986-87 levels by 1996-97. Since this ratio is influenced by shifts in enrolment, educator attrition and hiring rates, it is important to examine these trends when interpreting these data.

- Over the past decade, enrolment at all levels of education has increased and has generally outpaced population growth. In the mid-1990s, however, university participation has levelled off.

- In 1997, approximately 27% of the population between the ages of 25 and 54 participated in some form of job-related adult education and training. In Canada, the rate of participation in job-related training in 1994-95 was about average among the ten countries reported by the OECD, but well below that of the United States.

- In recent years, as governments in Canada have moved to reduce deficits, per capita expenditures on education have generally fallen. Overall per capita spending on education in Canada decreased 7% between 1994-95 and 1998-99—from $2,147 to $1,996. Over this period, expenditure on education fell by an estimated $1.9 billion (in constant 1998 dollars), which represents a 3% reduction.

- Comparative international data on education expenditures show that, in 1995, among G-7 countries, Canada had the second highest per student expenditure, below only that of the United States. The higher expenditure of Canada and the United States partly stems from their high rates of participation in postsecondary education. Since per student costs are higher at this level, the large proportion of postsecondary students in these countries raises their overall per student costs. It is worth noting that the comparative international data used here pre-date the recent decrease in education spending in Canada.

- In 1995, spending on education as a percentage of public expenditures ranged from 9.7% in Nova Scotia to 16.9% in Newfoundland and Labrador. The percentage of public spending devoted to education was below the OECD average in six of the 12 jurisdictions in Canada.

- Over the past ten years, debt levels among postsecondary students and recent graduates have risen substantially. While the percentage of graduates who relied on government student loan programs to help finance their education has remained just under 50%, those who do borrow are accumulating larger debt loads, and are paying them off over a longer period. In 1997, two years after graduation, those with loans owed on average $8,300—more than twice the amount of nine years earlier.

- Canada's education systems are making considerable strides in equipping elementary–secondary schools with computers. In January 1999, there was one computer for every nine elementary students, compared with one for every eight lower secondary students, and one for every seven upper secondary students. In January 1999, elementary schools representing 88% of enrolments, secondary schools representing 97% of enrolments were connected to the Internet for educational purposes. The majority of elementary and secondary students had used e-mail and had retrieved information from the World Wide Web for learning purposes. School principals identified the following obstacles to more fully achieving school computer-related goals: an insufficient number of computers; lack of time for teachers to prepare lessons using computers for learning purposes; and insufficient training opportunities for teachers to develop skills in using computers for learning purposes.

## 3.1 Schools and postsecondary institutions

### Policy context

Since elementary–secondary education is compulsory in all jurisdictions at least up to the age of 16, the capacity of the elementary–secondary school system in each jurisdiction, and in turn the number of schools is largely dependent on the size of the school-aged population. Schools open and close over time and this varies by jurisdiction. Comparing overall counts of schools by jurisdiction at different time points reveals only the net change, and does not reveal the extent to which schools are closed and new schools are opened within jurisdictions to replace obsolete facilities and to accommodate population shifts.

With declines in the youth population projected for many jurisdictions (see section 2.1), or areas within jurisdictions, some school districts will find themselves with schools that are not filled to capacity. Given fiscal constraints, school districts will need to plan carefully for anticipated growth and shrinkage in the student base and come up with alternative uses for underutilized or empty schools.

At the postsecondary level, the number and size of educational institutions (and consequently the programs and courses offered) are more a reflection of demand. Postsecondary institutions must remain attentive to student and labour market demands, not only in the type of courses and programs offered, but also in how they are delivered. With advances in technology, such as the Internet, video-conferencing and other forms of electronic communication, long-distance and correspondence education may continue to increase in importance.

### Findings

### Canada

In 1996-97, there were approximately 16,000 elementary and secondary schools in Canada, representing only a slight increase from 1995-96. More than 95% of these schools had an enrolment of less than 1,000 students.

In 1996-97, Canada had 204 colleges and most of these (90%) had an enrolment of less than 5,000 students.

Universities generally tend to be larger than other educational institutions. Of the 76 universities in Canada in 1996-97, only 43 had an enrolment of less than 5,000 students. Twenty-five universities had more than 10,000 full-time students, compared with only three colleges. At the other end of the spectrum, about 20% of universities and degree-granting institutions were small, with enrolments of less than 300 students. These institutions tend to specialize in one discipline, the most common being theology.

*Tables 3.1 and 3.2 show the number and distribution of educational institutions by size of full-time enrolment. Appendix 2 provides a list of colleges and universities.*

*Most colleges had less than 5,000 full-time students . . .*

*. . . and one-third of universities had more than 10,000 full-time students.*

### Jurisdictions

The relationship between the number of small schools with less than 50 students and the geography and population dispersion within jurisdictions is evident from the higher percentage of small schools found in Newfoundland and Labrador, the Western provinces and the territories. The size of schools and the areas served have an impact on the costs of education delivery as well as the extent to which specialized instruction and services can be offered.

*Smaller schools tend to be found in the more sparsely populated regions of the country.*

**The number and size of universities varies across jurisdictions . . . more but smaller universities are found in Nova Scotia . . . fewer but larger universities are found in Quebec.**

When we examine the number of colleges by jurisdiction, Quebec stands out with 90 colleges—more than double the number in Ontario. This reflects the higher college enrolment in Quebec's CEGEP system, which provides pre-university programs in addition to normal college curricula.

As one might expect, there are more universities in the more populated jurisdictions. Nova Scotia is a notable exception, with the second highest number of universities in Canada after Ontario. When we examine student mobility (section 5.3), we will see that Nova Scotia has one of the highest proportions of out-of-province students compared with other jurisdictions. Universities in Nova Scotia also tend to have smaller enrolments.

In contrast, Quebec has only seven universities—a relatively small number given its population—however, they are large. All but one have enrolments of more than 10,000 students; four have full-time enrolments exceeding 20,000 students. Many of these larger institutions are made up of a number of geographically separated campuses. For example, although the Université de Québec has several campuses throughout the province, it is counted as one institution.

## 3.2 Educators

### Policy context

> *"The importance of the role of the teacher as an agent of change, promoting understanding and tolerance, has never been more obvious than today."* Delors (1996).

The 268,000 full-time elementary and secondary educators, and the more than 60,000 faculty at universities and colleges, constitute the largest single distinctive category of people engaged in professional and technical occupations in Canada. The demographic composition of educators as a group is quite different than that of the work force as a whole with respect to age and gender. As a group, educators are older than the rest of the work force, and there are fewer men than women at the elementary–secondary level, and fewer women than men at postsecondary levels.

**Although retirements will increase the demand for elementary–secondary educators in the years ahead, there appears to be a sufficient supply at the pan-Canadian level.**

A look at the age distribution of the educator work force reveals that large cohorts currently aged 40 to 49 and 50 and over will be reaching retirement age in the next two decades. These older cohorts are considerably larger than the cohort aged 30 to 39, reflecting the recent levels of hiring and retention of educators. Therefore, the future demand for teachers is likely to increase above recent levels in order to replace the large older cohorts as they retire. This will be particularly true as the largest cohort, currently aged 40 to 49, moves into retirement. In a recent study of educator supply and demand, Tremblay (1997) concluded that at a pan-Canadian level the supply of educators is likely to be sufficient to replace those retiring in the years ahead. Using socio-demographic analysis, future requirements for new teachers were determined according to three scenarios regarding retirement age, namely, retirement at age 55, 60 or 65, assuming that the pupil–educator ratio will remain constant. There remains scope for further research on this topic to examine supply and demand issues by jurisdiction, grade level, and subject matter specialty.

The issue of ageing staff is perhaps most pronounced at the university level. It is already recognized as one of the most important issues currently facing the management of these institutions. The median age for full-time university faculty in 1997-98 was 49 years, up from 46 years a decade before. Professors hired during the rapid expansion period of the 1960s and early 1970s have begun to retire, and will continue to retire in greater numbers over the next ten years.

*There are likely to be large-scale retirements of university faculty in the years ahead, but the supply of replacements is less certain.*

In the last decade, the percentage of female educators has risen at all levels of education. However, women continue to be greatly outnumbered by men among full-time university faculty, accounting for 20% of faculty in 1996-97. In contrast, at the elementary–secondary level, over the past ten years, women have been making up a growing majority of educators—more than 60% in 1996-97. As well, work force demographics show that a significant percentage of male educators will be retiring over the next decade; if current patterns continue there will be fewer males in the younger cohorts replacing them.

*Women comprise an increasing majority of elementary and secondary educators, and men comprise a decreasing majority of university faculty.*

The overall increase in part-time employment experienced in the Canadian labour market during the 1990s has been paralleled by a rise in part-time employment among educators. There are many reasons, both economic and social, for the increase in part-time employment in this sector. While section 5.1 examines involuntary part-time employment issues for the entire work force, further research would be helpful to identify factors that influence this trend among educators.

There is a gender gap in earnings in the Canadian economy. Among full-time, full-year workers, the female-to-male earnings ratio in 1997-98 was 72.5%. In the work force as a whole, there was an earnings gap at all levels of education; for example, among university graduates, the female-to-male earnings ratio was 73.6% (Statistics Canada 1999). In this section we examine the extent to which there is an earnings gap among educators at the university level. Given that comparative pan-Canadian data for educators at other levels is not available, this is an area where further research is needed to determine if there is an earnings gap, and if so, how big it is, and to explore the implications for education systems.

The pupil–educator ratio is a measure that is affected by the trends in both enrolments and the number of educators. Demographic changes (and the resulting enrolment shifts), educator attrition rates, and the hiring of new educators all affect this ratio. Jurisdictional policy can also have an impact. Policy makers and educators must strive to find a desirable ratio that balances fiscal constraints and teacher workload in order to create an effective learning environment for students.

## FINDINGS

### A.  GENDER DISTRIBUTION

#### CANADA

The number of public full-time elementary–secondary educators in Canada has been falling, after peaking at approximately 285,000 in 1991-92. Much of this decline is seen in the drop in the number of male educators. By 1996-97, only 37% of educators were male, down from 43% a decade earlier.

While the proportion of female staff has been growing in recent years at all levels, women are in the majority only at the elementary–secondary level, accounting for 63% of full-time educators in 1996-97. In universities, women comprised 25% of full-time faculty in 1997-98, up from 17% in 1987-88. Women comprised 40% of full-time college teaching staff in 1996-97, up from 33% a decade earlier.

EDUCATION INDICATORS IN CANADA

Over the ten-year period in question, the number of full-time university faculty fell slightly, with a drop of 3,300 (11%) in the number of male faculty, and an increase of 2,600 (43%) in female faculty. Among colleges, the number of educators grew by 8,700 (42%), with increases in both male and female educators.

Tables 3.3 to 3.6 and Figures 3.1 to 3.3 show the number and percentage of full-time educators by gender for public elementary–secondary schools, community colleges, and universities.

FIGURE 3.1   NUMBER OF FULL-TIME EDUCATORS IN PUBLIC ELEMENTARY–SECONDARY SCHOOLS IN CANADA, 1986-87 TO 1996-97

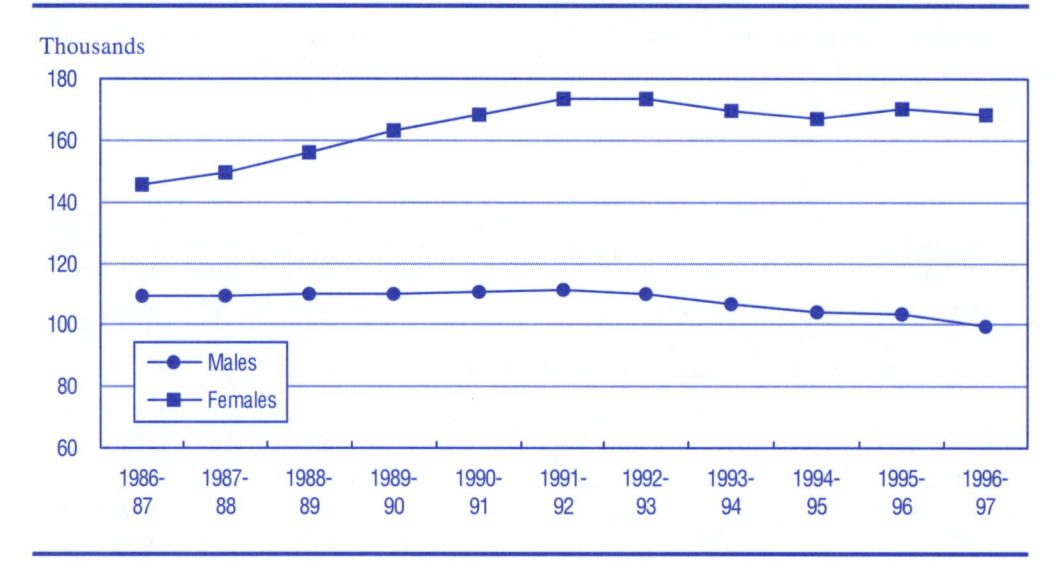

*Source:* Centre for Education Statistics, Statistics Canada; Statistiques de l'éducation - Enseignement primaire, secondaire, collégial et universitaire, *Gouvernement du Québec, Ministère de l'Éducation (for Quebec data).*

FIGURE 3.2   PERCENTAGE OF WOMEN AMONG FULL-TIME COMMUNITY COLLEGE EDUCATORS, CANADA AND JURISDICTIONS, 1986-87 AND 1996-97

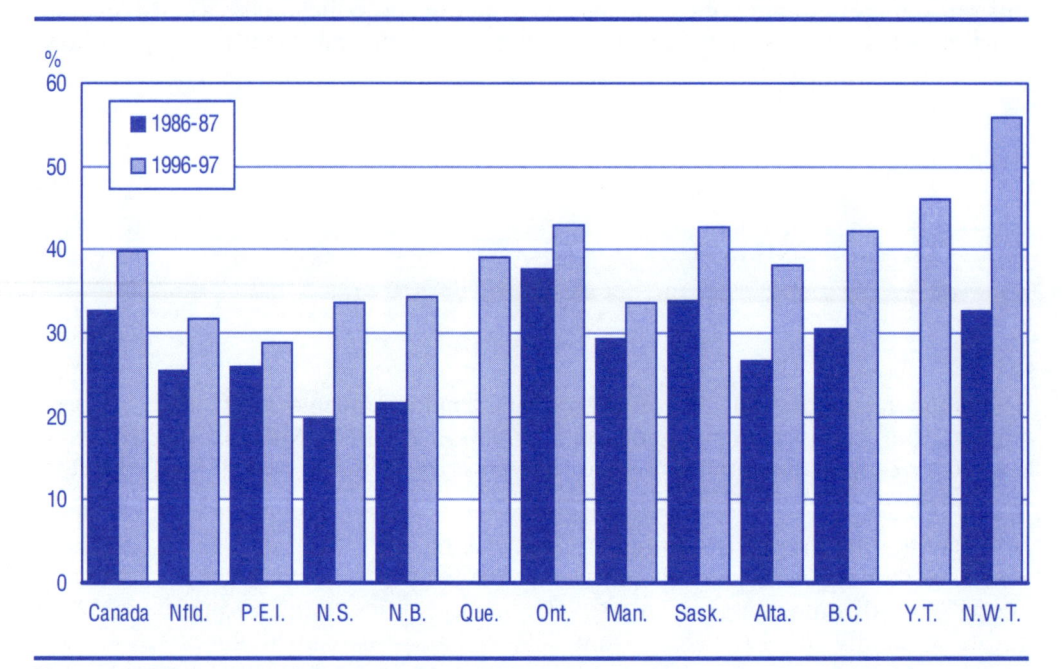

Note:    1986-87 data not available for Quebec and Yukon.
*Source:* Centre for Education Statistics, Statistics Canada.

CHARACTERISTICS AND FEATURES OF EDUCATION SYSTEMS

FIGURE 3.3   PERCENTAGE OF WOMEN AMONG FULL-TIME UNIVERSITY FACULTY BY RANK, CANADA AND PROVINCES, 1987-88 AND 1997-98

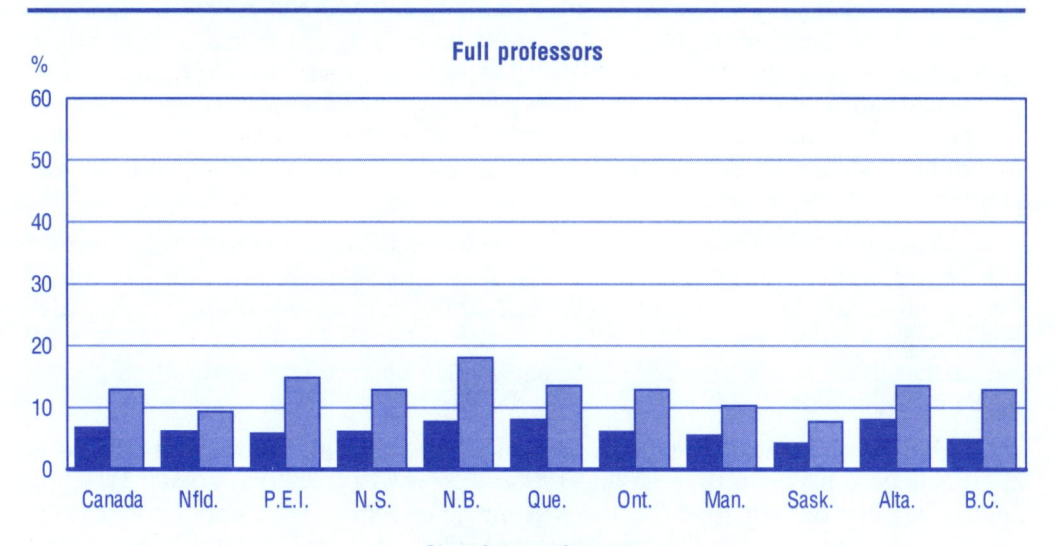

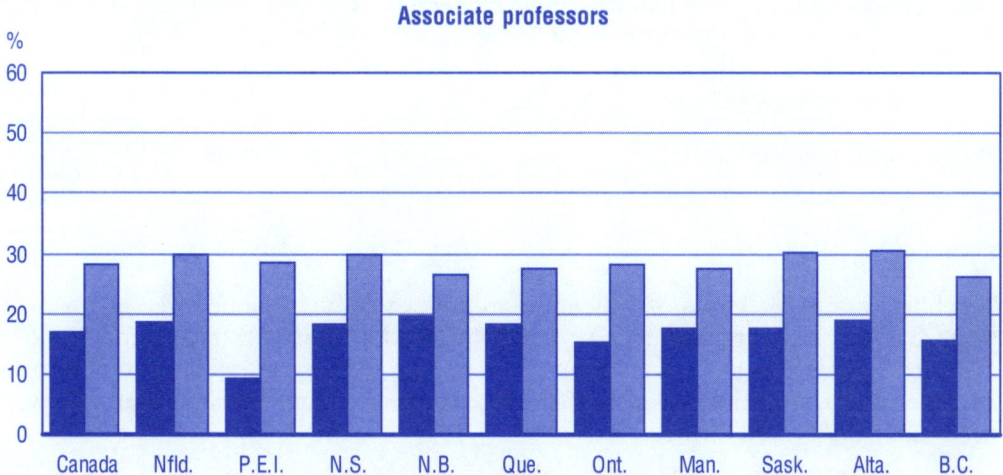

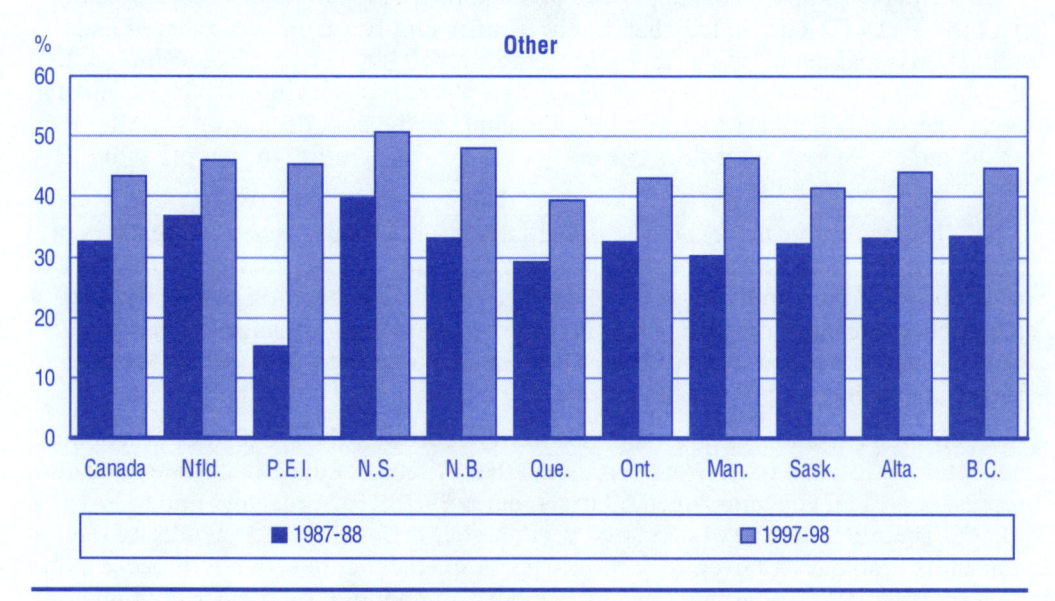

**Full professors**

**Associate professors**

**Other**

■ 1987-88    ■ 1997-98

Source:   Centre for Education Statistics, Statistics Canada.

## JURISDICTIONS

A decline in the number of public elementary–secondary educators from 1986-87 to 1996-97 occurred in Newfoundland and Labrador, Nova Scotia, Quebec, Manitoba, and Saskatchewan. The number remained stable in New Brunswick, while Prince Edward Island, Ontario, Alberta and British Columbia, experienced a slight increase. Yukon and Northwest Territories had larger percentage increases. By 1996-97, females comprised more than 55% of public teaching staff in Newfoundland and Labrador, Manitoba, and British Columbia, and 60% or more in the remaining jurisdictions (Table 3.3).

At the postsecondary level, trends reflect the national picture with little variation among jurisdictions. All jurisdictions experienced an increase in the proportion of female university staff between 1987-88 and 1997-98; in most jurisdictions, females represented approximately 25% of university full-time faculty in 1997-98, with Saskatchewan somewhat lower at 21% and Prince Edward Island slightly higher at 32% (Table 3.6).

At the college level, the proportion of female teaching staff also increased in all jurisdictions between 1986-87 and 1996-97; however, there was greater variation among jurisdictions. In 1996-97, the percentage of female educators exceeded the pan-Canadian average in Ontario, Saskatchewan, British Columbia, Yukon and Northwest Territories. The Northwest Territories was the only jurisdiction in which women accounted for the majority (56%) of educators at the college level.

## B. AGE DISTRIBUTION

### CANADA

Teaching staff at all levels of education are older than the labour force as a whole (Figure 3.4). Over the next decade, the field of education will have a much more significant replacement demand than other sectors, just to maintain current pupil–educator ratios. Additional demand from areas experiencing enrolment growth will necessitate even more hiring.

In his examination of supply and demand for elementary–secondary educators, Tremblay (1997) concluded that, if the future supply of university graduates in education is maintained at its current level of about 20,000 per year (see section 4.2B), the supply of educators would be sufficient to replace those retiring. At a pan-Canadian level, the supply is likely to exceed the demand for the next decade or so. After this, as the larger group of educators currently in their forties retire, the supply will likely be adequate to meet the demand.

There is scope, however, for research that explores these issues in greater depth. There is a particular need for research that examines the sensitivity of findings to assumptions about the average age of retirement and extends the analysis to a jurisdictional level where differences in patterns of population change (see section 2.1) might lead to different conclusions. There is also a need to consider differences in supply and demand by level and specialty.

*In elementary–secondary education, male educators are older and are retiring at a faster rate than they are being replaced.*

Moreover, among elementary–secondary educators, the age distribution of male educators reflects an older work force than that of female educators. Male educators represent 46% of educators aged 50 to 59, but only 28% of educators under 30 years of age. Their median age of 46 is two years higher than the median gender of female educators (Table 3.7). Given the retirements of the older cohort that will occur in the next ten years, if current rates of recruitment and retention by gender continue, the percentage of male educators will continue to fall over the next decade.

### CHARACTERISTICS AND FEATURES OF EDUCATION SYSTEMS

Teachers at the university level are somewhat older than at other levels of education; 50- to 59-year-olds comprised 38% of university teaching staff compared with 37% of college teachers and 28% of elementary–secondary staff. In contrast, the proportion of teaching staff under 40 years of age is 18%, 17% and 30%, for the university, college and elementary–secondary levels, respectively.

FIGURE 3.4  AGE DISTRIBUTION OF EDUCATORS BY LEVEL OF EDUCATION VERSUS THAT OF THE OVERALL LABOUR FORCE, CANADA, 1996

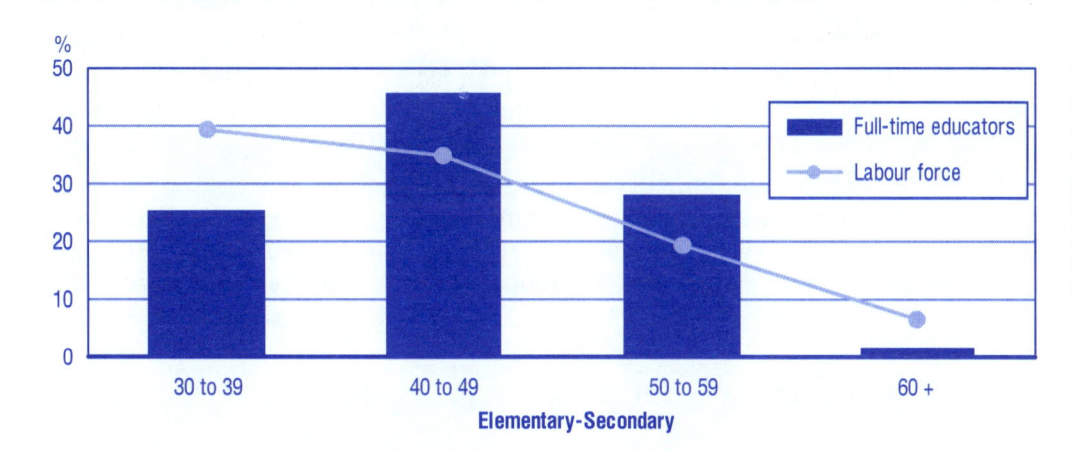

Tables 3.7 to 3.9 show the number and distribution of educators by gender and age in 1996, for public elementary–secondary schools, colleges and universities. Figure 3.4 compares the age distribution of educators to that of the work force as a whole.

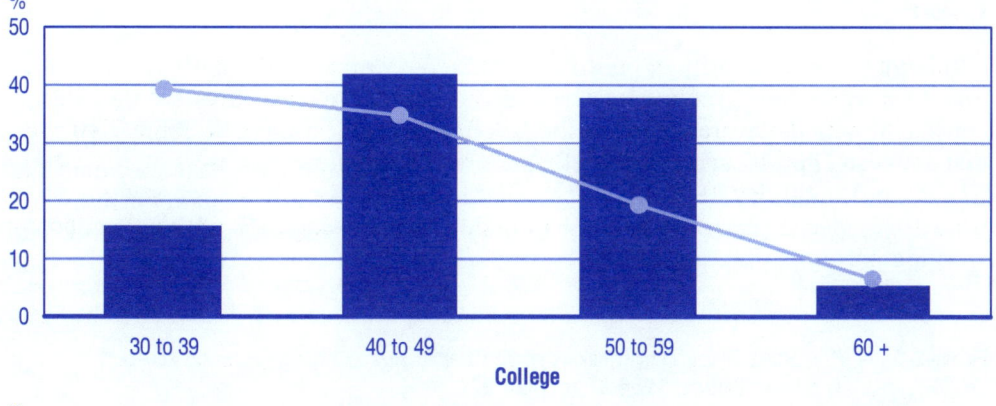

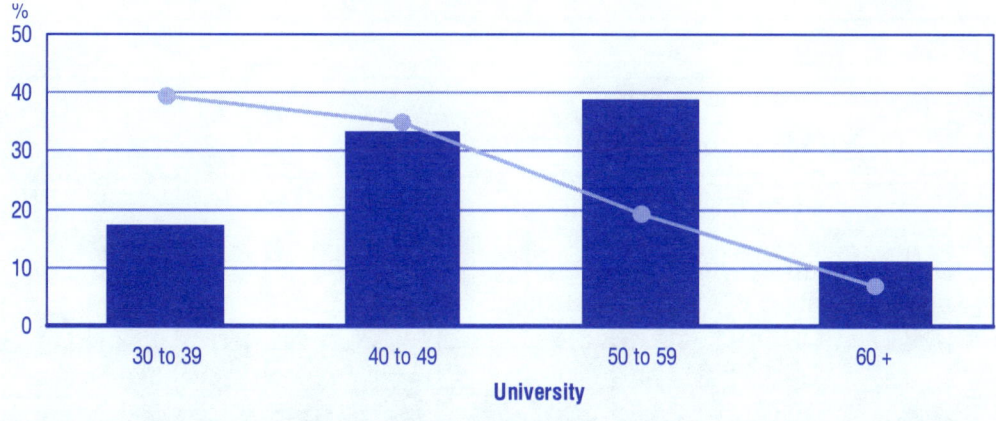

Note: Age distributions of educators and labour force are calculated as a percentage of the educator and labour force populations aged 30 and over.

Source: *Centre for Education Statistics, Statistics Canada; Statistiques de l'éducation - Enseignement primaire, secondaire, collégial et universitaire, Gouvernement du Québec, Ministère de l'Éducation (for Quebec data); Labour Force Survey, Statistics Canada.*

EDUCATION INDICATORS IN CANADA

**The age distribution of elementary–secondary educators varies across jurisdictions.**

## JURISDICTIONS

In general, while the same trends are found throughout all jurisdictions at all levels of education, there are some variations. The Northwest Territories has a significantly higher number of young educators compared with other jurisdictions. A total of 22% of teaching staff are between 20 and 29 years of age and a further 37% are between 30 and 39 years of age. Elementary–secondary educators are also slightly younger in Prince Edward Island, Saskatchewan, and Alberta—the only other jurisdictions where more than 10% of educators are aged 20 to 29. In contrast, Quebec, Ontario, Manitoba, Alberta, British Columbia, and Yukon are jurisdictions in which 25% or more of teaching staff are between the ages of 50 and 59 years of age. In Yukon, although the numbers are small, 24% of educators are 60 years of age or older (Table 3.7).

At the college level, the age distribution of teaching staff in 1996-97 was more consistent across jurisdictions, with the majority of staff between the ages of 40 and 59 years in all jurisdictions.

Finally, when examining university faculty, trends are also consistent among provinces. In general, faculty are older compared with those at other levels of education. Jurisdictions in which 40% or more of faculty are between the ages of 50 and 59 years include Newfoundland and Labrador, Nova Scotia, New Brunswick, and Manitoba.

### C. EMPLOYMENT STATUS OF ELEMENTARY–SECONDARY EDUCATORS

#### CANADA

Although the vast majority of public elementary–secondary educators work on a full-time basis, part-time employment has become more prevalent over the past decade, consistent with the overall trend in the labour market (section 5.1). Table 3.10 shows that between 1986-87 and 1996-97, the number of part-time educators increased from 27,200 to 55,300. By 1996-97, 17% of educators held part-time appointments, up from 10% a decade earlier, with 10% of male educators and 21% of female educators working part time (Table 3.11 and Figure 3.5).

FIGURE 3.5    PERCENTAGE OF EDUCATORS WORKING PART TIME IN PUBLIC ELEMENTARY–SECONDARY SCHOOLS, BY GENDER, CANADA, 1986-87 TO 1996-97

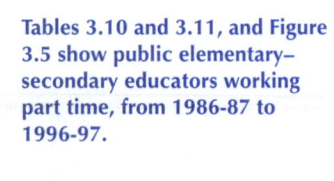

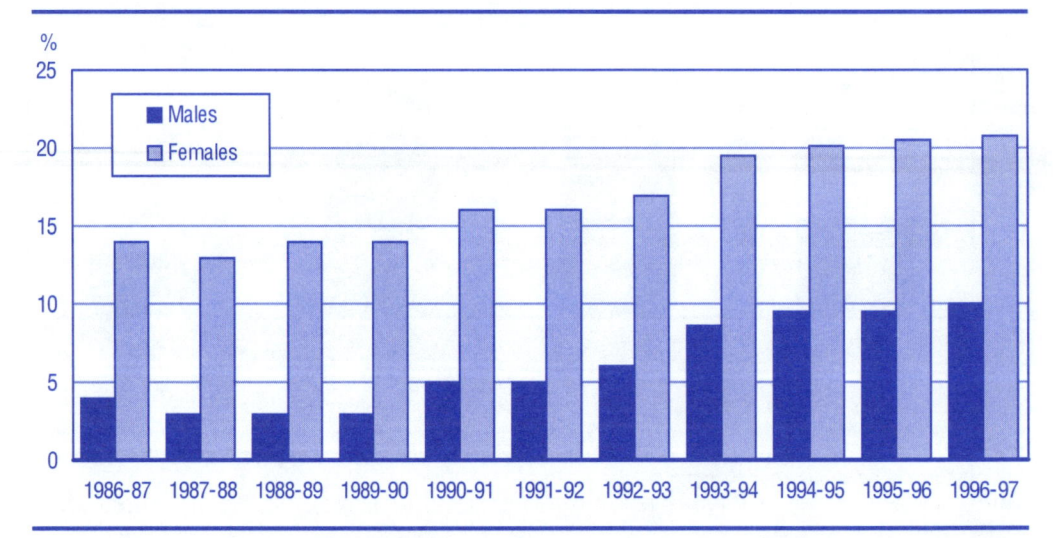

Tables 3.10 and 3.11, and Figure 3.5 show public elementary–secondary educators working part time, from 1986-87 to 1996-97.

Source: Centre for Education Statistics, Statistics Canada; Statistiques de l'éducation - Enseignement primaire, secondaire, collégial et universitaire, Gouvernement du Québec, Ministère de l'Éducation (for Quebec data).

## Jurisdictions

Trends in part-time employment were similar in most jurisdictions, with higher percentages of female educators working part time than males, and growth in part-time work over the last decade among both genders.

In Quebec and British Columbia, over the ten-year period, the rate of female part-time employment was somewhat higher than in other jurisdictions, at 28% in 1996-97.

## D. Salaries

### Canada

Between 1987-88 and 1997-98, average salaries (in constant 1997 dollars) of full-time university faculty rose 1.6% to $77,737 for male faculty, and rose 4.1% to $65,994 for female faculty.

Over the period, the gender gap in earnings narrowed slightly. Salaries of female faculty were 85% of those of males in 1997-98, up from 83% a decade earlier. Two-thirds of the earnings gap is a reflection of fewer women at higher professor and associate professor ranks at both time periods, despite some improvement in the representation of women in these positions over the period. Within ranks, the female-to-male earnings ratio varied from 94% to 96% in 1997-98. Some of these differences may be explained by the overrepresentation of females among new hires and new promotions. For further information on the wage gap by gender among university faculty see Ornstein (1998).

*Table 3.12 shows the average salaries (in constant 1997 dollars) of university faculty by rank and gender, for 1987-88 and 1997-98.*

*The gender gap in earnings within ranks has decreased.*

### Jurisdictions

Generally, the earnings gap by gender in jurisdictions mirrored the pan-Canadian situation, with some small differences. At the university level, there was only a minor variation in the salary gap across jurisdictions. In 1997-98, the gender gap was slightly larger in Manitoba, Saskatchewan, and Alberta than the pan-Canadian average.

## E. Pupil–educator ratio in elementary–secondary schools

### Canada

The pupil–educator ratio in elementary-secondary schools in Canada decreased from 1986-87 until 1991-92 then began to climb again. By 1996-97, it had returned to about the same level as in 1986-87.

### Jurisdictions

A similar pattern emerges in most jurisdictions, where a decline in the ratio from 1986-87 until the early 1990s has been offset by an increase since then. Newfoundland and Labrador, Yukon, and Northwest Territories are exceptions. The pupil–educator ratio continued to decline in Newfoundland and Labrador, down to 14.4 in 1996-97 from 16.5 in 1986-87. Newfoundland and Labrador experienced a decline in both full-time equivalent (FTE) enrolments and FTE educators during that period. The percentage decline in enrolments was larger, which led to lower pupil–educator ratios.

In contrast, Yukon and Northwest Territories have experienced lower pupil–educator ratios primarily as a result of an increasing number of educators coming into the system, outpacing the rate of growth in enrolments. The number of FTE educators increased in Yukon by 60% and in Northwest Territories by 94% during the period of analysis, while enrolments increased 33% and 36% respectively.

EDUCATION INDICATORS IN CANADA

FIGURE 3.6    PUPIL–EDUCATOR RATIO IN PUBLIC ELEMENTARY–SECONDARY SCHOOLS, CANADA AND JURISDICTIONS, 1986-87 TO 1996-97

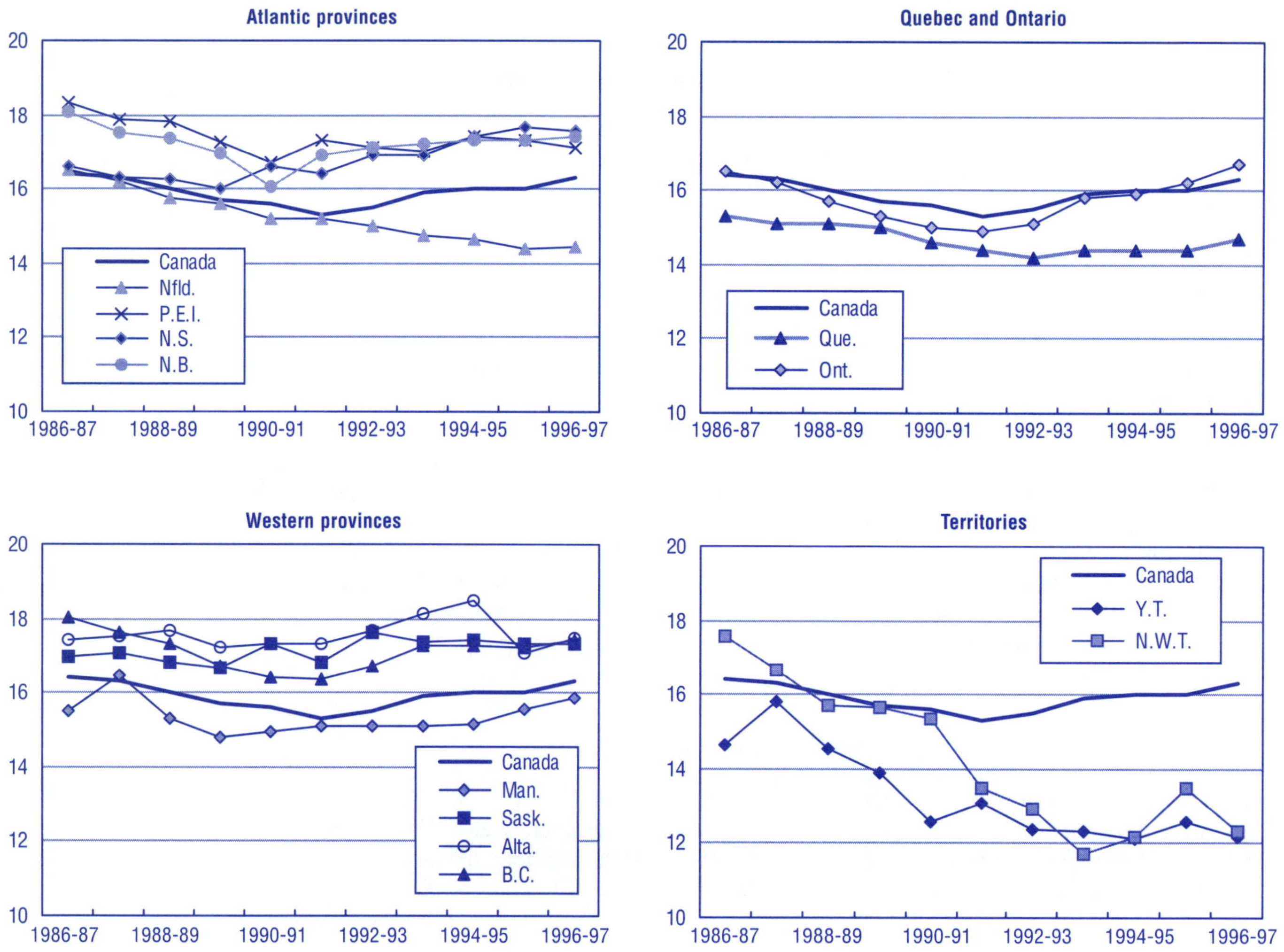

Source:  Centre for Education Statistics, Statistics Canada; Statistiques de l'éducation - Enseignement primaire, secondaire, collégial et universitaire, Gouvernement du Québec, Ministère de l'Éducation (for Quebec data).

Table 3.13 and Figure 3.6 show the pupil–educator ratio for public elementary–secondary education between 1986-87 and 1996-97.

## 3.3 PARTICIPATION IN FORMAL EDUCATION

### A.    PARTICIPATION IN EDUCATION BY YOUNG CHILDREN

#### POLICY CONTEXT

Data are presented on the extent to which 3- to 5-year-olds participate in the formal education system (Table 3.14).

The role of pre-elementary education is an issue of emerging importance in research. For example, "school readiness" is an important component of Cycle Four of the National Longitudinal Survey of Children and Youth (NLSCY) to be conducted in 2001. Pre-elementary education forms an important component of the lifelong learning policy framework recently adopted by the OECD.

Research has shown advantages for children who participate in some form of education at an early age, although some studies have concluded that a rich home environment may also play as significant a role (for example, see Browne 1996).

## FINDINGS

### CANADA

Despite policy differences between jurisdictions, between one-third and one-half of all 3- to 5-year-olds were attending a pre-elementary program in most jurisdictions over the period examined (Table 3.14).

Between 1986-87 and 1996-97 the enrolment rate for pre-elementary education increased by 3 percentage points, from 38.8% to 41.6%.

### JURISDICTIONS

Table 3.14 shows that, in 1996-97, enrolment rates were similar in most jurisdictions, at between 31% and 39%. Most jurisdictions experienced less than a 5% fluctuation throughout the decade shown, except for New Brunswick, which introduced public pre-elementary education in 1991-92. Prince Edward Island does not provide public pre-elementary education in its school system. In 1996-97, Ontario and Quebec provided two years of public pre-elementary education, while Saskatchewan provided three years. (See Appendix 1 for more detailed information on education systems in Canada.)

## B. ELEMENTARY–SECONDARY ENROLMENT

### POLICY CONTEXT

Enrolment figures at the elementary–secondary level tend to reflect demographic trends because of compulsory school attendance requirements, and are affected not only by the birth rate within a jurisdiction, but also by factors such as net in- or out-migration. Some portion of the increased enrolment in British Columbia, Ontario, and Alberta no doubt reflects their popularity as destinations over the past few years, while the declining enrolment in Newfoundland and Labrador reflects the out-migration the province has experienced (see section 2.1 for information on demographic trends and mobility).

Enrolment growth may also indicate a higher incidence of students remaining in school past the age for compulsory schooling. Sections 2.3 (on educational attainment) and 4.2A (on high-school completions), reveal that the number of people with high school completion or a higher level of education is increasing.

*Higher enrolment figures may reflect increases in high school completion.*

Population projections (see section 2.1) suggest that the Atlantic Provinces, Quebec, Manitoba, Saskatchewan, and Yukon are likely to face declines in enrolment. These jurisdictions may experience conflicting pressures both to maintain human and financial resources at present levels and to cut these resources in response to lower enrolment. However, jurisdictions such as Ontario, Alberta, British Columbia, and the Northwest Territories, where growth is projected for the population aged 5 to 24, may feel pressure to provide increased funding, in order to maintain a consistent per-student expenditure as enrolment rises. As was discussed in section 2.1, the movement of individuals and families within a jurisdiction and the concentration of immigration in larger centres, such as Toronto, Vancouver, and Montreal, mean that the effects described here may not apply equally to all regions within a jurisdiction.

*Future predictions of enrolment at this level can be based in part on population projections of increase and decline such as those in section 2.1.*

In 2002-03, Ontario will complete its shift from a five-year to a four-year high school program. In the next year, Ontario will face lower secondary school enrolments, because of this program change.

EDUCATION INDICATORS IN CANADA

## FINDINGS

### CANADA

Elementary–secondary enrolment grew steadily by approximately 1% per year between 1986-87 and 1995-96. In 1996-97, enrolment showed a marginal decrease of 0.3% (Table 3.15 and Figure 3.7).

### JURISDICTIONS

**Enrolment increased or remained stable in all jurisdictions except Newfoundland and Labrador, Nova Scotia, and New Brunswick, where it declined.**

Newfoundland and Labrador, Nova Scotia, and New Brunswick experienced a decline in elementary–secondary enrolment between 1986-87 and 1996-97. The greatest decrease was in Newfoundland and Labrador, which in 1996-97 had only 76% of the students it had in 1986-87. Enrolment was relatively stable in Prince Edward Island, Quebec, Manitoba, and Saskatchewan. Enrolment increased in Ontario, Alberta, British Columbia, and the Territories. In particular, British Columbia, Yukon, and Northwest Territories experienced increases of more than 25%. Despite its overall increase, Ontario experienced a 1.3% decline in 1996-97, because of changes in policy affecting pre-elementary programs (Figure 3.7).

FIGURE 3.7   ELEMENTARY-SECONDARY ENROLMENT INDEX[1], CANADA AND JURISDICTIONS, 1986-87 TO 1996-97[2]

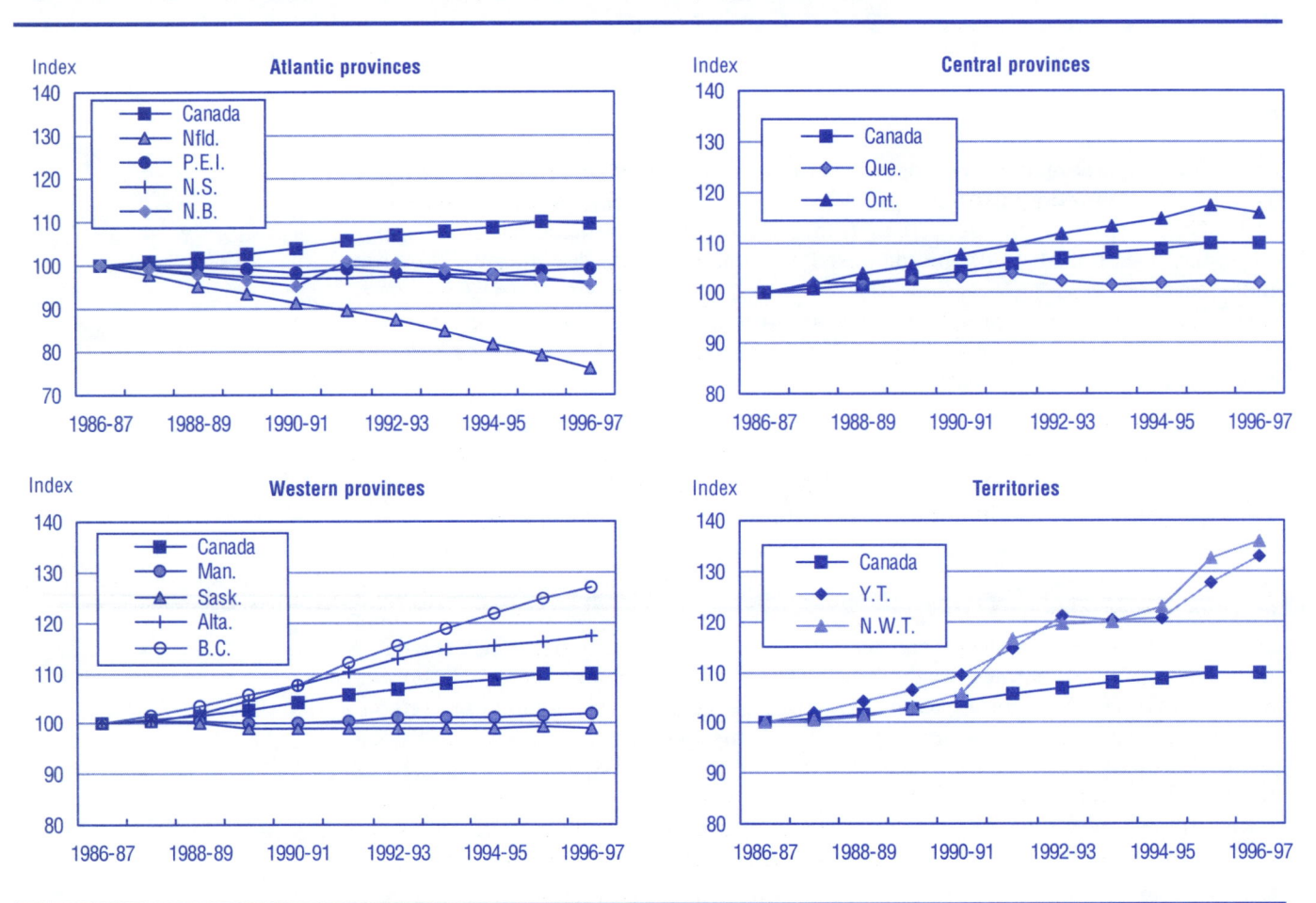

1   Includes students registered in public, private, and federal schools, and schools for the visually and hearing impaired. Coverage includes students registered in pre-primary programs offered by these schools.
2   Indices equal 100 in 1986-87.

Source: Centre for Education Statistics, Statistics Canada; Statistiques de l'éducation - Enseignement primaire, secondaire, collégial et universitaire, Gouvernement du Québec, Ministère de l'Éducation (for Quebec data).

## C. Trade–vocational enrolment

### Policy context

Enrolment in trade–vocational programs, especially in preparatory training such as academic upgrading, language training, job readiness and orientation programs, has historically increased during periods of recession.

Several provinces over the last few years have changed entrance requirements for programs. For example in the Atlantic Provinces, many programs which in 1987-88 did not require graduation from high school and were counted in the trade–vocational enrolments, required high school completion by 1997-98, and hence were included in the college enrolment figure. Such changes need to be kept in mind when comparing changes in trade-vocational and college enrolments over time.

The data presented here do not differentiate between apprenticeship and other trade–vocational programs, and the trends shown are those for all trade–vocational programs. In some jurisdictions, enrolment trends in apprenticeship programs may be different from those for other trade–vocational programs.

The percentage increase in full-time enrolment in New Brunswick (55%) between 1987-88 and 1995-96 likely results from provincial initiatives to improve and upgrade the work force in order to attract businesses and industry (Figure 3.9).

The decline in the percentage of females enrolled in trade–vocational programs (to 33.4% for full-time and 14.4% for part-time) in Newfoundland and Labrador possibly represents an increase in male enrolment during the early and mid-1990s (Figure 3.10). The decline coincides with the introduction of compensation and retraining programs following the restructuring of the fishing industry, and with a dramatic rise in private sector training, which enrolled more men than women.

*Trade–vocational programs include apprenticeship programs and other preparatory training programs. These programs generally do not require high school graduation.*

### Findings

#### Canada

Between 1987-88 and 1995-96, full-time enrolment decreased by 2% while part-time enrolment has increased by 4% in Canada (Figure 3.9). Full-time enrolment has remained fairly stable. After peaking in 1993-94, part-time enrolment declined close to 1987-88 levels (Table 3.16 and Figures 3.8 and 3.9). This pattern can also be seen in part-time enrolment at the college and university levels.

Women accounted for 41% of full-time enrollments in 1995-96, up 3 percentage points from 1987-88 (Figure 3.10).

*Since 1993–94, enrolment has declined.*

#### Jurisdictions

Only New Brunswick, Quebec, and Saskatchewan reported increases in full-time enrolment (Figure 3.9). Nova Scotia and Alberta have experienced significant decreases over the ten-year period. In addition to normal changes in enrolment, recent changes in the classification of some trade-vocational programs in some Atlantic Provinces, now considered as being college programs, may also account for the decrease in trade-vocational enrolment.

In 1995-96, women represented less than 50% of full-time enrolment in all provinces except New Brunswick, Quebec, Saskatchewan, and Alberta. While most provinces reported an increase in the percentage of women among full-time female enrolments between 1987-88 and 1995-96, Newfoundland and Labrador, Ontario and Alberta experienced a decline. Newfoundland and Labrador, experienced the greatest drop, of almost 20 percentage points (Figure 3.10).

In regards to part-time enrolment, Newfoundland and Labrador, New Brunswick, Quebec and British Columbia all experienced increases. Both New Brunswick and Quebec experienced significant increases over the period of analysis (Fig. 3.9) in both full- and part-time enrolment compared to other jurisdictions.

FIGURE 3.8   INDEX OF ENROLMENT IN TRADE-VOCATIONAL PROGRAMS[1] BY REGISTRATION STATUS, CANADA[2], 1987-88 TO 1995-96

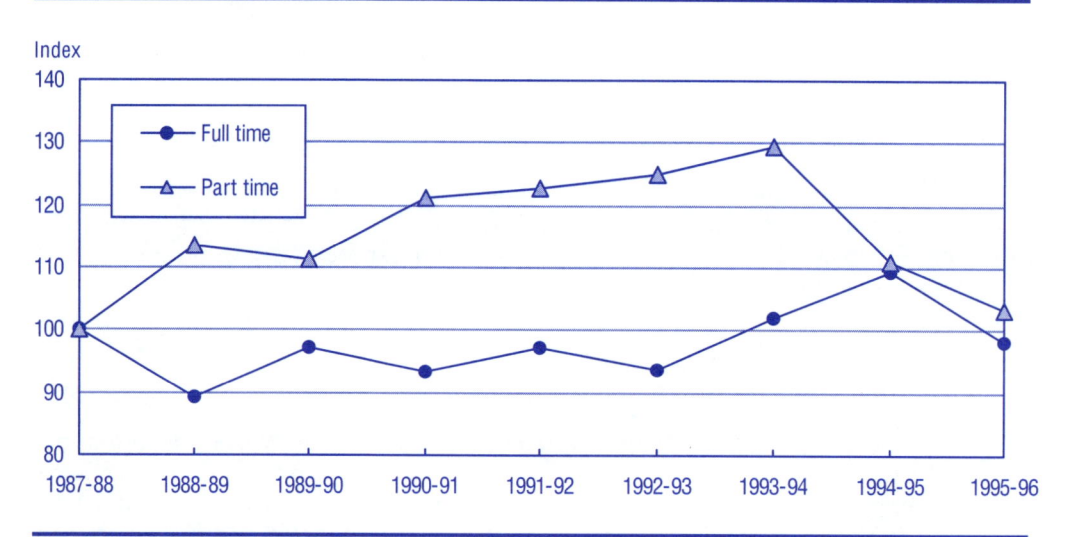

1   Indices equal 100 in 1987-88.
2   Index for part-time enrolment excludes Quebec, as Quebec data were not available in 1987-88.
Source:   Centre for Education Statistics, Statistics Canada; Statistiques de l'éducation - Enseignement primaire, secondaire, collégial et universitaire, Gouvernement du Québec, Ministère de l'Éducation (for Quebec data).

FIGURE 3.9   PERCENTAGE CHANGE IN ENROLMENT IN TRADE-VOCATIONAL PROGRAMS, BY REGISTRATION STATUS, CANADA AND PROVINCES[1], 1987-88 TO 1995-96

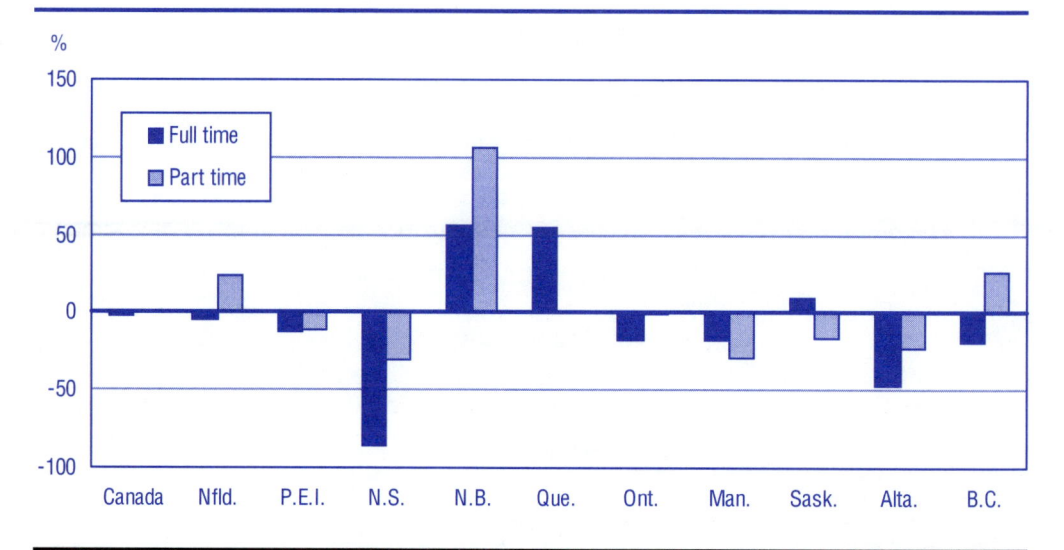

1   Part-time enrolment data not available for Quebec in 1987-88; hence percentage change in part-time enrolment is not available for Quebec and Canada.
Source:   Centre for Education Statistics, Statistics Canada; Statistiques de l'éducation - Enseignement primaire, secondaire, collégial et universitaire, Gouvernement du Québec, Ministère de l'Éducation (for Quebec data).

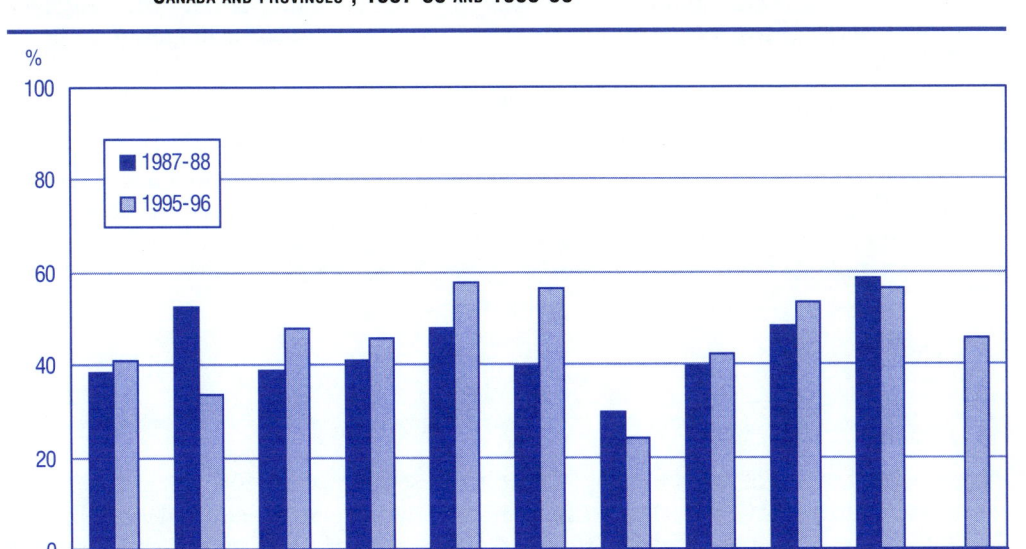

CHARACTERISTICS AND FEATURES OF EDUCATION SYSTEMS

FIGURE 3.10   PERCENTAGE OF WOMEN AMONG FULL-TIME ENROLMENTS IN TRADE-VOCATIONAL PROGRAMS[1], CANADA AND PROVINCES[2], 1987-88 AND 1995-96

1   Percentages are calculated based on reported gender counts.
2   The gender distribution is based on estimates for Ontario in 1995-96, and is not available for British Columbia in 1987-88.
Source:   Centre for Education Statistics, Statistics Canada; Statistiques de l'éducation - Enseignement primaire, secondaire, collégial et universitaire, Gouvernement du Québec, Ministère de l'Éducation (for Quebec data).

## D.   COLLEGE ENROLMENT

### POLICY CONTEXT

The period of economic recession in the early 1990s may have contributed to increased college enrolments, as more people chose to stay in school rather than look for work. The number of college graduates who report that they are working in a field related to their program of study (see section 5.2) suggests that programs designed to provide knowledge and skills that apply directly to the workplace are particularly important in the college setting.

The growing popularity of university transfer programs in British Columbia and Alberta indicates that such programs may provide a useful transition to the university environment for some students.

The decline in the percentage of women enrolled in college programs seen in some jurisdictions may be balanced by an increase in the percentage enrolled in university. This would be consistent with the pattern of rising educational attainment outlined in section 2.3.

Increases in enrolment in jurisdictions with declining populations of 18- to 21-year-olds demonstrate the growing importance of postsecondary education and training in today's society. The growth may reflect both higher participation rates among the 18 to 21 age group and the extension of learning beyond the "normal school age," as a higher proportion of students fall outside that age group. The number of places available limits increases in college enrolment. If the higher participation rate continues, it may produce enrolment pressure in jurisdictions with growing populations, and help offset the effects of declining populations in other jurisdictions.

In 1987-88, in the Atlantic Provinces, many programs that did not require graduation from high school were counted in the trade–vocational enrolments. These

**Data are reported here for two types of college programs: career technical programs, designed primarily to train students for a particular career or skill, and university transfer programs, which allow students to apply to transfer their college academic credits to a university after two years.
These programs are offered at postsecondary community colleges and similar institutions. For a list of colleges, see Appendix 2.**

programs are included in the college enrolment figures for 1997-98, resulting in significant increases when the two sets of figures are compared. The increases may also be explained by the entry into the system of greater numbers of older learners because of setbacks in their economic circumstances, as is the case in Newfoundland and Labrador.

The elimination of the fifth year of high school in Ontario, which will affect students graduating from high school in 2002-03, will be a key concern for postsecondary education planning in Ontario. The change also has potential implications for students across Canada who want to pursue higher education in Ontario, and for the other jurisdictions, which are likely to see an increase in the number of students from Ontario applying to study elsewhere.

## FINDINGS

### CANADA

Figure 3.11 shows that full-time enrolment increased between 1987-88 and 1997-98 except the Northwest Territories, while part-time enrolment rose until 1992-93, and then fell. Figure 3.12 shows that full-time career technical program enrolment increased by approximately 33%.

*Full-time career technical enrolment increased by almost a third. Part-time enrolment rose in the early 1990s, but has since declined.*

The number of full-time students as a proportion of the 18 to 21 age group increased from 19% to 25% between 1987-88 and 1997-98 (Figure 3.13). Students in the 18 to 21 age group continue to account for over half of career technical program enrolments. The percentage of students over 21 rose slightly between 1987-88 and 1997-98.

Female students accounted for more than 50% of both full- and part-time enrolment in both career technical and university transfer programs. The percentage of females enrolled in full- and part-time career technical programs fell slightly between 1987-88 and 1997-98, while female full- and part-time university transfer and university college enrolment rose in the same period (Figure 3.14 and Table 3.17).

### JURISDICTIONS

Enrolment in full-time career technical programs increased in all jurisdictions between 1987-88 and 1997-98. As noted above, increases in enrolment in the Atlantic Provinces may be largely due to changes in program entrance requirements. Outside the Atlantic Provinces, enrolment growth was strongest in Ontario, British Columbia and the Yukon by a substantial margin (Figure 3.12).

As can be seen in Figure 3.13, in 1997-98, the number of full-time college students as a proportion of the 18 to 21 age group was between 10% and 24% in most jurisdictions. The highest proportion was in Quebec (42.1%). This is likely a result of the CEGEP system, where students attend a college before moving on to university. In Manitoba, Saskatchewan, and the Northwest Territories, the number of full-time students as a proportion of the 18 to 21 age group was less than 6% in 1997-98. The Atlantic Provinces showed significant increases. Figure 3.13 only shows full-time enrolment. In jurisdictions such as British Columbia, the Yukon and Northwest Territories, which have more part-time students than full-time students, participation rates for both levels of enrolment combined would be higher. Changes in the size of the population aged 18 to 21 between 1987-88 and 1997-98 also affects the percentage shown.

*Women accounted for over 50% of enrolment*

Female enrolment as a percentage of total full-time career technical program enrolment rose slightly from 1987-88 to 1997-98 in Alberta and British Columbia and increased significantly in Yukon and Northwest Territories, both of which show 66% female enrolment (Figure 3.14). Female enrolment declined in all other jurisdictions, dropping to below 50% in the Atlantic Provinces.

CHARACTERISTICS AND FEATURES OF EDUCATION SYSTEMS

FIGURE 3.11  COLLEGE ENROLMENT[1] INDEX[2] BY REGISTRATION STATUS, AND INDEX OF THE POPULATION AGED 18-21, CANADA, 1987-88 TO 1997-98[e]

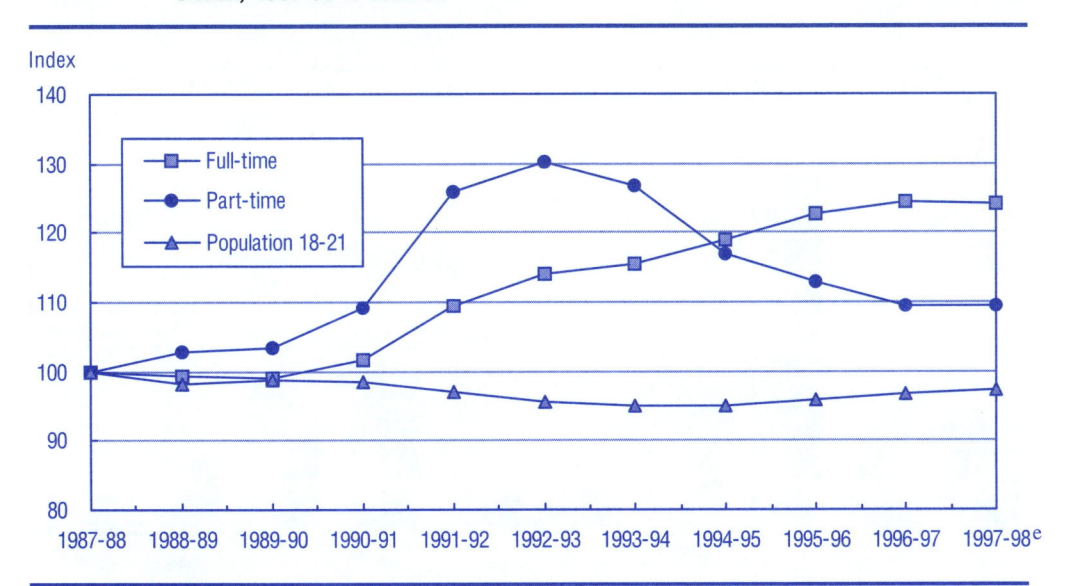

e   Preliminary data for full-time and previous year's data for part-time.
1   Includes career-technical, university transfer and university college.
2   Indices equal 100 in 1987-88.
*Source: Centre for Education Statistics, Statistics Canada.*

FIGURE 3.12  PERCENTAGE CHANGE IN FULL-TIME COLLEGE CAREER TECHNICAL ENROLMENT, CANADA AND JURISDICTIONS, 1987-88 TO 1997-98[p]

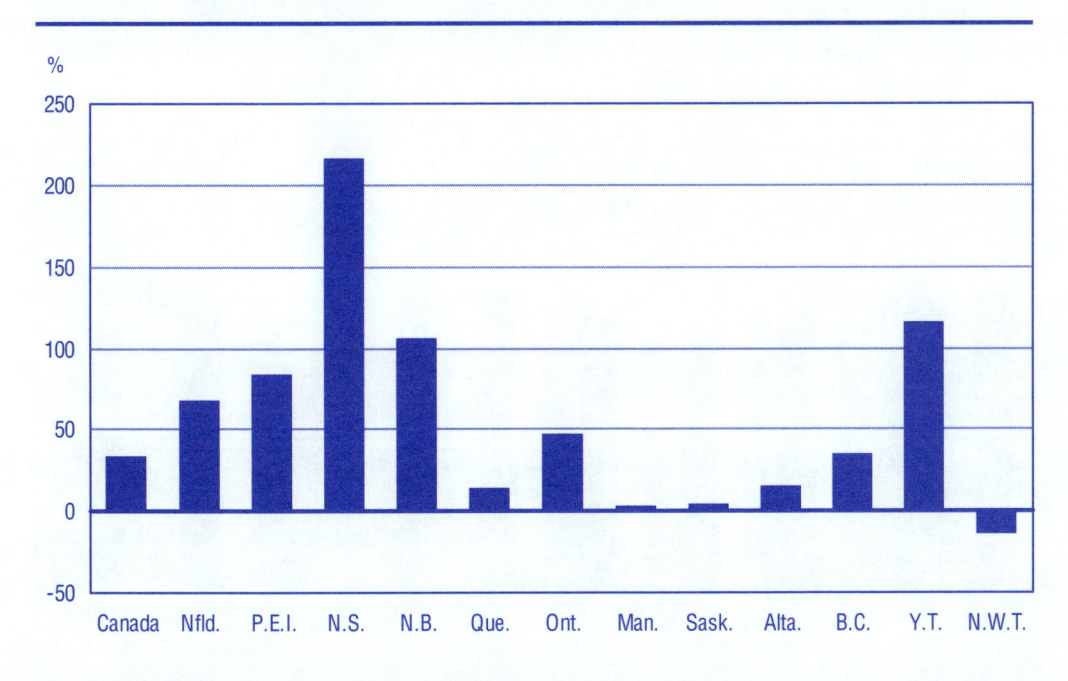

p   Preliminary data
*Source: Centre for Education Statistics, Statistics Canada.*

43

EDUCATION INDICATORS IN CANADA

FIGURE 3.13    FULL-TIME COLLEGE ENROLMENT[1] AS A PERCENTAGE OF THE POPULATION AGED 18 TO 21, CANADA AND JURISDICTIONS, 1987-88 AND 1997-98[p]

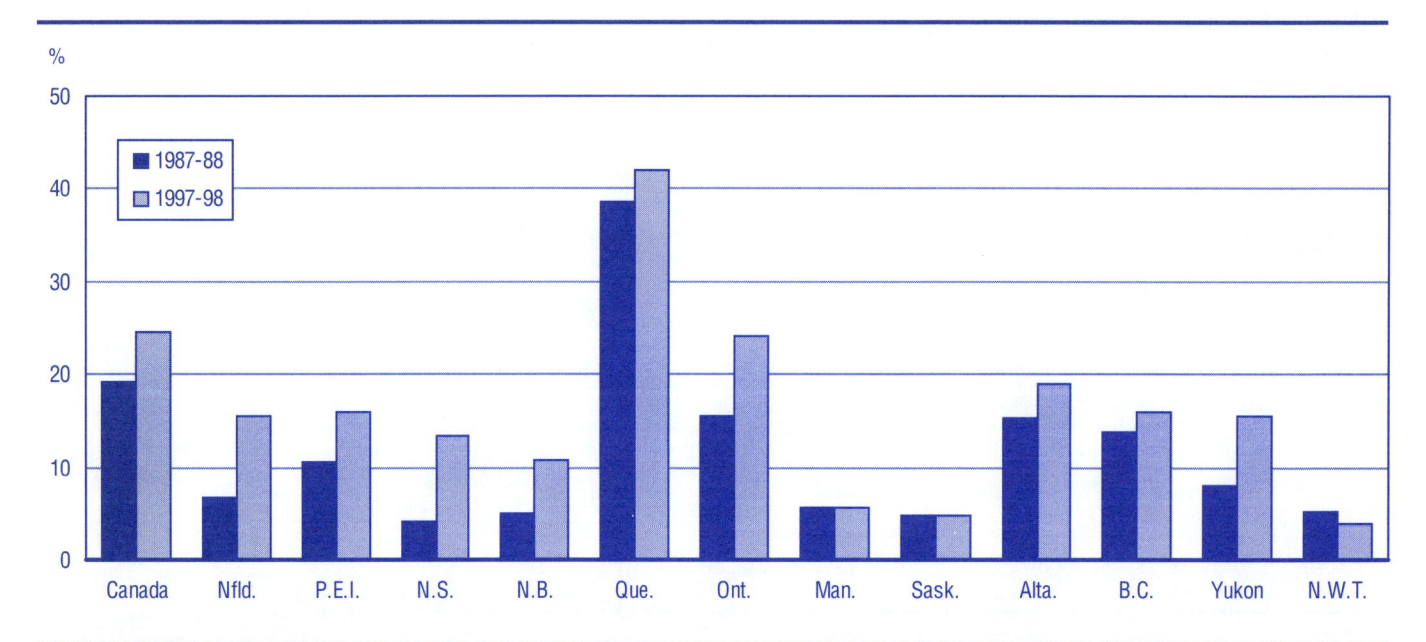

1   Includes career-technical, university transfer and university college courses.
p   Preliminary data.
*Source:*   *Centre for Education Statistics, Statistics Canada.*

FIGURE 3.14    PERCENTAGE OF WOMEN AMONG FULL-TIME COLLEGE CAREER TECHNICAL ENROLMENTS, CANADA AND JURISDICTIONS, 1987-88 AND 1997-98[p]

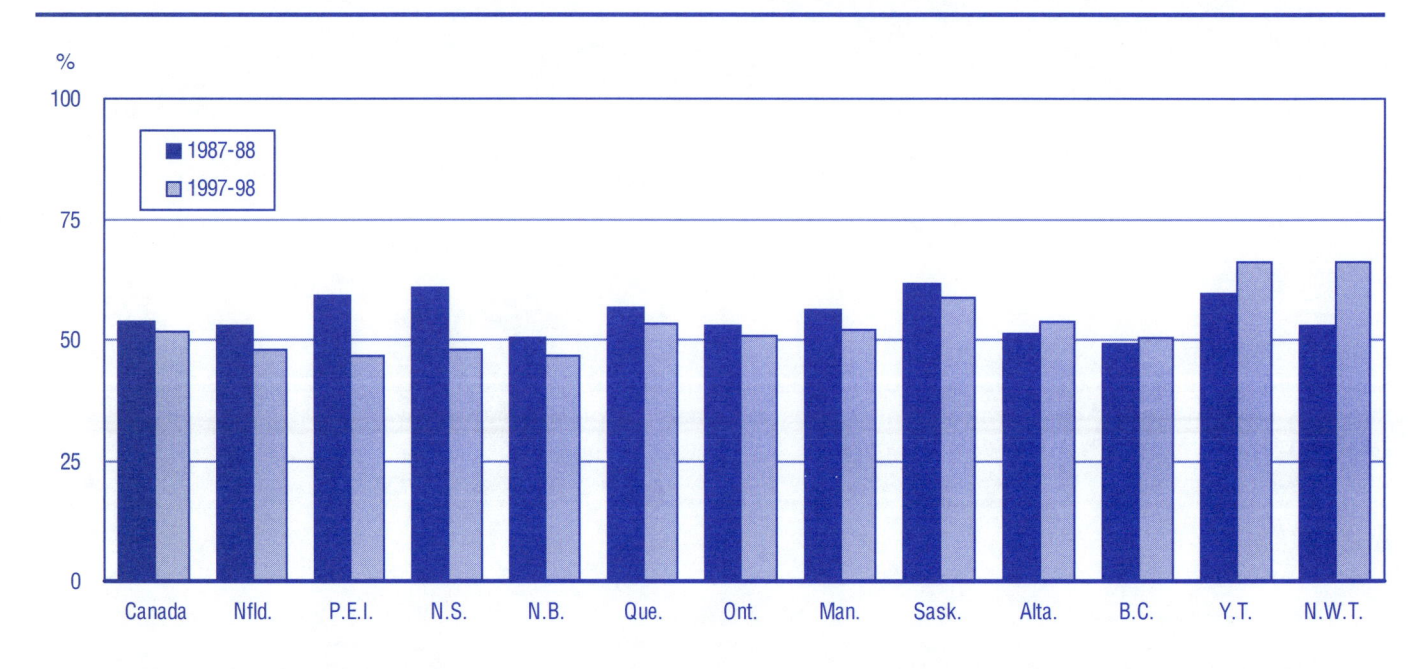

p   Preliminary data.
*Source:*   *Centre for Education Statistics, Statistics Canada.*

Not all jurisdictions offer university transfer and university college programs. Of those that do, Alberta's enrolments more than tripled, while British Columbia's increased by approximately 54%. In Quebec, enrolment fell by 8%. By 1997-98, women represented above 50% of enrolments in university transfer and university college programs in all jurisdictions except Manitoba (Table 3.17).

## E. University enrolment

### Policy context

The section on educational attainment (2.3) shows that between 1990 and 1998, the percentage of the population between the ages of 25 and 54 with a university education increased. The university enrolment index shows similar growth between 1987-88 and 1997-98, because of both increases in the population and higher participation rates. Population projections in section 2.1 suggest that in Canada overall, the population between the ages of 18 and 24—the typical ages for university enrolments—will remain relatively stable over the next few years.

Despite the overall increase in enrolment since 1987-88, both the participation rate and enrolment indices show little change from the early 1990s onward. Many factors, such as the cost of attending university, the availability of other educational programs, and the strength of the economy and number of job opportunities affect a student's decision to attend university, which in turn affects enrolment. Program size also has an impact, as some institutions may function at full capacity or face budgetary and other practical impediments to expansion. (See section 4.3C for information on university participation by socio-economic status, and section 3.3D and F.)

*The participation rate has flattened since the early 1990s.*

Part-time enrolment has shown a significant decrease since 1992-93. Further research is required to determine the cause of the decline and whether it reflects a shift in demand or whether changes to the part-time system would restore enrolments to previous levels.

A key factor affecting enrolments is the mobility of university students. The students are able to search for the best program available to them, not only within Canada, but also internationally. At the same time, students from other countries have the option to enrol at Canadian universities. Canadian university programs, therefore, need to be internationally competitive, to attract foreign students and retain Canadian students, as well as equitable, to ensure that domestic access to education is not compromised.

Women have traditionally had higher participation rates than men in part-time undergraduate studies, but are now also in the majority in full-time undergraduate studies. In graduate studies, female enrolment almost equals that of males. This suggests that, to some extent, earlier imbalances in female enrolment have now lessened. The data here, however, do not provide information about specific programs, and graduation data (section 4.2B) show that significant gender differences exist by field of study. It will continue to be important to monitor the gender breakdown, not only to inform policies designed to maintain strong female participation, but also to ensure that male enrolment levels do not drop.

As was mentioned in the college section, the elimination of the fifth year of high school in Ontario in 2002-03 will be a key concern for postsecondary education planning in Ontario. The change also has potential implications for students across Canada who want to pursue higher education in Ontario, and for the other jurisdictions, which are likely to see an increase in the number of students applying from Ontario to study.

## FINDINGS

### CANADA

For a list of universities, see Appendix 2.

Figures 3.15 and 3.16 show a clear levelling-off in full-time university enrolment rates since 1991-92. Two rates are shown: one covering all enrolment; and the other covering only new entrants (ie: first year enrolments). The levelling-off is seen more clearly in the new entrants' rate. The overall participation rate (Figure 3.16) has responded more slowly, as it reflects the size of entering cohorts over a number of years. It continued to grow up to 1993-94 but has decreased slightly since then. Overall, however, between 1987-88 and 1997-98, full-time enrolment increased by 18.0% (Figure 3.15). Part-time enrolment has been falling since 1992-93, with an even larger drop in the index for new entrants.

Participation among the 18 to 24 age group increased between 1987-88 and 1997-98. Full-time enrolment as a proportion of that age group increased from 15% to 20% (Figure 3.18).

By 1997–98 women represented 56% of full-time undergraduate enrolment.

The percentage of women among full-time undergraduate enrolment increased from 50% in 1987-88 to 56% in 1997-98. The percentage of women among graduate enrolment also increased, though it remained below 50% in 1997-98. Women account for a higher percentage of part-time than full-time enrolments at each level (Figures 3.19 and 3.20).

### JURISDICTIONS

All provinces reported increases in full-time enrolment.

In all provinces, full-time enrolment grew between 1987-88 and 1997-98 (Figure 3.17). At 42%, British Columbia reported the strongest growth in full-time enrolment, largely a reflection of the rapid population growth in the province. New Brunswick and Nova Scotia have high enrolment growth at 25% and 23%. At the lower end of the scale, full-time enrolment in Prince Edward Island, Quebec, Manitoba, Saskatchewan, and Alberta grew 13% to 14% (Figure 3.17).

Full-time enrolment as a proportion of the 18- to-24-year-old population increased in all jurisdictions between 1987-88 and 1997-98 (Figure 3.18). The lower rate of full-time enrolment in Alberta and British Columbia than in other provinces is in part due to sizeable enrolments in university transfer programs, which are reported as college enrolments (Table 3.17), and due to higher part-time enrolment.

Most provinces reported a decline in part-time undergraduate enrolment between 1987-88 and 1997-98. Only Alberta and British Columbia reported increases. Part-time graduate studies have become more popular, with enrolment increasing in all provinces except Ontario, and Manitoba (Table 3.18).

Male undergraduate enrolment was below 45% in all provinces.

The percentage of women among both undergraduate and graduate enrolments, rose in all provinces between 1987-88 and 1997-98 (Figures 3.19 and 3.20). Women accounted for more than 55% of undergraduate enrolment in 1997-98, with the highest percentage in Prince Edward Island, where 61% of undergraduates were female. Prince Edward Island's female enrolment was also particularly strong in graduate programs. It was the only province where more women than men were pursuing graduate studies. In all other provinces except Saskatchewan women represented close to 50% of graduate enrolments. The largest percentage increase was in New Brunswick (Figure 3.20).

In all provinces, women constitute a higher percentage of total part-time enrolment, both undergraduate and graduate, than full-time enrolment, except at the graduate level in Prince Edward Island (Table 3.18).

CHARACTERISTICS AND FEATURES OF EDUCATION SYSTEMS

FIGURE 3.15  INDICES OF UNIVERSITY ENROLMENT[1] BY REGISTRATION STATUS, AND INDICES OF POPULATION FOR SELECTED AGE GROUPS, CANADA, 1987-88 TO 1997-98[2]

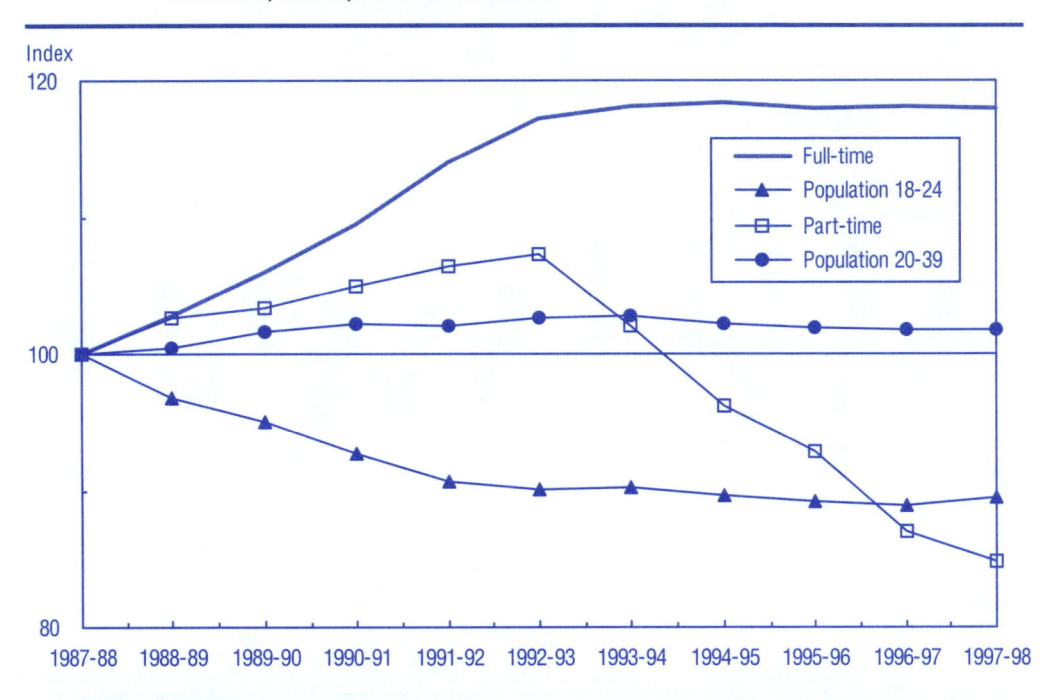

1 Includes undergraduate and graduate enrolments.
2 Indices equal 100 in 1987-88.
*Source: Centre for Education Statistics, Statistics Canada.*

FIGURE 3.16  INDICES OF PARTICIPATION RATES IN UNDERGRADUATE PROGRAMS[1], CANADA, 1987-88 TO 1997-98[2]

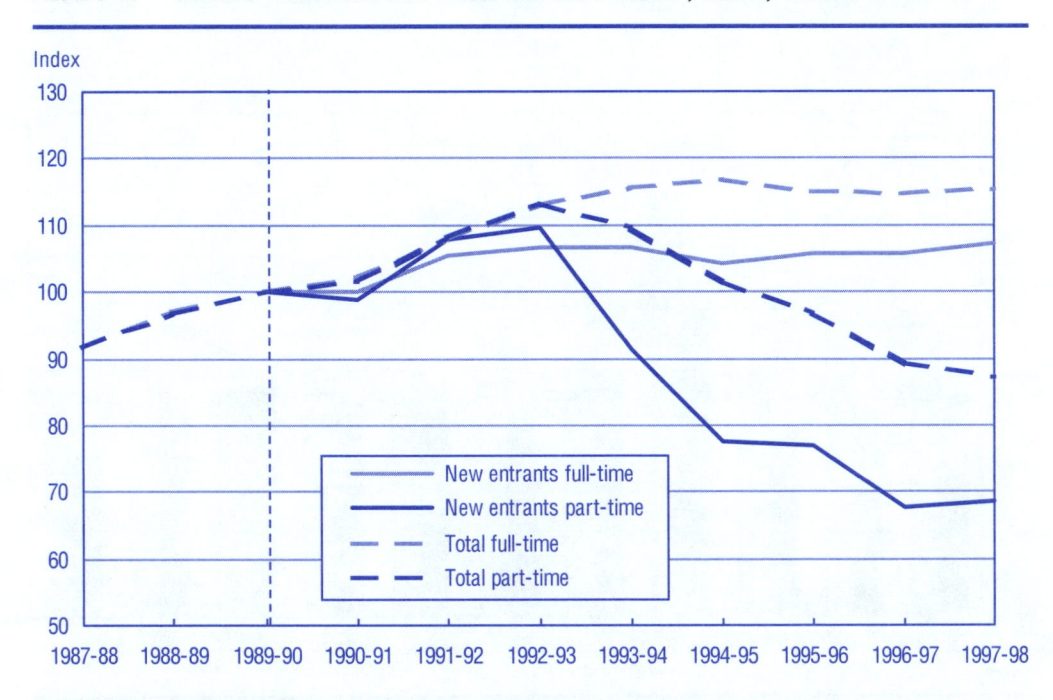

1 Includes only undergraduate programs leading to a bachelor's degree. Excludes undergraduate programs leading to certificates and diplomas.
2 Indices equal 100 in 1989-90.
*Source: Centre for Education Statistics, Statistics Canada.*

EDUCATION INDICATORS IN CANADA

FIGURE 3.17  PERCENTAGE CHANGE IN UNIVERSITY ENROLMENT[1] BY REGISTRATION STATUS, CANADA AND PROVINCES, 1987-88 TO 1997-98

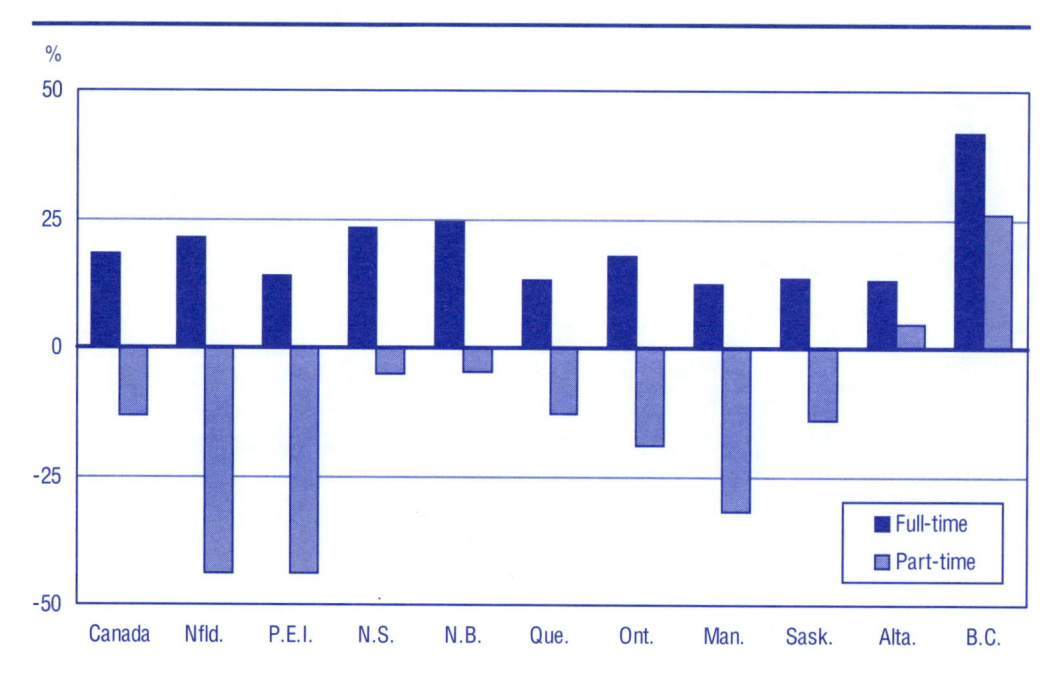

1 Includes undergraduate and graduate enrolments.
*Source: Centre for Education Statistics, Statistics Canada.*

FIGURE 3.18  FULL-TIME UNIVERSITY ENROLMENT[1] AS A PERCENTAGE OF THE POPULATION AGED 18 TO 24, CANADA AND PROVINCES, 1987-88 AND 1997-98

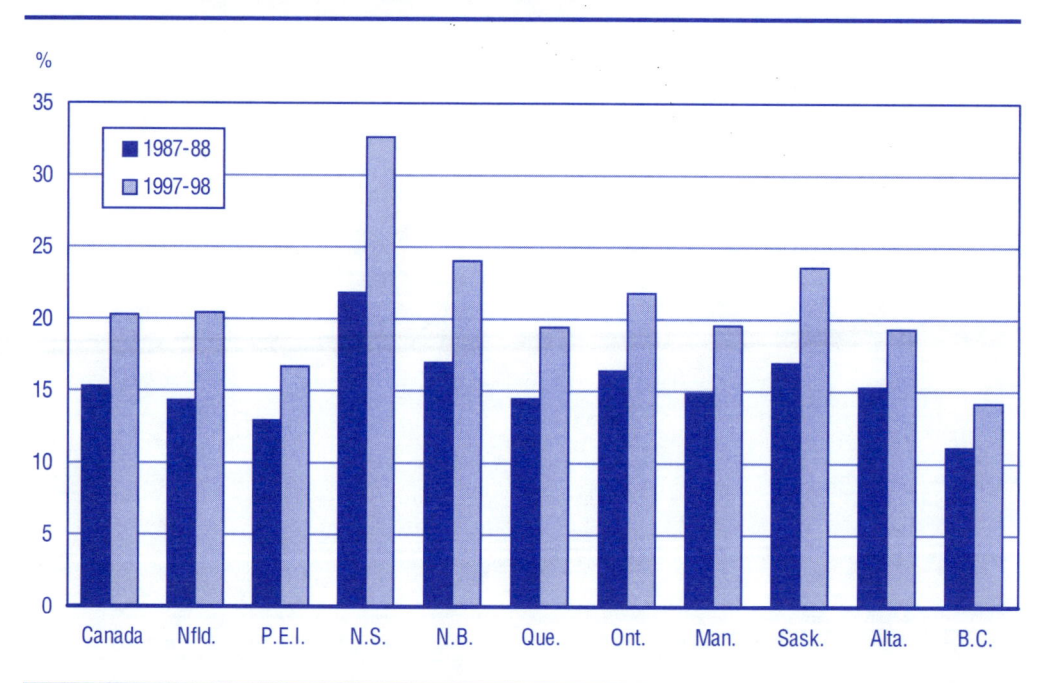

1 Includes undergraduate and graduate enrolments.
*Source: Centre for Education Statistics, Statistics Canada.*

CHARACTERISTICS AND FEATURES OF EDUCATION SYSTEMS

FIGURE 3.19   PERCENTAGE OF WOMEN AMONG FULL-TIME UNDERGRADUATE ENROLMENTS, CANADA AND PROVINCES, 1987-88 AND 1997-98

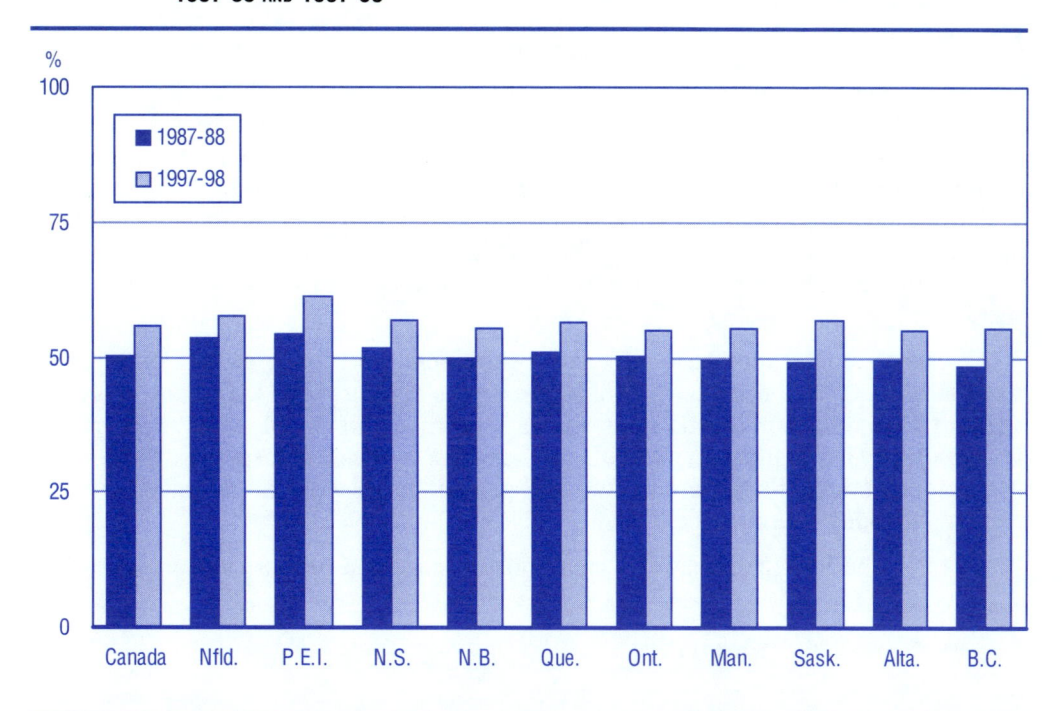

*Source:   Centre for Education Statistics, Statistics Canada.*

FIGURE 3.20   PERCENTAGE OF WOMEN AMONG FULL-TIME GRADUATE ENROLMENTS, CANADA AND PROVINCES, 1987-88 AND 1997-98

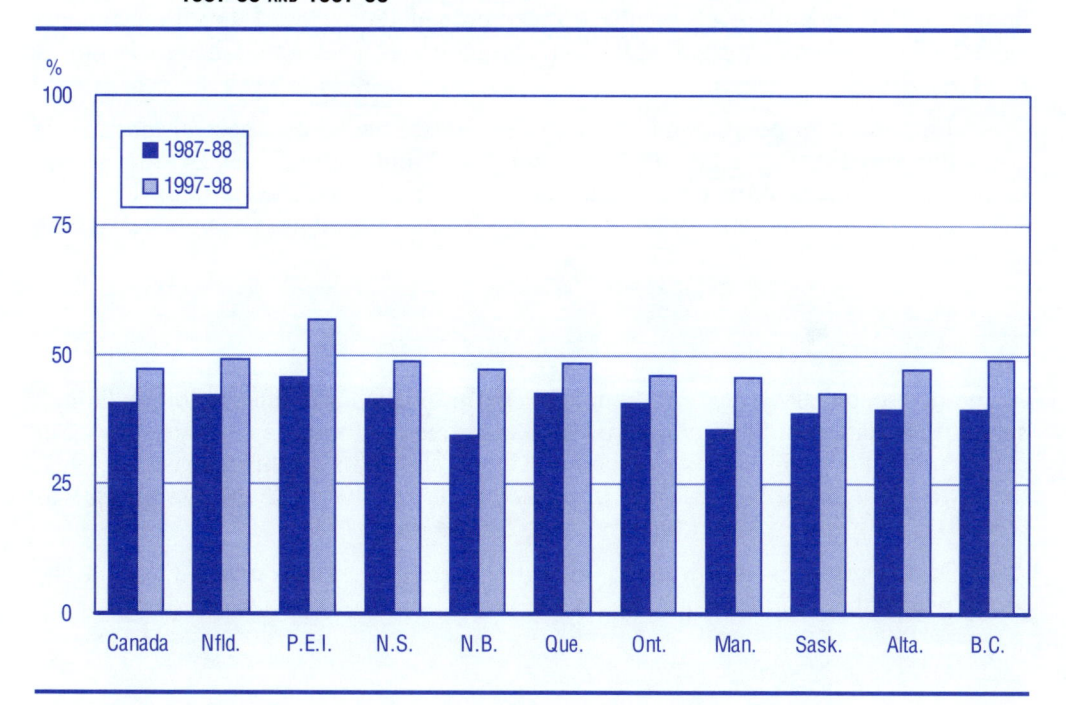

*Source:   Centre for Education Statistics, Statistics Canada.*

EDUCATION INDICATORS IN CANADA

## F. ADULT PARTICIPATION IN EDUCATION

### POLICY CONTEXT

**Formal education and training activities considered here are those with an identifiable structured plan and clear objectives geared to the development of the learner's skill and competence, where some kind of formal recognition of completion is received.**

Not all students attend formal education programs at a typical age. The data here provide information about the number of adults enrolled in part-time or full-time programs after the typical age of graduation. This provides an important reminder of the needs of students who fall outside the usual pattern of study. Some of these people will be returning to school to complete diplomas or degrees, others may be seeking to upgrade credentials or acquire new skills. Adult participation in education can also be seen through participation in job-related education and training programs (see section 3.4).

Older students may have different requirements and concerns than the younger population, such as a need for transition programs to assist with the return to school, support in balancing family and studies, or recognition of work experience. Postsecondary institutions, in particular, will need to continue to respond to the demand from older students for programs that will provide them with the skills and training needed for today's workplace.

In Quebec, adult education is an important part of secondary school education.

### FINDINGS

### CANADA

**Over 1 million people between the ages of 25 and 54 participated in a formal education program in 1997.**

Table 3.19 shows that the enrolment of adults in formal education rose slightly between 1991 and 1997. In both years, the participation rate of the 17 to 24 age group was significantly higher than that of the 25 to 54 age group. However, because the second group contains more people, the number of students in the 25 to 54 age group is much higher. In 1997, at both levels of education combined, there were 1.4 million students aged 25-54 enrolled in formal education, compared with 576,000 students in the 17 to 24 age group.

**The majority of this participation occurred in postsecondary programs.**

Enrolment in postsecondary programs constituted the largest proportion of adult participation by a considerable margin. Among the 17 to 24 age group, participation increased by 4 percentage points from 13% to 17% between 1991 and 1997. The participation rate for the 25 to 54 age group showed little change, remaining at about 9%.

### PROVINCES

At the postsecondary level, enrolment in most provinces remained stable, although some of the data should be compared with caution (see footnote to Table 3.19). For the 25 to 54 age group, Nova Scotia and Alberta showed a slight increase. In 1997, the province with the highest rate of participation for the 17 to 24 age group was Ontario (24%); it was Alberta for the 25 to 54 age group (11%).

In all provinces, and in both years, the participation rate of the 17 to 24 age group was higher than for the 25 to 54 age group.

CHARACTERISTICS AND FEATURES OF EDUCATION SYSTEMS

## 3.4 JOB-RELATED ADULT EDUCATION

### POLICY CONTEXT

In Canada, more and more people will need an increasing amount of training and retraining throughout their careers. As a country, we need an educated, skilled, and flexible work force to remain competitive. This can be achieved by directly promoting continuing education and training among employed and unemployed individuals. Such training is particularly important to unemployed people, since it can equip them with skills that are in demand in the labour market, thereby helping them to enter and succeed in the work force.

Unlike section 3.3F, which looked at adult participation in general formal education programs, this section examines trends in participation in job-related adult education and training in Canada and the provinces over time. It also includes international comparisons of the level and intensity of participation in job-related adult education and training among the ten countries that took part in the 1994-95 International Adult Literacy Survey.

### FINDINGS

### CANADA

While Canada has the highest participation rate in formal postsecondary education of the 10 countries studied, its participation in job-related adult education and training is about average. Moreover, pan-Canadian data show a slight drop in this participation between 1991 and 1997. Although small, there is perhaps a need to find out why this decline has occurred. Are fewer courses being offered? Are individuals replacing classroom training with other forms of learning, such as informal learning via the Internet? Is there less time available for training in a growing economy? Are individuals choosing other activities over further education and training?

Table 3.20 shows adult participation in job-related education and training, by gender and educational attainment, in 1991 and 1997.

FIGURE 3.21 PARTICIPATION IN JOB-RELATED TRAINING FOR ADULTS IN THE 25 TO 64 AGE GROUP, BY EMPLOYMENT STATUS, CANADA AND SELECTED COUNTRIES, 1994-95

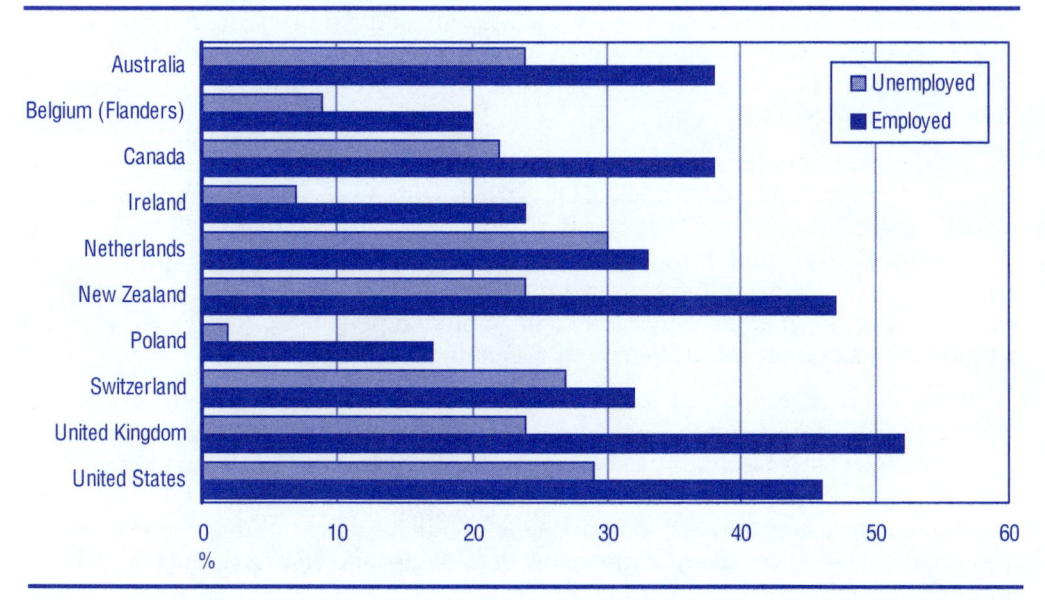

Table 3.21 and Figures 3.21 and 3.22 show international participation in job-related adult education and training, in 1994–95.

*Source:* Education at a Glance: OECD Indicators 1998, Table C5.2; and International Adult Literacy Survey 1994-95, Statistics Canada and OECD.

FIGURE 3.22   AVERAGE DURATION OF JOB-RELATED TRAINING UNDERTAKEN BY EMPLOYED ADULTS IN THE 25 TO 64 AGE GROUP, CANADA AND SELECTED COUNTRIES, 1994-95

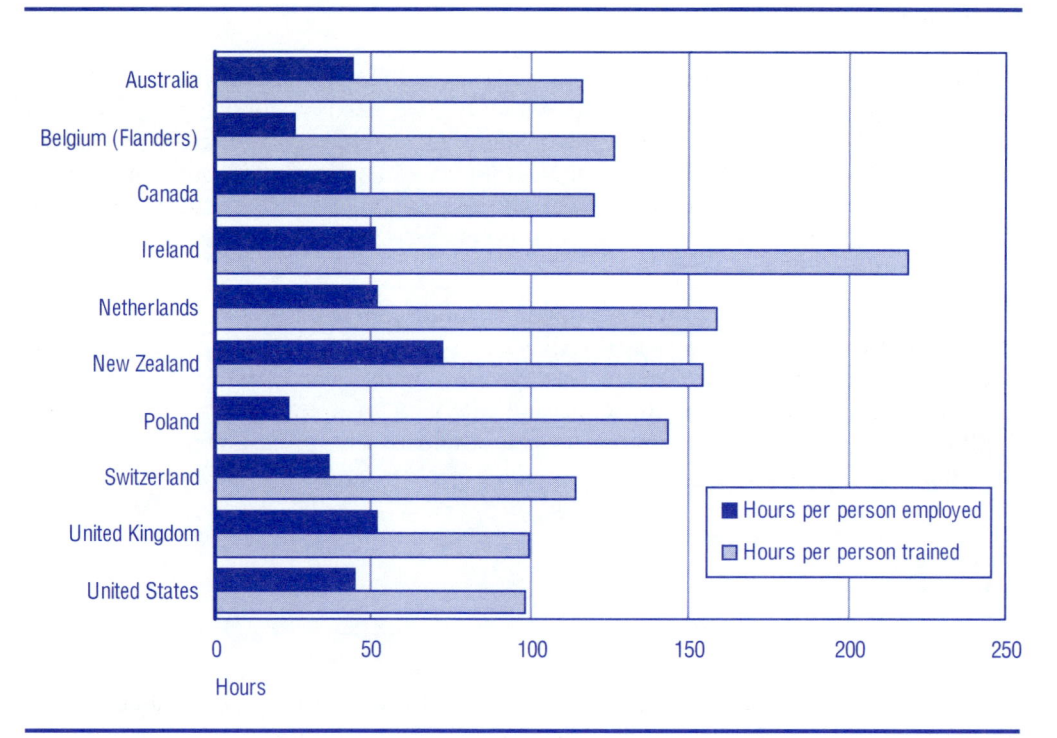

Source: Human Capital Investment: An International Comparison 1998, OECD, Table A3.4, and International Adult Literacy Survey 1994-95, Statistics Canada and OECD.

**In 1997, 27% of adults pursued job-related education and training.**

Approximately 27% of people between the ages of 25 and 54 pursued some form of job-related adult education and training in 1997, down slightly from 29% in 1991. There was little difference in the participation of men and women in 1997, in contrast with 1991, when men participated at a higher rate than women. Although the dip in participation occurred across all education levels, it was most pronounced for those with a university degree.

In general, the rate of participation for both males and females in job-related education and training increases with educational attainment. Adults with a postsecondary non-university education participated at twice the rate (31%) of those with only elementary or secondary education. University graduates participated at an even higher rate of 43%.

Of the ten countries that took part in the International Adult Literacy Survey in 1994-95, Canada fell in the middle of the group with respect to participation in job-related adult education and training. In Canada, 38% of employed persons pursued such training, compared with 22% of unemployed persons. Canada's participation rates were below those of the United Kingdom and the United States, and similar to those of Australia. The participation of unemployed persons in job-related training was lower in all countries, despite their arguably greater need for it.

On average, employed adults engaged in education and training in Canada took 120 hours of training; this was about average for the ten countries. A measure of the overall intensity of training can be constructed by averaging the duration of training over all employed persons (those who took training as well as those who did not). In Canada, this measure stood at 45 hours. Once again, Canada fell in the middle of the ten countries, with Poland recording a low of 23 hours and New Zealand a high of 72 hours (Table 3.21).

## PROVINCES

While the overall pattern of higher participation in adult education among individuals with higher levels of education generally held across provinces in 1997, there were some variations. For example, in Newfoundland and Labrador the participation rate of university graduates was nine times greater than that of adults with a high school education or less. In contrast, Saskatchewan and Alberta showed the smallest difference by level of education; the participation rate of university graduates was just over twice that of adults with a high school education or less.

Overall the participation rate rose between 1991 and 1997 in Ontario, Prince Edward Island, Nova Scotia, and New Brunswick. It fell in Newfoundland and Labrador, Quebec, Manitoba, Alberta, and British Columbia, while it remained the same in Saskatchewan.

In 1997, the participation rate of 25- to 54-year-olds was lowest in Newfoundland and Labrador, and Quebec (20%). Provinces with participation rates of 30% or more included Nova Scotia, Alberta, Saskatchewan, Ontario and British Columbia.

In 1991, in all provinces, men had higher overall rates of participation in job-related education and training than women. With few exceptions, this tended to be the case regardless of level of education. However, by 1997, women's participation rates in job-related adult education and training were similar to those of men. Among university graduates, women had even higher participation rates than men. At 75%, female university graduates in Newfoundland and Labrador had the highest participation rate—well above that in the rest of the country. Female rates were also higher at other levels of education in many provinces, for example, in Quebec and Alberta.

*Trends apparent at the pan-Canadian level were reflected at the jurisdictional level.*

*By 1997, women's participation in job-related education and training had caught up with that of men.*

## 3.5 EDUCATION FINANCES

### POLICY CONTEXT

The gross domestic product (GDP) measures the financial resources generated within a country or jurisdiction. How that wealth is used affects everyone's standard of living. What proportion of this wealth to devote to education is a key decision that each government must make.

Governments in Canada have always provided resources to ensure that citizens have educational services. The proportion of public funds allocated for this purpose is one indicator of the priority that governments place on education. Education represents the second largest category of public expenditures in Canada, exceeded only by spending on health. How much government invests in education depends on such factors as the demographic structure of the population, enrolment rates at the various levels of education, national costs for educational resources, and the strength of the economy.

For example, the relative size of the youth population shapes potential demand for initial education and training. Other factors being equal, the larger the proportion of young people, the more resources will be required for education. Higher participation rates will also create a need for more financial resources. Decisions about investment in education must also be made in light of competing demands for resources.

Once the overall level of public resources devoted to education has been established, the proportion given to each level of education must be determined. The particular areas that receive funding priority reflect government policy on educational development. The desire to achieve high rates of school attendance and completion, and support equality of opportunity and special education programs have all influenced resource allocation decisions in the past. Recent pedagogical studies point to the importance of the pre-elementary and elementary levels of education to learning later in life, and may result in increased pressure to fund these in the future.

*Expenditures reported in this section, unless otherwise noted, include both public and private expenditures. Public expenditures include those of provincial and territorial ministries responsible for education and training, as well as federal expenditures on education and training.*

Governments strive to improve the quality of education for their citizens. Although there are many ways to address this issue, many require spending more per student, or reallocating existing dollars to better reflect changing priorities. Yet, given the complexity of education, differences in spending do not necessarily translate into differences in the overall quality of education.

Particularly at higher levels of education, there is also the question of the appropriate mix between public versus private funding. There are positive returns on the investment in education to both individuals and to society (see OECD 1998) hence it is not unreasonable that both should contribute to the costs of the education. These debates are not unique to Canada; other OECD countries are grappling with the same issues. Presentation of financial indicators for the G-7 countries shows differences in how countries are approaching these issues and the financing of education.

In Canada, universities in recent years have been relying more on private funds from tuition fees and less on public funding from governments (Little 1997).

Finally, rising debt levels among postsecondary graduates, together with a widening gap in participation between people from low and middle–high socio-economic backgrounds (see section 4.3C), raise concerns about access to postsecondary education. In Canada, the fundamental principle that access to postsecondary education should be independent of an individual's financial situation underpins the student loan programs offered by the federal and provincial governments. Provincial and federal governments have recently undertaken initiatives to improve the affordability of postsecondary education, for example the Millenium Scholarship programs announced in the 1998 federal speech from the Throne. Whether the criteria for assessing need, loan limits and remissions, and grants have been keeping pace with the rapid increases in the cost of postsecondary education in recent years remain issues facing these programs.

## A. EXPENDITURES BY LEVEL OF EDUCATION

### FINDINGS

### CANADA

*Educational expenditure in Canada was estimated at $60.5 billion in 1998-99, or just under $2,000 per capita.*

Educational expenditure in Canada was estimated at 60.5 billion in 1998-99, or just under $2,000 per capita. Ten years earlier, in 1988-89, expenditure on education stood at $53.7 billion (in constant 1998-99 dollars); this represents an average increase of 1.3% per annum, keeping pace with the rate of population growth.

While current per capita expenditure ($1,996 in 1998-99) is about the same as it was ten years ago, there have been significant trends and changes over this period (Table 3.22). From 1988-89 to 1994-95, per capita expenditure rose 7% to $2,147. Annual decreases since 1994-95 have reduced per capita expenditure 7% to $1,996 in 1998-99. The estimated total expenditure in 1998-99 was $1.9 billion (or 3%) lower than the peak of $62.3 billion spent in 1994-95.

At the trade–vocational level, expenditure rose 43% between 1988-89 and 1998-99. Over the same period, expenditure at the college level grew 13%, matching the rate of population growth. Expenditures at the elementary–secondary and university levels grew 10%, less than the rate of population growth.

Expenditures on elementary–secondary education, which increased up to 1994-95, have since edged down 2%. Expenditures at the college and trade–vocational levels increased until 1995-96, and subsequently declined. At the university level, expenditures rose from 1988-89 through to 1991-92, levelled off for four years, and declined in the last three years.

CHARACTERISTICS AND FEATURES OF EDUCATION SYSTEMS

FIGURE 3.23    PER CAPITA EXPENDITURES ON EDUCATION[1] IN CONSTANT 1998 DOLLARS (THOUSANDS), CANADA AND JURISDICTIONS, 1988-89 TO 1998-99

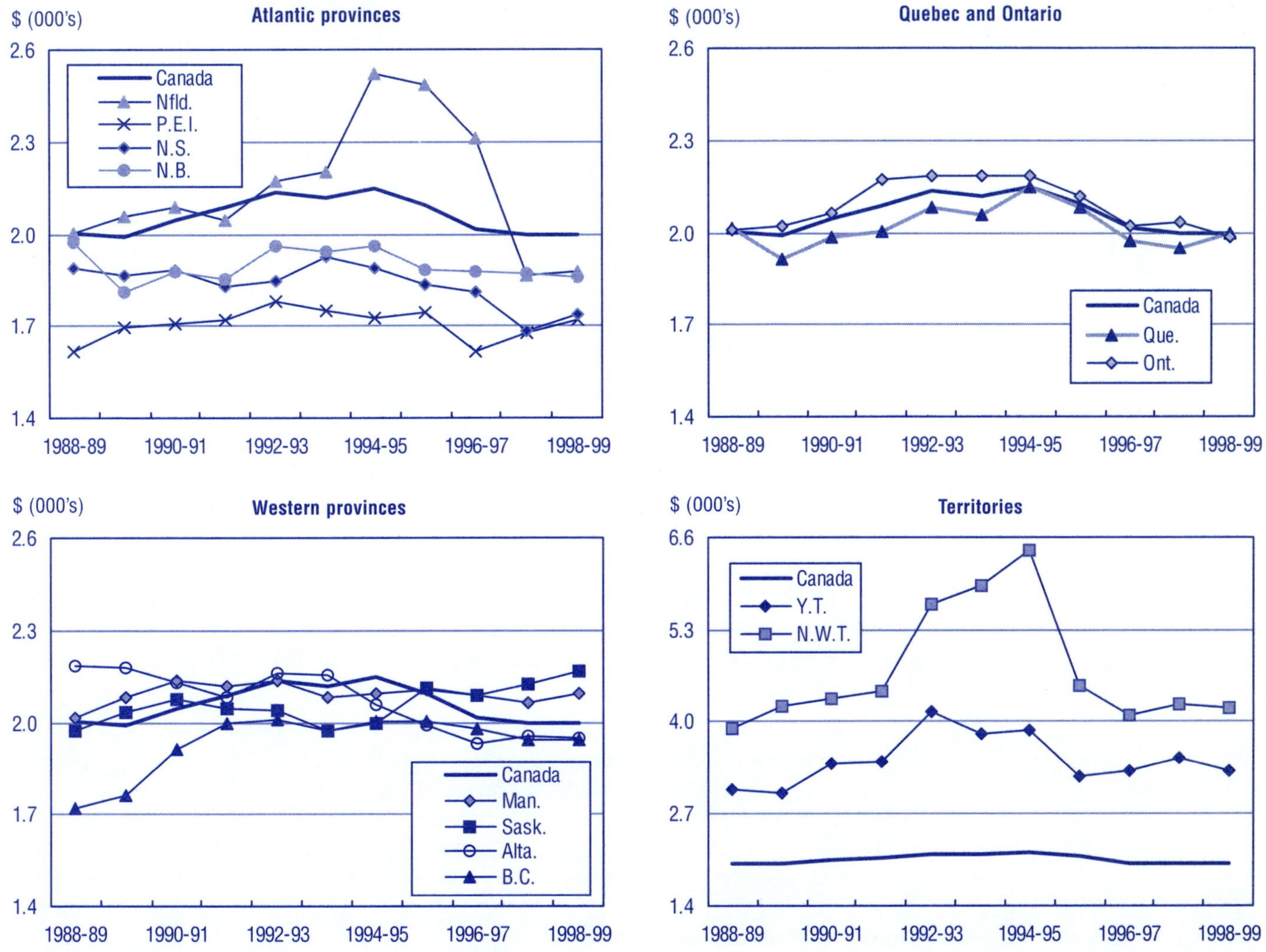

[1] Data for 1996-97, 1998-99, and 1998-98 are estimates.
Source: Centre for Education Statistics, Statistics Canada.

Table 3.22 and Figures 3.23 show expenditure and per capita expenditure on education from 1988-89 to 1998-99, expressed in 1998 constant dollars.

## JURISDICTIONS

In the last ten years, jurisdictions were evenly split between those in which per capita spending increased and those in which per capita spending decreased.

In Prince Edward Island, per capita spending increased 7% between 1988-89 and 1998-99. This was primarily the result of an increase in trade–vocational education spending. In Manitoba, per capita spending rose 4%, but this increase occurred in 1989-90, with little change since then. In Saskatchewan, per capita spending rose 10% over the ten-year period. The population changed little over this period, and most of the increased expenditure occurred at postsecondary levels.

In British Columbia, per capita expenditure went up 13% over the ten-year period. Per capita expenditure increased 17% between 1988-89 and 1995-96, and since then has fallen by 4 percentage points. Expenditure growth matched the population growth of 30% at the university level, but exceeded population growth at other levels. In Northwest Territories and Yukon, estimated per capita expenditures in 1998-99 were 7% and 9% higher than those of a decade earlier, respectively. In both

Per capita expenditures increased between 1988-89 and 1998-99 in Prince Edward Island, Manitoba, Saskatchewan, British Columbia, and Yukon and Northwest Territories.

**Per capita expenditures decreased between 1988-89 and 1998-99 in Newfoundland and Labrador, Nova Scotia, New Brunswick, Quebec, Ontario, and Alberta.**

territories, expenditures at the university level increased greatly from 1992-93 to 1994-95 as a result of a federal program, pushing up overall expenditures in those years.

In Newfoundland and Labrador, expenditures rose 11% from 1988-89 to 1993-94. Overall expenditures then jumped between 1994-95 and 1996-97 because of the increased spending on trade-vocational programs associated with retraining programs for those affected by the closure of the North Atlantic cod fisheries. With the expiry of those programs, expenditures have fallen in the last two years—to 11% below the level of ten years earlier, and 22% below the expenditures of five years ago. The largest decreases were in elementary-secondary education, where expenditure declines have matched the decline in the school-aged population (see section 2.1). At all levels of education combined, the 11% reduction in expenditures over the past ten years is just over twice the rate of population decrease (5%).

In Nova Scotia, per capita expenditures fell an estimated 8%, and actual expenditures decreased 4% over the last ten years. College and trade-vocational expenditures increased, at slightly less than the 4% population growth over the period, while expenditures at other levels decreased. In New Brunswick, per capita expenditures decreased 6% over the last ten years. College and university expenditures increased at a rate that outpaced the 3% population growth during the period, while expenditures at the elementary-secondary and trade-vocational levels decreased.

In Quebec, estimated per capita expenditures in 1998-99 were 1% less than ten years earlier. Per capita expenditures rose 7% during the first half of the ten-year period, and fell 8% from 1994-95 to 1998-99. Spending on trade-vocational programs increased significantly over the period, despite a good deal of year-to-year volatility. Spending on elementary-secondary education decreased 2% over the past ten years, while spending at the other levels increased, but at a slower rate than the population growth of 7%.

As in Quebec, per capita education expenditures in Ontario also fell 1% over the past ten years. Per capita expenditures increased early in this period, peaking at 9% above the 1988-89 level in 1992-93 and 1993-94, and have since fallen by 10%. Trade-vocational expenditures, which increased 57%, have significantly outpaced the 16% growth in population over the period. College expenditures kept pace with population growth, while expenditures at other levels did not. Since 1995-96, when Ontario moved to a new funding model, overall expenditures have increased 2%, while the population has grown 3%.

In Alberta, per capita expenditures decreased 11% over the period. In the late 1980s, Alberta's per capita expenditure had been among the highest in the country—the decreases over the last ten years have left Alberta's per capita expenditure in line with the pan-Canadian average. Expenditures dropped 20% at the college level and 9% at the university level over the period. On the other hand, expenditures at the elementary-secondary and trade-vocational levels increased, but more slowly than the rate of population growth (19%) over the period.

## B. Educational expenditure per student

**Table 3.23 and Figures 3.24 and 3.25 show expenditure per student in Canadian and in equivalent U.S. dollars by level of education, for Canada, its jurisdictions and the G-7 countries.**

Variations in expenditures per student reflect variations in financial resources available to schools from public and private sources, as well as levels of educator salaries and student enrolment. Expenditures per student are largely related to instructional cost and include all expenditures dealing with activities involved in the teaching process, such as salaries, fringe benefits and instructional supplies. The pupil–educator ratio (section 3.2E) also has an impact on expenditures per student: other things being equal, the higher the ratio, the lower the expenditures per student and vice versa. Additionally, qualifications and experience affect educators' salaries. In general, a more experienced work force—as is Canada's aging group of educators—will translate into higher salaries and hence contribute to higher expenditures per student.

## Characteristics and Features of Education Systems

**FIGURE 3.24**    Expenditure per student on public and private institutions, by level of education, Canada and jurisdictions, 1995, in Canadian dollars

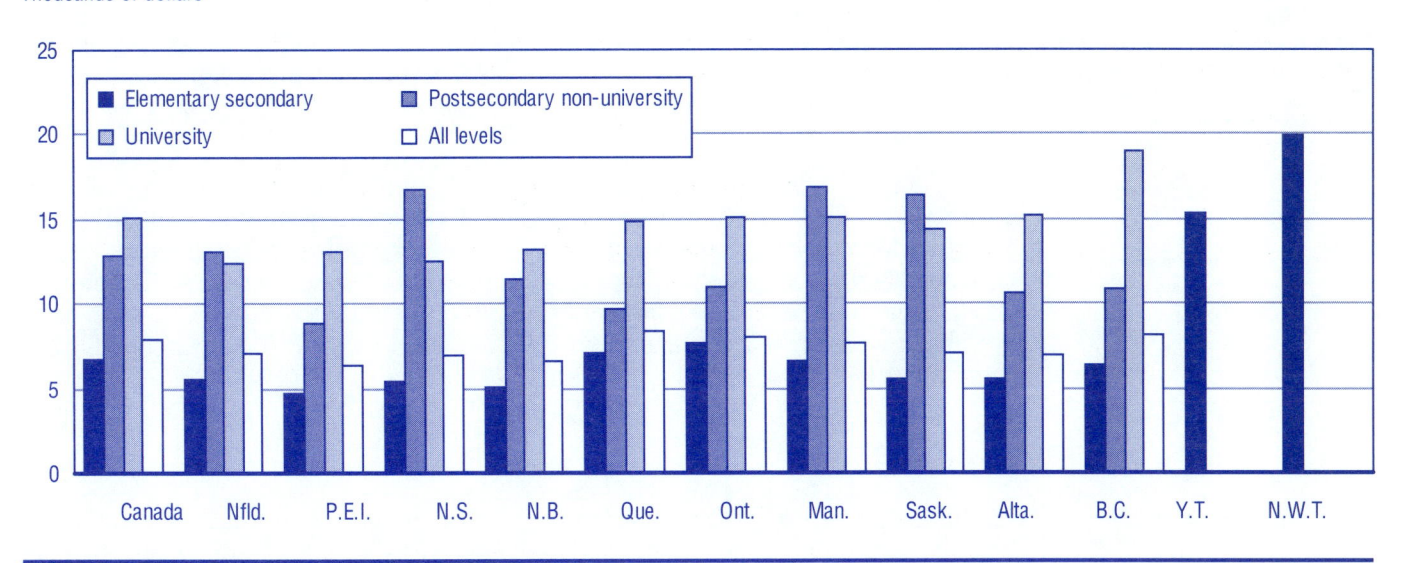

Thousands of dollars

- Elementary secondary
- Postsecondary non-university
- University
- All levels

Jurisdictions: Canada, Nfld., P.E.I., N.S., N.B., Que., Ont., Man., Sask., Alta., B.C., Y.T., N.W.T.

*Source:* Centre for Education Statistics, Statistics Canada.

**FIGURE 3.25**    Expenditure per student on public and private institutions, by level of education, Canada and G-7 countries, 1995, in U.S. dollars converted using PPPs[1]

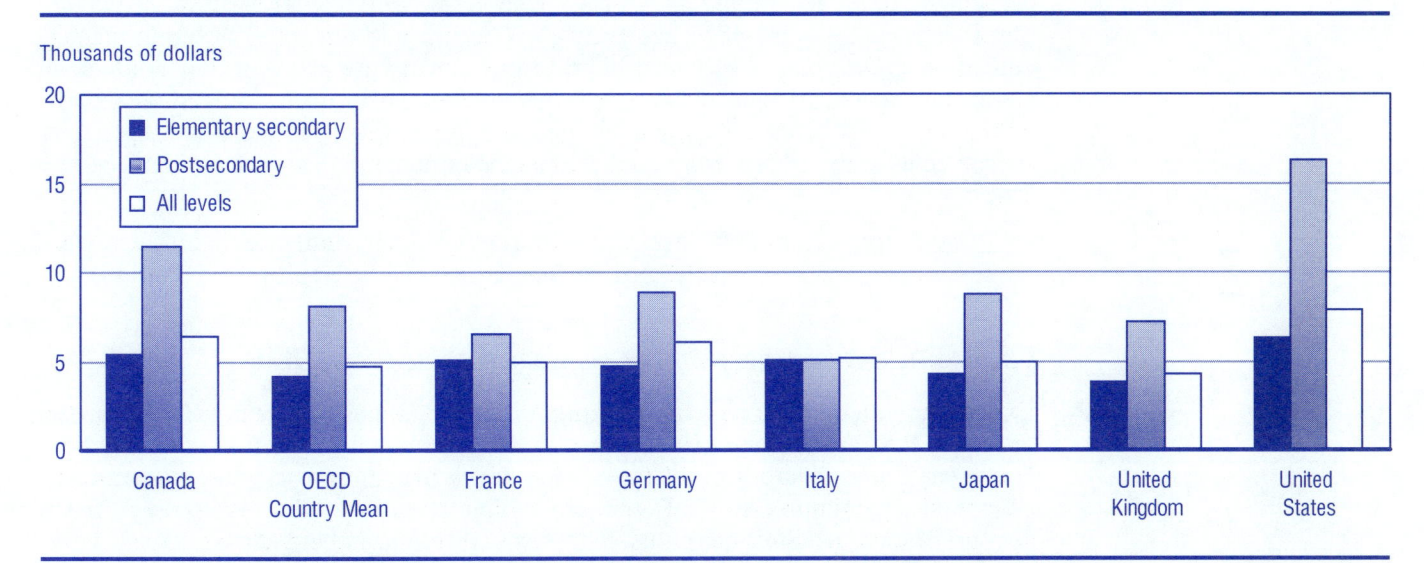

Thousands of dollars

- Elementary secondary
- Postsecondary
- All levels

Countries: Canada, OECD Country Mean, France, Germany, Italy, Japan, United Kingdom, United States

[1] Purchasing power parities (PPPs) are currency exchange rates that equalize the purchasing power of different currencies, expressed here in equivalent U.S. dollars.

*Source:* Centre for Education Statistics, Statistics Canada; Education at a Glance: OECD Indicators, 1998, Table B4.1.

## FINDINGS

### CANADA

In 1995, Canada ranked second among G-7 countries in education expenditures per student, behind only the United States.

In 1995, per student expenditures on education, from both public and private sources, were $6,396 in Canada, compared with $7,905 in the United States (all dollar expenditures are expressed in equivalent U.S. dollars). The OECD country mean was $4,717.

Canada's per student expenditures at both elementary-secondary and postsecondary levels ranked second among G-7 countries, behind the United States. The spread between countries in per student expenditures was larger at the postsecondary level: Canada spent $11,471, the United States spent $16,262 and the OECD mean was $8,134. Per student expenditures at the elementary-secondary level in Canada were $5,401, compared with $6,281 in the United States, and an OECD mean of $4,162.

### JURISDICTIONS

The indicator of expenditures per student exhibits a common pattern throughout Canada; expenditures per student increase with level of education. At a pan-Canadian level, and in most jurisdictions, the amount spent per student on postsecondary education was at least twice the amount spent per student on elementary-secondary education. The exceptions were Quebec and Ontario, which had higher per student expenditures on elementary-secondary education than the other jurisdictions and a ratio of postsecondary to elementary-secondary expenditure of just under 2 to 1.

Prince Edward Island recorded the lowest elementary-secondary expenditure per student of $4,761 (Table 3.23). The lower costs are likely a reflection of the fact that Prince Edward Island is the only jurisdiction without public pre-elementary education. Yukon and Northwest Territories spent twice as much per student on elementary-secondary education as the provinces. For the territories and remote regions within other jurisdictions, the impact of geography can be substantial, affecting factors such as school size, transportation needs, special remote living allowances, and energy costs.

At the postsecondary level, the differences in per student expenditures were not large; they ranged from $12,532 in New Brunswick to $15,615 in Manitoba.

### C. EDUCATION EXPENDITURE AS A PROPORTION OF GDP

Expenditure on education as a proportion of Gross Domestic Product (GDP) can be viewed as the relative share of wealth invested in education by a country or jurisdiction. However, this indicator should be interpreted with caution. Clearly, the ratio of education expenditures to GDP goes up as education expenditures increase, but it also goes down as GDP increases. Therefore, differences between ratios can be as much an indicator of differences in economic well-being between countries and jurisdictions as of different levels of commitment to education. Moreover, differences in spending do not necessarily translate into variations in the quality of education or to differences in levels of student performance.

# FINDINGS

## CANADA

In 1995, Canada spent 7.0% of GDP on education, the highest expenditure among the G-7 countries (Figure 3.27). The OECD country mean was 5.6%; at 6.7%, the United States had the second highest education expenditures as a percentage of GDP. The lower spending on education by the United States compared with Canada reflects the higher per capita GDP in the United States. As the earlier indicator on per student expenditures showed (see section 3.3B), the United States spends more per student than does Canada in equivalent U.S. dollars.

Spending in Canada on elementary and secondary education, at 4.3% of GDP, was about 16% higher than the OECD average of 3.7%, and about 10% higher than the United States figure of 3.9% of GDP. Spending on postsecondary education represented 2.5% of GDP in Canada compared with 2.4% in the United States. Both countries were well above the OECD average of 1.3%. This can be attributed to both the higher per student expenditure on post-secondary education in Canada and the United States (see section 3.3B) and the higher rates of participation in postsecondary education in both countries compared with other OECD countries.

Table 3.24 and Figures 3.26 and 3.27 show public and private expenditure on education as a percentage of GDP in 1995, for Canada, jurisdictions, G-7 countries and the mean across all OECD countries.

FIGURE 3.26  EDUCATIONAL EXPENDITURE FROM PUBLIC AND PRIVATE SOURCES FOR EDUCATIONAL INSTITUTIONS AS A PERCENTAGE OF GDP BY LEVEL OF EDUCATION, CANADA AND JURISDICTIONS, 1995

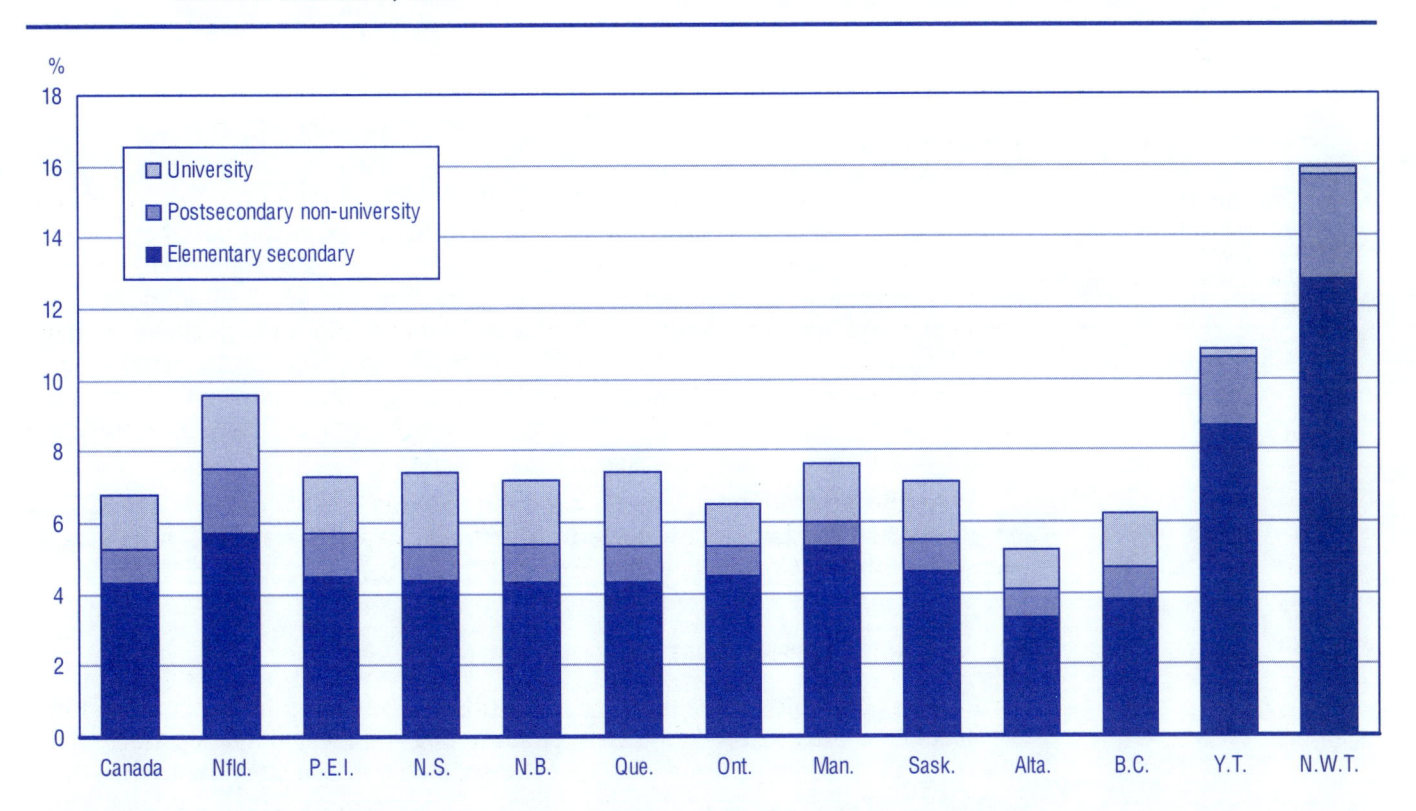

Source: Centre for Education Statistics, Statistics Canada; GDP from National Accounts, Statistics Canada.

EDUCATION INDICATORS IN CANADA

FIGURE 3.27　EDUCATIONAL EXPENDITURE FROM PUBLIC AND PRIVATE SOURCES FOR EDUCATIONAL INSTITUTIONS AS A PERCENTAGE OF GDP BY LEVEL OF EDUCATION, CANADA AND G-7 COUNTRIES, 1995

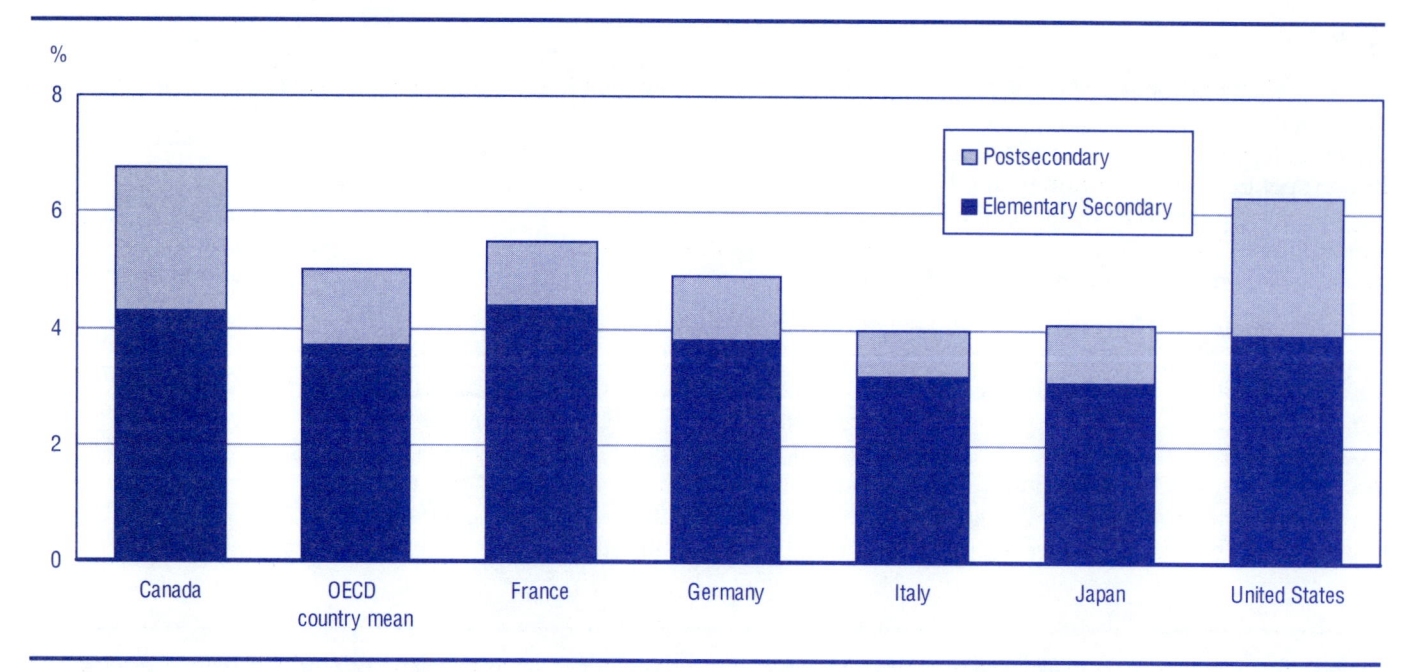

Source: Centre for Education Statistics, Statistics Canada; GDP from National Accounts, Statistics Canada; Education at a Glance: OECD Indicators, *1998*, Table B1.1d.

**A wide range existed across jurisdictions in expenditures on education as a percentage of GDP, which is partly explained by differences in GDP per capita.**

### JURISDICTIONS

Overall education expenditures as a percentage of GDP ranged from 11.3% and 16.6% in Yukon and Northwest Territories, to 5.4% in Alberta (Table 3.24). Higher expenditures in the territories reflect higher educational costs stemming from factors such as geography and population dispersion. Alberta's low expenditures as a percentage of GDP are more a function of its higher GDP. In both Newfoundland and Labrador and Prince Edward Island, education expenditures as a percentage of GDP were above the pan-Canadian average, a reflection of lower GDP in these provinces. In both provinces, education expenditures per student were below the pan-Canadian average.

At the postsecondary level, expenditures ranged from 3.9% of GDP in Newfoundland and Labrador to 1.9% in Alberta; the expenditures of all jurisdictions were above the OECD average of 1.3%.

### D.　PUBLIC EXPENDITURE ON EDUCATION

Two aspects of public expenditure on education are examined in this section. First, we look at the share of total public expenditure that is allocated to education, which illustrates the priority governments attach to spending on education relative to other areas such as health care, justice, and other social programs. When comparing this indicator internationally, the size of the public sector should be kept in mind. Generally, countries with smaller public sectors spend a larger percentage of public funds on education than countries with larger public sectors.

Second, we look at the distribution of funding to educational institutions from public and private sources before and after transfers of funds from the public to the private sector by means of subsidies, scholarships, and the like.

## Findings

### Canada

The United States has the highest expenditure on education as a percentage of public spending, at 14.4%, followed by Canada at 13.6% (Table 3.25). The OECD average was 12.7%.

Public expenditures on education can be broken into two principal components: direct expenditures for education services, and public subsidies to the private sector. Examples of the latter include government scholarships and bursaries, and loan subsidies and forgiveness. Direct expenditures are by far the largest category, accounting for 11.9% of overall public expenditures in Canada, versus 1.7% for public subsidies. While Canada's direct public expenditures were about the same as the OECD mean of 11.8%, public subsidies of education in Canada were about twice the OECD mean of 0.9%. Public subsidies in other G-7 countries were below the OECD average, at 0.5% or less.

*In 1995, 13.6% of public expenditures in Canada went to education, the second highest among G-7 countries.*

FIGURE 3.28  PUBLIC EXPENDITURE ON EDUCATION AS A PERCENTAGE OF TOTAL PUBLIC EXPENDITURE, BY LEVEL OF EDUCATION, CANADA AND JURISDICTIONS, 1995

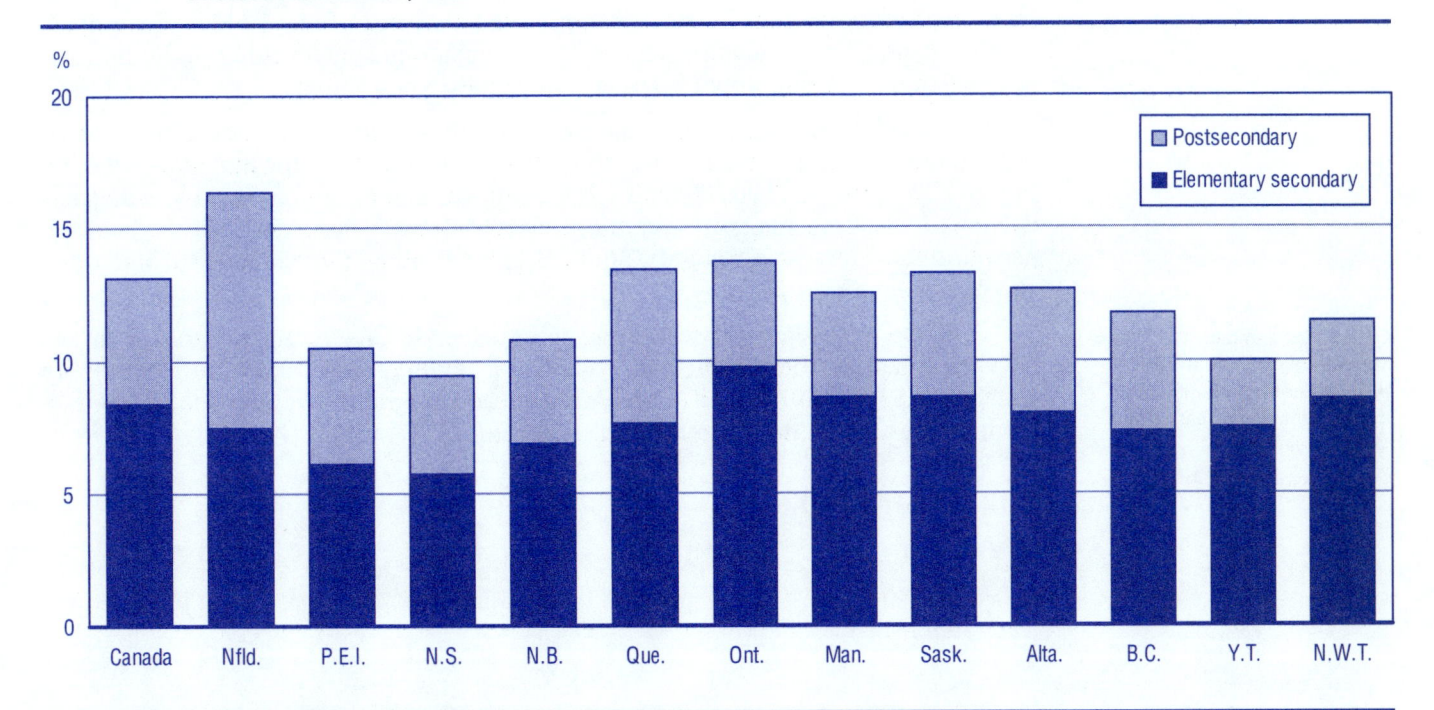

Source: Centre for Education Statistics, Statistics Canada.

EDUCATION INDICATORS IN CANADA

In 1995, almost two-thirds of public education expenditures in Canada were on elementary–secondary education, accounting for 8.4% of public expenditures. This was slightly below the OECD average of 8.7%, and less than the corresponding United States figure of 9.8%.

Spending on postsecondary education represented 4.8% of public expenditures in Canada, well above the OECD mean of 2.7% and higher than in other G-7 countries. The United States was next highest, at 3.6%. The larger share of public expenditures devoted to postsecondary education in both Canada and the United States would appear to reflect the high priority given to postsecondary education relative to other sectors in both these countries. This priority is also reflected in the higher participation and graduation rates in postsecondary education in both countries (see section 4.2B). Direct public expenditures on postsecondary education were comparable between Canada and the United States, with the differential in postsecondary expenditures arising from higher public subsidies in Canada (1.7%) than in the United States (0.4%).

*Table 3.26 shows the distribution of public and private sources of funds for educational institutions before (initial funds) and after (final funds) transfers from public sources in 1995 for Canada, jurisdictions and G-7 countries.*

Table 3.26 shows the percentage of funding to educational institutions that comes from the public and private sectors, and indicates the distribution before and after transfers between the two sectors. Before transfers, 90% of education spending in Canada was from public sources—about the same as the OECD average. This corresponded to 94% of expenditure for elementary–secondary education, and 82% for postsecondary expenditures. A net transfer from public to private sources occurred at the postsecondary level, increasing private spending from 18% before transfers to 39% after transfers. These transfers include the public expenditures to the private sector noted above (that is, scholarships, subsidies, etc.) Final funds from private sources capture all education fees paid to educational institutions, including the proportion that are supported by public subsidies to households.

Since the late 1980s, there has been a shift toward more private and less public expenditure on postsecondary education. This is illustrated for the university level by Figure 3.29. Between 1982-83 and 1998-99, government funding to universities has decreased as a percentage of operating revenue, from 74% to 55%. Over the same period, tuition fees have roughly doubled, increasing as a percentage of operating revenue, from 8% to 17%.

*Figure 3.30 and Table 3.27 show average undergraduate arts tuition fees in 1998 -99, and the percentage increase from 10 years earlier.*

Figure 3.30 shows that average tuition fees in undergraduate arts programs have more than doubled at the pan-Canadian level; they were $3,199 in 1998-99, up from about $1,500 in 1988-89. (Undergraduate arts programs were chosen to illustrate fee increases across the range of programs offered.)

## Characteristics and Features of Education Systems

FIGURE 3.29 TUITION FEES AND GOVERNMENT CONTRIBUTIONS AS A PERCENTAGE OF OPERATING REVENUE OF UNIVERSITIES, CANADA, 1982-83 TO 1998-99

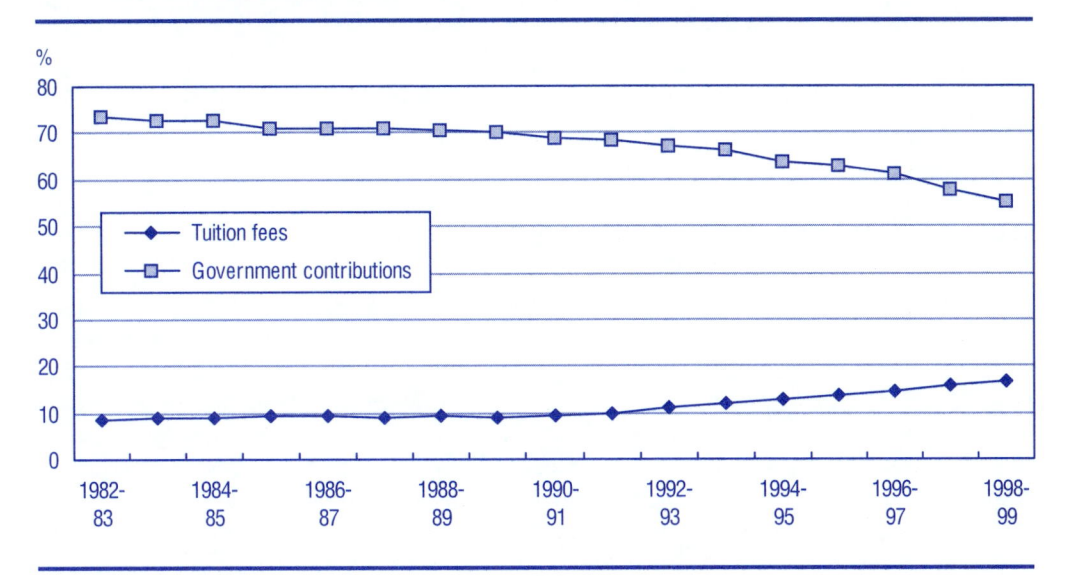

*Source: Centre for Education Statistics, Statistics Canada.*

FIGURE 3.30 AVERAGE TUITION FEES IN UNDERGRADUATE ARTS PROGRAMS AND PERCENTAGE CHANGE FROM 1988-89 TO 1998-99, CANADA AND PROVINCES

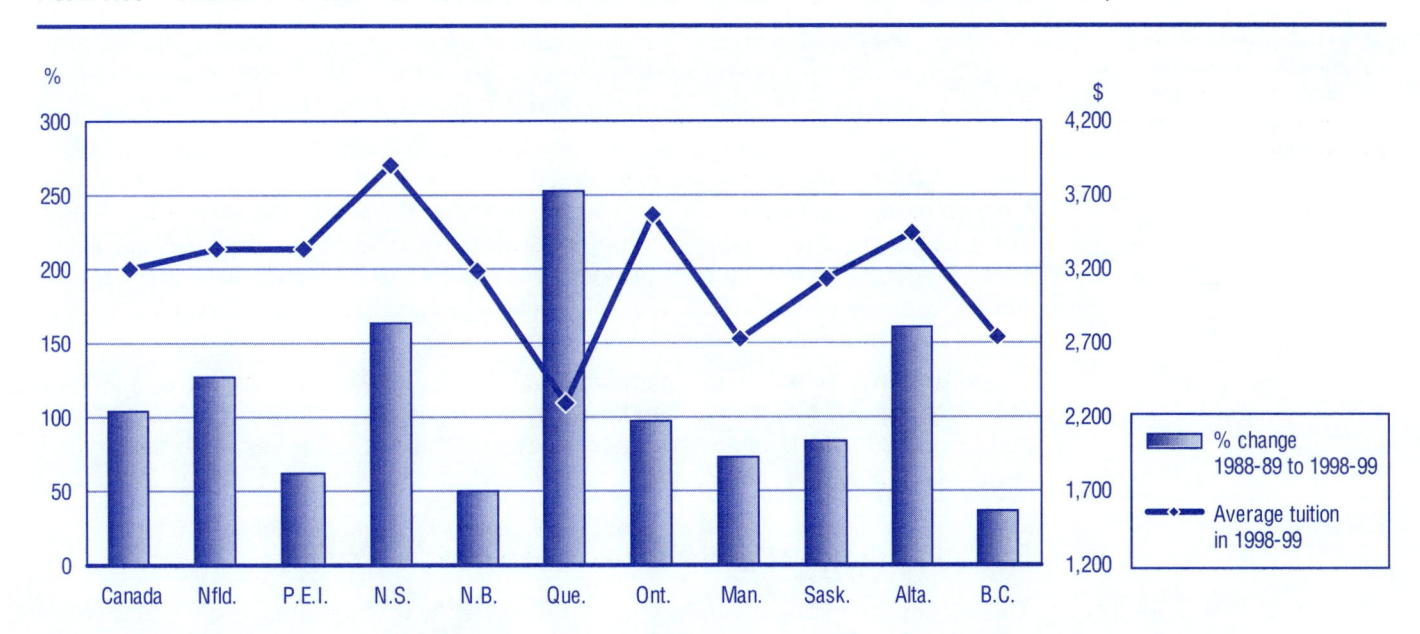

*Source: Centre for Education Statistics, Statistics Canada.*

## Jurisdictions

In 1995, public spending on education ranged from 9.7% of public expenditures in Nova Scotia to 16.9% in Newfoundland and Labrador (Table 3.25).

In 1995, public spending on elementary-secondary education ranged from 5.7% of public expenditures in Nova Scotia to 9.7% in Ontario.

Spending from private sources for elementary-secondary education varies considerably by jurisdiction, ranging from 1% in Prince Edward Island, New Brunswick, and Yukon, to 8%–9% in Quebec, Manitoba, and British Columbia (Table 3.26). This reflects the variability across jurisdictions in enrolments in private elementary and secondary schools.

Public spending on postsecondary education ranged from 2.5% of public expenditures in Yukon to 8.9% in Newfoundland and Labrador. The lower spending in Yukon and Northwest Territories may reflect a different structure in the postsecondary education sector, which includes colleges but no universities, as well as lower participation rates in postsecondary education. The higher spending in Newfoundland and Labrador in 1995 stemmed from the higher public subsidies to postsecondary education, which, at 5.7% of public expenditures, was over three times the pan-Canadian average. These expenditures were partly related to retraining programs associated with the closure of the Atlantic cod fishery.

Public expenditure on postsecondary education in Quebec was also above the pan-Canadian mean. The higher expenditure on postsecondary education and the lower than average expenditures on elementary-secondary education arise from the fact that the Quebec system has fewer years of elementary-secondary education prior to the commencement of postsecondary education in the CEGEP system. Also, a larger share of university revenues in Quebec is funded by the public sector, and university tuition fees are lower than in other jurisdictions (see below).

*At the university level, there is considerable variation in tuition fees, and the rate of increase in these fees has varied over the past ten years.*

In 1998-1999, university undergraduate tuition fees were well above the pan-Canadian average in Nova Scotia, Ontario, and Alberta, and well below the pan-Canadian average in Quebec, Manitoba, and British Columbia (Figure 3.30, Table 3.27).

Quebec had the lowest fees of any jurisdiction; average fees were $1,668 in 1998-99 for its own residents, unchanged from 1997-98. Quebec universities have been charging higher fees for out-of-province students since 1997-98—fees which are more comparable to those in other jurisdictions. In 1998-99, average fees in Quebec for all students (both in and out of province) were $2,292. Despite having the lowest tuition fees of any jurisdiction, Quebec has also had the largest percentage increase in fees of any jurisdiction in the past ten years.

Tuition fees in British Columbia have been frozen for the past five years, rising only 36% since 1989-90, the smallest increase of any jurisdiction. New Brunswick and Prince Edward Island experienced the next smallest increases, with tuition fees rising about 50% over the period.

## E. Educational expenditure by resource category

This section compares jurisdictions with respect to the way spending is divided between current and capital outlays, and the way current expenditure is distributed by resource category. Current expenditures are for goods and services consumed within the current year, which have to be made recurrently to sustain the production of educational services. Capital expenditures are for assets that last longer than one year, and include outlays for construction, renovation, major building repairs and expenditures for new or replacement equipment. They represent the value of educational capital acquired or created during the year in question.

# CHARACTERISTICS AND FEATURES OF EDUCATION SYSTEMS

In this particular indicator, as is the case for all finance indicators, neither current nor capital expenditures include expenditure for debt service, because of the international definitions used. As a result, the view of expenditures provided by these indicators is not as complete as it might be, since many jurisdictions finance their capital ventures. Additionally, capital expenditures can vary substantially from year to year, so that a single year's data may not be representative. For these reasons, while capital expenditures are shown in Tables 3.28 and 3.29, the focus of the analysis is on current expenditures. The proportions of current expenditure allocated to the compensation of educators, the compensation of other staff, total staff compensation, and other (non-personnel) current outlays are calculated by expressing the respective amounts as percentages of total current expenditure.

## FINDINGS

### CANADA

In elementary–secondary education, current expenditures accounted for 96% of overall expenditures in 1995. Staff compensation comprised by far the majority of current expenditures. In Canada, the salaries of all staff employed made up 81% of current expenditures, about the same as both the United States and the OECD average. Canada devoted more of its staff compensation to educators than the United States (65% of current expenditures versus 57% in the United States), but both countries were below the OECD average of 69%. Educator compensation per student in Canada was slightly higher than in the United States, at $3,405 versus $3,241. However, the United States spent more on non-teaching staff per student ($4,201 in Canada versus $4,554 in the United States). The United States also had higher capital spending per student at $559 versus $192 in Canada.

In postsecondary education, the percentage of current expenditures devoted to staff compensation was somewhat lower, averaging a little more than two-thirds across all OECD countries (69%). The variation between G-7 countries was rather wide, ranging from a low of 45% in the United Kingdom to a high of 76% in Germany. Staff compensation in Canada represented 72% of current expenditures, slightly above the OECD mean. However, the percentage of current expenditures devoted to the compensation of educators was less in Canada, at 39%, compared with the OECD mean of 44%. More was spent on non-teaching staff in Canada (33% versus the OECD mean of 22%).

Postsecondary spending per student was lower in Canada than the United States across all categories of resources. Compensation of teaching staff per student was almost 50% higher in the United States than in Canada ($6,100 versus $4,189); other current expenditures were almost double in the United States, and capital expenditures were 70% higher in the United States.

*Tables 3.28 and 3.29 show educational expenditure by resource category and level of education for public and private institutions.*

*In 1995, Canada devoted 65% of current expenditures to salaries of educators at the elementary–secondary level . . .*

*. . . and 39% of current expenditures to salaries of educators at the postsecondary level.*

EDUCATION INDICATORS IN CANADA

FIGURE 3.31  PERCENT DISTRIBUTION OF CURRENT EDUCATIONAL EXPENDITURE BY RESOURCE CATEGORY FOR PUBLIC AND PRIVATE INSTITUTIONS (1995), CANADA AND JURISDICTIONS

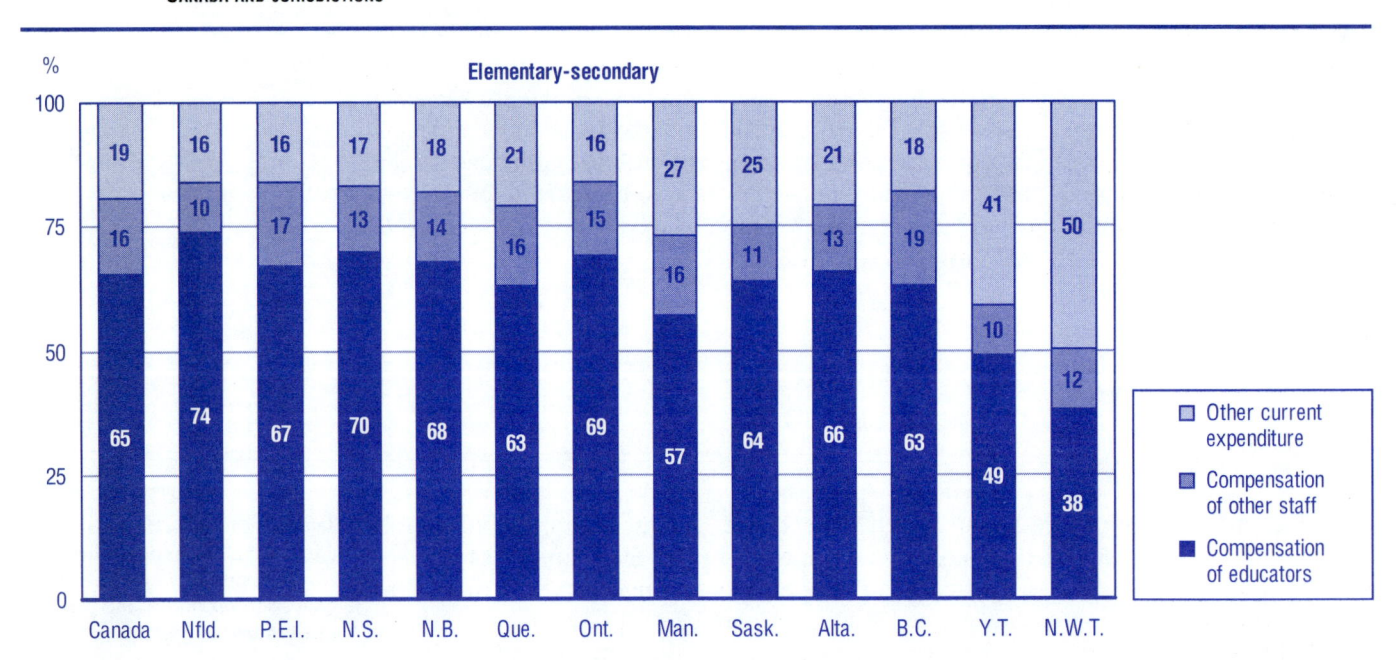

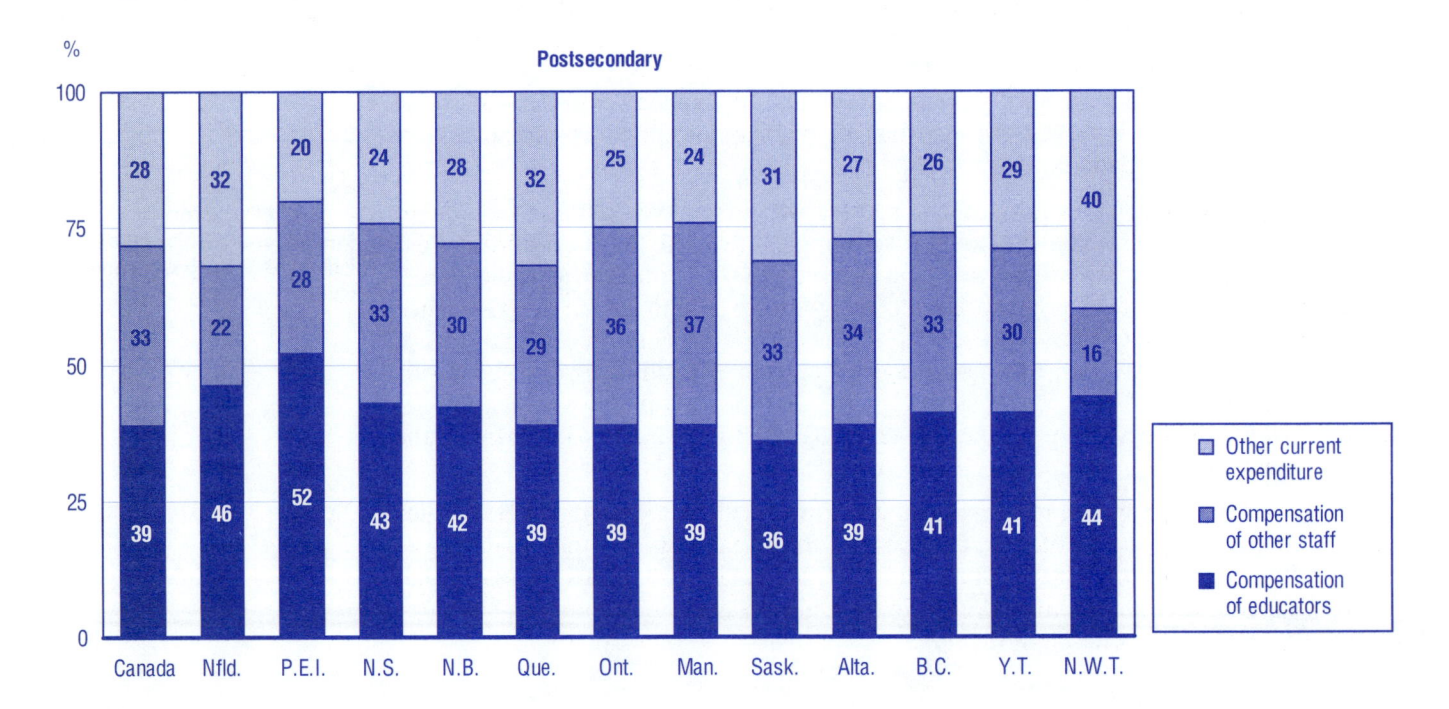

**Elementary-secondary**

| | Canada | Nfld. | P.E.I. | N.S. | N.B. | Que. | Ont. | Man. | Sask. | Alta. | B.C. | Y.T. | N.W.T. |
|---|---|---|---|---|---|---|---|---|---|---|---|---|---|
| Other current expenditure | 19 | 16 | 16 | 17 | 18 | 21 | 16 | 27 | 25 | 21 | 18 | 41 | 50 |
| Compensation of other staff | 16 | 10 | 17 | 13 | 14 | 16 | 15 | 16 | 11 | 13 | 19 | 10 | 12 |
| Compensation of educators | 65 | 74 | 67 | 70 | 68 | 63 | 69 | 57 | 64 | 66 | 63 | 49 | 38 |

**Postsecondary**

| | Canada | Nfld. | P.E.I. | N.S. | N.B. | Que. | Ont. | Man. | Sask. | Alta. | B.C. | Y.T. | N.W.T. |
|---|---|---|---|---|---|---|---|---|---|---|---|---|---|
| Other current expenditure | 28 | 32 | 20 | 24 | 28 | 32 | 25 | 24 | 31 | 27 | 26 | 29 | 40 |
| Compensation of other staff | 33 | 22 | 28 | 33 | 30 | 29 | 36 | 37 | 33 | 34 | 33 | 30 | 16 |
| Compensation of educators | 39 | 46 | 52 | 43 | 42 | 39 | 39 | 39 | 36 | 39 | 41 | 41 | 44 |

*Source: Centre for Education Statistics, Statistics Canada.*

## JURISDICTIONS

At the elementary–secondary level, the percentage of current expenditures devoted to staff compensation was close to the pan-Canadian mean of 81% in all jurisdictions except Manitoba, Saskatchewan, Yukon, and Northwest Territories. In the territories, there was a more even distribution between salaries and other current expenditures, reflecting different cost structures because of geographic differences that affect things such as school size, transportation, utilities, etc. Therefore, proportionately less was spent on the instruction function and more on the non-salary function. To a lesser extent, the same factors affected the cost structures in Manitoba and Saskatchewan.

Compensation of teaching staff ranged from 74% of current expenditures in Newfoundland and Labrador to 38% and 49% in Northwest Territories and Yukon, respectively, while compensation of non-teaching staff ranged from 19% of current expenditures in British Columbia to 10% in both the Yukon and Newfoundland and Labrador.

At the postsecondary level, compensation of staff was generally close to the pan-Canadian mean of 72%, ranging from 80% of current expenditures in Prince Edward Island to 60% in Northwest Territories. Compensation of educators was also close to the pan-Canadian mean of 39%, with Prince Edward Island and Newfoundland and Labrador somewhat higher at 52% and 46%, respectively.

## F. STUDENT DEBT

As the cost of postsecondary education has increased during the 1990s, so has public debate and concern about rising student indebtedness. Student debt is one component of private contributions to financing of education, and hence debates about student indebtedness are an element of the broader debate about public versus private contributions to the financing of postsecondary education. Is student assistance appropriate and sufficient? This section examines the evolution in student debt from government sponsored student loan programs among postsecondary graduates of colleges and universities.

## FINDINGS

## CANADA

While the use of government student loan programs to help finance college and university education has held fairly steady at just under 50% of graduates in 1986, 1990, and 1995, the amounts owing at the time of graduation and two years after graduation have increased over this period. Postsecondary graduates from the class of 1995 who took student loans owed an average of just over $11,000 at graduation. This was 39% more than the class of 1990 and 59% more than the class of 1986. Two years after graduation the 1995 class owed $8,300 on average, up 66% from the class of 1990 and 111% from the class of 1986. However this data pre-dates recent provincial and federal initiatives aimed at reducing student debt.

Graduates with master's and doctoral degrees had lower average debt on graduation and a faster rate of repayment than graduates with bachelor's degrees at all three time periods. (Debt figures refer to the accumulated debt incurred at all levels of study.)

EDUCATION INDICATORS IN CANADA

FIGURE 3.32 AVERAGE AMOUNT OWED TO STUDENT LOAN PROGRAMS, BY COLLEGE AND UNIVERSITY GRADUATES WHO BORROWED FROM STUDENT LOAN PROGRAMS, CANADA, 1986, 1990, AND 1995, IN CONSTANT 1995 DOLLARS

Table 3.30 and Figure 3.32 show average debt levels (in constant 1995 dollars) for 1986, 1990 and 1995 college and university graduates who borrowed from student loan programs.

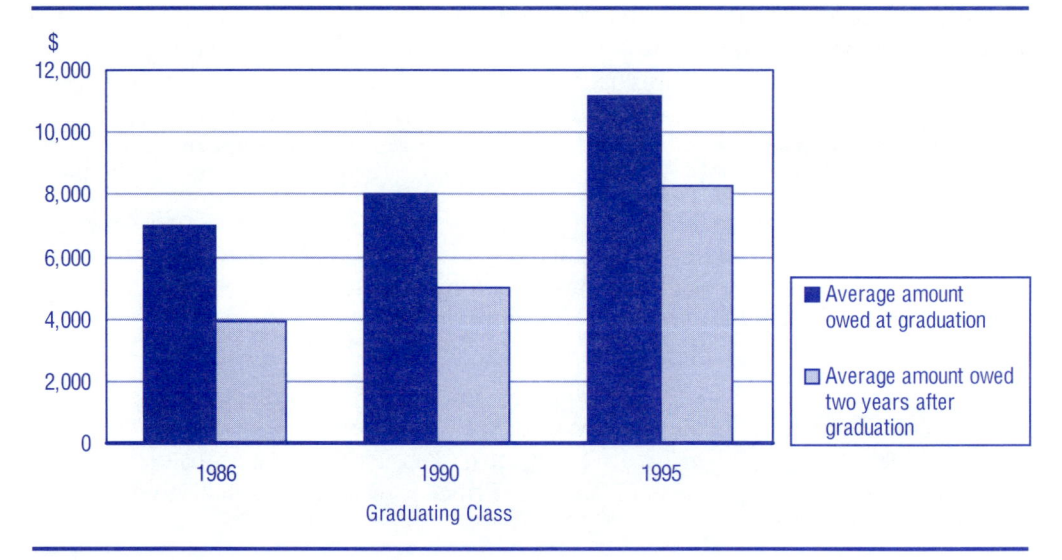

Source: National Graduates Surveys, 1988, 1992, and 1997, Statistics Canada.

Figure 3.33 shows indices of university tuition fees and median family incomes since 1988 (in constant 1999 dollars).

1995 graduates were paying off loans over a longer period than previous classes.

In part, the higher debt levels on graduation reflect increases in tuition and other costs, at a time when family income (in constant dollars) changed little (the 1990s). The changes in student aid policy with respect to grants and loans have likely had an impact as well, Plager (1999).

The 1995 cohort of postsecondary graduates in Canada lowered their debt on average by 25% within two years after graduation. This proportion was 38% for the 1990 cohort and 44% for the 1986 graduates. While the percentage of loan repayment was smaller for the recent cohort, the amount of loan repayment was similar, about $3,000, among all three classes. Changes in loan repayment schedules by both federal and provincial governments have without doubt had a direct bearing. Additionally, these findings are consistent with the slightly weaker labour market outcomes for 1995 graduates than 1986 graduates, as evident in lower rates of full-time employment and lower median earnings among the full-time employed (see section 5.2).

## PROVINCES

There has been a good deal of variation across provinces in the percentage of graduates who had borrowed to finance their education. The percentage borrowing exceeded the pan-Canadian average in the Atlantic Provinces and Alberta in all three graduating classes, and in Quebec for the two most recent classes. The percentage borrowing was generally less than the pan-Canadian average in Ontario, Manitoba, and British Columbia, and the same as the pan-Canadian average in Saskatchewan.

Debt at graduation, as well as two years after graduation, has increased in all provinces between 1986 and 1995. Postsecondary graduates in Quebec reported the lowest average amount owed at graduation of all provinces for the 1995 cohort ($9,575). However, they experienced the second highest rate of increase of average debt at graduation between the 1986 and 1995 cohorts, paralleling the large percentage increase in tuition fees in Quebec.

Saskatchewan had the largest increase in the average debt at graduation as well as two years after graduation, between the 1986 and 1995 cohorts, due to providing higher levels of assistance and the change from a provincial bursary to a provincial loan program.

FIGURE 3.33    INDICES OF MEDIAN FAMILY INCOME AND AVERAGE TUITION FEES IN UNDERGRADUATE ARTS PROGRAMS, CANADA, 1988 TO 1999, IN CONSTANT 1999 DOLLARS

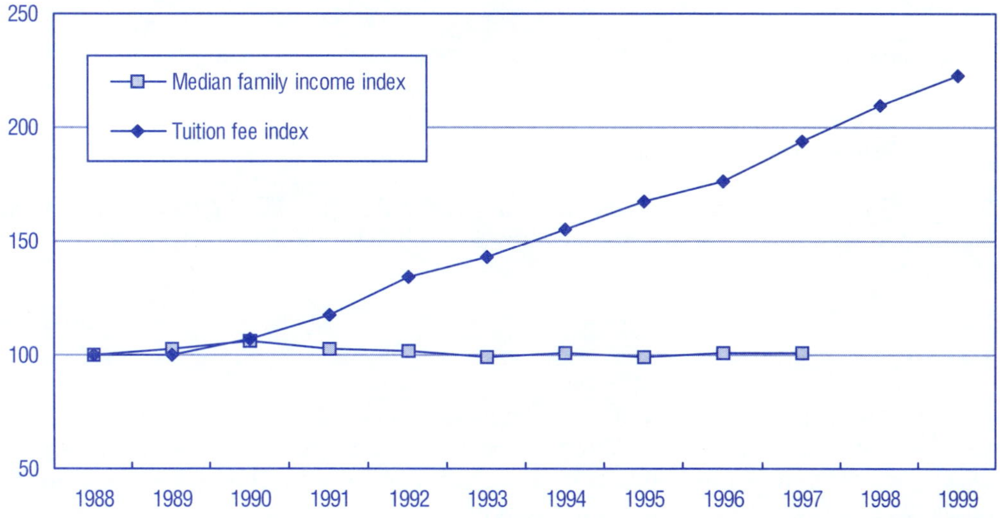

*Source:* Centre for Education Statistics, Statistics Canada, Income distribution by size in Canada *1997*, *Statistics Canada*, Catalogue no. 13-207.

Debt repayment took place over a longer period in all provinces for the 1995 graduates compared with the 1986 and 1990 cohorts. Two years after graduating, postsecondary graduates from the class of 1995 in the Atlantic Provinces and Quebec had lowered their debt between 15% and 21%. In Ontario and the Western provinces, 1995 graduates had lowered their debt between 27% and 33%. This may be due to the different economic conditions facing students and graduates across Canada.

## 3.6 INFORMATION AND COMMUNICATIONS TECHNOLOGIES IN SCHOOLS

### POLICY CONTEXT

All provincial and territorial ministries responsible for education have plans to use new information and communications technology (ICT) to help students acquire the skills needed for full participation in our increasingly complex knowledge-based environment. In addition, as part of a broader plan entitled Connecting Canadians, the federal government has introduced initiatives that promote the development and use of information technology in education. These include Industry Canada's SchoolNet and Computers for Schools programs.

The increasing amount of ICT hardware and software in Canada's school systems, coupled with the debates about how best to use them, has created a need for further study of this issue. In an effort to generate vital data, Canada, along with 27 countries in total, participated in the Second Information Technology in Education Study (SITES). (See Appendix 3 for a description of SITES.)

In an area that is changing as rapidly as ICT use in schools, SITES will provide valuable benchmark information against which future progress can be measured. The survey captures education systems at different stages in the implementation of their plans. The differences across provinces need to be viewed in this context.

EDUCATION INDICATORS IN CANADA

Findings presented include the number of computers in schools, the rates of connectivity of schools to the Internet, the learning activities of students that involve the Internet, and the perceived obstacles to fuller achievement of schools' computer-related goals.

## FINDINGS

### A. PUPIL-COMPUTER RATIO

Figure 3.34 shows the pupil–computer ratio by province in 1999.

The pupil-computer ratio is a proxy measure of the access or availability of computers to students in schools. Only computers used for educational purposes are included in the ratio.

### CANADA

In general, computers were more available to students in higher grades. When the survey was carried out, from January to February 1999, there was one computer for every nine elementary students, compared with one for every eight lower secondary students, and one for every seven upper secondary students.

### PROVINCES

The overall pattern of more availability of computers for students in higher grades was present in all provinces, with some variability in the actual ratios. Compared to pan-Canadian averages, at all grade levels ratios were higher in Nova Scotia and Quebec, and lower in Manitoba and Alberta. In Prince Edward Island, more emphasis has been placed on making computers available to students at the higher grade levels, with a ratio below that for Canada, while at the lower grade levels fewer computers were available, with a ratio above that for Canada.

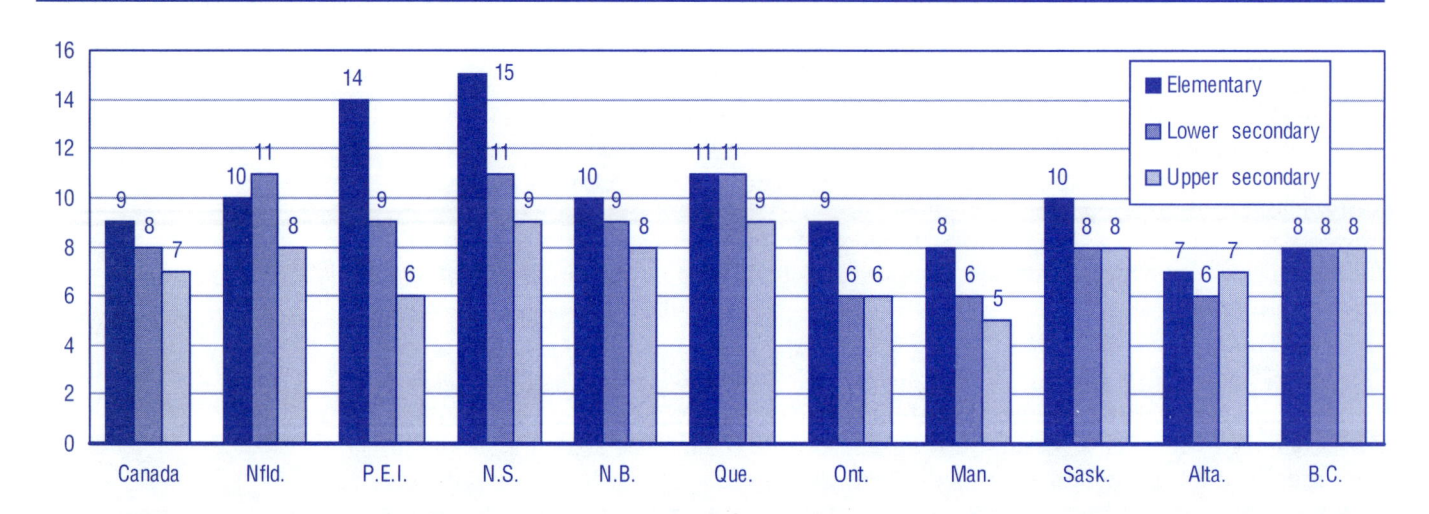

FIGURE 3.34    PUPIL-COMPUTER RATIO IN ELEMENTARY-SECONDARY SCHOOLS[1], CANADA AND PROVINCES, 1999

| Province | Elementary | Lower secondary | Upper secondary |
|---|---|---|---|
| Canada | 9 | 8 | 7 |
| Nfld. | 10 | 11 | 8 |
| P.E.I. | 14 | 9 | 6 |
| N.S. | 15 | 11 | 9 |
| N.B. | 10 | 9 | 8 |
| Que. | 11 | 11 | 9 |
| Ont. | 9 | 6 | 6 |
| Man. | 8 | 6 | 5 |
| Sask. | 10 | 8 | 8 |
| Alta. | 7 | 6 | 7 |
| B.C. | 8 | 8 | 8 |

1  Includes public and private elementary and secondary schools, classified into mutually exclusive groupings as follows:
    Elementary: schools in which grade 5 is taught.
    Lower secondary: schools in which grade 9 is taught.
    Upper secondary: schools in which the final grade of secondary is taught.

Source:  Second Information Technology in Education Study (SITES), 1999, Centre for Education Statistics, Statistic Canada, and International Association for the Evaluation of Educational Achievement (IEA).

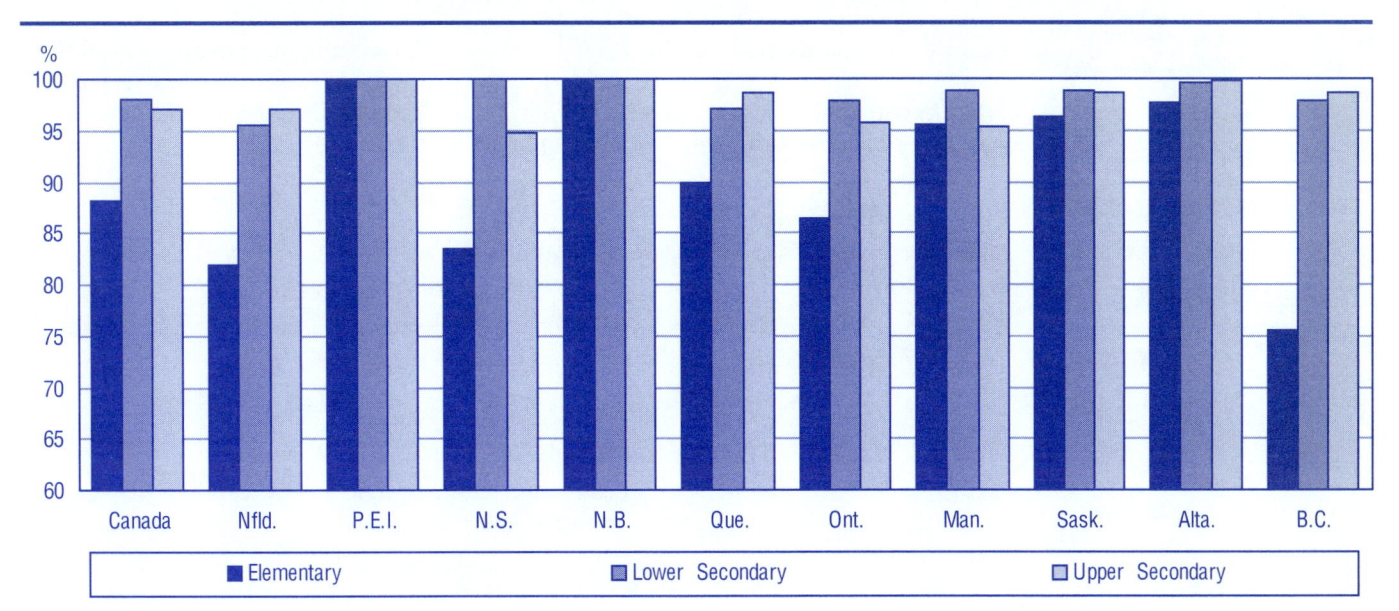

CHARACTERISTICS AND FEATURES OF EDUCATION SYSTEMS

FIGURE 3.35    PERCENTAGE OF STUDENTS IN ELEMENTARY-SECONDARY[1] SCHOOLS CONNECTED TO THE INTERNET, CANADA AND PROVINCES, 1999

■ Elementary   ■ Lower Secondary   □ Upper Secondary

1   Includes public and private elementary and secondary schools, classified into mutually exclusive groupings as follows:
    Elementary: schools in which grade 5 is taught.
    Lower secondary: schools in which grade 9 is taught.
    Upper secondary: schools in which the final grade of secondary is taught.
Source:   Second Information Technology in Education Study (SITES), 1999, Centre for Education Statistics, Statistic Canada, and International Association for the Evaluation of Educational Achievement (IEA).

## B.   INTERNET CONNECTIVITY

This is a measure of the percentage of students attending schools that were connected to the Internet for educational purposes at the time of the survey. Schools that were connected for administrative purposes only were excluded.

Figure 3.35 shows the percentage of students attending schools that are connected to the Internet for instructional purposes.

### CANADA

By the first two months of 1999, Canadian schools had widespread access to the Internet for instructional purposes. Eighty-eight percent of elementary students attended a school that had Internet access for instructional purposes, as did more than 97% of students in lower and upper secondary schools.

Close to 100% of intermediate and upper secondary schools were connected to the Internet.

### PROVINCES

The rate of connection to the Internet was uniformly high across provinces. In Prince Edward Island and New Brunswick, all schools were connected.

## C.   INTERNET ACTIVITIES OF STUDENTS

School ICT co-ordinators were questioned about instructional activities involving the use of the Internet. They were asked to identify typical activities that students at certain grade levels would have engaged in by the end of the school year.

Table 3.31 shows the percentage of students using the Internet for instructional purposes, by activity.

71

## CANADA

**One-third of students used e-mail and two-thirds used the World Wide Web for educational purposes.**

About one-third of elementary and lower secondary students and one-half of upper secondary students had used e-mail for different learning purposes. E-mail was commonly used to communicate with peers in other schools or other countries and to communicate with teachers for learning purposes. Students also used e-mail or bulletin boards to participate in group projects at school or with other schools.

In addition, 76% of elementary students, 80% of lower secondary and 87% of upper secondary students had, as part of their activities at school, extracted information from Web sites. Slightly more than one-third of all students had disseminated information on the Internet. The percentage of students who had designed or maintained a Web site ranged from 9% of elementary students to 53% of upper secondary students.

## PROVINCES

Use of the Internet varied across provinces. For example, the percentage of students that used e-mail in projects, and sent e-mail to peers and teachers, ranged from about two-thirds of students in Prince Edward Island to about one-third of students in New Brunswick. While a consistently high proportion of students in all provinces extracted information from the World Wide Web, there was a good deal of variation across provinces in other uses of the Internet, such as building or maintaining Web sites and disseminating information.

## D. OBSTACLES TO FULLER USE OF INFORMATION AND COMMUNICATIONS TECHNOLOGIES

**Table 3.32 reveals the major obstacles to greater use of ICT identified by principals.**

Principals were asked to identify the major barriers hindering the achievement of their school's computer-related goals for students. In this section we present items identified as major obstacles by principals of schools representing at least 50% of enrolments at each of the three levels of schools. The obstacles noted have been grouped into three categories: those relating to hardware and software, those relating to instruction, and those relating to the training of teachers.

## CANADA

**Obstacles included an insufficient number of computers, lack of teacher preparation time, lack of teacher skills in ICT, and lack of training opportunities for teachers.**

As regards hardware and software, an insufficient number of computers and insufficient variety of software were rated as major obstacles in schools representing the majority of enrolments. Obstacles relating to instruction included: insufficient time for teachers to prepare lessons in which computers are used, difficulty to integrate computers into the classroom, problems in scheduling computer time, and lack of time in teachers' schedules to explore the World Wide Web. Obstacles related to the training of teachers included a lack of skills or knowledge on the part of teachers about how to use computers for instructional purposes, and inadequate training opportunities for teachers.

An insufficient number of computers was more often perceived as a major obstacle for students in lower secondary and upper secondary schools than in elementary schools even though they have lower pupil-to-computer ratios than elementary schools. The perceived need for more computers for students in higher grades is possibly because the use of technology in these grades requires more direct use by students.

Difficulty scheduling enough computer time for different classes was also a significant issue in secondary schools where it was cited as a major obstacle in schools representing more than 60% of students. This was less of a concern in elementary schools, where the organisation of classes is not as highly structured.

## PROVINCES

In most provinces, not having enough computers was cited as a major problem in schools representing more than 60% of enrolments. An exception was Quebec, where an insufficient number of computers was less frequently cited as a major problem (in about 50% of cases), even though Quebec has one of the highest pupil-computer ratios. In contrast, Nova Scotia, the province with the highest pupil-computer ratio, was also the province where an insufficient number of computers was most frequently cited as a major obstacle.

*An insufficient number of computers was cited as an obstacle affecting over 60% of students.*

Insufficient teacher preparation time achieved a consistently high rating as a major obstacle across provinces. There was more variation across provinces in the frequency with which other instructional factors were perceived to be major obstacles. Difficulty scheduling computer time was less of an issue at all grade levels in Quebec. Lack of time for teachers to explore opportunities for using the Internet and the World Wide Web was less frequently cited as a major obstacle at all levels in Quebec and Manitoba, and at specific levels in other provinces.

Not enough opportunities for teacher training was generally cited as a major obstacle in schools representing well over 50% of enrolments in each province. Quebec and Manitoba were exceptions. In these provinces, lack of training opportunities was not as frequent an obstacle at all grade levels, especially at the upper secondary level, where it was rated a major obstacle in only about one-third of cases. Similarly, in upper secondary schools in Prince Edward Island, lack of training opportunities was an obstacle in only about one-third of cases.

*Insufficient teacher training opportunities were cited as an obstacle by principals of the majority of students except in Quebec and Manitoba.*

In most provinces, teachers' lack of knowledge or skills in using computers for instructional purposes was cited as a major obstacle in schools representing more than 50% of enrolments. Exceptions were lower secondary schools in Nova Scotia, and upper secondary schools in Manitoba. In both instances, this coincided with the less frequent citing of lack of training opportunities as an obstacle.

# REFERENCES

Browne, N. 1996. "English Early Years Education: Some Sociological Dimensions." *British Journal of Sociology of Education,* 17(3).

Delors, J. et. al. 1996. "Education: The Treasure Within." *Report to UNESCO of the International Commission on Education for the Twenty-first Century.* Paris: UNESCO, 141–142.

Little, D. 1997. "Financing Universities: Why are Students Paying More?" *Education Quarterly Review*, 4 (2): 10-26.

OECD 1998. "Human Capital Investment: An International Comparison" OECD Publications, Paris.

Ornstein, M. 1998. "The Status of Women Faculty in Canadian Universities." *Education Quarterly Review*, 5(2): 9-29.

Plager, L. and Chen, E. 1999. "Student debt from 1990-91 to 1995-96: An Analysis of Canada Student Loan Data." *Education Quarterly Review*, 5(4): 10-35.

Statistics Canada. 1999. *Earnings of Men and Women, 1997*. Ottawa: Minister responsible for Statistics Canada, 14.

Tremblay, A. 1997. "Are We Headed Toward a Teacher Surplus or a Teacher Shortage?" *Education Quarterly Review*, 4(1): 53-85.

# CHAPTER 4

## EDUCATION OUTCOMES

- Student achievement in pan-Canadian and international assessments
- Output rates
- Equity

## HIGHLIGHTS

- Pan-Canadian assessments in mathematics, science, and reading and writing show a learning gain for students between the ages of 13 and 16. Lower performance in reading and writing of francophone minorities and of male students suggests that both these groups need particular attention. In assessments of mathematics and science, there is little difference between the results achieved by males and females, or between results for francophone minority students and other students.

- Results of international assessments in mathematics and science carried out in 1994-95 show that the performance of Grade 8 students in Canada was above the international mean in both subjects. Performance of grade 4 students was above the international mean in science, and no different from the international mean in mathematics. For some jurisdictions, the performance was on par with the best in the world. A 1994-95 international literacy survey of adults placed Canada in the middle range of countries surveyed with respect to literacy skills.

- A higher percentage of females than males graduate from high school, and more females complete postsecondary education. Graduation rates from postsecondary programs increased considerably between 1976 and 1997 for both males and females.

- An examination of equity issues reveals that the educational attainment of the Aboriginal population is lower than that of the non-Aboriginal population. Compared with the non-Aboriginal population, a higher percentage of the Aboriginal population do not complete high school. Only a small percentage of Aboriginal peoples have obtained a university degree.

- Among linguistic minorities, individuals whose mother tongue is other than French or English (including those whose first language is an Aboriginal language) are less likely than francophones or anglophones to graduate from high school. However, people in this group are also more likely to have a university degree. Some of the differences for this group may be attributable to immigration policy rather than to Canadian education systems. Francophone and anglophone minorities generally have similar levels of educational attainment as the majority language group in their jurisdiction, despite the concerns arising from student assessment results noted above.

- There is a relationship between an individual's educational attainment and the socio-economic status (SES) of parents. People from low SES backgrounds are less likely to complete high school than those from high SES backgrounds. Between 1986 and 1994, university participation rates increased for persons from all SES backgrounds. The increase, however, was smallest for those from low SES backgrounds, which opened up a gap in participation between those from low and middle SES backgrounds.

EDUCATION OUTCOMES

# 4.1 STUDENT ACHIEVEMENT IN PAN-CANADIAN AND INTERNATIONAL ASSESSMENTS

Comparing student achievement over time and across jurisdictional and national boundaries is often regarded as a valuable way to assess the relative performance of education systems, although care must be taken when comparing education systems that have diverse needs and different local conditions. Large-scale assessments provide a mechanism for policy makers to determine whether provincial and territorial standards and programs are appropriate and effective. Test results also provide a way to measure variations in student achievement that can lead to inequalities that may last through adulthood.

On a pan-Canadian basis, student achievement is reported through the School Achievement Indicators Program (SAIP). At an international level, student achievement was assessed through the 1994-95 Third International Mathematics and Science Study (TIMSS), while the 1994 International Adult Literacy Survey (IALS) assessed the literacy skills of the adult population. Some provinces participating in the international assessments had sufficiently large samples to permit comparisons with other countries.

**Large-scale assessments help to measure the performance of students across Canada and internationally, in areas such as mathematics, science, and reading and writing.**

## A. SCHOOL ACHIEVEMENT INDICATORS PROGRAM

The School Achievement Indicators Program (SAIP) measures the achievements of a sample of 13- and 16-year-old students across Canada. The first assessment, in mathematics content and problem solving, was administered in 1993. This was followed by an assessment of reading and writing in 1994, and of science in 1996. A second cycle of assessments began in 1997 and was completed in 1999. SAIP results are reported according to the level achieved: level 1 being the lowest, level 5 being the highest. (See Appendix 3 for description of the different levels.)

In each assessment, both age groups write components of the same test. The developers of SAIP anticipated that the majority of 13-year-olds would achieve level 2 and the majority of 16-year-olds would achieve level 3 in each assessment. The SAIP data presented here show the percentage of each age group that achieved these levels or above. For example, discussion of the performance of 13-year-olds relates to the percentage that achieved level 2 or above.

**SAIP assessments are administered to a sample of 13- and 16-year-old students from each jurisdiction.**

Figures 4.1 and 4.2 show the performance of each jurisdiction compared with the results for Canada as a whole. For the reading and writing assessment, results for francophones by jurisdiction are compared with pan-Canadian francophone results, and results for anglophones by jurisdiction with pan-Canadian anglophone results.

As expected, in all assessments, significantly more of the 16-year-olds achieved the higher levels (4 and 5) than did the 13-year-olds. Results by level are not included in this report but are available in the SAIP reports.[1]

### POLICY CONTEXT

The higher achievement of 16-year-olds indicates that a learning gain and an associated increase in skills and knowledge takes place between the ages of 13 and 16. This is particularly evident in the substantial difference in achievement between the two age cohorts at levels 4 and 5.

The SAIP results raise a number of questions that merit further research in order to determine what is effective in improving student achievement. For example, what are the causes of the significantly lower percentage of male students who achieve advanced reading and writing levels in both age groups, and what can be done to increase their achievement? Research into the differences in results between jurisdictions would help to discover whether there are any relationships between the results of assessments such as SAIP, TIMSS and IALS and factors such as curriculum, class size, per student expenditure, and socio-economic and linguistic distribution.

EDUCATION INDICATORS IN CANADA

A comparison of results in reading and writing between francophone minorities and the pan-Canadian average for francophones suggests that policies may be needed to improve these skills for the francophone minority, along with research into the underlying reasons for their lower performance.

Many students in what is now Nunavut are educated in Inuktitut from kindergarten to Grade 3, with English instruction beginning in grade 4. Education in other aboriginal languages is also growing in the Northwest Territories. The results for students in the Northwest Territories in the reading and writing assessments should be interpreted accordingly.

FIGURE 4.1    PERFORMANCE OF JURISDICTIONS RELATIVE TO CANADA IN SAIP ASSESSMENTS, SHOWING PERCENTAGE OF 13-YEAR-OLDS AT LEVEL 2 OR ABOVE

|  | Mathematics content 1993 | Mathematics content 1997 | Mathematics problem solving 1997 | Reading 1994 | Reading 1998 | Writing 1994 | Writing 1998 | Written science 1996 |
|---|---|---|---|---|---|---|---|---|
| Newfoundland and Labrador | ▼ | o | ▼ | o | o | o | o | o |
| Prince Edward Island | ▼ | ▼ | o | ▼ | o | ▼ | o | ▲ |
| Nova Scotia | ▼ | ... | ... | o | ... | o | ... | ... |
| Nova Scotia (E) | ... | ▼ | ▼ | ... | ▼ | ... | o | o |
| Nova Scotia (F) | ... | ▲ | ▼ | ... | ▼ | ... | ▼ | ▲ |
| New Brunswick (E) | o | ▼ | ▼ | o | o | o | o | o |
| New Brunswick (F) | o | o | o | ▼ | ▼ | ▼ | ▼ | ▼ |
| Quebec (E) | o | ▲ | ▲ | o | o | o | o | o |
| Quebec (F) | ▲ | ▲ | ▲ | o | o | o | o | o |
| Ontario (E) | ▼ | ▼ | ▼ | o | o | o | o | ▼ |
| Ontario (F) | ▼ | ▼ | ▼ | ▼ | ▼ | ▼ | ▼ | ▼ |
| Manitoba (E) | ▼ | ▼ | ▼ | o | o | o | o | o |
| Manitoba (F) | o | o | o | o | ▼ | ▼ | ▼ | ▼ |
| Saskatchewan | ... | ▼ | o | ... | o | ... | o | ▲ |
| Alberta | ▲ | ▲ | ▲ | o | o | o | o | ▲ |
| British Columbia | o | o | ▼ | o | o | o | o | o |
| Yukon | ▼ | o | ▼ | ▼ | o | ▼ | o | o |
| Northwest Territories | ▼ | ▼ | ▼ | ▼ | ▼ | ▼ | ▼ | ▼ |

▲  Significantly higher than Canada.
o   No statistically significant difference from Canada.
▼  Significantly lower than Canada.

Note:   The terms "significantly higher" and "significantly lower" refer to statistically significant differences between the results of jurisdictions and the results at the Canada level. Results are statistically different with 95 % confidence if the relevant confidence intervals do not overlap.
The 1997 SAIP Mathematics Report was used as the source of data for the 1993 mathematics content results.
Comparisons between the 1993 and 1997 mathematics problem solving assessments are not shown in this report. Because only four questions on the 1997 mathematics problem solving assessment were the same as those used in the 1993 assessment, it is not appropriate to compare these assessments.
For the reading and writing assessments, anglophone and francophone populations in Nova Scotia, New Brunswick, Quebec, Ontario, and Manitoba were compared with the respective Canadian anglophone and francophone populations.
For the reading and writing assessments, results for Newfoundland and Labrador, Prince Edward Island, Nova Scotia (1994), Saskatchewan, Alberta, British Columbia, Yukon, and Northwest Territories were compared to Canada anglophone results.
Results for the written portion of the SAIP science assessment are shown in this report. The practical portion is not included because results are generally not available by jurisdiction.
Saskatchewan did not participate in SAIP in 1993 or 1994.
Nova Scotia did not sample English and French students separately in 1993 and 1994.

Source:  School Achievement Indicators Program (SAIP), Council of Ministers of Education, Canada.

EDUCATION OUTCOMES

FIGURE 4.2  PERFORMANCE OF JURISDICTIONS RELATIVE TO CANADA IN SAIP ASSESSMENTS, SHOWING PERCENTAGE OF 16-YEAR-OLDS AT LEVEL 3 OR ABOVE

|  | Mathematics content | | Mathematics problem solving | Reading | | Writing | | Written science |
|---|---|---|---|---|---|---|---|---|
|  | 1993 | 1997 | 1997 | 1994 | 1998 | 1994 | 1998 | 1996 |
| Newfoundland and Labrador | ▼ | ▼ | ▼ | o | o | o | o | ▼ |
| Prince Edward Island | ▼ | ▼ | ▼ | o | ▼ | o | o | o |
| Nova Scotia | o | ... | ... | o | ... | o | ... | ... |
| Nova Scotia (E) | ... | o | o | ... | o | ... | o | o |
| Nova Scotia (F) | ... | ▲ | ▲ | ... | ▼ | ... | ▼ | ▲ |
| New Brunswick (E) | ▼ | ▼ | ▼ | o | o | o | o | o |
| New Brunswick (F) | o | o | o | ▼ | ▼ | ▼ | ▼ | ▼ |
| Quebec (E) | o | ▲ | ▲ | o | o | o | o | o |
| Quebec (F) | ▲ | ▲ | ▲ | o | o | o | o | ▲ |
| Ontario (E) | ▼ | ▼ | ▼ | o | o | o | o | ▼ |
| Ontario (F) | ▼ | ▼ | ▼ | ▼ | ▼ | ▼ | ▼ | ▼ |
| Manitoba (E) | ▼ | ▼ | o | o | o | o | o | o |
| Manitoba (F) | o | o | o | ▼ | ▼ | ▼ | ▼ | o |
| Saskatchewan | ... | ▼ | o | ... | ▼ | ... | o | o |
| Alberta | o | o | ▲ | o | o | o | o | ▲ |
| British Columbia | o | ▼ | ▼ | o | o | o | o | o |
| Yukon | o | o | ▼ | ▼ | ▼ | o | o | o |
| Northwest Territories | ▼ | ▼ | ▼ | ▼ | ▼ | ▼ | ▼ | ▼ |

▲   Significantly higher than Canada.
o   No statistically significant difference from Canada.
▼   Significantly lower than Canada.

Notes:  The terms "significantly higher" and "significantly lower" refer to statistically significant differences between the results of jurisdictions and the results at the Canada level. Results are statistically different with 95 % confidence if the relevant confidence intervals do not overlap.
The 1997 SAIP Mathematics Report was used as the source of data for the 1993 mathematics content results.
Comparisons between the 1993 and 1997 mathematics problem solving assessments are not shown in this report. Because only four questions on the 1997 mathematics problem solving assessment were the same as those used in the 1993 assessment, it is not appropriate to compare these assessments.
For the reading and writing assessments, anglophone and francophone populations in Nova Scotia, New Brunswick, Quebec, Ontario, and Manitoba were compared with the respective Canadian anglophone and francophone populations.
For the reading and writing assessments, results for Newfoundland and Labrador, Prince Edward Island, Nova Scotia (1994), Saskatchewan, Alberta, British Columbia, Yukon, and Northwest Territories were compared to Canada anglophone results.
Results for the written portion of the SAIP science assessment are shown in this report. The practical portion is not included because results are generally not available by jurisdiction.
Saskatchewan did not participate in SAIP in 1993 or 1994.
Nova Scotia did not sample English and French students separately in 1993 and 1994.

Source:  *School Achievement Indicators Program (SAIP), Council of Ministers of Education, Canada.*

EDUCATION INDICATORS IN CANADA

## SAIP MATHEMATICS ASSESSMENTS

Two SAIP mathematics assessments have been completed, the first in 1993 and the second in 1997. Each assessment had two components: a section on mathematics content, which tested general mathematical knowledge, and a section that tested problem-solving skills. Given the changes made to the mathematics problem-solving component in 1997, comparisons between the 1993 and 1997 components would be inappropriate, and therefore only the 1997 results are included here.

## FINDINGS

### CANADA

**In 1997, more students in both age groups reached the upper levels in mathematics content than in problem solving.**

In mathematics content, the results for 13-year-olds were slightly lower in 1997 than in 1993. The performance of 16-year-olds remained stable. In 1997, 59% of 13 year olds achieved level 2 or above in mathematics content, compared with 52% in problem solving. The gap was wider for 16 year olds, approximately 60% achieved level 3 or above in mathematics content while only 40% achieved this in problem solving (Tables 4.1 and 4.2).

**The performance of male and female students was similar in mathematics.**

In both 1993 and 1997, results by gender showed little difference. Among 13-year-olds, the only statistically significant difference was in problem solving in 1997, with slightly more female than male students achieving level 2 or above (Table 4.3). Among 16-year-olds, the situation was reversed, with slightly more males than females achieving level 3 or above in mathematics content at both time periods (Table 4.4).

### JURISDICTIONS

In 1997, more than half of the 13-year-olds achieved level 2 or above in mathematics content in all jurisdictions except Saskatchewan and Northwest Territories. For problem solving, only New Brunswick (French), Quebec, Manitoba (French), Saskatchewan, and Alberta had half their 13-year-olds achieve level 2 or above. For 16-year-olds, over 50% achieved level 3 or more in mathematics content in 1997 except in Newfoundland and Labrador, Prince Edward Island, New Brunswick (English), Ontario (French), and Northwest Territories. The results of 16-year-olds were also not as strong in problem solving; there were only four jurisdictions in which more than 40% achieved level 3 or above. Only in Quebec (French) was the percentage higher than 50%.

**Students in Quebec, Alberta and Nova Scotia (French) achieved results that were generally higher than the overall pan-Canadian average.**

In Alberta, the results for 13-year-olds were above the pan-Canadian average in both the 1993 and 1997 mathematics assessments for both components, and the results for 16-year-olds were above the pan-Canadian average in problem solving in 1997. Quebec francophones in both age groups were above the pan-Canadian average in both assessments and both components, while Quebec anglophones of the same age were above the pan-Canadian average in both components in 1997. In Nova Scotia, francophone 16-year-olds were also above the pan-Canadian average on the 1997 assessment, while francophone 13-year-olds were above the pan-Canadian average in mathematics content.

The results for Ontario and Northwest Territories were lower than the pan-Canadian average in both assessments, for both age groups. In Manitoba, anglophone 13-year-olds were also below the pan-Canadian average in both assessments, as were 16-year-olds in Newfoundland and Labrador, Prince Edward Island, and New Brunswick (English).

Other jurisdictions were not consistently above or below the pan-Canadian average.

## SAIP READING AND WRITING ASSESSMENTS

Reading and writing assessments were carried out in 1994 and 1998. Despite the care taken to ensure equivalency, caution is advised when comparing achievement results based on assessment instruments of reading and writing prepared in different languages. The 1998 results are comparable to the 1994 results.

## FINDINGS

### CANADA

Between 1994 and 1998, the performance of both age groups in reading remained stable, but writing achievement increased (Tables 4.1 and 4.2).

In general, female students showed stronger performance in reading and writing than male students. In 1998, the differences ranged from approximately 5 percentage points for writing among 13-year-olds, to close to 22 percentage points for reading and 11 percentage points for writing among 16-year-olds (Tables 4.3 and 4.4). In both 1994 and 1998, significantly more females than males demonstrated advanced reading and writing skills (levels 3 and above for 13-year-olds and levels 4 and 5 for 16-year-olds).

*Significantly more female than male students demonstrated advanced reading and writing skills.*

### JURISDICTIONS

The reading achievement of 13-year-olds remained approximately the same from 1994 to 1998 in most jurisdictions, except Nova Scotia, where it decreased. The percentage of 16-year-olds at level 3 or above increased among New Brunswick francophone students, but remained relatively stable in the other jurisdictions. In writing, significant improvements occurred in the following jurisdictions between 1994 and 1998: among 13-year-olds, in New Brunswick (French), Ontario (French), Manitoba (French) and Yukon; among 16-year-olds, in New Brunswick (French) and Quebec (French) (Tables 4.1 and 4.2).

In 1998, over 70% of 13-year-olds achieved level 2 or higher in reading in most jurisdictions. The exceptions were Nova Scotia (French) and Northwest Territories. More than 65% of 16-year-olds in all jurisdictions except Prince Edward Island, Nova Scotia (French), Manitoba (French), Yukon, and Northwest Territories achieved level 3 or above. In the 1998 writing assessment, over 80% of students of both age groups met the expected levels. Among 13-year-olds, exceptions were Nova Scotia (French) and Northwest Territories, and among 16-year-olds, francophone minority students and students in Northwest Territories.

No jurisdiction showed results significantly above the pan-Canadian figures in either the 1994 or 1998 reading and writing assessments.

Francophone minorities achieved results below the pan-Canadian francophone average in all but one case. The exception was Manitoba, where, in reading, francophone 13-year-olds equalled the pan-Canadian figure in 1994. Anglophone students in Quebec matched the pan-Canadian anglophone averages in all assessments. Students in Northwest Territories, many of whom speak neither English nor French as a first language, performed below the pan-Canadian average on all assessments.

*Francophone minorities generally performed below the pan-Canadian francophone average.*

## SAIP SCIENCE ASSESSMENT

The SAIP science assessment was designed to test students' knowledge of scientific concepts. The assessment covered general science knowledge, as well as the nature of science, the relationship of science and technology to societal issues, and science inquiry skills. Only the results of the written component of the assessment in 1996 are reported here, because results are not available for all jurisdictions for the practical component. The second SAIP science assessment was completed in 1999. Results will be available in early 2000.

## FINDINGS

### CANADA

Close to 70% of 16-year-olds achieved level 3 or above in the 1996 written component of the SAIP science assessment. Approximately the same percentage of 13-year-olds achieved results at level 2 or above (Tables 4.1 and 4.2).

*Differences in results by gender were slight.*

A slight statistical difference existed in favour of 13-year-old female students when results are aggregated at level 2 and above and in favour of 16-year-old male students when results are aggregated at level 3 and above (Tables 4.3 and 4.4).

### JURISDICTIONS

Thirteen-year-olds in Prince Edward Island, Nova Scotia (French), Saskatchewan, and Alberta achieved results that were higher than the pan-Canadian average. Sixteen-year-olds in Nova Scotia (French), Quebec (French) and Alberta had results that exceeded the pan-Canadian average (Figures 4.1 and 4.2).

New Brunswick (French), Ontario, and the Northwest Territories fell below the pan-Canadian average in both age groups, as did 13-year-olds in Manitoba (French), and 16-year-olds in Newfoundland and Labrador.

## B. THIRD INTERNATIONAL MATHEMATICS AND SCIENCE STUDY (TIMSS)

### POLICY CONTEXT

*Data from the 1994-95 TIMSS assessment are presented for Population 1 (Grade 4) and Population 2 (Grade 8).*

In today's increasingly technological world, where many jobs require a firm foundation in the basic sciences, the ability to assess student achievement in mathematics and science is important. Canada needs a well-educated work force in order to maintain our standard of living, with its relatively high wages and earnings. International assessments complement results from pan-Canadian assessments, such as the SAIP mathematics and science assessments, by helping to measure how students in Canada are doing in relation to those in other countries. The results for provinces that produced separate samples for the Third International Mathematics and Science Study (TIMSS) are generally similar to their standing, relative to the result for Canada, on the SAIP assessments shown in Figures 4.1 and 4.2.

The extent of participation in TIMSS in 1994-95 demonstrates the importance countries place on mathematics and science assessments. For TIMSS, students were assessed in three population groups: Population 1 (grades 3 and 4), Population 2 (grades 7 and 8), and Population 3 (final year of secondary school). Twenty-six countries participated in TIMSS at the Population 1 level, of which 15 met all sampling requirements. Forty-one countries participated at the Population 2 level, with 19 meeting all sampling requirements.

Results are presented here for the countries that fully met the sampling requirements for Population 1 (referred to here as Grade 4) and Population 2 (Grade 8).[2] In addition to the nationally representative sample for Canada as a whole, Newfoundland and Labrador, New Brunswick, Quebec, Ontario, Alberta, and British Columbia had large enough samples to allow their results to be compared with those of other countries.

# EDUCATION OUTCOMES

Results for any country or province are likely to be affected by the extent to which the material presented in the assessment has been covered in the curriculum of that country or province. In part, this represents choices that are made about what areas to cover. It may also reflect the approach to curriculum planning in general. Some education systems focus on discrete subject areas in each grade, for example, physics one year, followed by biology the next, while other education systems cover a wider range of subject areas in each grade, dealing with both physics and biology in the same grade, but students study the material in less depth.

Results from TIMSS show that students in Canada, on average, performed at or above the international mean score. However, countries such as Japan and Korea produced results that were higher than Canada's in both subjects and for both Grade 4 and Grade 8, which indicates that we still have room to improve. It is also important to note that only a few of the G-7 countries are represented in the results, and that the international mean is based on all participating countries.

*Canadian students achieved results at or above the international mean.*

International assessments can be used to highlight countries (or jurisdictions) where performance is particularly strong. We can then study their education systems to identify the factors that contribute to high achievement. For example, is a country's performance related to the investment in education made per student? Is a particular curriculum structure used? At what age are students introduced to particular concepts? Although some aspects of foreign education systems that seem conducive to strong results may not fit the Canadian context, it is still useful to examine other systems. The differences provide a valuable stimulus to debate and enquiry. In-depth analysis is required for fuller interpretation of the TIMSS results (see for example, the TIMSS Canada Report, Robitaille et al., Lauzon; and Zhang[3]).

*In 1999, TIMSS-R (Repeat) was administered to Population 2 only. It involves a fresh sample of the cohort that wrote the 1994-95 test as Population 1.*

## FINDINGS

### CANADA

TIMSS scores represent the overall percent correct. Unlike SAIP, no division into levels is used for TIMSS (Figures 4.3 and 4.4).

Canada's score was above the international mean for both mathematics and science at the Grade 8 level. It was also above the international mean for science at the Grade 4 level, and was at the international mean for Grade 4 mathematics. For Grade 4 mathematics, five countries had significantly higher scores than Canada. For Grade 8 mathematics, seven countries were significantly higher than Canada. Three countries scored above Canada for Grade 4 science and four scored above Canada for Grade 8 science.

Japan, Korea, and Singapore showed the strongest overall results. Japan and Korea were among the top three countries in each assessment, while Singapore was in the top three in every assessment except Grade 4 science.

Among the G-7 countries, Japan scored significantly higher than Canada in both subjects and both grades. Results for the United States were not significantly different than those of Canada for mathematics, and were higher for science. (This applies to Grade 4 only; Grade 8 results are not presented because the United States did not meet all sampling requirements.) France's results were not significantly different than Canada's for Grade 8 mathematics, but were significantly lower for Grade 8 science.

Although data on gender differences are not presented in this report, no significant differences were found between male and female students in Canada in overall achievement in either mathematics or science (Robitaille et al., 1996-97). The provinces had similar results.

83

## Jurisdictions

In the Grade 4 assessments, in both subjects, all six Canadian provinces that showed separate results had scores that were either similar to or above those for Canada as a whole (Figures 4.3 and 4.4).

Alberta's performance in science was higher than that of Canada and not significantly different than that of Japan at both grade levels. Quebec ranked above Canada in mathematics at both grade levels. British Columbia's result was higher than Canada's for Grade 8 mathematics.

In Grade 8, in both subjects, Ontario's results were below those of Canada. New Brunswick ranked lower than Canada in Grade 8 mathematics.

**In both Grade 4 and Grade 8, Quebec ranked above the Canadian result for mathematics, and Alberta ranked above the Canadian result for science.**

FIGURE 4.3     TIMSS INTERNATIONAL, CANADIAN, AND PROVINCIAL ACHIEVEMENT SCORES IN MATHEMATICS, 1994-95

### Grade 4 mathematics

| Jurisdictions | Percent correct | Confidence interval |
|---|---|---|
| Korea | 76 | 0.8 |
| Singapore | 76 | 1.6 |
| Japan | 74 | 0.8 |
| Hong Kong | 73 | 1.8 |
| **Quebec** | **69** | **2.0** |
| Czech Republic | 66 | 1.2 |
| **Alberta** | **65** | **3.4** |
| Ireland | 63 | 1.6 |
| United States | 63 | 1.2 |
| **CANADA** | **60** | **2.0** |
| **British Columbia** | **59** | **4.8** |
| **Newfoundland and Labrador** | **58** | **2.8** |
| **New Brunswick (English)** | **58** | **4.0** |
| **Ontario** | **57** | **1.6** |
| Cyprus | 54 | 1.2 |
| Norway | 53 | 1.4 |
| New Zealand | 53 | 2.0 |
| Greece | 51 | 1.8 |
| Iceland | 50 | 1.6 |
| Portugal | 48 | 1.4 |
| Iran | 38 | 1.8 |
| **International mean** | **50** | **0.4** |

### Grade 8 mathematics

| Jurisdictions | Percent correct | Confidence interval |
|---|---|---|
| Singapore | 79 | 1.8 |
| Japan | 73 | 0.8 |
| Korea | 72 | 1.0 |
| Hong Kong | 70 | 2.8 |
| **Quebec** | **68** | **3.0** |
| Czech Republic | 66 | 2.2 |
| **British Columbia** | **63** | **3.0** |
| Slovak Republic | 62 | 1.6 |
| Hungary | 62 | 1.4 |
| France | 61 | 1.6 |
| **Alberta** | **61** | **2.0** |
| Russian Federation | 60 | 2.6 |
| **CANADA** | **59** | **1.0** |
| Ireland | 59 | 2.4 |
| **Newfoundland and Labrador** | **56** | **4.2** |
| Sweden | 56 | 1.4 |
| **New Brunswick (English)** | **54** | **2.6** |
| **Ontario** | **54** | **1.2** |
| New Zealand | 54 | 2.0 |
| Norway | 54 | 1.0 |
| Spain | 51 | 1.0 |
| Iceland | 50 | 2.2 |
| Cyprus | 48 | 1.0 |
| Portugal | 43 | 1.4 |
| Iran | 38 | 1.2 |
| **International mean** | **55** | **0.2** |

Results significantly higher than Canada
Results not statistically different from Canada
Results significantly lower than Canada

Notes: The terms "significantly higher" and "significantly lower" refer to statistically significant differences between the results of the jurisdictions or countries and the results at the Canada level. Results are statistically different with 95 % confidence if the relevant confidence intervals do not overlap.
The data represent mean scores, i.e., overall percent correct.
Countries that used replacement schools or did not meet all sampling requirements are not shown in this table.
The international mean includes countries not shown here.
Apparent contradictions in the placing of countries or provinces are due to the effects of rounding.
Results for Population 3 are omitted from this report, as Canada did not meet all sampling requirements for this population.

Source: Third International Mathematics and Science Study, 1994-95, International Association for the Evaluation of Educational Achievement (IEA); Robitaille et al., 1996-1997. Source for Quebec data is: Une comparaison internationale des résultats des élèves québécois en mathématique et en sciences, Bulletin statistique de l'éducation, no 6, août 1998, Ministère de l'Éducation du Québec.

# EDUCATION OUTCOMES

FIGURE 4.4　TIMSS INTERNATIONAL, CANADIAN, AND PROVINCIAL ACHIEVEMENT SCORES IN SCIENCE, 1994-95

**Grade 4 Science**

| Jurisdictions | Percent correct | Confidence interval |
|---|---|---|
| Korea | 74 | 0.8 |
| Japan | 70 | 0.6 |
| **Alberta** | **68** | **3.0** |
| United States | 66 | 1.0 |
| Czech Republic | 65 | 1.0 |
| **Quebec** | **65** | **1.4** |
| Singapore | 64 | 1.6 |
| **CANADA** | **64** | **1.2** |
| **British Columbia** | **64** | **3.4** |
| **Newfoundland and Labrador** | **62** | **1.8** |
| Hong Kong | 62 | 1.4 |
| **Ontario** | **62** | **1.4** |
| **New Brunswick (English)** | **61** | **2.6** |
| Ireland | 61 | 1.2 |
| Norway | 60 | 1.2 |
| New Zealand | 60 | 1.8 |
| Iceland | 55 | 1.4 |
| Greece | 54 | 1.6 |
| Cyprus | 51 | 1.0 |
| Portugal | 50 | 1.4 |
| Iran | 40 | 1.4 |
| **International mean** | **59** | **0.2** |

**Grade 8 Science**

| Jurisdictions | Percent correct | Confidence interval |
|---|---|---|
| Singapore | 70 | 2.0 |
| Korea | 66 | 0.6 |
| Japan | 65 | 0.6 |
| **Alberta** | **65** | **2.0** |
| Czech Republic | 64 | 1.6 |
| **British Columbia** | **62** | **3.4** |
| Hungary | 61 | 1.2 |
| Slovak Republic | 59 | 1.2 |
| Sweden | 59 | 1.2 |
| **CANADA** | **59** | **1.0** |
| **Quebec** | **59** | **2.6** |
| **Newfoundland and Labrador** | **59** | **3.2** |
| Ireland | 58 | 1.8 |
| Russian Federation | 58 | 1.6 |
| New Zealand | 58 | 1.6 |
| Norway | 58 | 0.8 |
| Hong Kong | 58 | 2.0 |
| **New Brunswick (English)** | **57** | **2.4** |
| **Ontario** | **56** | **1.4** |
| Spain | 56 | 0.8 |
| France | 54 | 1.2 |
| Iceland | 52 | 1.8 |
| Portugal | 50 | 1.2 |
| Iran | 47 | 1.2 |
| Cyprus | 47 | 0.8 |
| **International mean** | **56** | **0.2** |

Results significantly higher than Canada

Results not statistically different from Canada

Results significantly lower than Canada

Notes: The terms "significantly higher" and "significantly lower" refer to statistically significant differences between the results of the jurisdictions or countries and the results at the Canada level. Results are statistically different with 95 % confidence if the relevant confidence intervals do not overlap.
　The data represent mean scores, i.e., overall percent correct.
　Countries that used replacement schools or did not meet all sampling requirements are not shown in this table.
　The international mean includes countries not shown here.
　Apparent contradictions in the placing of countries or provinces are due to the effects of rounding.
　Results for Population 3 are omitted from this report, as Canada did not meet all sampling requirements for this population.

Source: *Third International Mathematics and Science Study, 1994-95, International Association for the Evaluation of Educational Achievement (IEA); Robitaille et al., 1996-1997.* Source for Quebec data is: *Une comparaison internationale des résultats des élèves québécois en mathématique et en sciences,* Bulletin statistique de l'éducation, *no 6, août 1998,* Ministère de l'Éducation du Québec.

EDUCATION INDICATORS IN CANADA

## C. INTERNATIONAL ADULT LITERACY SURVEY (IALS)

### POLICY CONTEXT

*IALS measured literacy and numeracy skills among the adult population of several countries.*

Literacy skills have never been more important to national economies. Information and communications technology, as well as globalization is forcing economies into a growing reliance on versatile and highly literate workers. Low levels of literacy affect an individual's ability to find a job and to perform well in that job. Low levels of literacy are likely to lead to lower-paying jobs, reinforcing inequities that may have contributed to the low literacy skills in the first place. Thus it is increasingly important to acknowledge low literacy skills as a barrier to advancement in the workplace. Literacy levels also have an impact on an individual's ability to participate in society and culture. Literacy is an important element in citizenship as well, because it influences an individual's ability to understand important issues.

Assessing literacy offers a measure of the effectiveness of education systems, although in a country such as Canada, which has a large immigrant population, not all people surveyed were necessarily educated here. Immigrants, who may be less fluent in English or French, face special challenges in literacy, which are addressed through English/French as a Second Language programs, for example.

Immigration is not equally distributed across the country (see section 2.1), and this may have affected IALS results for some provinces more than others. The provinces with the highest percentage of immigrants in the IALS sample were British Columbia (33%), Ontario (31%), and Alberta (21%). As was shown in section 2.1, these provinces tend to receive a larger percentage of immigrants than most other provinces.

The first International Adult Literacy Survey, conducted in 1994-95, measured the variation in basic literacy skills of adults aged 16 to 65 across diverse languages and cultures. In addition to Canada, six other countries were represented: the United States, Germany, the Netherlands, Sweden, Switzerland, and Poland. Canada's literacy levels were comparable to the international mean, though not as strong as those for some of the participating countries. Significant portions of Canadian adults were not able to perform the more complicated tasks in the test, suggesting that efforts to improve literacy should continue.

IALS used three scales or domains of literacy—prose (ordinary texts), document (forms or graphics, such as maps and timetables), and quantitative (e.g., calculating a tip)—to assess a common set of skills for various tasks. Based on their responses, participants were classified into one of five levels of proficiency for each of the three domains. Level 1 is the lowest level, level 5 the highest. Because only a small proportion of the population was at level 5, levels 4 and 5 are shown together. (See Appendix 3 for more details.)[4]

Like most skills, literacy skills tend to deteriorate when they are not used. Adult education programs, especially for people whose literacy skills are not challenged at work, can play an important role in counteracting this trend. It is important to consider the needs of individuals who do not perform well on assessments such as IALS, TIMSS, and SAIP. A lack of basic skills in literacy, science, and mathematics affects people's ability to find and keep jobs, as well as their ability to participate fully in society.

IALS was designed to provide literary measures in a stable and reliable way across national and linguistic boundaries; nevertheless, comparisons between countries should be made with some caution. Language and cultural values are closely allied, making neutral judgements extremely difficult. The participating countries are from Europe and North America, which share some common cultural and societal values.

The data are presented here at a regional level for most of the Canadian jurisdictions, because the samples were too small for stable estimates in all but the largest provinces.

## FINDINGS

### CANADA

In all countries except the United States, and for all domains, the 16 to 25 age group showed a higher percentage of people at level 3 and above than did the 26 to 65 age group. This may simply reflect the proximity of this age group to formal schooling and to more frequent use of the skills tested (some of this group had probably not yet left school). However, for Canada, it is also consistent with the rising level of educational attainment (see Table 4.5 and Figures 4.5 and 4.6).

Approximately two-thirds of 16- to 25-year-olds in Canada were at level 3 or above in the document and prose scales, and just over 60% were at level 3 in the quantitative scale. Canada's results put it in the middle range of the countries surveyed. Sweden and the Netherlands were the highest, with the United States and Poland showing significantly lower percentages than Canada (see Table 4.5).

For the Canadian population aged 26 to 65, between 55% and 56% were at level 3 or above in the three scales measured. The country with the highest percentage of people at level 3 or above, in all scales, was Sweden. The country with the lowest percentages was Poland.

Canada had a relatively large percentage of people at the outer levels (level 1 and level 4/5). This polarization between those who struggle with literacy tasks and those who are highly literate was also seen in the United States. The Netherlands and Germany, by contrast, show large percentages at level 3, the middle level.

### JURISDICTIONS

There were no statistically significant differences in the IALS results between Canada's results and those by jurisdiction.

*In all countries except the United States, a higher percentage of the 16 to 25 age group achieved level 3 or above than in the 26 to 65 age group.*

*In Canada, among the 26 to 65 age group, over half of the group achieved level 3 or above.*

EDUCATION INDICATORS IN CANADA

FIGURE 4.5   PERCENTAGE OF THE POPULATION AGED 16 TO 25 AND 26 TO 65 AT LEVEL 3 OR ABOVE IN THE IALS DOCUMENT, PROSE, QUANTITATIVE SCALES, CANADA AND OTHER IALS PARTICIPATING COUNTRIES, 1994-95

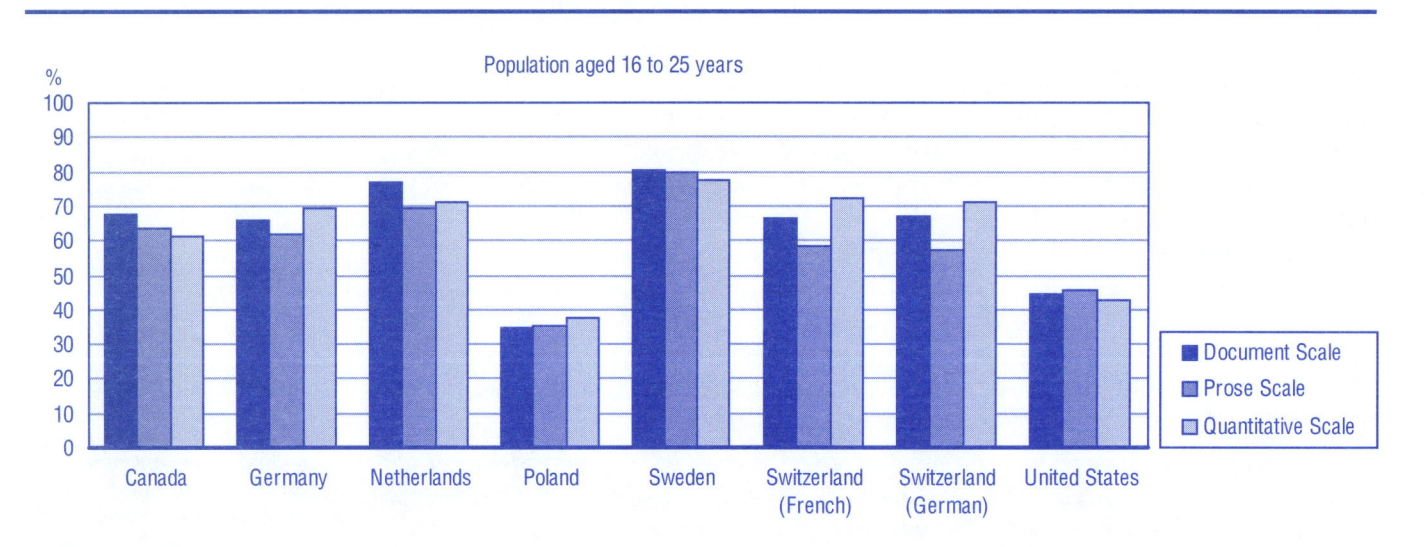

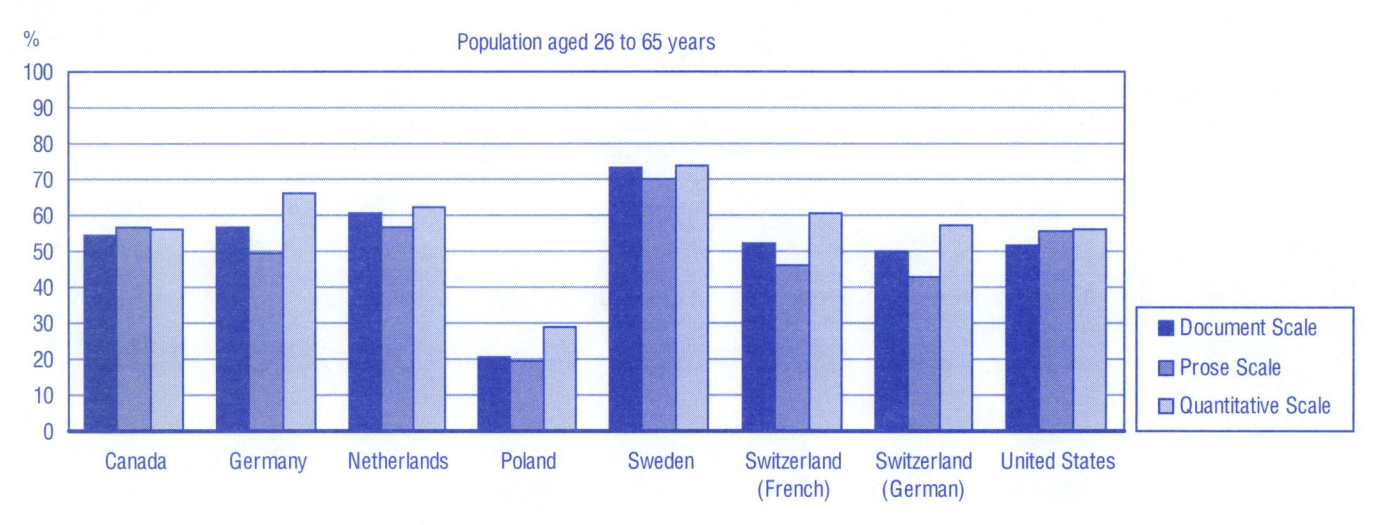

Notes: See Appendix 3 for a description of the scales and levels used in IALS.
The United States, because of a sampling anomoly, used data from the National Adult Literacy Survey (NALS) for the group aged 16-25. NALS measures a skill set comparable to IALS.

*Source: International Adult Literacy Survey, Statistics Canada and OECD, 1994-95.*

FIGURE 4.6  PERCENTAGE OF THE POPULATION AGED 16 TO 25 AND 26 TO 65 AT LEVEL 3 OR ABOVE IN THE IALS DOCUMENT, PROSE, QUANTITATIVE SCALES, CANADA AND REGIONS, 1994-95

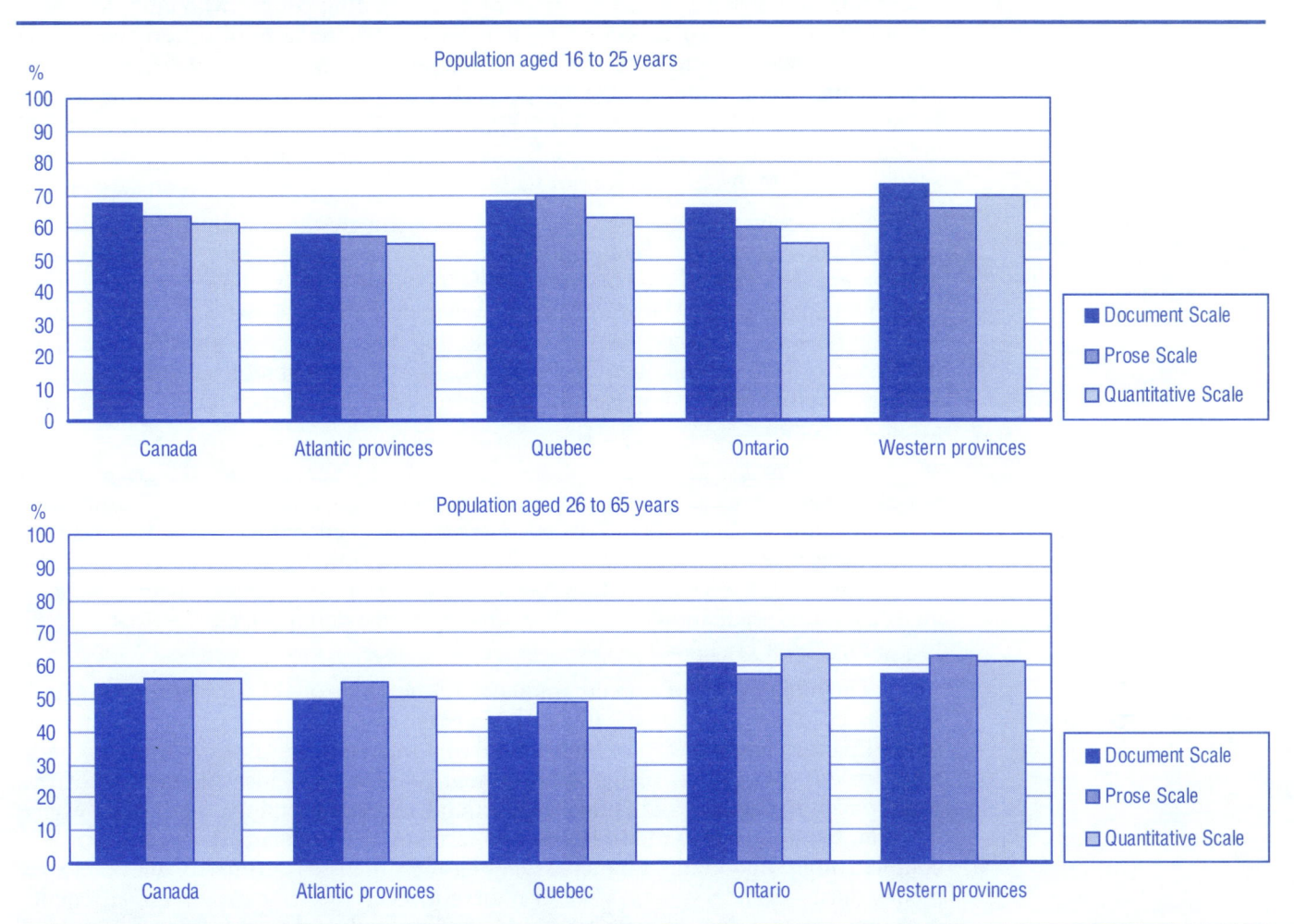

Notes: See Appendix 3 for a description of the scales and levels used in IALS.
The Atlantic provinces include Newfoundland and Labrador, Prince Edward Island, Nova Scotia, and New Brunswick.
The Western provinces include Manitoba, Saskatchewan, Alberta, and British Columbia.

*Source: International Adult Literacy Survey, Statistics Canada and OECD, 1994-95.*

## 4.2 OUTPUT RATES

### A. HIGH SCHOOL COMPLETIONS

**POLICY CONTEXT**

High school graduation rates have historically been a basic indicator of the outcomes of Canada's secondary school systems. A number of different methods exist for measuring high school graduation rates, two of which are presented here. The first rate, based on administrative data, is defined as the number of graduation certificates issued in a given year compared with the total population at a typical age of graduation, age 18. The rate shows all graduates, regardless of age. The second rate focuses on a specific age group, 19- to 20-year-olds, and examines what percentage of this group report that they have completed high school. This second measure is based on data from the Labour Force Survey.

*This indicator uses two measures—the rate of graduates to population aged 18 and the percentage of 19- to 20-year-olds who are high school graduates—to give a fuller picture of high school completions.*

EDUCATION INDICATORS IN CANADA

Because the two measures are derived from different sources and use different methodology, the rates reported will be somewhat different. The first measure may underestimate the true graduation rate, by not including people who complete high school outside the regular secondary school systems, because of differences in the coverage of data collected and reported to Statistics Canada by jurisdictions. Data on graduations from some secondary programs are not uniformly available across jurisdictions, and General Education Diplomas (GED), adult basic upgrading and education, and graduation from adult day school, which take place outside regular secondary school programs, are not included.

> The picture of high school completion can be expanded by looking at the 25 to 29 age group in the educational attainment data (section 2.3).

The second measure may somewhat overestimate the percentage of graduates of education systems in Canada among 19- to 20-year-olds because it is based on the achievement of all 19- to 20-year-olds and includes individuals who may have received their credentials outside Canada. The percentage may also be somewhat overestimated because it is self-reported data. By presenting both measures together, a clearer perspective on graduation rates can be gained. For a picture of high school completion among a slightly older group, see the educational attainment data on the 25 to 29 age group in section 2.3.

Comparison with other countries shows that Canada's ratio of graduates to population at a "typical age of graduation" is lower than in most other G-7 countries. This may indicate that further steps need to be taken to encourage students in Canada to complete high school. However, it should be noted that graduation requirements, which vary to some extent within Canada, can differ considerably internationally, and a country's graduation ratio will be affected by the definition used by that country for "high school graduate."

> Male students are less likely than female students to finish high school.

The higher ratio of female graduates to the 18-year-old population compared with males, combined with the higher percentage of female 19- to 20-year-olds who report that they have received a high school diploma, indicates that progress has been made in efforts to improve the achievement of females. Close monitoring of the situation among males would now be beneficial. (See also sections 4.1 and 2.3 where a similar trend has been noted.) Further research to help understand why fewer males complete high school might indicate whether the situation is primarily due to factors arising during high school, or whether intervention at an earlier stage might affect the outcome. Another area of research could explore the benefits of programs designed to help males who have dropped out complete high school at a later point in their lives. Such research might include action-oriented studies and interventions to promote improvements.

Policies to encourage students to remain in school at least long enough to complete high school remain important, since approximately 20% of 19- to 20-year-olds have not obtained a high school diploma. Without this credential, they face economic disadvantages, as shown in section 5.1. It is evident that people with less than high school education have more trouble finding and keeping jobs than those with higher levels of educational attainment.

In the Northwest Territories, a growing number of people aged 20 and older are returning to school and graduating, now that education to Grade 12 is available in most communities.

# FINDINGS

## CANADA

Compared with other G-7 nations, Canada's ratio of graduates to population aged 18 was the second lowest in 1996, fractionally higher than the United States, but four points lower than Italy, the next highest country. In all the G-7 countries except France and Germany, the ratio for women was at least six points higher than for men (Table 4.6). As noted above, this data should be interpreted with caution.

Overall, the data suggest that high school completion rates increase with age. Results from the Labour Force Survey show the average completion rate for 19- to 20-year-olds between 1995 and 1998 was 81%, rising to 87% among those aged 25 to 29 (Tables 4.7 and 4.8, and section 2.3).

Between 1991 to 1994 and 1995 to 1998, only a slight increase occurred in the rate of high school completion among 19- to 20-year-olds in Canada.

Figure 4.7 shows that in 1997, the ratio of graduates to population aged 18 was 11 percentage points higher among females than among males (81% for females, 70% for males). As can be seen in Figure 4.8, the percentage of 19- to 20-year-old females who reported having completed high school was also higher than for males, although not by as wide a margin (84% for females between 1995 and 1998, 78% for males).

## JURISDICTIONS

In 1997, in all jurisdictions, the ratio of graduates to population aged 18 was higher for females than for males (Figure 4.7). Likewise, the high school completion rate of female 19- to 20-year-olds was higher than the male rate in all the provinces (territorial information is not included in the Labour Force Survey). Between 1995 and 1998, the female high school completion rate was above 80% in all jurisdictions and above 85% in Newfoundland and Labrador, Prince Edward Island, New Brunswick and Saskatchewan. For males, the rate was between 74% and 83%, with only Newfoundland and Labrador, Prince Edward Island, New Brunswick, and Saskatchewan above 80% (Figure and Table 4.8).

In 1997, the ratio of graduates to population aged 18 ranged from 86% in Quebec and 85% in New Brunswick to 25% in Northwest Territories and 43% in the Yukon. Most provinces had a ratio in the 70s or low 80s, except Alberta and British Columbia, where lower results may be affected by net in-migration.

The percentage of the 19- to 20-year old population with a high school diploma has increased between 1991 to 1994 and 1995 to 1998 for all provinces except British Columbia, which remained relatively stable. In British Columbia, the completion rate decreased for males, while it increased for females. In the 1995 to 1998 period, all provinces had at least a 79% completion rate.

Ontario's results for the 19- to 20-year-old population may also be affected by its five-year high school program, which means that more 19-year-olds are still in high school than may be the case for other jurisdictions (see Appendix 1).

EDUCATION INDICATORS IN CANADA

FIGURE 4.7    RATIO OF SECONDARY GRADUATES TO THE POPULATION AT AGE 18 BY GENDER, CANADA AND JURISDICTIONS, 1997

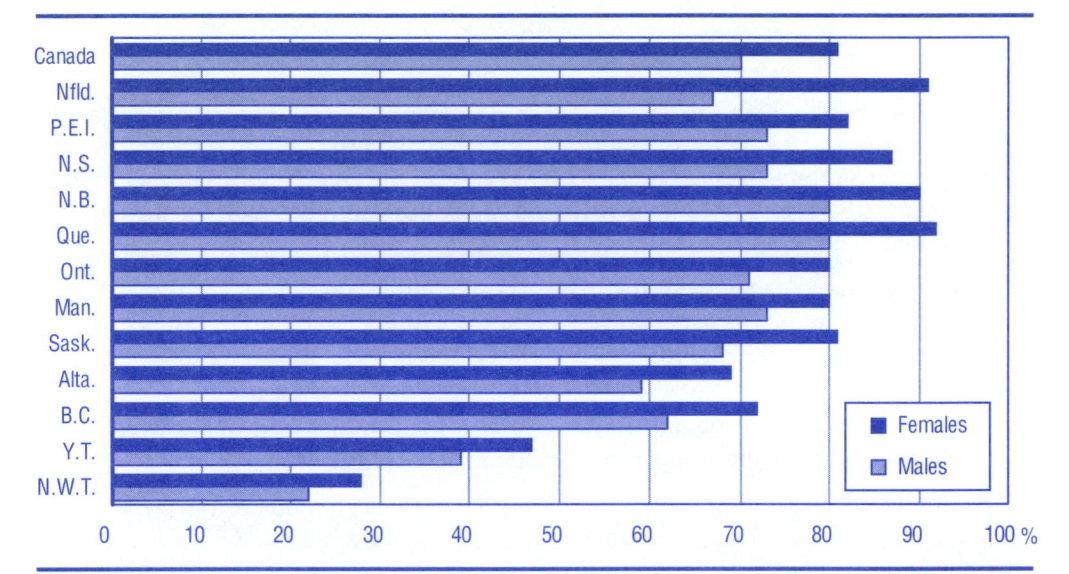

■ Females
☐ Males

Notes:  Ratio is calculated as the number of graduates (irrespective of age) as a percentage of the total 18-year-old population.
Secondary school graduates exclude General Education Diplomas (GED), adult basic upgrading and education, and graduation from adult day school which takes place outside regular secondary school programs.
Quebec data includes graduates of the "formation professionnelle" and adult education programs.

Source: Centre for Education Statistics, Statistics Canada; For Quebec data: Statistiques de l'éducation — Enseignement primaire, secondaire,collégial et universitaire, Gouvernement du Québec, Ministère de l'Éducation.

FIGURE 4.8    HIGH SCHOOL COMPLETION RATES OF THE POPULATION AGED 19 TO 20, BY GENDER, CANADA AND PROVINCES, 1991 TO 1994 AND 1995 TO 1998

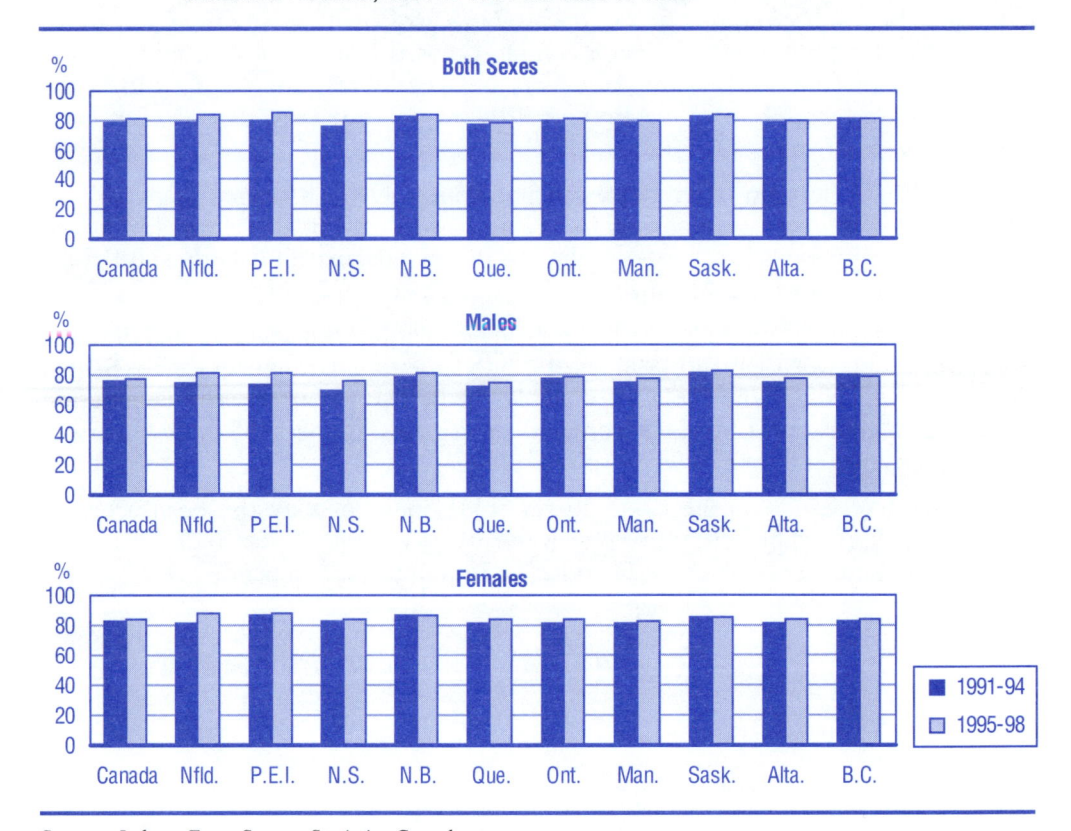

■ 1991-94
☐ 1995-98

Source: Labour Force Survey, Statistics Canada.

## B. POSTSECONDARY COMPLETIONS

### POLICY CONTEXT

Canada must position itself to remain competitive in the emerging information-based global economy. An educated work force is a key element in a strong economy. In addition, employers often now require a higher level of credentials for a job than in the past. The knowledge and training available through university and college programs contribute significantly to creating a work force capable of succeeding in and adapting to a climate of change. Well-educated citizens are also better equipped to contribute to society and participate more effectively in the democratic process.

Postsecondary education completion rates provide information about highly educated and skilled individuals—a potential supply of labour for many areas in the economy. The data in this indicator show an increase in the number of diplomas and degrees granted between 1976 and 1997. The same trend can be seen in the educational attainment of the adult population, and is reflected, over a shorter period, in the relevant student enrolment figures (see sections 2.3 and 3.3). Data on graduation by field of study provide information on the number of people graduating with specialized skills in areas such as science and technology. The data in this indicator do not include trade–vocational certificates and diplomas, or apprenticeship completions.

The increase in the number of credentials granted reflects the growing demand for postsecondary education in Canada, particularly at the university level. It may also reflect increased access to colleges and universities. However, university enrolments have levelled off in recent years (see section 3.3), a trend which is only beginning to be reflected in graduation data.

Two main gender issues emerge from the data. More women than men graduate from university. This is consistent with the data on educational attainment (see section 2.3) and with the data presented in section 4.2A on high school graduation rates. It is important to ascertain the reasons for this trend and to determine what effect it may have in the future. The other issue is that more men graduate with a degree in science. The gap between males and female science graduates has lessened over time. At the secondary level, the SAIP results (see section 4.1) show minimal gender differences in the mathematics and science assessments. Enrolment by gender and field of study, however, remains an area that requires further monitoring.

Science and technology play a central role in our world and an appropriately skilled and knowledgeable work force is essential to Canada's future. The percentage of graduates with science-related qualifications relative to the size of the labour force, showed Canada ranked below the OECD mean in 1995. Further research into this issue may help explain why students choose particular fields of study and how they use their degree after graduation.

*The qualifications required for many jobs have increased, creating a corresponding need for more education.*

*The data presented here are on college and university completion rates and on graduation by field of study at the university level. Apprenticeship and trade-vocational completions are not included.*

*More women than men are graduating from university, although male graduates continue to outnumber females in the sciences.*

### FINDINGS

#### CANADA

The total number of postsecondary credentials granted increased 67% between 1976 and 1997 (Table 4.9). The percentage varies significantly by type of credential. Figure 4.9 shows that, in 1997, the index for diplomas and degrees granted either levelled off or dropped slightly for all types of credentials.

In 1997, undergraduate degrees accounted for the largest portion (50%) of all the credentials granted, followed closely by community college diplomas (40%), and then master's degrees (8%) and doctorates (2%) (Table 4.9). Master's degrees and doctorates showed the highest rates of increase between 1976 and 1997, at 84% and

*The largest portion of post-secondary credentials granted in 1997 was for undergraduate degrees, followed by college diplomas.*

EDUCATION INDICATORS IN CANADA

**University graduation rates by jurisdiction of study provide a measure of the output of university systems within jurisdictions . . .**

**. . . while university graduation rates by jurisdiction of residence provide a measure of educational attainment of the population.**

136% respectively. While undergraduate degrees had the slowest growth rate, they still showed a substantial increase of 51%.

Two university graduation rates are presented. The first is defined as the number of degrees granted per jurisdiction as a percentage of the jurisdiction's population at a typical age of graduation (Table 4.10). This is a measure of the output of the university education system within each jurisdiction, relative to the size of the population. As with high school completion rates, postsecondary graduation rates may be affected by net in-migration.

The second rate is defined as the number of residents of a jurisdiction (based on residence prior to commencement of studies) that obtained a university degree as a percentage of the jurisdiction's population at the typical age of graduation (Table 4.11).

The two rates are very similar at the pan-Canadian level. The only difference is that the rates by jurisdiction of residence exclude foreign students and Canadian citizens living abroad, whereas the rates by jurisdiction of study include them. The graduation rate (based on jurisdiction of study) for bachelor's degrees increased from 27.8% in 1991 to 32.4% in 1996, before dropping to 30.4% in 1997. The drop in 1997 coincides, although with a lag of about four years, with the flattening of university enrolments during the mid-1990s. The comparable rate for master's degrees exhibits the same pattern as the rate for bachelor's degrees, increasing from 4.2% in 1991 to 5.3% in 1996, and then falling back to 5.2% in 1997. The comparable rate for doctorates was 0.6% in 1991, and after growth in the mid-1990s, it has been stable at 0.9% over the most recent three years.

Table 4.12 examines university graduation rates by field of study in Canada in 1987 and 1997. Rates are shown for three levels of university education and both sexes. Persons graduating with a diploma or certificate at the university level are not counted.

In 1987, social sciences and related fields of study had the highest rates of graduation at the undergraduate level, for both males and females. This was also the case at both the master's and doctorate levels. For women, the field with the second highest graduation rate was that of education while for men, it was engineering and applied sciences.

By 1997, social sciences and related fields continued to have the highest graduation rates, for both males and females, in Canada at all levels of university education. For women, the field with the second highest graduation rate continued to be that of education while for men, it was again engineering and applied sciences.

## JURISDICTIONS

**The number of college diplomas and university degrees granted grew or remained steady in most jurisdictions.**

Overall, the number of college diplomas and university degrees granted increased or remained stable in most jurisdictions between 1991 and 1997, except for declines at the college level in Manitoba and at the undergraduate level in Newfoundland and Labrador, and Saskatchewan (Table 4.13).

Data on university graduation by field of study (Tables 4.14 and 4.15) show that more people graduated in 1997 than in 1987 in most fields of study across jurisdictions. Fewer men graduated in 1997 in Manitoba and Saskatchewan. Female graduation figures increased in all provinces. Few consistent trends appear across all provinces because of differences in programs offered at various universities.

For women, increases in the number of graduates were concentrated in the humanities in most jurisdictions. The exceptions were Newfoundland and Labrador, where higher increases were shown in the number of female science and commerce graduates, and Prince Edward Island, where the increase in the number of female science graduates was higher than the increase in humanities graduates.

For male graduates, the pattern is more mixed. In New Brunswick, Quebec, Ontario, and British Columbia, the number of male humanities graduates increased more than for other programs. In Newfoundland and Labrador, Prince Edward Island, Nova Scotia, Manitoba, and Alberta, commerce and science programs showed increases in the number of male graduates. In Saskatchewan, the number of male graduates decreased with the largest decrease in the humanities.

In terms of graduation rates based on province of study, Nova Scotia had the highest rate at the bachelor's level (46.8%), well above the Canada average of 30.4%. This reflects the large number of universities in the province, and the sizeable in-migration of students to study at these institutions (see section 5.3). The graduation rates at the bachelor's level in Ontario, New Brunswick and Manitoba were also above the pan-Canadian average. The corresponding rate was lower in British Columbia, but as footnoted in the table, this is a reflection of a data problem. Since the early 1990s, British Columbia has had four degree-granting university colleges. However, degrees from these institutions are not covered by current statistics.

> High graduation rates in Nova Scotia reflect the large capacity of its system, which serves more than local needs.

In terms of rates by province of study, Nova Scotia and Quebec had the highest rates at the master's level, while Quebec had the highest rate at the doctoral level.

Despite having no universities, residents of Yukon and Northwest Territories have made great strides in obtaining university education during the 1990s. In Yukon, the bachelor's graduation rate has increased from 5.9%, about one-fifth the pan-Canadian rate in 1991, to 15.9%, over half of the pan-Canadian rate in 1997. Over the same period, the rate for Northwest Territories rose from 4.1% to 8.0%.

> The Yukon and Northwest Territories have experienced large percentage increases in bachelor's graduation rates based on jurisdiction of residence.

Rates by jurisdiction of residence at the bachelor's level showed a similar pattern to those based on jurisdiction of study. In Nova Scotia's case, the rate based on province of residence was still the highest of any jurisdiction at 36.9%. It would appear that the large capacity within the province might be contributing to a higher percentage of residents who pursue and obtain university degrees. Ontario had the next highest bachelor's rate. At 6.0%, Quebec was well above the pan-Canadian average at the master's level. At the PhD level, rates were similar across most jurisdictions, and lower in Newfoundland and Labrador and Prince Edward Island, and the territories.

FIGURE 4.9   INDEX OF DIPLOMAS AND DEGREES GRANTED, BY LEVEL OF EDUCATION, CANADA, 1976 TO 1997

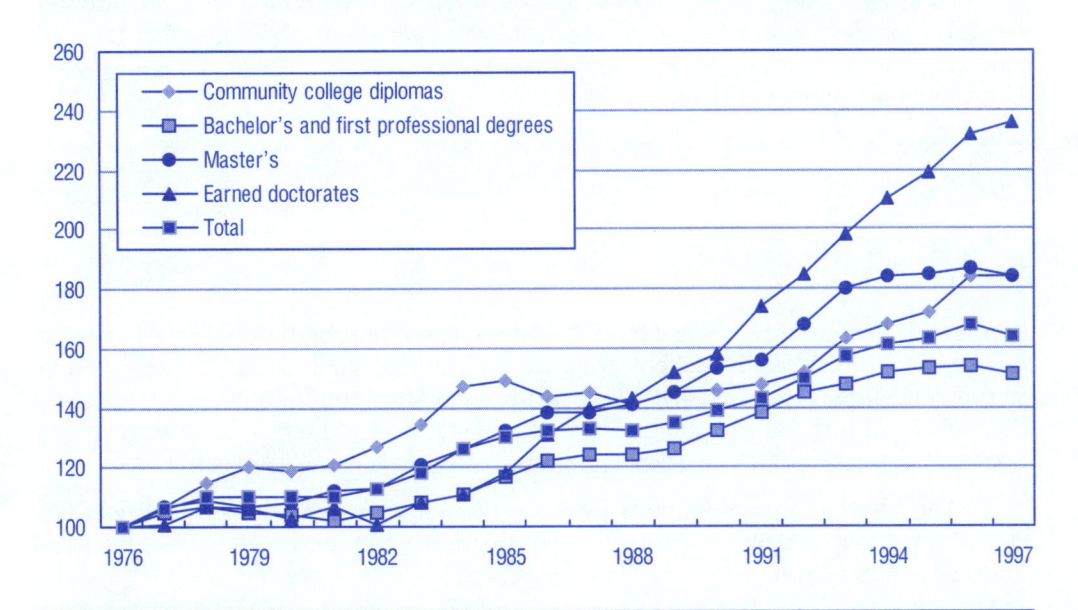

Note:   Index equals 100 in 1976.
Source: Centre for Education Statistics, Statistics Canada.

# 4.3 EQUITY

*This indicator examines three aspects of educational equity: educational attainment of the Aboriginal population, the educational attainment of linguistic minorities, and the effect of socio-economic status on participation in education.*

An important concern for any education system is the extent to which it serves the entire student population. Disparities in educational attainment affect the ability of individuals to compete for jobs, to participate in debate around issues that affect them, and to function fully and effectively in society. Our education systems are striving to support students who face additional challenges, through special needs programs, English/French as a Second Language programs, and through an increased sensitivity to and awareness of how the cultural and linguistic characteristics of systems may affect students.

## A. EDUCATIONAL ATTAINMENT OF THE ABORIGINAL POPULATION

### POLICY CONTEXT

Aboriginal people have historically faced many challenges in the predominantly non-Aboriginal education systems. One difficulty is language; the first language of many Aboriginal people is not the language (English or French) in which they have been expected to study. The role of language will be explored in section 4.3B. Other difficulties stem from cultural differences, or from negative stereotyping. Because relatively few Aboriginal people have pursued postsecondary education in the past, particularly at the university level, Aboriginal students have fewer role models to encourage them to continue their schooling. In addition, many Aboriginal communities are geographically remote and have found it difficult to attract and retain well-qualified teachers for their schools.

Governments have attempted to address some of the systemic issues. For example, students in the eastern part of the Northwest Territories (what is now Nunavut) are taught in an Aboriginal language for the first few grades, before switching to instruction in English around Grade 4. There is financial support for postsecondary tuition costs for Aboriginal students. Jurisdictions have also introduced programs aimed specifically at assisting Aboriginal students.

Data for two age groups are presented here. The population aged 25 to 54 represents the core working-age population, and will be referred to as the "working-age population." Within that group, the 25- to 29-year-old population has been through the education system the most recently. If the younger group show a higher level of educational attainment than the working-age population as a whole, it suggests that educational attainment is rising over time.

### FINDINGS

### CANADA

*The educational attainment of the Aboriginal population is well below that of the non-Aboriginal population.*

Aboriginal students are at a greater risk of dropping out of school than non-Aboriginal students. In 1996, 42% of the Aboriginal working-age population had less than a high school education, compared with 22% of the non-Aboriginal population. The 25 to 29-year-old Aboriginal population showed a higher rate of high school completions than did the total working-age Aboriginal population (Figures 4.10 and 4.11).

The Aboriginal population is less likely to hold a postsecondary qualification: 35% of this group had a postsecondary qualification, compared with 52% of the non-Aboriginal population.

EDUCATION OUTCOMES

Figure 4.12 shows the educational attainment of the Aboriginal and non-Aboriginal population aged 20 to 29 in 1986 and 1996 (see also Table 4.16). Among the Aboriginal population, the percentage with less than high school education decreased from 60% to 45% over this period. The largest increases among the Aboriginal population were in college and trade graduates, rising from 15% in 1986 to 20% in 1996, and persons with a high school diploma, which increased from 24% to 32%. This group includes persons who had some postsecondary education, but who did not obtain a postsecondary degree or diploma. The percentage of the Aboriginal population with a university degree, while more than doubling between 1986 and 1996, was nevertheless still small at about 4%. Despite the gains in educational attainment of the Aboriginal population over this period, in comparison to the non-Aboriginal population, the largest differences remained at the low and high ends of the education spectrum. At the low end, much more of the Aboriginal population had less than high school education (45% versus 17% of the non-Aboriginal population), while at the high end far fewer Aboriginal people had a university education (4% versus 19% of non-Aboriginal people).

*The educational attainment of the Aboriginal population improved between 1986 and 1996.*

Caution needs to be exercised, however, in interpreting the gains between 1986 and 1996 in the educational attainment of the Aboriginal population. Some of the gains in educational attainment can be attributed to the phenomenon of "ethnic mobility." A large increase in the Aboriginal population was reported in the 1996 Census that could not be attributed to natural increase. It appears that a number of persons who had not reported any Aboriginal connection in 1986, did so in 1996 as a result of heightened awareness of Aboriginal issues over time. This new group had better socio-economic conditions for the most part, and hence artificially raised education levels. While there has certainly been real improvement for the Aboriginal population over the period, the extent of the contribution as a result of ethnic mobility is not known. Another caution in comparing 1986 and 1996 Census results for the Aboriginal population relates to the fact that a number of reserves did not participate in the census. Some of those who did not participate in 1986 were the same as in 1996, while others were not.

Another way to examine evolution of educational attainment over time is to examine the educational attainment of different age cohorts for a single census. Younger cohorts are more representative of those who have gone through the education system most recently, while older cohorts tend to be more representative of the education system at earlier points in time. Examination of 1996 Census results shows little difference in the educational attainment of the Aboriginal population aged 25 to 29 when compared with the Aboriginal working-age population as a whole. Among the younger cohort aged 25 to 29, the percentage with a college or trade vocational education was 25% compared with 29% for the entire working-age population. Similarly, the percentage of the younger cohort with a university education was 5% versus 6% for the entire working-age population (Figure 4.10). The opposite pattern occurred among the non-Aboriginal population, where the younger group was the more likely of the two cohorts to have postsecondary qualifications (Figure 4.11). In part the similarity in educational attainment of the two Aboriginal cohorts might be a reflection of a significant amount of continuation of education among the adult Aboriginal population after the age of 29.

## JURISDICTIONS

The percentage of the Aboriginal population of working age not completing high school ranged from 28% in New Brunswick to 51% in Manitoba. The percentage not completing high school was higher among the Aboriginal than the non-Aboriginal population in all jurisdictions except New Brunswick (where this percentage was 29% among the non-Aboriginal population). For the non-Aboriginal working-age population, the range was between 12% and 34%. In several jurisdictions, the percentage of the Aboriginal population with less than high school education was larger than the percentages that had graduated from either high school or postsecondary programs (Tables 4.17 to 4.20, and Figure 4.13).

Between 11% and 26% of the working-age Aboriginal population held high school diplomas with no postsecondary qualification. The comparable percentages for the non-Aboriginal population ranged from 17% to 27%. In some jurisdictions, the percentage of the Aboriginal population with high school diplomas and no postsecondary qualifications was higher than for the non-Aboriginal population, but this is explained by the higher figures for postsecondary qualifications among the non-Aboriginal population.

The percentage of the working-age Aboriginal population with trade–vocational or college qualifications ranged from 23% to 42%. This percentage was higher for the Aboriginal population than the non-Aboriginal population in Newfoundland and Labrador, New Brunswick, and Yukon. The percentages were similar for the two populations in the remaining jurisdictions.

**At the university level, the educational attainment of the Aboriginal population is significantly lower in all jurisdictions than that of the non-Aboriginal population.**

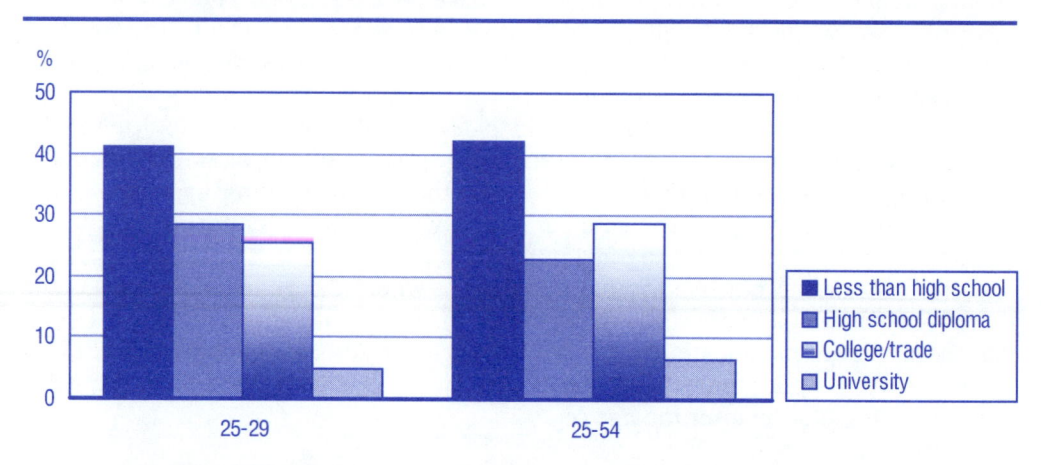

In 1996, between 3% and 10% of the Aboriginal working-age population had a university degree, with the lowest percentage living in the Northwest Territories and the highest in Nova Scotia and New Brunswick. Conversely, between 13% and 29% of the non-Aboriginal population had graduated from university.

The Aboriginal population in the 25 to 29 age group generally does not show higher levels of educational attainment when compared with the working-age Aboriginal population as a whole. In most jurisdictions, with the exception of Newfoundland and Labrador, Prince Edward Island, and Yukon, the Aboriginal population aged 25 to 29 was less likely than the working-age Aboriginal population as a whole to have a college degree, although in most jurisdictions the difference was less than 5 percentage points. The percentages for Aboriginal population aged 25 to 29 ranged from 21% to 65%. The trend was similar at the university level, where the percentages for the 25 to 29 age group ranged from 1% to 9%, which was lower than for the working-age population as a whole.

FIGURE 4.10  DISTRIBUTION OF THE ABORIGINAL POPULATION AGED 25 TO 29 AND 25 TO 54, BY HIGHEST LEVEL OF EDUCATION ATTAINED, CANADA, 1996

Notes: Aboriginal population refers to those persons who reported identifying with at least one Aboriginal group, i.e., North American Indian, Métis or Inuit (Eskimo) and/or who reported being a Treaty Indian or a Registered Indian as defined by the *Indian Act of Canada* and/or who were members of an Indian Band or First Nation.
"Less than high school" includes individuals having at least some pre-elementary, elementary or secondary education.
"High school diploma" includes high school graduates and individuals who have some postsecondary education (not completed).
"College/trade" includes graduates of college and trade-vocational programs.
"University" includes individuals with a university degree or certificate.

*Source: 1996 Census, Statistics Canada.*

EDUCATION OUTCOMES

FIGURE 4.11  DISTRIBUTION OF THE NON-ABORIGINAL POPULATION AGED 25 TO 29 AND 25 TO 54, BY HIGHEST LEVEL OF EDUCATION ATTAINED, CANADA, 1996

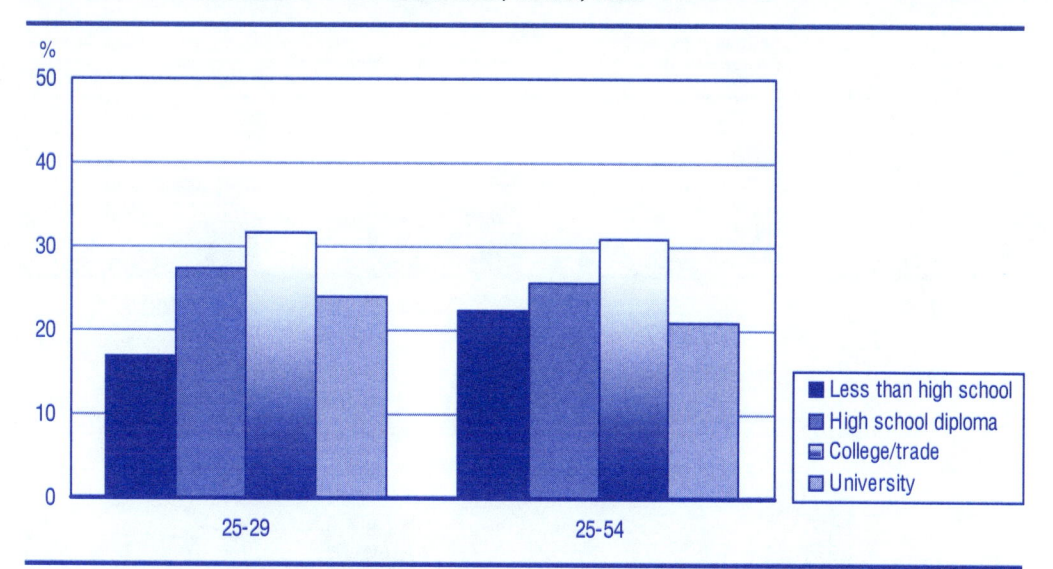

Notes: "Less than high school" includes individuals having at least some pre-elementary, elementary or secondary education.
"High school diploma" includes high school graduates and individuals who have some postsecondary education (not completed).
"College/trade" includes graduates of college and trade-vocational programs.
"University" includes individuals with a university degree or certificate.

*Source:* 1996 Census, Statistics Canada.

FIGURE 4.12  DISTRIBUTION OF THE POPULATION AGED 20 TO 29, BY HIGHEST LEVEL OF EDUCATION ATTAINED, ABORIGINAL AND NON-ABORIGINAL POPULATIONS, CANADA, 1986 AND 1996

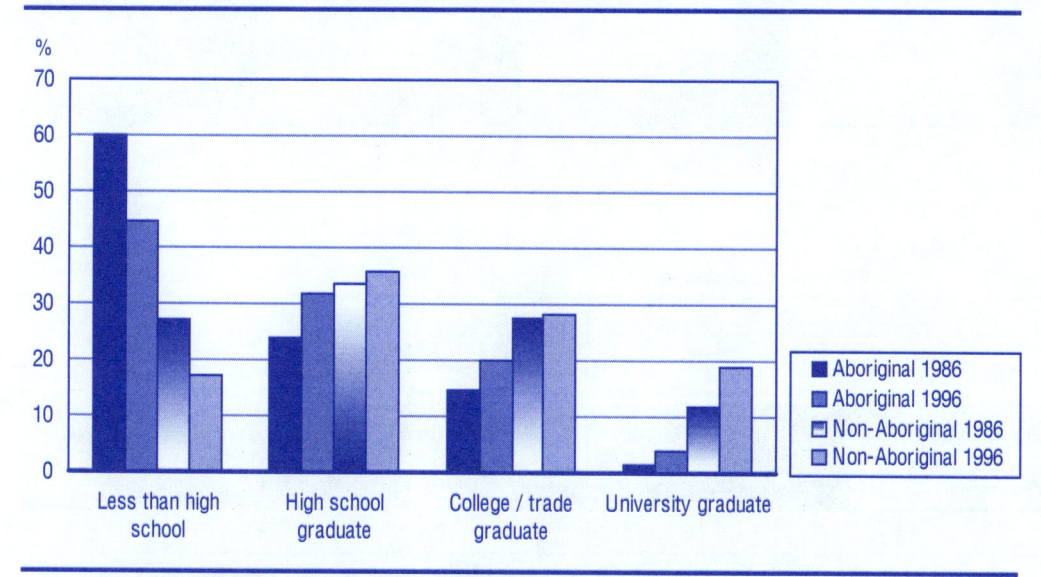

Notes: Aboriginal population refers to those persons who reported identifying with at least one Aboriginal group, i.e., North American Indian, Métis or Inuit (Eskimo) and/or who reported being a Treaty Indian or a Registered Indian as defined by the *Indian Act of Canada* and/or who were members of an Indian Band or First Nation.
"Less than high school" includes individuals having at least some pre-elementary, elementary or secondary education.
"High school diploma" includes high school graduates and individuals who have some postsecondary education (not completed).
"College/trade" includes graduates of college and trade-vocational programs.
"University" includes individuals with a university degree or certificate.

*Source:* 1986 and 1996 Census, Statistics Canada.

EDUCATION INDICATORS IN CANADA

**FIGURE 4.13   DISTRIBUTION OF THE ABORIGINAL POPULATION AGED 25 TO 54, BY HIGHEST LEVEL OF EDUCATION ATTAINED, CANADA AND JURISDICTIONS, 1996**

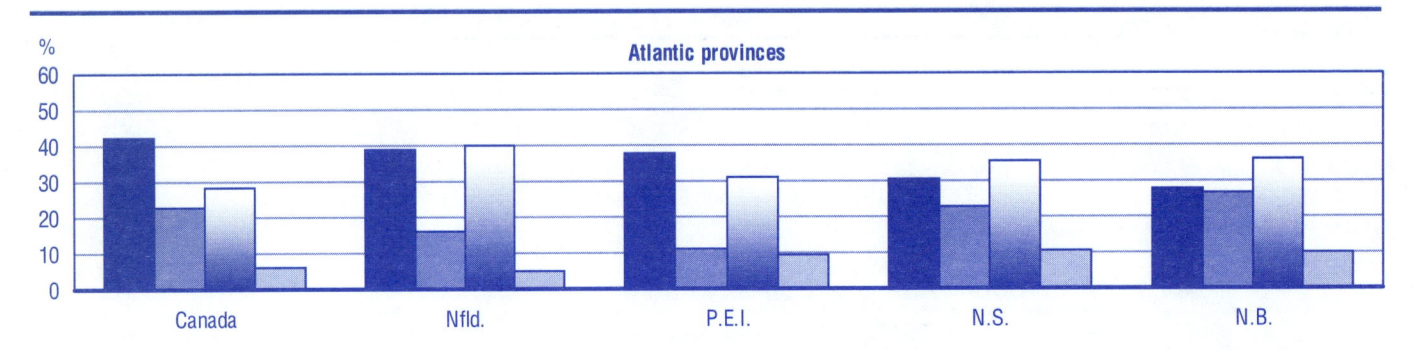

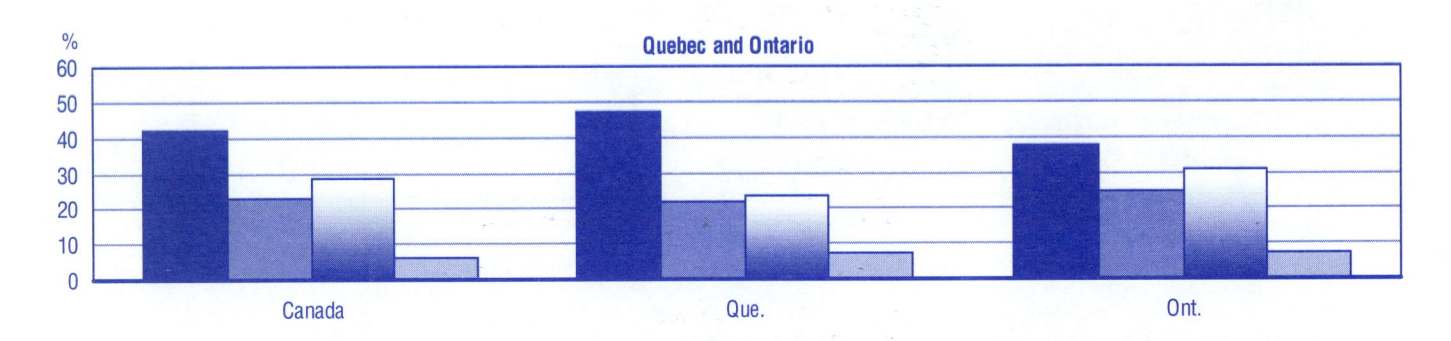

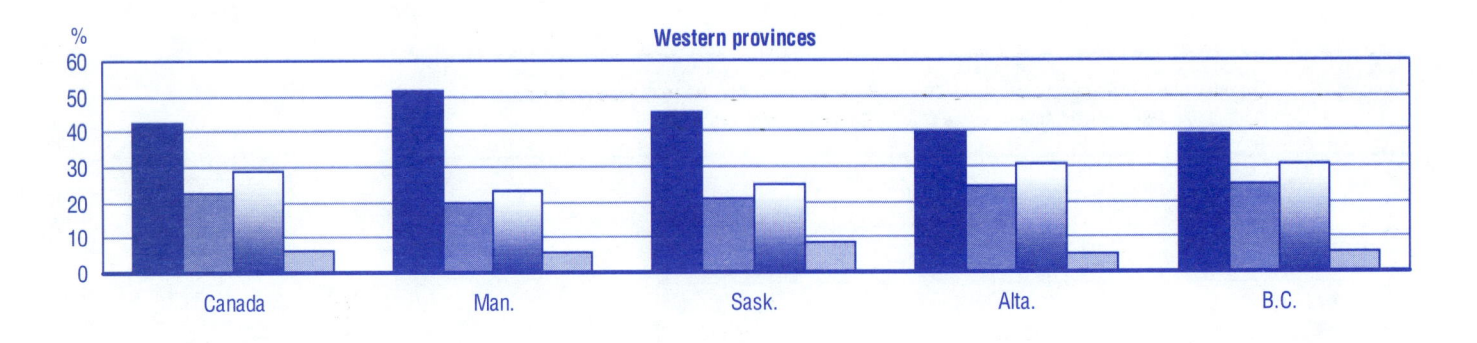

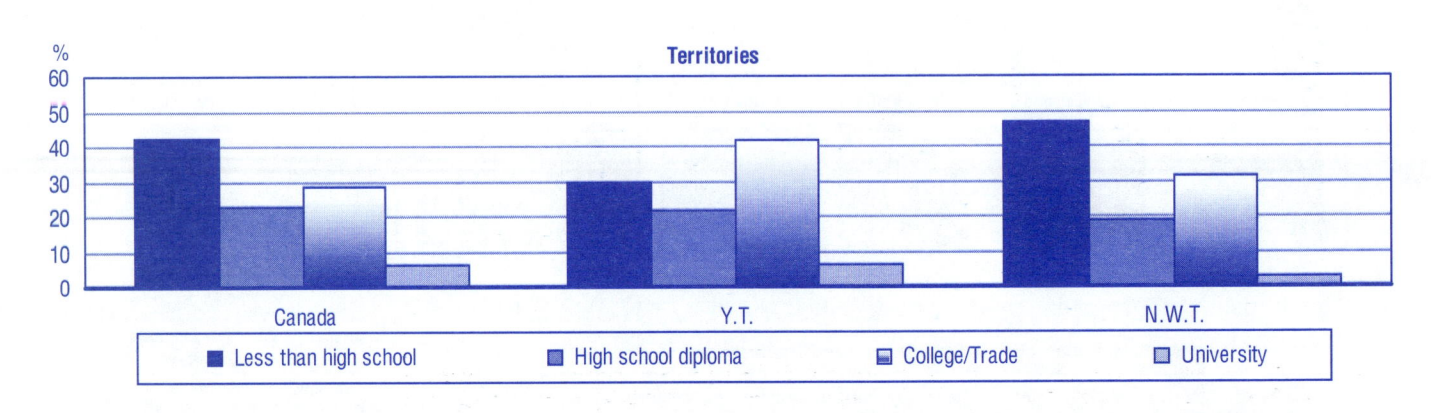

■ Less than high school     ■ High school diploma     ■ College/Trade     ■ University

Notes: Aboriginal population refers to those persons who reported identifying with at least one Aboriginal group, i.e., North American Indian, Métis or Inuit (Eskimo) and/or who reported being a Treaty Indian or a Registered Indian as defined by the *Indian Act of Canada* and/or who were members of an Indian Band or First Nation.
"Less than high school" includes individuals having at least some pre-elementary, elementary or secondary education.
"High school diploma" includes high school graduates and individuals who have some postsecondary education (not completed).
"College/trade" includes graduates of college and trade-vocational programs.
"University" includes individuals with a university degree or certificate.

*Source: 1996 Census, Statistics Canada.*

## B. EDUCATIONAL ATTAINMENT AMONG LINGUISTIC GROUPS

### POLICY CONTEXT

Table 4.21 shows the population distribution of francophones (persons with French as a mother tongue, that is the first language learned), anglophones (persons with English as a mother tongue) and a non-official language group whose first language is neither English nor French. The data that follow present the educational attainment for each group. Attainment at each educational level is shown as a percentage of the population of each linguistic group.

Three linguistic groups are examined: francophones, anglophones, and those whose first language is neither French nor English.

Some people whose mother tongue is neither English nor French (labelled "other" in the tables and charts) may have immigrated to Canada after receiving their education elsewhere. The high levels of education in this group in some jurisdictions may in part reflect immigration policies aimed at attracting individuals with higher levels of education.

Not all of the discrepancies that exist between the attainment of the non-official language group and the attainment of anglophones and francophones can be attributed to language barriers. Social and economic factors may also be involved. Immigrants who do not speak English or French well are more likely to have difficulty in securing employment, and their children may, therefore, experience the difficulties of children in situations of low income (see section 2.2). The situation of the Aboriginal population has already been examined (sections 4.3A). Aboriginal people whose first language was neither English nor French are included in the non-official language group.

The non-official language group includes immigrants and those whose first language was an Aboriginal language.

The fact that a significant proportion of the non-official language group are highly motivated to obtain an education is illustrated by the considerable percentage with a university degree. However, at the other end of the spectrum, this group is also more likely not to have completed high school. Research is needed to determine which people from this group are most likely to leave the education system without obtaining a high school diploma and what type of programs might help them overcome barriers that deter them from continuing.

People in the non-official language group are more likely to attend university, but are also more likely to have less than high school education than people in English and French language groups.

Where jurisdictions have large Aboriginal populations, the data on linguistic groups appear consistent with the information on the Aboriginal population already presented. In those jurisdictions, the non-official language group shows higher rates of less than high school education than do the other two linguistic groups.

### FINDINGS

#### CANADA

Figure 4.14 shows that among the population aged 25-29, at the time of the 1996 Census, the distribution of educational attainment of anglophones was similar to that of all linguistic groups combined. Francophones were more likely to be college–trade graduates, which may partly be due to the CEGEP program in Quebec. The non-official language group was more likely to have a university degree than anglophones or francophones, but was also more likely not to have completed high school.

The data show the educational attainment of the 25- to 29-year-old population.

EDUCATION INDICATORS IN CANADA

## JURISDICTIONS

In Ontario, Manitoba, Saskatchewan, Alberta, and Northwest Territories, all jurisdictions with relatively large Aboriginal populations, the percentage of the non-official language group who had less than a high school education was 5 percentage points or more above that of the majority language group. In most jurisdictions, those in the non-official language group were less likely to be college graduates. Levels of university graduation for this group are similar to the percentage for the majority linguistic group in many jurisdictions. The non-official language group had a considerably higher percentage of university graduates, compared with anglophones, in Newfoundland and Labrador, Nova Scotia, New Brunswick, and British Columbia, and a considerably lower percentage in Yukon, and Northwest Territories (Figures 4.15 to 4.18).

*The educational attainment of francophone and anglophone minorities is comparable with that of the majority language group in their jurisdictions.*

Francophone and anglophone minorities appeared for the most part to have educational attainment that is equal to or higher than the linguistic majority in their respective jurisdictions. Francophone minorities and anglophone majorities had similar levels of postsecondary graduation (within 5 percentage points). At the university level, the percentage of the population with a university degree was higher among francophones than anglophones in Prince Edward Island, Saskatchewan, British Columbia, Yukon, and Northwest Territories.

In Quebec, the anglophone minority had the smallest percentage with less than high school education and the highest percentage of university graduates among the three linguistic groups.

FIGURE 4.14  DISTRIBUTION OF THE POPULATION AGED 25 TO 29, BY HIGHEST LEVEL OF EDUCATION ATTAINED AND BY MOTHER TONGUE, CANADA, 1996

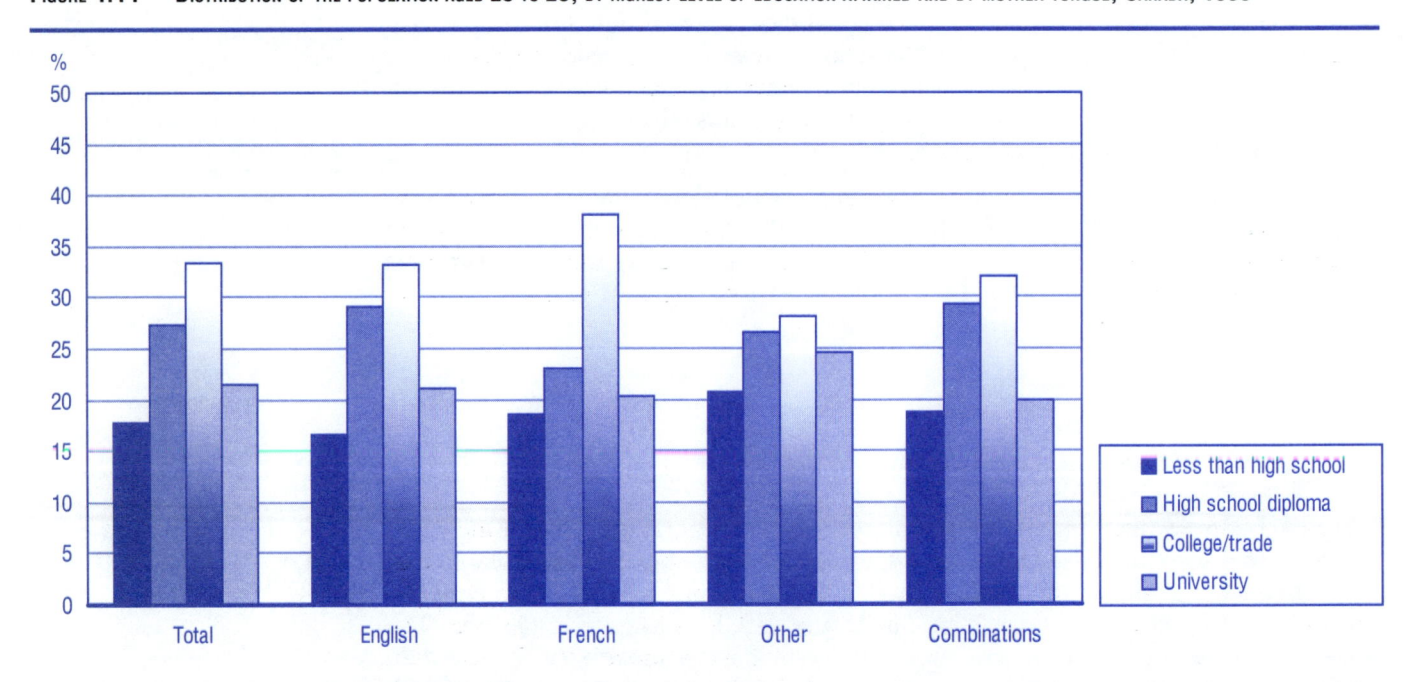

Notes: The "Other" category includes individuals whose first language is neither English nor French (including those whose first language is an Aboriginal language).
The "Combinations" category includes any of the following linguistic combinations: English and French; English and other; French and other; English, French, and other.
"Less than high school" includes individuals having at least some pre-elementary, elementary or secondary education.
"High school diploma" includes high school graduates and individuals who have some postsecondary education (not completed).
"College/trade" includes graduates of college and trade-vocational programs.
"University" includes individuals with a university degree or certificate.

Source: 1996 Census, Statistics Canada.

EDUCATION OUTCOMES

FIGURE 4.15   PERCENTAGE OF THE POPULATION AGED 25 TO 29 WITH LESS THAN HIGH SCHOOL EDUCATION BY MOTHER TONGUE, CANADA AND JURISDICTIONS, 1996

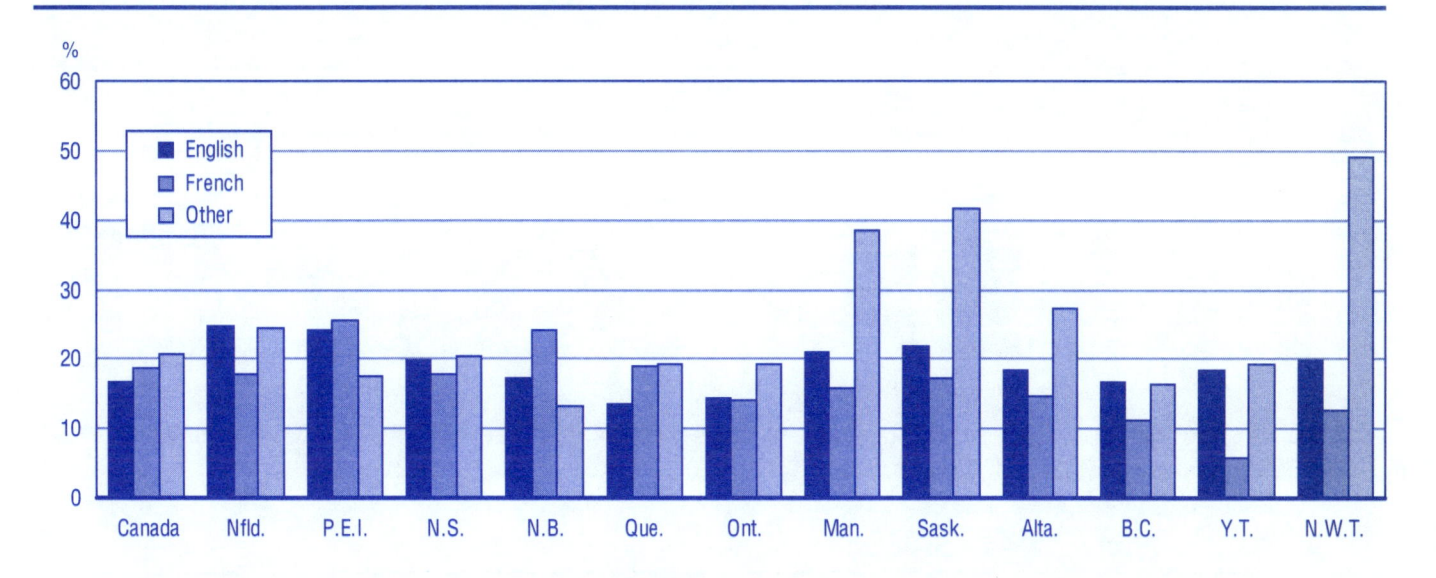

Notes: The "Other" category includes individuals whose first language is neither English nor French (including those whose first language is an Aboriginal language).
"Less than high school" includes individuals having at least some pre-elementary, elementary or secondary education.
*Source:* 1996 Census, Statistics Canada.

FIGURE 4.16   PERCENTAGE OF THE POPULATION AGED 25 TO 29 WITH HIGH SCHOOL EDUCATION BY MOTHER TONGUE, CANADA AND JURISDICTIONS, 1996

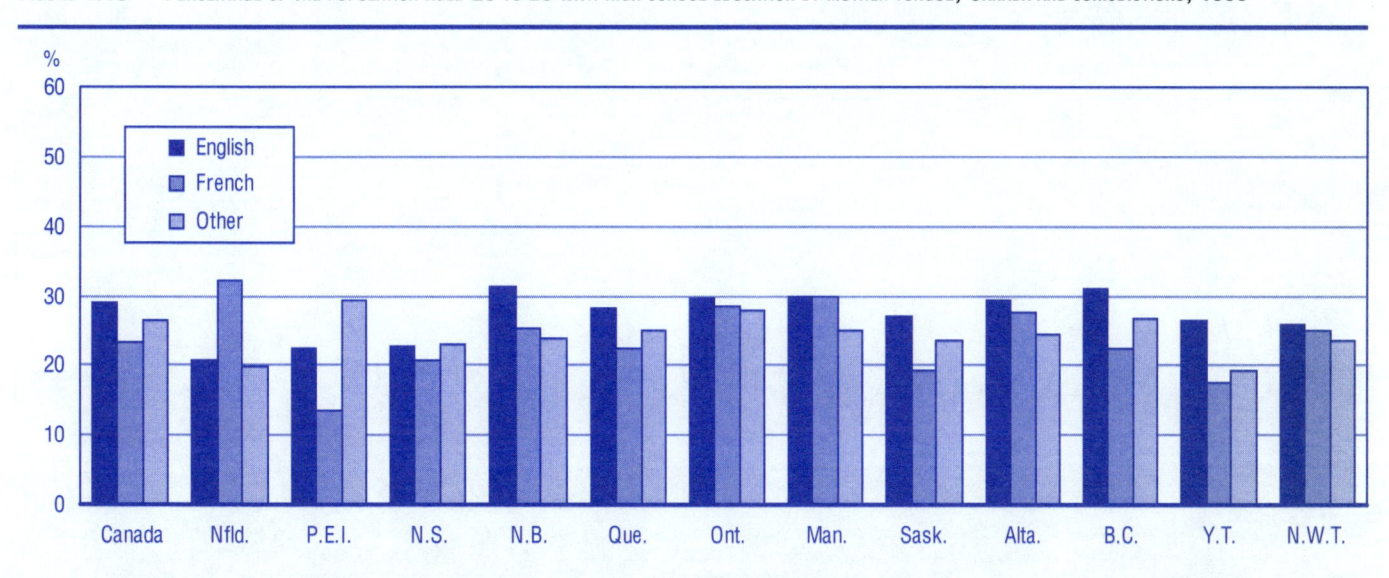

Notes: "High school education" includes high school graduates and individuals who have some postsecondary education (not completed).
The "Other" category includes individuals whose first language is neither English nor French (including those whose first language is an Aboriginal language).
*Source:* 1996 Census, Statistics Canada.

EDUCATION INDICATORS IN CANADA

FIGURE 4.17   PERCENTAGE OF THE POPULATION AGED 25 TO 29 WITH A COLLEGE/TRADE EDUCATION BY MOTHER TONGUE, CANADA AND JURISDICTIONS, 1996

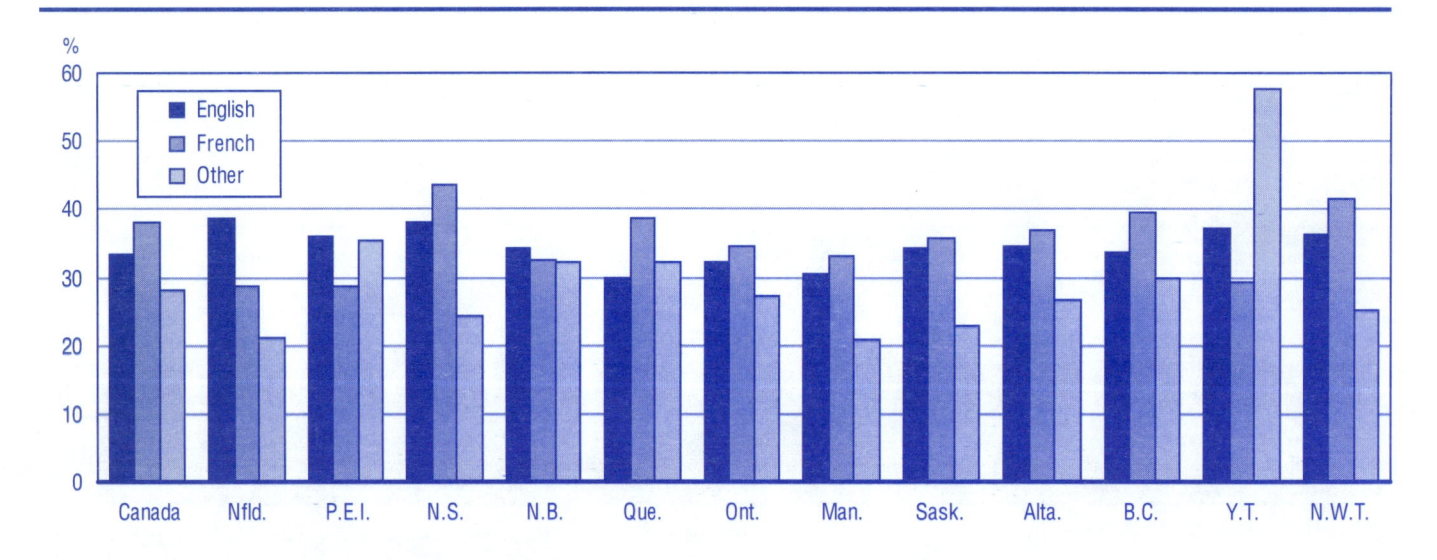

Notes:  The "Other" category includes individuals whose first language is neither English nor French (including those whose first language is an Aboriginal language).
"College/trade" includes graduates of college and trade-vocational programs.

*Source:* 1996 Census, Statistics Canada.

FIGURE 4.18   PERCENTAGE OF THE POPULATION AGED 25 TO 29 WITH A UNIVERSITY EDUCATION BY MOTHER TONGUE, CANADA AND JURISDICTIONS, 1996

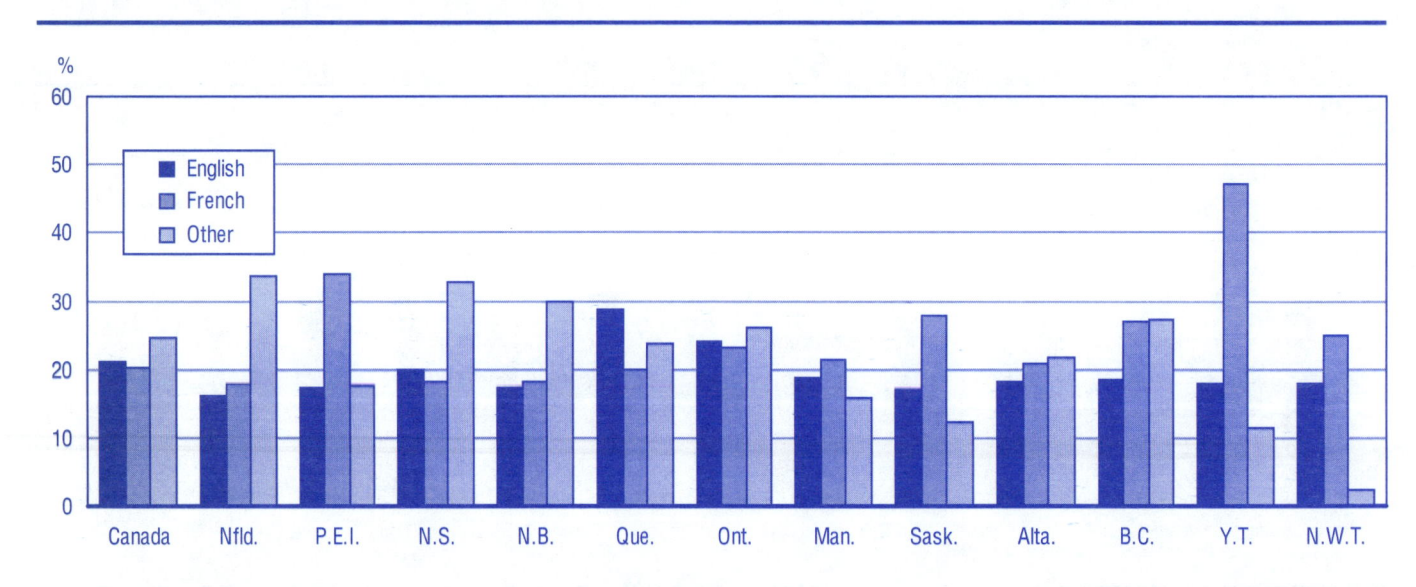

Notes:  The "Other" category includes individuals whose first language is neither English nor French (including those whose first language is an Aboriginal language).
"University" includes individuals with a university degree or certificate.

*Source:* 1996 Census, Statistics Canada.

## C. Participation in education by socio-economic status

### Policy context

Many social and economic factors, such as student achievement, parental educational attainment, and household income can influence the extent to which an individual participates in education. This section focuses on the socio-economic status (SES) backgrounds of 18- to 21-year-olds at the two extremes of the education spectrum—those with less than high school education and those in university. (See Appendix 4 for the definition of SES.)

People who do not complete high school have a much harder time finding and keeping work than do those with higher educational attainment (see section 5.1). Despite this, individuals from the lowest SES quartile may feel pressure to leave school to earn an income. Without at least a high school education, they are unlikely to be able to experience upward mobility in their socio-economic status. These are students who may need extra encouragement and assistance to complete high school and who could benefit from programs that facilitate upgrading after the "typical" graduation age.

The overall increase in university participation rates at all SES levels is consistent with the trend toward higher levels of educational attainment (see section 2.3). Those in the middle and lower SES groups must make a relatively greater financial sacrifice to attend university than individuals in the highest quartile. While the participation rate of the middle two quartiles has grown faster than for the highest quartile, the lowest quartile registered the smallest increase in participation.

In 1986, the participation rates of those from low and middle SES backgrounds were comparable, whereas by 1994, a gap existed with a lower participation rate for the low SES group. The emergence of this gap raises questions about equity of access. The appearance of this gap coincided with a period in which real family income generally showed little change, income inequality increased, and student assistance moved toward a more loan-based rather than grant-based approach (see also section 3.5F, student debt and tuition fees). The gap demonstrates the importance of ensuring that rising costs are matched by the availability of funding, through grants, loans, bursaries, or other means, for individuals from low-income backgrounds. Without such funding, inequities may result from financial circumstances, regardless of the ability of the student.

The most recent collection of data on educational attainment by family SES was in 1994. More regular monitoring of educational attainment by SES is needed, especially for university participation, in light of the substantial cost increases in postsecondary education in recent years. Such monitoring would allow policy makers to track and fine-tune programs aimed at ensuring that students who are academically capable of attending and benefiting from university are not prevented from participating because of low income.

## FINDINGS

### CANADA

By 1994, a gap existed in university participation rates between persons from low and middle SES backgrounds (Figure 4.19)

A higher percentage of 18 to 21-year-olds from each quartile was participating in university in 1994 than in 1986. However, the disparity between the participation of the lowest quartile and the other quartiles increased over the same period. In 1986, results from the General Social Survey showed no significant difference in participation rates among students from the lowest SES quartile and those in the middle two quartiles. By 1994, a gap of 7 percentage points had opened up, with participation rates of 18% and 25% respectively, as the considerable increase in participation among those in the middle quartiles outpaced the increase among the lowest SES quartile. Those in the highest SES quartile continued to show by far the highest university participation rate, at 40%.

In 1994, those in the lowest quartile were also most likely to have less than a high school education. About one-third of those in the lowest quartile had not completed high school (34%), compared with about one-quarter of those in the upper quartile (23%). Hence, the rate of high-school non-completion was about 50% higher in the lowest SES group than the highest SES group. It is worth noting that these figures may overstate the extent of high school non-completion, as some of the 18- to 21-year-old cohort who had not finished high school were still students at the time of the survey.

Results are presented for Canada only, and not by jurisdiction due to sample size limitations of the source data from Statistics Canada's General Social Survey.

EDUCATION OUTCOMES

FIGURE 4.19   PERCENTAGE OF THE POPULATION AGED 18 TO 21 ATTENDING UNIVERSITY, BY FAMILY SOCIO-ECONOMIC STATUS, CANADA, 1986 AND 1994

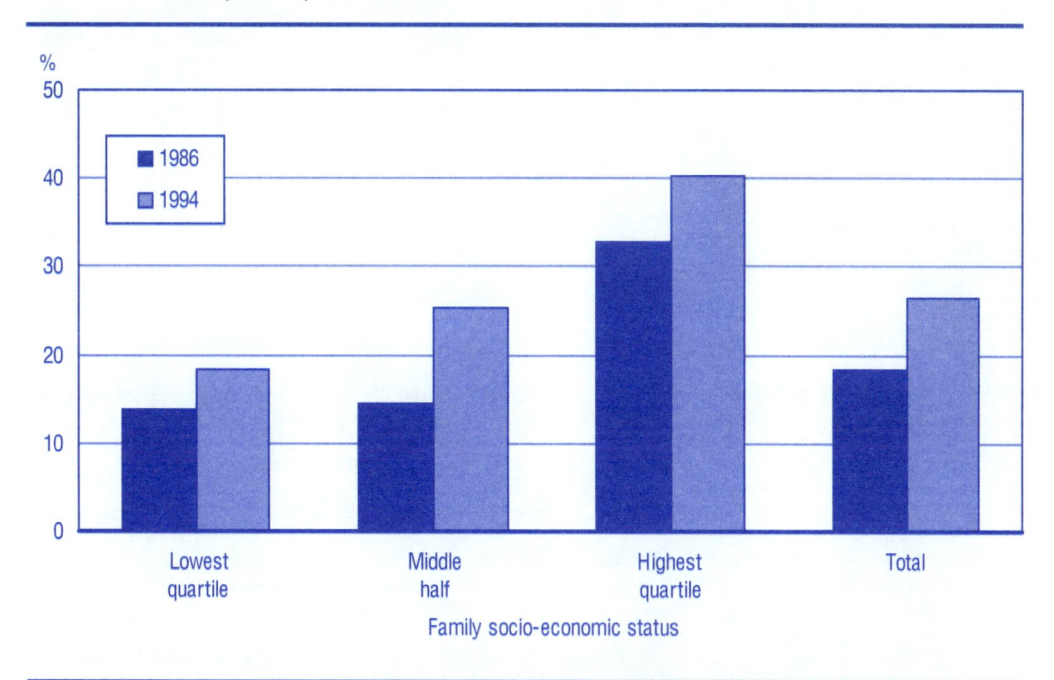

Note:   Due to sample size limitations of the General Social Survey, these data are not available by jurisdiction.
Source: *General Social Survey 1986 and 1994, and Centre for Education Statistics, Statistics Canada.*

FIGURE 4.20   PERCENTAGE OF THE POPULATION AGED 18 TO 21 WITH LESS THAN HIGH SCHOOL COMPLETION, BY FAMILY SOCIO-ECONOMIC STATUS, CANADA, 1994

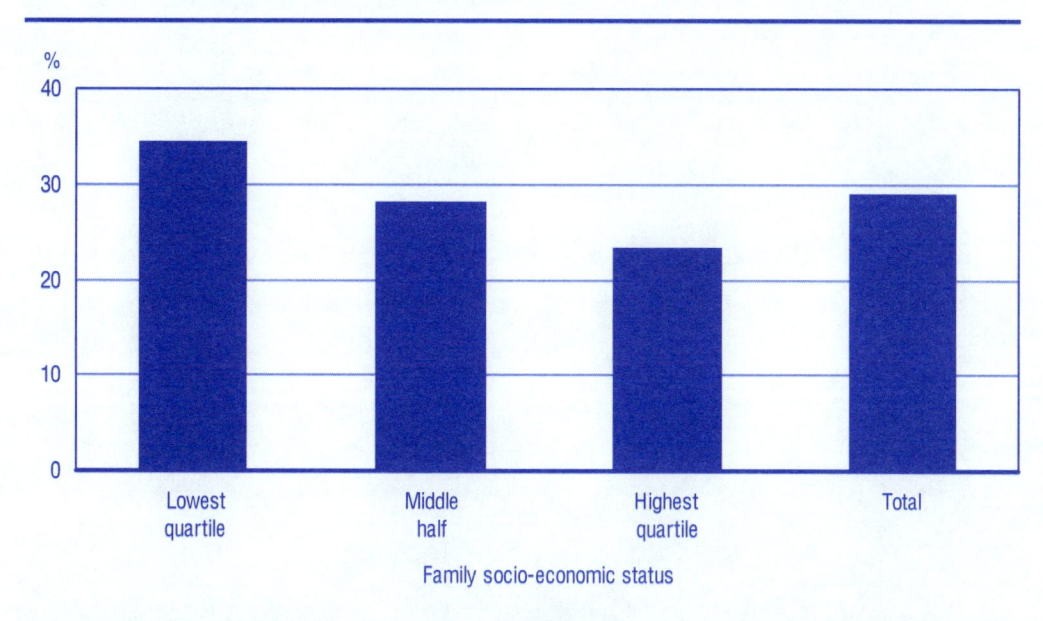

Note:   Due to sample size limitations of the General Social Survey, these data are not available by jurisdiction.
Source: *General Social Survey 1986 and 1994, and Centre for Education Statistics, Statistics Canada.*

# ENDNOTES

1. For more detail on the results of the SAIP assessments, consult the individual SAIP reports, published by Council of Ministers of Education, Canada (Toronto). See also <www.cmec.ca>.
2. Countries participating in TIMSS whose results have been omitted due to sampling issues include: the United States and Germany (Population 2), and the United Kingdom (Populations 1 and 2). France and Germany did not participate in the Population 1 study. Italy did not participate in either Population 1 or 2. Results for Population 3 are omitted from this report, as Canada did not meet all sampling requirements for this population.
3. David F. Robitaille, Alan R Taylor and Graham Orpwood, *TIMSS-Canada Report, Volume 2: Grade 4 (Volume 1: Grade 8)* 1996–97. See also *Selected research highlights: TIMSS Population 2 (13-year-olds)* (Toronto: Educational Quality and Accountability Office, 1998); Darren Lauzon, *Gender Differences in Science and Math Achievement in the Final Year of Secondary School: Evidence from the 1995 TIMSS* (Statistics Canada, 1999); and Yanhong Zhang, *Gender Differences in Mathematics and Science Achievement in the 8th Grade: The Role of Engagement in Out-of-School Activities and Experimentation in Science Lessons* (Statistics Canada, 1999).
4. See also *Reading the Future: A Portrait of Literacy in Canada* (Statistics Canada, 1996, Catalogue No.89-55-XPE).

# CHAPTER 5

## LABOUR MARKET OUTCOMES

- Labour force participation
- Flows between formal education and work
- Mobility of postsecondary students and graduates

## HIGHLIGHTS

- In Canada's labour force, a sizeable premium is attached to higher levels of educational attainment. Higher levels of education are associated with higher rates of employment and lower rates of unemployment.

- In the 1990s, labour market outcomes deteriorated for young people with low levels of educational attainment. This was particularly true for youth who did not complete high school, and, to a lesser extent, for high school graduates with no further education.

- Labour market outcomes vary less by jurisdiction and gender than by educational attainment.

- The overall incidence of underemployment—as measured by the number of persons working part time on an involuntary basis as a percentage of all persons in the labour force—has risen in the last two decades, and is higher among those with lower levels of educational attainment.

- Postsecondary graduates in the 1990s appear to be having slightly more difficulty making the transition from school to work than did graduates in the 1980s. Although unemployment rates were similar, they have lower rates of full-time employment two years after graduation, lower earnings, and, with the exception of university graduates, they report less education-to-job relevance.

- Interjurisdictional mobility of postsecondary students and graduates is an important phenomenon, particularly at the university level, where about 8% of the class of university graduates in both 1986 and 1995 had left their jurisdiction of residence to study. University graduates were also mobile after completing their studies, particularly 1986 graduates.

## 5.1 Labour force participation

### Policy context

The goals of education and training are broad and encompass many desired outcomes. These include developing well-rounded individuals capable of participating in and making positive contributions to society. From both an individual and societal perspective, good labour market outcomes are another important goal, especially in light of their impact on the current and future competitiveness of Canada's economy.

Labour force measures—including the employment rate, the unemployment rate and a measure of underemployment—can provide an overall reading on how labour market outcomes vary by level of education. Such information can help educators and education stakeholders understand the impact and benefits of higher levels of education, and point to areas where interventions are needed to improve labour market outcomes.

Examining these rates for younger people can indicate how youth are coping with the transition from school to work and reveal where measures may be needed to help them make this transition successfully. Examining these rates for the working-age population as a whole can paint a picture of the longer-term impacts of educational attainment on labour market outcomes.

The findings presented here show that individuals with higher levels of educational attainment have better labour market outcomes in all provinces. Also, it is evident that individuals with less than a high school education are having greater difficulties in the labour market, especially those who are younger and new to the labour force.

These findings argue in favour of a continued emphasis on the part of educational systems toward achieving high levels of high school completion, and ensuring opportunities for access to higher levels of education. New Brunswick offers one example of a strategy for doing this. The school year 1999-2000 will see the school-leaving age raised from 16 to 18—students will be able to leave earlier only if they have completed their graduating requirements.

Given the structural changes occurring in the economy and the rapid transition toward a knowledge-based economy, entering the labour market today requires ever-increasing levels of educational attainment. While there were well-paying jobs that required relatively little formal education in the past, there are fewer such jobs today, and this is also likely to be the case in the future.

The high proportion of youth (15 to 24 years of age) engaged in involuntary part-time work is one illustration of the difficulties young people experience in making the transition from school to work. Regardless of educational attainment, in many provinces youth are having a tougher time finding employment. This suggests the need for strategies to address these transitional difficulties—strategies that may call for partnerships between education and training systems, institutions, and business and industry. However, while promoting higher education and developing better transition strategies may be of some help in moving youth into full-time work, this is not likely to change what appears to be an ongoing restructuring of the labour market towards more part-time work.

LABOUR MARKET OUTCOMES

## A. EMPLOYMENT AND UNEMPLOYMENT RATES

### FINDINGS

#### CANADA

In general, higher levels of educational attainment are associated with improved labour market outcomes. Employment rates increase and unemployment rates decrease with higher levels of education.

In 1990, among men, the employment rate of high school graduates was about the same as that of university and college graduates, and well above the rate among men with less than high school education. Among women, the employment rate of high school graduates was somewhat lower than among postsecondary graduates, but well above the rate among those with less than high school education (Figures 5.1 to 5.4 and Tables 5.1 and 5.2 ).

**Definitions**
**Employment rate: the number of persons employed as a percentage of the population.**
**Unemployment rate: the number of persons unemployed expressed as a percentage of the labour force.**

**In the 1990s, in terms of finding employment, the largest premium has been associated with high school graduation.**

FIGURE 5.1    EMPLOYMENT RATE OF MALES IN THE 25 TO 54 AGE GROUP BY EDUCATIONAL ATTAINMENT, CANADA AND PROVINCES, 1990 AND 1998

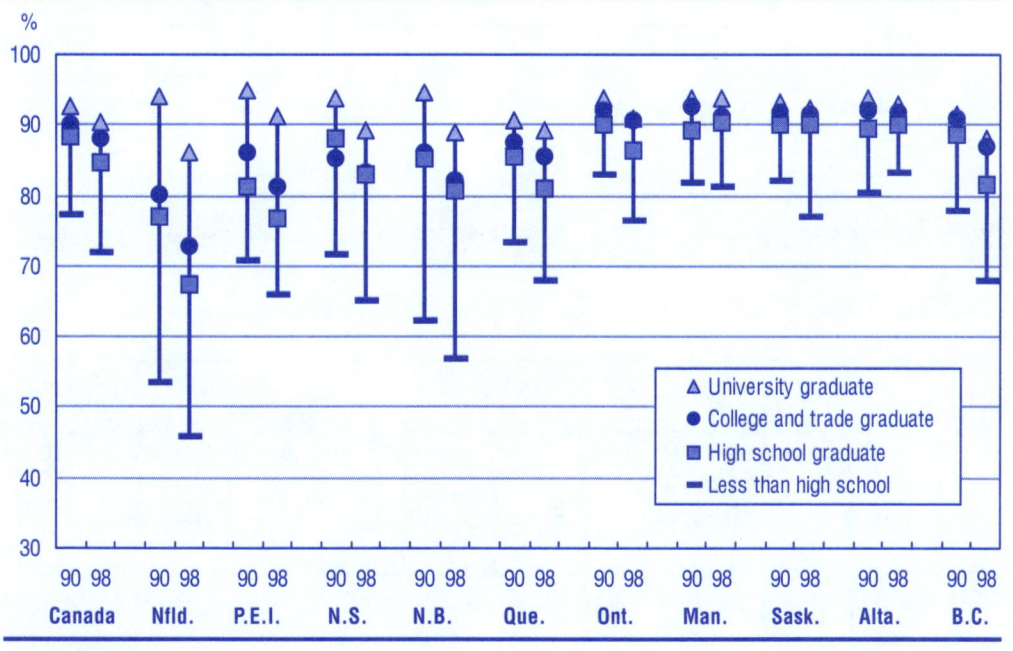

Table 5.1 and figures 5.1 and 5.2 show provincial employment rates by educational attainment for the 25 to 54 age group. Table 5.2 and figures 5.3 and 5.4 present the same data for the 25 to 29 age group.

*Source: Labour Force Survey, Statistics Canada.*

111

**FIGURE 5.2** EMPLOYMENT RATE OF FEMALES IN THE 25 TO 54 AGE GROUP BY EDUCATIONAL ATTAINMENT, CANADA AND PROVINCES, 1990 AND 1998

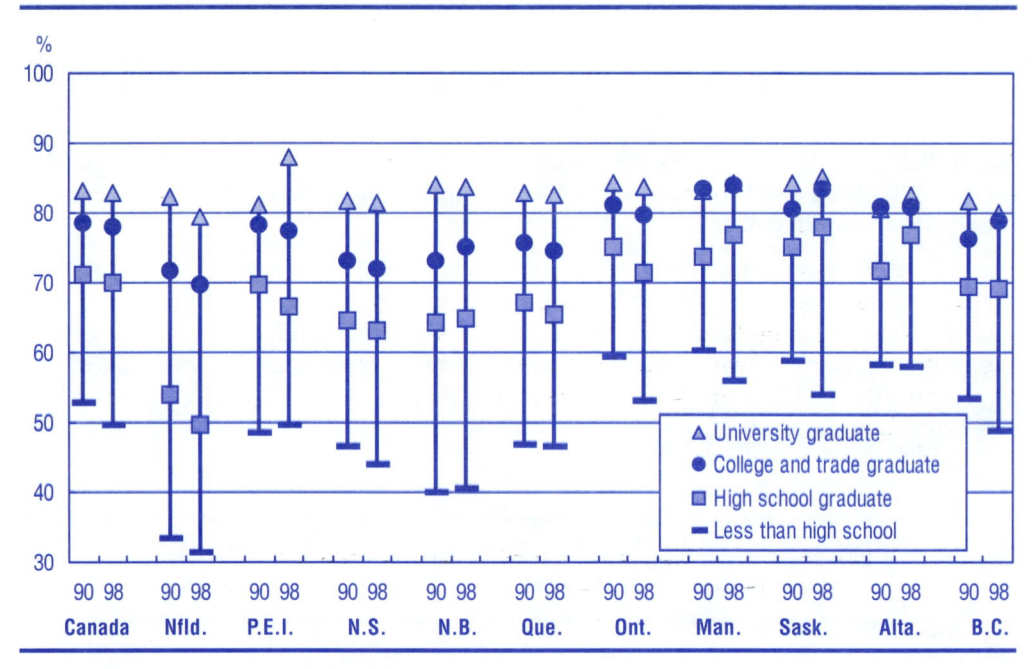

*Source: Labour Force Survey, Statistics Canada.*

**FIGURE 5.3** EMPLOYMENT RATE OF MALES IN THE 25 TO 29 AGE GROUP BY EDUCATIONAL ATTAINMENT, CANADA AND PROVINCES, 1990 AND 1998

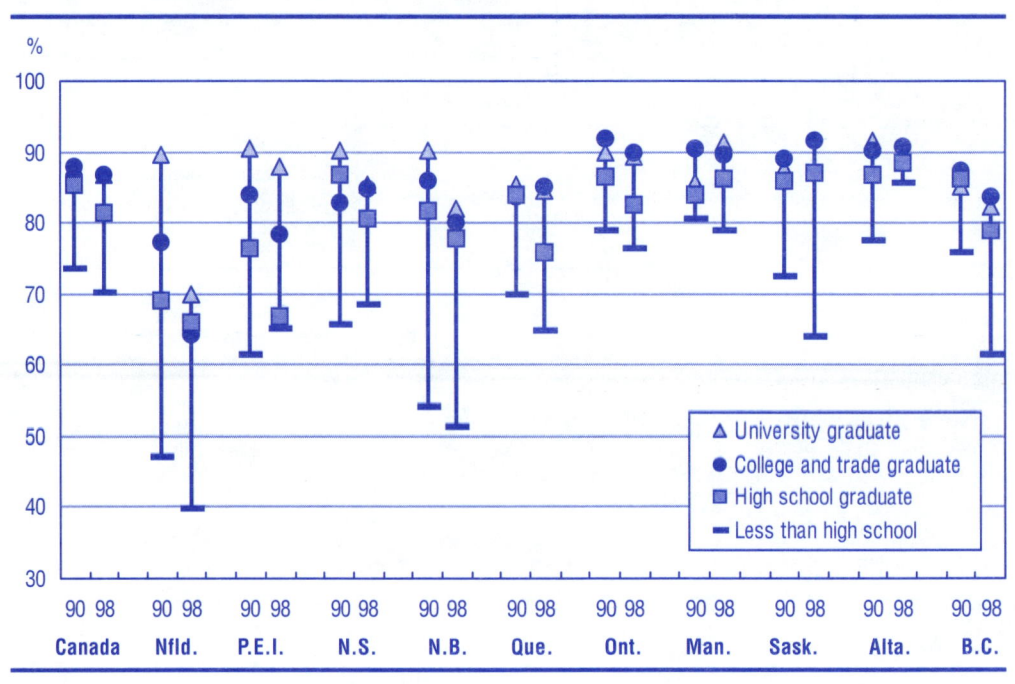

*Source: Labour Force Survey, Statistics Canada.*

## LABOUR MARKET OUTCOMES

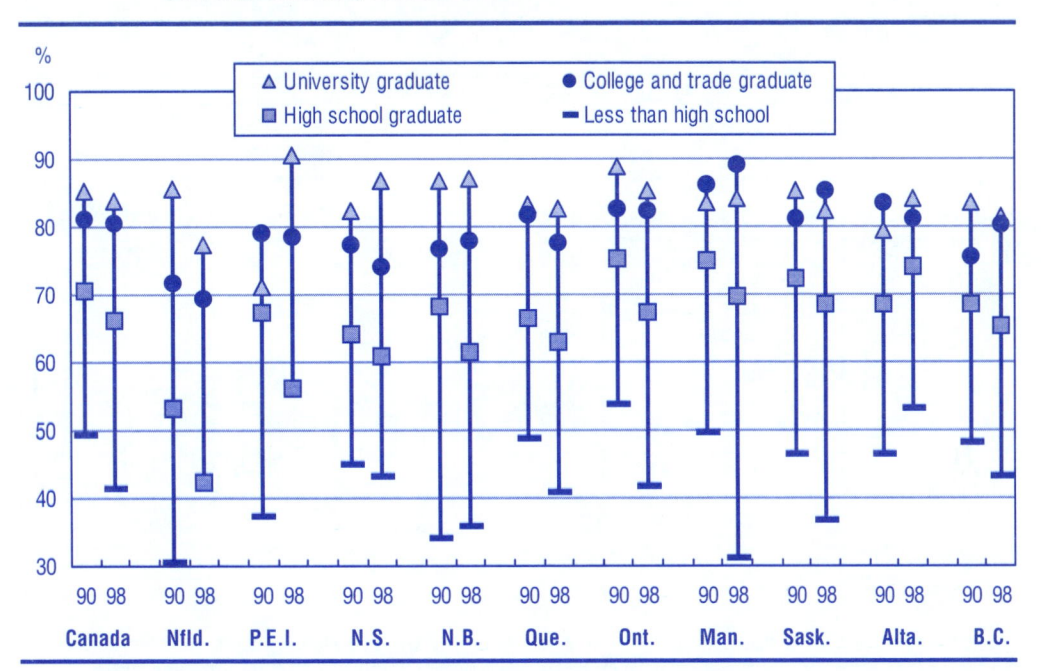

FIGURE 5.4  EMPLOYMENT RATE OF FEMALES IN THE 25 TO 29 AGE GROUP BY EDUCATIONAL ATTAINMENT, CANADA AND PROVINCES, 1990 AND 1998[1]

Legend:
- △ University graduate
- ● College and trade graduate
- ■ High school graduate
- — Less than high school

X-axis: 90 98 for Canada, Nfld., P.E.I., N.S., N.B., Que., Ont., Man., Sask., Alta., B.C.

1  A number of provincial estimates have been suppressed due to high sampling errors (see Table 5.2).
*Source: Labour Force Survey, Statistics Canada.*

By 1998, there had been an overall drop in employment rates. The recession of the early 1990s has had enduring effects as workplaces and industries have restructured taking advantage of new possibilities with advanced communication technologies, constrained by the competitive nature of global markets. In this context, during the 1990s, employment in low skill occupations has trended downward, while job growth has been concentrated in professional and managerial occupations requiring higher education and skill levels. Examining changes in employment rates by level of educational attainment, the drop was largest among those with less than high school education, and next largest among high school graduates. This served to widen the gap in employment rates between high school graduates and non-graduates and also gave rise to more differentiation in employment rates between high school and postsecondary graduates.

In 1998, among those aged 25 to 54 with less than high school education, 50% of women were employed, compared with more than 70% of men, constituting a gender gap of 20 percentage points. Among university graduates in this age group, the gap was less—7 percentage points. Among the younger age group, those aged 25 to 29, the gender gap in employment rates was comparable to that of the 25 to 54 age group among those with high school or less education. It was less among those with postsecondary education; the gap was only 3 percentage points among university graduates. The gender gap in employment rates by level of education for both age groups changed little between 1990 and 1998.

There were no significant gender differences in unemployment rates for either age group at either time. It should be noted that employment and unemployment rates provide only a partial view of labour market conditions. Other measures that are not examined here, such as the full-time employment rate and earnings, do reveal a gender gap.

**Gender differences in labour market outcomes lessen with increasing education levels.**

EDUCATION INDICATORS IN CANADA

FIGURE 5.5    UNEMPLOYMENT RATE OF MALES IN THE 25 TO 54 AGE GROUP BY EDUCATIONAL ATTAINMENT, CANADA AND PROVINCES, 1990 AND 1998[1]

Table 5.3 and figures 5.5 and 5.6 show provincial unemployment rates by educational attainment for males and females aged 25 to 54. Data for the 25-to-29 age group are presented in Table 5.4 and figures 5.7 and 5.8.

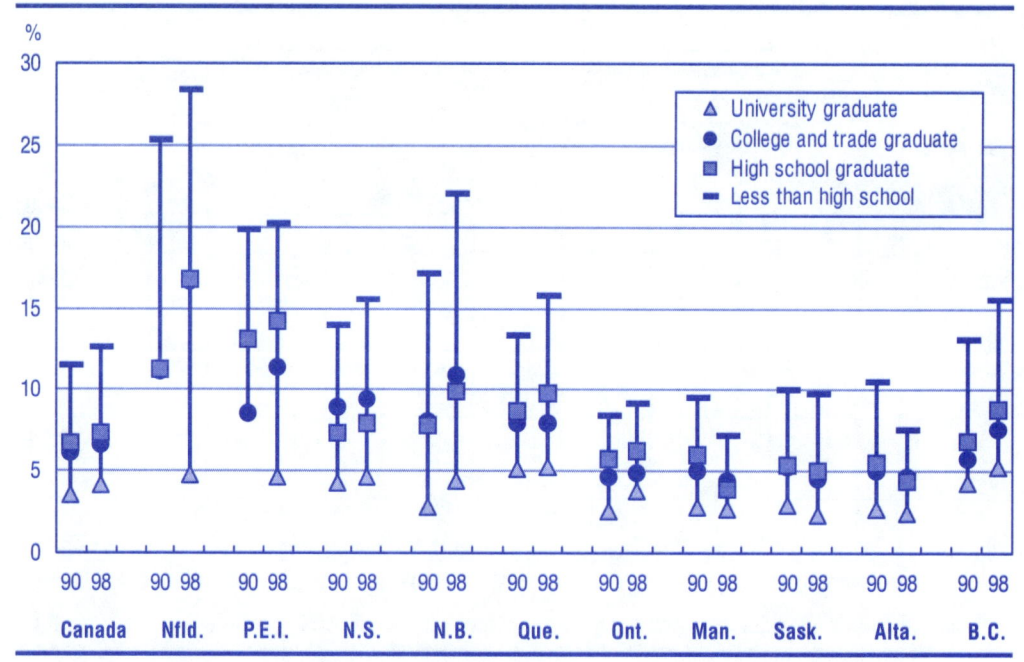

1  A number of provincial estimates have been suppressed due to high sampling errors (see Table 5.3).
*Source: Labour Force Survey, Statistics Canada.*

FIGURE 5.6    UNEMPLOYMENT RATE OF FEMALES IN THE 25 TO 54 AGE GROUP BY EDUCATIONAL ATTAINMENT, CANADA AND PROVINCES, 1990 AND 1998[1]

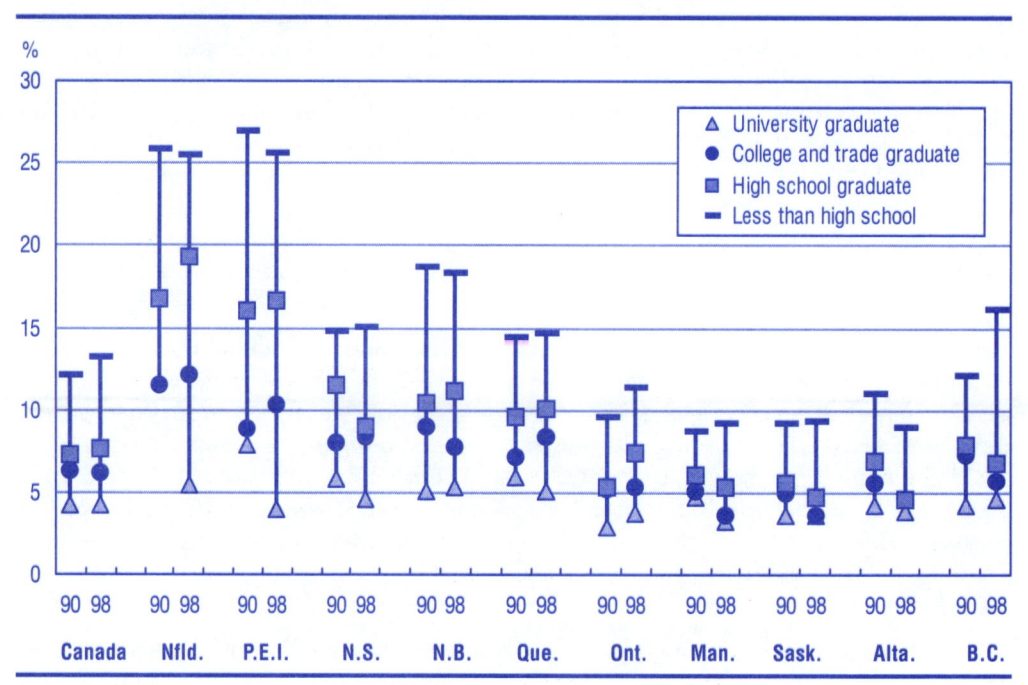

1  A number of provincial estimates have been suppressed due to high sampling errors (see Table 5.3).
*Source: Labour Force Survey, Statistics Canada.*

## Labour Market Outcomes

**FIGURE 5.7** UNEMPLOYMENT RATE OF MALES IN THE 25 TO 29 AGE GROUP BY EDUCATIONAL ATTAINMENT, CANADA AND PROVINCES, 1990 AND 1998[1]

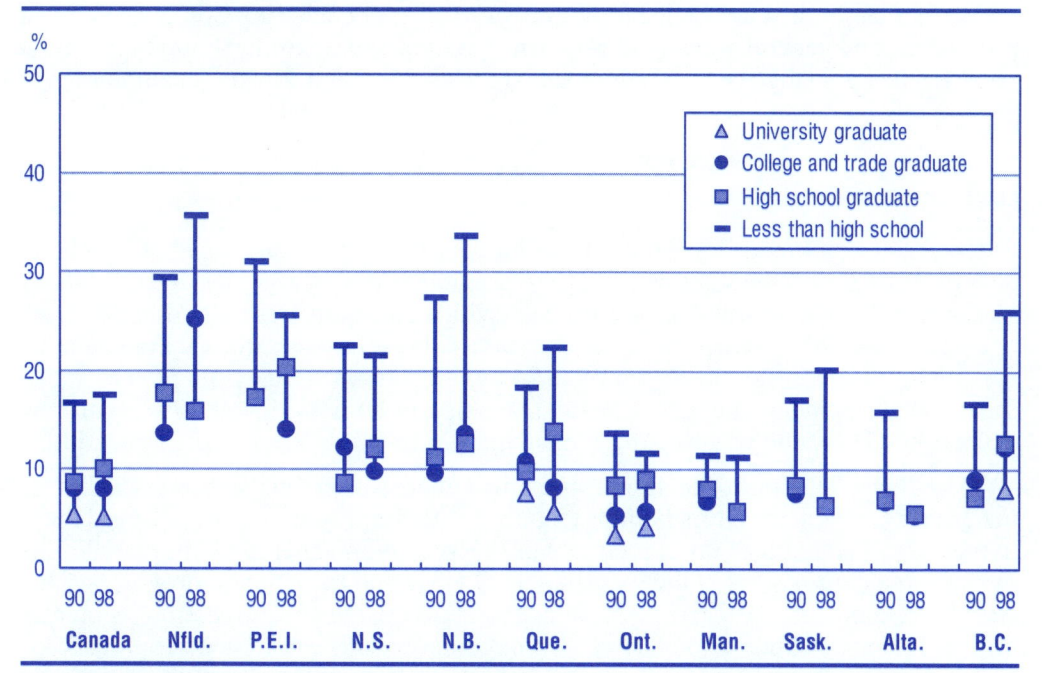

1 A number of provincial estimates have been suppressed due to high sampling errors (see Table 5.4).
*Source:* Labour Force Survey, Statistics Canada.

**FIGURE 5.8** UNEMPLOYMENT RATE OF FEMALES IN THE 25 TO 29 AGE GROUP BY EDUCATIONAL ATTAINMENT, CANADA AND PROVINCES, 1990 AND 1998[1]

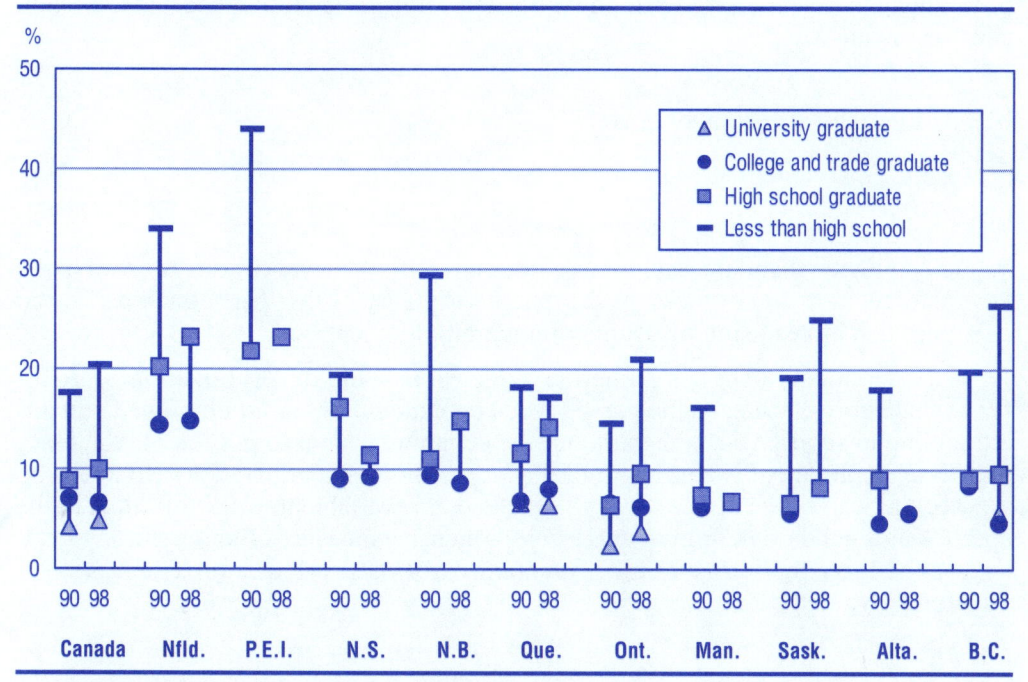

1 A number of provincial estimates have been suppressed due to high sampling errors (see Table 5.4).
*Source:* Labour Force Survey, Statistics Canada.

EDUCATION INDICATORS IN CANADA

**Young persons with low educational attainment are experiencing increased difficulty in the labour market.**

Young people with less than high school education are experiencing substantially lower employment rates and higher unemployment rates than those with higher educational attainment. In particular, the employment rates of women aged 25 to 29 with less than high school education are very low (between 30% and 50% in most provinces), and generally dropped between 1990 and 1998. Similarly, unemployment rates for these young women have risen significantly, with a pan-Canadian rate of 20% in 1998.

## JURISDICTIONS

**Labour market outcomes vary less by jurisdiction than by educational attainment.**

The premium on higher levels of education apparent at the pan-Canadian level can also be seen across jurisdictions. Despite sizeable differences in the overall labour market conditions of provinces, individuals with a university degree had higher rates of employment in all provinces, with little variability between provinces. For example, the employment rates of men aged 25 to 54 by jurisdiction were within plus or minus 3 percentage points of the pan-Canadian average in both 1990 and 1998, with few exceptions. The same was true of women aged 25 to 54 with university education.

**Labour market conditions vary more across jurisdictions among the young cohort, and have generally worsened between 1990 and 1998.**

At lower levels of educational attainment, there was greater variability in labour market outcomes across jurisdictions (figures 5.1 to 5.8). Outcomes were linked more to the overall strength of provincial labour markets, with generally better conditions in Ontario and provinces to the west than in Quebec and the Atlantic provinces. This was the case in both 1990 and 1998 for both age groups. In general, there was greater differentiation in labour market outcomes in provinces with less robust labour markets, with more spread between rates for those with lower versus higher levels of educational attainment.

The cohort aged 25 to 29 coincides with the population group that has recently completed school or is in the midst of the transition from school to work. Labour market outcomes are generally less favourable for this group than for the overall working-age population, the majority of whom are beyond the point of transition into the work force. In the younger age group, labour market outcomes are particularly poor among those with less than high school education in Newfoundland and Labrador, and New Brunswick.

## B. UNDEREMPLOYMENT RATE

### FINDINGS

**As a measure of underemployment, the involuntary part-time employment rate is defined as the number of persons working part time on an involuntary basis as a percentage of all persons in the labour force.**

While employment and unemployment rates quantify the level of participation in the labour force, they do not measure the extent or quality of that participation. We can examine such issues using measures of underemployment.

Underemployment has numerous dimensions—the underutilization of skills, for example, or, alternately, the gap between the amount of labour employed persons are willing to supply versus the amount the economy is able to provide. Involuntary part-time employment is a measure of the latter. This is experienced by persons who are working part time but who both want to and are available to work full time. In the absence of a standard definition and a comprehensive measure of underemployment, we use the economic measure of involuntary part-time work as a proxy measure of underemployment.

### CANADA

The involuntary part-time employment rate, like the unemployment rate, has risen and fallen in concert with changes in the business cycle. Both rates spiked upwards during the recessions of the early 1980s and 1990s. However, the reduction in the

## LABOUR MARKET OUTCOMES

involuntary part-time employment rate was generally not as pronounced as that of the unemployment rate in the periods of recovery and expansion that followed the recessions.

The involuntary part-time rate actually kept on increasing during the early stages of the 1990s recovery. Hence, the recessions had a ratcheting-up effect on the involuntary part-time employment rate, which was less evident in the unemployment rate. These trends are illustrated for persons with high school education or less in Figures 5.9 to 5.11.

*The involuntary part-time employment rate has been on an upward trend over the past two decades.*

FIGURE 5.9  INVOLUNTARY PART-TIME EMPLOYMENT RATE AND UNEMPLOYMENT RATE FOR PERSONS WITH HIGH SCHOOL COMPLETION OR LESS, 15 TO 24 AGE GROUP, CANADA, 1976 TO 1996

*Source: Labour Force Survey, Statistics Canada.*

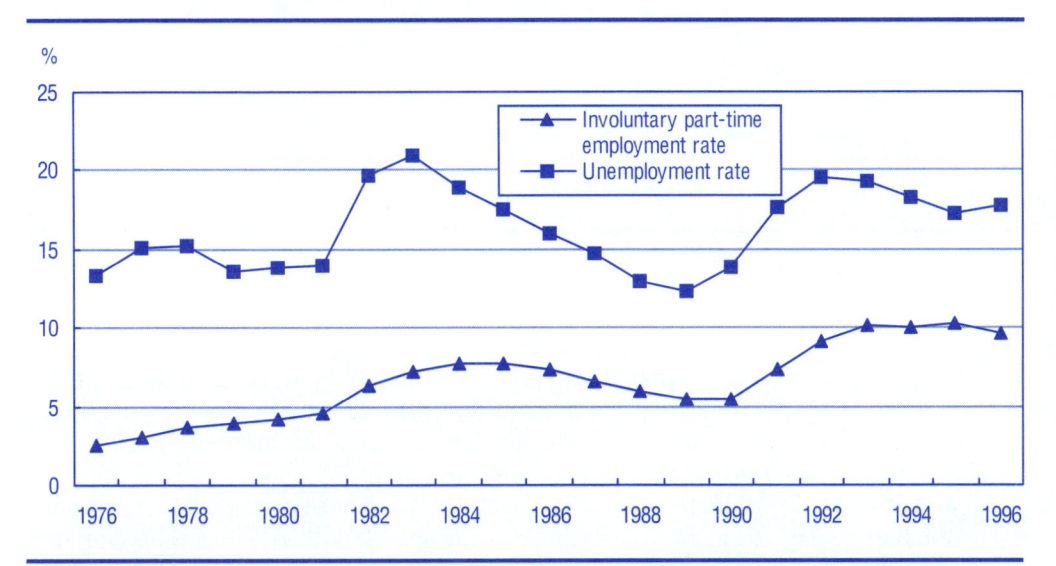

*Tables 5.5 and 5.6 show the involuntary part-time employment rate and unemployment rates for three age groups. Figures 5.9 to 5.11 graph these rates for individuals with a high school education or less. Results are presented for Canada only, as jurisdictional level data are not available.*

FIGURE 5.10  INVOLUNTARY PART-TIME EMPLOYMENT RATE AND UNEMPLOYMENT RATE FOR PERSONS WITH HIGH SCHOOL COMPLETION OR LESS, 25 TO 34 AGE GROUP, CANADA, 1976 TO 1996

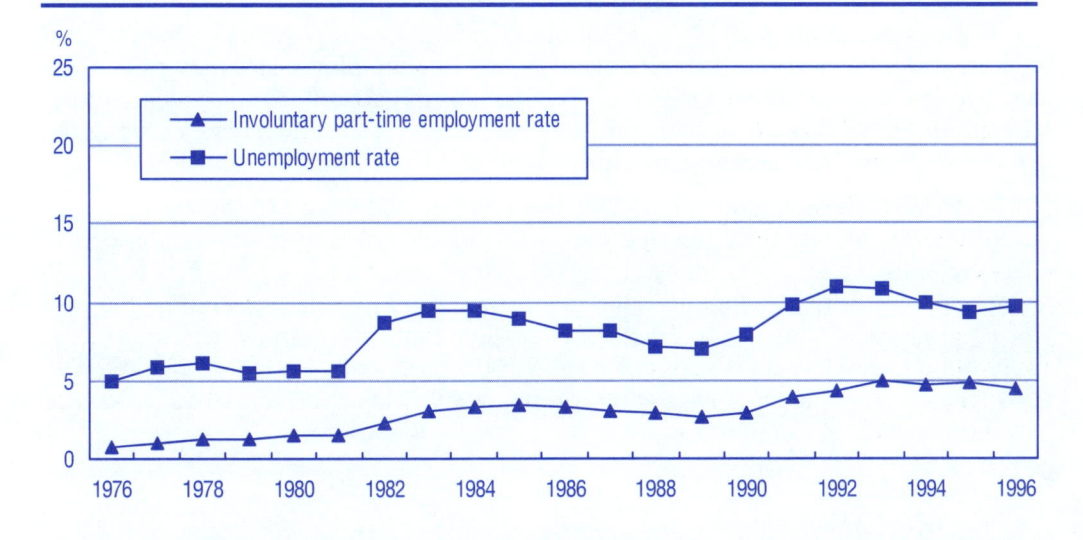

*Source: Labour Force Survey, Statistics Canada.*

EDUCATION INDICATORS IN CANADA

FIGURE 5.11  INVOLUNTARY PART-TIME EMPLOYMENT RATE AND UNEMPLOYMENT RATE FOR PERSONS WITH HIGH SCHOOL COMPLETION OR LESS, 35 TO 54 AGE GROUP, CANADA, 1976 TO 1996

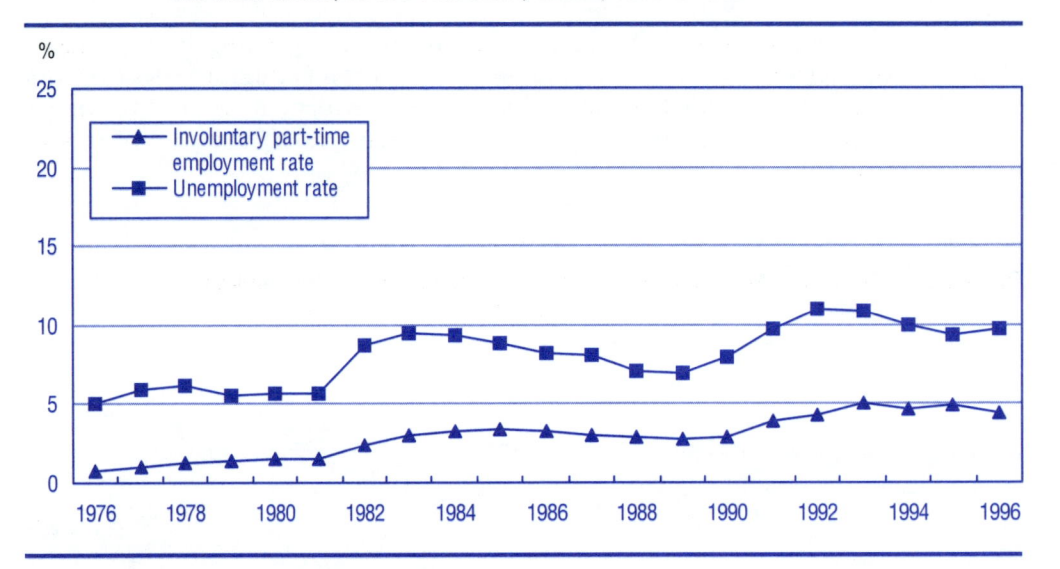

*Source:* Labour Force Survey, Statistics Canada.

**Underemployment has become an increasingly important phenomenon over the past two decades…**

The rate of involuntary part-time employment more than tripled between 1976 and 1996. In 1976, involuntary part-time employment was much less prevalent than unemployment. The unemployment rate was more than five times higher than the involuntary part-time rate for the three age groups examined, those aged 15 to 24, 25 to 34, and 35 to 54. By 1996, the unemployment rate was less than twice the involuntary part-time rate among 15- to 24-year-olds (16% compared with 10%), and about twice the involuntary part-time rate among the older groups (tables 5.5 and 5.6).

**…in large part because of structural changes in the economy, where full-time employment is increasingly difficult to find.**

As Table 5.7 shows, the incidence of part-time employment has increased substantially over the past 20 years. A sizeable portion of this increase has been involuntary in nature, particularly between 1976 and 1986. In this period, the increase in involuntary part-time employment matched the overall increase in part-time employment for the groups aged 25 to 34, and 35 to 54. It was half the overall increase in part-time employment for the youngest age group.

Between 1986 and 1996, involuntary part-time employment continued to represent a large portion of the increase in part-time employment among the older age groups, but accounted for less of the increase in part-time employment among the group aged 15 to 24. In part, this may reflect an increased tendency among the younger age group to combine part-time work and schooling.

**Table 5.7 shows the level and change in part-time and involuntary part-time employment rates for three age groups.**

**The involuntary part-time employment rate is higher among youth aged 15 to 24 than among the adult work force.**

In 1996, the involuntary part-time rate among youths aged 15 to 24 was 10%—twice the rate among the older age groups. Young people are in a transition period between school and work. Many are entering the labour force for the first time and may be having difficulty finding suitable full-time employment, especially if they are recent graduates or have lower levels of education. Part-time employment may be the only option available until they can establish themselves in the labour market. The involuntary part-time employment rate among youths was quite similar regardless of level of education.

# LABOUR MARKET OUTCOMES

In 1996, the involuntary part-time employment rate stood at 4% for those aged 25 to 34, and 4% for those aged 35 to 54. While the involuntary part-time rate has remained lower for these groups than for the younger age group, the gap has narrowed over time. The youth rate was three times as high as the rate for older workers in 1976, but was only twice as high by 1996.

## 5.2 FLOWS BETWEEN FORMAL EDUCATION AND WORK

### POLICY CONTEXT

In today's knowledge-based global economy, workers need more education and higher skill levels than ever to succeed. Prevailing economic conditions and the supply and demand characteristics of industries and occupations also have a bearing on the labour market outcomes of recent graduates. Postsecondary graduates represent a large investment in the development of human capital, therefore it is important to monitor their transition from school to the labour market.

The transition from school to work today is long and complex. More youth aged 15 to 24 are full-time students, and as part of the transition, many are combining work with education.

**FIGURE 5.12  EDUCATION AND EMPLOYMENT ACTIVITIES OF YOUTH AGED 15 TO 19 YEARS, CANADA, 1976, 1986, AND 1996**

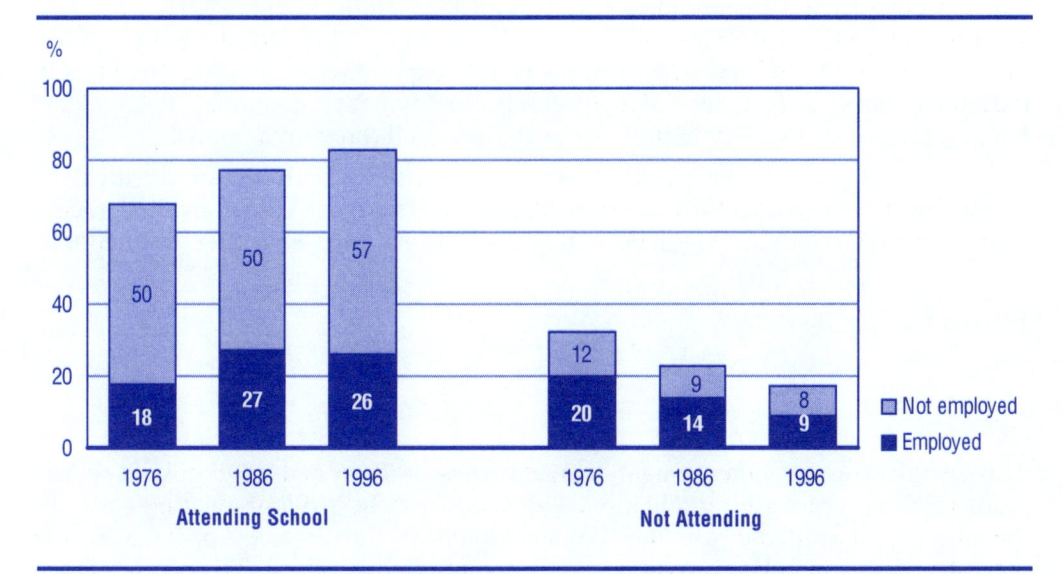

Figures 5.12 and 5.13 show the various ways in which individuals aged 15 to 19 and 20 to 24 combine education and employment activities.

*Source: Labour Force Survey, Statistics Canada.*

As might be expected, the predominant activity of the 15- to 19-year-old age group, by far, is attending school. In 1996, 83% were attending school, up from 68% in 1976. Among 15- to 19-year-olds attending school, the percentage working peaked in 1986, at more than 35% (i.e., in Figure 5.12, 27 out of 77), and fell to 31% in 1996. This may reflect the availability of fewer part-time jobs for students, or a shift on the part of students toward focusing more on their studies and less on part-time jobs, or a combination of both.

FIGURE 5.13    EDUCATION AND EMPLOYMENT ACTIVITIES OF YOUTH AGED 20 TO 24 YEARS, CANADA, 1976, 1986, AND 1996

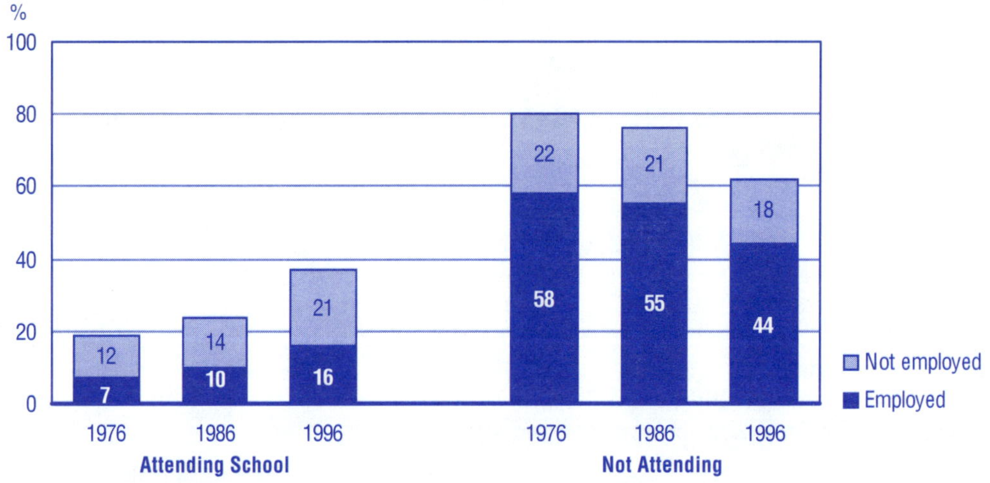

| | Attending School | | | Not Attending | | |
|---|---|---|---|---|---|---|
| Year | 1976 | 1986 | 1996 | 1976 | 1986 | 1996 |
| Employed | 7 | 10 | 16 | 58 | 55 | 44 |
| Not employed | 12 | 14 | 21 | 22 | 21 | 18 |

Source: Labour Force Survey, Statistics Canada.

Among the group aged 20 to 24, the percentage in school almost doubled over the 20-year period, from 19% to 37% (as reflected in section 3.3, student enrolments). Among those in school in this age group, the percentage working increased over the period, from 37% in 1976 to 43% in 1996.

Among 15- to 19-year-olds not attending school, employment rates have dropped sharply, from 60% in 1986 to 53% in 1996. This group, which for the most part has lower levels of educational attainment, is clearly experiencing greater difficulties in the labour market. Among the older age group, employment rates among non-students have remained consistently high—just over 70% at all three time points.

We can see that the transition from school to work increasingly involves combining these two activities. We now examine a later stage in the transition process for postsecondary graduates—labour market outcomes two years after graduation.

## FINDINGS

### CANADA

This section presents employment characteristics of 1986 and 1995 postsecondary graduates, two years after graduation. The results for the 1995 graduating class are the most recent available from the National Graduates Survey (see Appendix 3), and the 1986 graduating class provides a useful point of comparison. The two reference years are roughly 10 years apart and are at similar points in the business cycle—well into sustained periods of economic expansion.

**Overall, the labour market performance of 1995 post-secondary graduates two years after graduation was slightly worse than that achieved two years after graduation by 1986 graduates.**

Compared with the 1986 graduating class, 1995 graduates had lower rates of full-time employment, and the earnings (in constant 1997 dollars) of those employed full time were generally lower. However, unemployment rates were similar between the two graduating classes. These differences in labour market outcomes between the two graduating classes should be viewed in the context of differences in overall labour market conditions. While both 1988 and 1997 represent points well into periods of expansion following severe recessions, the recovery of the 1980s was accompanied by stronger employment growth than that of the 1990s.

LABOUR MARKET OUTCOMES

FIGURE 5.14    PERCENTAGE OF 1986 AND 1995 UNIVERSITY GRADUATES WORKING FULL TIME, TWO YEARS AFTER GRADUATION, BY GENDER AND FIELD OF STUDY, CANADA

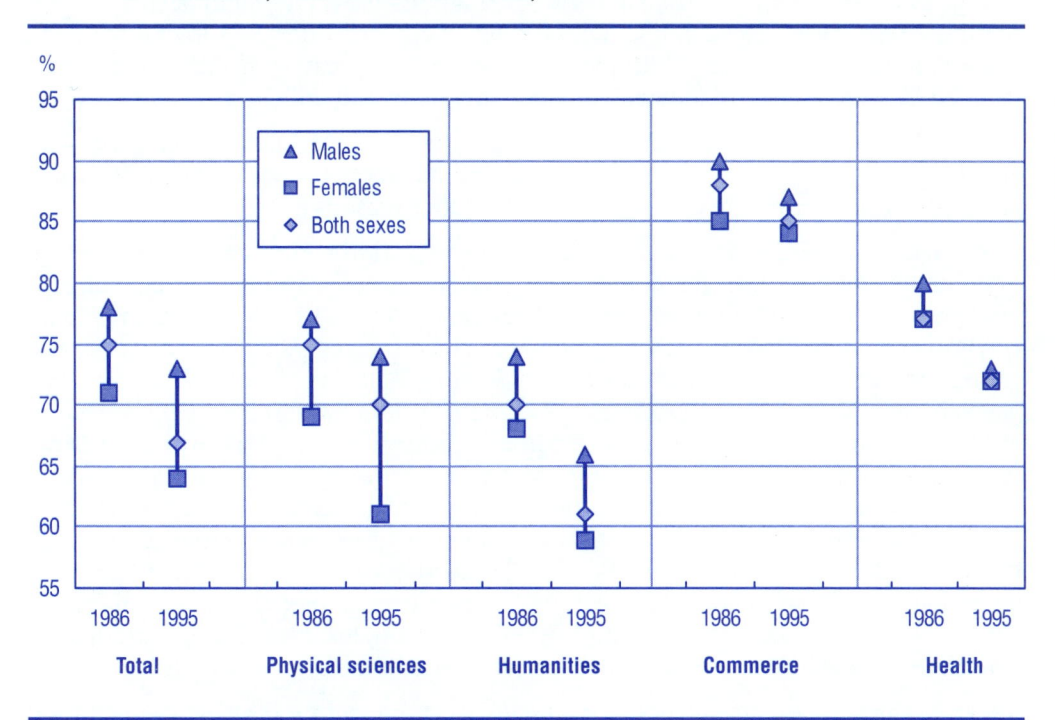

The percentage of graduates working full time is shown by gender and field of study in Table 5.8 and Figure 5.14, and by province of study and level of education in Table 5.9 and Figure 5.15.

Source: 1988 and 1997 National Graduates Surveys, Statistics Canada.

FIGURE 5.15    PERCENTAGE OF 1986 AND 1995 GRADUATES WORKING FULL TIME, TWO YEARS AFTER GRADUATION, BY LEVEL OF EDUCATION AND PROVINCE OF STUDY

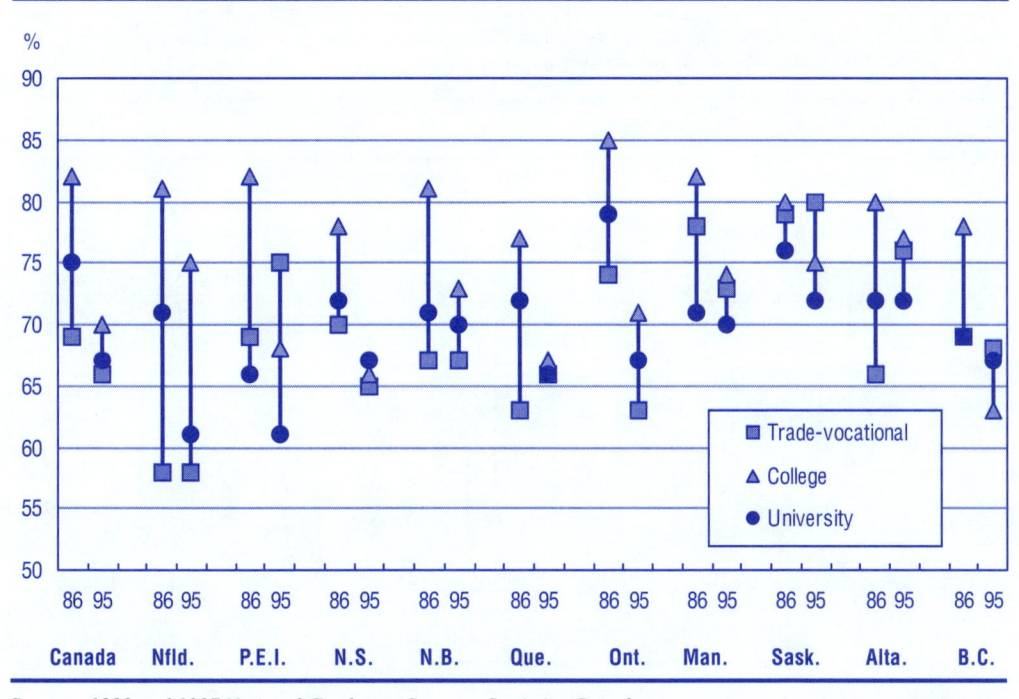

Source: 1988 and 1997 National Graduates Surveys, Statistics Canada.

EDUCATION INDICATORS IN CANADA

**The rate of full-time employment fell between the 1986 and 1995 classes of college graduates...**

Just over two-thirds of 1995 postsecondary graduates were employed full time two years after graduation. The rate of full-time employment was highest among college graduates at 70%, compared with 67% among university graduates, and 66% for trade–vocational graduates. These rates were considerably lower than the corresponding rates for the 1986 class. The drop was greatest at the college level, from 82%, which reduced the gap between university and college rates.

**...while the labour force participation rate increased for graduates at all levels (Table 5.10).**

Graduates not working full time include those in the labour force who were either working part time or unemployed, as well as graduates not in the labour force due to full-time enrolment as a student, or for other reasons.

**There is considerable variation in rates of full-time employment by field of study among university graduates.**

While the percentage of graduates employed full time dropped, the percentage of graduates who were in the labour force (that is, either working on a part-or full-time basis, or looking for work) increased between 1986 and 1995 for graduates at all levels of education (Table 5.10). The increase in labour force participation was largest among university graduates, rising from 85% to 91%. The increased labour force participation, despite fewer graduates working full time, in part may be a reflection of the overall trend in the labour market towards more part-time work over this period. Also, more graduates were working part time while pursuing further studies, particularly among university graduates. Results not shown here from the National Graduates Survey are consistent with this; while 6% of graduates with bachelor's or first professional degrees in the 1986 class pursued master's or doctoral studies, this increased to 13% among the class of 1995. At both time points, the pursuit of further studies was more prevalent among university graduates than college graduates, contributing to the lower percentage of university graduates employed full time.

The percentage of university graduates working full time by gender and field of study are examined in Table 5.8. In most fields of study, and at both time periods, a higher percentage of men than women were working full time. Between 1988 and 1997 the percentage working full time declined for both genders, with a slightly larger decline among women. There is considerable variation in rates by field of study, with the highest percentages employed full time among commerce, management

FIGURE 5.16  UNEMPLOYMENT RATE OF 1986 AND 1995 GRADUATES, TWO YEARS AFTER GRADUATION, BY LEVEL OF EDUCATION AND PROVINCE OF STUDY

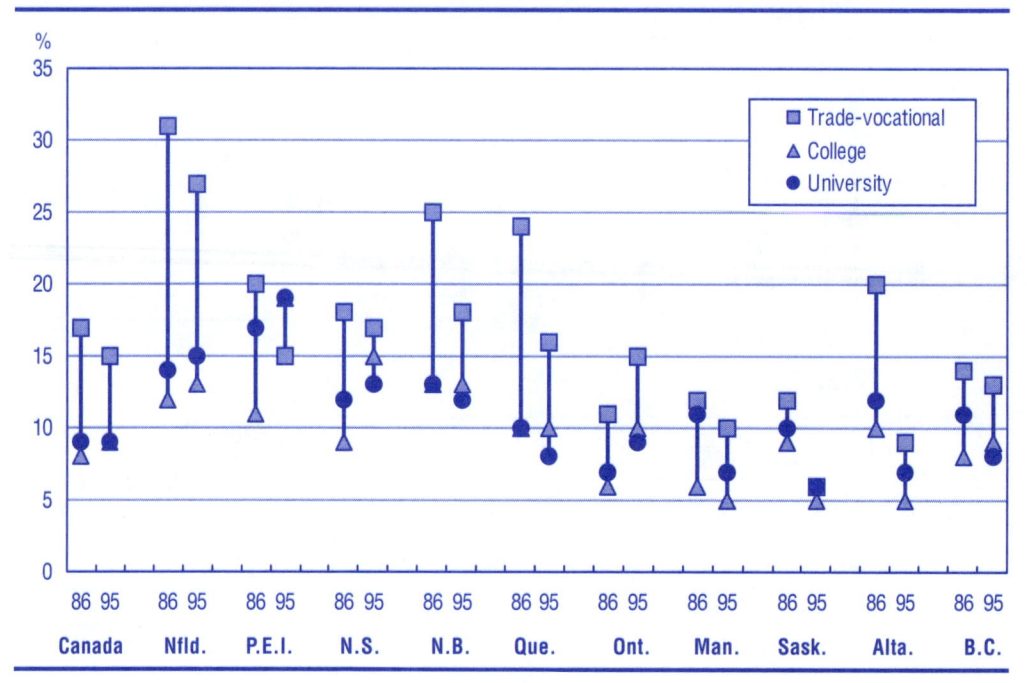

Table 5.11 and Figure 5.16 show the unemployment rates for graduates by level of education and province of study.

*Source: 1988 and 1997 National Graduates Surveys, Statistics Canada.*

122

and administration graduates, engineers, and health professionals. The lowest rates of full-time employment are among graduates of the humanities and social sciences, particularly fine and applied arts.

The unemployment rate in 1997 was highest for trade–vocational graduates, 15%, and the same, 9%, for both university and college graduates. These rates were little changed from the rates for 1986 graduates in 1988. Results presented earlier (see section 5.1) suggest that in the longer term, university graduates are more likely to have lower unemployment rates and experience less unemployment over the course of their careers.

University graduates had the highest median earnings, followed by college graduates, and then by trade–vocational graduates. While median earnings generally declined for graduates between 1988 and 1997, the difference in median earnings by level of education remained fairly constant. Table 5.13 and Figure 5.18 reveal that, among university graduates, median earnings generally decreased between 1988 and 1997 in most fields of study, for both men and women. Exceptions were physical, natural and applied sciences, in which median earnings of both men and women increased, and health professions, in which median earnings of women increased while those of men decreased. While female university graduates earned less than males in most fields, the gender gap in earnings between men and women narrowed over the period. There was also significant variation in median earnings by field of study (Table 5.13 and Figure 5.18). In 1997, median earnings ranged from approximately $25,000 for fine and applied arts graduates to $40,000 for graduates in engineering and applied sciences and $42,000 for graduates in the health professions.

**University graduates had the highest earnings, but with large variations by field of study.**

FIGURE 5.17    MEDIAN EARNINGS OF 1986 AND 1995 GRADUATES WORKING FULL TIME, TWO YEARS AFTER GRADUATION, BY LEVEL OF EDUCATION AND PROVINCE OF STUDY, (IN CONSTANT 1997 $000'S)

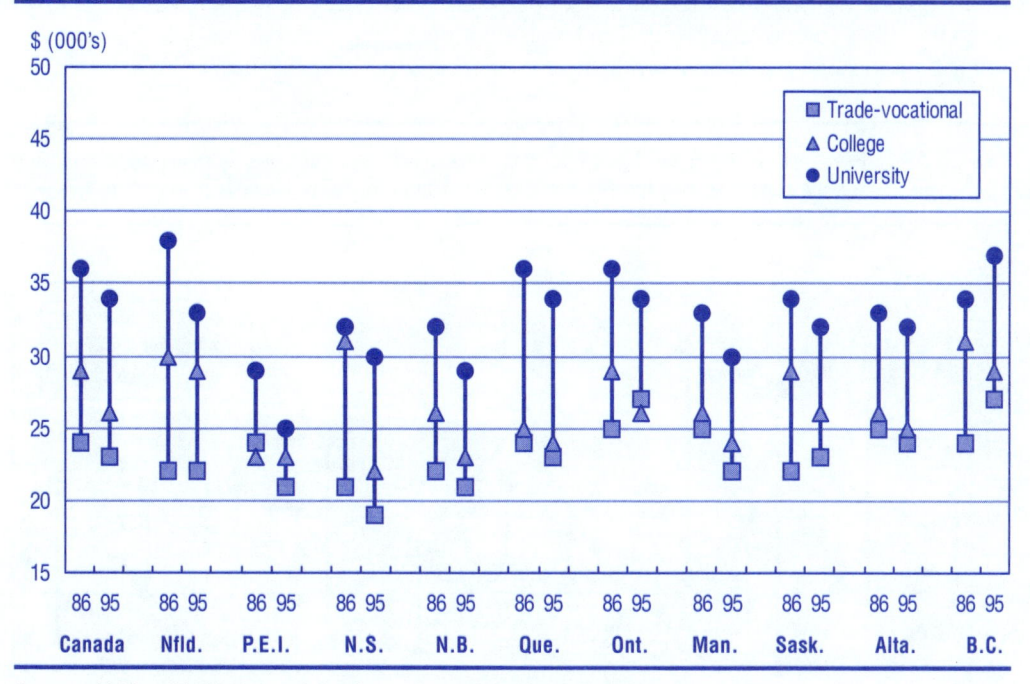

Table 5.12 and Figure 5.17 examine the earnings of graduates working full time by level of education and province of study. Earnings are expressed in constant 1997 dollars.

Source: 1988 and 1997 National Graduates Surveys, Statistics Canada.

EDUCATION INDICATORS IN CANADA

Table 5.13 and Figure 5.18 compare earnings of university graduates working full-time by field of study and gender. Earnings are expressed in constant 1997 dollars.

FIGURE 5.18  MEDIAN EARNINGS OF 1986 AND 1995 UNIVERSITY GRADUATES WORKING FULL TIME, TWO YEARS AFTER GRADUATION, BY GENDER AND FIELD OF STUDY, CANADA (IN CONSTANT 1997 $000's)

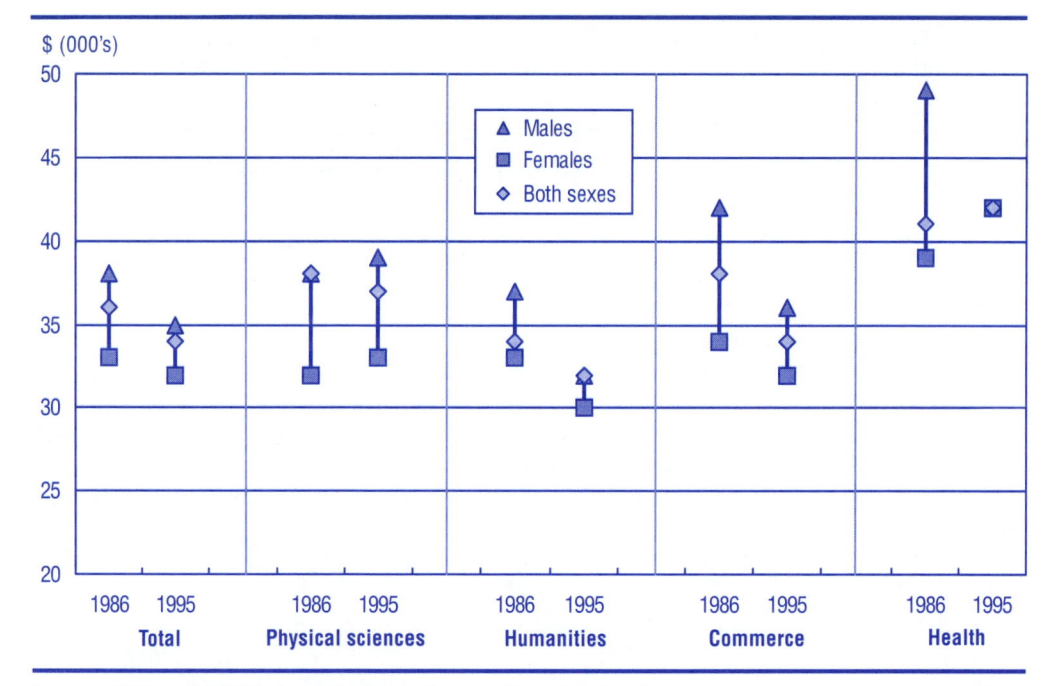

*Source: 1988 and 1997 National Graduates Surveys, Statistics Canada.*

In 1997, just over 50% of graduates who were working full time reported that their current job was closely related to their program of study.

At both time periods, college and trade–vocational graduates were more likely to be working in a job directly related to their education than were university graduates. This is not surprising given that many college and trade–vocational programs are more labour market oriented and occupationally specific. However, between 1988 and 1997 the gap between education levels declined, as the education–job fit improved among university graduates, while it worsened among other graduates.

FIGURE 5.19  PERCENTAGE OF 1986 AND 1995 GRADUATES WORKING FULL TIME TWO YEARS AFTER GRADUATION WHO ARE IN A JOB CLOSELY RELATED TO THEIR EDUCATION, BY PROVINCE OF STUDY AND LEVEL OF EDUCATION

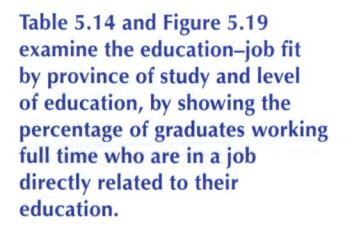

Table 5.14 and Figure 5.19 examine the education–job fit by province of study and level of education, by showing the percentage of graduates working full time who are in a job directly related to their education.

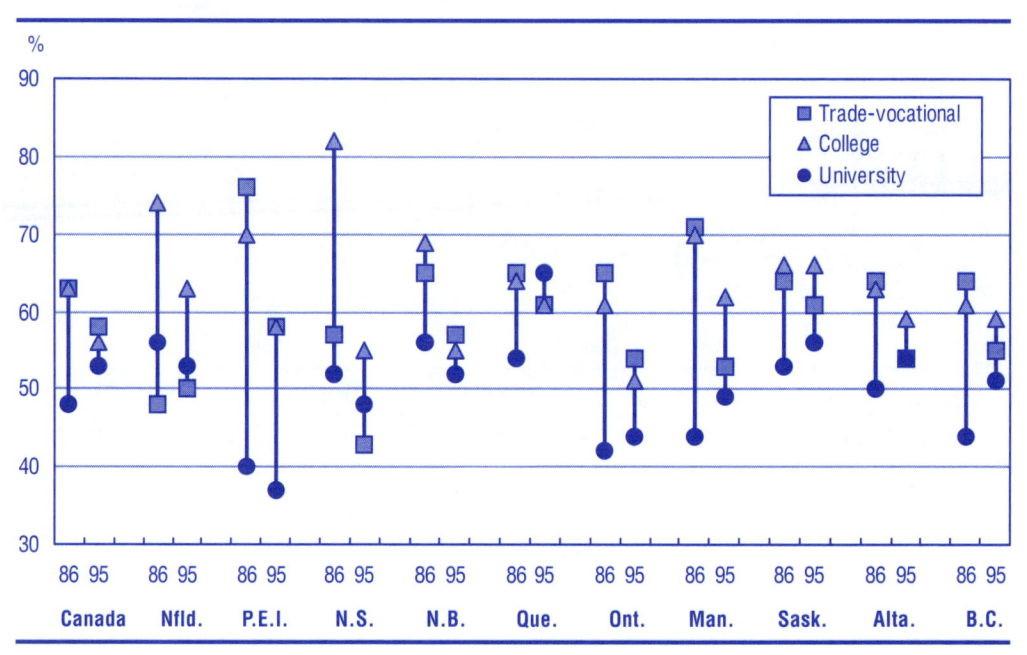

*Source: 1988 and 1997 National Graduates Surveys, Statistics Canada.*

LABOUR MARKET OUTCOMES

Among university graduates, the education–job fit was highest among graduates in the health professions, at 72% for the class of 1995; this had changed little from the 1986 class. The fit was also high and increasing among education graduates (Table 5.15). For both these fields of study, the programs are quite occupationally specific. The fit was also above average in both 1988 and 1997 among graduates of commerce, management and business administration; engineering and applied science; and math and physical science. The fit was lowest among graduates of fine and applied arts, and the humanities; the fit for both was less than 30% among the 1995 class—which is not surprising since these programs do not tend to be occupationally specific. Generally, there was a close relationship between education–job fit and median earnings. Those fields with higher education–job fits had higher earnings while those with lower education–job fits had lower earnings.

*The education–job fit was highest among university graduates in health professions and education, and lowest among graduates in fine and applied arts, and humanities (Table 5.15).*

FIGURE 5.20  PERCENTAGE OF **1986** AND **1995** UNIVERSITY GRADUATES WORKING FULL TIME TWO YEARS AFTER GRADUATION WHO ARE IN A JOB CLOSELY RELATED TO THEIR EDUCATION, BY GENDER AND FIELD OF STUDY, CANADA

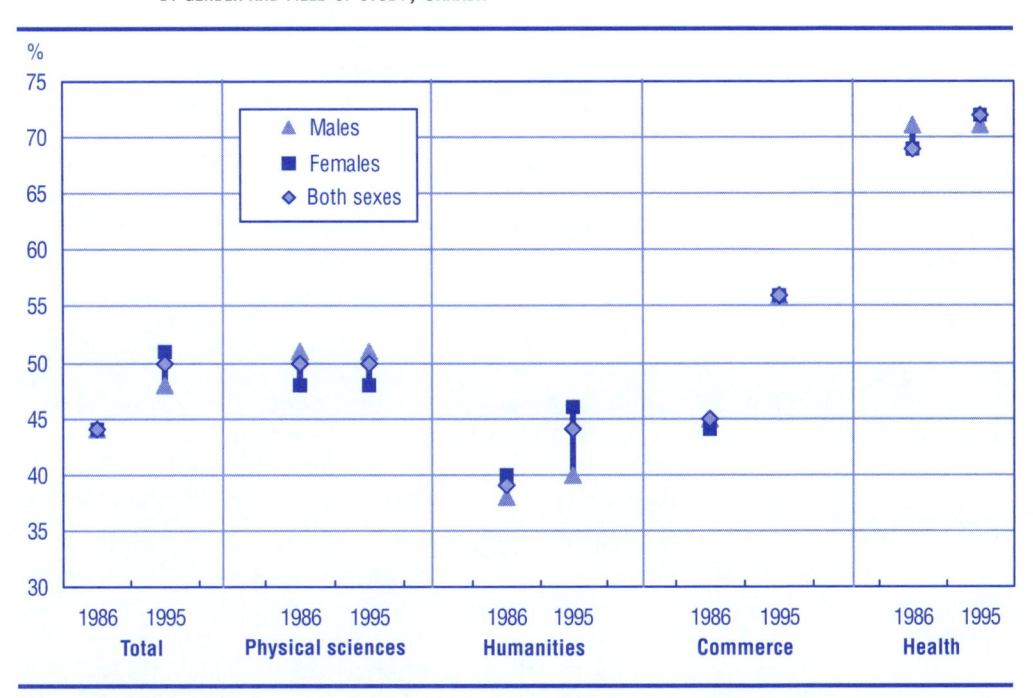

*Table 5.15 and Figure 5.20 examine the education–job fit among university graduates by gender and field of study.*

Source: 1988 and 1997 National Graduates Surveys, Statistics Canada.

## JURISDICTIONS

Generally, many of the same trends were evident across jurisdictions as were observed at the pan-Canadian level.

Among the 1986 class, the percentage employed full time was generally highest among college graduates, followed by university graduates and then trade–vocational graduates. Although this pattern continued to hold for the 1995 class, the gap between levels of education has declined across jurisdictions (see Table 5.9).

*For all provinces, there was a decline in full-time employment among graduates between the two classes, mirroring the drop at the pan-Canadian level.*

In all jurisdictions except British Columbia, graduates working full time experienced a decline in median earnings between 1988 and 1997. The pattern of higher earnings among university graduates, followed by college and then trade–vocational graduates, held across most jurisdictions (see Table 5.12 and Figure 5.17).

*Graduates working full time in most jurisdictions experienced a decline in median earnings.*

Across jurisdictions, in general, the education–job fit declined, and the gap in the fit by level of education narrowed between the two time periods (see Figure 5.19 and Table 5.14).

EDUCATION INDICATORS IN CANADA

**Unemployment rates of trade–vocational graduates were generally higher than those of university and college graduates at both time periods and across jurisdictions.**

While the unemployment rates of trade–vocational graduates were higher than other graduates in both classes, the gap narrowed between 1988 and 1997, as the unemployment rates of trade–vocational graduates fell in most jurisdictions. Two years after graduation, unemployment rates were similar for college and university graduates; between 1988 and 1997, rates had generally increased in the Atlantic provinces and Ontario, had changed little in Quebec, and had decreased in the western provinces (see Table 5.11 and Figure 5.16.). The gap in unemployment rates by level of education was more pronounced in 1988 among graduates who studied in Newfoundland and Labrador, New Brunswick, and Quebec, but this gap had also narrowed by 1997.

## 5.3 Mobility of postsecondary students and graduates

### Policy context

**This section presents results from the National Graduates Survey relating to the migration characteristics of graduates. (It should be noted that the definition of graduate migration includes students returning to their original jurisdiction of residence.)**

In this section we examine the migration of postsecondary students and graduates, using results from the National Graduates Survey. The NGS collects information on residence of graduates of postsecondary programs at three points in time: one year before enrolment, at the time of graduation (that is, the jurisdiction of study), and two years after graduation. Hence the NGS provides information on the migration that graduates undertook prior to enrolment in the postsecondary program, as well as their migration after graduation. In the analysis, we refer to these two types of migration as "student mobility" and "graduate mobility". (This measure of "student mobility" is based on those students who went on to graduate as opposed to all students.)

Student mobility may help offset some of the pressures brought about by varying rates of population change. Institutions in jurisdictions experiencing slower population growth are likely to have more capacity to accept out-of-jurisdiction students, relieving some of the pressures on capacity within jurisdictions experiencing population growth. The resultant flexibility is an important consideration, given the fluctuations and unpredictability of population change (see section 2.1).

**The National Graduates Survey to date has included only graduates who remained in Canada. Beginning in 2001, it will also include graduates who left Canada for the United States, which will yield results on the international migration of graduates and shed light on the "brain drain" phenomenon.**

The movement of graduates away from their province of study, on the other hand, is more likely tied to such considerations as labour market opportunities, and closeness to family and friends. The mobility of both students and graduates tends to be higher at the university level than at college and trade–vocational levels. This may be an indication that community colleges often set their programs to satisfy the employment needs of their local community. Among university graduates, it may reflect a greater demand for certain university qualifications that require greater mobility. Likewise, the economic conditions of jurisdictions greatly affect the mobility of graduates at all levels; this is even more the case at the university level.

In the future, "virtual programs" offered over the Internet may have a significant impact on student mobility, and on the delivery of postsecondary education in general, as more institutions in Canada and abroad offer programs students can take without leaving home.

With the shift to a knowledge-based global economy, the human capital invested in populations has become an increasingly valuable resource. In this environment, the mobility of highly educated segments of the population—recent postsecondary graduates in particular—has become increasingly important. A well-educated and highly skilled work force has become crucial to competitiveness in this new economic environment.

# FINDINGS

## CANADA

About 8% of the 1986 and 1995 classes of university graduates had left their province of residence to study at a university in another jurisdiction. This was more than twice the rate of student mobility among college graduates, and more than three times the rate among trade–vocational graduates.

Among the 1995 class of university graduates, the percentage of students who had left their jurisdiction of residence to study (8%) exceeded the percentage of graduates who had left their jurisdiction of study two years after graduation (4%). Student migration was also higher than graduate migration at the college level, while the levels of migration were comparable at the trade–vocational level. The implication of this lower graduate mobility among the class of 1995 is that the majority of university and college graduates who moved to another jurisdiction to study remained in that jurisdiction two years after graduation. Hence, students who were attracted to a jurisdiction's educational institutions became an important source of graduates for its labour market. Among the class of 1986 and 1990 (not shown here), the situation was reversed, however; the mobility of graduates was higher than the mobility of students. The reasons for the differences between classes are not well understood and could benefit from further research.

*Both students and graduates of universities are more mobile compared to students and graduates at other levels of education.*

*In the class of 1995, graduate mobility was less than student mobility.*

FIGURE 5.21   MOBILITY CHARACTERISTICS OF THE CLASS OF 1995, UNIVERSITY GRADUATES, CANADA AND PROVINCES

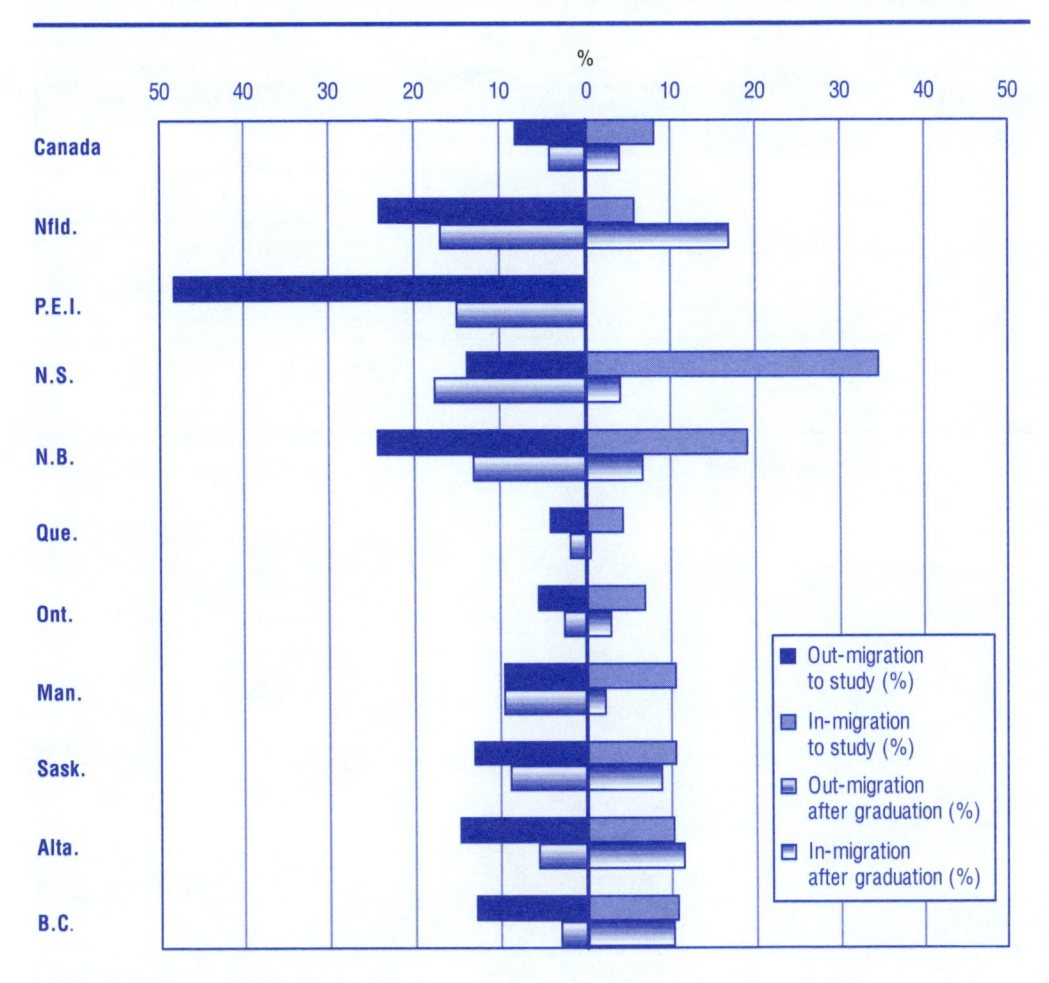

*Tables 5.16 and 5.17 and Figure 5.21 show the migration characteristics of 1986 and 1995 graduates before and after graduation.*

*Source: 1997 National Graduates Survey, Statistics Canada.*

## JURISDICTIONS

**Quebec and Ontario have had the lowest rates of both student and graduate migration.**

Lower rates of student and graduate mobility were evident in Quebec and Ontario among both graduating classes at all levels of education. This is likely a reflection of both the number of institutions and the variety of programs offered in these provinces, as well as generally favourable economic and lifestyle considerations. In Quebec, language is also an important factor in determining student and graduate flows. Despite low percentage flows, Ontario has gained overall from mobility. At university and college levels, this is mostly the result of the net in-migration of students, and at the trade–vocational level, this is mostly the result of the net in-migration of graduates. Quebec had net losses at both time periods, but with no consistent pattern between student versus graduate mobility.

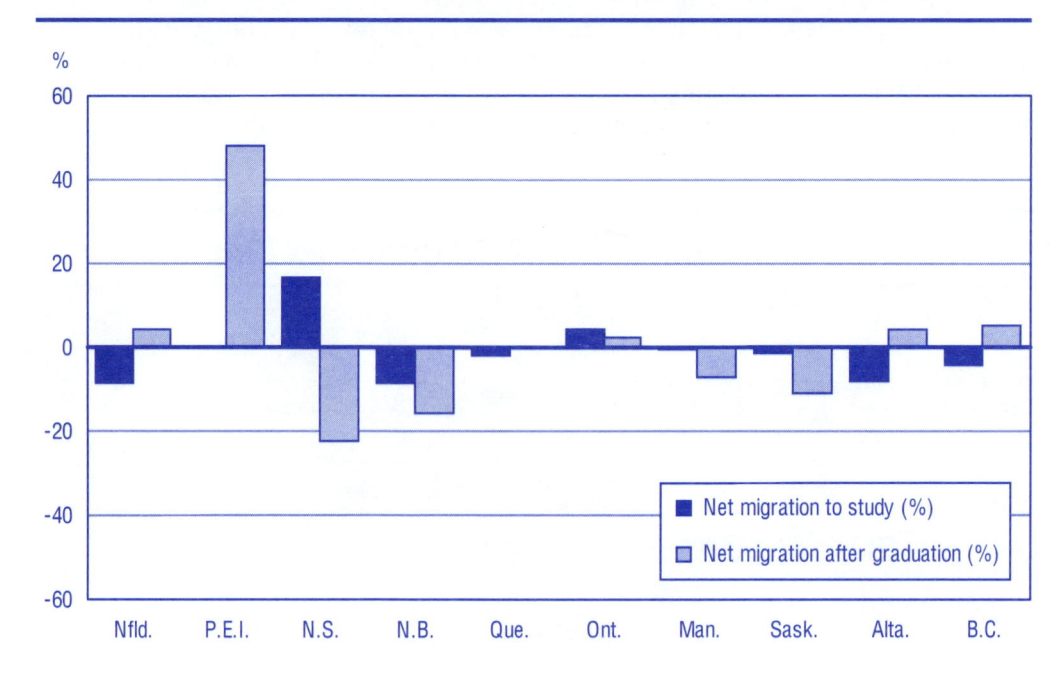

**Figures 5.22 and 5.23 show the net migration rates of students and graduates for the university classes of 1986 and 1995.**

FIGURE 5.22  NET MIGRATION OF THE CLASS OF 1986, UNIVERSITY GRADUATES, BY PROVINCE OF STUDY

*Source: 1988 National Graduates Survey, Statistics Canada.*

LABOUR MARKET OUTCOMES

FIGURE 5.23   NET MIGRATION OF THE CLASS OF 1995, UNIVERSITY GRADUATES, BY PROVINCE OF STUDY

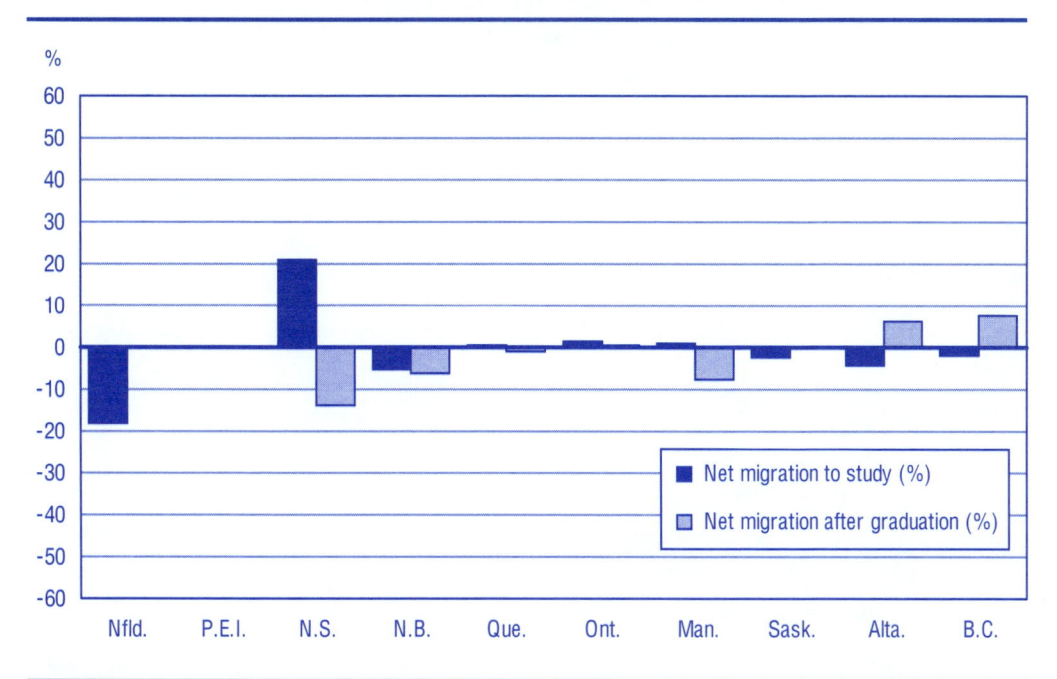

■ Net migration to study (%)
□ Net migration after graduation (%)

Source: 1997 National Graduates Survey, Statistics Canada.

Among the class of 1986, the Atlantic provinces experienced net overall losses because of combined student and graduate mobility. These overall losses occurred at all levels of education with the exception of the trade–vocational level in Prince Edward Island. Nova Scotia was the only Atlantic province where there was a net gain of university students because of student mobility. This occurred at both time periods. Nova Scotia has a large number of universities with the capacity to handle more students than just for its own needs. In 1986, the net in-migration of students was more than offset by losses from the mobility of university graduates. Among the class of 1995, the Atlantic provinces continued to experience overall losses to mobility, but with more exceptions. Prince Edward Island had an overall gain at both the trade–vocational and college levels, and Nova Scotia gained at the university level, as the net inflow of students exceeded the net losses from graduate mobility.

**The Atlantic provinces generally had overall losses from mobility of students and graduates...**

Among the class of 1986, Manitoba and Saskatchewan experienced overall losses because of student and graduate mobility, with the exception of the college level in Manitoba. There was no common pattern to the losses, which resulted from different combinations of student and/or graduate mobility.

**...as did Manitoba and Saskatchewan.**

At the university level and at both time periods, Alberta and British Columbia experienced net losses from student mobility, and net gains from graduate mobility. The losses from student mobility may reflect a situation where the capacity in other jurisdictions has helped to meet the increase in demand for university education in Alberta and British Columbia stemming from rapid population growth. In British Columbia, at both time periods, and in Alberta among the class of 1995, the gain of graduates exceeded the loss of students, resulting in an overall gain from mobility. In Alberta, among the class of 1986, the situation was reversed, with a smaller gain of graduates than loss of students, leading to an overall loss from mobility.

**Alberta and British Columbia had net outflows of university students, and net inflows of university graduates.**

# Appendices

# APPENDIX 1

## STRUCTURE OF EDUCATION AND TRAINING IN CANADA

Education in Canada is the responsibility of the 10 provinces and three territories. While educational structures and institutions across the country are similar in many ways, they have been developed by each jurisdiction to respond to the particular circumstances and historical and cultural heritage of the population they serve. The chart that follows shows the various structures of education and training in Canada today.

### PRE-ELEMENTARY PROGRAMS

Most jurisdictions offer pre-school or kindergarten programs that are operated by the local education authorities, providing pre-grade one education.

### ELEMENTARY AND SECONDARY EDUCATION

Public education is provided free to all Canadian citizens and permanent residents until the end of secondary school – normally at age 18. The ages for compulsory schooling vary from one jurisdiction to another; generally, schooling is required from age 6 or 7 to age 16.

Elementary schools in most jurisdictions cover the first six to eight years of compulsory schooling. Afterwards, children proceed to a secondary education program. A great variety of programs – vocational (job training) as well as academic – are offered at the secondary level. Secondary school diplomas are granted to students who pass the compulsory and optional courses of their programs.

The point of transition from elementary to secondary school may vary from jurisdiction to jurisdiction (see chart). The elementary-secondary continuum can be broken up into different grade combinations. In many northern and rural communities, schools offer all grades (K to 11/12). In Quebec, secondary schooling ends after 11 years of study. In Ontario, students usually complete the secondary school diploma requirements, including Ontario Academic Courses, in four to five years. However, Ontario students entering Grade 9 in 1999 will follow a new four-year programe.

### POSTSECONDARY EDUCATION

Once secondary school has been successfully completed, students may apply to a college career program or to a university. Enrolment in trade-vocational programs, such as apprenticeship or other programs geared towards preparation for employment in an occupation or trade, generally does not require graduation from secondary school.

Not all students who attend postsecondary institutions do so directly from high school, for example, a student may enter a college program after obtaining a university degree. Postsecondary education is available in both government-supported and private institutions, some of which award degrees.

After completing 11 years of elementary-secondary schooling, Quebec students must obtain a diploma from a *CEGEP (collège d'enseignement général et professionel)* in order to continue to the university level. *CEGEPs* offer both a general program that leads to university admission and a vocational program that prepares students for the labour force.

Colleges, such as technical and vocational institutes, community colleges, regional colleges, *CEGEPs*, and institutes of technology, offer programs for continuing education aimed at adults in the community and for developing skills for careers in business, the applied arts, technology, social services, and health sciences. Programs vary in length from six months to three years.

In general, colleges award diplomas or certificates only; they do not award degrees. However, the university transfer programs in the community college system in Alberta and British Columbia, and, to a lesser extent Manitoba and the Northwest Territories allows students to complete two years of academic course work toward bachelor's degrees. These programs allow students to complete the third or fourth years at a university-college or university, and receive a degree. In many provinces and territories, students must apply for admission and have their college studies evaluated before being granted credit for completed courses.

Programs leading to degrees are offered in universities or degree-granting institutions. Most Canadian universities, especially the larger ones, offer a complete range of programs. Others are more specialized, and have developed areas of excellence. There are some specialized institutions that are not campus-based that offer university programs through correspondence courses and distance education.

It is possible to study at three different levels, leading to either a bachelor's, master's, or doctoral degree. Not all universities offer graduate programs (master's and doctorates). In addition to degree programs, most universities offer diploma and certificate programs. These programs can be at either the undergraduate or graduate level, and can range from one to three years in duration.

APPENDIX 1

LEVELS WITHIN ELEMENTARY-SECONDARY SCHOOLS, BY JURISDICTION

| Jurisdiction | Levels |
|---|---|
| Newfoundland and Labrador | P, 1, 2, 3, 4, 5, 6, 7, 8, 9, 10, 11, 12 |
| Prince Edward Island | 1, 2, 3, 4, 5, 6, 7, 8, 9, 10, 11, 12 |
| Nova Scotia | P, 1, 2, 3, 4, 5, 6, 7, 8, 9, 10, 11, 12 |
| New Brunswick – English | P, 1, 2, 3, 4, 5, 6, 7, 8, 9, 10, 11, 12 |
| New Brunswick – French | P, 1, 2, 3, 4, 5, 6, 7, 8, 9, 10, 11, 12 |
| Quebec – General | P, P, 1, 2, 3, 4, 5, 6, 7, 8, 9, 10, 11 |
| Quebec – Vocational | 10, 11, 12, 13 |
| Ontario | P, P, 1, 2, 3, 4, 5, 6, 7, 8, 9, 10, 11, 12* |
| Manitoba | P, 1, 2, 3, 4, 5, 6, 7, 8, 9, 10, 11, 12 |
| Saskatchewan | P, P, P, 1, 2, 3, 4, 5, 6, 7, 8, 9, 10, 11, 12 |
| Alberta | P, 1, 2, 3, 4, 5, 6, 7, 8, 9, 10, 11, 12 |
| British Columbia | P, 1, 2, 3, 4, 5, 6, 7, 8, 9, 10, 11, 12 |
| Yukon | P, 1, 2, 3, 4, 5, 6, 7, 8, 9, 10, 11, 12 |
| Northwest Territories | P, 1, 2, 3, 4, 5, 6, 7, 8, 9, 10, 11, 12 |
| Nunavut | P, 1, 2, 3, 4, 5, 6, 7, 8, 9, 10, 11, 12 |

Legend:
- P: Pre-grade 1
- Elementary/Primary
- Junior high/Middle
- Senior high
- Secondary

\* includes Ontario Academic Course (OAC).

# APPENDIX 2

UNIVERSITIES[1] BY JURISDICTION AND SIZE OF FULL-TIME ENROLMENT

| Province/Institution | | Main Institutions | All Institutions | Enrolment 1996-97 | Enrolment 1997-98 |
|---|---|---|---|---|---|
| **Canada** | | **76** | **135** | **573,635** | **573,099** |
| **Newfoundland and Labrador** | | **1** | **3** | **13,193** | **13,115** |
| Memorial University of Newfoundland | | 1 | 3 | | |
| | Memorial University of Nfld. | | | 11,661 | 11,510 |
| | Memorial University Off Campus Centres | | | 481 | 484 |
| | Sir Wilfred Grenfell College | | | 1,051 | 1,121 |
| **Prince Edward Island** | | **1** | **1** | **2,313** | **2,452** |
| University of Prince Edward Island | | 1 | 1 | 2,313 | 2,452 |
| **Nova Scotia** | | **13** | **15** | **29,941** | **30,077** |
| Acadia University | | 1 | 2 | | |
| | Acadia Divinity College | | | 84 | 56 |
| | Acadia University | | | 3,657 | 3,563 |
| Atlantic School of Theology | | 1 | 1 | 61 | 56 |
| Dalhousie University | | 1 | 1 | 9,488 | 9,717 |
| Mount St. Vincent University | | 1 | 1 | 2,216 | 2,059 |
| Nova Scotia Agricultural College | | 1 | 1 | 907 | 876 |
| Nova Scotia College of Art and Design | | 1 | 1 | 582 | 668 |
| Nova Scotia Teachers' College | | 1 | 1 | 99 | .. |
| Saint Mary's University | | 1 | 1 | 5,008 | 5,108 |
| St. Francis Xavier University | | 1 | 2 | | |
| | Coady International Inst. | | | 47 | 55 |
| | St. Francis Xavier University | | | 3,227 | 3,407 |
| Technical University of Nova Scotia | | 1 | 1 | 1,330 | 1,277 |
| Université Sainte-Anne | | 1 | 1 | 337 | 264 |
| University College of Cape Breton | | 1 | 1 | 2,118 | 2,126 |
| University of King's College | | 1 | 1 | 780 | 845 |
| **New Brunswick** | | **5** | **8** | **18,931** | **18,503** |
| Bethany Bible College | | 1 | 1 | 168 | 185 |
| Mount Allison University | | 1 | 1 | 2,209 | 2,146 |
| St. Thomas University | | 1 | 1 | 1,897 | 1,970 |
| Université de Moncton | | 1 | 3 | | |
| | Centre Université de Moncton | | | 3,751 | 3,565 |
| | Centre Université de Shippegan | | | 408 | 380 |
| | Centre Université Saint-Louis-Maillet | | | 624 | 648 |
| University of New Brunswick | | 1 | 2 | | |
| | U.N.B. - Fredericton | | | 7,905 | 7,569 |
| | U.N.B. - Saint John | | | 1,969 | 2,040 |

# EDUCATION INDICATORS IN CANADA

## UNIVERSITIES[1] BY JURISDICTION AND SIZE OF FULL-TIME ENROLMENT

| Province/Institution | | Main Institutions | All Institutions | Enrolment 1996-97 | Enrolment 1997-98 |
|---|---|---|---|---|---|
| **Quebec** | | **7** | **20** | **132,054** | **131,074** |
| Bishop's University | | 1 | 2 | | |
| | Bishop's University | | | 1,844 | 1,788 |
| | Thomas Moore Inst. for Adult Ed. | | | 3 | 3 |
| Concordia University | | 1 | 1 | 13,752 | 14,093 |
| McGill University | | 1 | 1 | 22,385 | 21,425 |
| Université de Montreal | | 1 | 3 | | |
| | École polytechnique | | | 3,355 | 3,447 |
| | Facultés, écoles de l'U. de Montréal | | | 19,519 | 19,300 |
| | Hautes études commerciales | | | 3,796 | 4,027 |
| Université de Sherbrooke | | 1 | 1 | 10,589 | 10,547 |
| Université du Québec | | 1 | 11 | | |
| | École de technologie supérieure | | | 1,373 | 1,488 |
| | École nat. d'administration publique | | | 150 | 114 |
| | Inst. nat. recherche scient. | | | 109 | 126 |
| | Institute Armand Frappier | | | 34 | 112 |
| | Télé-Université | | | 308 | 306 |
| | Université du Québec - Abitibi-Témiscamingue | | | 793 | 728 |
| | Université du Québec à Chicoutimi | | | 3,083 | 2,901 |
| | Université du Québec à Hull | | | 2,117 | 2,037 |
| | Université du Québec à Montréal | | | 18,113 | 17,975 |
| | Université du Québec à Trois-Rivières | | | 5,764 | 5,526 |
| | Université du Québec à Rimouski | | | 1,945 | 1,787 |
| Université Laval | | 1 | 1 | 23,022 | 23,344 |
| **Ontario** | | **21** | **45** | **226,998** | **227,153** |
| Brock University | | 1 | 2 | | |
| | Brock College of Education | | | 360 | 354 |
| | Brock University | | | 7,070 | 7,159 |
| Carleton University | | 1 | 1 | 13,743 | 13,104 |
| Collège dominicain de philosophie et de théologie | | 1 | 2 | | |
| | Coll. domin. de philosophie et théologie | | | 81 | 77 |
| | Coll. dominicain - Montréal | | | 11 | 9 |
| Lakehead University | | 1 | 1 | 5,572 | 5,487 |
| Laurentian University of Sudbury/ Université laurentienne de Sudbury | | 1 | 3 | | |
| | Algoma College | | | 567 | 505 |
| | Collège de Hearst | | | 61 | 59 |
| | Laurentian University | | | 4,529 | 4,249 |
| McMaster University | | 1 | 2 | | |
| | McMaster Divinity College | | | 56 | 43 |
| | McMaster University | | | 13,736 | 13,601 |
| Nipissing University | | 1 | 1 | 1,584 | 1,755 |
| Queen's University at Kingston | | 1 | 2 | | |
| | Queen's Theological College | | | 34 | 25 |
| | Queen's University | | | 13,201 | 13,305 |
| Redeemer College | | 1 | 1 | 432 | 440 |
| Royal Military College of Canada | | 1 | 1 | 1,108 | 1,019 |
| Ryerson Polytechnic University | | 1 | 1 | 10,774 | 10,494 |
| Trent University | | 1 | 1 | 4,052 | 4,049 |
| Tyndale College and Seminary | | 1 | 2 | | |
| | Ontario Bible College | | | 239 | 208 |
| | Ontario Theological Seminary | | | 225 | 222 |
| University of Guelph | | 1 | 1 | 12,066 | 12,031 |
| University of Ottawa - Université d'Ottawa | | 1 | 2 | | |
| | Université St.-Paul | | | 344 | 393 |
| | University of Ottawa | | | 16,218 | 16,321 |

APPENDIX 2

Universities[1] by jurisdiction and size of full-time enrolment

| Province/Institution | | Main Institutions | All Institutions | Enrolment 1996-97 | Enrolment 1997-98 |
|---|---|---|---|---|---|
| University of Toronto | | 1 | 9 | | |
| | Emmanuel College | | | 138 | 109 |
| | Knox College | | | 78 | 62 |
| | Ontario Institute for Studies in Education | | | 917 | 985 |
| | Regis College | | | 87 | 95 |
| | St. Augustine College | | | 51 | 56 |
| | University of St. Michael's College | | | 129 | 108 |
| | University of Toronto | | | 36,851 | 37,273 |
| | University of Trinity College | | | 48 | 42 |
| | Wycliffe College | | | 74 | 80 |
| University of Waterloo | | 1 | 3 | | |
| | Renison College | | | 319 | 332 |
| | University of Waterloo | | | 15,703 | 16,113 |
| | University of St. Jerome's College | | | 683 | 704 |
| University of Western Ontario | | 1 | 4 | | |
| | Brescia College | | | 609 | 572 |
| | Huron College | | | 780 | 824 |
| | King's College | | | 1,805 | 1,739 |
| | University of Western Ontario | | | 18,262 | 18,803 |
| University of Windsor | | 1 | 1 | 10,243 | 9,573 |
| Wilfrid Laurier University | | 1 | 2 | | |
| | Wilfred Laurier University | | | 5,667 | 5,865 |
| | Wilfrid Laurier Seminary | | | 60 | 53 |
| York University | | 1 | 3 | | |
| | Atkinson College | | | 2,033 | 2,366 |
| | Glendon College | | | 1,583 | 1,441 |
| | York University | | | 24,815 | 25,049 |
| **Manitoba** | | **6** | **8** | **22,024** | **21,024** |
| Brandon University | | 1 | 1 | 2,103 | 1,728 |
| Canadian Mennonite Bible College | | 1 | 1 | 132 | 130 |
| Catherine Booth Bible College | | 1 | 1 | 74 | 70 |
| Concord College | | 1 | 1 | 59 | 43 |
| University of Manitoba | | 1 | 3 | | |
| | Collège Saint-Boniface | | | 378 | 313 |
| | St. Andrew's College | | | 13 | 13 |
| | University of Manitoba | | | 16,680 | 16,206 |
| University of Winnipeg | | 1 | 1 | 2,585 | 2,521 |
| **Saskatchewan** | | **4** | **13** | **23,571** | **23,864** |
| Canadian Bible College | | 1 | 1 | 271 | 314 |
| Canadian Theological College | | 1 | 1 | 45 | 47 |
| University of Regina | | 1 | 4 | | |
| | Campion College | | | 1,057 | 1,090 |
| | Luther College | | | 839 | 911 |
| | Saskatchewan Indian College | | | 817 | 832 |
| | University of Regina | | | 5,620 | 5,695 |
| University of Saskatchewan | | 1 | 7 | | |
| | Central Pentecostal College | | | 58 | 64 |
| | Coll. Emmanuel & St. Chad | | | 21 | 22 |
| | Lutheran Theological Seminary | | | 43 | 32 |
| | St. Andrew's College | | | 31 | 29 |
| | St. Peter's College | | | 57 | 57 |
| | St. Thomas More College | | | 1,131 | 1,179 |
| | University of Saskatchewan | | | 13,581 | 13,592 |

## Education Indicators in Canada

### Universities[1] by jurisdiction and size of full-time enrolment

| Province/Institution | | Main Institutions | All Institutions | Enrolment 1996-97 | Enrolment 1997-98 |
|---|---|---|---|---|---|
| **Alberta** | | **10** | **11** | **53,044** | **52,824** |
| Athabaska University | (No full-time enrolment) | 1 | 1 | | |
| Augustana University College | | 1 | 1 | 710 | 710 |
| Canadian Nazarene College | | 1 | 1 | 67 | 73 |
| Canadian University College | | 1 | 1 | 283 | 244 |
| Concordia College | | 1 | 1 | 620 | 997 |
| King's University College | | 1 | 1 | 468 | 473 |
| Newman Theological College | | 1 | 1 | 64 | 71 |
| University of Alberta | | 1 | 2 | | |
| | North American Baptist College | | | 228 | 216 |
| | University of Alberta | | | 26,121 | 25,829 |
| University of Calgary | | 1 | 1 | 20,034 | 19,617 |
| University of Lethbridge | | 1 | 1 | 4,449 | 4,594 |
| **British Columbia** | | **8** | **11** | **51,566** | **53,013** |
| Northwest Baptist Theological College | | 1 | 1 | 121 | 172 |
| Royal Roads University | | 1 | 1 | 206 | 286 |
| Seminary of Christ the King | | 1 | 1 | 34 | 28 |
| Simon Fraser University | | 1 | 1 | 10,603 | 10,534 |
| Trinity Western University | | 1 | 2 | | |
| | Canadian Baptist Seminary | | | 13 | 18 |
| | Trinity Western College | | | 1,708 | 1,572 |
| University of British Columbia | | 1 | 3 | | |
| | Regent College | | | 394 | 406 |
| | University of British Columbia | | | 25,624 | 26,544 |
| | Vancouver School of Theology | | | 62 | 76 |
| University of Northern British Columbia | | 1 | 1 | 1,623 | 1,960 |
| University of Victoria | | 1 | 1 | 11,178 | 11,417 |
| **Yukon** | | - | - | - | - |
| **Northwest Territories** | | - | - | - | - |

1 List of universities includes religious-based institutions that grant recognized university level degrees and that are currently reported to Statistics Canada. Coverage of these types of institutions may not be complete in all jurisdictions.

## APPENDIX 2

COMMUNITY COLLEGES AND RELATED INSTITUTIONS[1] BY JURISDICTION AND SIZE OF FULL-TIME ENROLMENT

| Province/Institution | Main Institutions | All Institutions | Enrolment 1996-97 |
|---|---|---|---|
| **Canada** | **204** | **277** | **395,326** |
| **Newfoundland and Labrador** | **10** | **27** | **5,704** |
| Fisheries and Marine Institute of Memorial University | 1 | 1 | 591 |
| Cabot College of Applied Arts, Tech. & Cont. Ed. | 1 | 5 | 2,117 |
|     Cabot College, Parade Street Campus | | | |
|     Cabot College, Bell Island Campus | | | |
|     Cabot College, Seal Cove Campus | | | |
|     Cabot College, Topsail Road Campus | | | |
|     Cabot College, Prince Phillip Drive Campus | | | |
| Westviking College | 1 | 5 | |
|     Westviking College, Stephenville Campus | | | .. |
|     Westviking College, Bay St. George Campus | | | 593 |
|     Westviking College, Port aux Basques Campus | | | 12 |
|     Westviking College, St. Anthony Campus | | | 29 |
|     Westviking College, Corner Brook Campus | | | 744 |
| Eastern College | 1 | 5 | |
|     Eastern College, Clarenville Campus | | | 134 |
|     Eastern College, Burin Campus | | | 150 |
|     Eastern College, Bonavista Campus | | | 71 |
|     Eastern College, Carbonear Campus | | | 147 |
|     Eastern College, Placentia Campus | | | 65 |
| Central Nfld. College | 1 | 5 | |
|     Central Nfld. College, Grand Falls-Windsor Campus | | | 263 |
|     Central Nfld. College, Gander Campus | | | 120 |
|     Central Nfld. College, Lewisporte Campus | | | 26 |
|     Central Nfld. College, Springdale Campus | | | .. |
|     Central Nfld. College, Baie Verte Campus | | | 102 |
| Labrador College | 1 | 2 | |
|     Labrador College, West Campus | | | 53 |
|     Labrador College, Happy Valley Campus | | | 78 |
| Western Memorial Regional Hospital, School of Nursing | 1 | 1 | 102 |
| St. Clare's Mercy Hospital, School of Nursing | 1 | 1 | 116 |
| The General Hospital, School of Nursing | 1 | 1 | 96 |
| Salvation Army Grace General Hospital, School of Nursing | 1 | 1 | 95 |
| **Prince Edward Island** | **2** | **4** | **1,275** |
| Holland College | 1 | 3 | 1,269 |
|     Holland College, Charlottetown Centre | | | |
|     Holland College, Summerside Centre | | | |
|     Holland College, Royalty Centre | | | |
| School of Radiography, Queen Elizabeth Hospital | 1 | 1 | 6 |
| **Nova Scotia** | **8** | **31** | **6,956** |
| Nova Scotia Community College | 1 | 18 | |
|     N.S.C.C., Lunenburg Campus | | | 389 |
|     N.S.C.C., Lunenburg Campus | | | 389 |
|     N.S.C.C., I.W. Akerly Campus | | | 853 |
|     N.S.C.C., Halifax Campus | | | 653 |
|     N.S.C.C., Annapolis Campus | | | 339 |
|     N.S.C.C., Colchester Campus | | | .. |
|     N.S.C.C., Strait Campus | | | 276 |
|     N.S.C.C., Shelburne Campus | | | 71 |
|     N.S.C.C., Cumberland Campus | | | 158 |
|     N.S.C.C., Pictou Campus | | | 465 |
|     N.S.C.C., Sydney Campus | | | .. |
|     N.S.C.C., Kingstec Campus | | | 566 |
|     N.S.C.C., Hants Campus | | | .. |
|     N.S.C.C., Burridge Campus | | | 374 |
|     N.S.C.C., Institute of Technology Campus | | | 549 |
|     N.S.C.C., College of Geographic Science | | | 382 |
|     N.S.C.C., Adult Vocational Training Campus, Dartmouth | | | .. |
|     N.S.C.C., Adult Vocational Training Campus, Cape Breton | | | 341 |
|     N.S.C.C., Truro Campus | | | 300 |

EDUCATION INDICATORS IN CANADA

COMMUNITY COLLEGES AND RELATED INSTITUTIONS[1] BY JURISDICTION AND SIZE OF FULL-TIME ENROLMENT

| Province/Institution | | Main Institutions | All Institutions | Enrolment 1996-97 |
|---|---|---|---|---|
| N.S. School of Fisheries | (Trade vocational only) | | | |
| University College of Cape Breton | | 1 | 1 | 831 |
| Institute for Early Childhood Ed. & Developmental Services | | 1 | 1 | 191 |
| Canadian Coast Guard College | | 1 | 1 | 27 |
| Collège de l'Acadie | | 1 | 2 | 85 |
| | Collège de l'Acadie, Sociétè d'éducation de l'Î.-P.-É. | | | 16 |
| Victoria General Hospital | | 1 | 6 | |
| | Victoria Gen. Hosp., School of Radiological Technology | | | 7 |
| | Victoria Gen. Hosp.,School of Nuclear Medicine Technology | | | 6 |
| | Victoria Gen. Hosp.,School of Diagnostic Cytology | | | 10 |
| | Victoria Gen. Hosp.,School of Respiratory Therapy | | | 22 |
| | Victoria Gen. Hosp.,School of Diagnostic Ultrasound | | | 4 |
| | Victoria Gen. Hosp.,School of Pre-Hospital Care | | | 19 |
| Halifax Infirmary Hosp., School of Health Records Science | | 1 | 1 | 13 |
| School of Radiation Therapy, Cancer Treatment & Research | | 1 | 1 | 9 |
| **New Brunswick** | | **4** | **14** | **4,808** |
| New Brunswick School of Fisheries | (Trade vocational only) | | | |
| Maritime Forest Ranger School | | 1 | 1 | 88 |
| New Brunswick Community College | | 1 | 10 | |
| | New Brunswick College of Craft & Design | | | 120 |
| | N.B.C.C., Edmundston Campus | | | 254 |
| | N.B.C.C., Bathurst Campus | | | 551 |
| | N.B.C.C., Campbellton Campus | | | 310 |
| | N.B.C.C., Moncton Campus | | | 947 |
| | N.B.C.C., Saint John Campus | | | 977 |
| | N.B.C.C., St. Andrew's Campus | | | 284 |
| | N.B.C.C., Woodstock Campus | | | 315 |
| | N.B.C.C., Miramichi Campus | | | 475 |
| | N.B.C.C., Dieppe Campus | | | 461 |
| School of Rad. Tech., Moncton Hospital | | 1 | 1 | 10 |
| Saint John Regional Hospital | | 1 | 2 | |
| | School of Rad. Tech., Saint John Regional Hospital | | | 9 |
| | Saint John Regional Hospital Radiation Therapy Technology | | | 7 |
| **Quebec** | | **90** | **97** | **166,858** |
| CEGEP Collège d'Abitibi-Témiscamingue | | 1 | 1 | 2 630 |
| CEGEP Collège Ahuntsic | | 1 | 1 | 6 405 |
| CEGEP d'Alma | | 1 | 1 | 1 251 |
| CEGEP André-Laurendeau | | 1 | 1 | 2 933 |
| CEGEP Collège Bois-de-Boulogne | | 1 | 1 | 2 775 |
| CEGEP de Chicoutimi | | 1 | 1 | 3 328 |
| CEGEP Dawson College | | 1 | 1 | 6 641 |
| CEGEP de Drummondville | | 1 | 1 | 1 781 |
| CEGEP Collège Edouard-Montpetit, Longueuil | | 1 | 1 | 7 023 |
| CEGEP François-Xavier-Garneau | | 1 | 1 | 5 204 |
| CEGEP de la Gaspésie et des Îles | | 1 | 1 | 1 215 |
| CEGEP de Granby-Haute Yamaska | | 1 | 1 | 1 398 |
| CEGEP de Baie Comeau | | 1 | 1 | 857 |
| CEGEP John Abbott College | | 1 | 1 | 4 606 |
| CEGEP Joliette-de Lanaudière | | 1 | 1 | 2 216 |
| CEGEP de Jonquière | | 1 | 1 | 3 628 |
| CEGEP Collège de La Pocatière | | 1 | 1 | 1 155 |
| CEGEP Lennoxville Campus | | 1 | 1 | 2 097 |
| CEGEP de Lévis-Lauzon | | 1 | 1 | 3 179 |
| CEGEP Collège de Limoilou | | 1 | 1 | 6 026 |
| CEGEP Collège Lionel-Groulx | | 1 | 1 | 3 494 |
| CEGEP Collège de Maisonneuve | | 1 | 1 | 5 592 |
| CEGEP Collège de Matane | | 1 | 1 | 719 |
| CEGEP Collège Montmorency | | 1 | 1 | 4 364 |
| CEGEP Collège de l'Outaouais | | 1 | 1 | 3 866 |
| CEGEP Collège de la région de l'Amiante | | 1 | 1 | 1 183 |

APPENDIX 2

COMMUNITY COLLEGES AND RELATED INSTITUTIONS[1] BY JURISDICTION AND SIZE OF FULL-TIME ENROLMENT

| Province/Institution | Main Institutions | All Institutions | Enrolment 1996-97 |
|---|---|---|---|
| CEGEP de Rimouski | 1 | 1 | 3 633 |
| CEGEP de Rivière-du-Loup | 1 | 1 | 1 532 |
| CEGEP Collège de Rosemont | 1 | 1 | 3 298 |
| CEGEP de Sainte-Foy | 1 | 1 | 5 816 |
| CEGEP de St-Félicien | 1 | 1 | 1 233 |
| CEGEP Collège de Saint-Hyacinthe | 1 | 1 | 2 773 |
| CEGEP Collège Saint-Jean-sur-Richelieu | 1 | 1 | 2 325 |
| CEGEP Collège de Saint-Jérôme | 1 | 1 | 3 277 |
| CEGEP de Saint-Laurent | 1 | 3 | |
| CEGEP St-Lambert Campus | | | 2 248 |
| CEGEP de Saint-Laurent, St-Lambert Campus | | | 3 372 |
| CEGEP St-Lawrence Campus | | | 702 |
| CEGEP de Sept-Îles | 1 | 1 | 745 |
| CEGEP de Shawinigan | 1 | 1 | 1 381 |
| CEGEP Collège de Sherbrooke | 1 | 1 | 5 574 |
| CEGEP de Sorel-Tracy | 1 | 1 | 1 065 |
| CEGEP de Trois-Rivières | 1 | 1 | 4 603 |
| CEGEP Collège de Valleyfield | 1 | 1 | 1 882 |
| CEGEP Vanier College | 1 | 1 | 4 824 |
| CEGEP de Victoriaville | 1 | 1 | 1 447 |
| CEGEP du Vieux-Montréal | 1 | 1 | 6 361 |
| CEGEP Beauce-Appalaches | 1 | 1 | 1 408 |
| CEGEP Heritage | 1 | 1 | 695 |
| CEGEP Marie Victorin | 1 | 1 | 3 630 |
| Centennial College/Collège Centennal | 1 | 1 | 180 |
| Collège d'Affaires Ellis | 1 | 1 | 299 |
| Collège André-Grasset | 1 | 1 | 981 |
| Collège de l'Assomption | 1 | 1 | 1 238 |
| Collège Bart | 1 | 1 | 199 |
| Conservatoire Lasalle | 1 | 1 | 225 |
| École de Musique Vincent D'indy | 1 | 1 | 87 |
| Collège Français | 1 | 1 | 487 |
| Institut Teccart Inc. | 1 | 1 | 609 |
| Collège Jean-de-Brébeuf | 1 | 1 | 1 426 |
| Collège Laflèche | 1 | 1 | 1 178 |
| Collège La Salle | 1 | 1 | 2 317 |
| Le Petit Séminaire de Québec | 1 | 1 | 413 |
| Collège de Lévis | 1 | 1 | 263 |
| Marianopolis | 1 | 1 | 1 513 |
| Collège Merici | 1 | 1 | 933 |
| Campus Notre-Dame-de-Foy | 1 | 1 | 1 136 |
| Collège de Secrétariat Notre-Dame/Notre Dame Secrétariat | 1 | 1 | 4 |
| Collège O'Sullivan | 1 | 2 | |
| Collège O'Sullivan | | | 450 |
| Collège O'Sullivan de Québec | | | 171 |
| Séminaire de Sherbrooke | 1 | 1 | 364 |
| Séminaire Saint-Augustin | 1 | 1 | .. |
| Inst. Informatique du Québec | 1 | 1 | 31 |
| Collège Technique de Montréal | 1 | 1 | 7 |
| École Sup. de Danse du Québec | 1 | 1 | 1 |
| Inst. Superieur d'électronique, Montréal | 1 | 1 | 104 |
| Collège Informatique Marsan | 1 | 1 | 7 |
| Informatique Multi Hexa | 1 | 1 | 29 |
| Collège Moderne de Trois-Rivières | 1 | 1 | 138 |
| Collège Inter dec | 1 | 1 | 44 |
| Sous-Centre des Îles | 1 | 1 | 137 |
| École de Mode Chatelaine Inc | 1 | 1 | 26 |
| Institut Demers Inc. | 1 | 1 | 52 |
| École de Dance de Québec | 1 | 1 | .. |
| Collège Radio-Télé du Québec Inc. | 1 | 1 | .. |
| Collège Photographie Marsan | 1 | 1 | .. |
| École Nationale du Cirque | 1 | 1 | .. |
| Collège Marie-de-France | 1 | 1 | 180 |
| Collège Stanislas | 1 | 1 | 244 |
| Conservatoire de Musique | 1 | 4 | |

## Education Indicators in Canada
### Community Colleges and Related Institutions[1] by Jurisdiction and Size of Full-time Enrolment

| Province/Institution | | Main Institutions | All Institutions | Enrolment 1996-97 |
|---|---|---|---|---|
| | Conservatoire de Musique de Chicoutimi | | | .. |
| | Conservatoire de Musique de Montréal | | | 82 |
| | Conservatoire de Musique de Québec | | | 31 |
| | Conservatoire de Musique de Trois-Rivières | | | .. |
| Institut de Tourisme et d'Hôtellerie | | 1 | 1 | 506 |
| Institut de Tech. Agr. | | 1 | 2 | |
| Institut de Tech. Agr.(St-Hyacinthe) | | | | 615 |
| Institut de Tech. Agr.(La Pocatière) | | | | 432 |
| Centre Specialisé de Pêche | | 1 | 1 | 17 |
| École Commerciale du Cap | | 1 | 1 | 167 |
| COFI Alain-Grandbois | (Trade-vocational only) | | | |
| COFI Maurice-Lefebvre | (Trade-vocational only) | | | |
| COFI Nord | (Trade-vocational only) | | | |
| COFI Olivar-Asselin | (Trade-vocational only) | | | |
| COFI Saint-Charles | (Trade-vocational only) | | | |
| COFI Centre régional du Parc | (Trade-vocational only) | | | |
| COFI Québec | (Trade-vocational only) | | | |
| COFI Estrie | (Trade-vocational only) | | | |
| COFI Outaouais | (Trade-vocational only) | | | |
| **Ontario** | | **41** | **43** | **141,257** |
| East. Ont. School of X-Ray Tech., Kingston General Hospital | | 1 | 1 | 32 |
| O'Brien Institute of Medical Technology | | 1 | 1 | 10 |
| Ontario School of Radiation Therapy, Ontario Cancer Inst. | | 1 | 1 | 20 |
| La Cité Collégiale | | 1 | 1 | 3,586 |
| Algonquin College of Applied Arts & Tech. | | 1 | 1 | 9,598 |
| Cambrian College | | 1 | 1 | 3,910 |
| Centennial College of Applied Arts & Tech. | | 1 | 1 | 10,219 |
| Conestoga College of Applied Arts & Tech. | | 1 | 1 | 4,126 |
| Confederation College of Applied Arts & Tech. | | 1 | 1 | 3,191 |
| Durham College of Applied Arts & Tech. | | 1 | 1 | 4,201 |
| Fanshawe College of Applied Arts & Tech. | | 1 | 1 | 8,267 |
| George Brown College of Applied Arts And Tech. | | 1 | 1 | 8,257 |
| Georgian College of Applied Arts & Tech., Barrie Campus | | 1 | 1 | 6,305 |
| Loyalist College of Applied Arts & Tech. | | 1 | 1 | 3,065 |
| Mohawk College of Applied Arts & Tech. | | 1 | 1 | 8,139 |
| Niagara College of Applied Arts & Tech. | | 1 | 1 | 5,654 |
| Niagara Parks Commission, School of Horticulture | | 1 | 1 | 40 |
| Lambton College of Applied Arts & Tech. | | 1 | 1 | 2,492 |
| Kemptville College of Agricultural Tech. | | 1 | 1 | 290 |
| Humber College of Applied Arts & Tech., North Campus | | 1 | 1 | 11,387 |
| Northern College of Applied Arts & Tech. | | 1 | 1 | 1,491 |
| Collège Boréal | | 1 | 1 | 1,166 |
| Ontario College of Art | | 1 | 1 | 1,621 |
| Ridgetown College of Agricultural Technology | | 1 | 1 | 292 |
| Collège des Grands-Lacs | | 1 | 1 | 111 |
| St. Clair College of Applied Arts & Tech. | | 1 | 1 | 5,640 |
| St. Lawrence College / Collège Saint-Laurent | | 1 | 3 | 3,251 |
| | St. Lawrence Coll. / Coll. Saint-Laurent, Brockville | | | 657 |
| | St. Lawrence Coll. / Coll. Saint-Laurent, Cornwall | | | 839 |
| Seneca College of Applied Arts & Tech. | | 1 | 1 | 11,464 |
| Sheridan College of Applied Arts & Tech. | | 1 | 1 | 9,359 |
| Sir Sandford Fleming College of Applied Arts & Tech. | | 1 | 1 | 5,285 |
| Collège de Tech. Agricole et Alimentaire d'Alfred | | 1 | 1 | 107 |
| Michener Institute of Applied Health Sciences | | 1 | 1 | 500 |
| Canadian Memorial Chiropratic College | | 1 | 1 | 612 |
| Canadore College of Applied Arts & Tech. | | 1 | 1 | 3,216 |
| Sault College of Applied Arts & Tech. | | 1 | 1 | 2,793 |
| Ont. Cancer Found. Sch. Rad. Ther., Hamilton | | 1 | 1 | 17 |
| Ont. Cancer Found. Sch. Rad. Ther., London | | 1 | 1 | 17 |
| Ont. Cancer Found. Sch. Rad. Ther., Ottawa | | 1 | 1 | 14 |
| Ont. Cancer Found. Sch. Rad. Ther., Thunder Bay | | 1 | 1 | 6 |
| Ont. Cancer Found. Sch. Rad. Ther., Windsor | | 1 | 1 | 3 |
| Ont. Cancer Found. Sch. Rad. Ther., Kingston | | 1 | 1 | 7 |

APPENDIX 2

COMMUNITY COLLEGES AND RELATED INSTITUTIONS[1] BY JURISDICTION AND SIZE OF FULL-TIME ENROLMENT

| Province/Institution | | Main Institutions | All Institutions | Enrolment 1996-97 |
|---|---|---|---|---|
| **Manitoba[2]** | | **5** | **8** | **3,598** |
| Assiniboine Community College | | 1 | 1 | 602 |
| Red River Community College | | 1 | 3 | 2,655 |
| | Red River Community College, Medical Lab. Technology | | | .. |
| | Red River Community College, Radiotherapy Technology | | | 21 |
| Keewatin Community College | | 1 | 1 | 276 |
| Stevenson Aviation Tech. Training Centre | Trade vocational institution only | | | |
| Manitoba Cancer Treatment & Research Foundation | | 1 | 1 | 12 |
| Winnipeg Technical College | Trade vocational institution only | | | |
| Health Sciences Centre | | 1 | 2 | |
| | Health Sciences Centre, School of Respiratory Therapy | | | 30 |
| | Health Sciences Centre, School of Cytotechnology | | | 2 |
| **Saskatchewan** | | **4** | **9** | **2,787** |
| Saskatchewan Institute of Applied Science and Technology | | 1 | 6 | |
| | Sask. Inst. of Appl. Science And Tech., Woodland Institute | | | 297 |
| | Sask. Inst. of Appl. Science And Tech., Kesley Institute | | | 735 |
| | Kelsey Inst., Dept. of Radiology Technology | | | 14 |
| | Kelsey Inst., Dept. of Medical Laboratory Technology | | | .. |
| | Sask. Inst. of Appl. Science And Tech., Palliser Institute | | | 1,282 |
| | Sask. Inst. of Appl. Science And Tech., Wascana Institute | | | 448 |
| Regional Colleges | Trade vocational institutions only | | | |
| | Carlton Trail Regional College | | | |
| | Cumberland Regional College | | | |
| | Cypress Hills Regional College | | | |
| | Northwest Career College | | | |
| | Parkland Career College | | | |
| | Prairie West Regional College | | | |
| | Saskatchewan Indian Career College | | | |
| | Lakeland Lloydminster Career College | | | |
| | Southeast Regional College | | | |
| | Northlands Career College | | | |
| School of Rad. Therapy Tech., Allan Blair Memorial Hospital | | 1 | 1 | 5 |
| Saskatoon Cancer Centre Radiation Therapy Program | | 1 | 1 | 4 |
| School of Cytotechnology, Pasqua | | 1 | 1 | 2 |
| **Alberta** | | **16** | **16** | **29,366** |
| Olds College | | 1 | 1 | 670 |
| Lakeland College (at Vermilion) | | 1 | 1 | 956 |
| Fairview College | | 1 | 1 | 219 |
| Grande Prairie Regional College | | 1 | 1 | 1,083 |
| Lethbridge Community College | | 1 | 1 | 2,253 |
| Medicine Hat College | | 1 | 1 | 1,240 |
| Mount Royal College | | 1 | 1 | 5,331 |
| Grant Macewan Community College, Main Campus | | 1 | 1 | 4,461 |
| Keyano College | | 1 | 1 | 515 |
| Red Deer College | | 1 | 1 | 2,905 |
| Northern Alberta Institute of Technology | | 1 | 1 | 4,846 |
| Southern Alberta Institute of Technology | | 1 | 1 | 4,113 |
| Alberta College of Art | | 1 | 1 | 729 |
| Alberta Vocational Colleges | (Trade vocational only) | | | |
| | Alberta Vocational College, Calgary | | | |
| | Alberta Vocational College, Edmonton | | | |
| | Alberta Vocational Centre, Grouard | | | |
| | Alberta Vocational College, Lac La Biche | | | |
| School of Psychiatric Nursing, Alberta Hospital, Ponoka | | 1 | 1 | 34 |
| School of Radiation Therapy, Cross Cancer Institute | | 1 | 1 | 7 |
| School of Radiation Therapy, Tom Baker Cancer Centre | | 1 | 1 | 4 |

# Education Indicators in Canada

## Community colleges and related institutions[1] by jurisdiction and size of full-time enrolment

| Province/Institution | Main Institutions | All Institutions | Enrolment 1996-97 |
|---|---|---|---|
| **British Columbia** | **21** | **21** | **32,279** |
| British Columbia Institute of Technology | 1 | 1 | 4,357 |
| Capilano College | 1 | 1 | 3,663 |
| College of New Caledonia | 1 | 1 | 898 |
| Columbia College | 1 | 1 | 256 |
| Douglas College | 1 | 1 | 2,755 |
| Institute of Indigenous Government *(no enrolment in 1996-97)* | | | - |
| Justice Institute of British Columbia *(no enrolment in 1996-97)* | | | - |
| Malaspina University-College | 1 | 1 | 2,116 |
| Nicola Valley Institute of Technology *(no enrolment in 1996-97)* | | | - |
| Okanagan University College | 1 | 1 | 2,392 |
| Selkirk College | 1 | 1 | 850 |
| Vancouver Community College | 1 | 1 | 306 |
| Northern Lights College | 1 | 1 | 115 |
| Camosun College | 1 | 1 | 2,394 |
| North Island College | 1 | 1 | 459 |
| Northwest Community College | 1 | 1 | 343 |
| University College of the Cariboo | 1 | 1 | 2,981 |
| University College of the Fraser Valley | 1 | 1 | 1,477 |
| College of the Rockies | 1 | 1 | 350 |
| Emily Carr Institute of Art & Design | 1 | 1 | 804 |
| Kwantlen University College | 1 | 1 | 2,854 |
| Langara College | 1 | 1 | 2,899 |
| Open Learning Agency | 1 | 1 | .. |
| Cancer Control Agency of B.C. | 1 | 1 | 10 |
| **Yukon** | **1** | **1** | **272** |
| Yukon College | 1 | 1 | 272 |
| **Northwest Territories** | **2** | **6** | **166** |
| Nunavut Arctic College | 1 | 3 | |
|     Nunavut Arctic College, Keewatin Campus | | | 18 |
|     Nunavut Arctic College, Kitikmeot Campus | | | .. |
|     Nunavut Arctic College, Numatta Campus | | | 95 |
| Aurora College | 1 | 3 | |
|     Aurora College, Aurora Campus | | | 22 |
|     Aurora College, Thebacha Campus | | | 12 |
|     Aurora College, Yellowknife Campus | | | 19 |

1 Includes health sciences centres offering medical programs, whether or not they are affiliated with a hospital.

2 Statistics Canada began only in 1998 to collect data for postsecondary non-university programs at Saint Boniface College. Consequently they are not reflected in these data.

# APPENDIX 3

## DATA SOURCES USED IN THIS PUBLICATION

### ADULT EDUCATION AND TRAINING SURVEY, 1992 AND 1998

The Adult Education and Training Survey (AETS), initiated by Human Resources Development Canada (HRDC) to determine the importance of adult education and training in Canada, was conducted by Statistics Canada in 1984, 1986, 1990, 1992, 1994 and 1998. The objective of the AETS is to gather information on the incidence and nature of adult education and training, and the socio-economic and demographic profile of persons who have and have not participated in education or training programs. Data are also collected on barriers to adult education and training and employer involvement.

The AETS has a sample size of approximately 50,000 households and covers household members 17 years of age or older. One respondent in the target age range is surveyed in each of the sampled households. To ensure accurate reporting of education or training incidences, no proxy responses are permitted. Residents of the territories, persons living on Indian reserves, full-time members of the Canadian Armed Forces, and residents of institutions are excluded from the survey. The survey is conducted as a supplement to the Labour Force Survey.

### CANADIAN SOCIO-ECONOMIC INFORMATION MANAGEMENT SYSTEM

The Canadian Socio-Economic Information Management System (CANSIM) is a Statistics Canada time series database containing more than 650,000 items. Selected data are provided by various Statistics Canada divisions and compiled into the CANSIM database. Time series included provide a wide range of demographic, social, and economic statistics. Education statistics available on CANSIM include time series relating to enrolment and degrees, finances, teachers, and language education and literacy.

### CENSUS OF POPULATION AND HOUSING, 1986, 1991 AND 1996

Conducted every five years, the Census provides extensive and detailed demographic, social, economic and cultural information on the Canadian population. All Canadian citizens and landed immigrants are surveyed in the Census; a 20% sub-sample of the census population receives a more extensive questionnaire. Variables covered in the detailed Census questionnaire include age, sex, education and major field of study, marital status, household relationship, ethnic and cultural origin, mother tongue, language spoken at home, knowledge of official languages, place of birth, citizenship, period or year of immigration and disability. Information is also collected on respondents' occupation, place of work, type of employment (paid worker, self-employed, unpaid family worker), number of weeks worked (full- or part-time) in the year, labour market activities in the week preceding the census, employment income, government transfer payments, other money income (from investments, pensions, etc.) and total income.

## CENTRE FOR EDUCATION STATISTICS, STATISTICS CANADA

The purpose of the Centre for Education Statistics (CES) is to develop and carry out a comprehensive program of pan-Canadian education statistics and analysis to support policy decisions and program management, while ensuring that accurate and relevant information concerning education is available to the Canadian public and to other educational stakeholders.

The CES conducts much of its work in consultation with the Canadian Education Statistics Council (CESC), which comprises the Chief Statistician of Canada and the provincial deputy ministers responsible for education. This arrangement recognizes the provincial and territorial responsibility for education, and Statistics Canada's mandate under the Statistics Act for the collection, analysis and dissemination of information on education. It also acknowledges the value and need for close collaboration and partnership between jurisdictions and Statistics Canada in ensuring that the goals of accuracy and relevance of information are met. Statistics Canada is responsible for the management of the Centre's program as well as for its outputs.

The CES reports on students, staff and finances at elementary, secondary and postsecondary levels of education using administrative data collected from ministries and educational institutions as well as data generated from sample surveys. In this report, administrative data gathered by the CES have been used to produce the statistics on enrolment, diplomas and degrees granted, tuition fees and finances at the elementary, secondary and postsecondary levels of education. Sample surveys conducted by the CES have also been used to generate statistics on the number of persons participating in adult education, the employment characteristics and earnings of postsecondary graduates, and the use of communications technology in schools.

Throughout this document the CES is cited as the source of statistics generated from the Centre's holdings of administrative data. For statistics generated from sample surveys, the actual survey is cited as the source. A description of the sample surveys used in the 1999 PCEIP report is provided in this appendix. For information on the administrative data used in this report contact the Centre for Education Statistics.

## DEMOGRAPHY DIVISION, STATISTICS CANADA

The Demography Division of Statistics Canada is responsible for various surveys and research relating to demography, including population, household and family projections, population estimates and migration data.

The following table summarizes the assumptions for the Medium Growth Model used for population projections in section 2.1. Flow data presented on immigration, emigration, returning Canadians, and net internal migration refer to the periods 1990-91, 1992-93, 2000-01, and 2015-16. The number of returning Canadians is derived using 50% of emigrants over a 10-year period based on medium assumption, and the stock number of non-permanent residents is kept constant after 1995; in other words, net flows equal zero from 1995-96 onward. The medium scenario for interprovincial migration is generally the average of the Western scenario— westward migration, mainly to British Columbia, which is the most favourable scenario for the Atlantic provinces, Alberta and British Columbia—and the Central scenario (Ontario as main destination for interprovincial migrants), which is most favourable for Quebec, Ontario, Manitoba and Saskatchewan.

## Assumptions for the Medium-Growth Model Used for Population Projections

| | Estimates | | Projections | |
|---|---|---|---|---|
| Components | 1991 | 1993 | 2001 | 2016 |
| **Mortality** (life expectancy in years) | | | | |
| **Males** | 74.6 | 74.8 | 76.2 | 78.5 |
| **Females** | 80.9 | 81.3 | 82.1 | 84.0 |
| **Fertility** (births per woman) | 1.70 | 1.70 | 1.70 | 1.70 |
| **Immigration** | 219,300 | 257,500 | 250,000 | 250,000 |
| **Emigration** | 43,700 | 46,400 | 48,760 | 53,970 |
| **Returning Canadians** | 18,500 | 21,800 | 23,100 | 25,630 |
| **Non-permanent residents** | 381,000 | 208,500 | 149,600 | 149,600 |
| **Net interprovincial migration** | Interprovincial scenario | | Medium scenario | |

## Organisation for Economic Co-operation and Development

*Education at a Glance – OECD Indicators* (EAG) is an annual publication that was first released by the Organisation for Economic Co-operation and Development (OECD) in 1992. The publication contains data and analysis for over 30 indicators. These indicators are designed to provide insight into the functioning of the education systems of OECD member countries and to allow international comparisons that illustrate the strengths and weaknesses of different education systems.

EAG data are obtained directly from member countries. For all nations covered, EAG data include all types of students and all age groups. Thus, child, adult, national and foreign students are included, as well as students in open distance learning and special education programs. All educational programs, whether organized by ministries responsible for education or by other government ministries or by the private sector are covered. Levels of education are defined according to the International Standard Classification of Education (ISCED).

## General Social Survey

GSS Cycle 2, 1986
GSS Cycle 9, 1994

In 1994, Cycle 9 of the General Social Survey (GSS) collected information relating to education, work and retirement and examined the relationship between these three main activities. Data collected relating to education included educational attainment and intentions, reason for leaving school, province and language of elementary and secondary education, spouse's years of schooling and main activity. Particular data collected relating to work included occupation of parents, employment history, job characteristics (including satisfaction), income and income source, unpaid work and total income of household members. The survey also collected data on social mobility, and records general demographic detail, such as age, sex, marital status, religion, mother tongue, health and immigration status.

The sample size for the GSS Cycle 9 is approximately 10,000 respondents. They are selected by a random-digit dialing technique and interviewed by telephone. The survey excludes persons younger than 15 years of age, residents of the Northwest Territories and Yukon, as well as individuals belonging to households without a telephone, persons incapable of answering the telephone, and persons who speak neither English nor French.

## INTERNATIONAL ADULT LITERACY SURVEY, 1994-1995

The International Adult Literacy Survey (IALS) was initially carried out in seven countries with the goal of directly measuring the literacy skills of the adult population of participating countries in order to create comparable literacy profiles across national, linguistic and cultural boundaries. The seven countries that took part in this survey are: Canada, Germany, the Netherlands, Poland, Sweden, Switzerland and the United States. In addition, a number of provinces provided funding for a larger sample in order to allow for analysis of their results.

In Canada, IALS assessed literacy skills and the proficiency levels of these skills in each of the official languages. IALS measured three types of literacy:

1. prose literacy—the knowledge and skills needed to understand and use information from texts, including editorials, news stories, poems, and fiction;
2. document literacy—the knowledge and skills required to locate and use information contained in various formats such as job applications, payroll forms, transportation schedules, maps, tables, and graphics;
3. quantitative literacy—the knowledge and skills required to apply arithmetic operations to numbers embedded in printed materials, such as balancing a cheque-book, figuring out a tip, completing an order form, or determining the amount of interest on a loan from an advertisement.

The level of proficiency in each skill was determined using a five-point scale, which assessed abilities and strategies required to succeed at various literacy tasks. For example, a level 3 performance would be the minimum for efficient day-to-day living in an advanced democratic country.

The survey combined educational testing techniques with those of household survey research to measure literacy and to provide the information necessary to make these measures meaningful. Respondents were asked a series of questions to obtain background and demographic information on educational attainment, literacy practices at work and at home, labour force information, adult education participation and literacy self-assessment.

The Canadian portion of the study involved a sample of about 5,700 individuals. This sample was drawn from the Labour Force Survey. The sample consisted of the civilian, non-institutionalized population aged 16 to 69. Excluded from the survey's coverage are residents of the Yukon and Northwest Territories, persons living on Indian reserves, full-time members of the Canadian Armed Forces and inmates of institutions, and Francophone residents of the province of Ontario who lived in geographic regions where less than 20 persons were Francophone.

## LABOUR FORCE SURVEY

The Labour Force Survey (LFS) is a household survey carried out each month by Statistics Canada to provide timely, accurate and consistent estimates of the labour market aspects of the economy. The survey divides the population aged 15 and over into three mutually exclusive groups: those who are employed, those who are unemployed and those who are not in the labour force. In addition, data are collected on a wide range of variables concerning the respondents' household, family and individual characteristics including educational attainment, school attendance and number of students.

The sample size of the survey is approximately 58,000 households (or about 110,000 persons) across Canada each month. The survey sample size is large enough to provide accurate and reliable estimates at the jurisdictional and metropolitan levels.

Persons younger than 15 years of age, persons living in the Yukon and Northwest Territories, persons living on Indian reserves, full-time members of the Canadian Armed Forces, and residents of institutions are excluded from the survey.

## NATIONAL GRADUATES SURVEY 1988, 1992 AND 1997

The purpose of the National Graduates Survey (NGS), conducted by Statistics Canada under the sponsorship of Human Resources Development Canada (HRDC), is to provide information on the integration of recent postsecondary education graduates into the labour market. Information is collected on numerous issues relating to education–training and the labour market. This included the program or field of study, characteristics of the graduate, characteristics and duration of all jobs held since graduation, employment characteristics, length of job search, match between education and employment, additional education or training that a graduate may have taken since graduating, and the graduate's earnings, finances and/or loans.

The sample of graduates is designed to provide accurate estimates by province, program and field of study. The 1997 NGS involved 43,000 trade–vocational, college and university graduates. Surveys have been conducted for the 1976, 1980, 1986, 1990 and 1995 graduating classes. Graduates are interviewed two years after graduation and are asked to provide information relating to the period from one year prior to enrolment to the time of interview, two years after graduation. Follow-up surveys are also conducted five years after graduation to provide data on the longer-term outcomes for graduates.

## DEFINITION OF GRADUATES

The NGS defines graduates as students who completed the requirements for a degree, diploma or certificate in trade–vocational, college or university programs during the reference year (for example, during the 1995 calendar year for the class of '95). Specifically, individuals included are:

i) graduates of university programs that lead to bachelor's, master's or doctoral degrees, or to specialized certificates or diplomas;

ii) graduates of postsecondary programs (of at least one year in duration and normally requiring secondary school completion or equivalent for admission) in Colleges of Applied Arts and Technology (CAAT), Collèges d'enseignement général et professionnel (CEGEP), community colleges, technical schools, or similar institutions;

iii) graduates of skilled trade pre-employment programs (with a normal duration of at least three months) which lead to a certificate or diploma at the trade level and are offered at trade–vocational schools, as well as many community colleges and technical institutes.

Excluded from the definition of graduates are:

i) graduates from private postsecondary institutions such as computer training schools or commercial secretarial schools;

ii) individuals who completed continuing education courses, at universities and colleges, that do not lead to degrees or diplomas;

iii) individuals who completed part-time trade courses, such as adult education evening courses, while employed full-time;

iv) individuals who completed vocational programs that were not in the skilled trades and/or were less than three months in duration;

v) individuals in apprenticeship programs.

## SCHOOL ACHIEVEMENT INDICATORS PROGRAM, 1993, 1994, 1996, 1997 AND 1998

The School Achievement Indicators Program (SAIP) was developed by the provinces and territories through the Council of Ministers of Education, Canada for the purpose of assessing the academic performance of 13- and 16-year-old students across Canada in mathematics content and problem solving, reading and writing, and science. SAIP presents achievement results for Canada as a whole and for each participating province and territory. SAIP also provides results for the English and French school systems within a jurisdiction. In SAIP, the achievement of individual students is not identified, and no attempt is made to relate an individual's achievement to that of other students. Similarly, results are not available by school or school district.

The first SAIP assessment, in mathematics content and problem solving, was administered in 1993, followed by an assessment of reading and writing in 1994 and of science in 1996. A second cycle of assessments began in 1997 and was completed in 1999. Future assessments include mathematics in 2001; reading, writing and science will follow.

All assessments carried out to date, with the exception of the mathematics assessment in 1993, and reading and writing in 1994, have been administered to a random sample of students drawn from all jurisdictions. The 1993 and 1994 assessments excluded Saskatchewan, as the province chose to concentrate on its own assessment and indicators programs.

To date, two mathematics assessments have been completed, the first in 1993 and the second in 1997. Each mathematics assessment had two components: a section on mathematics content and a section on problem solving skills. The mathematics content component focused on assessing students' understanding and knowledge of numbers and operations, algebra and functions, measurement and geometry, and data management and statistics. While the goal of the 1997 mathematics content assessment was to measure the same concepts and skills in the same manner as the 1993 assessment, some slight modifications were made to the 1997 mathematics content assessment in order to update the test materials and to address comments arising from the 1993 administration. It was determined that the changed items did not alter the measuring characteristics of the instrument, hence the 1997 mathematics content results are comparable to the 1993 results.

In the case of the 1997 problem solving assessment, the magnitude of the changes over the 1993 assessment lead SAIP assessment developers to indicate that both assessments are not completely comparable. This report focuses on the results from the 1997 mathematics problem-solving assessment.

In 1997, the SAIP mathematics assessment was administered to a random sample of about 48,000 students—26,000 13-year-olds and 22,000 16-year-olds. Students were randomly assigned to an assessment of either mathematics content or problem solving. About 36,000 completed the assessment in English and 12,000 in French. In the 1993 SAIP mathematics assessment, the number of 13- and 16-year-olds writing the assessment was similar to the number writing in 1997, again with students randomly assigned to write the mathematics content or problem-solving test.

Two SAIP reading and writing assessments have been completed, the first in 1994, and the second in 1998. The instruments used to assess reading and writing in 1994 and 1998 were essentially the same. Students in the reading assessment were presented with a booklet of readings from recognized literature, essays and newspaper articles. The students were asked to read the material and answer multiple-choice questions as well as to respond in writing to specific questions. The written responses required the students to express opinions about the texts, explain something in the texts, make judgements about textual information, extract ideas from the texts or relate concepts in the texts to their personal experiences.

APPENDIX 3

The writing assessment followed typical writing processes. It was structured so that students had the opportunity to read textual material on a theme, make notes about the text material, discuss their ideas with peers in the classroom, write first drafts, and revise or edit their drafts using reference books that are normally available, such as dictionaries.

The reading and writing assessments used comparable instruments in both English and French. However, caution is advised when comparing achievement results based on assessment instruments prepared in different languages, despite the care taken to ensure equivalency. Every language has unique features that are optimal for speaking, writing or reading, but these features are not easy to equate. While the writing assessment task was the same in English and French, pedagogical differences relating to differences in language structure render comparisons between languages inherently more difficult.

In 1998, approximately 24,000 13-year-old students and 22,000 16-year-old students were selected to participate in the SAIP reading and writing assessment. Students were randomly assigned to either the reading or the writing assessment. Students completed the assessment in their first official language; about 34,000 students wrote in English and about 12,000 in French. Students in French immersion wrote in English. In 1994, approximately 29,000 13-year-olds and 29,000 16-year-olds were chosen to take the SAIP reading and writing assessment, with about half of these students taking the reading test and the other half taking the writing test. Of the approximately 58,000 students writing the assessment in 1994, about 43,000 completed the reading and writing tasks in English, and about 15,000 completed them in French.

In the SAIP science assessment, students were asked to complete only one assessment, focusing on either (a) their understanding of science concepts, the nature of science, and the relationship of science to technology and societal issues (written assessment) or (b) their science inquiry skills (practical tasks). Only the results of the written assessment are reported in this document.

In 1996, approximately 19,500 13-year-old students and 18,000 16-year-old students were chosen to take the SAIP science assessment. About 70% of these students participated in the written assessment and 30% in the practical tasks. Of the approximately 37,500 students, 26,500 completed the science assessments in English, and about 11,000 completed them in French.

In each assessment both age groups write components of the same test. SAIP results are reported according to the level achieved: level 1 is the lowest, level 5 the highest. An expectation-setting process was carried out as part of the development of the SAIP assessments, and it was determined that 13-year-olds should be able to achieve at least level 2, and that 16-year-olds should achieve level 3 or above. In the 1999 PCEIP report, all references to the results achieved by each age cohort are in the context of these guidelines, unless specified otherwise. For example, discussion of the performance of 13-year-olds related to the percentage that achieved level 2 or above.

The summary criteria for the SAIP assessment levels are presented below. Although these may be used to gain a general impression of the levels of difficulty, they are by no means a complete list.

## SUMMARY CRITERIA FOR THE MATHEMATICS CONTENT ASSESSMENT

A student at level 2 can:
- use the four basic operations with natural numbers
- use patterns and classifications in real-life situations and plot points on a grid
- calculate dimensions and areas of plane figures, classify solid forms, and use single geometric transformations
- extract and represent data using tables and diagrams

A student at level 3 can:
- use the four basic operations with integers
- use monomial algebraic expressions and plot points on a Cartesian grid
- use length, angle measure, area, and volume involving various plane geometric figures and repetitions of the same geometric transformation
- use information from various sources and calculate arithmetic mean and simple probabilities

## SUMMARY CRITERIA FOR THE MATHEMATICS PROBLEM-SOLVING ASSESSMENT

A student at level 2 can:
- make a choice of algorithms to find a solution to (a) multi-step problems, using a limited range of whole numbers or (b) one-step problems, using rational numbers
- use more than one particular case to establish a proof
- use common vocabulary to present solutions

A student at level 3 can:
- choose from two algorithms to find solutions to multi-step problems, using a limited range of rational numbers
- use necessary and sufficient cases to establish a proof
- use mathematical vocabulary imprecisely to present solutions

## SUMMARY CRITERIA FOR THE WRITING ASSESSMENT

Level 2

The writer demonstrates an uneven and/or uncertain grasp of the elements of writing. Integration of some of the elements is apparent, but development is sketchy and/or inconsistently maintained. The writing conveys simple and/or uneven meaning.

- TThe writer's voice/tone/stance are discernible but may be inconsistent or uneven.
- The writer demonstrates some evidence of engagement with the subject and superficial awareness of the reader.
- The controlling idea and its development are limited but discernible.
- Grasp of conventional syntax and rules of language are limited. Errors are distracting and interfere with communication.

Level 3

The writer demonstrates a control of the elements of writing. The writing is generally integrated, and development is generalized, functional and usually maintained throughout. The writing conveys a clear perspective.

- The writer's voice/tone/stance are clear and appropriate. It is apparent that the writer is interested in the subject and in communication with the reader.
- The controlling idea and its development are straightforward, clear and appropriate, if overgeneralized.
- Control of conventional style, syntax and rules of language is evident. Errors do not unduly affect the reader.

APPENDIX 3

## SUMMARY CRITERIA FOR THE READING ASSESSMENT

Level 2

The student interprets, evaluates, explores surface and/or indirectly implied meanings from straightforward texts and some meaning from more complex texts by:

- responding to concrete details, strongly implied ideas, or key points
- making supported judgements about purpose, content, or relationships
- exploring in the context of personal experience and understanding.

Level 3

The student interprets, evaluates, explores complex meanings in complex texts and some meaning from sophisticated texts by:

- responding to more abstract language, details, and ideas
- making informed judgements about purpose, content, or relationship among elements
- exploring and demonstrating personal understanding and appreciation.

## SUMMARY CRITERIA FOR THE SCIENCE ASSESSMENT

A student at level 2 can:

- classify substances according to their physical properties
- compare various plant and animal adaptations
- know that the amount of energy in the universe is conserved but that it can change form and be transferred
- know that the movement and tilt of Earth affects cycles such as years, days and seasons
- explain that there are different forms of scientific investigations and that their results may contradict each other
- identify technologies that influence science, and science knowledge that leads to new technologies.

A student at level 3 can:

- use chemical properties to compare and classify substances
- know that some life forms are unicellular and others are multi-cellular, and that life forms are involved in the transfer of energy
- compare gravitational and electrical forces
- compare changes in Earth's surface and their causes
- analyse experiments and judge their validity
- identify areas where science knowledge and technologies address societal problems.

## Note on Confidence Intervals Used in SAIP Assessments

In this assessment, the percentages calculated are based on samples of students. Therefore, these are only estimates of the actual achievement students would have demonstrated if all of the students in the population had taken the assessment. Because an estimate based on a sample is rarely exact, it is common practice to provide a range of percentages within which the actual achievement is likely to fall. This range of percentage values is called a confidence interval. The confidence interval represents high- and low-end points between which the actual achievement would fall 95% of the time. In other words, one can be confident that the actual achievement level of all students would fall somewhere into the established range 19 times out of 20, if the assessment were repeated with different samples from the same student population.

Confidence intervals are given in the tables showing the SAIP results. If the confidence intervals overlap, the differences are not statistically significant. It should be noted that the size of the confidence interval depends upon the size of the sample. In smaller jurisdictions, a large interval may indicate difficulties in achieving a large sample, and does not necessarily reflect on the competency of the students who were administered the assessment.

As an example, a score of 65 with a confidence interval of 2.5 would mean that the actual score would fall between 62.5 and 67.5.

## Second Information Technology in Education Study

The Second Information Technology in Education Study (SITES) was designed as an international evaluation of the use of new information and communications technology in elementary and secondary schools. It was conducted in a total of 27 nations, including Canada. In Canada, data collection occurred in January and February 1999.

In Canada, Statistics Canada, under the auspices of the International Association for the Evaluation of Educational Achievement, conducted the survey. A number of partners were involved in either the funding and/or the conduct of the survey, including provincial ministries of education; the Council of Ministers of Education, Canada; Industry Canada; and Human Resources Development Canada. As international results were not available at the time this report was being prepared, only results for Canada and the provinces are presented.

The Canadian survey involved 4,000 schools, each of which received two questionnaires, one to be completed by the principal and another to be completed by an individual responsible for technology in the school. Both questionnaires included questions on the school, the use of communication technology, the training and professional development of teachers, and obstacles to the use of technology at the school.

Data are available for both Canada and the provinces for three specific population groups of students: elementary (up to Grade 5), intermediate (up to Grade 9) and secondary (up to Grade 12). The territories did not participate in the survey.

## Survey of Consumer Finances

The purpose of the Survey of Consumer Finances (SCF), conducted annually since 1971, is to collect information on individual and family income. The survey produces data on income distributions for families and individuals, the earnings of men and women, and the income of dual-earner families. The information gathered enables governments to establish low-income cut-offs.

# Third International Mathematics and Science Study, 1994-1995

The Third International Mathematics and Science Study (TIMSS) was conducted in order to compare the teaching and learning of mathematics and science at the elementary and secondary school levels on an international level. It was conducted in 1995, under the auspices of the International Association for the Evaluation of Educational Achievement (IEA). Over 50 countries, including Canada, participated in one or more aspects of the study.

About half a million students in more than 15,000 schools participated in TIMSS. Students were assessed in three population groups: Population 1 (grades 3 and 4), Population 2 (grades 7 and 8), Population 3 (final year of secondary school).

This report does not present results for Population 3 (final year of secondary school) because for the mathematics, science, and literacy components of the study, Canada did not meet all the sampling criteria established. In order to meet the study sampling criteria, national samples had to meet three criteria: 85 percent of the schools selected had to agree to participate, 85 percent of the students in those schools who were selected had to write the test, and the product of those two percentages had to be at least 75 percent. For the mathematics, science and literacy components, the student participation rate fell below the 85 percent criterion. The general rule established for TIMMS is that if a country fails to meet these criteria, the results should be interpreted with caution because they might be biased. For the advanced mathematics component of the study, only a limited number of jurisdictions participated.

All students wrote a 90-minute test in mathematics and science, and responded to a questionnaire about their opinions, attitudes, and interests. Teachers completed questionnaires about their academic and professional preparation, their teaching approaches, and the material taught. Principals provided information about schools, students, and teachers.

In Canada, a nationally representative sample of schools and classrooms was selected by Statistics Canada. The sample included public, separate, and private schools. The sample included both French-speaking and English-speaking schools. In six provinces (British Columbia, Alberta, Ontario, Quebec, New Brunswick – English-speaking schools, and Newfoundland and Labrador), the samples chosen were large enough to allow comparisons to be made at the provincial level.

Twenty-six countries participated in TIMSS at Population 1, of which 15 met all sampling requirements or did not use replacement schools in producing their sample. The Canadian sample for Population 1 included more than 16,000 students, evenly divided between grades 3 and 4. Forty-one countries participated at the Population 2 level, of which 19 met all sampling requirements or did not use replacement schools in producing their sample. The Canadian sample for Population 2 included more than 17,000 students from grades 7 and 8.

All of the data collection instruments for the study, including questionnaires and test booklets, were produced in both French and English.

# APPENDIX 4

## GLOSSARY OF TERMS USED IN THIS PUBLICATION

**Academic rank:** This refers to a classification of university teaching staff according to level of academic appointment. Generally, the ranking consists of "full professor" at the top, followed by "associate professor." The other category refers to "assistant professors", "lecturers" and "instructors".

**Adult participation in formal education:** Participation in formal education and training for accreditation by persons aged 17 years and over on a part-time or full-time basis. However, unless sponsored by an employer, it excludes persons aged 17 to 19 who are enrolled full-time in elementary or secondary programs as well as persons aged 17 to 24 who are enrolled full-time in postsecondary programs without employer support.

**Apprenticeship enrolment:** Registered apprenticeship programs consist of both in-class and on-the-job training. The enrolment data in this report covers only the programs' in-class training, required to be taken at a designated community college or similar institution. The province of Quebec differs from the other jurisdictions in that its registered apprenticeship training involves only on-the-job training. As a result, its enrolment figures for in-class apprenticeship training are almost non-existent.

**Apprenticeship programs:** Apprenticeship programs provide training and experience for employment in the trades. Apprentices and employers sign contracts that are registered with the provinces and territories. Programs vary in length from one to five years, depending on the trade. Registered apprenticeship combines on-the-job experience with six- to eight-week periods of in-class training. In most jurisdictions, the in-class portion is usually taken at a postsecondary institution during the apprenticeship training. In Quebec, however, the in-class training is taken prior to beginning the apprenticeship program. Depending on the jurisdiction and trade, graduates of apprenticeship programs can receive both a Certificate of Apprenticeship and a Certificate of Qualification.

**Bachelor's and first professional degrees:** These include all bachelor's degrees so named, whether specialized or general, and all professional degrees that are neither bachelor's nor master's degrees (such as M.D., D.M.D, D.D.S. and D.V.M.).

**Capital expenditures:** Capital expenditures are for assets that last longer than one year. These include outlays for construction, renovation, major building repairs and expenditures for new or replacement equipment. They represent the value of educational capital acquired or created during the year in question. Capital expenditures reported do not include expenditure for debt service because of the international definitions used.

**Career–technical programs:** These programs, which are offered at community colleges, prepare students to enter occupations at a level between that of the university-trained professional and the skilled tradesman. Secondary school completion or equivalent is a normal prerequisite for entry. These programs require at least one school year of 24 weeks or more for completion. Most take two or three years and some take longer. One-year programs lead to a certificate and the longer ones lead to a diploma.

**Census subdivision:** This is a census term that applies to municipalities (as determined by jurisdictional legislation) or their equivalent (for example, Indian reserves, Indian settlements and unorganized territories).

**Community college diplomas:** These include all diplomas and certificates granted for completion of career–technical programs and two-year general courses at CEGEPs in Quebec. Data are shown for academic years.

**Community college enrolment:** This includes enrolment in career-technical and university transfer programs of postsecondary non-university institutions as well as enrolment in radiography, medical technology, health records and RN programs in hospital schools.

**Community colleges:** The term "community college" refers to community colleges, CEGEPs, technical institutes, hospital and regional schools of nursing, and establishments providing technological training in specialized fields. In counting the number of institutions, hospital schools of radiography, medical technology and health records are included.

**Constant dollars:** Constant dollars are derived by applying a price deflator to convert expenditures displayed in a time series to a price level that existed at a certain point in time (the base year). Constant dollars eliminate the changes in the purchasing power of the dollar over time. The result is a series as it would exist if the dollar had a purchasing power equal to the purchasing power in the base year.

**Core working-age population:** The core working-age population has been defined as persons aged 25 to 54. This is a subset of the entire working age population, consisting of persons aged 15 and over. The core working-age population excludes youth aged 15 to 24, many of whom are students, and excludes persons aged 55 and over, since a significant percentage of this age group has retired or withdrawn from the labour force.

APPENDIX 4

**Current expenditures:** Current expenditures are for goods and services consumed within the current year, which have to be made recurrently to sustain the production of educational services. Current expenditures reported do not include expenditure for debt service because of the international definitions used.

**Direct public expenditure:** Public expenditures on education can be divided into two main components: direct expenditures for education services and public subsidies to the private sector. Examples of the latter include government scholarships and bursaries, and loan subsidies and forgiveness.

**Doctorates:** These are the highest academic degree conferred by a university. Only earned doctorates are included in these statistics. First professional degrees with "doctor" in the title, such as M.D. and D.D.S. are not included here; they are included under bachelor's and first professional degrees.

**Educational attainment:** This is defined as the highest level of formal education completed by an individual according to the following categories:

Less than high school includes individuals having completed pre-school, elementary school and those with less than high school completion.

High school graduate includes individuals who have obtained high school graduation and includes persons who have some postsecondary education, albeit uncompleted.

Trade–vocational graduate includes individuals who have obtained a trade certificate or diploma from a vocational or apprenticeship training program.

College graduate includes individuals who have obtained a non-university certificate or diploma from a community college.

University graduate includes individuals who have obtained a university certificate, diploma or degree.

**Elementary–secondary educators:** This refers to teaching staff and non-teaching academic staff (principals, vice-principals and department heads), as well as school board based instructional staff employed as of September 30 of a school year (October 31 for Ontario). Staff on leave are excluded; their replacements are included.

**Elementary–secondary enrolment:** The head count of students enrolled in elementary–secondary schools as of September 30 of the school year (October 31 for Ontario). Coverage extends to students in public schools, private schools, federal schools, and schools for the visually and hearing impaired, including students enrolled in pre-elementary programs offered by these schools.

| | |
|---|---|
| **Elementary–secondary schools:** | Elementary–secondary schools include public, private, federal institutions and schools for the visually and hearing impaired. Schools are classified as elementary if they provide Grade 6 and under or a majority of elementary grades, and secondary if they offer Grade 7 and over or a majority of secondary grades. |
| **Employed:** | Employed persons are those who, during the reference week, did any work for pay or profit, or had a job and were absent from work. |
| **Employment rate:** | The number of persons employed as a percentage of the population. |
| **English (French) as a second language programs (ESL) (FSL):** | These are programs offered to students to improve their language skills in the official language of the regular program in which they are enrolled. |
| **Expenditure on elementary–secondary education:** | This includes expenditures on public schools, federal schools, special education programs (for example, for students with special needs) and private (academic) schools. Also included are expenditures by provincial, territorial and federal departments such as program administration and contributions to teachers' pension funds. |
| **Expenditure on postsecondary non-university institutions:** | This includes the operating and capital expenditures of all institutions that provide postsecondary education programs but do not grant degrees (CAATs, CEGEPs, technical institutes, agricultural colleges, schools of art, hospital schools). Also included is government spending on student aid and on other departmental administrative programs. |
| **Expenditure on trade-vocational education:** | This includes expenditures on all vocational training programs offered by public and private trade–vocational schools, community colleges, institutes of technology, etc. They include spending on human resource programs such as apprenticeships and training in industries, as well as allowances paid to trainees. Also included in this category are the training costs of nursing assistants and aides in hospitals, government language courses, vocational training in provincial reform schools and federal penitentiaries, and other training expenditures by provincial and federal departments, private business colleges and trade schools, and other private schools. |
| **Expenditure on universities:** | This includes the operating, capital and sponsored research expenditures of all degree-granting institutions and their affiliates. Also included is government spending on student aid and on other departmental administrative programs. |
| **Expenditure per student:** | This is calculated by dividing the total expenditure of a particular level of education by the corresponding full-time equivalent enrolment. For international comparisons, the result in national currency is then converted into equivalent U.S. dollars by dividing the national currency figure by the purchasing power parity (PPP) index produced by the World Bank. (See purchasing power parity.) |

# APPENDIX 4

**Federal schools:** These include schools administered directly by the federal government, overseas schools operated by the Department of National Defence for dependants of Canadian Forces personnel, and schools operated by Indian and Northern Affairs Canada or by local band councils.

**Field of study:** The predominant discipline, area of learning, or subject specialization of studies.

**Foreign students:** Students studying in Canada with a student authorization or special visa. Students with permanent resident (landed immigrant) status are not included in this category.

**Formal education:** Education and training activities with an identifiable structured plan and clear objectives geared to the development of the learner's skill and competence, from which accreditation or some kind of formal recognition of completion is received.

**Full-time community college educator:** This refers to all teaching staff, academic administrators, guidance counsellors employed full-time, as defined by the institution, with a contract of seven months or more. Educators on leave, presidents and principals are excluded. Teaching staff who spend at least 50% of their time teaching at the college level are classified as college educators; those who spend more than 50% of their time teaching at the trade-vocational level are classified as trade educators.

**Full-time elementary–secondary educators:** This refers to all teaching and non-teaching academic staff (principals, vice-principals, department heads and subject supervisors) employed full time as defined by the jurisdiction. Those on leave are excluded.

**Full-time equivalent elementary–secondary educators:** All full-time educators plus the full-time equivalent of part-time educators. For example, a part-time educator employed for 60% of a "normal workload" is equal to 0.60 of a full-time educator.

**Full-time university educators:** All academic staff and senior administrators whose term of appointment is four months or more. Presidents and vice-presidents are excluded.

**Full-time/part-time students:** Given that there is no commonly accepted definition of a part-time student, Statistics Canada reports full-time or part-time registration status as supplied by each respondent.

**Graduate diplomas and certificates:** University qualifications awarded after a master's degree, after a first professional degree, or after a first degree in the same field of study.

**Graduate enrolment:** This includes university students in master's and doctoral degree programs or in graduate diploma and certificate programs. Full-time graduate enrolment also includes hospital residents, and since 1980, interns.

**Gross Domestic Product (GDP):** The GDP measures the unduplicated value of production originating within the geographical boundaries of Canada, regardless of whether the factors of production are resident or non-resident.

| | |
|---|---|
| **Immigrant:** | An immigrant is a person from another country admitted to Canada as a "permanent resident" (also called a landed immigrant) under one of the Government of Canada's immigration programs. |
| **Index:** | Annual cumulative percentage changes in a variable from a given base year, expressed as an index with the base year equal to 100. An index value of 140, for example, 10 years after the base year, would indicate a 40% increase in the variable over that time period. |
| **Inter-jurisdictional migrants:** | Individuals who, on census day, were residing in a different jurisdiction than they were one year earlier. |
| **Intra-jurisdictional migrants:** | Individuals, who on census day, were residing in a different census subdivision within the same jurisdiction than they were one year earlier. |
| **Involuntary part-time employment:** | Persons working part time for economic reasons, not out of personal choice. These are persons working part time who would prefer to be working full time and are available to work full time. Part-time employment is defined by usual hours of work per week being less than 30. |
| **Involuntary part-time employment rate:** | The number of persons working part time on an involuntary basis as a percentage of all persons in the labour force. |
| **Job-related adult education and training:** | Any education or training activities undertaken by adults for the development or upgrading of skills to be used in a present or future career/employment position. Job-related training can be either formal (for accreditation) or non-formal (not for accreditation). |
| **Labour force:** | The labour force is composed of that portion of the civilian, non-institutional population 15 years of age and over who are actively participating in the labour force. For the reference period in question, it includes employed and unemployed persons. Employed persons are those with a job or business, and unemployed persons are those without a job or business who are looking for work. |
| **Labour force participation rate:** | The labour force participation rate represents the labour force expressed as a percentage of the population 15 years of age and over. |
| **Low-income cut-offs (LICOs):** | Income levels used to delineate family units into "low income" and "other" groups. A family unit is considered to be a "low-income" family if its income is below the estimated cut-off for its family size and for its urban (or rural) area of residence . A family with income equal to or above the cut-off is considered to be in the "other" category. |
| | The LICOs were first introduced in Canada in 1968 based on 1961 census income data and 1959 family expenditure patterns. At that time, expenditure patterns indicated that Canadian families spent about 50% of their income on food, shelter and clothing. It was arbitrarily estimated that families spending 70% or more of their income on these basic necessities would be in "straitened" circumstances. With this assumption, low- |

APPENDIX 4

income cut-off points were set for five different sizes of families.

Subsequently, revised low-income cut-offs were established, based on national data from the Family Expenditure Surveys (FAMEX) of 1969, 1978, 1986 and 1992. These data indicated that Canadian families spent, on average, 42% of their income on basic necessities in 1969 (38.5% in 1978, 36.2% in 1986, and 34.7% in 1992). By adding the original difference of 20 percentage points to the overall Canada level of expenditure on necessities, new low-income cut-offs were set. The FAMEX data are then analysed to determine the income levels where families spend this percentage (that is, the overall Canada percentage plus 20 percentage points) on the basic necessities. These income levels, differentiated by size of urban area of residence and by family size, become the base year low-income cut-offs. Low-income cut-offs are updated yearly by changes in the consumer price index.

The following is the 1996 matrix of low-income cut-offs:

**Low-Income Cut-offs (in Canadian Dollars) for Economic Families and Unattached Individuals, 1996**

| Family size | 500,000 or more | 100,000 to 499,999 | 30,000 to 99,999 | Small urban Regions | Rural (farm and non-farm) |
|---|---|---|---|---|---|
| 1 | 17,132 | 14,694 | 14,591 | 13,577 | 11,839 |
| 2 | 21,414 | 18,367 | 18,239 | 16,971 | 14,799 |
| 3 | 26,633 | 22,844 | 22,684 | 21,107 | 18,406 |
| 4 | 32,238 | 27,651 | 27,459 | 25,551 | 22,279 |
| 5 | 36,036 | 30,910 | 30,695 | 28,562 | 24,905 |
| 6 | 39,835 | 34,168 | 33,930 | 31,571 | 27,530 |
| 7+ | 43,634 | 37,427 | 37,166 | 34,581 | 30,156 |

Size of area of residence

**Low-income families:** A family unit with income below a certain level, established by Statistics Canada's low-income cut-offs. These low-income cut-offs are differentiated by family size and by size of urban (or rural) area of residence. For a detailed explanation of how low-income cut-offs are established, see the definition for "Low income cut-offs (LICOs).

**Master's degree:** These include all university degrees so named except the Master's of Divinity, which is considered a first professional degree.

**Median family income:** The amount of income that divides family income size distribution into two halves. The incomes of the first half of the families or non-family persons are below the median, while those of the second half are above the median.

**Minority language education programs:** The minority language education program is designed to offer persons in minority language groups (English in Quebec, French outside of Quebec) education in their mother tongue. In these programs minority language is used as the language of instruction for at least 25% of the school day.

**Mobility:** Student mobility—The movement of students between jurisdictions for the purpose of pursuing postsecondary studies.

Graduate mobility—The movement of graduates away from their province of study.

**Non-university postsecondary:** An aggregation including trade–vocational and community college.

**Participation rate:** This is calculated by taking the total enrolment of a particular level of education as a percentage of a specified population group. For example, the participation rate in full-time bachelor's programs is commonly calculated as total enrolment in bachelor's programs divided by the total population aged 18 to 24. In this example, the reference population is set as persons aged 18 to 24, since this age group has traditionally accounted for most bachelor's students.

**Personal income:** The sum of all incomes received by persons resident in Canada regardless of whether these incomes represent factor earnings of persons from current production or whether they are received as current transfers of income from government and other sectors. It also includes investment income accumulated on behalf of persons by life insurance companies, private pension plans and similar institutions as well as transactions of private non-commercial institutions such as universities, labour unions, political and charitable organizations.

**Pre-elementary enrolment:** The head count of students registered in pre-Grade 1 programs offered by public, private and federal schools, as well as schools for the visually and hearing impaired.

**Pre-vocational programs:** Pre-vocational programs provide students with the prerequisites needed to enter a trade–vocational or postsecondary program of study. They include language training, basic training in skill development and academic upgrading.

**Private elementary–secondary schools:** These schools, whether church-affiliated or non-sectarian, are operated and administered by private individuals or groups.

**Programs for registered apprentices:** These combine on-the-job experience with short periods of formal technical instruction in provincially and territorially designated trades. Depending upon the trade, apprenticeship terms may vary from one to five years in length. The apprenticeship data in this publication reflect enrolments in the theoretical aspects of instruction and not the practical training component.

**Public elementary–secondary schools:** These are established and operated by local educational authorities according to the public school act of the jurisdiction. Also included in this category are Protestant and Roman Catholic separate schools, and schools operated in Canada by the Department of National Defence within the framework of the public school system.

**Public subsidies to the private sector:** These include government scholarships and bursaries, loan subsidies and forgiveness, and education-related tax credits.

**Pupil–computer ratio:** The pupil-computer ratio is a proxy measure of the access or availability of computers to students in elementary and secondary schools. Based on the Second Information Technology in Education Study (SITES)—the estimate of full-time equivalent enrolment is divided by the estimated number of computers used for educational purposes.

**Pupil–educator ratio:** Full-time equivalent enrolment (in grades 1 to 12, and OAC in Ontario) and ungraded programs plus pre-elementary full-time equivalent enrolment, divided by the full-time equivalent number of educators.

**Purchasing Power Parities (PPPs):** Purchasing Power Parities, developed by the World Bank, are the current exchange rates that equalize the purchasing power of different currencies, so that a given amount of money, when converted to various currencies using PPPs, will buy the same goods and services in all countries. The PPP exchange rate gives the amount of a national currency that will buy the same basket of goods and services in a country as the U.S. dollar amount will in the United States. The PPP exchange rate is used because the currency exchange rate is affected by many factors (such as interest rates, trade policies, expectations of economic growth) that have little to do with current, relative domestic purchasing power in different countries.

**Registration status:** A classification of enrolment as either full time or part time according to institutional definitions. Since standard national definitions of full-time and part-time enrolment do not exist, one can expect that the definitions used by institutions will vary somewhat from jurisdiction to jurisdiction.

**Schools for students who are visually and hearing impaired:** These schools provide special facilities and training for students who are visually and hearing impaired. Most of these institutions are under direct provincial government administration.

**Second language education programs:** Second language education programs are designed to offer instruction in the minority language (English in Quebec, French outside Quebec) for children of the majority language group. There are two types of second language programs:

Regular second language courses—programs where students take the second language as a "subject" for less than 25% of the school day;

Second language immersion programs—programs where students learn the second language by receiving a minimum of 25% of their education in that language.

**Secondary graduation rate:** Secondary graduates (regardless of age) as a percentage of the 18-year-old population. In theory, all secondary graduates ought to be included, but because of coverage problems in the data collected by jurisdictions, and in processing procedures at Statistics Canada, some programs are excluded from these rates. For example, graduates from upgrading programs for out-of-school adults, which sometimes lead to equivalency certification but in other cases lead to regular high school graduation certification, are not uniformly included.

**Secondary school graduates:** Secondary school graduation refers to completion of Grade 12 (OAC in Ontario) in all jurisdictions except Quebec (Secondary V) and Newfoundland and Labrador before 1983–84 (Grade 11). Secondary school graduate statistics are presented for academic years.

**Skills upgrading programs:** These have as their objective instruction in new occupational methods and techniques. Students engaged in skills upgrading have usually had prior training and work experience in their occupation, but have fallen behind in their qualifications due to technological changes or other developments. Programs within this category may range from 2 to 20 weeks.

**Socio-economic status:** An individual's or a family's relative position in society. Depending on the purpose of its usage in analysis, this relative position is operationally defined using variables such as educational attainment, occupation, income, or a combination of such variables. In indicator 4.3C, the family socio-economic status is operationally defined as the Blishen socio-economic index for father's occupation. Father's occupation was preferred to mother's occupation since relatively fewer mothers are in the labour force. The Blishen socio-economic index has been shown to have high concurrent validity with both education and income and is well accepted in social research.

**Trade-vocational programs:** Trade–vocational programs at community colleges and similar institutions are those that do not require secondary school completion and do not include continuing education or general interest programs. Trade–vocational programs include apprenticeship programs, and preparation programs for employment in an occupation or trade, including pre-employment/pre-apprenticeship programs, academic and skill upgrading programs, language training, job readiness and orientation to work programs. Programs of 25 weeks or more are identified as full time and those that are 24 weeks or less are considered part time. A large portion of the in-class training for apprenticeship programs is structured in study blocks of four to eight weeks, and would be classified as part time, even though the length of the apprenticeship program itself may be from two to five years. However, some jurisdictions, notably Ontario, identified the total weeks of in-class training over the whole apprenticeship period, and as a result, a large portion of the registered apprenticeship enrolments are included in the full-time data rather than the part-time. Full-time enrolment includes, for example, most of the pre-employment/pre-apprenticeship programs and some of the longer programs in academic upgrading, language and job readiness training. Part-time enrolment includes, in addition to the registered apprenticeship programs, most of the programs in skill-upgrading, orientation, job readiness and special training.

Language training—These programs offer a basic knowledge of English or French. As second language programs, they are primarily aimed at recent immigrants and others whose first language is neither English nor French.

Job readiness—These programs attempt to give students the knowledge and skills required to search for a job or explore career options.

Orientation programs—These programs present the basic knowledge and skills, in many cases for a range of occupations, to help participants decide whether or not they wish to pursue their training in a chosen occupation.

Pre-employment or pre-apprenticeship programs—These programs provide basic training in a particular occupation, offering entry-level skills for employment. These programs also offer the knowledge and skills required to enter an apprenticeship program.

**Undergraduate diplomas and certificates:** Diplomas and certificates conferred by degree-granting institutions with entry conditions similar to those for bachelor's degree candidates (for example, Diploma in Physiotherapy.) Diplomas and certificates earned after a first degree but in a different field of study are also classified as undergraduate.

**Undergraduate enrolment:** University students in bachelor's and first professional degree programs, undergraduate diploma and certificate programs, and non-university courses offered in universities. In the 1970s full-time undergraduate enrolment also included medical interns. Since 1980, interns have been classified as graduate students.

**Unemployed:** Unemployed persons are those who, during the reference week, did not have a job or business and who were available for work and were either on temporary layoff, had looked for work in the past four weeks or had a job to start within the next four weeks.

**Unemployment rate:** The unemployment rate represents the number of unemployed persons expressed as a percentage of the labour force. The unemployment rate for a particular group (such as age or sex) is the number of unemployed in that group expressed as a percentage of the labour force for that group.

**Universities and other degree-granting institutions:** These include:
Universities—independent institutions granting degrees in at least arts and sciences.

Colleges of theology—independent institutions granting degrees only in theology.

Liberal arts colleges—independent institutions granting degrees in only in arts.

Other—independent institutions granting degrees in specialized fields other than theology (such as engineering, fine arts).

**University college programs:** These refer to degree-granting programs offered by community colleges. These differ from university transfer programs also offered by some community colleges, as the college offers the degree-granting program in its entirety (that is, all the years of the degree-granting program). Community colleges offering these programs are able to do so as they have been awarded degree-granting powers in certain fields or programs of study by the jurisdiction. University college programs exist in British Columbia and to a lesser extent in Alberta. Statistics on university college enrolments are not captured and reported by Statistics Canada as part of its university statistics program, but rather with its college statistics program. As of the date of production of this report, data on university college graduation were not available. However, these degrees will be captured in the near future by Statistics Canada through the Enhanced Student Information System (ESIS), scheduled for implementation at the national level beginning in the year 2000.

**University transfer programs:** Programs of postsecondary non-university institutions that require secondary school completion to enter and which provide a student with standing equivalent to the first or second year of a university degree program with which one can apply for admission to subsequent senior years at a degree-granting institution. The "général" programs of the Quebec CEGEPs, completion of which is a prerequisite for entry into Quebec universities, are included in this classification.

# APPENDIX 5

## THE PCEIP INDICATORS SET

The following is a list of PCEIP indicators and components proposed for development. Indicators/components that are included in whole or in part in *Education Indicators in Canada: Report of the Pan-Canadian Education Indicators Program 1999* are indicated below by ✓ .

### INDICATORS AND COMPONENTS:

| Context | | Section |
|---|---|---|
| | **Demographics: Population Dynamics** | |
| ✓ | Population, distribution and forecasts of the school age population | 2.1 |
| ✓ | Immigration of the school-age population | 2.1 |
| ✓ | Interprovincial migration of the school-age population | 2.1 |
| | **Demographics: Educational Attainment** | |
| ✓ | Educational attainment of the adult population | 2.3 |
| | **Economic and Social Context: Labour Force Participation** | |
| | Labour force participation rate | |
| ✓ | Employment rate by educational attainment | 5.1 |
| ✓ | Unemployment rate by educational attainment | 5.1 |
| ✓ | Underemployment rate by educational attainment | 5.1 |
| | **Economic and Social Context: Socioeconomic Status** | |
| ✓ | Percentage of the school-age population living in low income family units | 2.2 |
| | **Economic and Social Context: Equity of Socioeconomic Status** | |
| | Family status of students | |
| | Health status of pre-school and school age youth | |
| | School Readiness | |
| **Features and Characteristics of Education Systems** | | |
| | **Learner/Student Inputs: Participation in and Access to Formal Education** | |
| ✓ | Student enrolment | 3.3 |
| ✓ | Adult participation in formal education | 3.3 |
| ✓ | Participation in education by young children | 3.3 |
| | Interjurisdictional distribution of PSE students | |
| | Entry Rate | |
| | **Learner/Student Inputs: Opportunity for Specific Groups** | |
| | Enrolment in specialized programs | |
| | Number and percentage of K-12 students accessing special education services | |
| | Participation rates in special purpose schools and programs | |

EDUCATION INDICATORS IN CANADA

| Indicator and Components | Section |
|---|---|
| **Learner Progression, Transitions and Choices: Learner Flows and Progression** <br> Cohort retention rates through K-PSE systems <br> Cohort drop out rates through K-PSE systems <br> Persistence Rate at all levels of education <br> Proportion of graduates who progress to PSE | |
| **Learner Progression, Transitions, and Choices: Learner Flows between Formal Education and Work/Home** <br> Number of students (aged 16-20) moving to the work force with or without completion of credential <br> ✓ Participation of adult learners in education <br> ✓ Employment Rate for graduates and leavers <br> Duration of unemployment for graduates and leavers <br> ✓ Earnings (average or median) of graduates and leavers | <br><br><br>3.3<br>5.2<br><br>5.2 |
| **Human Resources: Learner Interaction with Educators** <br> ✓ Pupil-educator ratio <br> Class size: average and distribution <br> Access to PSE teaching faculty (time) <br> Composite indicator of learner interaction with educators | <br>3.2 |
| **Human Resources: Characteristics of Educators** <br> ✓ Characteristics of educators | <br>3.2 |
| **Human Resources: Characteristics of Educational Staff** <br> Proportion of school personnel (by position and gender) | |
| **Technology and Innovation: Technology Use and Availability** <br> ✓ Pupil-to-computer ratio <br> ✓ Internet connectivity <br> ✓ Internet activities of students <br> ✓ Obstacles to fuller use of ICT <br> Enrolment rates in programs delivered through off-site delivery <br> Completion rates in programs delivered through off-site delivery | <br>3.6<br>3.6<br>3.6<br>3.6 |
| **Technology and Innovation: Innovation** <br> Components to be developed | |
| **Physical Environment: Characteristics and Use** <br> ✓ Number of schools | <br>3.1 |
| **Role of Institutions and Schools: Institutional Mandate and Instructional Delivery Style** <br> Distribution of faculty time among instruction, research and service (PSE) <br> Instructional hours (average per week/student) | |
| **Financial Efficiency and Productivity: Cost per Unit** <br> Cost per graduate and non-graduate (total and by object of expenditure) <br> Cost per student | |
| **Financial Inputs: Revenue Profiles** <br> ✓ Tuition income as a proportion of total budget | <br>3.5 |
| **Financial Inputs: Expenditure Profiles** <br> ✓ Public expenditure on education <br> ✓ Educational expenditure per student <br> ✓ Educational expenditure by resource category <br> ✓ Education expenditure as a proportion of GDP | <br>3.5<br>3.5<br>3.5<br>3.5 |
| **Financial Inputs: Learner Financing** <br> ✓ Total cost to learner <br> ✓ Student debt | <br>3.5<br>3.5 |
| **Sustainability: Sustaining Public Support** <br> Components to be developed | |
| **Sustainability: Capacity of Learner to Pay** <br> Components to be developed | |
| **Partnership and Linkages: Business and Government** <br> Number and breadth of academic inclusion in co-operative education and other work related programs <br> Participation in co-operative education and other work related programs | |
| **Partnership and Linkages: Parents and other Societal Groups** <br> Components to be developed | |

APPENDIX 5

| | Indicator and Components | Section |
|---|---|---|
| | **Post-School Learning: Individual Learner Patterns**<br>Percentage of adults (aged 17+) who return to formal education after having been out of the system for 1 or more years<br>Proportion of students moving directly from grade 12 or equivalent to PSE or successful employment | |
| ✓ | Participation in job-related education and training | 3.4 |
| | **Post-School Learning: Institutional Activities**<br>Hours or credits of continuing education or professional development offerings | |
| | **Structure and Goals of the Education Systems: Structure**<br>Activity: number of institutions by International Standard Classification of Education (ISCED) level<br>Activity: student enrolment by ISCED level<br>Activity public funding by ISCED level<br>Participation in education by education sector | |

**Outputs and Outcomes**

| | | |
|---|---|---|
| ✓ | **Achievement and Effectiveness: Learning Experience and Achievement**<br>Student achievement and attainment by key stage assessments of student performance in pan-Canadian (SAIP) and international (TIMSS) exams/tests (by age and/or grade)<br>Learner achievement on externally set standardized examinations<br>Learning gained | 4.1 |
| | **Achievement and Effectiveness: Research Intensity and Output**<br>PSE Research Intensity and Output | |
| | **Efficiency and Productivity: Output Levels** | |
| ✓ | Number of completions | 4.2 |
| ✓ | Ratio of upper secondary graduates to population at a typical age of graduation | 4.2 |
| | **Efficiency and Productivity: Output Rates** | |
| ✓ | The percentage of 19 - 20 year olds who have a high school leaving credential | 4.2 |
| | Proportion of completions versus entry relative to standard program duration | |
| | Percentage of former grade 2 students completing grade 12 within normal time frame | |
| | **Responsiveness and Relevance: Employability, Employment and Citizenship Activities of Graduates**<br>Proportion of secondary school and postsecondary graduates who obtain employment of more than 6 months duration within set time period | |
| ✓ | Percentage of graduates and local graduates retained in jurisdiction | 5.3 |
| | Duration of underemployment of graduates and leavers | |
| | **Equity**<br>Rates of completion of credential relative to norms<br>Time to completion of credential relative to norms | |
| ✓ | Disparities in educational achievement and attainment of First Nation peoples and linguistic minorities | 4.3 |
| ✓ | Highest level of schooling of 19-24 year old persons reporting aboriginal ancestry | 4.3 |
| ✓ | Participation in education by socioeconomic status | 4.3 |

# TABLES

# CHAPTER 2 TABLES

TABLE 2.1  ESTIMATES AND PROJECTIONS[1] OF THE POPULATION BY SELECTED AGE GROUPS, AND THE RATIOS OF YOUTH AND SENIORS TO THE WORKING-AGE POPULATION[2], CANADA AND JURISDICTIONS, 1986 TO 2016

|  | \multicolumn{8}{c|}{Population estimates and projections} | \multicolumn{2}{c|}{Ratios} |
|---|---|---|---|---|---|---|---|---|---|---|
|  | \multicolumn{8}{c|}{Age groups} | Youth to working-age Population | Senior to working-age Population |
|  | 0-4 | 5-14 | 15-19 | 20-24 | 15-24 | 5-24 | 25-64 | 65 + |  |  |
| **Canada** |  |  |  |  |  |  |  |  |  |  |
| 1986 | 1,844,736 | 3,651,895 | 1,995,404 | 2,474,002 | 4,469,406 | 8,121,301 | 13,495,508 | 2,742,274 | 0.60 | 0.20 |
| 1991 | 1,953,346 | 3,866,160 | 1,926,090 | 2,109,452 | 4,035,542 | 7,901,702 | 15,054,004 | 3,211,013 | 0.52 | 0.21 |
| 1996 | 1,991,543 | 4,072,100 | 1,996,299 | 2,027,000 | 4,023,299 | 8,095,399 | 16,218,787 | 3,657,969 | 0.50 | 0.23 |
| 2001 | 1,924,342 | 4,206,978 | 2,124,450 | 2,115,169 | 4,239,619 | 8,446,597 | 17,475,686 | 4,030,703 | 0.48 | 0.23 |
| 2006 | 1,924,563 | 4,186,092 | 2,213,717 | 2,242,892 | 4,456,609 | 8,642,701 | 18,710,928 | 4,399,296 | 0.46 | 0.24 |
| 2011 | 1,980,148 | 4,121,441 | 2,259,161 | 2,332,291 | 4,591,452 | 8,712,893 | 19,746,106 | 4,981,122 | 0.44 | 0.25 |
| 2016 | 2,052,815 | 4,177,895 | 2,194,828 | 2,378,218 | 4,573,046 | 8,750,941 | 20,421,717 | 5,894,292 | 0.43 | 0.29 |
| **Nfld.** |  |  |  |  |  |  |  |  |  |  |
| 1986 | 43,510 | 104,085 | 58,901 | 54,150 | 113,051 | 217,136 | 267,053 | 50,384 | 0.81 | 0.19 |
| 1991 | 37,542 | 91,252 | 54,579 | 50,676 | 105,255 | 196,507 | 290,621 | 55,657 | 0.68 | 0.19 |
| 1996 | 35,787 | 82,094 | 44,897 | 47,484 | 92,381 | 174,475 | 311,042 | 60,766 | 0.56 | 0.20 |
| 2001 | 31,651 | 74,897 | 40,803 | 38,689 | 79,492 | 154,389 | 325,744 | 65,561 | 0.47 | 0.20 |
| 2006 | 27,830 | 68,528 | 35,856 | 34,815 | 70,671 | 139,199 | 328,005 | 71,165 | 0.42 | 0.22 |
| 2011 | 24,583 | 60,599 | 33,474 | 30,482 | 63,956 | 124,555 | 320,050 | 81,683 | 0.39 | 0.26 |
| 2016 | 22,133 | 54,047 | 29,439 | 28,072 | 57,511 | 111,558 | 301,143 | 98,429 | 0.37 | 0.33 |
| **P.E.I.** |  |  |  |  |  |  |  |  |  |  |
| 1986 | 9,698 | 19,825 | 10,878 | 11,989 | 22,867 | 42,692 | 60,169 | 16,273 | 0.71 | 0.27 |
| 1991 | 9,547 | 19,889 | 10,052 | 9,653 | 19,705 | 39,594 | 64,571 | 17,114 | 0.61 | 0.27 |
| 1996 | 9,205 | 19,721 | 9,546 | 9,409 | 18,955 | 38,676 | 68,512 | 17,783 | 0.56 | 0.26 |
| 2001 | 8,724 | 19,250 | 9,656 | 8,954 | 18,610 | 37,860 | 72,739 | 18,752 | 0.52 | 0.26 |
| 2006 | 8,396 | 18,445 | 9,476 | 9,025 | 18,501 | 36,946 | 76,044 | 19,822 | 0.49 | 0.26 |
| 2011 | 8,221 | 17,584 | 9,147 | 8,824 | 17,971 | 35,555 | 78,169 | 21,790 | 0.45 | 0.28 |
| 2016 | 8,097 | 17,056 | 8,602 | 8,474 | 17,076 | 34,132 | 77,844 | 25,643 | 0.44 | 0.33 |
| **N.S.** |  |  |  |  |  |  |  |  |  |  |
| 1986 | 60,858 | 128,622 | 73,318 | 86,421 | 159,739 | 288,361 | 438,087 | 104,834 | 0.66 | 0.24 |
| 1991 | 61,713 | 124,695 | 67,882 | 71,117 | 138,999 | 263,694 | 478,348 | 114,191 | 0.55 | 0.24 |
| 1996 | 57,983 | 124,569 | 62,582 | 66,941 | 129,523 | 254,092 | 502,152 | 122,124 | 0.51 | 0.24 |
| 2001 | 52,861 | 119,878 | 63,302 | 62,549 | 125,851 | 245,729 | 524,771 | 129,427 | 0.47 | 0.25 |
| 2006 | 49,626 | 111,163 | 62,477 | 63,110 | 125,587 | 236,750 | 540,059 | 137,656 | 0.44 | 0.25 |
| 2011 | 47,942 | 103,060 | 58,949 | 62,003 | 120,952 | 224,012 | 546,413 | 153,140 | 0.41 | 0.28 |
| 2016 | 46,713 | 98,246 | 54,105 | 58,692 | 112,797 | 211,043 | 537,760 | 180,090 | 0.39 | 0.33 |
| **N.B.** |  |  |  |  |  |  |  |  |  |  |
| 1986 | 50,469 | 112,290 | 61,263 | 68,812 | 130,075 | 242,365 | 355,015 | 79,811 | 0.68 | 0.22 |
| 1991 | 48,870 | 106,131 | 59,445 | 58,132 | 117,577 | 223,708 | 386,621 | 89,346 | 0.58 | 0.23 |
| 1996 | 46,049 | 101,177 | 52,860 | 56,054 | 108,914 | 210,091 | 407,190 | 96,093 | 0.52 | 0.24 |
| 2001 | 42,231 | 95,773 | 50,965 | 49,986 | 100,951 | 196,724 | 427,481 | 101,609 | 0.46 | 0.24 |
| 2006 | 39,195 | 89,187 | 48,335 | 48,123 | 96,458 | 185,645 | 438,410 | 108,035 | 0.42 | 0.25 |
| 2011 | 37,054 | 82,299 | 45,701 | 45,684 | 91,385 | 173,684 | 440,220 | 120,236 | 0.39 | 0.27 |
| 2016 | 35,536 | 77,582 | 41,917 | 43,349 | 85,266 | 162,848 | 428,858 | 142,831 | 0.38 | 0.33 |
| **Que.** |  |  |  |  |  |  |  |  |  |  |
| 1986 | 437,473 | 922,908 | 487,252 | 633,347 | 1,120,599 | 2,043,507 | 3,594,031 | 658,771 | 0.57 | 0.18 |
| 1991 | 453,853 | 948,772 | 463,718 | 505,641 | 969,359 | 1,918,131 | 3,927,547 | 781,073 | 0.49 | 0.20 |
| 1996 | 467,308 | 943,075 | 503,194 | 478,395 | 981,589 | 1,924,664 | 4,124,476 | 897,208 | 0.47 | 0.22 |
| 2001 | 432,402 | 970,751 | 488,422 | 519,330 | 1,007,752 | 1,978,503 | 4,323,800 | 992,315 | 0.46 | 0.23 |
| 2006 | 425,475 | 949,827 | 502,609 | 506,298 | 1,008,907 | 1,958,734 | 4,537,563 | 1,082,415 | 0.43 | 0.24 |
| 2011 | 428,929 | 909,701 | 515,286 | 520,596 | 1,035,882 | 1,945,583 | 4,647,510 | 1,235,512 | 0.42 | 0.27 |
| 2016 | 434,623 | 907,000 | 482,966 | 532,876 | 1,015,842 | 1,922,842 | 4,691,904 | 1,441,745 | 0.41 | 0.31 |
| **Ont.** |  |  |  |  |  |  |  |  |  |  |
| 1986 | 647,745 | 1,269,373 | 723,864 | 906,668 | 1,630,532 | 2,899,905 | 4,918,565 | 1,010,966 | 0.59 | 0.21 |
| 1991 | 731,545 | 1,387,442 | 707,274 | 808,808 | 1,516,082 | 2,903,524 | 5,633,846 | 1,202,551 | 0.52 | 0.21 |
| 1996 | 761,145 | 1,534,132 | 723,419 | 766,923 | 1,490,342 | 3,024,474 | 6,141,421 | 1,386,928 | 0.49 | 0.23 |
| 2001 | 753,383 | 1,638,940 | 810,275 | 798,424 | 1,608,699 | 3,247,639 | 6,733,502 | 1,539,512 | 0.48 | 0.23 |
| 2006 | 762,700 | 1,670,888 | 878,873 | 886,055 | 1,764,928 | 3,435,816 | 7,330,468 | 1,691,563 | 0.47 | 0.23 |
| 2011 | 798,411 | 1,676,657 | 917,022 | 954,093 | 1,871,115 | 3,547,772 | 7,900,958 | 1,917,754 | 0.45 | 0.24 |
| 2016 | 847,504 | 1,723,404 | 911,755 | 992,016 | 1,903,771 | 3,627,175 | 8,353,999 | 2,278,126 | 0.43 | 0.27 |

**TABLE 2.1** ESTIMATES AND PROJECTIONS[1] OF THE POPULATION BY SELECTED AGE GROUPS, AND THE RATIOS OF YOUTH AND SENIORS TO THE WORKING-AGE POPULATION[2], CANADA AND JURISDICTIONS, **1986** TO **2016** (concluded)

|  | \multicolumn{8}{c}{Population estimates and projections} | \multicolumn{2}{c}{Ratios} |
|---|---|---|---|---|---|---|---|---|---|---|
|  | \multicolumn{8}{c}{Age groups} | Youth to working-age Population | Senior to working-age Population |
|  | 0-4 | 5-14 | 15-19 | 20-24 | 15-24 | 5-24 | 25-64 | 65 + |  |  |
| **Man.** |  |  |  |  |  |  |  |  |  |  |
| 1986 | 80,793 | 158,750 | 84,969 | 103,812 | 188,781 | 347,531 | 530,060 | 135,665 | 0.66 | 0.26 |
| 1991 | 83,364 | 159,641 | 81,662 | 83,033 | 164,695 | 324,336 | 557,228 | 147,540 | 0.58 | 0.26 |
| 1996 | 82,220 | 163,090 | 77,103 | 80,089 | 157,192 | 320,282 | 575,113 | 154,497 | 0.56 | 0.27 |
| 2001 | 76,801 | 162,500 | 80,570 | 77,337 | 157,907 | 320,407 | 602,368 | 159,162 | 0.53 | 0.26 |
| 2006 | 75,298 | 156,228 | 81,757 | 81,097 | 162,854 | 319,082 | 627,193 | 164,087 | 0.51 | 0.26 |
| 2011 | 75,945 | 150,258 | 80,375 | 82,200 | 162,575 | 312,833 | 647,223 | 176,428 | 0.48 | 0.27 |
| 2016 | 76,907 | 149,535 | 76,030 | 80,911 | 156,941 | 306,476 | 654,594 | 200,959 | 0.47 | 0.31 |
| **Sask.** |  |  |  |  |  |  |  |  |  |  |
| 1986 | 87,011 | 161,955 | 80,351 | 95,997 | 176,348 | 338,303 | 477,742 | 129,823 | 0.71 | 0.27 |
| 1991 | 78,890 | 160,886 | 74,255 | 68,034 | 142,289 | 303,175 | 483,311 | 140,938 | 0.63 | 0.29 |
| 1996 | 72,243 | 156,439 | 75,261 | 67,555 | 142,816 | 299,255 | 483,630 | 148,259 | 0.62 | 0.31 |
| 2001 | 66,671 | 144,741 | 76,920 | 69,405 | 146,325 | 291,066 | 497,374 | 151,169 | 0.59 | 0.30 |
| 2006 | 65,202 | 133,746 | 72,707 | 71,397 | 144,104 | 277,850 | 514,961 | 152,464 | 0.54 | 0.3 |
| 2011 | 65,327 | 127,835 | 67,386 | 68,216 | 135,602 | 263,437 | 529,778 | 158,695 | 0.50 | 0.30 |
| 2016 | 64,336 | 126,808 | 63,049 | 63,863 | 126,912 | 253,720 | 530,247 | 176,349 | 0.48 | 0.33 |
| **Alta.** |  |  |  |  |  |  |  |  |  |  |
| 1986 | 208,290 | 362,646 | 187,865 | 246,027 | 433,892 | 796,538 | 1,240,113 | 193,762 | 0.64 | 0.16 |
| 1991 | 211,426 | 399,470 | 181,665 | 204,034 | 385,699 | 785,169 | 1,371,984 | 232,710 | 0.57 | 0.17 |
| 1996 | 207,865 | 423,862 | 197,002 | 197,680 | 394,682 | 818,544 | 1,489,166 | 273,881 | 0.55 | 0.18 |
| 2001 | 201,388 | 425,105 | 217,957 | 210,621 | 428,578 | 853,683 | 1,609,881 | 312,501 | 0.53 | 0.19 |
| 2006 | 204,799 | 418,412 | 221,921 | 231,829 | 453,750 | 872,162 | 1,735,293 | 351,683 | 0.50 | 0.20 |
| 2011 | 214,406 | 416,370 | 221,413 | 236,577 | 457,990 | 874,360 | 1,852,373 | 407,478 | 0.47 | 0.22 |
| 2016 | 223,327 | 428,233 | 216,208 | 236,506 | 452,714 | 880,947 | 1,926,239 | 496,760 | 0.46 | 0.26 |
| **B.C.** |  |  |  |  |  |  |  |  |  |  |
| 1986 | 209,983 | 396,667 | 219,476 | 258,485 | 477,961 | 874,628 | 1,576,339 | 359,424 | 0.55 | 0.23 |
| 1991 | 226,095 | 451,407 | 218,568 | 242,075 | 460,643 | 912,050 | 1,814,565 | 427,117 | 0.50 | 0.24 |
| 1996 | 241,767 | 504,915 | 242,528 | 248,598 | 491,126 | 996,041 | 2,063,587 | 496,556 | 0.48 | 0.24 |
| 2001 | 248,350 | 535,926 | 276,450 | 271,285 | 547,735 | 1,083,661 | 2,300,151 | 555,320 | 0.47 | 0.24 |
| 2006 | 255,573 | 551,158 | 289,722 | 301,421 | 591,143 | 1,142,301 | 2,519,988 | 613,486 | 0.45 | 0.24 |
| 2011 | 267,985 | 558,202 | 300,855 | 313,130 | 613,985 | 1,172,187 | 2,715,677 | 699,504 | 0.43 | 0.26 |
| 2016 | 281,567 | 575,929 | 301,285 | 323,201 | 624,486 | 1,200,415 | 2,847,775 | 841,530 | 0.42 | 0.30 |
| **Y.T.** |  |  |  |  |  |  |  |  |  |  |
| 1986 | 2,341 | 3,759 | 1,943 | 2,302 | 4,245 | 8,004 | 13,494 | 922 | 0.59 | 0.07 |
| 1991 | 2,565 | 4,556 | 1,946 | 2,209 | 4,155 | 8,711 | 16,746 | 1,127 | 0.52 | 0.07 |
| 1996 | 2,630 | 5,399 | 2,325 | 2,507 | 4,832 | 10,231 | 20,266 | 1,604 | 0.50 | 0.08 |
| 2001 | 2,452 | 5,307 | 2,761 | 2,629 | 5,390 | 10,697 | 22,034 | 2,103 | 0.49 | 0.10 |
| 2006 | 2,489 | 4,930 | 2,788 | 2,958 | 5,746 | 10,676 | 23,130 | 2,675 | 0.46 | 0.12 |
| 2011 | 2,615 | 4,724 | 2,648 | 2,976 | 5,624 | 10,348 | 23,911 | 3,393 | 0.43 | 0.14 |
| 2016 | 2,716 | 4,744 | 2,462 | 2,850 | 5,312 | 10,056 | 23,913 | 4,389 | 0.42 | 0.18 |
| **N.W.T.** |  |  |  |  |  |  |  |  |  |  |
| 1986 | 6,565 | 11,015 | 5,324 | 5,992 | 11,316 | 22,331 | 24,840 | 1,639 | 0.90 | 0.07 |
| 1991 | 7,936 | 12,019 | 5,044 | 6,040 | 11,084 | 23,103 | 28,616 | 1,649 | 0.81 | 0.06 |
| 1996 | 7,341 | 13,627 | 5,582 | 5,365 | 10,947 | 24,574 | 32,232 | 2,270 | 0.76 | 0.07 |
| 2001 | 7,428 | 13,910 | 6,369 | 5,960 | 12,329 | 26,239 | 35,841 | 3,272 | 0.73 | 0.09 |
| 2006 | 7,980 | 13,580 | 7,196 | 6,764 | 13,960 | 27,540 | 39,814 | 4,245 | 0.69 | 0.11 |
| 2011 | 8,730 | 14,152 | 6,905 | 7,510 | 14,415 | 28,567 | 43,824 | 5,509 | 0.65 | 0.13 |
| 2016 | 9,356 | 15,311 | 7,010 | 7,408 | 14,418 | 29,729 | 47,441 | 7,441 | 0.63 | 0.16 |

1 Projections are based on a medium growth model. The assumptions underlying this model are outlined in Appendix 3.
2 Definitions are as follows: "youth" is the population aged 5 to 24, "working age population" is the population aged 25 to 64, and "senior" is the population aged 65 and over.

Source: *Demography Division, Statistics Canada. 1994. Population Projections for Canada, Provinces and Territories, 1993-2016, Statistics Canada Catalogue No. 91-520 (Occasional), December 1994.*

CHAPTER 2 TABLES

TABLE 2.2  NUMBER OF IMMIGRANT ARRIVALS AND IMMIGRANT ARRIVALS AS A PERCENTAGE OF THE POPULATION, SELECTED AGE GROUPS, CANADA, 1976 TO 1997

|  | Number of immigrant arrivals ||||||  Immigrant arrivals as a percentage of the population ||||||
|  | Age group |||||| Age group ||||||
|  | 4 to 5 | 6 to 15 | 16 to 19 | 20 to 24 | 4 to 24 | All ages | 4 to 5 | 6 to 15 | 16 to 19 | 20 to 24 | 4 to 24 | All ages |
|---|---|---|---|---|---|---|---|---|---|---|---|---|
| 1976 | 7,212 | 28,507 | 12,494 | 26,770 | 74,983 | **170,028** | 1.0 | 0.7 | 0.7 | 1.2 | 0.8 | **0.7** |
| 1977 | 5,143 | 21,034 | 10,476 | 21,209 | 57,862 | **130,931** | 0.7 | 0.5 | 0.5 | 0.9 | 0.6 | **0.6** |
| 1978 | 3,462 | 15,280 | 8,468 | 16,783 | 43,993 | **100,967** | 0.5 | 0.4 | 0.4 | 0.7 | 0.5 | **0.4** |
| 1979 | 2,514 | 12,672 | 8,236 | 13,638 | 37,060 | **84,518** | 0.4 | 0.3 | 0.4 | 0.6 | 0.4 | **0.3** |
| 1980 | 4,930 | 23,924 | 14,639 | 22,303 | 65,796 | **143,616** | 0.7 | 0.6 | 0.7 | 0.9 | 0.7 | **0.6** |
| 1981 | 3,689 | 19,785 | 11,728 | 18,550 | 53,752 | **126,995** | 0.5 | 0.5 | 0.6 | 0.7 | 0.6 | **0.5** |
| 1982 | 3,805 | 19,186 | 10,683 | 19,105 | 52,779 | **135,148** | 0.5 | 0.5 | 0.6 | 0.8 | 0.6 | **0.5** |
| 1983 | 2,711 | 14,003 | 8,491 | 14,550 | 39,755 | **101,234** | 0.4 | 0.4 | 0.5 | 0.6 | 0.5 | **0.4** |
| 1984 | 2,145 | 11,503 | 7,895 | 13,753 | **35,296** | **88,318** | 0.3 | 0.3 | 0.5 | 0.5 | 0.4 | **0.3** |
| 1985 | 2,004 | 11,148 | 7,035 | 12,872 | **33,059** | **83,691** | 0.3 | 0.3 | 0.4 | 0.5 | 0.4 | **0.3** |
| 1986 | 2,209 | 12,228 | 7,410 | 13,137 | 34,984 | **88,639** | 0.3 | 0.3 | 0.5 | 0.5 | 0.4 | **0.3** |
| 1987 | 3,517 | 17,213 | 9,446 | 19,043 | 49,219 | **130,813** | 0.5 | 0.5 | 0.6 | 0.8 | 0.6 | **0.5** |
| 1988 | 5,012 | 24,539 | 11,168 | 18,030 | 58,749 | **152,413** | 0.7 | 0.7 | 0.7 | 0.8 | 0.7 | **0.6** |
| 1989 | 5,996 | 28,474 | 12,105 | 20,879 | 67,454 | **178,152** | 0.8 | 0.8 | 0.8 | 1.0 | 0.8 | **0.7** |
| 1990 | 6,800 | 31,669 | 12,853 | 24,332 | 75,654 | **202,979** | 0.9 | 0.8 | 0.8 | 1.1 | 0.9 | **0.7** |
| 1991 | 6,629 | 31,679 | 12,088 | 24,519 | 74,915 | **219,250** | 0.9 | 0.8 | 0.8 | 1.2 | 0.9 | **0.8** |
| 1992 | 6,371 | 32,201 | 13,348 | 29,029 | 80,949 | **241,810** | 0.8 | 0.8 | 0.9 | 1.4 | 1.0 | **0.9** |
| 1993 | 6,234 | 36,766 | 15,980 | 26,150 | 85,130 | **234,457** | 0.8 | 0.9 | 1.0 | 1.3 | 1.0 | **0.8** |
| 1994 | 6,270 | 35,062 | 14,370 | 20,796 | 76,498 | **220,123** | 0.8 | 0.9 | 0.9 | 1.0 | 0.9 | **0.8** |
| 1995 | 6,398 | 35,338 | 13,449 | 19,524 | 74,709 | **216,988** | 0.8 | 0.9 | 0.8 | 1.0 | 0.9 | **0.7** |
| 1996 | 7,106 | 37,465 | 12,757 | 18,263 | 75,591 | **224,870** | 0.9 | 0.9 | 0.8 | 0.9 | 0.9 | **0.8** |
| 1997 | 5,906 | 32,789 | 11,301 | 16,220 | 66,216 | **194,351** | 0.7 | 0.8 | 0.7 | 0.8 | 0.8 | **0.6** |

Source: Citizenship and Immigration Canada, and Demography Division, Statistics Canada.

TABLE 2.3  NUMBER OF IMMIGRANT ARRIVALS AND IMMIGRANT ARRIVALS AS A PERCENTAGE OF THE POPULATION, SELECTED AGE GROUPS, CANADA AND JURISDICTIONS, 1996

|  | Number of immigrant arrivals |||||| Immigrant arrivals as a percentage of the population ||||||
|  | Age group |||||| Age group ||||||
|  | 4 to 5 | 6 to 15 | 16 to 19 | 20 to 24 | 4 to 24 | All ages | 4 to 5 | 6 to 15 | 16 to 19 | 20 to 24 | 4 to 24 | All ages |
|---|---|---|---|---|---|---|---|---|---|---|---|---|
| **Canada** | **7,106** | **37,465** | **12,757** | **18,263** | **75,591** | **224,870** | **0.9** | **0.9** | **0.8** | **0.9** | **0.9** | **0.8** |
| Nfld. | 17 | 62 | 19 | 32 | 130 | **480** | 0.1 | 0.1 | 0.1 | 0.1 | 0.1 | **0.1** |
| P.E.I. | 5 | 39 | 8 | 13 | 65 | **186** | 0.1 | 0.2 | 0.1 | 0.1 | 0.2 | **0.1** |
| N.S. | 128 | 750 | 223 | 205 | 1,306 | **3,208** | 0.5 | 0.6 | 0.4 | 0.3 | 0.5 | **0.3** |
| N.B. | 20 | 108 | 25 | 57 | 210 | **690** | 0.1 | 0.1 | 0.1 | 0.1 | 0.1 | **0.1** |
| Que. | 878 | 4,690 | 1,628 | 2,751 | 9,947 | **27,631** | 0.4 | 0.5 | 0.4 | 0.6 | 0.5 | **0.4** |
| Ont. | 3,769 | 19,881 | 6,806 | 9,705 | 40,161 | **119,378** | 1.2 | 1.3 | 1.2 | 1.3 | 1.3 | **1.1** |
| Man. | 140 | 687 | 202 | 380 | 1,409 | **4,166** | 0.4 | 0.4 | 0.3 | 0.5 | 0.4 | **0.4** |
| Sask. | 78 | 309 | 113 | 143 | 643 | **1,802** | 0.3 | 0.2 | 0.2 | 0.2 | 0.2 | **0.2** |
| Alta. | 443 | 2,191 | 793 | 1,218 | 4,645 | **13,949** | 0.5 | 0.5 | 0.5 | 0.6 | 0.5 | **0.5** |
| B.C. | 1,624 | 8,714 | 2,928 | 3,749 | 17,015 | **53,193** | 1.6 | 1.7 | 1.4 | 1.4 | 1.6 | **1.4** |
| Y.T. | .. | 10 | .. | 8 | 21 | **92** | .. | 0.2 | .. | 0.4 | 0.2 | **0.3** |
| N.W.T. | .. | 24 | 11 | .. | 39 | **95** | .. | 0.2 | 0.2 | .. | 0.1 | **0.1** |

Source: Citizenship and Immigration Canada, and Demography Division, Statistics Canada.

TABLE 2.4  NET NUMBER OF INTERJURISDICTIONAL MIGRANTS[1] AND INTERJURISDICTIONAL MIGRANTS AS A PERCENTAGE OF THE POPULATION, JURISDICTIONS, 1971 TO 1997

|  | Newfoundland and Labrador | Prince Edward Island | Nova Scotia | New Brunswick | Quebec | Ontario | Manitoba | Saskatchewan | Alberta | British Columbia | Yukon | Northwest Territories |
|---|---|---|---|---|---|---|---|---|---|---|---|---|
| | | Net number of interjurisdictional migrants |
| 1971 to 1979 | -1,929 | 466 | 763 | 1,236 | -23,462 | -7,679 | -6,684 | -5,164 | 22,869 | 19,862 | -28 | -249 |
| 1980 to 1989 | -3,122 | -31 | 235 | -931 | -13,136 | 17,208 | -4,048 | -6,178 | -3,891 | 14,668 | -338 | -436 |
| 1990 to 1997 | -5,549 | 96 | -1,448 | -859 | -12,411 | -5,328 | -5,441 | -5,502 | 11,124 | 25,881 | -48 | -511 |
| 1990 | -711 | -544 | 573 | 928 | -13,093 | -10,947 | -7,687 | -11,783 | 8,647 | 34,108 | 477 | 32 |
| 1991 | -1,669 | -237 | 306 | -253 | -12,552 | -11,045 | -7,641 | -8,481 | 2,983 | 38,004 | 645 | -60 |
| 1992 | -3,078 | 654 | 96 | -1,402 | -8,420 | -14,189 | -5,544 | -6,348 | -1,181 | 40,099 | -265 | -422 |
| 1993 | -4,952 | 622 | -1,887 | -671 | -8,758 | -9,420 | -4,614 | -5,431 | -1,630 | 37,871 | -1,094 | -36 |
| 1994 | -6,974 | 349 | -2,741 | -813 | -8,947 | -2,841 | -3,220 | -3,652 | -556 | 29,291 | 269 | -165 |
| 1995 | -7,436 | 638 | -1,245 | -369 | -12,626 | -2,822 | -3,566 | -2,161 | 7,656 | 22,025 | 564 | -658 |
| 1996 | -8,134 | 136 | -1,648 | -1,236 | -17,436 | 1,977 | -5,873 | -2,794 | 26,282 | 9,880 | -54 | -1,073 |
| 1997 | -11,434 | -851 | -5,040 | -3,056 | -17,454 | 6,662 | -5,383 | -3,367 | 46,787 | -4,230 | -929 | -1,705 |
| | | Interjurisdictional migrants as a percentage of the population |
| 1971 to 1979 | -0.3 | 0.4 | 0.1 | 0.2 | -0.4 | -0.1 | -0.7 | -0.6 | 1.2 | 0.8 | - | -0.5 |
| 1980 to 1989 | -0.5 | - | - | -0.1 | -0.2 | 0.2 | -0.4 | -0.6 | -0.1 | 0.5 | -1.4 | -0.8 |
| 1990 to 1997 | -1.0 | 0.1 | -0.2 | -0.1 | -0.2 | -0.1 | -0.5 | -0.5 | 0.4 | 0.7 | -0.1 | -0.8 |
| 1990 | -0.1 | -0.4 | 0.1 | 0.1 | -0.2 | -0.1 | -0.7 | -1.2 | 0.3 | 1.0 | 1.7 | 0.1 |
| 1991 | -0.3 | -0.2 | - | - | -0.2 | -0.1 | -0.7 | -0.8 | 0.1 | 1.1 | 2.2 | -0.1 |
| 1992 | -0.5 | 0.5 | - | -0.2 | -0.1 | -0.1 | -0.5 | -0.6 | - | 1.2 | -0.9 | -0.7 |
| 1993 | -0.9 | 0.5 | -0.2 | -0.1 | -0.1 | -0.1 | -0.4 | -0.5 | -0.1 | 1.1 | -3.6 | -0.1 |
| 1994 | -1.2 | 0.3 | -0.3 | -0.1 | -0.1 | - | -0.3 | -0.4 | - | 0.8 | 0.9 | -0.3 |
| 1995 | -1.3 | 0.5 | -0.1 | - | -0.2 | - | -0.3 | -0.2 | 0.3 | 0.6 | 1.8 | -1.0 |
| 1996 | -1.5 | 0.1 | -0.2 | -0.2 | -0.2 | - | -0.5 | -0.3 | 0.9 | 0.3 | -0.2 | -1.6 |
| 1997 | -2.1 | -0.6 | -0.5 | -0.4 | -0.2 | 0.1 | -0.5 | -0.3 | 1.6 | -0.1 | -2.9 | -2.5 |

1  For the net number of interjurisdictional migrants, figures for decades represent the average annual number of interjurisdictional migrants over that time period, (i.e., the count for 1971 to 1979 is the net sum of interjurisdictional migrants for those years divided by the number of years in the time period).

*Source: Demography Division, Statistics Canada.*

TABLE 2.5   NUMBER AND PERCENTAGE OF THE POPULATION WHO MIGRATED WITHIN AND BETWEEN JURISDICTIONS, BY AGE GROUP, CANADA AND JURISDICTIONS, 1995 TO 1996

|  | Total population | Inter-jurisdictional migrants[1] | % inter-jurisdictional migrants | Intra-jurisdictional migrants[2] | % intra-jurisdictional migrants |
|---|---|---|---|---|---|
| **Canada** | | | | | |
| All ages | 28,155,225 | 293,340 | 1.0 | 1,290,150 | 4.6 |
| 0-14 | 5,531,680 | 55,090 | 1.0 | 242,790 | 4.4 |
| 15-24 | 3,848,350 | 68,835 | 1.8 | 278,925 | 7.2 |
| **Newfoundland and Labrador** | | | | | |
| All ages | 541,630 | 7,285 | 1.3 | 18,410 | 3.4 |
| 0-14 | 104,380 | 1,280 | 1.2 | 3,360 | 3.2 |
| 15-24 | 88,230 | 1,995 | 2.3 | 5,120 | 5.8 |
| **Prince Edward Island** | | | | | |
| All ages | 131,050 | 3,440 | 2.6 | 3,795 | 2.9 |
| 0-14 | 27,325 | 665 | 2.4 | 820 | 3.0 |
| 15-24 | 19,350 | 830 | 4.3 | 845 | 4.4 |
| **Nova Scotia** | | | | | |
| All ages | 888,835 | 17,155 | 1.9 | 28,470 | 3.2 |
| 0-14 | 169,145 | 3,215 | 1.9 | 5,020 | 3.0 |
| 15-24 | 123,530 | 3,935 | 3.2 | 6,890 | 5.6 |
| **New Brunswick** | | | | | |
| All ages | 721,070 | 12,710 | 1.8 | 24,330 | 3.4 |
| 0-14 | 136,215 | 2,495 | 1.8 | 4,500 | 3.3 |
| 15-24 | 105,545 | 2,735 | 2.6 | 6,260 | 5.9 |
| **Quebec** | | | | | |
| All ages | 6,958,710 | 25,410 | 0.4 | 352,880 | 5.1 |
| 0-14 | 1,286,170 | 4,215 | 0.3 | 59,025 | 4.6 |
| 15-24 | 945,245 | 5,955 | 0.6 | 78,285 | 8.3 |
| **Ontario** | | | | | |
| All ages | 10,496,475 | 67,080 | 0.6 | 479,750 | 4.6 |
| 0-14 | 2,070,510 | 12,715 | 0.6 | 92,175 | 4.5 |
| 15-24 | 1,399,130 | 14,925 | 1.1 | 94,650 | 6.8 |
| **Manitoba** | | | | | |
| All ages | 1,084,900 | 15,615 | 1.4 | 30,220 | 2.8 |
| 0-14 | 229,105 | 3,255 | 1.4 | 7,190 | 3.1 |
| 15-24 | 152,995 | 3,615 | 2.4 | 7,985 | 5.2 |
| **Saskatchewan** | | | | | |
| All ages | 963,305 | 18,255 | 1.9 | 40,300 | 4.2 |
| 0-14 | 215,245 | 4,370 | 2.0 | 9,635 | 4.5 |
| 15-24 | 141,185 | 4,625 | 3.3 | 11,940 | 8.5 |
| **Alberta** | | | | | |
| All ages | 2,631,835 | 54,690 | 2.1 | 112,285 | 4.3 |
| 0-14 | 577,035 | 10,315 | 1.8 | 24,975 | 4.3 |
| 15-24 | 375,690 | 13,865 | 3.7 | 27,315 | 7.3 |
| **British Columbia** | | | | | |
| All ages | 3,644,505 | 66,205 | 1.8 | 196,280 | 5.4 |
| 0-14 | 690,060 | 11,515 | 1.7 | 35,160 | 5.1 |
| 15-24 | 483,035 | 15,100 | 3.1 | 38,975 | 8.1 |
| **Yukon** | | | | | |
| All ages | 30,220 | 2,360 | 7.8 | 745 | 2.5 |
| 0-14 | 6,960 | 470 | 6.8 | 140 | 2.0 |
| 15-24 | 4,110 | 545 | 13.3 | 115 | 2.8 |
| **Northwest Territories** | | | | | |
| All ages | 62,680 | 3,130 | 5.0 | 2,670 | 4.3 |
| 0-14 | 19,535 | 575 | 2.9 | 795 | 4.1 |
| 15-24 | 10,305 | 715 | 6.9 | 540 | 5.2 |

1   Inter-jurisdictional migrants are individuals who, on Census day, were residing in a different jurisdiction than they were one year earlier.
2   Intra-jurisdictional migrants are individuals, who on Census day, were residing in a different Census Subdivision within the same jurisdiction than they were one year earlier.

*Source: 1996 Census, Statistics Canada.*

TABLE 2.6  CHILDREN 15 YEARS OF AGE AND YOUNGER LIVING IN LOW INCOME FAMILIES[1], CANADA AND PROVINCES, 1980 TO 1996

|        | 1980 | 1981 | 1982 | 1983 | 1984 | 1985 | 1986 | 1987 | 1988 | 1989 | 1990 | 1991 | 1992 | 1993 | 1994 | 1995 | 1996 |
|--------|------|------|------|------|------|------|------|------|------|------|------|------|------|------|------|------|------|
| **Number (000s)** ||||||||||||||||||
| Canada | 932 | 975 | 1,133 | 1,159 | 1,232 | 1,145 | 1,036 | 1,063 | 974 | 942 | 1,092 | 1,170 | 1,219 | 1,375 | 1,247 | 1,351 | 1,365 |
| Nfld.  | 55 | 38 | 46 | 53 | 47 | 46 | 41 | 40 | 32 | 28 | 30 | 29 | 37 | 29 | 30 | 33 | 24 |
| P.E.I. | 5  | 7  | 6  | 5  | 6  | 5  | 5  | 5  | 4  | 4  | 4  | 5  | 4  | 4  | 4  | 5  | 6  |
| N.S.   | 34 | 37 | 46 | 46 | 42 | 41 | 36 | 33 | 29 | 33 | 33 | 40 | 37 | 47 | 41 | 44 | 47 |
| N.B.   | 38 | 44 | 48 | 50 | 47 | 37 | 32 | 35 | 32 | 30 | 31 | 31 | 26 | 30 | 29 | 39 | 32 |
| Que.   | 290 | 299 | 319 | 311 | 347 | 307 | 287 | 308 | 283 | 244 | 286 | 303 | 301 | 333 | 299 | 342 | 330 |
| Ont.   | 298 | 287 | 361 | 354 | 346 | 330 | 282 | 282 | 270 | 261 | 340 | 397 | 386 | 501 | 439 | 468 | 504 |
| Man.   | 46 | 49 | 59 | 58 | 52 | 57 | 57 | 58 | 55 | 58 | 60 | 78 | 61 | 67 | 58 | 59 | 67 |
| Sask.  | 29 | 49 | 46 | 57 | 62 | 55 | 64 | 50 | 55 | 55 | 53 | 56 | 60 | 63 | 57 | 53 | 55 |
| Alta.  | 68 | 72 | 81 | 117 | 141 | 125 | 99 | 126 | 111 | 122 | 130 | 127 | 165 | 138 | 123 | 147 | 137 |
| B.C.   | 70 | 91 | 120 | 107 | 141 | 142 | 132 | 125 | 103 | 106 | 126 | 104 | 143 | 163 | 166 | 163 | 163 |
| **Percentage** ||||||||||||||||||
| Canada | 16 | 17 | 20 | 20 | 22 | 20 | 18 | 18 | 17 | 16 | 18 | 19 | 20 | 22 | 20 | 22 | 22 |
| Nfld.  | 30 | 22 | 27 | 31 | 29 | 29 | 26 | 26 | 21 | 20 | 21 | 21 | 28 | 23 | 24 | 27 | 21 |
| P.E.I. | 16 | 24 | 21 | 23 | 22 | 21 | 19 | 17 | 13 | 13 | 14 | 16 | 14 | 12 | 14 | 15 | 20 |
| N.S.   | 17 | 19 | 23 | 23 | 22 | 21 | 19 | 17 | 15 | 17 | 17 | 21 | 20 | 24 | 21 | 23 | 25 |
| N.B.   | 20 | 24 | 27 | 28 | 28 | 22 | 19 | 21 | 19 | 18 | 19 | 20 | 16 | 19 | 19 | 25 | 21 |
| Que.   | 19 | 20 | 22 | 21 | 24 | 22 | 20 | 22 | 20 | 17 | 19 | 21 | 20 | 22 | 20 | 23 | 23 |
| Ont.   | 15 | 14 | 18 | 18 | 17 | 16 | 14 | 14 | 13 | 12 | 15 | 18 | 17 | 22 | 19 | 20 | 21 |
| Man.   | 19 | 21 | 25 | 24 | 22 | 24 | 21 | 22 | 23 | 24 | 25 | 32 | 25 | 28 | 24 | 24 | 28 |
| Sask.  | 12 | 20 | 19 | 23 | 25 | 22 | 26 | 20 | 23 | 23 | 22 | 23 | 25 | 26 | 24 | 23 | 24 |
| Alta.  | 12 | 12 | 14 | 20 | 24 | 21 | 17 | 21 | 19 | 20 | 21 | 20 | 26 | 21 | 19 | 23 | 21 |
| B.C.   | 11 | 15 | 19 | 17 | 22 | 22 | 21 | 19 | 16 | 16 | 18 | 15 | 20 | 22 | 22 | 21 | 21 |

1  Estimates based on Low Income Cut-offs, 1992 base; See Appendix 4.
*Source: Survey of Consumer Finances, Statistics Canada.*

**TABLE 2.7**    PERCENTAGE DISTRIBUTION OF THE POPULATION AGED 25 TO 54, BY HIGHEST COMPLETED LEVEL OF EDUCATION AND GENDER, CANADA AND PROVINCES, 1990 AND 1998

|  | Both sexes ||||  Males |||| Females ||||
|---|---|---|---|---|---|---|---|---|---|---|---|---|
| | Less than high school | High school graduate | College and trade graduate | University graduate | Less than high school | High school graduate | College and trade graduate | University graduate | Less than high school | High school graduate | College and trade graduate | University graduate |
| **1990** | | | | | | | | | | | | |
| **Canada** | 27 | 31 | 25 | 18 | 27 | 28 | 25 | 19 | 26 | 34 | 24 | 16 |
| Nfld. | 38 | 22 | 29 | 11 | 36 | 21 | 30 | 13 | 39 | 22 | 29 | 9 |
| P.E.I. | 37 | 25 | 26 | 12 | 42 | 24 | 21 | 13 | 32 | 27 | 30 | 11 |
| N.S. | 30 | 23 | 30 | 17 | 32 | 21 | 29 | 18 | 29 | 25 | 31 | 15 |
| N.B. | 34 | 29 | 25 | 12 | 36 | 26 | 25 | 13 | 32 | 31 | 25 | 12 |
| Que. | 32 | 28 | 24 | 17 | 32 | 25 | 25 | 19 | 32 | 30 | 22 | 15 |
| Ont. | 25 | 32 | 24 | 19 | 25 | 29 | 25 | 21 | 24 | 34 | 24 | 17 |
| Man. | 29 | 32 | 23 | 17 | 30 | 30 | 22 | 18 | 28 | 34 | 23 | 15 |
| Sask. | 27 | 33 | 24 | 15 | 30 | 33 | 22 | 16 | 25 | 34 | 27 | 15 |
| Alta. | 21 | 34 | 28 | 18 | 21 | 31 | 29 | 19 | 20 | 37 | 26 | 17 |
| B.C. | 19 | 38 | 26 | 18 | 20 | 34 | 27 | 19 | 19 | 41 | 24 | 16 |
| **1998** | | | | | | | | | | | | |
| **Canada** | 18 | 29 | 31 | 23 | 18 | 27 | 31 | 23 | 17 | 30 | 31 | 22 |
| Nfld. | 29 | 21 | 37 | 14 | 29 | 20 | 37 | 14 | 29 | 22 | 37 | 13 |
| P.E.I. | 26 | 24 | 33 | 18 | 31 | 23 | 29 | 16 | 20 | 25 | 36 | 20 |
| N.S. | 22 | 22 | 36 | 21 | 24 | 20 | 35 | 21 | 19 | 23 | 37 | 21 |
| N.B. | 22 | 30 | 30 | 17 | 24 | 29 | 31 | 16 | 21 | 32 | 30 | 17 |
| Que. | 22 | 24 | 31 | 23 | 22 | 22 | 32 | 24 | 22 | 25 | 31 | 22 |
| Ont. | 16 | 30 | 30 | 24 | 16 | 29 | 29 | 25 | 16 | 32 | 30 | 23 |
| Man. | 21 | 29 | 28 | 22 | 23 | 28 | 27 | 22 | 18 | 31 | 29 | 22 |
| Sask. | 18 | 32 | 31 | 19 | 22 | 32 | 28 | 19 | 15 | 33 | 34 | 19 |
| Alta. | 14 | 30 | 34 | 21 | 15 | 28 | 35 | 22 | 13 | 33 | 34 | 21 |
| B.C. | 13 | 33 | 31 | 23 | 14 | 31 | 31 | 24 | 12 | 35 | 30 | 22 |

Note:    The category "High school graduate" includes individuals who have some postsecondary education (not completed).
*Source:* Labour Force Survey, Statistics Canada.

**TABLE 2.8** PERCENTAGE DISTRIBUTION OF THE POPULATION AGED 25 TO 29, BY HIGHEST COMPLETED LEVEL OF EDUCATION AND GENDER, CANADA AND PROVINCES, 1990 AND 1998

|  | \multicolumn{4}{c}{Both sexes} | \multicolumn{4}{c}{Males} | \multicolumn{4}{c}{Females} |
|---|---|---|---|---|---|---|---|---|---|---|---|---|
|  | Less than high school | High school graduate | College and trade graduate | University graduate | Less than high school | High school graduate | College and trade graduate | University graduate | Less than high school | High school graduate | College and trade graduate | University graduate |
| **1990** | | | | | | | | | | | | |
| **Canada** | **20** | **36** | **27** | **17** | **21** | **35** | **27** | **17** | **19** | **37** | **27** | **17** |
| Nfld. | 28 | 24 | 35 | 13 | 30 | 24 | 33 | 13 | 26 | 25 | 36 | 13 |
| P.E.I. | 30 | 33 | 26 | 10 | 36 | 30 | 22 | 11 | 24 | 36 | 31 | 10 |
| N.S. | 24 | 26 | 33 | 18 | 27 | 23 | 30 | 19 | 20 | 28 | 35 | 17 |
| N.B. | 23 | 38 | 27 | 13 | 27 | 36 | 24 | 13 | 19 | 40 | 29 | 12 |
| Que. | 21 | 32 | 29 | 18 | 24 | 28 | 30 | 18 | 18 | 35 | 29 | 18 |
| Ont. | 19 | 36 | 26 | 18 | 20 | 35 | 27 | 18 | 18 | 37 | 26 | 18 |
| Man. | 23 | 40 | 22 | 16 | 24 | 41 | 20 | 16 | 23 | 38 | 23 | 16 |
| Sask. | 19 | 41 | 26 | 14 | 21 | 42 | 24 | 14 | 18 | 40 | 28 | 14 |
| Alta. | 19 | 41 | 26 | 15 | 19 | 40 | 27 | 14 | 18 | 42 | 25 | 15 |
| B.C. | 16 | 44 | 26 | 14 | 16 | 44 | 26 | 14 | 17 | 44 | 26 | 14 |
| **1998** | | | | | | | | | | | | |
| **Canada** | **13** | **29** | **32** | **26** | **14** | **31** | **30** | **25** | **12** | **28** | **33** | **28** |
| Nfld. | 17 | 27 | 38 | 18 | 20 | 28 | 37 | 16 | 14 | 26 | 39 | 20 |
| P.E.I. | 17 | 27 | 33 | 22 | 23 | 27 | 33 | 17 | 11 | 28 | 33 | 28 |
| N.S. | 15 | 25 | 35 | 25 | 18 | 24 | 34 | 24 | 11 | 25 | 37 | 27 |
| N.B. | 15 | 33 | 29 | 23 | 18 | 35 | 27 | 20 | 12 | 30 | 31 | 26 |
| Que. | 15 | 20 | 37 | 28 | 16 | 21 | 38 | 25 | 15 | 20 | 35 | 31 |
| Ont. | 11 | 30 | 30 | 28 | 12 | 32 | 28 | 28 | 10 | 29 | 33 | 29 |
| Man. | 15 | 33 | 27 | 25 | 17 | 36 | 24 | 23 | 13 | 30 | 30 | 28 |
| Sask. | 14 | 33 | 32 | 21 | 15 | 37 | 28 | 20 | 13 | 29 | 36 | 21 |
| Alta. | 12 | 33 | 32 | 22 | 13 | 36 | 30 | 21 | 12 | 30 | 35 | 23 |
| B.C. | 11 | 36 | 28 | 25 | 11 | 38 | 27 | 24 | 10 | 34 | 29 | 27 |

Note: The category "High school graduate" includes individuals who have some postsecondary education (not completed).
Source: Labour Force Survey, Statistics Canada.

# Chapter 3 Tables

## CHAPTER 3 TABLES

**TABLE 3.1    INSTITUTIONS[1], BY LEVEL AND SIZE OF FULL-TIME ENROLMENT, CANADA AND JURISDICTIONS, 1996-97**

| Level and size of institution | Canada | Nfld. | P.E.I. | N.S. | N.B. | Que. | Ont. | Man.[2] | Sask. | Alta. | B.C. | Y.T. | N.W.T. | Overseas |
|---|---|---|---|---|---|---|---|---|---|---|---|---|---|---|
| **Elementary-secondary[3]** | | | | | | | | | | | | | | |
| 49 and less | 1,963 | 63 | 3 | 38 | 29 | 260 | 664 | 169 | 157 | 286 | 276 | 3 | 14 | 1 |
| 50 – 99 | 1,150 | 66 | 4 | 39 | 43 | 246 | 276 | 68 | 84 | 158 | 151 | 5 | 9 | 1 |
| 100 – 199 | 2,655 | 110 | 13 | 94 | 71 | 494 | 799 | 154 | 226 | 320 | 343 | 9 | 22 | - |
| 200 – 299 | 2,907 | 90 | 16 | 84 | 76 | 516 | 1,048 | 162 | 208 | 316 | 366 | 6 | 19 | - |
| 300 – 399 | 2,538 | 61 | 9 | 81 | 65 | 531 | 907 | 110 | 115 | 285 | 358 | 4 | 12 | - |
| 400 – 499 | 1,741 | 28 | 11 | 61 | 46 | 321 | 703 | 79 | 64 | 200 | 221 | 1 | 6 | - |
| 500 – 999 | 2,368 | 43 | 12 | 79 | 61 | 493 | 1,026 | 90 | 56 | 257 | 246 | 2 | 3 | - |
| 1,000 – 1,499 | 535 | 1 | 2 | 17 | 8 | 127 | 256 | 17 | 9 | 28 | 70 | - | - | - |
| 1,500 – 1,999 | 135 | - | - | 1 | 3 | 35 | 63 | 1 | 1 | 13 | 18 | - | - | - |
| 2,000 – and over | 41 | - | - | - | 1 | 24 | 10 | - | - | 2 | 4 | - | - | - |
| **Total** | 16,033 | 462 | 70 | 494 | 403 | 3,047 | 5,752 | 850 | 920 | 1,865 | 2,053 | 30 | 85 | 2 |
| **Community colleges and related institutions[4]** | | | | | | | | | | | | | | |
| 99 and less | 46 | 2 | 1 | 4 | 3 | 15 | 10 | 2 | 3 | 3 | 2 | - | 1 | - |
| 100 – 299 | 27 | 3 | - | 2 | - | 12 | 4 | 1 | - | 1 | 2 | 1 | 1 | - |
| 300 – 499 | 7 | - | - | - | - | 3 | - | - | - | - | 4 | - | - | - |
| 500 – 999 | 23 | 3 | - | 1 | - | 9 | 2 | 1 | - | 4 | 3 | - | - | - |
| 1,000 – 2,999 | 49 | 2 | 1 | - | - | 27 | 5 | 1 | 1 | 4 | 8 | - | - | - |
| 3,000 – 4,999 | 29 | - | - | - | 1 | 15 | 8 | - | - | 3 | 2 | - | - | - |
| 5,000 – 9,999 | 20 | - | - | 1 | - | 9 | 9 | - | - | 1 | - | - | - | - |
| 10,000 – 19,999 | 3 | - | - | - | - | - | 3 | - | - | - | - | - | - | - |
| 20,000 – 29,999 | - | - | - | - | - | - | - | - | - | - | - | - | - | - |
| 30,000 – and over | - | - | - | - | - | - | - | - | - | - | - | - | - | - |
| **Total** | 204 | 10 | 2 | 8 | 4 | 90 | 41 | 5 | 4 | 16 | 21 | - | 2 | - |
| **Universities and other degree-granting institutions[5]** | | | | | | | | | | | | | | |
| 99 and less | 10 | - | - | 2 | - | - | 1 | 2 | 1 | 3 | 1 | - | - | - |
| 100 – 299 | 6 | - | - | - | 1 | - | - | 1 | 1 | 1 | 2 | - | - | - |
| 300 – 499 | 4 | - | - | 1 | - | - | 2 | - | - | 1 | - | - | - | - |
| 500 – 999 | 5 | - | - | 3 | - | - | - | - | - | 2 | - | - | - | - |
| 1,000 – 2,999 | 13 | - | 1 | 3 | 2 | 1 | 2 | 2 | - | - | 2 | - | - | - |
| 3,000 – 4,999 | 5 | - | - | 2 | 1 | - | 1 | - | - | 1 | - | - | - | - |
| 5,000 – 9,999 | 8 | - | - | 2 | 1 | - | 4 | - | 1 | - | - | - | - | - |
| 10,000 – 19,999 | 15 | 1 | - | - | - | 2 | 8 | 1 | 1 | - | 2 | - | - | - |
| 20,000 – 29,999 | 8 | - | - | - | - | 3 | 2 | - | - | 2 | 1 | - | - | - |
| 30,000 – and over | 2 | - | - | - | - | 1 | 1 | - | - | - | - | - | - | - |
| **Total** | 76 | 1 | 1 | 13 | 5 | 7 | 21 | 6 | 4 | 10 | 8 | - | - | - |

1   See Appendix 2 for lists of community colleges and related institutions, and universities and other degree-granting institutions.
2   Statistics Canada only began collecting data from St. Boniface College in 1998-99 (non-university postsecondary programs) and as a consequence it is not included in the count of community colleges.
3   Includes all public, private and federal schools, and schools for the visually and hearing impaired.
4   Includes health-science centres which offer medical type programs, whether or not they are associated with a hospital.
5   Includes religious-based institutions that grant recognized university level degrees. The reporting of these institutions may not be complete in all jurisdictions.

*Source:   Centre for Education Statistics, Statistics Canada.*

TABLE 3.2    PERCENTAGE DISTRIBUTION OF INSTITUTIONS[1], BY LEVEL AND SIZE OF FULL-TIME ENROLMENT, CANADA AND JURISDICTIONS, 1996-97

| Level and size of institution | Canada | Nfld. | P.E.I. | N.S. | N.B. | Que. | Ont. | Man.[2] | Sask. | Alta. | B.C. | Y.T. | N.W.T. | Overseas |
|---|---|---|---|---|---|---|---|---|---|---|---|---|---|---|
| **Elementary-secondary**[3] | | | | | | | | | | | | | | |
| 49 and less | 12 | 14 | 4 | 8 | 7 | 9 | 12 | 20 | 17 | 15 | 13 | 10 | 16 | 50 |
| 50 – 99 | 7 | 14 | 6 | 8 | 11 | 8 | 5 | 8 | 9 | 8 | 7 | 17 | 11 | 50 |
| 100 – 199 | 17 | 24 | 19 | 19 | 18 | 16 | 14 | 18 | 25 | 17 | 17 | 30 | 26 | - |
| 200 – 299 | 18 | 19 | 23 | 17 | 19 | 17 | 18 | 19 | 23 | 17 | 18 | 20 | 22 | - |
| 300 – 399 | 16 | 13 | 13 | 16 | 16 | 17 | 16 | 13 | 13 | 15 | 17 | 13 | 14 | - |
| 400 – 499 | 11 | 6 | 16 | 12 | 11 | 11 | 12 | 9 | 7 | 11 | 11 | 3 | 7 | - |
| 500 – 999 | 15 | 9 | 17 | 16 | 15 | 16 | 18 | 11 | 6 | 14 | 12 | 7 | 4 | - |
| 1,000 – 1,499 | 3 | - | 3 | 3 | 2 | 4 | 4 | 2 | 1 | 2 | 3 | - | - | - |
| 1,500 – 1,999 | 1 | - | - | - | 1 | 1 | 1 | - | - | 1 | 1 | - | - | - |
| 2,000 – and over | - | - | - | - | - | 1 | - | - | - | - | - | - | - | - |
| **Community college and related institutions**[4] | | | | | | | | | | | | | | |
| 99 and less | 23 | 20 | 50 | 50 | 75 | 17 | 24 | 40 | 75 | 19 | 10 | - | 50 | - |
| 100 – 299 | 13 | 30 | - | 25 | - | 13 | 10 | 20 | - | 6 | 10 | 100 | 50 | - |
| 300 – 499 | 3 | - | - | - | - | 3 | - | - | - | - | 19 | - | - | - |
| 500 – 999 | 11 | 30 | - | 13 | - | 10 | 5 | 20 | - | 25 | 14 | - | - | - |
| 1,000 – 2,999 | 24 | 20 | 50 | - | - | 30 | 12 | 20 | 25 | 25 | 38 | - | - | - |
| 3,000 – 4,999 | 14 | - | - | - | 25 | 17 | 20 | - | - | 19 | 10 | - | - | - |
| 5,000 – 9,999 | 10 | - | - | 13 | - | 10 | 22 | - | - | 6 | - | - | - | - |
| 10,000 – 19,999 | 1 | - | - | - | - | - | 7 | - | - | - | - | - | - | - |
| 20,000 – 29,999 | - | - | - | - | - | - | - | - | - | - | - | - | - | - |
| 30,000 – and over | - | - | - | - | - | - | - | - | - | - | - | - | - | - |
| **Universities and other degree-granting institutions**[5] | | | | | | | | | | | | | | |
| 99 and less | 13 | - | - | 15 | - | - | 5 | 33 | 25 | 30 | 13 | - | - | - |
| 100 – 299 | 8 | - | - | - | 20 | - | - | 17 | 25 | 10 | 25 | - | - | - |
| 300 – 499 | 5 | - | - | 8 | - | - | 10 | - | - | 10 | - | - | - | - |
| 500 – 999 | 7 | - | - | 23 | - | - | - | - | - | 20 | - | - | - | - |
| 1,000 – 2,999 | 17 | - | 100 | 23 | 40 | 14 | 10 | 33 | - | - | 25 | - | - | - |
| 3,000 – 4,999 | 7 | - | - | 15 | 20 | - | 5 | - | - | 10 | - | - | - | - |
| 5,000 – 9,999 | 11 | - | - | 15 | 20 | - | 19 | - | 25 | - | - | - | - | - |
| 10,000 – 19,999 | 20 | 100 | - | - | - | 29 | 38 | 17 | 25 | - | 25 | - | - | - |
| 20,000 – 29,999 | 11 | - | - | - | - | 43 | 10 | - | - | 20 | 13 | - | - | - |
| 30,000 – and over | 3 | - | - | - | - | 14 | 5 | - | - | - | - | - | - | - |

1   See Appendix 2 for lists of community colleges and related institutions, and universities and other degree-granting institutions.
2   Statistics Canada only began collecting data from St. Boniface College in 1998-99 (non-university postsecondary programs) and as a consequence it is not included in the count of community colleges.
3   Includes all public, private and federal schools, and schools for the visually and hearing impaired.
4   Includes health-science centres which offer medical type programs, whether or not they are associated with a hospital.
5   Includes religious-based institutions that grant recognized university level degrees. The reporting of these institutions may not be complete in all jurisdictions.

*Source:* Centre for Education Statistics, Statistics Canada.

TABLE 3.3  NUMBER OF FULL-TIME EDUCATORS IN PUBLIC ELEMENTARY–SECONDARY SCHOOLS BY GENDER, CANADA AND JURISDICTIONS, 1986-87 TO 1996-97

|  | Canada | Nfld. | P.E.I. | N.S. | N.B. | Que. | Ont. | Man. | Sask. | Alta. | B.C. | Y.T. | N.W.T. |
|---|---|---|---|---|---|---|---|---|---|---|---|---|---|
| **Both sexes** | | | | | | | | | | | | | |
| 1986-87 | **254,862** | 8,059 | 1,283 | 9,930 | 7,479 | 60,557 | 96,519 | 11,483 | 10,736 | 23,864 | 23,954 | 292 | 706 |
| 1987-88 | **259,331** | 8,019 | 1,310 | 10,015 | 7,658 | 60,110 | 101,434 | 10,847 | 10,688 | 23,643 | 24,588 | 275 | 744 |
| 1988-89 | **265,913** | 8,034 | 1,322 | 9,918 | 7,630 | 59,685 | 106,701 | 11,538 | 10,789 | 23,792 | 25,394 | 307 | 803 |
| 1989-90 | **272,833** | 7,932 | 1,375 | 10,031 | 7,707 | 59,024 | 111,352 | 11,889 | 10,740 | 24,806 | 26,834 | 319 | 824 |
| 1990-91 | **279,740** | 7,956 | 1,364 | 9,680 | 8,026 | 60,120 | 116,203 | 11,711 | 10,303 | 25,411 | 27,722 | 373 | 871 |
| 1991-92 | **284,843** | 7,741 | 1,352 | 9,776 | 8,104 | 59,794 | 119,824 | 11,465 | 10,529 | 26,044 | 28,747 | 376 | 1,091 |
| 1992-93 | **283,215** | 7,699 | 1,361 | 9,498 | 7,973 | 59,333 | 119,769 | 11,406 | 10,004 | 25,909 | 28,676 | 416 | 1,171 |
| 1993-94 | **276,366** | 7,630 | 1,351 | 9,495 | 7,854 | 58,726 | 114,176 | 11,402 | 10,116 | 25,516 | 28,378 | 428 | 1,294 |
| 1994-95 | **271,058** | 7,359 | 1,327 | 8,996 | 7,677 | 58,085 | 111,132 | 11,186 | 10,034 | 24,867 | 28,686 | 430 | 1,279 |
| 1995-96 | **273,748** | 7,233 | 1,334 | 8,724 | 7,583 | 57,510 | 112,640 | 10,883 | 10,064 | 26,961 | 29,149 | 430 | 1,237 |
| 1996-97 | **267,808** | 6,939 | 1,361 | 8,799 | 7,427 | 56,528 | 108,737 | 10,618 | 9,745 | 26,482 | 29,330 | 450 | 1,392 |
|  | Canada | Nfld. | P.E.I. | N.S. | N.B. | Que. | Ont. | Man. | Sask. | Alta. | B.C. | Y.T. | N.W.T. |
| **Males** | | | | | | | | | | | | | |
| 1986-87 | **109,452** | 3,853 | 571 | 4,208 | 3,052 | 21,876 | 42,686 | 5,474 | 4,908 | 10,218 | 12,165 | 130 | 311 |
| 1987-88 | **109,459** | 3,820 | 577 | 4,222 | 3,071 | 21,491[e] | 43,609 | 5,208 | 4,850 | 10,068 | 12,103 | 112 | 328 |
| 1988-89 | **109,878** | 3,808 | 575 | 4,149 | 3,051 | 21,114 | 44,354 | 5,366 | 4,817 | 9,992 | 12,194 | 120 | 338 |
| 1989-90 | **110,005** | 3,733 | 579 | 4,177 | 3,039 | 20,645 | 44,632 | 5,419 | 4,713 | 10,198 | 12,426 | 127 | 317 |
| 1990-91 | **110,961** | 3,676 | 572 | 4,048 | 3,173 | 20,908 | 45,361 | 5,272 | 4,635 | 10,285 | 12,563 | 142 | 326 |
| 1991-92 | **111,283** | 3,589 | 575 | 3,979 | 2,975 | 20,675 | 46,043 | 5,169 | 4,500 | 10,417 | 12,838 | 140 | 383 |
| 1992-93 | **109,961** | 3,508 | 576 | 3,901 | 2,922 | 20,444 | 45,613 | 5,067 | 4,237 | 10,350 | 12,783 | 150 | 410 |
| 1993-94 | **107,014** | 3,447 | 561 | 3,852 | 2,855 | 20,188 | 43,631 | 5,001 | 4,224 | 10,093 | 12,558 | 154 | 450 |
| 1994-95 | **103,998** | 3,292 | 543 | 3,602 | 2,786 | 19,854 | 41,941 | 4,844 | 4,132 | 9,855 | 12,539 | 155 | 455 |
| 1995-96 | **103,177** | 3,309 | 544 | 3,457 | 2,689 | 19,419 | 41,682 | 4,689 | 4,070 | 10,204 | 12,545 | 155 | 414 |
| 1996-97 | **99,544** | 3,124 | 549 | 3,365 | 2,593 | 18,810 | 39,517 | 4,572 | 3,929 | 9,958 | 12,484 | 166 | 477 |
|  | Canada | Nfld. | P.E.I. | N.S. | N.B. | Que. | Ont. | Man. | Sask. | Alta. | B.C. | Y.T. | N.W.T. |
| **Females** | | | | | | | | | | | | | |
| 1986-87 | **145,410** | 4,206 | 712 | 5,722 | 4,427 | 38,681 | 53,833 | 6,009 | 5,828 | 13,646 | 11,789 | 162 | 395 |
| 1987-88 | **149,872** | 4,199 | 733 | 5,793 | 4,587 | 38,619[e] | 57,825 | 5,639 | 5,838 | 13,575 | 12,485 | 163 | 416 |
| 1988-89 | **156,035** | 4,226 | 747 | 5,769 | 4,579 | 38,571 | 62,347 | 6,172 | 5,972 | 13,800 | 13,200 | 187 | 465 |
| 1989-90 | **162,828** | 4,199 | 796 | 5,854 | 4,668 | 38,379 | 66,720 | 6,470 | 6,027 | 14,608 | 14,408 | 192 | 507 |
| 1990-91 | **168,779** | 4,280 | 792 | 5,632 | 4,853 | 39,212 | 70,842 | 6,439 | 5,668 | 15,126 | 15,159 | 231 | 545 |
| 1991-92 | **173,560** | 4,152 | 777 | 5,797 | 5,129 | 39,119 | 73,781 | 6,296 | 6,029 | 15,627 | 15,909 | 236 | 708 |
| 1992-93 | **173,249** | 4,191 | 785 | 5,597 | 5,051 | 38,889 | 74,156 | 6,334 | 5,767 | 15,559 | 15,893 | 266 | 761 |
| 1993-94 | **169,351** | 4,183 | 790 | 5,643 | 4,999 | 38,538 | 70,545 | 6,400 | 5,892 | 15,423 | 15,820 | 274 | 844 |
| 1994-95 | **167,056** | 4,067 | 784 | 5,394 | 4,891 | 38,231 | 69,191 | 6,338 | 5,902 | 15,012 | 16,147 | 275 | 824 |
| 1995-96 | **170,571** | 3,924 | 790 | 5,267 | 4,894 | 38,091 | 70,958 | 6,194 | 5,994 | 16,757 | 16,604 | 275 | 823 |
| 1996-97 | **168,264** | 3,815 | 812 | 5,434 | 4,834 | 37,718 | 69,220 | 6,046 | 5,816 | 16,524 | 16,846 | 284 | 915 |

*Source:* Centre for Education Statistics, Statistics Canada; Statistiques de l'éducation - Enseignement primaire, secondaire, collégial et universitaire, Gouvernement du Québec, Ministère de l'Éducation (for Quebec data).

EDUCATION INDICATORS IN CANADA

**TABLE 3.4  GENDER DISTRIBUTION OF FULL-TIME EDUCATORS IN PUBLIC ELEMENTARY–SECONDARY SCHOOLS, CANADA AND JURISDICTIONS, 1986-87 TO 1996-97**

|  | Canada | Nfld. | P.E.I. | N.S. | N.B. | Que. | Ont. | Man. | Sask. | Alta. | B.C. | Y.T. | N.W.T. |
|---|---|---|---|---|---|---|---|---|---|---|---|---|---|
| **Males** | | | | | | | | | | | | | |
| 1986-87 | **43** | 48 | 45 | 42 | 41 | 36 | 44 | 48 | 46 | 43 | 51 | 45 | 44 |
| 1987-88 | **42** | 48 | 44 | 42 | 40 | 36 e | 43 | 48 | 45 | 43 | 49 | 41 | 45 |
| 1988-89 | **41** | 47 | 43 | 42 | 40 | 35 | 42 | 47 | 45 | 42 | 48 | 39 | 42 |
| 1989-90 | **40** | 47 | 42 | 42 | 39 | 35 | 40 | 46 | 44 | 41 | 46 | 40 | 38 |
| 1990-91 | **40** | 46 | 42 | 42 | 40 | 35 | 39 | 45 | 45 | 40 | 45 | 38 | 37 |
| 1991-92 | **39** | 46 | 43 | 41 | 37 | 35 | 38 | 45 | 43 | 40 | 45 | 37 | 35 |
| 1992-93 | **39** | 46 | 42 | 41 | 37 | 34 | 38 | 44 | 42 | 40 | 45 | 36 | 35 |
| 1993-94 | **39** | 45 | 42 | 41 | 36 | 34 | 38 | 44 | 42 | 40 | 44 | 36 | 35 |
| 1994-95 | **38** | 45 | 41 | 40 | 36 | 34 | 38 | 43 | 41 | 40 | 44 | 36 | 36 |
| 1995-96 | **38** | 46 | 41 | 40 | 35 | 34 | 37 | 43 | 40 | 38 | 43 | 36 | 33 |
| 1996-97 | **37** | 45 | 40 | 38 | 35 | 33 | 36 | 43 | 40 | 38 | 43 | 37 | 34 |
|  | Canada | Nfld. | P.E.I. | N.S. | N.B. | Que. | Ont. | Man. | Sask. | Alta. | B.C. | Y.T. | N.W.T. |
| **Females** | | | | | | | | | | | | | |
| 1986-87 | **57** | 52 | 55 | 58 | 59 | 64 | 56 | 52 | 54 | 57 | 49 | 55 | 56 |
| 1987-88 | **58** | 52 | 56 | 58 | 60 | 64 e | 57 | 52 | 55 | 57 | 51 | 59 | 56 |
| 1988-89 | **59** | 53 | 57 | 58 | 60 | 65 | 58 | 53 | 55 | 58 | 52 | 61 | 58 |
| 1989-90 | **60** | 53 | 58 | 58 | 61 | 65 | 60 | 54 | 56 | 59 | 54 | 60 | 62 |
| 1990-91 | **60** | 54 | 58 | 58 | 60 | 65 | 61 | 55 | 55 | 60 | 55 | 62 | 63 |
| 1991-92 | **61** | 54 | 57 | 59 | 63 | 65 | 62 | 55 | 57 | 60 | 55 | 63 | 65 |
| 1992-93 | **61** | 54 | 58 | 59 | 63 | 66 | 62 | 56 | 58 | 60 | 55 | 64 | 65 |
| 1993-94 | **61** | 55 | 58 | 59 | 64 | 66 | 62 | 56 | 58 | 60 | 56 | 64 | 65 |
| 1994-95 | **62** | 55 | 59 | 60 | 64 | 66 | 62 | 57 | 59 | 60 | 56 | 64 | 64 |
| 1995-96 | **62** | 54 | 59 | 60 | 65 | 66 | 63 | 57 | 60 | 62 | 57 | 64 | 67 |
| 1996-97 | **63** | 55 | 60 | 62 | 65 | 67 | 64 | 57 | 60 | 62 | 57 | 63 | 66 |

Source:  Centre for Education Statistics, Statistics Canada; Statistiques de l'éducation - Enseignement primaire, secondaire, collégial et universitaire, Gouvernement du Québec, Ministère de l'Éducation (for Quebec data).

**TABLE 3.5  FULL-TIME COMMUNITY COLLEGE EDUCATORS BY GENDER, CANADA AND JURISDICTIONS, 1986-87[1] AND 1996-97**

|  | Canada | | Newfoundland and Labrador | | Prince Edward Island | | Nova Scotia | | New Brunswick | | Quebec | | Ontario | |
|---|---|---|---|---|---|---|---|---|---|---|---|---|---|---|
|  | 1986-87 | 1996-97 | 1986-87 | 1996-97 | 1986-87 | 1996-97 | 1986-87 | 1996-97 | 1986-87 | 1996-97 | 1986-87 | 1996-97 | 1986-87 | 1996-97 |
| Both sexes | .. | 29,813 | 745 | 654 | 135 | 87 | 872 | 535 | 577 | 797 | .. | 12,940 | 10,614 | 7,153 |
| % Female | .. | **40** | 26 | 32 | 26 | 29 | 20 | 34 | 21 | 34 | .. | 39 | 38 | 43 |
| % Male | .. | **60** | 74 | 68 | 74 | 71 | 80 | 66 | 79 | 66 | .. | 61 | 62 | 57 |

|  | Manitoba | | Saskatchewan | | Alberta | | British Columbia | | Yukon | | Northwest Territories | |
|---|---|---|---|---|---|---|---|---|---|---|---|---|
|  | 1986-87 | 1996-97 | 1986-87 | 1996-97 | 1986-87 | 1996-97 | 1986-87 | 1996-97 | 1986-87 | 1996-97 | 1986-87 | 1996-97 |
| Both sexes | 688 | 694 | 788 | 808 | 3,475 | 2,158 | 2,875 | 3,810 | .. | 91 | 86 | 86 |
| % Female | 29 | 34 | 34 | 43 | 27 | 38 | 30 | 42 | .. | 46 | 33 | 56 |
| % Male | 71 | 66 | 66 | 57 | 73 | 62 | 70 | 58 | .. | 54 | 67 | 44 |

1  1986-87 data not available for Quebec and Yukon, Canada totals are therefore not available.
Source:  Centre for Education Statistics, Statistics Canada.

TABLE 3.6    FULL-TIME UNIVERSITY FACULTY BY GENDER, CANADA AND JURISDICTIONS, 1987-88 AND 1997-98

|  | Total 1987-88 | Total 1997-98 | Full professor 1987-88 | Full professor 1997-98 | Associate professor 1987-88 | Associate professor 1997-98 | Other 1987-88 | Other 1997-98 |
|---|---|---|---|---|---|---|---|---|
| **Canada** | **34,651** | **33,925** | **12,829** | **13,910** | **12,650** | **12,095** | **9,172** | **7,817** |
| % Females | 17 | 25 | 7 | 13 | 17 | 28 | 32 | 44 |
| % Males | 83 | 75 | 93 | 87 | 83 | 72 | 68 | 56 |
| **Newfoundland and Labrador** | 944 | 865 | 279 | 296 | 372 | 380 | 293 | 189 |
| % Females | 21 | 26 | 6 | 9 | 19 | 30 | 37 | 46 |
| % Males | 79 | 74 | 94 | 91 | 81 | 70 | 63 | 54 |
| **Prince Edward Island** | 132 | 180 | 35 | 47 | 64 | 56 | 33 | 77 |
| % Females | 10 | 32 | 6 | 15 | 9 | 29 | 15 | 45 |
| % Males | 90 | 68 | 94 | 85 | 91 | 71 | 85 | 55 |
| **Nova Scotia** | 1,973 | 1,910 | 550 | 681 | 766 | 714 | 657 | 515 |
| % Females | 22 | 29 | 6 | 13 | 18 | 30 | 40 | 51 |
| % Males | 78 | 71 | 94 | 87 | 82 | 70 | 60 | 49 |
| **New Brunswick** | 1,149 | 1,146 | 432 | 516 | 397 | 339 | 320 | 291 |
| % Females | 19 | 28 | 8 | 18 | 20 | 27 | 33 | 48 |
| % Males | 81 | 72 | 92 | 82 | 80 | 73 | 67 | 52 |
| **Quebec[1]** | 8,001 | 8,705 | 2,926 | 3,512 | 3,346 | 3,267 | 1,729 | 1,568 |
| % Females | 17 | 23 | 8 | 14 | 18 | 27 | 29 | 39 |
| % Males | 83 | 77 | 92 | 86 | 82 | 73 | 71 | 61 |
| **Ontario** | 13,389 | 12,346 | 4,719 | 4,888 | 4,616 | 4,397 | 4,054 | 3,061 |
| % Females | 17 | 26 | 6 | 13 | 15 | 28 | 32 | 43 |
| % Males | 83 | 74 | 94 | 87 | 85 | 72 | 68 | 57 |
| **Manitoba** | 1,630 | 1,506 | 654 | 633 | 567 | 495 | 409 | 378 |
| % Females | 16 | 25 | 6 | 10 | 17 | 27 | 30 | 47 |
| % Males | 84 | 75 | 94 | 90 | 83 | 73 | 70 | 53 |
| **Saskatchewan** | 1,491 | 1,034 | 680 | 664 | 480 | 423 | 331 | 202 |
| % Females | 15 | 21 | 4 | 8 | 18 | 30 | 32 | 42 |
| % Males | 85 | 79 | 96 | 92 | 82 | 70 | 68 | 58 |
| **Alberta** | 3,004 | 2,940 | 1,417 | 1,303 | 1,030 | 961 | 557 | 676 |
| % Females | 16 | 26 | 8 | 13 | 19 | 30 | 33 | 44 |
| % Males | 84 | 74 | 92 | 87 | 81 | 70 | 67 | 56 |
| **British Columbia** | 2,938 | 3,293 | 1,137 | 1,370 | 1,012 | 1,063 | 789 | 860 |
| % Females | 16 | 25 | 5 | 13 | 16 | 26 | 34 | 45 |
| % Males | 84 | 75 | 95 | 87 | 84 | 74 | 66 | 55 |

1   1996-97 data were used for Quebec, as 1997-98 data were not available.

*Source: Centre for Education Statistics, Statistics Canada.*

EDUCATION INDICATORS IN CANADA

**TABLE 3.7** FULL-TIME EDUCATORS IN ELEMENTARY–SECONDARY SCHOOLS, NUMBER AND DISTRIBUTION (%) BY AGE AND GENDER, AND MEDIAN AGE, CANADA AND JURISDICTIONS, 1996-97

| Age group | Canada | Nfld. | P.E.I. | N.S. | N.B. | Que. | Ont. | Man. | Sask. | Alta. | B.C. | Y.T. | N.W.T. |
|---|---|---|---|---|---|---|---|---|---|---|---|---|---|
| **Number of educators** ||||||||||||||
| **Both sexes** ||||||||||||||
| All Ages[1] | 267,808 | 6,939 | 1,361 | 8,799 | 7,427 | 56,528 | 108,737 | 10,618 | 9,745 | 26,482 | 29,330 | 450 | 1,392 |
| 20–29 | 21,043 | 618 | 138 | 694 | 670 | 3,575 | 7,445 | 988 | 1,312 | 2,757 | 2,550 | 2 | 294 |
| 30–39 | 59,025 | 1,890 | 291 | 1,780 | 1,675 | 10,158 | 24,783 | 2,453 | 2,586 | 6,672 | 6,218 | 34 | 485 |
| 40–49 | 109,906 | 3,675 | 599 | 4,681 | 3,324 | 21,959 | 44,691 | 4,396 | 4,082 | 10,021 | 11,936 | 182 | 360 |
| 50–59 | 74,163 | 750 | 325 | 1,611 | 1,716 | 20,100 | 30,239 | 2,643 | 1,728 | 6,575 | 8,180 | 123 | 173 |
| 60 + | 3,142 | 6 | 8 | 33 | 42 | 736 | 1,130 | 130 | 37 | 457 | 445 | 109 | 9 |
| **Males** ||||||||||||||
| All ages[1] | 99,544 | 3,124 | 549 | 3,365 | 2,593 | 18,810 | 39,517 | 4,572 | 3,929 | 9,958 | 12,484 | 166 | 477 |
| 20–29 | 5,373 | 182 | 43 | 198 | 147 | 705 | 1,820 | 306 | 446 | 685 | 747 | 1 | 93 |
| 30–39 | 20,054 | 736 | 99 | 550 | 467 | 2,698 | 8,397 | 988 | 952 | 2,410 | 2,570 | 15 | 172 |
| 40–49 | 40,068 | 1,789 | 244 | 1,795 | 1,189 | 7,298 | 15,305 | 1,828 | 1,731 | 3,753 | 4,961 | 63 | 112 |
| 50–59 | 32,477 | 414 | 159 | 809 | 781 | 7,749 | 13,341 | 1,388 | 787 | 2,922 | 4,017 | 40 | 70 |
| 60 + | 1,344 | 3 | 4 | 13 | 9 | 360 | 453 | 62 | 13 | 188 | 188 | 47 | 4 |
| **Females** ||||||||||||||
| All ages[1] | 168,264 | 3,815 | 812 | 5,434 | 4,834 | 37,718 | 69,220 | 6,046 | 5,816 | 16,524 | 16,846 | 284 | 915 |
| 20–29 | 15,670 | 436 | 95 | 496 | 523 | 2,870 | 5,625 | 682 | 866 | 2,072 | 1,803 | 1 | 201 |
| 30–39 | 38,971 | 1,154 | 192 | 1,230 | 1,208 | 7,460 | 16,386 | 1,465 | 1,634 | 4,262 | 3,648 | 19 | 313 |
| 40–49 | 69,838 | 1,886 | 355 | 2,886 | 2,135 | 14,661 | 29,386 | 2,568 | 2,351 | 6,268 | 6,975 | 119 | 248 |
| 50–59 | 41,686 | 336 | 166 | 802 | 935 | 12,351 | 16,898 | 1,255 | 941 | 3,653 | 4,163 | 83 | 103 |
| 60 + | 1,798 | 3 | 4 | 20 | 33 | 376 | 677 | 68 | 24 | 269 | 257 | 62 | 5 |
| **Distribution of educators[2] (%)** ||||||||||||||
| **Both sexes** ||||||||||||||
| 20–29 | 8 | 9 | 10 | 8 | 9 | 6 | 7 | 9 | 13 | 10 | 9 | - | 22 |
| 30–39 | 22 | 27 | 21 | 20 | 23 | 18 | 23 | 23 | 27 | 25 | 21 | 8 | 37 |
| 40–49 | 41 | 53 | 44 | 53 | 45 | 39 | 41 | 41 | 42 | 38 | 41 | 40 | 27 |
| 50–59 | 28 | 11 | 24 | 18 | 23 | 36 | 28 | 25 | 18 | 25 | 28 | 27 | 13 |
| 60 + | 1 | - | 1 | - | 1 | 1 | 1 | 1 | - | 2 | 2 | 24 | 1 |
| **Males** ||||||||||||||
| 20–29 | 5 | 6 | 8 | 6 | 6 | 4 | 5 | 7 | 11 | 7 | 6 | 1 | 21 |
| 30–39 | 20 | 24 | 18 | 16 | 18 | 14 | 21 | 22 | 24 | 24 | 21 | 9 | 38 |
| 40–49 | 40 | 57 | 44 | 53 | 46 | 39 | 39 | 40 | 44 | 38 | 40 | 38 | 25 |
| 50–59 | 33 | 13 | 29 | 24 | 30 | 41 | 34 | 30 | 20 | 29 | 32 | 24 | 16 |
| 60 + | 1 | - | 1 | - | - | 2 | 1 | 1 | - | 2 | 2 | 28 | 1 |
| **Females** ||||||||||||||
| 20–29 | 9 | 11 | 12 | 9 | 11 | 8 | 8 | 11 | 15 | 13 | 11 | - | 23 |
| 30–39 | 23 | 30 | 24 | 23 | 25 | 20 | 24 | 24 | 28 | 26 | 22 | 7 | 36 |
| 40–49 | 42 | 49 | 44 | 53 | 44 | 39 | 43 | 43 | 40 | 38 | 41 | 42 | 29 |
| 50–59 | 25 | 9 | 20 | 15 | 19 | 33 | 24 | 21 | 16 | 22 | 25 | 29 | 12 |
| 60 + | 1 | - | - | - | 1 | 1 | 1 | 1 | - | 2 | 2 | 22 | 1 |
| **Median age of educators** ||||||||||||||
| Both sexes | 45 | 43 | 45 | 45 | 45 | 47 | 46 | 45 | 42 | 44 | 45 | 50 | 37 |
| Males | 46 | 44 | 46 | 46 | 47 | 48 | 47 | 46 | 44 | 45 | 46 | 50 | 37 |
| Females | 44 | 42 | 44 | 44 | 44 | 46 | 45 | 44 | 41 | 43 | 45 | 50 | 37 |

1 Includes a small number of cases for which age is not reported.
2 Percentage distribution is based on educators for which age is reported.
Source: Centre for Education Statistics, Statistics Canada; Statistiques de l'éducation - Enseignement primaire, secondaire, collégial et universitaire, Gouvernement du Québec, Ministère de l'Éducation (for Quebec data).

## Chapter 3 Tables

**TABLE 3.8** FULL-TIME EDUCATORS IN COMMUNITY COLLEGES, NUMBER AND DISTRIBUTION (%) BY AGE AND GENDER, AND MEDIAN AGE, CANADA AND JURISDICTIONS, 1996-97

| Age group | Canada | Nfld. | P.E.I. | N.S. | N.B. | Que. | Ont. | Man. | Sask. | Alta. | B.C. | Y.T. | N.W.T. |
|---|---|---|---|---|---|---|---|---|---|---|---|---|---|
| **Number of educators** ||||||||||||||
| **Both Sexes** ||||||||||||||
| All Ages[1] | 29,813 | 654 | 87 | 535 | 797 | 12,940 | 7,153 | 694 | 808 | 2,158 | 3,810 | 91 | 86 |
| 20–29 | 452 | 13 | - | 10 | 19 | 267 | 58 | 14 | 13 | 29 | 24 | 2 | 3 |
| 30–39 | 4,153 | 137 | 21 | 109 | 168 | 1,963 | 666 | 121 | 107 | 302 | 527 | 13 | 19 |
| 40–49 | 11,092 | 297 | 30 | 240 | 332 | 4,896 | 2,319 | 265 | 355 | 946 | 1,332 | 43 | 37 |
| 50–59 | 10,014 | 160 | 32 | 161 | 238 | 4,221 | 2,532 | 253 | 260 | 781 | 1,336 | 21 | 19 |
| 60 + | 1,414 | 11 | 4 | 15 | 40 | 429 | 498 | 39 | 41 | 97 | 227 | 7 | 6 |
| **Males** ||||||||||||||
| All ages[1] | 17,899 | 447 | 62 | 355 | 524 | 7,880 | 4,080 | 460 | 463 | 1,337 | 2,204 | 49 | 38 |
| 20–29 | 211 | 8 | - | 5 | 12 | 122 | 25 | 8 | 8 | 13 | 9 | - | 1 |
| 30–39 | 2,272 | 100 | 19 | 63 | 93 | 1,107 | 304 | 75 | 61 | 169 | 267 | 8 | 6 |
| 40–49 | 6,142 | 194 | 16 | 161 | 203 | 2,711 | 1,217 | 159 | 192 | 544 | 705 | 25 | 15 |
| 50–59 | 6,665 | 110 | 24 | 114 | 184 | 2,976 | 1,536 | 183 | 164 | 534 | 822 | 8 | 10 |
| 60 + | 1,045 | 10 | 3 | 12 | 32 | 318 | 368 | 34 | 21 | 75 | 163 | 3 | 6 |
| **Females** ||||||||||||||
| All ages[1] | 11,914 | 207 | 25 | 180 | 273 | 5,060 | 3,073 | 234 | 345 | 821 | 1,606 | 42 | 48 |
| 20–29 | 241 | 5 | - | 5 | 7 | 145 | 33 | 6 | 5 | 16 | 15 | 2 | 2 |
| 30–39 | 1,881 | 37 | 2 | 46 | 75 | 856 | 362 | 46 | 46 | 133 | 260 | 5 | 13 |
| 40–49 | 4,950 | 103 | 14 | 79 | 129 | 2,185 | 1,102 | 106 | 163 | 402 | 627 | 18 | 22 |
| 50–59 | 3,349 | 50 | 8 | 47 | 54 | 1,245 | 996 | 70 | 96 | 247 | 514 | 13 | 9 |
| 60 + | 369 | 1 | 1 | 3 | 8 | 111 | 130 | 5 | 20 | 22 | 64 | 4 | - |
| **Distribution of educators[2] (%)** ||||||||||||||
| **Both sexes** ||||||||||||||
| 20–29 | 2 | 2 | - | 2 | 2 | 2 | 1 | 2 | 2 | 1 | 1 | 2 | 4 |
| 30–39 | 15 | 22 | 24 | 20 | 21 | 17 | 11 | 17 | 14 | 14 | 15 | 15 | 23 |
| 40–49 | 41 | 48 | 34 | 45 | 42 | 42 | 38 | 38 | 46 | 44 | 39 | 50 | 44 |
| 50–59 | 37 | 26 | 37 | 30 | 30 | 36 | 42 | 37 | 34 | 36 | 39 | 24 | 23 |
| 60 + | 5 | 2 | 5 | 3 | 5 | 4 | 8 | 6 | 5 | 5 | 7 | 8 | 7 |
| **Males** ||||||||||||||
| 20–29 | 1 | 2 | - | 1 | 2 | 2 | 1 | 2 | 2 | 1 | - | - | 3 |
| 30–39 | 14 | 24 | 31 | 18 | 18 | 15 | 9 | 16 | 14 | 13 | 14 | 18 | 16 |
| 40–49 | 38 | 46 | 26 | 45 | 39 | 37 | 35 | 35 | 43 | 41 | 36 | 57 | 39 |
| 50–59 | 41 | 26 | 39 | 32 | 35 | 41 | 45 | 40 | 37 | 40 | 42 | 18 | 26 |
| 60 + | 6 | 2 | 5 | 3 | 6 | 4 | 11 | 7 | 5 | 6 | 8 | 7 | 16 |
| **Females** ||||||||||||||
| 20–29 | 2 | 3 | - | 3 | 3 | 3 | 1 | 3 | 2 | 2 | 1 | 5 | 4 |
| 30–39 | 17 | 19 | 8 | 26 | 27 | 19 | 14 | 20 | 14 | 16 | 18 | 12 | 28 |
| 40–49 | 46 | 53 | 56 | 44 | 47 | 48 | 42 | 45 | 49 | 49 | 42 | 43 | 48 |
| 50–59 | 31 | 26 | 32 | 26 | 20 | 27 | 38 | 30 | 29 | 30 | 35 | 31 | 20 |
| 60 + | 3 | 1 | 4 | 2 | 3 | 2 | 5 | 2 | 6 | 3 | 4 | 10 | - |
| **Median age of educators** ||||||||||||||
| Both Sexes | 47 | 44 | 45 | 45 | 46 | 47 | 49 | 47 | 46 | 47 | 48 | .. | 44 |
| Males | 48 | 45 | 45 | 46 | 47 | 48 | 50 | 48 | 47 | 48 | 49 | .. | 48 |
| Females | 45 | 44 | 45 | 43 | 44 | 45 | 48 | 45 | 46 | 46 | 46 | .. | 42 |

1 Includes cases for which age is not reported.
2 Percentage distribution is based on educators for which age is reported.

Source: Centre for Education Statistics, Statistics Canada; Statistiques de l'éducation - Enseignement primaire, secondaire, collégial et universitaire, Gouvernement du Québec, Ministère de l'Éducation (for Quebec data).

TABLE 3.9  FULL-TIME EDUCATORS IN UNIVERSITIES, NUMBER AND DISTRIBUTION (%) BY AGE AND GENDER, AND MEDIAN AGE, CANADA AND JURISDICTIONS, 1996-97

| | Canada | Nfld. | P.E.I. | N.S. | N.B. | Que. | Ont. | Man. | Sask. | Alta. | B.C. |
|---|---|---|---|---|---|---|---|---|---|---|---|
| **Number of educators** | | | | | | | | | | | |
| **Both sexes** | | | | | | | | | | | |
| All ages[1] | 34,613 | 885 | 188 | 1,950 | 1,160 | 8,705 | 12,539 | 1,575 | 1,410 | 2,852 | 3,349 |
| 20–29 | 189 | 6 | 2 | 14 | 10 | 39 | 82 | 7 | 5 | 13 | 11 |
| 30–39 | 5,842 | 143 | 56 | 307 | 210 | 1,532 | 2,072 | 227 | 234 | 464 | 597 |
| 40–49 | 11,449 | 314 | 57 | 686 | 401 | 2,869 | 4,064 | 470 | 473 | 1,015 | 1,100 |
| 50–59 | 13,276 | 356 | 55 | 781 | 459 | 3,180 | 4,931 | 637 | 506 | 1,121 | 1,250 |
| 60 + | 3,819 | 66 | 18 | 143 | 80 | 1,085 | 1,375 | 234 | 192 | 236 | 390 |
| **Males** | | | | | | | | | | | |
| All ages[1] | 26,172 | 659 | 135 | 1,391 | 842 | 6,740 | 9,376 | 1,216 | 1,117 | 2,173 | 2,523 |
| 20–29 | 112 | 2 | 0 | 8 | 7 | 28 | 46 | 4 | 4 | 5 | 8 |
| 30–39 | 3,845 | 94 | 31 | 194 | 140 | 1,036 | 1,331 | 144 | 155 | 321 | 399 |
| 40–49 | 8,018 | 226 | 37 | 449 | 279 | 2,060 | 2,810 | 313 | 354 | 726 | 764 |
| 50–59 | 10,810 | 289 | 50 | 614 | 349 | 2,663 | 3,963 | 545 | 425 | 906 | 1,006 |
| 60 + | 3,364 | 48 | 17 | 115 | 67 | 953 | 1,215 | 210 | 179 | 214 | 346 |
| **Females** | | | | | | | | | | | |
| All ages[1] | 8,441 | 226 | 53 | 559 | 318 | 1,965 | 3,163 | 359 | 293 | 679 | 826 |
| 20–29 | 77 | 4 | 2 | 6 | 3 | 11 | 36 | 3 | 1 | 8 | 3 |
| 30–39 | 1,997 | 49 | 25 | 113 | 70 | 496 | 741 | 83 | 79 | 143 | 198 |
| 40–49 | 3,431 | 88 | 20 | 237 | 122 | 809 | 1,254 | 157 | 119 | 289 | 336 |
| 50–59 | 2,466 | 67 | 5 | 167 | 110 | 517 | 968 | 92 | 81 | 215 | 244 |
| 60 + | 455 | 18 | 1 | 28 | 13 | 132 | 160 | 24 | 13 | 22 | 44 |
| **Distribution of educators[2] (%)** | | | | | | | | | | | |
| **Both sexes** | | | | | | | | | | | |
| 20–29 | 1 | 1 | 1 | 1 | 1 | – | 1 | – | – | – | – |
| 30–39 | 17 | 16 | 30 | 16 | 18 | 18 | 17 | 14 | 17 | 16 | 18 |
| 40–49 | 33 | 35 | 30 | 36 | 35 | 33 | 32 | 30 | 34 | 36 | 33 |
| 50–59 | 38 | 40 | 29 | 40 | 40 | 37 | 39 | 40 | 36 | 39 | 37 |
| 60 + | 11 | 7 | 10 | 7 | 7 | 12 | 11 | 15 | 14 | 8 | 12 |
| **Males** | | | | | | | | | | | |
| 20–29 | – | – | – | 1 | 1 | – | – | – | – | – | – |
| 30–39 | 15 | 14 | 23 | 14 | 17 | 15 | 14 | 12 | 14 | 15 | 16 |
| 40–49 | 31 | 34 | 27 | 33 | 33 | 31 | 30 | 26 | 32 | 33 | 30 |
| 50–59 | 41 | 44 | 37 | 44 | 41 | 40 | 42 | 45 | 38 | 42 | 40 |
| 60 + | 13 | 7 | 13 | 8 | 8 | 14 | 13 | 17 | 16 | 10 | 14 |
| **Females** | | | | | | | | | | | |
| 20–29 | 1 | 2 | 4 | 1 | 1 | 1 | 1 | 1 | – | 1 | – |
| 30–39 | 24 | 22 | 47 | 21 | 22 | 25 | 23 | 23 | 27 | 21 | 24 |
| 40–49 | 41 | 39 | 38 | 43 | 38 | 41 | 40 | 44 | 41 | 43 | 41 |
| 50–59 | 29 | 30 | 9 | 30 | 35 | 26 | 31 | 26 | 28 | 32 | 30 |
| 60 + | 5 | 8 | 2 | 5 | 4 | 7 | 5 | 7 | 4 | 3 | 5 |
| **Median age of educators** | | | | | | | | | | | |
| Both sexes | 49 | 49 | 45 | 49 | 48 | 49 | 50 | 51 | 49 | 49 | 49 |
| Males | 50 | 50 | 49 | 50 | 49 | 50 | 51 | 52 | 50 | 50 | 51 |
| Females | 46 | 47 | 39 | 46 | 47 | 46 | 46 | 45 | 45 | 46 | 46 |

1  Includes a small number of cases for which age is not reported.
2  Percentage distribution is based on educators for which age is reported.

Source: Centre for Education Statistics, Statistics Canada; Statistiques de l'éducation - Enseignement primaire, secondaire, collégial et universitaire, Gouvernement du Québec, Ministère de l'Éducation (for Quebec data).

## CHAPTER 3 TABLES

**TABLE 3.10** NUMBER OF EDUCATORS WORKING PART TIME IN PUBLIC ELEMENTARY–SECONDARY SCHOOLS, BY GENDER, CANADA AND JURISDICTIONS, 1986-87 TO 1996-97

|  | Canada | Nfld. | P.E.I. | N.S. | N.B. | Que. | Ont. | Man. | Sask. | Alta. | B.C. | Y.T. | N.W.T. |
|---|---|---|---|---|---|---|---|---|---|---|---|---|---|
| **Both sexes** | | | | | | | | | | | | | |
| 1986-87 | **27,195** | 213 | 127 | 492 | 427 | 5,758 | 11,096 | 1,523 | 1,381 | 2,334 | 3,774 | 40 | 30 |
| 1987-88 | **26,825** | 218 | 128 | 508 | 430 | 6,235 | 9,851 | 1,395 | 1,380 | 2,565 | 4,033 | 39 | 43 |
| 1988-89 | **28,109** | 221 | 124 | 541 | 409 | 6,997 | 9,818 | 1,680 | 1,467 | 2,542 | 4,248 | 38 | 24 |
| 1989-90 | **30,202** | 225 | 95 | 616 | 419 | 8,228 | 9,985 | 1,664 | 1,514 | 2,880 | 4,509 | 45 | 22 |
| 1990-91 | **38,011** | 231 | 119 | 572 | 428 | 15,378 | 10,225 | 1,693 | 1,428 | 2,924 | 4,957 | 46 | 10 |
| 1991-92 | **40,243** | 244 | 119 | 603 | 388 | 16,824 | 10,313 | 1,774 | 1,526 | 3,058 | 5,339 | 47 | 8 |
| 1992-93 | **42,447** | 260 | 108 | 580 | 401 | 18,487 | 10,324 | 1,835 | 1,511 | 3,109 | 5,770 | 55 | 7 |
| 1993-94 | **50,948** | 277 | 122 | 621 | 385 | 18,790 | 17,880 | 1,843 | 1,631 | 3,346 | 5,984 | 51 | 18 |
| 1994-95 | **53,170** | 299 | 107 | 696 | 385 | 19,085 | 18,706 | 1,923 | 1,622 | 3,687 | 6,590 | 62 | 8 |
| 1995-96 | **54,656** | 307 | 122 | 698 | 410 | 19,796 | 17,192 | 1,996 | 1,612 | 5,475 | 6,972 | 62 | 14 |
| 1996-97 | **55,264** | 333 | 113 | 721 | 385 | 19,646 | 17,173 | 1,997 | 1,626 | 5,822 | 7,350 | 83 | 15 |
|  | Canada | Nfld. | P.E.I. | N.S. | N.B. | Que. | Ont. | Man. | Sask. | Alta. | B.C. | Y.T. | N.W.T. |
| **Males** | | | | | | | | | | | | | |
| 1986-87 | **3,975** | 22 | 18 | 41 | 44 | 1,178 | 1,934 | 155 | 102 | 155 | 323 | 2 | 1 |
| 1987-88 | **3,496** | 26 | 16 | 40 | 59 | 1,338[e] | 1,258 | 119 | 90 | 191 | 357 | 1 | 1 |
| 1988-89 | **3,644** | 34 | 16 | 43 | 41 | 1,559 | 1,155 | 171 | 85 | 188 | 346 | 5 | 1 |
| 1989-90 | **3,934** | 26 | 21 | 39 | 46 | 1,868 | 1,146 | 159 | 109 | 184 | 332 | 4 | - |
| 1990-91 | **5,797** | 26 | 22 | 44 | 38 | 3,584 | 1,209 | 160 | 86 | 199 | 427 | 1 | 1 |
| 1991-92 | **6,451** | 30 | 16 | 50 | 39 | 4,046 | 1,242 | 188 | 123 | 248 | 465 | 2 | 2 |
| 1992-93 | **7,093** | 37 | 14 | 40 | 48 | 4,568 | 1,269 | 196 | 127 | 249 | 541 | 4 | - |
| 1993-94 | **10,097** | 31 | 19 | 52 | 41 | 4,735 | 3,984 | 185 | 158 | 295 | 589 | 5 | 3 |
| 1994-95 | **10,949** | 39 | 21 | 64 | 41 | 4,867 | 4,485 | 219 | 154 | 326 | 726 | 6 | 1 |
| 1995-96 | **10,786** | 48 | 26 | 74 | 63 | 5,109 | 3,669 | 239 | 150 | 654 | 746 | 6 | 2 |
| 1996-97 | **11,039** | 49 | 16 | 75 | 53 | 5,129 | 3,748 | 263 | 171 | 700 | 822 | 10 | 3 |
|  | Canada | Nfld. | P.E.I. | N.S. | N.B. | Que. | Ont. | Man. | Sask. | Alta. | B.C. | Y.T. | N.W.T. |
| **Females** | | | | | | | | | | | | | |
| 1986-87 | **23,220** | 191 | 109 | 451 | 383 | 4,580 | 9,162 | 1,368 | 1,279 | 2,179 | 3,451 | 38 | 29 |
| 1987-88 | **23,329** | 192 | 112 | 468 | 371 | 4,897[e] | 8,593 | 1,276 | 1,290 | 2,374 | 3,676 | 38 | 42 |
| 1988-89 | **24,465** | 187 | 108 | 498 | 368 | 5,438 | 8,663 | 1,509 | 1,382 | 2,354 | 3,902 | 33 | 23 |
| 1989-90 | **26,268** | 199 | 74 | 577 | 373 | 6,360 | 8,839 | 1,505 | 1,405 | 2,696 | 4,177 | 41 | 22 |
| 1990-91 | **32,214** | 205 | 97 | 528 | 390 | 11,794 | 9,016 | 1,533 | 1,342 | 2,725 | 4,530 | 45 | 9 |
| 1991-92 | **33,792** | 214 | 103 | 553 | 349 | 12,778 | 9,071 | 1,586 | 1,403 | 2,810 | 4,874 | 45 | 6 |
| 1992-93 | **35,354** | 223 | 94 | 540 | 353 | 13,919 | 9,055 | 1,639 | 1,384 | 2,860 | 5,229 | 51 | 7 |
| 1993-94 | **40,851** | 246 | 103 | 569 | 344 | 14,055 | 13,896 | 1,658 | 1,473 | 3,051 | 5,395 | 46 | 15 |
| 1994-95 | **42,221** | 260 | 86 | 632 | 344 | 14,218 | 14,221 | 1,704 | 1,468 | 3,361 | 5,864 | 56 | 7 |
| 1995-96 | **43,870** | 259 | 96 | 624 | 347 | 14,687 | 13,523 | 1,757 | 1,462 | 4,821 | 6,226 | 56 | 12 |
| 1996-97 | **44,225** | 284 | 97 | 646 | 332 | 14,517 | 13,425 | 1,734 | 1,455 | 5,122 | 6,528 | 73 | 12 |

*Source:* Centre for Education Statistics, Statistics Canada; Statistiques de l'éducation - Enseignement primaire, secondaire, collégial et universitaire, Gouvernement du Québec, Ministère de l'Éducation (for Quebec data).

TABLE 3.11  PERCENTAGE OF EDUCATORS WORKING PART TIME IN PUBLIC ELEMENTARY–SECONDARY SCHOOLS, BY GENDER, CANADA AND JURISDICTIONS, **1986-87** TO **1996-97**

|  | Canada | Nfld. | P.E.I. | N.S. | N.B. | Que. | Ont. | Man. | Sask. | Alta. | B.C. | Y.T. | N.W.T. |
|---|---|---|---|---|---|---|---|---|---|---|---|---|---|
| **Both sexes** | | | | | | | | | | | | | |
| 1986-87 | **10** | 3 | 9 | 5 | 5 | 9 | 10 | 12 | 11 | 9 | 14 | 12 | 4 |
| 1987-88 | **9** | 3 | 9 | 5 | 5 | 9 | 9 | 11 | 11 | 10 | 14 | 12 | 5 |
| 1988-89 | **10** | 3 | 9 | 5 | 5 | 10 | 8 | 13 | 12 | 10 | 14 | 11 | 3 |
| 1989-90 | **10** | 3 | 6 | 6 | 5 | 12 | 8 | 12 | 12 | 10 | 14 | 12 | 3 |
| 1990-91 | **12** | 3 | 8 | 6 | 5 | 20 | 8 | 13 | 12 | 10 | 15 | 11 | 1 |
| 1991-92 | **12** | 3 | 8 | 6 | 5 | 22 | 8 | 13 | 13 | 11 | 16 | 11 | 1 |
| 1992-93 | **13** | 3 | 7 | 6 | 5 | 24 | 8 | 14 | 13 | 11 | 17 | 12 | 1 |
| 1993-94 | **16** | 4 | 8 | 6 | 5 | 24 | 14 | 14 | 14 | 12 | 17 | 11 | 1 |
| 1994-95 | **16** | 4 | 7 | 7 | 5 | 25 | 14 | 15 | 14 | 13 | 19 | 13 | 1 |
| 1995-96 | **17** | 4 | 8 | 7 | 5 | 26 | 13 | 15 | 14 | 17 | 19 | 13 | 1 |
| 1996-97 | **17** | 5 | 8 | 8 | 5 | 26 | 14 | 16 | 14 | 18 | 20 | 16 | 1 |
|  | Canada | Nfld. | P.E.I. | N.S. | N.B. | Que. | Ont. | Man. | Sask. | Alta. | B.C. | Y.T. | N.W.T. |
| **Males** | | | | | | | | | | | | | |
| 1986-87 | **4** | 1 | 3 | 1 | 1 | 5 | 4 | 3 | 2 | 1 | 3 | 2 | - |
| 1987-88 | **3** | 1 | 3 | 1 | 2 | 6 [e] | 3 | 2 | 2 | 2 | 3 | 1 | - |
| 1988-89 | **3** | 1 | 3 | 1 | 1 | 7 | 3 | 3 | 2 | 2 | 3 | 4 | - |
| 1989-90 | **3** | 1 | 4 | 1 | 1 | 8 | 3 | 3 | 2 | 2 | 3 | 3 | - |
| 1990-91 | **5** | 1 | 4 | 1 | 1 | 15 | 3 | 3 | 2 | 2 | 3 | 1 | - |
| 1991-92 | **5** | 1 | 3 | 1 | 1 | 16 | 3 | 4 | 3 | 2 | 3 | 1 | 1 |
| 1992-93 | **6** | 1 | 2 | 1 | 2 | 18 | 3 | 4 | 3 | 2 | 4 | 3 | - |
| 1993-94 | **9** | 1 | 3 | 1 | 1 | 19 | 8 | 4 | 4 | 3 | 4 | 3 | 1 |
| 1994-95 | **10** | 1 | 4 | 2 | 1 | 20 | 10 | 4 | 4 | 3 | 5 | 4 | - |
| 1995-96 | **9** | 1 | 5 | 2 | 2 | 21 | 8 | 5 | 4 | 6 | 6 | 4 | - |
| 1996-97 | **10** | 2 | 3 | 2 | 2 | 21 | 9 | 5 | 4 | 7 | 6 | 6 | 1 |
|  | Canada | Nfld. | P.E.I. | N.S. | N.B. | Que. | Ont. | Man. | Sask. | Alta. | B.C. | Y.T. | N.W.T. |
| **Females** | | | | | | | | | | | | | |
| 1986-87 | **14** | 4 | 13 | 7 | 8 | 11 | 15 | 19 | 18 | 14 | 23 | 19 | 7 |
| 1987-88 | **13** | 4 | 13 | 7 | 7 | 11 [e] | 13 | 18 | 18 | 15 | 23 | 19 | 9 |
| 1988-89 | **14** | 4 | 13 | 8 | 7 | 12 | 12 | 20 | 19 | 15 | 23 | 15 | 5 |
| 1989-90 | **14** | 5 | 9 | 9 | 7 | 14 | 12 | 19 | 19 | 16 | 22 | 18 | 4 |
| 1990-91 | **16** | 5 | 11 | 9 | 7 | 23 | 11 | 19 | 19 | 15 | 23 | 16 | 2 |
| 1991-92 | **16** | 5 | 12 | 9 | 6 | 25 | 11 | 20 | 19 | 15 | 23 | 16 | 1 |
| 1992-93 | **17** | 5 | 11 | 9 | 7 | 26 | 11 | 21 | 19 | 16 | 25 | 16 | 1 |
| 1993-94 | **19** | 6 | 12 | 9 | 6 | 27 | 16 | 21 | 20 | 17 | 25 | 14 | 2 |
| 1994-95 | **20** | 6 | 10 | 10 | 7 | 27 | 17 | 21 | 20 | 18 | 27 | 17 | 1 |
| 1995-96 | **20** | 6 | 11 | 11 | 7 | 28 | 16 | 22 | 20 | 22 | 27 | 17 | 1 |
| 1996-97 | **21** | 7 | 11 | 11 | 6 | 28 | 16 | 22 | 20 | 24 | 28 | 20 | 1 |

Source: Centre for Education Statistics, Statistics Canada; Statistiques de l'éducation - Enseignement primaire, secondaire, collégial et universitaire, Gouvernement du Québec, Ministère de l'Éducation (for Quebec data).

TABLE 3.12  NUMBER AND AVERAGE SALARY OF FULL-TIME UNIVERSITY FACULTY, BY RANK AND GENDER, CANADA AND PROVINCES, 1987-88 AND 1997-98, IN CONSTANT 1997 DOLLARS

|  | Canada 1987-88 | Canada 1997-98 | Newfoundland and Labrador 1987-88 | Newfoundland and Labrador 1997-98 | Prince Edward Island 1987-88 | Prince Edward Island 1997-98 | Nova Scotia 1987-88 | Nova Scotia 1997-98 | New Brunswick 1987-88 | New Brunswick 1997-98 | Quebec[2] 1987-88 | Quebec[2] 1997-98 |
|---|---|---|---|---|---|---|---|---|---|---|---|---|
| **All teaching faculty** | | | | | | | | | | | | |
| Males | 28,672 | 25,396 | 750 | 637 | 119 | 122 | 1,539 | 1,349 | 932 | 823 | 6,641 | 6,740 |
| Females | 5,979 | 8,529 | 194 | 228 | 13 | 58 | 434 | 561 | 217 | 323 | 1,360 | 1,965 |
| Both sexes | 34,651 | 33,925 | 944 | 865 | 132 | 180 | 1,973 | 1,910 | 1,149 | 1,146 | 8,001 | 8,705 |
| **Average salary:** | | | | | | | | | | | | |
| Males | 76,479 | 77,737 | 61,344 | 64,888 | 68,400 | 67,996 | 69,557 | 68,524 | 67,595 | 71,487 | 73,871 | 75,151 |
| Females | 63,406 | 65,994 | 50,606 | 56,672 | 63,533 | 59,173 | 55,208 | 57,857 | 57,621 | 60,524 | 64,214 | 65,720 |
| Both sexes | 74,236 | 74,800 | 59,208 | 62,761 | 67,955 | 65,121 | 66,389 | 65,407 | 65,713 | 68,434 | 72,230 | 73,022 |
| Gender gap (%)[1] | 83 | 85 | 82 | 87 | 93 | 87 | 79 | 84 | 85 | 85 | 87 | 87 |
| **Full professors** | | | | | | | | | | | | |
| Males | 11,980 | 12,110 | 262 | 268 | 33 | 40 | 517 | 594 | 399 | 423 | 2,686 | 3,031 |
| Females | 849 | 1,800 | 17 | 28 | 2 | 7 | 33 | 87 | 33 | 93 | 240 | 481 |
| Both sexes | 12,829 | 13,910 | 279 | 296 | 35 | 47 | 550 | 681 | 432 | 516 | 2,926 | 3,512 |
| **Average salary:** | | | | | | | | | | | | |
| Males | 90,132 | 89,463 | 75,045 | 74,537 | 81,295 | 82,100 | 84,087 | 80,018 | 80,272 | 82,792 | 84,631 | 84,220 |
| Females | 84,790 | 84,118 | 65,697 | 76,073 | 78,831 | 76,351 | 77,645 | 73,217 | 77,224 | 75,953 | 81,530 | 81,302 |
| Both sexes | 89,781 | 88,775 | 74,501 | 74,675 | 81,154 | 81,244 | 83,698 | 79,156 | 80,044 | 81,554 | 84,377 | 83,820 |
| Gender gap (%)[1] | 94 | 94 | 88 | 102 | 97 | 93 | 92 | 92 | 96 | 92 | 96 | 97 |
| **Associate professors** | | | | | | | | | | | | |
| Males | 10,500 | 8,694 | 303 | 267 | 58 | 40 | 627 | 502 | 319 | 249 | 2,732 | 2,370 |
| Females | 2,150 | 3,401 | 69 | 113 | 6 | 16 | 139 | 212 | 78 | 90 | 614 | 897 |
| Both sexes | 12,650 | 12,095 | 372 | 380 | 64 | 56 | 766 | 714 | 397 | 339 | 3,346 | 3,267 |
| **Average salary:** | | | | | | | | | | | | |
| Males | 72,150 | 71,215 | 57,760 | 61,478 | 66,872 | 68,928 | 67,255 | 63,142 | 64,383 | 64,791 | 71,840 | 69,173 |
| Females | 68,732 | 67,664 | 55,866 | 59,543 | 66,095 | 67,903 | 62,582 | 61,608 | 62,753 | 63,343 | 67,979 | 65,968 |
| Both sexes | 71,571 | 70,219 | 57,417 | 60,903 | 66,799 | 68,624 | 66,400 | 62,689 | 64,063 | 64,425 | 71,132 | 68,293 |
| Gender gap (%)[1] | 95 | 95 | 97 | 97 | 99 | 99 | 93 | 98 | 97 | 98 | 95 | 95 |
| **Other ranks** | | | | | | | | | | | | |
| Males | 6,192 | 4,412 | 185 | 102 | 28 | 42 | 395 | 253 | 214 | 151 | 1,223 | 951 |
| Females | 2,980 | 3,405 | 108 | 87 | 5 | 35 | 262 | 262 | 106 | 140 | 506 | 617 |
| Both sexes | 9,172 | 7,817 | 293 | 189 | 33 | 77 | 657 | 515 | 320 | 291 | 1,729 | 1,568 |
| **Average salary:** | | | | | | | | | | | | |
| Males | 57,215 | 57,122 | 47,864 | 48,311 | 56,369 | 53,721 | 53,878 | 51,976 | 48,366 | 49,919 | 54,789 | 55,295 |
| Females | 53,411 | 54,591 | 44,834 | 46,545 | 52,041 | 51,746 | 48,392 | 49,768 | 47,840 | 48,277 | 51,410 | 52,500 |
| Both sexes | 55,982 | 56,020 | 46,783 | 47,516 | 55,829 | 52,823 | 51,671 | 50,855 | 48,189 | 49,118 | 53,800 | 54,195 |
| Gender gap (%)[1] | 93 | 96 | 94 | 96 | 92 | 96 | 90 | 96 | 99 | 97 | 94 | 95 |

TABLE 3.12    NUMBER AND AVERAGE SALARY OF FULL-TIME UNIVERSITY FACULTY, BY RANK AND GENDER, CANADA AND PROVINCES, 1987-88 AND 1997-98, IN CONSTANT 1997 DOLLARS (Concluded)

|  | Ontario 1987-88 | Ontario 1997-98 | Manitoba 1987-88 | Manitoba 1997-98 | Saskatchewan 1987-88 | Saskatchewan 1997-98 | Alberta 1987-88 | Alberta 1997-98 | British Columbia 1987-88 | British Columbia 1997-98 |
|---|---|---|---|---|---|---|---|---|---|---|
| **All teaching faculty** | | | | | | | | | | |
| Males | 11,078 | 9,147 | 1,371 | 1,128 | 1,271 | 818 | 2,510 | 2,175 | 2,461 | 2,457 |
| Females | 2,311 | 3,199 | 259 | 378 | 220 | 216 | 494 | 765 | 477 | 836 |
| **Both sexes** | **13,389** | **12,346** | **1,630** | **1,506** | **1,491** | **1,034** | **3,004** | **2,940** | **2,938** | **3,293** |
| **Average salary:** | | | | | | | | | | |
| Males | 78,657 | 80,313 | 79,322 | 76,666 | 80,634 | 89,429 | 81,622 | 76,642 | 77,750 | 84,019 |
| Females | 64,957 | 68,510 | 63,759 | 61,854 | 61,267 | 71,813 | 67,575 | 63,170 | 64,700 | 70,490 |
| **Both sexes** | **76,320** | **77,261** | **76,855** | **72,996** | **77,812** | **85,902** | **79,334** | **73,199** | **75,613** | **80,569** |
| Gender gap (%)[1] | 83 | 85 | 80 | 81 | 76 | 80 | 83 | 82 | 83 | 84 |
| **Full professors** | | | | | | | | | | |
| Males | 4,430 | 4,252 | 618 | 567 | 651 | 612 | 1,302 | 1,128 | 1,082 | 1,195 |
| Females | 289 | 636 | 36 | 66 | 29 | 52 | 115 | 175 | 55 | 175 |
| **Both sexes** | **4,719** | **4,888** | **654** | **633** | **680** | **664** | **1,417** | **1,303** | **1,137** | **1,370** |
| **Average salary:** | | | | | | | | | | |
| Males | 93,515 | 92,462 | 95,633 | 89,774 | 93,331 | 96,637 | 95,176 | 90,561 | 90,546 | 98,189 |
| Females | 87,293 | 86,182 | 88,366 | 83,834 | 83,137 | 82,299 | 88,873 | 83,347 | 89,251 | 97,240 |
| **Both sexes** | **93,143** | **91,656** | **95,235** | **89,153** | **92,913** | **95,548** | **94,662** | **89,589** | **90,482** | **98,068** |
| Gender gap (%)[1] | 93 | 93 | 92 | 93 | 89 | 85 | 93 | 92 | 99 | 99 |
| **Associate professors** | | | | | | | | | | |
| Males | 3,907 | 3,157 | 468 | 359 | 395 | 296 | 836 | 668 | 855 | 786 |
| Females | 709 | 1,240 | 99 | 136 | 85 | 127 | 194 | 293 | 157 | 277 |
| **Both sexes** | **4,616** | **4,397** | **567** | **495** | **480** | **423** | **1,030** | **961** | **1,012** | **1,063** |
| **Average salary:** | | | | | | | | | | |
| Males | 74,379 | 75,132 | 73,382 | 68,795 | 72,873 | 75,871 | 72,412 | 66,646 | 72,630 | 75,595 |
| Females | 71,581 | 70,932 | 69,988 | 65,567 | 67,778 | 71,705 | 68,173 | 64,421 | 71,453 | 70,416 |
| **Both sexes** | **73,951** | **73,946** | **72,790** | **67,909** | **72,002** | **74,645** | **71,625** | **65,975** | **72,447** | **74,239** |
| Gender gap (%)[1] | 96 | 94 | 95 | 95 | 93 | 95 | 94 | 97 | 98 | 93 |
| **Other ranks** | | | | | | | | | | |
| Males | 2,741 | 1,738 | 285 | 202 | 225 | 118 | 372 | 379 | 524 | 476 |
| Females | 1,313 | 1,323 | 124 | 176 | 106 | 84 | 185 | 297 | 265 | 384 |
| **Both sexes** | **4,054** | **3,061** | **409** | **378** | **331** | **202** | **557** | **676** | **789** | **860** |
| **Average salary:** | | | | | | | | | | |
| Males | 60,575 | 59,601 | 54,426 | 53,683 | 57,244 | 65,531 | 53,715 | 52,999 | 59,170 | 61,911 |
| Females | 56,425 | 57,789 | 51,696 | 50,325 | 50,642 | 64,067 | 53,217 | 49,450 | 55,654 | 58,461 |
| **Both sexes** | **59,243** | **58,812** | **53,607** | **52,150** | **55,098** | **64,947** | **53,547** | **51,486** | **57,965** | **60,353** |
| Gender gap (%)[1] | 93 | 97 | 95 | 94 | 88 | 98 | 99 | 93 | 94 | 94 |

1  Gender gap is defined as the average salary of females as a percentage of the average salary of males.
2  1996-97 data used for Quebec, as 1997-98 data were not available.

*Source: Centre for Education Statistics, Statistics Canada.*

**CHAPTER 3 TABLES**

**TABLE 3.13** PUPIL–EDUCATOR RATIO IN PUBLIC ELEMENTARY–SECONDARY SCHOOLS, CANADA AND JURISDICTIONS, **1986-87** TO **1996-97**

| Year | Canada | Nfld. | P.E.I. | N.S. | N.B. | Que. | Ont. | Man. | Sask. | Alta. | B.C. | Y.T. | N.W.T. |
|---|---|---|---|---|---|---|---|---|---|---|---|---|---|
| 1986-87 | **16.4** | 16.5 | 18.3 | 16.6 | 18.1 | 15.3 | 16.5 | 15.5 | 17.0 | 17.4 | 18.0 | 14.6 | 17.6 |
| 1987-88 | **16.3** | 16.2 | 17.9 | 16.3 | 17.5 | 15.1 | 16.2 | 16.5 | 17.1 | 17.5 | 17.6 | 15.8 | 16.7 |
| 1988-89 | **16.0** | 15.8 | 17.8 | 16.3 | 17.4 | 15.1 | 15.7 | 15.3 | 16.8 | 17.7 | 17.3 | 14.6 | 15.7 |
| 1989-90 | **15.7** | 15.6 | 17.3 | 16.0 | 17.0 | 15.0 | 15.3 | 14.8 | 16.7 | 17.2 | 16.7 | 13.9 | 15.7 |
| 1990-91 | **15.6** | 15.2 | 16.7 | 16.6 | 16.1 | 14.6 | 15.0 | 15.0 | 17.3 | 17.3 | 16.4 | 12.6 | 15.4 |
| 1991-92 | **15.3** | 15.2 | 17.3 | 16.4 | 16.9 | 14.4 | 14.9 | 15.1 | 16.8 | 17.3 | 16.3 | 13.1 | 13.5 |
| 1992-93 | **15.5** | 15.0 | 17.1 | 16.9 | 17.1 | 14.2 | 15.1 | 15.1 | 17.6 | 17.7 | 16.7 | 12.4 | 12.9 |
| 1993-94 | **15.9** | 14.7 | 17.0 | 16.9 | 17.2 | 14.4 | 15.8 | 15.1 | 17.4 | 18.1 | 17.2 | 12.3 | 11.7 |
| 1994-95 | **16.0** | 14.7 | 17.4 | 17.4 | 17.3 | 14.4 | 15.9 | 15.2 | 17.4 | 18.5 | 17.3 | 12.1 | 12.2 |
| 1995-96 | **16.0** | 14.4 | 17.3 | 17.7 | 17.3 | 14.4 | 16.2 | 15.5 | 17.3 | 17.1 | 17.2 | 12.6 | 13.5 |
| 1996-97 | **16.3** | 14.4 | 17.1 | 17.6 | 17.4 | 14.7 | 16.7 | 15.9 | 17.3 | 17.5 | 17.4 | 12.2 | 12.3 |

Source: *Centre for Education Statistics, Statistics Canada;* Statistiques de l'éducation - Enseignement primaire, secondaire, collégial et universitaire, *Gouvernement du Québec, Ministère de l'éducation (for Quebec data).*

**TABLE 3.14** PRE-ELEMENTARY ENROLMENT[1] AND ENROLMENT RATE[2], CANADA AND JURISDICTIONS, **1986-87** TO **1996-97**

|  | Canada[3] Enrolment | Canada[3] Enrolment rate | Newfoundland and Labrador Enrolment | Newfoundland and Labrador Enrolment rate | Prince Edward Island[4] Enrolment | Prince Edward Island[4] Enrolment rate | Nova Scotia Enrolment | Nova Scotia Enrolment rate | New Brunswick Enrolment | New Brunswick Enrolment rate | Quebec Enrolment | Quebec Enrolment rate | Ontario Enrolment | Ontario Enrolment rate |
|---|---|---|---|---|---|---|---|---|---|---|---|---|---|---|
| 1986-87 | **430,128** | **38.8** | 9,355 | 34.0 | 66 | 1.1 | 12,830 | 35.1 | 546 | 1.8 | 100,261 | 36.4 | 192,347 | 50.3 |
| 1987-88 | **441,041** | **39.6** | 9,153 | 34.3 | 61 | 1.1 | 12,938 | 35.3 | 599 | 2.0 | 96,261 | 35.8 | 202,580 | 51.7 |
| 1988-89 | **458,759** | **40.7** | 8,974 | 34.6 | 66 | 1.1 | 13,109 | 35.6 | 394 | 1.3 | 94,369 | 35.7 | 219,103 | 54.1 |
| 1989-90 | **472,447** | **41.2** | 8,811 | 35.0 | 25 | 0.4 | 13,085 | 35.3 | 558 | 1.8 | 95,209 | 36.0 | 229,015 | 54.6 |
| 1990-91 | **472,802** | **41.0** | 8,502 | 35.0 | 18 | 0.3 | 13,222 | 35.6 | 379 | 1.3 | 93,512 | 35.7 | 235,685 | 55.2 |
| 1991-92 | **486,609** | **42.5** | 8,057 | 34.6 | 24 | 0.4 | 13,060 | 35.4 | 9,237 | 31.2 | 92,874 | 35.8 | 237,792 | 55.9 |
| 1992-93 | **482,446** | **41.7** | 7,700 | 34.1 | 31 | 0.5 | 12,794 | 34.9 | 9,556 | 32.8 | 91,532 | 34.9 | 236,051 | 54.6 |
| 1993-94 | **489,398** | **41.2** | 7,475 | 32.9 | 35 | 0.6 | 12,710 | 34.2 | 9,627 | 32.9 | 92,467 | 33.8 | 241,797 | 54.4 |
| 1994-95 | **507,437** | **41.6** | 7,626 | 34.0 | 30 | 0.5 | 12,831 | 34.1 | 9,699 | 33.0 | 103,935 | 36.2 | 253,282 | 55.3 |
| 1995-96 | **536,536** | **43.5** | 7,522 | 34.7 | 49 | 0.8 | 13,224 | 35.5 | 9,866 | 33.8 | 112,935 | 38.4 | 273,787 | 58.9 |
| 1996-97 | **507,837** | **41.6** | 6,867 | 34.1 | 32 | 0.6 | 12,568 | 34.6 | 9,636 | 33.7 | 113,381 | 38.9 | 245,882 | 53.0 |

|  | Manitoba Enrolment | Manitoba Enrolment rate | Saskatchewan Enrolment | Saskatchewan Enrolment rate | Alberta Enrolment | Alberta Enrolment rate | British Columbia Enrolment | British Columbia Enrolment rate | Yukon Enrolment | Yukon Enrolment rate | Northwest Territories[5] Enrolment | Northwest Territories[5] Enrolment rate |
|---|---|---|---|---|---|---|---|---|---|---|---|---|
| 1986-87 | 18,889 | 39.5 | 18,239 | 35.4 | 33,347 | 27.7 | 41,444 | 33.3 | 451 | 34.6 | 1,214 | 32.3 |
| 1987-88 | 19,300 | 40.0 | 18,618 | 35.9 | 34,633 | 28.4 | 44,081 | 34.7 | 446 | 30.7 | 1,256 | 32.8 |
| 1988-89 | 19,821 | 40.8 | 18,344 | 35.7 | 36,325 | 29.4 | 45,134 | 34.7 | 508 | 33.8 | 1,292 | 33.3 |
| 1989-90 | 20,064 | 40.9 | 18,110 | 35.7 | 37,371 | 29.7 | 47,267 | 35.4 | 501 | 33.7 | 1,286 | 33.0 |
| 1990-91 | 20,261 | 40.9 | 17,899 | 36.4 | 37,985 | 30.0 | 42,185 | 31.0 | 495 | 33.9 | 1,254 | 30.7 |
| 1991-92 | 20,340 | 41.4 | 17,496 | 36.7 | 37,579 | 29.8 | 47,041 | 34.4 | 480 | 33.2 | 1,447 | 33.4 |
| 1992-93 | 20,339 | 41.4 | 17,094 | 36.3 | 37,741 | 29.8 | 46,949 | 33.7 | 484 | 32.2 | 1,428 | 31.3 |
| 1993-94 | 20,492 | 41.0 | 16,884 | 35.6 | 38,304 | 29.8 | 48,312 | 33.8 | 503 | 33.0 | 1,315 | 27.9 |
| 1994-95 | 20,811 | 40.9 | 17,248 | 36.2 | 38,496 | 29.9 | 48,575 | 33.0 | 457 | 29.8 | 1,383 | 29.1 |
| 1995-96 | 21,114 | 41.3 | 17,261 | 36.7 | 38,211 | 29.8 | 50,502 | 33.9 | 531 | 34.1 | 1,640 | 34.5 |
| 1996-97 | 21,133 | 42.1 | 16,533 | 36.1 | 39,560 | 31.7 | 50,197 | 33.8 | 535 | 35.0 | 1,640 | 34.5 |

1 Defined as the headcount of individuals registered in pre-grade 1 programs offered by public, private, and federal schools, and schools for the visually and hearing impaired.
2 Calculated as the headcount of individuals enrolled in pre-elementary education divided by the population aged 3 to 5.
3 Enrolments in Department of National Defence overseas schools are included in the Canada total.
4 Prince Edward Island does not provide public pre-elementary education in its school system.
5 Data for the Northwest Territories were estimated for 1996-97.

Source: *Centre for Education Statistics, Statistics Canada;* Statistiques de l'éducation - Enseignement primaire, secondaire, collégial et universitaire, *Gouvernement du Québec, Ministère de l'Éducation (for Quebec data).*

TABLE 3.15    ELEMENTARY-SECONDARY ENROLMENT[1] AND PERCENTAGE ANNUAL CHANGE IN ENROLMENT, CANADA AND JURISDICTIONS, 1986-87 TO 1996-97

### Enrolment

|  | Canada | Nfld. | P.E.I. | N.S. | N.B. | Que. | Ont. | Man. | Sask. | Alta. | B.C. | Y.T. | N.W.T. | DND[2] |
|---|---|---|---|---|---|---|---|---|---|---|---|---|---|---|
| 1986-87 | 4,937,991 | 139,821 | 25,004 | 174,308 | 141,350 | 1,347,305 | 1,866,900 | 219,184 | 214,530 | 471,530 | 524,697 | 4,805 | 13,296 | 3,587 |
| 1987-88 | 4,972,883 | 136,675 | 24,872 | 172,959 | 140,353 | 1,371,710 | 1,896,253 | 220,192 | 215,334 | 473,421 | 532,244 | 4,896 | 13,386 | 3,633 |
| 1988-89 | 5,024,117 | 133,420 | 24,937 | 170,991 | 138,269 | 1,376,109 | 1,937,022 | 219,878 | 214,608 | 481,674 | 542,023 | 5,006 | 13,449 | 3,758 |
| 1989-90 | 5,075,277 | 130,503 | 24,804 | 169,630 | 136,527 | 1,384,450 | 1,967,497 | 219,245 | 212,676 | 492,910 | 555,546 | 5,113 | 13,732 | 3,722 |
| 1990-91 | 5,141,003 | 127,400 | 24,523 | 169,170 | 134,761 | 1,389,525 | 2,009,090 | 219,859 | 212,278 | 507,460 | 564,627 | 5,266 | 14,079 | 3,720 |
| 1991-92 | 5,218,237 | 125,492 | 24,754 | 168,897 | 142,687 | 1,396,871 | 2,046,492 | 220,515 | 212,071 | 519,936 | 587,920 | 5,516 | 15,515 | 3,376 |
| 1992-93 | 5,284,145 | 122,125 | 24,596 | 169,755 | 141,722 | 1,376,962 | 2,085,395 | 221,578 | 212,386 | 531,783 | 604,740 | 5,811 | 15,872 | 1,894 |
| 1993-94 | 5,327,826 | 118,595 | 24,483 | 169,805 | 140,378 | 1,368,721 | 2,113,813 | 222,038 | 212,677 | 540,230 | 623,069 | 5,777 | 15,921 | 613 |
| 1994-95 | 5,362,799 | 114,445 | 24,481 | 168,507 | 138,306 | 1,373,321 | 2,140,085 | 221,747 | 212,666 | 544,561 | 638,111 | 5,792 | 16,338 | 200 |
| 1995-96 | 5,430,836 | 110,901 | 24,704 | 167,960 | 136,776 | 1,379,523 | 2,189,029 | 223,045 | 212,986 | 548,459 | 654,351 | 6,132 | 17,625 | 191 |
| 1996-97 | 5,414,344 | 106,494 | 24,814 | 167,162 | 135,254 | 1,374,893 | 2,161,488 | 223,826 | 212,725 | 553,726 | 667,070 | 6,378 | 18,047 | 238 |

### Annual change in enrolment (%)

|  | Canada | Nfld. | P.E.I. | N.S. | N.B. | Que. | Ont. | Man. | Sask. | Alta. | B.C. | Y.T. | N.W.T. | DND[2] |
|---|---|---|---|---|---|---|---|---|---|---|---|---|---|---|
| 1987-88 | 0.7 | -2.3 | -0.5 | -0.8 | -0.7 | 1.8 | 1.6 | 0.5 | 0.4 | 0.4 | 1.4 | 1.9 | 0.7 | 1.3 |
| 1988-89 | 1.0 | -2.4 | 0.3 | -1.1 | -1.5 | 0.3 | 2.1 | -0.1 | -0.3 | 1.7 | 1.8 | 2.2 | 0.5 | 3.4 |
| 1989-90 | 1.0 | -2.2 | -0.5 | -0.8 | -1.3 | 0.6 | 1.6 | -0.3 | -0.9 | 2.3 | 2.5 | 2.1 | 2.1 | -1.0 |
| 1990-91 | 1.3 | -2.4 | -1.1 | -0.3 | -1.3 | 0.4 | 2.1 | 0.3 | -0.2 | 3.0 | 1.6 | 3.0 | 2.5 | -0.1 |
| 1991-92 | 1.5 | -1.5 | 0.9 | -0.2 | 5.9 | 0.5 | 1.9 | 0.3 | -0.1 | 2.5 | 4.1 | 4.7 | 10.2 | -9.2 |
| 1992-93 | 1.3 | -2.7 | -0.6 | 0.5 | -0.7 | -1.4 | 1.9 | 0.5 | 0.1 | 2.3 | 2.9 | 5.3 | 2.3 | -43.9 |
| 1993-94 | 0.8 | -2.9 | -0.5 | - | -0.9 | -0.6 | 1.4 | 0.2 | 0.1 | 1.6 | 3.0 | -0.6 | 0.3 | -67.6 |
| 1994-95 | 0.7 | -3.5 | - | -0.8 | -1.5 | 0.3 | 1.2 | -0.1 | - | 0.8 | 2.4 | 0.3 | 2.6 | -67.4 |
| 1995-96 | 1.3 | -3.1 | 0.9 | -0.3 | -1.1 | 0.5 | 2.3 | 0.6 | 0.2 | 0.7 | 2.5 | 5.9 | 7.9 | -4.5 |
| 1996-97 | -0.3 | -4.0 | 0.4 | -0.5 | -1.1 | -0.3 | -1.3 | 0.4 | -0.1 | 1.0 | 1.9 | 4.0 | 2.4 | 24.6 |

1  Includes students registered in public, private, and federal schools, and schools for the visually and hearing impaired. Coverage includes students registered in pre-elementary programs offered by these schools.
2  DND refers to Department of National Defence overseas schools.

Source:  *Centre for Education Statistics, Statistics Canada;* Statistiques de l'éducation - Enseignement primaire, secondaire, collégial et universitaire, *Gouvernement du Québec, Ministère de l'Éducation (for Quebec data).*

TABLE 3.16  TRADE-VOCATIONAL ENROLMENT BY REGISTRATION STATUS AND GENDER, CANADA AND JURISDICTIONS, 1987-88 AND 1995-96

|  | Both sexes 1987-88 | Both sexes 1995-96 | Males 1987-88 | Males 1995-96 | Females 1987-88 | Females 1995-96 | Gender not reported 1987-88 | Gender not reported 1995-96 |
|---|---|---|---|---|---|---|---|---|
| **Full-time** | | | | | | | | |
| Canada | 148,673 | 145,879 | 62,160 | 81,023 | 42,367 | 58,723 | 44,146 | 6,133 |
| Nfld. | 4,430 | 4,210 | 2,024 | 2,803 | 2,255 | 1,407 | 151 | - |
| P.E.I. | 918 | 810 | 507 | 422 | 323 | 388 | 88 | - |
| N.S. | 6,490 | 946 | 3,743 | 515 | 2,604 | 431 | 143 | - |
| N.B. | 4,593 | 7,142 | 2,154 | 3,022 | 1,970 | 4,120 | 469 | - |
| Que. | 38,509 | 59,450 | 21,118 | 32,205 | 16,844 | 27,087 | 547 | 158 |
| Ont.[1] | 39,378 | 32,340 | 25,673 | 23,179 | 10,902 | 7,331 | 2,803 | 1,830 |
| Man. | 2,932 | 2,403 | 1,587 | 1,363 | 1,045 | 992 | 300 | 48 |
| Sask. | 4,958 | 5,408 | 2,458 | 2,483 | 2,306 | 2,850 | 194 | 75 |
| Alta.[3] | 15,228 | 7,987 | 2,896 | 3,494 | 4,118 | 4,493 | 8,214 | - |
| B.C. | 31,237 | 25,183 | .. | 11,537 | .. | 9,624 | 31,237 | 4,022 |
| Y.T. | .. | .. | .. | .. | .. | .. | .. | .. |
| N.W.T. | .. | .. | .. | .. | .. | .. | .. | .. |
| **Part-time** | | | | | | | | |
| Canada[2] | .. | 146,057 | .. | 91,292 | .. | 47,187 | .. | 7,578 |
| Nfld. | 2,693 | 3,339 | 1,709 | 2,858 | 920 | 481 | 64 | - |
| P.E.I. | 870 | 768 | 287 | 436 | 213 | 332 | 370 | - |
| N.S. | 3,003 | 2,108 | 2,687 | 1,699 | 262 | 409 | 54 | - |
| N.B. | 6,120 | 12,612 | 4,066 | 7,964 | 1,803 | 4,648 | 251 | - |
| Que.[2] | .. | 40,400 | .. | 23,815 | .. | 14,244 | - | 2,341 |
| Ont.[1] | 35,942 | 35,771 | 18,614 | 20,603 | 15,390 | 13,247 | 1,938 | 1,921 |
| Man. | 5,040 | 3,597 | 3,323 | 2,622 | 1,571 | 953 | 146 | 22 |
| Sask.[3] | 4,203 | 3,540 | 3,008 | 2,631 | 955 | 908 | 240 | 1 |
| Alta. | 23,053 | 17,894 | 7,193 | 14,660 | 5,180 | 3,234 | 10,680 | - |
| B.C. | 20,527 | 26,028 | .. | 14,004 | .. | 8,731 | 20,527 | 3,293 |
| Y.T. | .. | .. | .. | .. | .. | .. | .. | .. |
| N.W.T. | .. | .. | .. | .. | .. | .. | .. | .. |

1  Gender distribution is based on estimates for 1995-96.
2  Data not available for Quebec for 1987-88; the Canada total therefore is not available.
3  Data are not strictly comparable over time due to improvements in reporting arrangements.
*Source:* Centre for Education Statistics, Statistics Canada; Statistiques de l'éducation - Enseignement primaire, secondaire, collégial et universitaire, Gouvernement du Québec, Ministère de l'Éducation (for Quebec data).


TABLE 3.17  COLLEGE ENROLMENT BY REGISTRATION STATUS[1] AND GENDER, CANADA AND JURISDICTIONS, 1987-88 AND 1997-98[E]

|  | Both sexes 1987-88 | Both sexes 1997-98 | Males 1987-88 | Males 1997-98 | Females 1987-88 | Females 1997-98 |
|---|---|---|---|---|---|---|
| **Total full-time** | | | | | | |
| Canada | 319,548 | 396,667 | 149,404 | 185,671 | 170,144 | 210,996 |
| Newfoundland and Labrador | 3,003 | 5,030 | 1,409 | 2,621 | 1,594 | 2,409 |
| Prince Edward Island | 907 | 1,663 | 371 | 885 | 536 | 778 |
| Nova Scotia | 2,435 | 7,696 | 957 | 3,995 | 1,478 | 3,701 |
| New Brunswick | 2,383 | 4,889 | 1,181 | 2,606 | 1,202 | 2,283 |
| Quebec | 159,940 | 162,270 | 73,170 | 72,493 | 86,770 | 89,777 |
| Ontario | 95,029 | 139,792 | 44,949 | 68,638 | 50,080 | 71,154 |
| Manitoba | 3,839 | 3,923 | 1,696 | 1,892 | 2,143 | 2,031 |
| Saskatchewan | 3,030 | 3,131 | 1,164 | 1,294 | 1,866 | 1,837 |
| Alberta | 24,000 | 32,501 | 11,806 | 14,494 | 12,194 | 18,007 |
| British Columbia | 24,634 | 35,319 | 12,553 | 16,596 | 12,081 | 18,723 |
| Yukon | 126 | 249 | 44 | 86 | 82 | 163 |
| Northwest Territories | 222 | 204 | 104 | 71 | 118 | 133 |

TABLE 3.17  COLLEGE ENROLMENT BY REGISTRATION STATUS[1] AND GENDER, CANADA AND JURISDICTIONS, 1987-88 AND 1997-98[E] (continued)

|  | Both sexes 1987-88 | Both sexes 1997-98 | Males 1987-88 | Males 1997-98 | Females 1987-88 | Females 1997-98 |
|---|---|---|---|---|---|---|
| **Full-time career technical** | | | | | | |
| **Canada** | 218,160 | 290,931 | 100,690 | 140,628 | 117,470 | 150,303 |
| Newfoundland and Labrador | 3,003 | 5,030 | 1,409 | 2,621 | 1,594 | 2,409 |
| Prince Edward Island | 907 | 1,663 | 371 | 885 | 536 | 778 |
| Nova Scotia | 2,435 | 7,696 | 957 | 3,995 | 1,478 | 3,701 |
| New Brunswick | 2,383 | 4,889 | 1,181 | 2,606 | 1,202 | 2,283 |
| Quebec | 72,598 | 82,092 | 31,641 | 38,337 | 40,957 | 43,755 |
| Ontario | 95,029 | 139,792 | 44,949 | 68,638 | 50,080 | 71,154 |
| Manitoba | 3,748 | 3,857 | 1,645 | 1,848 | 2,103 | 2,009 |
| Saskatchewan | 3,030 | 3,131 | 1,164 | 1,294 | 1,866 | 1,837 |
| Alberta | 21,400 | 24,573 | 10,474 | 11,402 | 10,926 | 13,171 |
| British Columbia | 13,356 | 17,905 | 6,775 | 8,899 | 6,581 | 9,006 |
| Yukon | 52 | 112 | 21 | 38 | 31 | 74 |
| Northwest Territories | 219 | 191 | 103 | 65 | 116 | 126 |
| **Full-time university transfer and university college** | | | | | | |
| **Canada** | 101,388 | 105,736 | 48,714 | 45,043 | 52,674 | 60,693 |
| Newfoundland and Labrador | ... | ... | ... | ... | ... | ... |
| Prince Edward Island | ... | ... | ... | ... | ... | ... |
| Nova Scotia | ... | ... | ... | ... | ... | ... |
| New Brunswick | ... | ... | ... | ... | ... | ... |
| Quebec | 87,342 | 80,178 | 41,529 | 34,156 | 45,813 | 46,022 |
| Ontario | ... | ... | ... | ... | ... | ... |
| Manitoba | 91 | 66 | 51 | 44 | 40 | 22 |
| Saskatchewan | ... | ... | ... | ... | ... | ... |
| Alberta | 2,600 | 7,928 | 1,332 | 3,092 | 1,268 | 4,836 |
| British Columbia | 11,278 | 17,414 | 5,778 | 7,697 | 5,500 | 9,717 |
| Yukon | 74 | 137 | 23 | 48 | 51 | 89 |
| Northwest Territories | 3 | 13 | 1 | 6 | 2 | 7 |
| **Total part-time** | | | | | | |
| **Canada** | 141,402 | 154,496 | 54,302 | 62,123 | 87,100 | 92,373 |
| Newfoundland and Labrador | 179 | 107 | 118 | 69 | 61 | 38 |
| Prince Edward Island | .. | 144 | .. | 83 | .. | 61 |
| Nova Scotia | 537 | 287 | 90 | 38 | 447 | 249 |
| New Brunswick | 26 | 170 | 14 | 81 | 12 | 89 |
| Quebec | 20,476 | 11,009 | 8,121 | 5,178 | 12,355 | 5,831 |
| Ontario | 76,498 | 78,619 | 29,587 | 32,580 | 46,911 | 46,039 |
| Manitoba | 2,126 | 2,145 | 752 | 937 | 1,374 | 1,208 |
| Saskatchewan | 524 | 159 | 51 | 42 | 473 | 117 |
| Alberta | 8,056 | 15,402 | 2,680 | 5,605 | 5,376 | 9,797 |
| British Columbia | 32,503 | 45,562 | 12,765 | 17,279 | 19,738 | 28,283 |
| Yukon | 338 | 382 | 86 | 116 | 252 | 266 |
| Northwest Territories | 139 | 510 | 38 | 115 | 101 | 395 |
| **Part-time career technical** | | | | | | |
| **Canada** | 116,958 | 121,738 | 45,257 | 49,391 | 71,701 | 72,347 |
| Newfoundland and Labrador | 179 | 107 | 118 | 69 | 61 | 38 |
| Prince Edward Island | .. | 144 | .. | 83 | .. | 61 |
| Nova Scotia | 537 | 287 | 90 | 38 | 447 | 249 |
| New Brunswick | 26 | 170 | 14 | 81 | 12 | 89 |
| Quebec | 10,769 | 5,355 | 4,296 | 2,501 | 6,473 | 2,854 |
| Ontario | 76,498 | 78,619 | 29,587 | 32,580 | 46,911 | 46,039 |
| Manitoba | 2,125 | 2,138 | 752 | 932 | 1,373 | 1,206 |
| Saskatchewan | 524 | 159 | 51 | 42 | 473 | 117 |
| Alberta | 7,350 | 14,145 | 2,381 | 5,154 | 4,969 | 8,991 |
| British Columbia | 18,532 | 19,924 | 7,856 | 7,749 | 10,676 | 12,175 |
| Yukon | 279 | 227 | 74 | 62 | 205 | 165 |
| Northwest Territories | 139 | 463 | 38 | 100 | 101 | 363 |

CHAPTER 3 TABLES

TABLE 3.17  COLLEGE ENROLMENT BY REGISTRATION STATUS[1] AND GENDER, CANADA AND JURISDICTIONS, 1987-88 AND 1997-98[e] (concluded)

|  | Both sexes | | Males | | Females | |
|---|---|---|---|---|---|---|
|  | 1987-88 | 1997-98 | 1987-88 | 1997-98 | 1987-88 | 1997-98 |
|  | Part-time university transfer and university college | | | | | |
| Canada | 24,444 | 32,758 | 9,045 | 12,732 | 15,399 | 20,026 |
| Newfoundland and Labrador | ... | ... | ... | ... | ... | ... |
| Prince Edward Island | ... | ... | ... | ... | ... | ... |
| Nova Scotia | ... | ... | ... | ... | ... | ... |
| New Brunswick | ... | ... | ... | ... | ... | ... |
| Quebec | 9,707 | 5,654 | 3,825 | 2,677 | 5,882 | 2,977 |
| Ontario | ... | ... | ... | ... | ... | ... |
| Manitoba | 1 | 7 | .. | 5 | 1 | 2 |
| Saskatchewan | ... | ... | ... | ... | ... | ... |
| Alberta | 706 | 1,257 | 299 | 451 | 407 | 806 |
| British Columbia | 13,971 | 25,638 | 4,909 | 9,530 | 9,062 | 16,108 |
| Yukon | 59 | 155 | 12 | 54 | 47 | 101 |
| Northwest Territories | .. | 47 | .. | 15 | .. | 32 |

1  See Appendix 2 for 1996-97 full-time enrolment by institution.
e  Data for 1997-98 are preliminary for full-time and previous year's data for part-time.
Source:  Centre for Education Statistics, Statistics Canada.


TABLE 3.18  UNIVERSITY ENROLMENT BY REGISTRATION STATUS[1] AND GENDER, CANADA AND PROVINCES, 1987-88, 1991-92 AND 1997-98

|  | Both sexes | | | Females | | | Males | | |
|---|---|---|---|---|---|---|---|---|---|
|  | 1987-88 | 1991-92 | 1997-98 | 1987-88 | 1991-92 | 1997-98 | 1987-88 | 1991-92 | 1997-98 |
|  | Total full-time (undergraduate and graduate) | | | | | | | | |
| Canada | 486,009 | 553,953 | 573,099 | 238,844 | 286,308 | 312,663 | 247,165 | 267,645 | 260,436 |
| Nfld. | 10,872 | 12,912 | 13,115 | 5,758 | 7,011 | 7,442 | 5,114 | 5,901 | 5,673 |
| P.E.I. | 2,030 | 2,609 | 2,452 | 1,099 | 1,435 | 1,504 | 931 | 1,174 | 948 |
| N.S. | 24,307 | 28,601 | 30,077 | 12,354 | 15,337 | 16,906 | 11,953 | 13,264 | 13,171 |
| N.B. | 15,200 | 18,096 | 18,503 | 7,475 | 9,552 | 10,138 | 7,725 | 8,544 | 8,365 |
| Que. | 116,623 | 129,993 | 131,074 | 57,940 | 67,634 | 72,063 | 58,683 | 62,359 | 59,011 |
| Ont. | 192,717 | 225,525 | 227,153 | 94,746 | 115,931 | 122,599 | 97,971 | 109,594 | 104,554 |
| Man. | 19,567 | 20,571 | 21,024 | 9,330 | 10,371 | 11,430 | 10,237 | 10,200 | 9,594 |
| Sask. | 20,729 | 22,392 | 23,864 | 10,062 | 11,514 | 13,324 | 10,667 | 10,878 | 10,540 |
| Alta. | 46,614 | 48,791 | 52,824 | 22,572 | 25,166 | 28,531 | 24,042 | 23,625 | 24,293 |
| B.C. | 37,350 | 44,463 | 53,013 | 17,508 | 22,357 | 28,726 | 19,842 | 22,106 | 24,287 |
|  | Full-time undergraduate | | | | | | | | |
| Canada | 427,807 | 485,461 | 497,072 | 215,217 | 257,749 | 276,763 | 212,590 | 227,712 | 220,309 |
| Nfld. | 10,208 | 11,909 | 11,749 | 5,478 | 6,622 | 6,772 | 4,730 | 5,287 | 4,977 |
| P.E.I. | 2,019 | 2,574 | 2,415 | 1,094 | 1,417 | 1,483 | 925 | 1,157 | 932 |
| N.S. | 22,214 | 26,258 | 27,865 | 11,491 | 14,311 | 15,830 | 10,723 | 11,947 | 12,035 |
| N.B. | 14,467 | 17,114 | 17,576 | 7,223 | 9,179 | 9,702 | 7,244 | 7,935 | 7,874 |
| Que. | 98,568 | 109,739 | 108,103 | 50,269 | 58,852 | 61,009 | 48,299 | 50,887 | 47,094 |
| Ont. | 170,665 | 199,494 | 199,009 | 85,837 | 105,244 | 109,644 | 84,828 | 94,250 | 89,365 |
| Man. | 17,201 | 18,093 | 18,637 | 8,494 | 9,461 | 10,339 | 8,707 | 8,632 | 8,298 |
| Sask. | 19,356 | 20,886 | 22,129 | 9,530 | 10,968 | 12,587 | 9,826 | 9,918 | 9,542 |
| Alta. | 41,414 | 43,146 | 46,598 | 20,516 | 22,842 | 25,600 | 20,898 | 20,304 | 20,998 |
| B.C. | 31,695 | 36,248 | 42,991 | 15,285 | 18,853 | 23,797 | 16,410 | 17,395 | 19,194 |

TABLE 3.18  UNIVERSITY ENROLMENT BY REGISTRATION STATUS AND GENDER, CANADA AND PROVINCES, 1987-88, 1991-92 AND 1997-98 (concluded)

| | Both sexes 1987-88 | Both sexes 1991-92 | Both sexes 1997-98 | Females 1987-88 | Females 1991-92 | Females 1997-98 | Males 1987-88 | Males 1991-92 | Males 1997-98 |
|---|---|---|---|---|---|---|---|---|---|
| **Full-time graduate** | | | | | | | | | |
| Canada | 58,202 | 68,492 | 76,027 | 23,627 | 28,559 | 35,900 | 34,575 | 39,933 | 40,127 |
| Nfld. | 664 | 1,003 | 1,366 | 280 | 389 | 670 | 384 | 614 | 696 |
| P.E.I. | 11 | 35 | 37 | 5 | 18 | 21 | 6 | 17 | 16 |
| N.S. | 2,093 | 2,343 | 2,212 | 863 | 1,026 | 1,076 | 1,230 | 1,317 | 1,136 |
| N.B. | 733 | 982 | 927 | 252 | 373 | 436 | 481 | 609 | 491 |
| Que. | 18,055 | 20,254 | 22,971 | 7,671 | 8,782 | 11,054 | 10,384 | 11,472 | 11,917 |
| Ont. | 22,052 | 26,031 | 28,144 | 8,909 | 10,687 | 12,955 | 13,143 | 15,344 | 15,189 |
| Man. | 2,366 | 2,478 | 2,387 | 836 | 910 | 1,091 | 1,530 | 1,568 | 1,296 |
| Sask. | 1,373 | 1,506 | 1,735 | 532 | 546 | 737 | 841 | 960 | 998 |
| Alta. | 5,200 | 5,645 | 6,226 | 2,056 | 2,324 | 2,931 | 3,144 | 3,321 | 3,295 |
| B.C. | 5,655 | 8,215 | 10,022 | 2,223 | 3,504 | 4,929 | 3,432 | 4,711 | 5,093 |
| **Total part-time (undergraduate and graduate)** | | | | | | | | | |
| Canada | 294,462 | 313,328 | 249,673 | 181,140 | 194,628 | 151,695 | 113,322 | 118,700 | 97,978 |
| Nfld. | 5,097 | 4,753 | 2,683 | 3,092 | 2,865 | 1,660 | 2,005 | 1,888 | 1,023 |
| P.E.I. | ... | 951 | 482 | ... | ... | 344 | ... | 293 | 138 |
| N.S. | 7,265 | 8,694 | 7,006 | 4,649 | 5,597 | 4,389 | 2,616 | 3,097 | 2,617 |
| N.B. | 4,923 | 5,702 | 4,181 | 3,209 | 3,842 | 2,794 | 1,714 | 1,860 | 1,387 |
| Que. | 118,658 | 119,722 | 101,021 | 71,485 | 73,587 | 61,113 | 47,173 | 46,135 | 39,908 |
| Ont. | 98,569 | 109,050 | 76,255 | 61,929 | 68,587 | 46,103 | 36,640 | 40,463 | 30,152 |
| Man. | 14,725 | 16,612 | 9,796 | 8,863 | 9,711 | 5,825 | 5,862 | 6,901 | 3,971 |
| Sask. | 9,001 | 9,435 | 7,364 | 5,645 | 5,801 | 4,583 | 3,356 | 3,634 | 2,781 |
| Alta. | 17,782 | 17,155 | 18,594 | 11,286 | 11,119 | 11,572 | 6,496 | 6,036 | 7,022 |
| B.C. | 17,689 | 21,254 | 22,291 | 10,499 | 12,861 | 13,312 | 7,190 | 8,393 | 8,979 |
| **Part-time undergraduate** | | | | | | | | | |
| Canada | 257,785 | 271,886 | 207,900 | 162,905 | 173,333 | 129,166 | 94,880 | 98,553 | 78,734 |
| Nfld. | 4,481 | 4,227 | 2,051 | 2,799 | 2,588 | 1,308 | 1,682 | 1,639 | 743 |
| P.E.I. | 753 | 948 | 477 | 483 | 658 | 343 | 270 | 290 | 134 |
| N.S. | 5,890 | 7,084 | 5,533 | 3,875 | 4,622 | 3,456 | 2,015 | 2,462 | 2,077 |
| N.B. | 4,408 | 5,075 | 3,578 | 2,968 | 3,511 | 2,463 | 1,440 | 1,564 | 1,115 |
| Que. | 102,421 | 100,402 | 79,358 | 63,643 | 63,956 | 49,690 | 38,778 | 36,446 | 29,668 |
| Ont. | 86,756 | 96,274 | 66,224 | 56,188 | 62,138 | 40,837 | 30,568 | 34,136 | 25,387 |
| Man. | 13,197 | 15,189 | 8,843 | 7,928 | 8,888 | 5,252 | 5,269 | 6,301 | 3,591 |
| Sask. | 8,277 | 8,524 | 6,042 | 5,320 | 5,352 | 3,885 | 2,957 | 3,172 | 2,157 |
| Alta. | 15,493 | 14,895 | 15,615 | 10,069 | 9,843 | 9,889 | 5,424 | 5,052 | 5,726 |
| B.C. | 16,109 | 19,268 | 20,179 | 9,632 | 11,777 | 12,043 | 6,477 | 7,491 | 8,136 |
| **Part-time graduate** | | | | | | | | | |
| Canada | 36,677 | 41,442 | 41,773 | 18,235 | 21,295 | 22,529 | 18,442 | 20,147 | 19,244 |
| Nfld. | 616 | 526 | 632 | 293 | 277 | 352 | 323 | 249 | 280 |
| P.E.I. | .. | 3 | 5 | .. | .. | 1 | .. | 3 | 4 |
| N.S. | 1,375 | 1,610 | 1,473 | 774 | 975 | 933 | 601 | 635 | 540 |
| N.B. | 515 | 627 | 603 | 241 | 331 | 331 | 274 | 296 | 272 |
| Que. | 16,237 | 19,320 | 21,663 | 7,842 | 9,631 | 11,423 | 8,395 | 9,689 | 10,240 |
| Ont. | 11,813 | 12,776 | 10,031 | 5,741 | 6,449 | 5,266 | 6,072 | 6,327 | 4,765 |
| Man. | 1,528 | 1,423 | 953 | 935 | 823 | 573 | 593 | 600 | 380 |
| Sask. | 724 | 911 | 1,322 | 325 | 449 | 698 | 399 | 462 | 624 |
| Alta. | 2,289 | 2,260 | 2,979 | 1,217 | 1,276 | 1,683 | 1,072 | 984 | 1,296 |
| B.C. | 1,580 | 1,986 | 2,112 | 867 | 1,084 | 1,269 | 713 | 902 | 843 |

1  See Appendix 2 for 1996-97 full-time enrolment by institution.
*Source: Centre for Education Statistics, Statistics Canada.*

**TABLE 3.19** PARTICIPATION OF ADULTS IN FORMAL EDUCATION AT ELEMENTARY-SECONDARY AND POSTSECONDARY LEVELS[1], BY AGE GROUP, CANADA AND PROVINCES, 1991 AND 1997

| Provinces | Age groups | 1991 Number[2] | 1991 Participation Rate (%) | 1997 Number[2] | 1997 Participation Rate (%) |
|---|---|---|---|---|---|
| | | Elementary-secondary programs | | | |
| **Canada** | 17–24 | **176,269** | **10** | **228,325** | **11** |
| | 25–54 | **164,362** | **1** | **123,281** | **1** |
| | | Postsecondary programs | | | |
| **Canada** | 17–24 | **226,317** | **13** | **348,052** | **17** |
| | 25–54 | **1,088,324** | **9** | **1,284,818** | **9** |
| Nfld. | 17–24 | -- | -- | -- | -- |
| | 25–54 | 18,598 | 8 | 21,566 | 8 |
| P.E.I. | 17–24 | -- | -- | -- | -- |
| | 25–54 | 4,148 * | 8* | -- | -- |
| N.S. | 17–24 | -- | -- | 8,318* | 13* |
| | 25–54 | 27,553 | 7 | 35,716 | 9 |
| N.B. | 17–24 | 6,009 * | 10* | 6,790* | 12* |
| | 25–54 | 23,993 | 8 | 27,615 | 8 |
| Que. | 17–24 | 59,244 * | 16* | 37,809* | 9* |
| | 25–54 | 288,956 | 9 | 312,023 | 9 |
| Ont. | 17–24 | 75,019 | 11 | 189,399 | 24 |
| | 25–54 | 411,860 | 9 | 493,450 | 9 |
| Man. | 17–24 | 18,668 | 23 | 14,300* | 19* |
| | 25–54 | 48,148 | 11 | 49,326 | 10 |
| Sask. | 17–24 | 7,388 * | 12* | 11,324* | 15* |
| | 25–54 | 33,824 | 9 | 34,397 | 9 |
| Alta. | 17–24 | 25,934 | 12 | 27,361* | 12* |
| | 25–54 | 97,544 | 9 | 139,810 | 11 |
| B.C. | 17–24 | 26,784 * | 12* | 48,780* | 19* |
| | 25–54 | 133,699 | 9 | 167,205 | 9 |

1  This table includes only adults enrolled in a program of study leading to a certificate, a diploma or a degree.
2  Excludes individuals who were (1) 17-19 years old and enrolled full-time in a non-employer sponsored elementary or secondary program or (2) 17-24 years old and enrolled full-time in a non-employer-sponsored postsecondary program.
*  Estimate has a coefficient of variation between 16% and 33% and as such is not as reliable as other values.

*Source: Adult Education and Training Survey, 1992 and 1998, Statistics Canada.*

TABLE 3.20  PERCENTAGE OF THE POPULATION AGED 25-54 PARTICIPATING IN JOB-RELATED ADULT EDUCATION AND TRAINING[1], BY GENDER AND EDUCATIONAL ATTAINMENT, CANADA AND JURISDICTIONS, 1991 AND 1997

|  | 1991 ||||||  1997 ||||||
|  | Participation (000s) ||| Participation rate (%) ||| Participation (000s) ||| Participation rate (%) |||
|  | Both sexes | Males | Female | Both sexes | Males | Females | Both sexes | Males | Females | Both Total | Males | Females |
|---|---|---|---|---|---|---|---|---|---|---|---|---|
| **Canada** | 3,475 | 1,809 | 1,665 | 29 | 31 | 28 | 3,757 | 1,870 | 1,888 | 27 | 27 | 27 |
| High school or less | 1,009 | 522 | 488 | 18 | 19 | 16 | 759 | 389 | 370 | 15 | 15 | 14 |
| Postsecondary non-university | 1,513 | 772 | 742 | 35 | 36 | 35 | 1,811 | 879 | 932 | 31 | 31 | 32 |
| University | 952 | 516 | 436 | 50 | 50 | 51 | 1,188 | 602 | 586 | 43 | 41 | 45 |
| **Newfoundland and Labrador** | 52 | 30 | 22 | 21 | 25 | 18 | 51 | 27 | 24 | 20 | 21 | 18 |
| High school or less | 9* | 5* | 4* | 8* | 10* | 6* | 6* | -- | -- | 6* | -- | -- |
| Postsecondary non-university | 30 | 19 | 11* | 30 | 34 | 25* | 27 | 16* | 11* | 24 | 26* | 22* |
| University | 13 | 6* | 6* | 57 | 55* | 58* | 17* | 7* | 10* | 52* | 36* | 75* |
| **Prince Edward Island** | 11 | 5* | 5 | 21 | 21* | 21 | 14 | 6 | 8 | 23 | 20 | 26 |
| High school or less | 3* | 2* | 1* | 10* | 10* | 11* | -- | -- | -- | -- | -- | -- |
| Postsecondary non-university | 5 | 3* | 3* | 27 | 30* | 26* | 8* | 4* | 4* | 33* | 32* | 34* |
| University | 3* | 1* | 1* | 48* | 52* | 44* | 4* | -- | 3* | 46* | -- | 57* |
| **Nova Scotia** | 91 | 48 | 42 | 24 | 26 | 22 | 129 | 69 | 60 | 31 | 34 | 28 |
| High school or less | 20 | 12* | 8* | 12 | 15* | 9* | 24 | 17* | 7* | 16 | 23* | 10* |
| Postsecondary non-university | 46 | 23 | 23 | 28 | 30 | 27 | 66 | 33* | 32 | 34 | 37* | 32 |
| University | 25 | 14* | 11* | 45 | 46* | 45* | 39 | 19* | 20* | 50 | 45* | 55* |
| **New Brunswick** | 65 | 36 | 30 | 21 | 23 | 19 | 76 | 40 | 36 | 22 | 23 | 21 |
| High school or less | 18 | 11* | 7* | 10 | 13* | 8* | 16 | 9* | 7* | 10 | 12* | 9* |
| Postsecondary non-university | 35 | 19 | 16 | 34 | 36 | 31 | 37 | 19 | 18 | 27 | 29 | 25 |
| University | 13 | 6* | 7* | 40 | 42* | 38* | 22 | 11* | 11* | 44 | 42* | 47* |
| **Quebec** | 802 | 407 | 395 | 25 | 26 | 25 | 680 | 327 | 353 | 20 | 19 | 21 |
| High school or less | 235 | 121 | 113 | 15 | 16 | 14 | 147 | 66 | 80 | 11 | 10 | 12 |
| Postsecondary non-university | 373 | 181 | 192 | 34 | 33 | 35 | 324 | 154 | 170 | 23 | 22 | 24 |
| University | 195 | 105 | 90 | 43 | 43 | 43 | 210 | 107 | 103 | 32 | 30 | 34 |
| **Ontario** | 1,320 | 690 | 629 | 30 | 32 | 28 | 1,602 | 800 | 802 | 31 | 31 | 30 |
| High school or less | 395 | 208 | 187 | 19 | 21 | 16 | 313 | 164 | 148 | 16 | 16 | 15 |
| Postsecondary non-university | 521 | 269 | 252 | 35 | 35 | 34 | 754 | 365 | 389 | 36 | 36 | 35 |
| University | 404 | 213 | 191 | 50 | 48 | 52 | 535 | 270 | 265 | 46 | 45 | 47 |
| **Manitoba** | 145 | 79 | 66 | 33 | 36 | 30 | 135 | 70 | 65 | 28 | 29 | 28 |
| High school or less | 41 | 23 | 19 | 19 | 22 | 17 | 32 | 18* | 14* | 15 | 16* | 14* |
| Postsecondary non-university | 66 | 34 | 32 | 41 | 44 | 37 | 62 | 31 | 31 | 33 | 34 | 32 |
| University | 38 | 22 | 15* | 59 | 61 | 57* | 41 | 21* | 20* | 52 | 51* | 53* |
| **Saskatchewan** | 118 | 61 | 57 | 31 | 32 | 30 | 124 | 63 | 61 | 31 | 31 | 30 |
| High school or less | 36 | 21 | 15 | 19 | 21 | 17 | 32 | 19 | 13* | 21 | 24 | 17* |
| Postsecondary non-university | 51 | 22 | 29 | 37 | 37 | 38 | 61 | 29 | 32 | 34 | 34 | 34 |
| University | 31 | 18 | 12 | 59 | 63 | 54 | 31 | 14* | 16* | 46 | 41* | 51* |
| **Alberta** | 408 | 213 | 195 | 36 | 38 | 35 | 414 | 206 | 207 | 32 | 31 | 32 |
| High school or less | 125 | 59 | 66 | 25 | 25 | 26 | 90 | 43* | 47 | 19 | 19* | 20 |
| Postsecondary non-university | 180 | 98 | 82 | 41 | 42 | 39 | 211 | 105 | 106 | 36 | 35 | 37 |
| University | 103 | 56 | 47 | 55 | 58 | 52 | 113 | 59 | 54 | 44 | 44 | 45 |
| **British Columbia** | 463 | 238 | 225 | 33 | 34 | 32 | 534 | 263 | 272 | 30 | 29 | 30 |
| High school or less | 126 | 59 | 67 | 20 | 21 | 19 | 97 | 47* | 49* | 16 | 16* | 16* |
| Postsecondary non-university | 207 | 105 | 103 | 37 | 36 | 39 | 261 | 123 | 138 | 32 | 30 | 33 |
| University | 130 | 74 | 55 | 60 | 60 | 59 | 177 | 92 | 84 | 46 | 46 | 47 |

1  Job-related education or training activities refers to any education or training activites taken for the development or upgrading skills to be used in a present or future career/employment position.
*  Estimate has a coefficient of variation between 16% and 33% and as such is not as reliable as other values.
Source: Adult Education and Training Survey, 1992 and 1998, Statistics Canada.

TABLE 3.21  PARTICIPATION RATE AND DURATION OF JOB-RELATED TRAINING UNDERTAKEN BY ADULTS AGED 25 TO 64, CANADA AND SELECTED COUNTRIES, 1994-95

| Country | Participation Rate (%) Employed | Participation Rate (%) Unemployed | Average duration (hrs) Per person employed | Average duration (hrs) Per person trained |
|---|---|---|---|---|
| Australia | 38 | 24 | 44.2 | 115.9 |
| Belgium (Flanders) | 20 | 9 | 25.2 | 126.2 |
| **Canada** | **38** | **22** | **44.9** | **119.8** |
| Ireland | 24 | 7 | 51.2 | 218.7 |
| Netherlands | 33 | 30 | 51.7 | 159.0 |
| New Zealand | 47 | 24 | 72.2 | 154.1 |
| Poland | 17 | 2 | 23.6 | 143.2 |
| Switzerland | 32 | 27 | 36.2 | 114.1 |
| United Kingdom | 52 | 24 | 51.6 | 99.5 |
| United States | 46 | 29 | 44.6 | 98.1 |

*Source:* Education at a Glance: OECD Indicators, *1998, Table C5.2;* Human Capital Investment: An International Comparison, *OECD, 1998, Table A3.4; and International Adult Literacy Survey, 1994-95, Statistics Canada and OECD.*

TABLE 3.22  EXPENDITURES ON EDUCATION AND INDEX OF EXPENDITURES BY LEVEL OF EDUCATION (CONSTANT $ 1998 IN MILLIONS), POPULATION (IN THOUSANDS), AND PER CAPITA EXPENDITURES ON EDUCATION (IN CONSTANT $ 1998), AND INDICES, CANADA AND JURISDICTIONS, 1988-89 TO 1998-99

| Jurisdiction and fiscal year | Total $ | Total Index | Elementary–secondary $ | Elementary–secondary Index | Postsecondary Trade–vocational $ | Trade–vocational Index | Community college $ | Community college Index | University $ | University Index | Sub–total $ | Sub–total Index | Population (000s) Count | Population Index | Expenditure per capita ($) $ | Expenditure per capita Index |
|---|---|---|---|---|---|---|---|---|---|---|---|---|---|---|---|---|
| **Canada** | | | | | | | | | | | | | | | | |
| 1988-89 | 53,735 | 100 | 34,156 | 100 | 4,417 | 100 | 4,134 | 100 | 11,028 | 100 | 19,580 | 100 | 26,798 | 100 | 2,005 | 100 |
| 1989-90 | 54,339 | 101 | 34,488 | 101 | 4,330 | 98 | 4,065 | 98 | 11,455 | 104 | 19,850 | 101 | 27,286 | 102 | 1,991 | 99 |
| 1990-91 | 56,662 | 105 | 35,714 | 105 | 4,679 | 106 | 4,152 | 100 | 12,118 | 110 | 20,948 | 107 | 27,701 | 103 | 2,046 | 102 |
| 1991-92 | 58,594 | 109 | 36,874 | 108 | 5,043 | 114 | 4,268 | 103 | 12,409 | 113 | 21,719 | 111 | 28,031 | 105 | 2,090 | 104 |
| 1992-93 | 60,599 | 113 | 37,765 | 111 | 5,844 | 132 | 4,426 | 107 | 12,565 | 114 | 22,834 | 117 | 28,377 | 106 | 2,136 | 107 |
| 1993-94 | 60,867 | 113 | 37,959 | 111 | 6,007 | 136 | 4,380 | 106 | 12,521 | 114 | 22,908 | 117 | 28,703 | 107 | 2,121 | 106 |
| 1994-95 | 62,349 | 116 | 38,261 | 112 | 6,983 | 158 | 4,479 | 108 | 12,625 | 114 | 24,088 | 123 | 29,036 | 108 | 2,147 | 107 |
| 1995-96 | 61,433 | 114 | 37,963 | 111 | 6,446 | 146 | 4,723 | 114 | 12,300 | 112 | 23,470 | 120 | 29,354 | 110 | 2,093 | 104 |
| 1996-97 e | 59,737 | 111 | 37,672 | 110 | 5,469 | 124 | 4,659 | 113 | 11,937 | 108 | 22,065 | 113 | 29,672 | 111 | 2,013 | 100 |
| 1997-98 e | 59,922 | 112 | 37,770 | 111 | 5,799 | 131 | 4,653 | 113 | 11,700 | 106 | 22,152 | 113 | 30,011 | 112 | 1,997 | 100 |
| 1998-99 e | 60,492 | 113 | 37,736 | 110 | 6,298 | 143 | 4,669 | 113 | 11,789 | 107 | 22,756 | 116 | 30,301 | 113 | 1,996 | 100 |
| **Nfld.** | | | | | | | | | | | | | | | | |
| 1988-89 | 1,150 | 100 | 697 | 100 | 183 | 100 | 44 | 100 | 226 | 100 | 453 | 100 | 575 | 100 | 2,000 | 100 |
| 1989-90 | 1,185 | 103 | 713 | 102 | 186 | 102 | 48 | 110 | 238 | 105 | 473 | 104 | 576 | 100 | 2,056 | 103 |
| 1990-91 | 1,208 | 105 | 701 | 101 | 207 | 113 | 51 | 116 | 248 | 110 | 506 | 112 | 578 | 101 | 2,089 | 104 |
| 1991-92 | 1,186 | 103 | 683 | 98 | 213 | 116 | 41 | 93 | 249 | 110 | 503 | 111 | 580 | 101 | 2,047 | 102 |
| 1992-93 | 1,260 | 110 | 704 | 101 | 264 | 144 | 36 | 82 | 257 | 113 | 557 | 123 | 580 | 101 | 2,173 | 109 |
| 1993-94 | 1,277 | 111 | 695 | 100 | 305 | 167 | 32 | 74 | 245 | 108 | 582 | 129 | 580 | 101 | 2,202 | 110 |
| 1994-95 | 1,448 | 126 | 650 | 93 | 522 | 285 | 33 | 76 | 243 | 107 | 798 | 176 | 575 | 100 | 2,519 | 126 |
| 1995-96 | 1,413 | 123 | 607 | 87 | 515 | 281 | 42 | 97 | 249 | 110 | 806 | 178 | 568 | 99 | 2,488 | 124 |
| 1996-97 e | 1,296 | 113 | 606 | 87 | 421 | 230 | 38 | 88 | 231 | 102 | 690 | 152 | 561 | 97 | 2,313 | 116 |
| 1997-98 e | 1,034 | 90 | 571 | 82 | 210 | 115 | 37 | 85 | 216 | 96 | 464 | 102 | 554 | 96 | 1,866 | 93 |
| 1998-99 e | 1,021 | 89 | 556 | 80 | 212 | 116 | 39 | 90 | 214 | 94 | 465 | 103 | 544 | 95 | 1,878 | 94 |
| **P.E.I.** | | | | | | | | | | | | | | | | |
| 1988-89 | 209 | 100 | 125 | 100 | 26 | 100 | 13 | 100 | 44 | 100 | 84 | 100 | 129 | 100 | 1,615 | 100 |
| 1989-90 | 221 | 106 | 127 | 101 | 27 | 104 | 13 | 97 | 54 | 122 | 94 | 112 | 130 | 101 | 1,697 | 105 |
| 1990-91 | 223 | 107 | 130 | 104 | 32 | 121 | 13 | 99 | 48 | 109 | 93 | 111 | 131 | 101 | 1,705 | 106 |
| 1991-92 | 224 | 107 | 132 | 105 | 32 | 121 | 13 | 100 | 47 | 107 | 92 | 110 | 130 | 101 | 1,721 | 107 |
| 1992-93 | 233 | 112 | 136 | 109 | 37 | 141 | 10 | 78 | 49 | 112 | 97 | 116 | 131 | 101 | 1,782 | 110 |
| 1993-94 | 232 | 111 | 139 | 111 | 36 | 135 | 11 | 82 | 46 | 104 | 92 | 110 | 132 | 102 | 1,751 | 108 |
| 1994-95 | 230 | 110 | 135 | 108 | 40 | 151 | 9 | 70 | 47 | 106 | 96 | 114 | 134 | 103 | 1,724 | 107 |
| 1995-96 | 235 | 112 | 124 | 99 | 55 | 207 | 13 | 99 | 43 | 98 | 111 | 132 | 135 | 104 | 1,742 | 108 |
| 1996-97 e | 220 | 105 | 119 | 95 | 39 | 147 | 15 | 108 | 47 | 108 | 101 | 120 | 136 | 105 | 1,616 | 100 |
| 1997-98 e | 230 | 110 | 127 | 102 | 45 | 171 | 13 | 99 | 44 | 101 | 103 | 122 | 137 | 106 | 1,677 | 104 |
| 1998-99 e | 235 | 113 | 133 | 106 | 45 | 171 | 13 | 99 | 44 | 100 | 102 | 122 | 137 | 106 | 1,722 | 107 |

**TABLE 3.22 EXPENDITURES ON EDUCATION AND INDEX OF EXPENDITURES BY LEVEL OF EDUCATION (CONSTANT $ 1998 IN MILLIONS), POPULATION (IN THOUSANDS), AND PER CAPITA EXPENDITURES ON EDUCATION (IN CONSTANT $ 1998), AND INDICES, CANADA AND JURISDICTIONS, 1988-89 TO 1998-99** (continued)

| Jurisdiction and fiscal year | Total | | Elementary–secondary | | Postsecondary: Trade–vocational | | Postsecondary: Community college | | Postsecondary: University | | Postsecondary: Sub–total | | Population (000s) | | Expenditure per capita ($) | |
|---|---|---|---|---|---|---|---|---|---|---|---|---|---|---|---|---|
| | $ | Index | $ | Index | $ | Index | $ | Index | $ | Index | $ | Index | Count | Index | $ | Index |
| **N.S.** | | | | | | | | | | | | | | | | |
| 1988-89 | 1,694 | 100 | 1,015 | 100 | 167 | 100 | 43 | 100 | 469 | 100 | 679 | 100 | 897 | 100 | 1,887 | 100 |
| 1989-90 | 1,687 | 100 | 1,007 | 99 | 159 | 95 | 45 | 106 | 475 | 101 | 680 | 100 | 904 | 101 | 1,866 | 99 |
| 1990-91 | 1,710 | 101 | 1,007 | 99 | 178 | 106 | 46 | 109 | 479 | 102 | 703 | 104 | 910 | 101 | 1,880 | 100 |
| 1991-92 | 1,674 | 99 | 970 | 96 | 175 | 105 | 42 | 99 | 487 | 104 | 704 | 104 | 915 | 102 | 1,829 | 97 |
| 1992-93 | 1,699 | 100 | 966 | 95 | 202 | 121 | 47 | 109 | 485 | 103 | 733 | 108 | 919 | 102 | 1,848 | 98 |
| 1993-94 | 1,780 | 105 | 1,026 | 101 | 211 | 126 | 46 | 107 | 498 | 106 | 754 | 111 | 924 | 103 | 1,927 | 102 |
| 1994-95 | 1,751 | 103 | 1,006 | 99 | 228 | 136 | 56 | 131 | 462 | 98 | 746 | 110 | 926 | 103 | 1,891 | 100 |
| 1995-96 | 1,701 | 100 | 961 | 95 | 228 | 137 | 50 | 118 | 461 | 98 | 740 | 109 | 928 | 103 | 1,834 | 97 |
| 1996-97 [e] | 1,685 | 99 | 954 | 94 | 208 | 124 | 49 | 114 | 474 | 101 | 730 | 108 | 931 | 104 | 1,809 | 96 |
| 1997-98 [e] | 1,572 | 93 | 914 | 90 | 166 | 99 | 44 | 104 | 448 | 95 | 658 | 97 | 935 | 104 | 1,681 | 89 |
| 1998-99 [e] | 1,623 | 96 | 951 | 94 | 172 | 103 | 44 | 104 | 457 | 97 | 673 | 99 | 934 | 104 | 1,738 | 92 |
| **N.B.** | | | | | | | | | | | | | | | | |
| 1988-89 | 1,442 | 100 | 859 | 100 | 250 | 100 | 42 | 100 | 290 | 100 | 583 | 100 | 730 | 100 | 1,975 | 100 |
| 1989-90 | 1,332 | 92 | 831 | 97 | 174 | 70 | 41 | 96 | 286 | 99 | 502 | 86 | 735 | 101 | 1,812 | 92 |
| 1990-91 | 1,389 | 96 | 840 | 98 | 167 | 67 | 90 | 213 | 292 | 100 | 550 | 94 | 740 | 101 | 1,877 | 95 |
| 1991-92 | 1,379 | 96 | 845 | 98 | 154 | 62 | 83 | 194 | 297 | 102 | 534 | 92 | 746 | 102 | 1,850 | 94 |
| 1992-93 | 1,469 | 102 | 878 | 102 | 197 | 79 | 80 | 187 | 315 | 108 | 591 | 101 | 748 | 102 | 1,963 | 99 |
| 1993-94 | 1,455 | 101 | 871 | 101 | 211 | 84 | 64 | 150 | 309 | 106 | 583 | 100 | 750 | 103 | 1,941 | 98 |
| 1994-95 | 1,475 | 102 | 868 | 101 | 219 | 88 | 61 | 145 | 326 | 112 | 606 | 104 | 751 | 103 | 1,964 | 99 |
| 1995-96 | 1,417 | 98 | 852 | 99 | 190 | 76 | 61 | 143 | 315 | 108 | 565 | 97 | 752 | 103 | 1,885 | 95 |
| 1996-97 [e] | 1,414 | 98 | 858 | 100 | 170 | 68 | 61 | 144 | 324 | 112 | 556 | 95 | 753 | 103 | 1,878 | 95 |
| 1997-98 [e] | 1,411 | 98 | 837 | 97 | 196 | 78 | 64 | 151 | 313 | 108 | 573 | 98 | 754 | 103 | 1,871 | 95 |
| 1998-99 [e] | 1,401 | 97 | 846 | 98 | 188 | 75 | 61 | 143 | 306 | 106 | 555 | 95 | 753 | 103 | 1,861 | 94 |
| **Que.** | | | | | | | | | | | | | | | | |
| 1988-89 | 13,780 | 100 | 8,690 | 100 | 623 | 100 | 1,714 | 100 | 2,752 | 100 | 5,090 | 100 | 6,840 | 100 | 2,015 | 100 |
| 1989-90 | 13,271 | 96 | 8,185 | 94 | 607 | 97 | 1,623 | 95 | 2,857 | 104 | 5,086 | 100 | 6,930 | 101 | 1,915 | 95 |
| 1990-91 | 13,918 | 101 | 8,391 | 97 | 716 | 115 | 1,737 | 101 | 3,074 | 112 | 5,527 | 109 | 7,004 | 102 | 1,987 | 99 |
| 1991-92 | 14,132 | 103 | 8,454 | 97 | 765 | 123 | 1,732 | 101 | 3,182 | 116 | 5,679 | 112 | 7,065 | 103 | 2,000 | 99 |
| 1992-93 | 14,818 | 108 | 8,752 | 101 | 976 | 157 | 1,757 | 103 | 3,332 | 121 | 6,066 | 119 | 7,113 | 104 | 2,083 | 103 |
| 1993-94 | 14,743 | 107 | 8,562 | 99 | 973 | 156 | 1,862 | 109 | 3,345 | 122 | 6,181 | 121 | 7,165 | 105 | 2,058 | 102 |
| 1994-95 | 15,478 | 112 | 8,894 | 102 | 1,076 | 173 | 2,037 | 119 | 3,471 | 126 | 6,584 | 129 | 7,207 | 105 | 2,147 | 107 |
| 1995-96 | 15,081 | 109 | 8,760 | 101 | 952 | 153 | 2,003 | 117 | 3,366 | 122 | 6,321 | 124 | 7,241 | 106 | 2,083 | 103 |
| 1996-97 [e] | 14,336 | 104 | 8,534 | 98 | 747 | 120 | 1,932 | 113 | 3,124 | 113 | 5,802 | 114 | 7,274 | 106 | 1,971 | 98 |
| 1997-98 [e] | 14,256 | 103 | 8,479 | 98 | 1,048 | 168 | 1,809 | 106 | 2,919 | 106 | 5,777 | 113 | 7,308 | 107 | 1,951 | 97 |
| 1998-99 [e] | 14,664 | 106 | 8,510 | 98 | 1,499 | 241 | 1,784 | 104 | 2,871 | 104 | 6,155 | 121 | 7,335 | 107 | 1,999 | 99 |
| **Ont.** | | | | | | | | | | | | | | | | |
| 1988-89 | 19,800 | 100 | 13,492 | 100 | 1,062 | 100 | 1,271 | 100 | 3,976 | 100 | 6,308 | 100 | 9,844 | 100 | 2,011 | 100 |
| 1989-90 | 20,413 | 103 | 14,052 | 104 | 997 | 94 | 1,242 | 98 | 4,122 | 104 | 6,361 | 101 | 10,110 | 103 | 2,019 | 100 |
| 1990-91 | 21,264 | 107 | 14,543 | 108 | 1,125 | 106 | 1,203 | 95 | 4,393 | 111 | 6,721 | 107 | 10,300 | 105 | 2,065 | 103 |
| 1991-92 | 22,629 | 114 | 15,538 | 115 | 1,296 | 122 | 1,290 | 102 | 4,504 | 113 | 7,091 | 112 | 10,428 | 106 | 2,170 | 108 |
| 1992-93 | 23,114 | 117 | 15,687 | 116 | 1,522 | 143 | 1,420 | 112 | 4,485 | 113 | 7,427 | 118 | 10,570 | 107 | 2,187 | 109 |
| 1993-94 | 23,332 | 118 | 15,928 | 118 | 1,773 | 167 | 1,237 | 97 | 4,394 | 111 | 7,404 | 117 | 10,690 | 109 | 2,183 | 109 |
| 1994-95 | 23,615 | 119 | 15,822 | 117 | 2,156 | 203 | 1,205 | 95 | 4,432 | 111 | 7,793 | 124 | 10,828 | 110 | 2,181 | 108 |
| 1995-96 | 23,190 | 117 | 15,624 | 116 | 1,923 | 181 | 1,367 | 108 | 4,276 | 108 | 7,566 | 120 | 10,965 | 111 | 2,115 | 105 |
| 1996-97 [e] | 22,466 | 113 | 15,479 | 115 | 1,420 | 134 | 1,368 | 108 | 4,199 | 106 | 6,987 | 111 | 11,101 | 113 | 2,024 | 101 |
| 1997-98 [e] | 22,885 | 116 | 15,521 | 115 | 1,648 | 155 | 1,462 | 115 | 4,254 | 107 | 7,363 | 117 | 11,264 | 114 | 2,032 | 101 |
| 1998-99 [e] | 22,680 | 115 | 15,183 | 113 | 1,672 | 157 | 1,487 | 117 | 4,337 | 109 | 7,496 | 119 | 11,414 | 116 | 1,987 | 99 |
| **Man.** | | | | | | | | | | | | | | | | |
| 1988-89 | 2,218 | 100 | 1,513 | 100 | 175 | 100 | 70 | 100 | 461 | 100 | 705 | 100 | 1,102 | 100 | 2,013 | 100 |
| 1989-90 | 2,299 | 104 | 1,569 | 104 | 186 | 106 | 70 | 100 | 474 | 103 | 730 | 103 | 1,104 | 100 | 2,083 | 103 |
| 1990-91 | 2,361 | 106 | 1,604 | 106 | 189 | 109 | 72 | 104 | 495 | 107 | 757 | 107 | 1,106 | 100 | 2,135 | 106 |
| 1991-92 | 2,348 | 106 | 1,592 | 105 | 188 | 108 | 62 | 89 | 506 | 110 | 756 | 107 | 1,110 | 101 | 2,116 | 105 |
| 1992-93 | 2,377 | 107 | 1,592 | 105 | 214 | 122 | 62 | 88 | 509 | 110 | 785 | 111 | 1,113 | 101 | 2,135 | 106 |
| 1993-94 | 2,331 | 105 | 1,584 | 105 | 201 | 115 | 56 | 81 | 490 | 106 | 747 | 106 | 1,118 | 101 | 2,084 | 104 |
| 1994-95 | 2,349 | 106 | 1,593 | 105 | 214 | 123 | 47 | 68 | 495 | 107 | 756 | 107 | 1,124 | 102 | 2,091 | 104 |
| 1995-96 | 2,378 | 107 | 1,640 | 108 | 182 | 104 | 70 | 101 | 486 | 105 | 738 | 105 | 1,130 | 103 | 2,105 | 105 |
| 1996-97 [e] | 2,367 | 107 | 1,629 | 108 | 177 | 102 | 79 | 113 | 481 | 104 | 738 | 105 | 1,134 | 103 | 2,087 | 104 |
| 1997-98 [e] | 2,348 | 106 | 1,614 | 107 | 186 | 107 | 79 | 114 | 469 | 102 | 734 | 104 | 1,137 | 103 | 2,065 | 103 |
| 1998-99 [e] | 2,383 | 107 | 1,631 | 108 | 190 | 109 | 80 | 115 | 482 | 104 | 752 | 107 | 1,139 | 103 | 2,093 | 104 |

TABLE 3.22  EXPENDITURES ON EDUCATION AND INDEX OF EXPENDITURES BY LEVEL OF EDUCATION (CONSTANT $ 1998 IN MILLIONS), POPULATION (IN THOUSANDS), AND PER CAPITA EXPENDITURES ON EDUCATION (IN CONSTANT $ 1998), AND INDICES, CANADA AND JURISDICTIONS, 1988-89 TO 1998-99  (continued)

| Jurisdiction and fiscal year | Total $ | Total Index | Elementary–secondary $ | Elementary–secondary Index | Postsecondary Trade–vocational $ | Trade–vocational Index | Community college $ | Community college Index | University $ | University Index | Sub-total $ | Sub-total Index | Population (000s) Count | Population Index | Expenditure per capita ($) $ | Expenditure per capita Index |
|---|---|---|---|---|---|---|---|---|---|---|---|---|---|---|---|---|
| **Sask.** | | | | | | | | | | | | | | | | |
| 1988-89 | 2,027 | 100 | 1,312 | 100 | 216 | 100 | 52 | 100 | 447 | 100 | 715 | 100 | 1,028 | 100 | 1,972 | 100 |
| 1989-90 | 2,070 | 102 | 1,292 | 98 | 218 | 101 | 58 | 113 | 501 | 112 | 777 | 109 | 1,019 | 99 | 2,031 | 103 |
| 1990-91 | 2,088 | 103 | 1,293 | 99 | 220 | 102 | 59 | 114 | 516 | 115 | 795 | 111 | 1,007 | 98 | 2,073 | 105 |
| 1991-92 | 2,051 | 101 | 1,274 | 97 | 223 | 103 | 45 | 87 | 508 | 114 | 776 | 109 | 1,003 | 98 | 2,045 | 104 |
| 1992-93 | 2,045 | 101 | 1,291 | 98 | 234 | 109 | 49 | 95 | 471 | 105 | 754 | 106 | 1,004 | 98 | 2,037 | 103 |
| 1993-94 | 1,985 | 98 | 1,250 | 95 | 228 | 106 | 46 | 89 | 461 | 103 | 735 | 103 | 1,007 | 98 | 1,971 | 100 |
| 1994-95 | 2,016 | 99 | 1,255 | 96 | 244 | 113 | 44 | 86 | 472 | 106 | 761 | 106 | 1,010 | 98 | 1,997 | 101 |
| 1995-96 | 2,139 | 106 | 1,326 | 101 | 239 | 111 | 57 | 110 | 518 | 116 | 813 | 114 | 1,014 | 99 | 2,110 | 107 |
| 1996-97 [e] | 2,125 | 105 | 1,320 | 101 | 246 | 114 | 57 | 110 | 503 | 112 | 805 | 113 | 1,019 | 99 | 2,085 | 106 |
| 1997-98 [e] | 2,169 | 107 | 1,337 | 102 | 276 | 128 | 56 | 108 | 500 | 112 | 832 | 116 | 1,022 | 99 | 2,122 | 108 |
| 1998-99 [e] | 2,217 | 109 | 1,339 | 102 | 303 | 141 | 55 | 107 | 519 | 116 | 878 | 123 | 1,024 | 100 | 2,164 | 110 |
| **Alta.** | | | | | | | | | | | | | | | | |
| 1988-89 | 5,365 | 100 | 3,154 | 100 | 586 | 100 | 482 | 100 | 1,142 | 100 | 2,211 | 100 | 2,455 | 100 | 2,186 | 100 |
| 1989-90 | 5,437 | 101 | 3,187 | 101 | 606 | 103 | 480 | 100 | 1,164 | 102 | 2,250 | 102 | 2,496 | 102 | 2,178 | 100 |
| 1990-91 | 5,428 | 101 | 3,268 | 104 | 628 | 107 | 378 | 78 | 1,154 | 101 | 2,161 | 98 | 2,548 | 104 | 2,131 | 97 |
| 1991-92 | 5,397 | 101 | 3,328 | 106 | 624 | 106 | 327 | 68 | 1,117 | 98 | 2,069 | 94 | 2,593 | 106 | 2,082 | 95 |
| 1992-93 | 5,688 | 106 | 3,482 | 110 | 720 | 123 | 359 | 74 | 1,126 | 99 | 2,205 | 100 | 2,634 | 107 | 2,159 | 99 |
| 1993-94 | 5,745 | 107 | 3,549 | 113 | 683 | 116 | 372 | 77 | 1,141 | 100 | 2,196 | 99 | 2,671 | 109 | 2,151 | 98 |
| 1994-95 | 5,571 | 104 | 3,444 | 109 | 719 | 123 | 325 | 67 | 1,083 | 95 | 2,128 | 96 | 2,705 | 110 | 2,060 | 94 |
| 1995-96 | 5,459 | 102 | 3,369 | 107 | 690 | 118 | 339 | 70 | 1,061 | 93 | 2,090 | 95 | 2,740 | 112 | 1,992 | 91 |
| 1996-97 [e] | 5,360 | 100 | 3,396 | 108 | 638 | 109 | 331 | 69 | 996 | 87 | 1,965 | 89 | 2,781 | 113 | 1,928 | 88 |
| 1997-98 [e] | 5,554 | 104 | 3,512 | 111 | 633 | 108 | 375 | 78 | 1,034 | 91 | 2,042 | 92 | 2,839 | 116 | 1,957 | 90 |
| 1998-99 [e] | 5,686 | 106 | 3,629 | 115 | 632 | 108 | 384 | 80 | 1,040 | 91 | 2,057 | 93 | 2,915 | 119 | 1,951 | 89 |
| **B.C.** | | | | | | | | | | | | | | | | |
| 1988-89 | 5,348 | 100 | 3,338 | 100 | 584 | 100 | 356 | 100 | 1,070 | 100 | 2,010 | 100 | 3,116 | 100 | 1,717 | 100 |
| 1989-90 | 5,634 | 105 | 3,540 | 106 | 594 | 102 | 401 | 113 | 1,098 | 103 | 2,093 | 104 | 3,199 | 103 | 1,761 | 103 |
| 1990-91 | 6,285 | 118 | 3,912 | 117 | 662 | 113 | 458 | 129 | 1,254 | 117 | 2,374 | 118 | 3,291 | 106 | 1,910 | 111 |
| 1991-92 | 6,727 | 126 | 4,075 | 122 | 741 | 127 | 570 | 160 | 1,342 | 125 | 2,652 | 132 | 3,373 | 108 | 1,994 | 116 |
| 1992-93 | 6,977 | 130 | 4,217 | 126 | 850 | 146 | 540 | 152 | 1,369 | 128 | 2,760 | 137 | 3,470 | 111 | 2,010 | 117 |
| 1993-94 | 7,049 | 132 | 4,246 | 127 | 789 | 135 | 577 | 162 | 1,437 | 134 | 2,802 | 139 | 3,572 | 115 | 1,974 | 115 |
| 1994-95 | 7,377 | 138 | 4,449 | 133 | 913 | 156 | 592 | 166 | 1,423 | 133 | 2,928 | 146 | 3,682 | 118 | 2,004 | 117 |
| 1995-96 | 7,582 | 142 | 4,633 | 139 | 892 | 153 | 667 | 187 | 1,390 | 130 | 2,949 | 147 | 3,784 | 121 | 2,004 | 117 |
| 1996-97 [e] | 7,675 | 144 | 4,729 | 142 | 836 | 143 | 683 | 192 | 1,427 | 133 | 2,947 | 147 | 3,882 | 125 | 1,977 | 115 |
| 1997-98 [e] | 7,688 | 144 | 4,752 | 142 | 883 | 151 | 667 | 187 | 1,386 | 130 | 2,935 | 146 | 3,962 | 127 | 1,941 | 113 |
| 1998-99 [e] | 7,798 | 146 | 4,848 | 145 | 884 | 151 | 670 | 188 | 1,396 | 130 | 2,949 | 147 | 4,009 | 129 | 1,945 | 113 |
| **Y.T.** | | | | | | | | | | | | | | | | |
| 1988-89 | 81 | 100 | 56 | 100 | 15 | 100 | 7 | 100 | 3 | 100 | 25 | 100 | 27 | 100 | 3,038 | 100 |
| 1989-90 | 81 | 101 | 58 | 103 | 17 | 109 | 5 | 73 | 2 | 75 | 24 | 95 | 27 | 102 | 3,000 | 99 |
| 1990-91 | 94 | 117 | 67 | 120 | 20 | 131 | 5 | 80 | 2 | 67 | 27 | 110 | 28 | 104 | 3,401 | 112 |
| 1991-92 | 100 | 123 | 74 | 132 | 16 | 108 | 6 | 89 | 3 | 116 | 26 | 104 | 29 | 109 | 3,446 | 113 |
| 1992-93 | 125 | 155 | 95 | 170 | 17 | 109 | 6 | 93 | 7 | 245 | 30 | 120 | 30 | 114 | 4,144 | 136 |
| 1993-94 | 117 | 145 | 87 | 155 | 17 | 113 | 6 | 91 | 7 | 252 | 31 | 123 | 31 | 115 | 3,829 | 126 |
| 1994-95 | 116 | 144 | 87 | 155 | 16 | 105 | 5 | 81 | 8 | 274 | 29 | 118 | 30 | 113 | 3,874 | 128 |
| 1995-96 | 100 | 124 | 75 | 134 | 15 | 96 | 7 | 96 | 4 | 148 | 25 | 102 | 31 | 116 | 3,242 | 107 |
| 1996-97 [e] | 106 | 131 | 80 | 142 | 15 | 97 | 7 | 98 | 5 | 157 | 26 | 104 | 32 | 120 | 3,309 | 109 |
| 1997-98 [e] | 113 | 139 | 82 | 146 | 19 | 124 | 7 | 103 | 5 | 163 | 31 | 123 | 32 | 121 | 3,491 | 115 |
| 1998-99 [e] | 105 | 130 | 74 | 133 | 19 | 123 | 7 | 103 | 5 | 163 | 31 | 122 | 32 | 119 | 3,308 | 109 |
| **N.W.T.** | | | | | | | | | | | | | | | | |
| 1988-89 | 218 | 100 | 156 | 100 | 26 | 100 | 33 | 100 | 3 | 100 | 62 | 100 | 56 | 100 | 3,908 | 100 |
| 1989-90 | 240 | 110 | 170 | 109 | 27 | 101 | 40 | 123 | 3 | 115 | 70 | 113 | 57 | 102 | 4,211 | 108 |
| 1990-91 | 255 | 117 | 187 | 120 | 24 | 90 | 40 | 123 | 4 | 133 | 68 | 109 | 59 | 106 | 4,328 | 111 |
| 1991-92 | 271 | 124 | 200 | 128 | 23 | 86 | 40 | 123 | 8 | 284 | 71 | 114 | 61 | 109 | 4,443 | 114 |
| 1992-93 | 354 | 162 | 266 | 171 | 21 | 80 | 40 | 123 | 26 | 916 | 87 | 141 | 62 | 112 | 5,664 | 145 |
| 1993-94 | 377 | 173 | 277 | 178 | 25 | 95 | 48 | 148 | 26 | 905 | 99 | 160 | 64 | 114 | 5,928 | 152 |
| 1994-95 | 418 | 192 | 306 | 197 | 29 | 112 | 53 | 160 | 30 | 1,038 | 112 | 180 | 65 | 117 | 6,411 | 164 |
| 1995-96 | 300 | 138 | 217 | 139 | 36 | 136 | 42 | 128 | 5 | 187 | 83 | 134 | 67 | 120 | 4,506 | 115 |
| 1996-97 [e] | 277 | 127 | 209 | 134 | 24 | 93 | 40 | 123 | 4 | 128 | 68 | 110 | 68 | 121 | 4,097 | 105 |
| 1997-98 [e] | 287 | 132 | 216 | 139 | 24 | 93 | 42 | 129 | 5 | 163 | 71 | 115 | 68 | 122 | 4,240 | 108 |
| 1998-99 [e] | 283 | 130 | 211 | 135 | 25 | 94 | 43 | 131 | 5 | 166 | 72 | 117 | 67 | 121 | 4,197 | 107 |

EDUCATION INDICATORS IN CANADA

**TABLE 3.22**  EXPENDITURES ON EDUCATION AND INDEX OF EXPENDITURES BY LEVEL OF EDUCATION (CONSTANT $ 1998 IN MILLIONS), POPULATION (IN THOUSANDS), AND PER CAPITA EXPENDITURES ON EDUCATION (IN CONSTANT $ 1998), AND INDICES, CANADA AND JURISDICTIONS, 1988-89 TO 1998-99 (concluded)

| Jurisdiction and fiscal year | Total $ | Total Index | Elementary–secondary $ | Elementary–secondary Index | Trade–vocational $ | Trade–vocational Index | Community college $ | Community college Index | University $ | University Index | Sub-total $ | Sub-total Index | Population (000s) Count | Population Index | Expenditure per capita ($) $ | Expenditure per capita Index |
|---|---|---|---|---|---|---|---|---|---|---|---|---|---|---|---|---|
| **Other[1]** | | | | | | | | | | | | | | | | |
| 1988-89 | 445 | 100 | 59 | 100 | 229 | 100 | 2 | 100 | 155 | 100 | 386 | 100 | … | … | … | … |
| 1989-90 | 562 | 126 | 80 | 134 | 280 | 123 | 2 | 112 | 200 | 129 | 482 | 125 | … | … | … | … |
| 1990-91 | 543 | 122 | 52 | 88 | 307 | 134 | 3 | 123 | 180 | 117 | 490 | 127 | … | … | … | … |
| 1991-92 | 518 | 116 | 47 | 80 | 305 | 134 | 3 | 134 | 163 | 105 | 471 | 122 | … | … | … | … |
| 1992-93 | 522 | 117 | 44 | 75 | 331 | 145 | 3 | 156 | 144 | 93 | 477 | 124 | … | … | … | … |
| 1993-94 | 481 | 108 | 35 | 59 | 318 | 139 | 4 | 187 | 124 | 80 | 446 | 116 | … | … | … | … |
| 1994-95 | 522 | 117 | 27 | 46 | 350 | 153 | 6 | 294 | 138 | 89 | 494 | 128 | … | … | … | … |
| 1995-96 | 440 | 99 | 26 | 43 | 281 | 123 | 2 | 81 | 132 | 85 | 415 | 108 | … | … | … | … |
| 1996-97 e | 447 | 101 | 23 | 39 | 290 | 127 | 2 | 88 | 132 | 85 | 424 | 110 | … | … | … | … |
| 1997-98 e | 399 | 90 | 23 | 38 | 262 | 114 | 2 | 75 | 114 | 73 | 377 | 98 | … | … | … | … |
| 1998-99 e | 397 | 89 | 23 | 39 | 260 | 114 | 2 | 74 | 113 | 73 | 374 | 97 | … | … | … | … |

1  "Other" refers to expenditures which cannot be attributed to any one province. One example of this is spending by the federal government on overseas schools.

e  For 1996-97, estimates are based on information from the Provincial Public Accounts (actual) and the Centre for Education Statistics; for 1997-98 and 1998-99, estimates are based on information from the Provincial Public Accounts (estimates) and the Centre for Education Statistics.

Source:  Centre for Education Statistics, Statistics Canada; Provincial Public Accounts.

**TABLE 3.23**  EXPENDITURE PER STUDENT (U.S. DOLLARS CONVERTED USING PPPs[1] AND CANADIAN DOLLARS) ON PUBLIC AND PRIVATE INSTITUTIONS BY LEVEL OF EDUCATION (BASED ON FULL-TIME EQUIVALENTS), CANADA, JURISDICTIONS AND G-7 COUNTRIES, 1995

| | Pre-elementary | Elementary | Secondary | Elem–sec All PPPs | Elem–sec All Canadian | Postsec All PPPs | Postsec All Canadian | Non-university PPPs | Non-university Canadian | University PPPs | University Canadian | All levels PPPs | All levels[2] Canadian |
|---|---|---|---|---|---|---|---|---|---|---|---|---|---|
| **Canada** | … | … | … | 5,401 | 6,677 | 11,471 | 14,182 | 10,434 | 12,899 | 12,217 | 15,105 | 6,396 | 7,907 |
| Newfoundland and Labrador | … | … | … | 4,462 | 5,516 | 10,292 | 12,724 | 10,575 | 13,074 | 10,061 | 12,439 | 5,726 | 7,079 |
| Prince Edward Island | … | … | … | 3,851 | 4,761 | 11,138 | 13,770 | 7,117 | 8,799 | 10,623 | 13,133 | 5,118 | 6,327 |
| Nova Scotia | … | … | … | 4,363 | 5,394 | 10,890 | 13,463 | 13,579 | 16,788 | 10,065 | 12,443 | 5,642 | 6,975 |
| New Brunswick | … | … | … | 4,141 | 5,120 | 10,137 | 12,532 | 9,229 | 11,410 | 10,694 | 13,221 | 5,357 | 6,623 |
| Quebec | … | … | … | 5,713 | 7,063 | 10,262 | 12,687 | 7,793 | 9,635 | 11,986 | 14,818 | 6,799 | 8,406 |
| Ontario | … | … | … | 6,161 | 7,617 | 10,614 | 13,122 | 8,903 | 11,007 | 12,177 | 15,055 | 6,441 | 7,963 |
| Manitoba | … | … | … | 5,387 | 6,660 | 12,630 | 15,615 | 13,661 | 16,889 | 12,224 | 15,113 | 6,219 | 7,689 |
| Saskatchewan | … | … | … | 4,454 | 5,507 | 12,174 | 15,051 | 13,224 | 16,349 | 11,623 | 14,370 | 5,688 | 7,032 |
| Alberta | … | … | … | 4,465 | 5,520 | 10,510 | 12,994 | 8,624 | 10,662 | 12,346 | 15,263 | 5,606 | 6,931 |
| British Columbia | … | … | … | 5,176 | 6,399 | 11,921 | 14,738 | 8,807 | 10,888 | 15,311 | 18,929 | 6,602 | 8,162 |
| Yukon | … | … | … | 12,397 | 15,327 | … | … | … | … | … | … | .. | .. |
| Northwest Territories | … | … | … | 16,107 | 19,913 | … | … | … | … | … | … | .. | .. |
| **G-7 countries** | | | | | | | | | | | | | |
| **Canada** | … | … | … | 5,401 | | 11,471 | | 10,434 | | 12,217 | | 6,396 | |
| France | 3,242 | 3,379 | 6,182 | 5,041 | | 6,569 | | … | | … | | 5,001 | |
| Germany[3] | 5,277 | 3,361 | 6,254 | 4,690 | | 8,897 | | 6,817 | | 9,001 | | 6,057 | |
| Italy[3] | 3,316 | 4,673 | 5,348 | 5,099 | | 5,013 | | 6,705 | | 4,932 | | 5,157 | |
| Japan | 2,476 | 4,065 | 4,465 | 4,282 | | 8,768 | | 6,409 | | 9,337 | | 4,991 | |
| United Kingdom[4] | 5,049 | 3,328 | 4,246 | 3,810 | | 7,225 | | … | | … | | 4,222 | |
| United States | .. | 5,371 | 6,812 | 6,281 | | 16,262 | | 7,973 | | 19,965 | | 7,905 | |
| **OECD country mean** | **3,224** | **3,546** | **4,606** | **4,162** | | **8,134** | | **6,016** | | **8,781** | | **4,717** | |

1  Purchasing power parities (PPPs) are currency exchange rates that equalize the purchasing power of different currencies, expressed here in equivalent U.S. dollars.
2  Canada total not as originally published by OECD due to data revisions.
3  Public institutions.
4  Public and government-dependent private institutions.

Source:  Centre for Education Statistics, Statistics Canada; Education at a Glance: OECD Indicators, 1998, Table B4.1.

CHAPTER 3 TABLES

TABLE 3.24    EDUCATIONAL EXPENDITURE FROM PUBLIC AND PRIVATE SOURCES FOR EDUCATIONAL INSTITUTIONS AS A PERCENTAGE OF GDP BY LEVEL OF EDUCATION, CANADA, JURISDICTIONS, AND G-7 COUNTRIES, 1995

|  | Elementary–secondary | | | Postsecondary | | | All levels of education combined (including preprimary and undistributed) |
|---|---|---|---|---|---|---|---|
|  | All | Elementary | Secondary | All | Non-university | University-level |  |
| **Canada** | 4.3 | .. | .. | 2.5 | 0.9 | 1.5 | 7.0 |
| Newfoundland and Labrador | 5.7 | .. | .. | 3.9 | 1.8 | 2.1 | 9.9 |
| Prince Edward Island | 4.5 | .. | .. | 2.9 | 1.2 | 1.6 | 7.6 |
| Nova Scotia | 4.4 | .. | .. | 3.0 | 0.9 | 2.1 | 7.6 |
| New Brunswick | 4.3 | .. | .. | 2.9 | 1.1 | 1.8 | 7.4 |
| Quebec | 4.3 | .. | .. | 3.1 | 1.0 | 2.1 | 7.6 |
| Ontario | 4.5 | .. | .. | 2.1 | 0.8 | 1.2 | 6.8 |
| Manitoba | 5.3 | .. | .. | 2.3 | 0.7 | 1.6 | 7.8 |
| Saskatchewan | 4.6 | .. | .. | 2.5 | 0.9 | 1.6 | 7.4 |
| Alberta | 3.3 | .. | .. | 1.9 | 0.8 | 1.1 | 5.4 |
| British Columbia | 3.8 | .. | .. | 2.5 | 0.9 | 1.5 | 6.5 |
| Yukon | 8.7 | .. | .. | 2.1 | 1.9 | 0.2 | 11.3 |
| Northwest Territories | 12.8 | .. | .. | 3.1 | 2.9 | 0.2 | 16.6 |
| **G-7 Countries** | | | | | | | |
| **Canada** | 4.3 | .. | .. | 2.5 | 0.9 | 1.5 | 7.0 |
| France | 4.4 | 1.2 | 3.2 | 1.1 | .. | .. | 6.3 |
| Germany | 3.8 | .. | .. | 1.1 | -- | 1.0 | 5.8 |
| Italy | 3.2 | 1.1 | 2.1 | 0.8 | -- | 0.8 | 4.7 |
| Japan | 3.1 | 1.3 | 1.7 | 1.0 | 0.1 | 0.9 | 4.7 |
| United Kingdom | .. | .. | .. | 1.0 | .. | .. | .. |
| United States | 3.9 | 1.8 | 2.0 | 2.4 | 0.4 | 2.0 | 6.7 |
| **OECD country mean** | 3.7 | 1.5 | 2.2 | 1.3 | 0.2 | 1.1 | 5.6 |

Source: Centre for Education Statistics, Statistics Canada; GDP from National Accounts, Statistics Canada; Education at a Glance: OECD Education Indicators, *1998, Table B1.1d.*

TABLE 3.25    PUBLIC EXPENDITURE ON EDUCATION AS A PERCENTAGE OF TOTAL PUBLIC EXPENDITURE BY LEVEL OF EDUCATION, CANADA, JURISDICTIONS AND G-7 COUNTRIES, 1995

|  | Total: direct expenditure plus public subsidies to the private sector | | | Direct public expenditure for educational services | | | Public subsidies to the private sector | | |
|---|---|---|---|---|---|---|---|---|---|
|  | Elementary-secondary | Post-secondary | All levels of education combined | Elementary-secondary | Post-secondary | All levels of education combined | Elementary-secondary | Post-secondary | All levels of education combined |
| **Canada** | 8.4 | 4.8 | 13.6 | 8.4 | 3.1 | 11.9 | .. | 1.7 | 1.7 |
| Newfoundland and Labrador | 7.5 | 8.9 | 16.9 | 7.5 | 3.2 | 11.2 | .. | 5.7 | 5.7 |
| Prince Edward Island | 6.1 | 4.4 | 10.8 | 6.1 | 2.4 | 8.8 | .. | 1.9 | 1.9 |
| Nova Scotia | 5.7 | 3.7 | 9.7 | 5.7 | 2.4 | 8.4 | .. | 1.3 | 1.3 |
| New Brunswick | 6.9 | 3.9 | 11.2 | 6.9 | 2.6 | 9.9 | .. | 1.3 | 1.3 |
| Quebec | 7.6 | 5.8 | 13.8 | 7.6 | 4.4 | 12.4 | .. | 1.4 | 1.4 |
| Ontario | 9.7 | 4.0 | 14.2 | 9.7 | 2.6 | 12.9 | .. | 1.4 | 1.4 |
| Manitoba | 8.6 | 3.9 | 12.9 | 8.6 | 2.3 | 11.4 | .. | 1.6 | 1.6 |
| Saskatchewan | 8.6 | 4.7 | 13.8 | 8.6 | 3.0 | 12.1 | .. | 1.7 | 1.7 |
| Alberta | 8.0 | 4.7 | 13.2 | 8.0 | 3.1 | 11.6 | .. | 1.6 | 1.6 |
| British Columbia | 7.3 | 4.5 | 12.2 | 7.3 | 2.9 | 10.6 | .. | 1.6 | 1.6 |
| Yukon | 7.5 | 2.5 | 10.4 | 7.5 | 1.4 | 9.2 | .. | 1.1 | 1.1 |
| Northwest Territories | 8.5 | 3.0 | 12.0 | 8.5 | 0.9 | 9.9 | .. | 2.1 | 2.1 |
| **G-7 countries** | | | | | | | | | |
| **Canada** | 8.4 | 4.8 | 13.6 | 8.4 | 3.1 | 11.9 | .. | 1.7 | 1.7 |
| France | 7.8 | 2.0 | 11.1 | 7.5 | 1.8 | 10.6 | 0.3 | 0.2 | 0.5 |
| Germany | 6.0 | 2.2 | 9.5 | 5.8 | 2.0 | 9.1 | 0.2 | 0.2 | 0.4 |
| Italy | 6.3 | 1.4 | 9.0 | 6.2 | 1.3 | 8.7 | 0.1 | 0.1 | 0.3 |
| Japan | 7.8 | 1.2 | 9.8 | 7.8 | 1.2 | 9.8 | .. | .. | .. |
| United Kingdom | .. | .. | .. | .. | .. | .. | .. | .. | .. |
| United States | 9.8 | 3.6 | 14.4 | 9.8 | 3.2 | 14.0 | .. | 0.4 | 0.4 |
| **OECD country mean** | 8.7 | 2.7 | 12.7 | 8.4 | 2.2 | 11.8 | 0.4 | 0.5 | 0.9 |

Source: Centre for Education Statistics, Statistics Canada; Education at a Glance: OECD Indicators, *1998, Table B2.1.*

EDUCATION INDICATORS IN CANADA

TABLE 3.26  DISTRIBUTION OF PUBLIC AND PRIVATE SOURCES OF FUNDS FOR EDUCATIONAL INSTITUTIONS BEFORE (INITIAL FUNDS) AND AFTER (FINAL FUNDS) TRANSFERS FROM PUBLIC SOURCES, BY LEVEL OF EDUCATION, CANADA, JURISDICTIONS AND G-7 COUNTRIES, 1995

|  | \multicolumn{6}{c|}{Initial funds (the orginal source of funds spent on education)} | \multicolumn{6}{c|}{Final funds (after public-to-private or private-to-public transfers have occured)} |
|---|---|---|---|---|---|---|---|---|---|---|---|---|
|  | \multicolumn{2}{c|}{Elementary–secondary} | \multicolumn{2}{c|}{Post-secondary} | \multicolumn{2}{c|}{All levels of education combined} | \multicolumn{2}{c|}{Elementary–secondary} | \multicolumn{2}{c|}{Post-secondary} | \multicolumn{2}{c|}{All levels of education combined} |
|  | Public | Private | Public | Private | Public | Private | Public | Private | Public | Private | Public | Private |
| **Canada** | **94** | **6** | **82** | **18** | **90** | **10** | **94** | **6** | **61** | **39** | **82** | **18** |
| Newfoundland and Labrador | 97 | 3 | 93 | 7 | 96 | 4 | 97 | 3 | 61 | 39 | 83 | 17 |
| Prince Edward Island | 99 | 1 | 90 | 10 | 95 | 5 | 99 | 1 | 60 | 40 | 84 | 16 |
| Nova Scotia | 97 | 3 | 78 | 22 | 90 | 10 | 97 | 3 | 60 | 40 | 83 | 17 |
| New Brunswick | 99 | 1 | 69 | 31 | 88 | 12 | 99 | 1 | 56 | 44 | 82 | 18 |
| Quebec | 92 | 8 | 88 | 12 | 90 | 10 | 92 | 8 | 74 | 26 | 84 | 16 |
| Ontario | 95 | 5 | 77 | 23 | 89 | 11 | 95 | 5 | 56 | 44 | 83 | 17 |
| Manitoba | 91 | 9 | 86 | 14 | 90 | 10 | 91 | 9 | 56 | 44 | 81 | 19 |
| Saskatchewan | 97 | 3 | 91 | 9 | 95 | 5 | 97 | 3 | 63 | 37 | 85 | 15 |
| Alberta | 95 | 5 | 81 | 19 | 90 | 10 | 95 | 5 | 64 | 36 | 84 | 16 |
| British Columbia | 91 | 9 | 78 | 22 | 86 | 14 | 91 | 9 | 56 | 44 | 78 | 22 |
| Yukon | 99 | 1 | .. | .. | .. | .. | 99 | 1 | 74 | 26 | 94 | 6 |
| Northwest Territories | 98 | 2 | .. | .. | .. | .. | 98 | 2 | 43 | 57 | 88 | 12 |
| **G-7 countries** | | | | | | | | | | | | |
| **Canada** | **94** | **6** | **82** | **18** | **90** | **10** | **94** | **6** | **61** | **39** | **82** | **18** |
| France | 93 | 7 | 84 | 16 | 91 | 9 | 93 | 7 | 84 | 16 | 91 | 9 |
| Germany | 76 | 24 | 93 | 7 | 78 | 22 | 76 | 24 | 92 | 8 | 78 | 22 |
| Italy | 100 | - | 91 | 9 | 100 | - | 100 | - | 84 | 16 | 97 | 3 |
| Japan | .. | .. | .. | .. | .. | .. | 92 | 8 | 43 | 57 | 75 | 25 |
| United Kingdom | .. | .. | 90 | 10 | .. | .. | .. | .. | 72 | 28 | .. | .. |
| United States | .. | .. | .. | .. | .. | .. | 90 | 10 | 48 | 52 | 75 | 25 |
| OECD country mean | 93 | 7 | 87 | 13 | 91 | 9 | 91 | 9 | 75 | 25 | 86 | 14 |

Source: Centre for Education Statistics, Statistics Canada; Education at a Glance: OECD Indicators, *1998, Table B3.1.*

TABLE 3.27  AVERAGE TUITION FEES IN UNDERGRADUATE ARTS PROGRAMS, CANADA AND PROVINCES, 1988-89 TO 1998-99, IN CONSTANT 1998 DOLLARS

| Year | Canada | Nfld. | P.E.I. | N.S. | N.B. | Que. | Ont. | Man. | Sask. | Alta. | B.C. |
|---|---|---|---|---|---|---|---|---|---|---|---|
| 1988-89 | **1,568** | 1,464 | 2,055 | 1,481 | 2,128 | 649 | 1,809 | 1,579 | 1,705 | 1,322 | 2,008 |
| 1989-90 | **1,615** | 1,554 | 2,077 | 2,196 | 2,141 | 623 | 1,850 | 1,659 | 1,723 | 1,366 | 2,067 |
| 1990-91 | **1,741** | 1,563 | 2,113 | 2,252 | 2,187 | 1,049 | 1,905 | 1,705 | 1,813 | 1,479 | 2,056 |
| 1991-92 | **1,890** | 1,691 | 2,265 | 2,405 | 2,188 | 1,417 | 1,964 | 1,988 | 2,048 | 1,710 | 2,159 |
| 1992-93 | **2,039** | 1,843 | 2,417 | 2,621 | 2,401 | 1,548 | 2,080 | 2,286 | 2,346 | 1,999 | 2,339 |
| 1993-94 | **2,161** | 2,132 | 2,590 | 2,858 | 2,498 | 1,623 | 2,185 | 2,334 | 2,503 | 2,374 | 2,389 |
| 1994-95 | **2,361** | 2,265 | 2,731 | 3,097 | 2,485 | 1,804 | 2,402 | 2,421 | 2,619 | 2,671 | 2,565 |
| 1995-96 | **2,486** | 2,401 | 2,894 | 3,284 | 2,594 | 1,772 | 2,579 | 2,476 | 2,709 | 2,891 | 2,638 |
| 1996-97 | **2,725** | 2,730 | 2,942 | 3,597 | 2,834 | 1,640 | 3,019 | 2,580 | 2,727 | 3,062 | 2,664 |
| 1997-98 | **3,019** | 3,156 | 3,135 | 3,748 | 3,015 | 2,223 | 3,292 | 2,621 | 3,010 | 3,229 | 2,724 |
| 1998-99 | **3,199** | 3,330 | 3,331 | 3,903 | 3,193 | 2,292 | 3,564 | 2,723 | 3,128 | 3,447 | 2,736 |

Source: Centre for Education Statistics, Statistics Canada.

TABLE 3.28  EDUCATIONAL EXPENDITURE ON PRE-ELEMENTARY AND ELEMENTARY–SECONDARY EDUCATION BY RESOURCE CATEGORY FOR PUBLIC AND PRIVATE INSTITUTIONS, CANADA, JURISDICTIONS AND G-7 COUNTRIES, 1995

|  | Percentage of total expenditure ||  Percentage of current expenditure ||||  Average expenditure per student (in equivalent U.S. dollars) |||||
|---|---|---|---|---|---|---|---|---|---|---|---|
|  |  |  | Compensation ||| Other current expenditure | Compensation ||| |  |
|  | Current | Capital | Educators | Other staff | All staff |  | Educators | Other staff | Other current expenditure | Current | Capital |
| Canada[1] | 96 | 4 | 65 | 16 | 81 | 19 | 3,405 | 4,201 | 1,008 | 5,209 | 192 |
| Newfoundland and Labrador | 96 | 4 | 74 | 10 | 84 | 16 | .. | .. | .. | .. | .. |
| Prince Edward Island | 98 | 2 | 67 | 17 | 84 | 16 | .. | .. | .. | .. | .. |
| Nova Scotia | 98 | 2 | 70 | 13 | 83 | 17 | .. | .. | .. | .. | .. |
| New Brunswick | 99 | 1 | 68 | 14 | 82 | 18 | .. | .. | .. | .. | .. |
| Quebec | 99 | 1 | 63 | 16 | 79 | 21 | .. | .. | .. | .. | .. |
| Ontario | 94 | 6 | 69 | 15 | 84 | 16 | .. | .. | .. | .. | .. |
| Manitoba | 97 | 3 | 57 | 16 | 73 | 27 | .. | .. | .. | .. | .. |
| Saskatchewan | 99 | 1 | 64 | 11 | 75 | 25 | .. | .. | .. | .. | .. |
| Alberta | 97 | 3 | 66 | 13 | 79 | 21 | .. | .. | .. | .. | .. |
| British Columbia | 97 | 3 | 63 | 19 | 82 | 18 | .. | .. | .. | .. | .. |
| Yukon | 92 | 8 | 49 | 10 | 59 | 41 | .. | .. | .. | .. | .. |
| Northwest Territories | 85 | 15 | 38 | 12 | 50 | 50 | .. | .. | .. | .. | .. |
| **G-7 countries** | | | | | | | | | | | |
| Canada[1] | 96 | 4 | 65 | 16 | 81 | 19 | 3,405 | 4,201 | 1,008 | 5,209 | 192 |
| France | 91 | 9 | .. | .. | 79 | 21 | .. | 3,617 | 975 | 4,592 | 449 |
| Germany[2] | 92 | 8 | .. | .. | 76 | 24 | .. | 3,262 | 1,057 | 4,319 | 371 |
| Italy[2] | 96 | 4 | 71 | 18 | 89 | 11 | 3,501 | 4,380 | 532 | 4,912 | 187 |
| Japan | 85 | 15 | .. | .. | 87 | 13 | .. | 3,182 | 479 | 3,661 | 621 |
| United Kingdom[3] | 95 | 5 | 54 | 16 | 70 | 30 | 1,940 | 2,522 | 1,092 | 3,614 | 196 |
| United States[2] | 91 | 9 | 57 | 23 | 80 | 20 | 3,241 | 4,554 | 1,168 | 5,722 | 559 |
| OECD country mean | 92 | 8 | 69 | 13 | 82 | 19 | 2,745 | 3,063 | 822 | 3,847 | 315 |

1 Canada total not as originally published by OECD due to data revisions.
2 Public institutions.
3 Public and government-dependent private institutions.

Source: Centre for Education Statistics, Statistics Canada; Education at a Glance: OECD Indicators, *1998, Table B5.1a.*

EDUCATION INDICATORS IN CANADA

TABLE 3.29  EDUCATIONAL EXPENDITURE ON POSTSECONDARY EDUCATION BY RESOURCE CATEGORY FOR PUBLIC AND PRIVATE INSTITUTIONS, CANADA, JURISDICTIONS AND G-7 COUNTRIES, 1995

|  | Percentage of total expenditure || Percentage of current expenditure |||| Average expenditure per student (in equivalent U.S. dollars) |||||
|---|---|---|---|---|---|---|---|---|---|---|---|
|  |  |  | Compensation ||| Other current expenditure | Compensation || Other current expenditure |  |  |
|  | Current | Capital | Educators | Other staff | All staff |  | Educators | Other staff |  | Current | Capital |
| **Canada** | **94** | **6** | **39** | **33** | **72** | **28** | **4,189** | **7,714** | **3,061** | **10,775** | **696** |
| Newfoundland and Labrador | 97 | 3 | 46 | 22 | 68 | 32 | .. | .. | .. | .. | .. |
| Prince Edward Island | 95 | 5 | 52 | 28 | 80 | 20 | .. | .. | .. | .. | .. |
| Nova Scotia | 98 | 2 | 43 | 33 | 76 | 24 | .. | .. | .. | .. | .. |
| New Brunswick | 95 | 5 | 42 | 30 | 72 | 28 | .. | .. | .. | .. | .. |
| Quebec | 91 | 9 | 39 | 29 | 68 | 32 | .. | .. | .. | .. | .. |
| Ontario | 97 | 3 | 39 | 36 | 75 | 25 | .. | .. | .. | .. | .. |
| Manitoba | 97 | 3 | 39 | 37 | 76 | 24 | .. | .. | .. | .. | .. |
| Saskatchewan | 97 | 3 | 36 | 33 | 69 | 31 | .. | .. | .. | .. | .. |
| Alberta | 95 | 5 | 39 | 34 | 73 | 27 | .. | .. | .. | .. | .. |
| British Columbia | 86 | 14 | 41 | 33 | 74 | 26 | .. | .. | .. | .. | .. |
| Yukon | 98 | 2 | 41 | 30 | 71 | 29 | .. | .. | .. | .. | .. |
| Northwest Territories | 99 | 1 | 44 | 16 | 60 | 40 | .. | .. | .. | .. | .. |
| **G-7 countries** |||||||||||||
| **Canada** | **94** | **6** | **39** | **33** | **72** | **28** | **4,189** | **7,714** | **3,061** | **10,775** | **696** |
| France | 88 | 12 | .. | .. | 69 | 31 | .. | 3,985 | 1,803 | 5,788 | 781 |
| Germany[1] | 89 | 11 | .. | .. | 76 | 24 | .. | 5,967 | 1,912 | 7,879 | 1,017 |
| Italy[1] | 79 | 21 | 46 | 26 | 72 | 28 | 1,834 | 2,876 | 1,104 | 3,980 | 1,033 |
| Japan | 79 | 21 | .. | .. | 67 | 33 | .. | 4,642 | 2,244 | 6,886 | 1,882 |
| United Kingdom[2] | 94 | 6 | 30 | 15 | 45 | 55 | 2,020 | 3,033 | 3,738 | 6,770 | 454 |
| United States | 93 | 7 | 41 | 20 | 60 | 40 | 6,100 | 9,071 | 5,987 | 15,059 | 1,203 |
| **OECD country mean** | **88** | **12** | **44** | **22** | **69** | **31** | **3,636** | **5,058** | **2,308** | **7,365** | **870** |

1  Public institutions.
2  Public and government-dependent private institutions.
*Source:* Centre for Education Statistics, Statistics Canada; Education at a Glance: OECD Indicators, *1998, Table B5.1b.*

TABLE 3.30  PERCENTAGE OF COLLEGE AND UNIVIVERSITY GRADUATES WHO BORROWED FROM STUDENT LOAN PROGRAMS, AND AVERAGE AMOUNT OWING AMONG BORROWERS AT GRADUATION AND TWO YEARS AFTER GRADUATION (IN CONSTANT $ 1995), BY LEVEL OF EDUCATION, CANADA AND PROVINCES, GRADUATING CLASSES OF 1986, 1990 AND 1995

|  | Percentage of graduates who borrowed ||| Amount owing at time of graduation ||| Amount owing two years after graduation |||
|---|---|---|---|---|---|---|---|---|---|
| Province of study and level of education | 1986 | 1990 | 1995 | 1986 | 1990 | 1995 | 1986 | 1990 | 1995 |
| **Canada** | 45 | 48 | 47 | 7,010 | 8,010 | 11,138 | 3,940 | 5,010 | 8,306 |
| College | 44 | 46 | 46 | 6,040 | 6,320 | 9,080 | 3,250 | 3,710 | 6,780 |
| Bachelor | 47 | 50 | 49 | 7,850 | 9,140 | 12,339 | 4,580 | 5,890 | 9,305 |
| Master's | 45 | 47 | 43 | 6,190 | 7,330 | 11,363 | 3,140 | 4,440 | 7,648 |
| Doctorate | 38 | 40 | 31 | 5,060 | 6,190 | 10,381 | 2,170 | 2,860 | 5,694 |
| All University | 46 | 49 | 48 | 7,590 | 8,820 | 12,188 | 4,360 | 5,610 | 9,040 |
| **Newfoundland and Labrador** | 61 | 69 | 57 | 8,930 | 10,300 | 12,986 | 5,650 | 6,350 | 10,534 |
| College | 59 | 69 | 49 | 6,100 | 6,970 | 10,787 | 3,870 | 3,730 | 9,048 |
| Bachelor | 65 | 73 | 66 | 10,880 | 12,060 | 14,193 | 6,800 | 7,680 | 11,542 |
| Master's | 40 | 43 | 33 | -- | 4,380 | 7,455 | -- | 1,880 | 5,232 |
| Doctorate | -- | -- | -- | -- | -- | -- | -- | -- | -- |
| All University | 62 | 69 | 61 | 10,440 | 11,570 | 13,636 | 6,560 | 7,280 | 10,985 |

TABLE 3.30  PERCENTAGE OF COLLEGE AND UNIVERSITY GRADUATES WHO BORROWED FROM STUDENT LOAN PROGRAMS, AND AVERAGE AMOUNT OWING AMONG BORROWERS AT GRADUATION AND TWO YEARS AFTER GRADUATION (IN CONSTANT $ 1995), BY LEVEL OF EDUCATION, CANADA AND PROVINCES, GRADUATING CLASSES OF 1986, 1990 AND 1995 (concluded)

| Province of study and level of education | Percentage of graduates who borrowed 1986 | 1990 | 1995 | Amount owing at time of graduation 1986 | 1990 | 1995 | Amount owing two years after graduation 1986 | 1990 | 1995 |
|---|---|---|---|---|---|---|---|---|---|
| **Prince Edward Island** | 52 | 63 | 53 | 6,300 | 7,340 | 9,728 | 3,700 | 5,110 | 8,259 |
| College | 51 | 59 | 46 | 5,560 | 5,520 | 6,974 | 2,890 | 3,720 | 5,500 |
| Bachelor | 54 | 69 | 59 | 7,680 | 10,050 | 11,722 | 5,240 | 7,070 | 10,057 |
| Master's | ... | -- | -- | ... | -- | -- | ... | -- | -- |
| Doctorate | ... | ... | ... | ... | ... | ... | ... | ... | ... |
| All University | 54 | 69 | 59 | 7,680 | 9,950 | 11,722 | 5,240 | 7,010 | 10,057 |
| **Nova Scotia** | 67 | 64 | 50 | 10,010 | 10,150 | 12,508 | 6,590 | 6,930 | 10,513 |
| College | 74 | 61 | 44 | 8,890 | 7,920 | 9,065 | 5,660 | 5,520 | 7,636 |
| Bachelor | 67 | 66 | 54 | 10,960 | 11,010 | 13,575 | 7,260 | 7,660 | 11,540 |
| Master's | 54 | 54 | 40 | 5,540 | 7,400 | 11,356 | 3,700* | 4,280 | 8,195 |
| Doctorate | -- | -- | -- | ... | -- | -- | -- | -- | -- |
| All University | 65 | 64 | 51 | 10,310 | 10,470 | 13,275 | 6,850 | 7,120 | 11,108 |
| **New Brunswick** | 64 | 64 | 53 | 8,530 | 8,750 | 11,963 | 5,650 | 6,400 | 9,970 |
| College | 63 | 59 | 47 | 7,510 | 7,520 | 9,027 | 4,750 | 4,920 | 6,139 |
| Bachelor | 65 | 69 | 57 | 9,480 | 9,550 | 13,264 | 6,440 | 7,210 | 11,451 |
| Master's | 55 | 53 | 40 | 4,360 | 5,610 | 9,280 | 2,010 | 3,460 | 7,213 |
| Doctorate | -- | -- | -- | ... | -- | -- | -- | -- | -- |
| All University | 64 | 66 | 55 | 8,980 | 9,080 | 12,915 | 6,010 | 6,740 | 11,069 |
| **Quebec** | 47 | 57 | 52 | 5,920 | 7,770 | 9,575 | 3,530 | 5,380 | 7,603 |
| College | 50 | 54 | 57 | 4,880 | 6,270 | 7,483 | 2,760 | 4,080 | 6,107 |
| Bachelor | 44 | 58 | 50 | 6,500 | 8,770 | 10,262 | 4,060 | 6,380 | 8,425 |
| Master's | 54 | 62 | 57 | 6,310 | 7,700 | 11,117 | 3,300 | 4,840 | 7,274 |
| Doctorate | 61 | 54 | 53 | 5,600 | 6,410 | 11,326 | 2,020 | 3,140 | 6,394 |
| All University | 46 | 58 | 51 | 6,460 | 8,510 | 10,426 | 3,920 | 6,010 | 8,192 |
| **Ontario** | 40 | 37 | 45 | 7,190 | 6,830 | 11,314 | 3,720 | 3,690 | 8,256 |
| College | 36 | 36 | 45 | 6,260 | 4,710 | 9,892 | 3,330 | 2,330 | 7,320 |
| Bachelor | 44 | 37 | 48 | 8,070 | 7,990 | 12,424 | 4,180 | 4,350 | 9,011 |
| Master's | 39 | 38 | 37 | 7,120 | 7,300 | 11,223 | 3,220 | 4,320 | 7,840 |
| Doctorate | 33 | 37 | 25 | 4,260 | 7,220 | 9,198 | 1,740 | 3,360 | 4,598 |
| All University | 43 | 37 | 46 | 7,860 | 7,870 | 12,244 | 4,000 | 4,320 | 8,818 |
| **Manitoba** | 39 | 47 | 34 | 7,380 | 8,160 | 10,164 | 3,770 | 4,950 | 6,774 |
| College | 46 | 49 | 26 | 7,180 | 7,060 | 7,259 | 3,790 | 4,440 | 4,837 |
| Bachelor | 36 | 48 | 40 | 7,690 | 8,720 | 11,075 | 3,910 | 5,280 | 7,314 |
| Master's | 33 | 39 | 28 | 5,870 | 6,870 | -- | 2,610* | 3,770 | -- |
| Doctorate | -- | -- | -- | -- | -- | -- | -- | -- | -- |
| All University | 36 | 47 | 38 | 7,470 | 8,500 | 11,020 | 3,750 | 5,100 | 7,283 |
| **Saskatchewan** | 43 | 52 | 46 | 5,860 | 9,910 | 14,953 | 3,230 | 6,380 | 10,466 |
| College | 45 | 61 | 50 | 6,110 | 8,420 | 10,894 | 3,340 | 4,740 | 7,326 |
| Bachelor | 42 | 51 | 48 | 5,990 | 10,930 | 16,526 | 3,360 | 7,260 | 11,663 |
| Master's | 38 | 37 | 28 | 3,010* | 5,110 | 11,144 | 1,150* | 3,610 | 7,422 |
| Doctorate | -- | -- | -- | -- | -- | -- | -- | -- | -- |
| All University | 42 | 49 | 46 | 5,780 | 10,400 | 16,120 | 3,190 | 6,910 | 11,334 |
| **Alberta** | 56 | 60 | 51 | 7,290 | 8,890 | 12,022 | 3,860 | 5,120 | 8,140 |
| College | 56 | 58 | 48 | 6,180 | 7,550 | 8,971 | 2,850 | 4,320 | 5,687 |
| Bachelor | 59 | 66 | 59 | 8,950 | 10,220 | 14,535 | 5,190 | 5,890 | 10,023 |
| Master's | 39 | 37 | 33 | 4,630 | 6,530 | 12,127 | -- | 4,060 | 8,620 |
| Doctorate | -- | 29 | 20 | -- | 3,210* | 10,919* | -- | -- | 6,864** |
| All University | 56 | 61 | 54 | 8,470 | 9,840 | 14,269 | 4,940 | 5,680 | 9,852 |
| **British Columbia** | 39 | 41 | 37 | 8,350 | 9,160 | 13,583 | 5,010 | 6,010 | 9,602 |
| College | 33 | 33 | 30 | 8,110 | 8,840 | 10,342 | 4,570 | 5,190 | 7,989 |
| Bachelor | 44 | 47 | 44 | 9,230 | 9,680 | 15,562 | 5,790 | 6,890 | 10,792 |
| Master's | 40 | 42 | 34 | 4,600 | 7,860 | 14,101 | 2,400* | 4,380 | 8,769 |
| Doctorate | 39 | 29 | 22 | 6,310 | 3,700* | 11,338 | 3,700* | 1,250** | 5,382 * |
| All University | 43 | 46 | 42 | 8,470 | 9,310 | 15,310 | 5,240 | 6,390 | 10,452 |

\* Estimate has a coefficient of variation between 16% and 24% and as such is not as reliable as other values.
\*\* Estimate has a coefficient of variation between 25% and 33% and as such is much less reliable than other values.
*Source: National Graduates Surveys, 1988, 1992, and 1997, Statistics Canada.*

TABLE 3.31 PERCENTAGE OF STUDENTS IN ELEMENTARY-SECONDARY SCHOOLS[1] USING THE INTERNET, BY TYPE OF ACTIVITY, CANADA AND PROVINCES, 1999

| Provinces | E-mail within/outside school — with teachers | with peers | for projects | World Wide Web — Retrieve information from WWW | Design or maintain WEB sites | Disseminating information |
|---|---|---|---|---|---|---|
| **Canada** | | | | | | |
| Elementary | 34 | 41 | 25 | 76 | 9 | 33 |
| Lower secondary | 35 | 45 | 23 | 80 | 23 | 31 |
| Upper secondary | 46 | 61 | 38 | 87 | 54 | 39 |
| **Newfoundland and Labrador** | | | | | | |
| Elementary | 46 | 61 | 23 | 62 | 33 | 37 |
| Lower secondary | 54 | 74 | 26 | 83 | 39 | 42 |
| Upper secondary | 52 | 82 | 45 | 94 | 56 | 53 |
| **Prince Edward Island** | | | | | | |
| Elementary | 52 | 69 | 27 | 57 | 0 | 28 |
| Lower secondary | 75 | 90 | 61 | 86 | 42 | 43 |
| Upper secondary | 69 | 100 | 50 | 100 | 86 | 50 |
| **Nova Scotia** | | | | | | |
| Elementary | 44 | 62 | 24 | 69 | 8 | 29 |
| Lower secondary | 57 | 79 | 30 | 74 | 39 | 44 |
| Upper secondary | 56 | 77 | 45 | 91 | 49 | 41 |
| **New Brunswick** | | | | | | |
| Elementary | 21 | 28 | 25 | 80 | 5 | 34 |
| Lower secondary | 45 | 25 | 2 | 100 | 15 | 44 |
| Upper secondary | 32 | 63 | 31 | 79 | 38 | 13 |
| **Quebec** | | | | | | |
| Elementary | 39 | 31 | 40 | 80 | 10 | 40 |
| Lower secondary | 48 | 53 | 26 | 76 | 24 | 35 |
| Upper secondary | 51 | 67 | 36 | 83 | 51 | 44 |
| **Ontario** | | | | | | |
| Elementary | 34 | 42 | 24 | 72 | 8 | 24 |
| Lower secondary | 21 | 29 | 21 | 86 | 14 | 28 |
| Upper secondary | 38 | 54 | 36 | 89 | 65 | 39 |
| **Manitoba** | | | | | | |
| Elementary | 26 | 60 | 28 | 77 | 9 | 27 |
| Lower secondary | 35 | 61 | 34 | 80 | 31 | 31 |
| Upper secondary | 62 | 85 | 50 | 85 | 50 | 53 |
| **Saskatchewan** | | | | | | |
| Elementary | 28 | 44 | 14 | 84 | 3 | 38 |
| Lower secondary | 39 | 71 | 38 | 60 | 10 | 15 |
| Upper secondary | 60 | 70 | 40 | 98 | 31 | 43 |
| **Alberta** | | | | | | |
| Elementary | 22 | 32 | 18 | 82 | 10 | 45 |
| Lower secondary | 39 | 57 | 19 | 75 | 34 | 41 |
| Upper secondary | 62 | 65 | 42 | 86 | 31 | 41 |
| **British Columbia** | | | | | | |
| Elementary | 41 | 54 | 22 | 73 | 8 | 32 |
| Lower secondary | 36 | 39 | 17 | 74 | 33 | 21 |
| Upper secondary | 48 | 61 | 39 | 77 | 33 | 26 |

1 Includes public and private elementary and secondary schools, classified into mutually exclusive groupings as follows:
Elementary: schools in which grade 5 is taught.
Lower secondary: schools in which grade 9 is taught.
Upper secondary: schools in which the final grade of secondary is taught.

Source: Second Information Technology in Education Study (SITES), 1999, Centre for Education Statistics, Statistic Canada, and International Association for the Evaluation of Educational Achievement (IEA).

**TABLE 3.32**  PERCENTAGE OF STUDENTS ATTENDING ELEMENTARY-SECONDARY SCHOOLS[1] AFFECTED BY SELECTED OBSTACLES[2] TO FULLER USE OF INFORMATION AND COMMUNICATIONS TECHNOLOGIES IN SCHOOLS, BY LEVEL OF SCHOOL, CANADA AND PROVINCES, **1999**

|  | Hardware | Software | Instruction | | | | Educator Training | |
|---|---|---|---|---|---|---|---|---|
| Provinces | Insufficient numbers of computers | Not enough types of software | Insufficient time to prepare lessons | Difficult to integrate computers into classroom | Problems scheduling computer time | No time in teacher schedules to explore WWW | Teachers lack of ICT knowledge/ skills | Not enough training opportunities |
| **Canada** | | | | | | | | |
| Elementary | 67 | 60 | 77 | 54 | 53 | 64 | 67 | 62 |
| Lower secondary | 69 | 54 | 69 | 56 | 67 | 60 | 64 | 61 |
| Upper secondary | 72 | 52 | 73 | 58 | 73 | 64 | 61 | 66 |
| **Newfoundland and Labrador** | | | | | | | | |
| Elementary | 55 | 53 | 72 | 40 | 31 | 53 | 66 | 85 |
| Lower secondary | 80 | 84 | 81 | 39 | 86 | 78 | 85 | 69 |
| Upper secondary | 75 | 49 | 81 | 58 | 80 | 34 | 50 | 88 |
| **Prince-Edward-Island** | | | | | | | | |
| Elementary | 59 | 78 | 83 | 72 | 40 | 75 | 84 | 90 |
| Lower secondary | 81 | 68 | 60 | 84 | 89 | 71 | 53 | 56 |
| Upper secondary | 100 | 21 | 21 | 41 | 86 | 10 | 56 | 35 |
| **Nova Scotia** | | | | | | | | |
| Elementary | 89 | 82 | 83 | 67 | 58 | 69 | 73 | 77 |
| Lower secondary | 89 | 78 | 70 | 43 | 75 | 71 | 48 | 59 |
| Upper secondary | 85 | 81 | 59 | 55 | 77 | 49 | 81 | 79 |
| **New Brunswick** | | | | | | | | |
| Elementary | 56 | 62 | 75 | 54 | 32 | 71 | 60 | 63 |
| Lower secondary | 89 | 76 | 56 | 43 | 87 | 55 | 82 | 82 |
| Upper secondary | 84 | 52 | 61 | 48 | 63 | 65 | 52 | 73 |
| **Quebec** | | | | | | | | |
| Elementary | 55 | 67 | 72 | 56 | 37 | 53 | 70 | 56 |
| Lower secondary | 47 | 54 | 60 | 62 | 45 | 46 | 84 | 57 |
| Upper secondary | 48 | 51 | 63 | 60 | 46 | 42 | 62 | 37 |
| **Ontario** | | | | | | | | |
| Elementary | 78 | 50 | 83 | 55 | 68 | 71 | 65 | 67 |
| Lower secondary | 76 | 52 | 78 | 52 | 77 | 75 | 54 | 69 |
| Upper secondary | 79 | 56 | 83 | 59 | 83 | 76 | 61 | 80 |
| **Manitoba** | | | | | | | | |
| Elementary | 63 | 59 | 70 | 41 | 55 | 58 | 61 | 51 |
| Lower secondary | 73 | 47 | 70 | 55 | 65 | 41 | 52 | 45 |
| Upper secondary | 77 | 51 | 51 | 44 | 81 | 32 | 45 | 35 |
| **Saskatchewan** | | | | | | | | |
| Elementary | 60 | 62 | 73 | 55 | 54 | 65 | 82 | 63 |
| Lower secondary | 72 | 76 | 63 | 51 | 80 | 55 | 71 | 70 |
| Upper secondary | 66 | 28 | 59 | 53 | 65 | 58 | 71 | 50 |
| **Alberta** | | | | | | | | |
| Elementary | 59 | 60 | 75 | 49 | 50 | 68 | 75 | 55 |
| Lower secondary | 62 | 43 | 67 | 66 | 63 | 57 | 52 | 42 |
| Upper secondary | 71 | 48 | 75 | 48 | 83 | 71 | 67 | 67 |
| **British Columbia** | | | | | | | | |
| Elementary | 61 | 67 | 75 | 54 | 43 | 61 | 56 | 61 |
| Lower secondary | 77 | 46 | 61 | 57 | 68 | 49 | 69 | 59 |
| Upper secondary | 70 | 41 | 56 | 65 | 62 | 63 | 60 | 56 |

1  Includes public and private elementary and secondary schools, classified into mutually exclusive groupings as follows:
   Elementary: schools in which grade 5 is taught.
   Lower secondary: schools in which grade 9 is taught.
   Upper secondary: schools in which the final grade of secondary is taught.
2  Includes only items rated as major obstacles by principals of schools representing 50% or more of enrolments at each of the three levels of schools, at the Canada level.

Source:  Second Information Technology in Education Study (SITES), 1999, Centre for Education Statistics, Statistic Canada, and International Association for the Evaluation of Educational Achievement (IEA).

# Chapter 4 Tables

## Chapter 4 Tables

**TABLE 4.1** PERCENTAGE OF 13-YEAR-OLDS AT PERFORMANCE LEVEL 2 OR ABOVE IN SAIP ASSESSMENTS, CANADA AND JURISDICTIONS

|  | Mathematics content 1993 % | +/- | Mathematics content 1997 % | +/- | Mathematics problem solving 1997 % | +/- | Reading 1994 % | +/- | Reading 1998 % | +/- | Writing 1994 % | +/- | Writing 1998 % | +/- | Written science 1996 % | +/- |
|---|---|---|---|---|---|---|---|---|---|---|---|---|---|---|---|---|
| Nfld. | 54.0 | 3.2 | 56.9 | 3.3 | 43.6 | 3.3 | 78.5 | 4.9 | 78.2 | 2.9 | 92.4 | 4.1 | 96.1 | 1.4 | 71.4 | 3.0 |
| P.E.I. | 54.9 | 3.4 | 53.6 | 3.2 | 49.3 | 3.2 | 75.3 | 4.1 | 77.3 | 2.9 | 92.0 | 2.7 | 94.9 | 1.6 | 76.4 | 2.7 |
| N.S. | 54.3 | 3.1 | ... | ... | ... | ... | 78.0 | 3.7 | ... | ... | 92.9 | 2.3 | ... | ... | ... | ... |
| N.S.(e) | ... | ... | 53.0 | 3.3 | 46.0 | 3.3 | ... | ... | 71.4 | 2.5 | ... | ... | 94.4 | 1.3 | 73.3 | 2.9 |
| N.S.(f) | ... | ... | 66.0 | ... | 48.1 | ... | ... | ... | 58.4 | ... | ... | ... | 71.2 | ... | 73.7 | ... |
| N.B. (e) | 60.5 | 3.2 | 54.6 | 3.3 | 47.2 | 3.3 | 74.7 | 4.0 | 76.1 | 3.0 | 92.8 | 2.4 | 95.0 | 1.6 | 70.6 | 2.9 |
| N.B. (f) | 66.9 | 3.1 | 63.2 | 3.0 | 53.2 | 3.1 | 65.9 | 4.2 | 72.8 | 2.9 | 74.1 | 3.9 | 87.7 | 2.1 | 60.4 | 2.9 |
| Que. (e) | 68.0 | 3.1 | 65.3 | 3.3 | 57.9 | 3.4 | 79.3 | 3.7 | 77.6 | 2.9 | 93.9 | 2.1 | 94.7 | 1.6 | 72.6 | 2.8 |
| Que. (f) | 83.4 | 2.2 | 78.3 | 2.6 | 66.8 | 3.0 | 82.0 | 4.2 | 83.7 | 2.5 | 90.5 | 4.1 | 95.3 | 1.4 | 73.3 | 2.6 |
| Ont. (e) | 56.0 | 2.8 | 50.0 | 3.1 | 45.4 | 3.1 | 79.2 | 3.8 | 77.8 | 2.7 | 93.3 | 4.0 | 96.6 | 1.2 | 67.4 | 2.8 |
| Ont. (f) | 57.2 | 3.0 | 51.9 | 3.0 | 43.0 | 3.0 | 72.9 | 5.4 | 72.4 | 3.2 | 69.5 | 6.2 | 80.8 | 2.8 | 57.1 | 3.1 |
| Man. (e) | 48.2 | 3.1 | 51.9 | 3.3 | 45.2 | 3.3 | 74.4 | 5.7 | 73.4 | 3.1 | 94.0 | 4.4 | 94.3 | 1.7 | 72.9 | 2.8 |
| Man (f) | 61.2 | 2.7 | 61.9 | 3.2 | 52.1 | 3.3 | 78.8 | 6.4 | 70.5 | 6.7 | 70.2 | 7.3 | 80.1 | 1.7 | 59.8 | 3.4 |
| Sask. | ... | ... | 47.9 | 3.2 | 51.2 | 3.2 | ... | ... | 76.1 | 2.8 | ... | ... | 95.9 | 1.4 | 76.1 | 2.7 |
| Alta. | 68.3 | 2.7 | 64.7 | 3.0 | 57.8 | 3.1 | 79.4 | 4.3 | 78.2 | 2.6 | 94.0 | 4.5 | 95.3 | 1.4 | 83.0 | 2.2 |
| B.C. | 62.2 | 2.9 | 56.9 | 3.0 | 47.8 | 3.1 | 75.4 | 4.1 | 74.9 | 2.9 | 92.6 | 4.3 | 94.5 | 1.6 | 74.9 | 2.6 |
| Y.T. | 53.8 | 6.4 | 65.4 | 5.2 | 40.7 | 5.2 | 64.2 | 9.0 | 77.5 | 5.3 | 82.0 | 6.9 | 93.9 | 3.0 | 76.2 | 3.7 |
| N.W.T. | 32.8 | 5.2 | 31.4 | 4.2 | 27.5 | 4.1 | 53.1 | 8.2 | 47.4 | 2.0 | 77.2 | 6.2 | 67.2 | 4.0 | 40.6 | 5.0 |
| Canada (e) | ... | ... | ... | ... | ... | ... | 78.0 | 1.3 | 76.7 | 0.9 | 93.2 | 0.8 | 95.6 | 0.4 | ... | ... |
| Canada (f) | ... | ... | ... | ... | ... | ... | 80.5 | 2.0 | 82.3 | 1.3 | 88.2 | 1.6 | 93.8 | 0.9 | ... | ... |
| Canada | 64.4 | 0.8 | 59.4 | 0.8 | 52.2 | 0.9 | 78.6 | 1.1 | 78.0 | 0.7 | 92.0 | 0.7 | 95.2 | 0.4 | 71.9 | 0.8 |

Notes: This table shows the cumulative percentages of students at or above level 2, and the confidence intervals for the percentages. Results are statistically different with 95% confidence if confidence intervals do not overlap.
The 1997 SAIP Mathematics report was used as the source of data for the 1993 mathematics content results.
Comparisons between the 1993 and 1997 problem solving assessments are not shown in this report. Because only four questions on the 1997 mathematics problem assessment were the same as those used in the 1993 assessment, it is not appropriate to compare both assessments in their entirety.
For the reading and writing assessments, caution is advised when comparing results based on instruments prepared in different languages. Every language has unique features that are optimal for speaking, reading, or writing, which are not easy to compare.
Results for the written portion of the SAIP science assessment are shown in this report. The practical portion is not included because results are generally not available by jurisdiction.
Saskatchewan did not participate in SAIP in 1993 and 1994. Nova Scotia did not sample English and French students separately in 1993 and 1994.
Nova Scotia francophone has no confidence interval because all students in that population were tested.

*Source:* School Achievement Indicators Program (SAIP), Council of Ministers of Education, Canada.

EDUCATION INDICATORS IN CANADA

TABLE 4.2   PERCENTAGE OF 16 YEAR OLDS AT PERFORMANCE LEVEL 3 OR ABOVE IN SAIP ASSESSMENTS, CANADA AND JURISDICTIONS

|  | Mathematics content 1993 % | +/- | Mathematics content 1997 % | +/- | Mathematics problem solving 1997 % | +/- | Reading 1994 % | +/- | Reading 1998 % | +/- | Writing 1994 % | +/- | Writing 1998 % | +/- | Written science 1996 % | +/- |
|---|---|---|---|---|---|---|---|---|---|---|---|---|---|---|---|---|
| Nfld. | 46.6 | 3.4 | 43.0 | 3.4 | 30.8 | 3.2 | 74.0 | 5.6 | 71.4 | 3.2 | 82.1 | 4.5 | 88.8 | 2.3 | 64.4 | 3.2 |
| P.E.I. | 48.5 | 3.8 | 48.5 | 3.6 | 27.5 | 3.2 | 69.6 | 4.8 | 63.9 | 3.5 | 81.3 | 4.2 | 85.1 | 2.7 | 68.6 | 3.3 |
| N.S. | 60.5 | 3.2 | ... | ... | ... | ... | 73.1 | 4.2 | ... | ... | 83.5 | 3.5 | ... | ... | ... | ... |
| N.S.(e) | ... | ... | 57.3 | 3.5 | 36.8 | 3.5 | ... | ... | 66.4 | 3.0 | ... | ... | 88.5 | 2.1 | 68.5 | 3.4 |
| N.S.(f) | ... | ... | 76.1 | ... | 44.2 | ... | ... | ... | 62.0 | ... | ... | ... | 44.8 | ... | 80.3 | ... |
| N.B. (e) | 54.2 | 3.4 | 47.3 | 3.5 | 33.6 | 3.3 | 69.1 | 4.4 | 65.9 | 3.5 | 82.1 | 3.7 | 87.5 | 2.5 | 69.8 | 3.1 |
| N.B. (f) | 60.1 | 3.2 | 63.4 | 3.2 | 37.1 | 3.2 | 59.8 | 4.5 | 68.1 | 3.2 | 52.5 | 4.8 | 61.2 | 3.4 | 58.0 | 3.1 |
| Que. (e) | 63.0 | 3.4 | 74.3 | 3.2 | 46.5 | 3.6 | 73.5 | 4.1 | 71.9 | 3.2 | 83.9 | 3.4 | 87.6 | 2.5 | 65.6 | 3.0 |
| Que. (f) | 77.8 | 2.4 | 81.0 | 2.7 | 57.0 | 3.4 | 80.4 | 5.5 | 79.4 | 2.7 | 78.5 | 4.9 | 87.0 | 2.3 | 73.4 | 2.6 |
| Ont. (e) | 55.8 | 3.0 | 52.0 | 3.2 | 33.0 | 3.0 | 68.7 | 4.9 | 71.6 | 3.0 | 81.0 | 5.1 | 87.5 | 2.3 | 64.9 | 3.0 |
| Ont. (f) | 52.9 | 3.3 | 49.2 | 3.3 | 27.8 | 3.0 | 61.3 | 4.9 | 65.0 | 3.4 | 46.8 | 5.1 | 50.8 | 3.5 | 51.4 | 3.3 |
| Man. (e) | 51.4 | 3.3 | 53.4 | 3.5 | 40.2 | 3.5 | 71.1 | 4.4 | 65.5 | 3.4 | 84.4 | 5.5 | 86.4 | 2.6 | 67.8 | 3.0 |
| Man (f) | 63.6 | 4.6 | 61.2 | 5.5 | 45.3 | 5.5 | 62.3 | 9.2 | 59.9 | 7.6 | 42.9 | 9.2 | 56.8 | 7.7 | 67.8 | 4.4 |
| Sask. | ... | ... | 50.0 | 3.3 | 38.6 | 3.3 | ... | ... | 64.9 | 3.2 | ... | ... | 84.2 | 2.5 | 71.0 | 3.1 |
| Alta. | 63.3 | 3.0 | 61.4 | 3.2 | 44.8 | 3.3 | 74.3 | 4.8 | 67.4 | 3.1 | 83.5 | 4.0 | 83.8 | 2.5 | 78.6 | 2.4 |
| B.C. | 58.7 | 3.1 | 54.6 | 3.2 | 31.2 | 3.0 | 68.4 | 6.0 | 67.9 | 3.3 | 78.5 | 5.4 | 83.6 | 2.8 | 69.2 | 2.9 |
| Y.T. | 62.6 | 8.1 | 59.2 | 7.7 | 30.8 | 6.9 | 54.3 | 12.8 | 55.3 | 7.9 | 69.4 | 11.5 | 83.3 | 6.4 | 73.9 | 6.3 |
| N.W.T. | 36.0 | 7.3 | 37.8 | 5.8 | 18.5 | 4.8 | 50.5 | 8.3 | 41.1 | 2.9 | 65.7 | 8.3 | 51.7 | 5.9 | 44.4 | 7.1 |
| Canada (e) | ... | ... | ... | ... | ... | ... | 70.1 | 1.5 | 69.3 | 1.0 | 81.4 | 1.2 | 86.0 | 0.8 | ... | ... |
| Canada (f) | ... | ... | ... | ... | ... | ... | 78.2 | 2.2 | 78 | 1.5 | 75.1 | 2.4 | 83.7 | 1.4 | ... | ... |
| Canada | 61.6 | 0.9 | 59.8 | 0.9 | 39.8 | 0.9 | 72.3 | 1.2 | 71.5 | 0.8 | 79.6 | 1.1 | 85.4 | 0.7 | 69.0 | 0.8 |

Notes:  This table shows the cumulative percentages of students at or above level 3, and the confidence intervals for the percentages. Results are statistically different with 95% confidence if confidence intervals do not overlap.
The 1997 SAIP Mathematics report was used as the source of data for the 1993 mathematics content results.
Comparisons between the 1993 and 1997 problem solving assessments are not shown in this report. Because only four questions on the 1997 mathematics problem assessment were the same as those used in the 1993 assessment, it is not appropriate to compare both assessments in their entirety.
For the reading and writing assessments, caution is advised when comparing results based on instruments prepared in different languages. Every language has unique features that are optimal for speaking, reading, or writing, which are not easy to compare.
Results for the written portion of the SAIP science assessment are shown in this report. The practical portion is not included because results are generally not available by jurisdiction.
Saskatchewan did not participate in SAIP in 1993 and 1994. Nova Scotia did not sample English and French students separately in 1993 and 1994. Nova Scotia francophone has no confidence interval because all students in that population were tested.

*Source:*  School Achievement Indicators Program (SAIP), Council of Ministers of Education, Canada.

## Chapter 4 Tables

**TABLE 4.3**    PERCENTAGE OF 13-YEAR-OLDS AT PERFORMANCE LEVEL 2 OR ABOVE IN SAIP ASSESSMENTS, BY GENDER, CANADA

|  | Mathematics content 1993 % | +/- | Mathematics content 1997 % | +/- | Mathematics problem solving 1997 % | +/- | Reading 1994 % | +/- | Reading 1998 % | +/- | Writing 1994 % | +/- | Writing 1998 % | +/- | Written science 1996 % | +/- |
|---|---|---|---|---|---|---|---|---|---|---|---|---|---|---|---|---|
| **Both sexes** | 64.4 | 0.8 | 59.4 | 0.8 | 52.2 | 0.9 | 78.6 | 1.1 | 78.1 | 0.7 | 92.0 | 0.7 | 95.2 | 0.4 | 71.9 | 0.8 |
| Males | 65.1 | 1.2 | 59.7 | 1.2 | 50.0 | 1.2 | 70.9 | 1.7 | 70.1 | 1.2 | 89.0 | 1.1 | 92.5 | 0.7 | 70.9 | 1.1 |
| Females | 63.9 | 1.2 | 59.5 | 1.2 | 54.5 | 1.2 | 87.5 | 1.2 | 85.8 | 0.9 | 95.5 | 0.8 | 97.7 | 0.4 | 73.3 | 1.1 |

Notes: This table shows the cumulative percentages of students at or above level 2 by gender, and the confidence intervals for the percentages. Results are statistically different with 95% confidence if confidence intervals do not overlap.
The 1997 SAIP Mathematics report was used as the source of data for the 1993 mathematics content results.
Comparisons between the 1993 and 1997 problem solving assessments are not shown in this report. Because only four questions on the 1997 mathematics problem assessment were the same as those used in the 1993 assessment, it is not appropriate to compare both assessments in their entirety.
Results for the written portion of the SAIP science assessment are shown in this report. The practical portion is not included because results are generally not available by jurisdiction.

Source: School Achievement Indicators Program (SAIP), Council of Ministers of Education, Canada.


**TABLE 4.4**    PERCENTAGE OF 16-YEAR-OLDS AT PERFORMANCE LEVEL 3 OR ABOVE IN SAIP ASSESSMENTS, BY GENDER, CANADA

|  | Mathematics content 1993 % | +/- | Mathematics content 1997 % | +/- | Mathematics problem solving 1997 % | +/- | Reading 1994 % | +/- | Reading 1998 % | +/- | Writing 1994 % | +/- | Writing 1998 % | +/- | Written science 1996 % | +/- |
|---|---|---|---|---|---|---|---|---|---|---|---|---|---|---|---|---|
| **Both sexes** | 61.6 | 0.9 | 59.8 | 0.9 | 39.8 | 0.9 | 72.3 | 1.2 | 71.5 | 0.8 | 79.6 | 1.1 | 85.4 | 0.7 | 69.0 | 0.8 |
| Males | 63.0 | 1.3 | 61.8 | 1.3 | 40.3 | 1.3 | 63.6 | 1.9 | 60.0 | 1.3 | 74.2 | 1.7 | 79.9 | 1.1 | 70.5 | 1.1 |
| Females | 60.3 | 1.3 | 57.8 | 1.3 | 39.5 | 1.3 | 81.7 | 1.5 | 81.9 | 1.0 | 85.5 | 1.4 | 90.5 | 0.8 | 68.0 | 1.2 |

Notes: This table shows the cumulative percentages of students at or above level 3 by gender, and the confidence intervals for the percentages. Results are statistically different with 95% confidence if confidence intervals do not overlap.
The 1997 SAIP Mathematics report was used as the source of data for the 1993 mathematics content results.
Comparisons between the 1993 and 1997 problem solving assessments are not shown in this report. Because only four questions on the 1997 mathematics problem assessment were the same as those used in the 1993 assessment, it is not appropriate to compare both assessments in their entirety.
Results for the written portion of the SAIP science assessment are shown in this report. The practical portion is not included because results are generally not available by jurisdiction.

Source: School Achievement Indicators Program (SAIP), Council of Ministers of Education, Canada.

TABLE 4.5  PERCENTAGE OF THE POPULATION AGED 16 TO 25 AND 26 TO 65 AT EACH LITERACY LEVEL IN THE IALS DOCUMENT, PROSE, AND QUANTITATIVE SCALES[1], CANADA, REGIONS, AND OTHER IALS PARTICIPATING COUNTRIES

|  | Document scale ||||| Prose scale ||||| Quantitative scale |||||
|---|---|---|---|---|---|---|---|---|---|---|---|---|---|---|---|
|  | 1 | 2 | 3 | 4/5 | 3 or above | 1 | 2 | 3 | 4/5 | 3 or above | 1 | 2 | 3 | 4/5 | 3 or above |
| **16 to 25 years** | | | (%) | | | | | (%) | | | | | (%) | | |
| **Canada** | 10 | 22 | 36 | 31 | 67 | 11 | 26 | 44 | 20 | 64 | 10 | 29 | 45 | 17 | 61 |
| Atlantic provinces[2] | 14 | 29 | 40 | 18 | 58 | 11 | 32 | 42 | 15 | 57 | 11 | 34 | 43 | 12 | 55 |
| Quebec | -- | 20 | 40 | 28 | 68 | -- | 22 | 56 | 14 | 70 | -- | 29 | 54 | 9 | 63 |
| Ontario | -- | 22 | 34 | 32 | 66 | 17 | 24 | 39 | 21 | 60 | 13 | 32 | 37 | 18 | 55 |
| Western provinces[3] | -- | 22 | 36 | 37 | 73 | -- | 28 | 41 | 25 | 66 | 7 | 23 | 47 | 23 | 70 |
| **Participating countries** | | | | | | | | | | | | | | | |
| **Canada** | 10 | 22 | 36 | 31 | 67 | 11 | 26 | 44 | 20 | 64 | 10 | 29 | 45 | 17 | 61 |
| Germany | 5 | 29 | 43 | 23 | 66 | 9 | 30 | 46 | 15 | 62 | 4 | 26 | 47 | 22 | 69 |
| Netherlands | 6 | 17 | 51 | 26 | 77 | 8 | 22 | 50 | 20 | 70 | 8 | 21 | 50 | 21 | 71 |
| Poland | 32 | 33 | 26 | 9 | 35 | 27 | 38 | 29 | 6 | 35 | 30 | 33 | 31 | 7 | 38 |
| Sweden | 3 | 17 | 40 | 41 | 80 | 4 | 17 | 40 | 40 | 80 | 5 | 18 | 39 | 38 | 77 |
| Switzerland (French) | 9 | 25 | 40 | 26 | 66 | 11 | 31 | 43 | 15 | 59 | 6 | 21 | 47 | 25 | 72 |
| Switzerland (German) | 7 | 26 | 41 | 26 | 67 | 7 | 36 | 43 | 14 | 57 | 7 | 22 | 48 | 23 | 71 |
| United States[4] | 25 | 31 | 28 | 16 | 45 | 24 | 31 | 33 | 13 | 46 | 27 | 31 | 29 | 14 | 43 |
| **26 to 65 years** | | | | | | | | | | | | | | | |
| **Canada** | 20 | 25 | 31 | 24 | 55 | 18 | 26 | 33 | 23 | 56 | 19 | 26 | 33 | 24 | 56 |
| Atlantic provinces[2] | 25 | 26 | 33 | 16 | 49 | 22 | 23 | 38 | 17 | 55 | 20 | 29 | 30 | 20 | 50 |
| Quebec | 25 | 30 | 32 | 13 | 45 | 24 | 27 | 41 | 8 | 49 | 24 | 35 | 30 | 12 | 41 |
| Ontario | 18 | 21 | 31 | 29 | 61 | 15 | 28 | 26 | 31 | 57 | 17 | 19 | 35 | 29 | 64 |
| Western provinces[3] | 16 | 27 | 29 | 29 | 58 | 15 | 22 | 34 | 29 | 63 | 15 | 24 | 32 | 29 | 61 |
| **Participating countries** | | | | | | | | | | | | | | | |
| **Canada** | 20 | 25 | 31 | 24 | 55 | 18 | 26 | 33 | 23 | 56 | 19 | 26 | 33 | 24 | 56 |
| Germany | 10 | 34 | 39 | 18 | 57 | 16 | 35 | 36 | 13 | 49 | 7 | 27 | 42 | 24 | 66 |
| Netherlands | 11 | 28 | 42 | 18 | 61 | 11 | 32 | 43 | 14 | 57 | 11 | 27 | 43 | 20 | 62 |
| Poland | 49 | 30 | 16 | 5 | 21 | 47 | 34 | 17 | 2 | 19 | 42 | 29 | 22 | 7 | 29 |
| Sweden | 7 | 20 | 39 | 34 | 73 | 9 | 21 | 40 | 30 | 70 | 7 | 19 | 39 | 35 | 74 |
| Switzerland (French) | 18 | 30 | 39 | 14 | 52 | 19 | 34 | 38 | 9 | 46 | 14 | 25 | 41 | 19 | 60 |
| Switzerland (German) | 20 | 30 | 36 | 14 | 50 | 22 | 36 | 35 | 8 | 43 | 16 | 27 | 39 | 18 | 57 |
| United States | 24 | 25 | 32 | 20 | 51 | 20 | 25 | 32 | 23 | 55 | 20 | 24 | 32 | 25 | 56 |

1 See Appendix 3 for a description of the scales and levels used in IALS. Levels 4 and 5 have been combined due to the small proportion of the population at level 5.
2 The Atlantic provinces include Newfoundland and Labrador, Prince Edward Island, Nova Scotia, and New Brunswick.
3 The Western provinces include Manitoba, Saskatchewan, Alberta, and British Columbia.
4 Because of a sampling anomaly, *National Adult Literacy Survey (NALS)* data have been used for the group aged 16-25. NALS measures a skill set comparable to IALS.

*Source: International Adult Literacy Survey, Statistics Canada and OECD, 1994-95.*

CHAPTER 4 TABLES

TABLE 4.6  RATIO (TIMES 100) OF UPPER SECONDARY GRADUATES TO POPULATION AT A TYPICAL AGE OF GRADUATION (FROM FIRST EDUCATIONAL PROGRAM[1]), G-7 COUNTRIES[2], 1996

| Country | Both sexes | Males | Females |
|---|---|---|---|
| United Kingdom | .. | .. | .. |
| Japan[3] | 99 | 96 | 102 |
| Germany | 86 | 86 | 86 |
| France | 85 | 85 | 86 |
| Italy | 79 | 76 | 82 |
| Canada[4] | 75 | 70 | 81 |
| United States | 72 | 69 | 76 |

1. The typical graduation age is the age at the end of the last school/academic year when the degree is obtained. The typical age is based on the assumption of full-time attendance in the regular education system without grade repetition. For Canada, the typical age used is 18.
2. The definition of an upper secondary graduate differs by country.
3. It should be noted that differences in the reference dates between graduation data and population data can lead this ratio to exceed 100 percent.
4. The numbers for Canada differ slightly from those published in *Education at a Glance* due to changes in the method of calculation.

*Source:* Education at a Glance: OECD Indicators, *1998, Table C2.3, and Centre for Education Statistics, Statistics Canada.*

TABLE 4.7  RATIO[1] OF SECONDARY GRADUATES[2] TO POPULATION AT AGE 18, BY GENDER, CANADA AND JURISDICTIONS, 1995 TO 1997

|  | 1995 |  |  | 1996 |  |  | 1997 |  |  |
|---|---|---|---|---|---|---|---|---|---|
|  | Both sexes | Males | Females | Both sexes | Males | Females | Both sexes | Males | Females |
| **Canada** | **75** | **69** | **81** | **75** | **70** | **81** | **75** | **70** | **81** |
| Nfld. | 76 | 70 | 82 | 80 | 75 | 85 | 79 | 67 | 91 |
| P.E.I. | 80 | 74 | 87 | 80 | 73 | 88 | 78 | 73 | 82 |
| N.S. | 75 | 71 | 79 | 74 | 69 | 79 | 80 | 73 | 87 |
| N.B. | 83 | 78 | 88 | 84 | 80 | 90 | 85 | 80 | 90 |
| Que.[3] | 88 | 80 | 96 | 91 | 84 | 98 | 86 | 80 | 92 |
| Ont. | 76 | 71 | 81 | 74 | 69 | 79 | 75 | 71 | 80 |
| Man. | 76 | 72 | 80 | 75 | 69 | 82 | 76 | 73 | 80 |
| Sask. | 73 | 69 | 78 | 71 | 66 | 77 | 74 | 68 | 81 |
| Alta. | 65 | 60 | 70 | 64 | 61 | 68 | 64 | 59 | 69 |
| B.C. | 66 | 61 | 72 | 67 | 63 | 72 | 67 | 62 | 72 |
| Y.T. | 44 | 40 | 48 | 45 | 44 | 46 | 43 | 39 | 47 |
| N.W.T. | 27 | 25 | 30 | 23 | 21 | 25 | 25 | 22 | 28 |

1. Calculated as the number of graduates (irrespective of age) as a percentage of the total 18-year-old population.
2. Excludes General Education Diplomas (GED), adult basic upgrading and education, and graduation from adult day school which takes place outside regular secondary school programs.
3. Includes graduates of the "formation professionnelle" and adult education programs.

*Source:* Centre for Education Statistics, Statistics Canada; *For Quebec data:* Statistiques de l'éducation — Enseignement primaire, secondaire,collégial et universitaire, *Gouvernement du Québec, Ministère de l'Éducation.*

EDUCATION INDICATORS IN CANADA

TABLE 4.8  HIGH SCHOOL COMPLETION RATES OF THE POPULATION AGED 19 TO 20, BY GENDER, CANADA AND PROVINCES, 1991 TO 1994 AND 1995 TO 1998

|  | 1991 to 1994 ||| 1995 to 1998 |||
|---|---|---|---|---|---|---|
|  | Both sexes | Males | Females | Both sexes | Males | Females |
| **Canada** | 79 | 76 | 82 | 81 | 78 | 84 |
| Nfld. | 78 | 75 | 82 | 84 | 82 | 87 |
| P.E.I. | 80 | 73 | 87 | 85 | 82 | 88 |
| N.S. | 76 | 69 | 83 | 80 | 77 | 84 |
| N.B. | 83 | 79 | 87 | 84 | 82 | 87 |
| Que. | 77 | 72 | 82 | 79 | 74 | 84 |
| Ont. | 79 | 77 | 81 | 81 | 79 | 84 |
| Man. | 78 | 75 | 81 | 80 | 77 | 83 |
| Sask. | 83 | 81 | 85 | 84 | 83 | 86 |
| Alta. | 78 | 75 | 81 | 80 | 77 | 83 |
| B.C. | 82 | 80 | 83 | 82 | 79 | 84 |

*Source: Labour Force Survey, Statistics Canada.*

TABLE 4.9  NUMBER OF DIPLOMAS AND DEGREES GRANTED, BY LEVEL OF EDUCATION, CANADA, 1976 TO 1997

|  | Community college diplomas | Bachelor's and first professional degrees | Master's degrees | Earned doctorates | Total |
|---|---|---|---|---|---|
| 1976 | 56,655 | 83,292 | 11,555 | 1,693 | 153,195 |
| 1977 | 60,687 | 87,356 | 12,375 | 1,702 | 162,120 |
| 1978 | 64,891 | 89,349 | 12,637 | 1,819 | 168,696 |
| 1979 | 67,883 | 87,238 | 12,351 | 1,803 | 169,275 |
| 1980 | 67,343 | 86,410 | 12,432 | 1,738 | 167,923 |
| 1981 | 68,744 | 84,926 | 12,903 | 1,816 | 168,389 |
| 1982 | 71,818 | 87,106 | 13,110 | 1,715 | 173,749 |
| 1983 | 75,776 | 89,770 | 13,925 | 1,821 | 181,292 |
| 1984 | 83,557 | 92,856 | 14,568 | 1,878 | 192,859 |
| 1985 | 84,281 | 97,551 | 15,208 | 2,004 | 199,044 |
| 1986 | 81,761 | 101,670 | 15,948 | 2,220 | 201,599 |
| 1987 | 82,419 | 103,078 | 15,968 | 2,375 | 203,840 |
| 1988 | 80,096 | 103,606 | 16,320 | 2,418 | 202,440 |
| 1989 | 82,190 | 104,981 | 16,750 | 2,573 | 206,494 |
| 1990 | 82,506 | 109,777 | 17,653 | 2,673 | 212,609 |
| 1991 | 83,824 | 114,820 | 18,033 | 2,947 | 219,624 |
| 1992 | 85,949 | 120,745 | 19,435 | 3,136 | 229,265 |
| 1993 | 92,515 | 123,202 | 20,818 | 3,356 | 239,891 |
| 1994 | 95,296 | 126,538 | 21,292 | 3,552 | 246,678 |
| 1995 | 97,195 | 127,331 | 21,356 | 3,716 | 249,598 |
| 1996 | 104,202 | 127,989 | 21,558 | 3,928 | 257,677 |
| 1997 | 104,202 e | 125,729 | 21,254 | 3,996 | 255,181 |

e   1996 data has been used as an estimate for 1997.
*Source: Centre for Education Statistics, Statistics Canada.*

**TABLE 4.10** RATIO OF UNIVERSITY GRADUATES TO THE POPULATION AT THE TYPICAL AGE OF GRADUATION[1] (TIMES 100), BY LEVEL OF EDUCATION AND BY JURISDICTION OF STUDY, CANADA AND JURISDICTIONS, 1991 TO 1997

| Level and year | Canada | Nfld. | P.E.I. | N.S. | N.B. | Que.[1] | Ont. | Man. | Sask. | Alta. | B.C.[2] | Y.T. | N.W.T. |
|---|---|---|---|---|---|---|---|---|---|---|---|---|---|
| **Bachelor's and first professional degrees:** | | | | | | | | | | | | | |
| 1991 | **27.8** | 22.4 | 21.4 | 38.8 | 26.2 | 27.6 | 31.4 | 30.5 | 30.8 | 23.3 | 18.3 | - | - |
| 1992 | **28.7** | 21.3 | 23.8 | 41.7 | 26.4 | 28.4 | 32.3 | 30.2 | 32.2 | 23.3 | 20.5 | - | - |
| 1993 | **29.4** | 22.3 | 22.5 | 42.2 | 26.9 | 29.8 | 33.0 | 30.5 | 32.7 | 23.3 | 20.6 | - | - |
| 1994 | **31.5** | 23.7 | 25.1 | 45.1 | 27.7 | 31.9 | 35.6 | 33.4 | 29.1 | 26.0 | 22.1 | - | - |
| 1995 | **32.1** | 23.7 | 26.9 | 46.1 | 30.0 | 32.1 | 36.8 | 34.0 | 31.3 | 25.9 | 22.2 | - | - |
| 1996 | **32.4** | 25.4 | 24.0 | 46.5 | 32.7 | 31.9 | 37.8 | 32.3 | 31.1 | 26.4 | 21.3 | - | - |
| 1997 | **30.4** | 25.5 | 26.6 | 46.8 | 31.9 | 29.2 | 35.8 | 31.3 | 27.9 | 26.4 | 21.4 | - | - |
| **Master's degrees:** | | | | | | | | | | | | | |
| 1991 | **4.2** | 2.1 | 0.3 | 6.3 | 2.9 | 5.0 | 4.7 | 2.8 | 2.8 | 3.1 | 3.2 | - | - |
| 1992 | **4.6** | 2.2 | 0.5 | 7.6 | 3.3 | 5.8 | 5.1 | 3.4 | 3.5 | 3.1 | 3.2 | - | - |
| 1993 | **5.0** | 2.7 | 0.8 | 7.6 | 3.6 | 6.1 | 5.4 | 3.5 | 3.2 | 3.6 | 3.7 | - | - |
| 1994 | **5.0** | 2.4 | 0.6 | 7.8 | 3.3 | 6.5 | 5.3 | 3.2 | 3.2 | 3.6 | 3.6 | - | - |
| 1995 | **5.0** | 2.8 | 0.2 | 7.8 | 3.6 | 6.6 | 5.3 | 3.6 | 3.9 | 3.6 | 3.7 | - | - |
| 1996 | **5.3** | 2.8 | 0.5 | 7.4 | 3.8 | 7.2 | 5.7 | 3.5 | 3.6 | 3.3 | 3.8 | - | - |
| 1997 | **5.2** | 3.3 | 0.3 | 7.8 | 3.8 | 7.2 | 5.6 | 3.6 | 3.5 | 3.3 | 3.8 | - | - |
| **Earned doctorates:** | | | | | | | | | | | | | |
| 1991 | **0.6** | 0.3 | - | 0.5 | 0.1 | 0.6 | 0.6 | 0.4 | 0.4 | 0.6 | 0.5 | - | - |
| 1992 | **0.6** | 0.2 | - | 0.4 | 0.2 | 0.7 | 0.7 | 0.5 | 0.5 | 0.7 | 0.5 | - | - |
| 1993 | **0.7** | 0.3 | - | 0.5 | 0.3 | 0.8 | 0.8 | 0.6 | 0.6 | 0.8 | 0.7 | - | - |
| 1994 | **0.8** | 0.3 | - | 0.5 | 0.3 | 0.9 | 0.9 | 0.8 | 0.6 | 0.9 | 0.7 | - | - |
| 1995 | **0.9** | 0.3 | - | 0.7 | 0.4 | 1.0 | 0.9 | 0.6 | 0.8 | 0.9 | 0.8 | - | - |
| 1996 | **0.9** | 0.4 | - | 0.6 | 0.5 | 1.1 | 1.0 | 0.7 | 0.8 | 0.9 | 0.8 | - | - |
| 1997 | **0.9** | 0.4 | - | 0.6 | 0.4 | 1.2 | 0.9 | 0.7 | 0.8 | 0.9 | 0.8 | - | - |

1 Typical age at graduation is 22 for Bachelor's and first professional degrees, 24 for Master's and 27 for Earned doctorates.
2 Postsecondary degrees granted by university colleges have not been captured historically and are therefore not reflected in these data. However these degrees will be captured in the near future by Statistics Canada through the Enhanced Student Information System (ESIS), scheduled for implementation at the national level beginning in the year 2000.

*Source: Centre for Education Statistics, Statistics Canada.*

TABLE 4.11  RATIO OF UNIVERSITY GRADUATES TO THE POPULATION AT THE TYPICAL AGE OF GRADUATION[1] (TIMES 100), BY LEVEL OF EDUCATION AND BY JURISDICTIONS OF RESIDENCE, CANADA AND JURISDICTIONS, 1991 TO 1997

| Level and year | Canada | Nfld. | P.E.I. | N.S. | N.B. | Que.[1] | Ont. | Man. | Sask. | Alta. | B.C.[2] | Y.T. | N.W.T. |
|---|---|---|---|---|---|---|---|---|---|---|---|---|---|
| **Bachelor's and first professional degrees:** | | | | | | | | | | | | | |
| 1991 | **26.8** | 24.3 | 33.2 | 30.5 | 25.9 | 28.0 | 29.6 | 28.1 | 28.3 | 23.2 | 17.2 | 5.9 | 4.1 |
| 1992 | **27.6** | 24.3 | 32.9 | 31.3 | 27.4 | 28.3 | 30.3 | 27.8 | 30.4 | 22.8 | 21.1 | 7.2 | 4.4 |
| 1993 | **28.2** | 26.0 | 33.6 | 31.8 | 27.7 | 30.0 | 31.1 | 27.8 | 31.7 | 23.0 | 19.4 | 7.9 | 5.8 |
| 1994 | **30.1** | 27.4 | 36.1 | 34.9 | 27.9 | 32.0 | 33.6 | 29.8 | 28.7 | 25.6 | 20.3 | 19.1 | 5.9 |
| 1995 | **30.9** | 27.8 | 36.2 | 34.2 | 32.7 | 31.1 | 35.3 | 30.4 | 31.5 | 25.7 | 20.9 | 12.7 | 5.6 |
| 1996 | **31.3** | 30.4 | 34.0 | 36.9 | 31.8 | 30.7 | 36.5 | 29.4 | 31.2 | 26.5 | 20.7 | 11.7 | 7.5 |
| 1997 | **29.7** | 31.3 | 34.3 | 36.9 | 31.0 | 28.1 | 34.6 | 29.0 | 27.9 | 23.1 | 22.2 | 15.9 | 8.0 |
| **Master's degrees:** | | | | | | | | | | | | | |
| 1991 | **3.5** | 2.8 | 3.4 | 4.9 | 3.1 | 4.4 | 3.7 | 2.6 | 1.8 | 3.0 | 2.4 | 1.1 | 0.9 |
| 1992 | **3.9** | 2.4 | 4.5 | 5.5 | 4.0 | 5.0 | 4.0 | 3.0 | 1.8 | 2.9 | 3.1 | 1.5 | 0.5 |
| 1993 | **4.1** | 3.2 | 4.8 | 5.3 | 4.0 | 5.5 | 4.3 | 3.3 | 2.0 | 3.3 | 2.3 | 0.5 | 1.2 |
| 1994 | **4.2** | 3.2 | 3.5 | 5.4 | 3.7 | 5.8 | 4.3 | 3.1 | 2.1 | 3.2 | 2.2 | 1.9 | 1.4 |
| 1995 | **4.3** | 3.9 | 6.7 | 5.2 | 3.7 | 5.5 | 4.5 | 3.5 | 3.7 | 3.2 | 2.4 | 3.1 | 0.7 |
| 1996 | **4.6** | 4.1 | 3.2 | 5.4 | 4.4 | 6.2 | 5.0 | 3.5 | 3.7 | 3.2 | 2.7 | 3.0 | 1.7 |
| 1997 | **4.7** | 4.4 | 2.8 | 5.1 | 4.7 | 6.0 | 4.9 | 3.9 | 3.5 | 3.3 | 3.4 | 1.5 | 1.0 |
| **Earned doctorates:** | | | | | | | | | | | | | |
| 1991 | **0.4** | 0.3 | - | 0.4 | 0.3 | 0.5 | 0.4 | 0.3 | 0.2 | 0.4 | 0.3 | - | 0.2 |
| 1992 | **0.4** | 0.1 | 0.2 | 0.4 | 0.1 | 0.5 | 0.5 | 0.3 | 0.2 | 0.4 | 0.4 | - | 0.1 |
| 1993 | **0.3** | 0.1 | 0.3 | 0.4 | 0.2 | 0.2 | 0.4 | 0.4 | 0.2 | 0.5 | 0.1 | - | 0.1 |
| 1994 | **0.5** | 0.2 | 0.2 | 0.4 | 0.4 | 0.6 | 0.6 | 0.6 | 0.3 | 0.6 | 0.2 | - | 0.2 |
| 1995 | **0.5** | 0.2 | 0.2 | 0.6 | 0.3 | 0.6 | 0.6 | 0.5 | 0.7 | 0.5 | 0.3 | - | 0.1 |
| 1996 | **0.6** | 0.2 | 0.4 | 0.5 | 0.5 | 0.6 | 0.7 | 0.6 | 0.7 | 0.6 | 0.3 | - | - |
| 1997 | **0.6** | 0.4 | 0.3 | 0.6 | 0.6 | 0.7 | 0.7 | 0.6 | 0.7 | 0.5 | 0.5 | - | 0.1 |

1  Typical age at graduation is 22 for Bachelor's and first professional degrees, 24 for Master's and 27 for Earned doctorates.
2  Postsecondary degrees granted by university colleges have not been captured historically and are therefore not reflected in these data. However these degrees will be captured in the near future by Statistics Canada through the Enhanced Student Information System (ESIS), scheduled for implementation at the national level beginning in the year 2000.

*Source:* Centre for Education Statistics, Statistics Canada.

TABLE 4.12   RATIO OF UNIVERSITY GRADUATES[1] TO THE POPULATION AT THE TYPICAL AGE[2] OF GRADUATION (TIMES 100), BY GENDER, FIELD OF STUDY AND LEVEL OF EDUCATION, CANADA, 1987 AND 1997

|  | Bachelor's and first professional degrees |  | Master's degrees |  | Earned doctorates |  |
|---|---|---|---|---|---|---|
|  | 1987 | 1997 | 1987 | 1997 | 1987 | 1997 |
| **Both sexes** | | | | | | |
| Agricultural and biological sciences | 1.3 | 2.3 | 0.2 | 0.2 | 0.1 | 0.1 |
| Arts and science | 1.4 | 0.9 | - | - | - | - |
| Education | 3.3 | 5.0 | 0.6 | 0.8 | - | 0.1 |
| Engineering and applied sciences | 1.8 | 2.2 | 0.3 | 0.5 | 0.1 | 0.2 |
| Fine and applied arts | 0.7 | 1.0 | 0.1 | 0.1 | - | - |
| Health professions and occupations | 1.4 | 2.1 | 0.2 | 0.4 | - | 0.1 |
| Humanities and related | 2.3 | 3.6 | 0.4 | 0.7 | 0.1 | 0.1 |
| Mathematics and physical sciences | 1.6 | 1.7 | 0.2 | 0.3 | 0.1 | 0.2 |
| Social sciences and related | 7.5 | 11.5 | 1.2 | 2.1 | 0.1 | 0.2 |
| **Total** | **21.2** | **30.4** | **3.1** | **5.2** | **0.5** | **0.9** |
| **Males** | | | | | | |
| Agricultural and biological sciences | 1.1 | 1.8 | 0.2 | 0.2 | 0.1 | 0.1 |
| Arts and science | 1.2 | 0.6 | - | - | - | - |
| Education | 1.9 | 2.8 | 0.4 | 0.5 | - | 0.1 |
| Engineering and applied sciences | 3.0 | 3.4 | 0.5 | 0.8 | 0.1 | 0.3 |
| Fine and applied arts | 0.5 | 0.7 | - | 0.1 | - | - |
| Health professions and occupations | 0.8 | 1.1 | 0.1 | 0.2 | 0.1 | 0.1 |
| Humanities and related | 1.7 | 2.6 | 0.3 | 0.6 | 0.1 | 0.1 |
| Mathematics and physical sciences | 2.2 | 2.3 | 0.3 | 0.5 | 0.2 | 0.3 |
| Social sciences and related | 7.1 | 9.3 | 1.3 | 2.2 | 0.1 | 0.2 |
| **Total** | **19.5** | **24.5** | **3.3** | **5.0** | **0.7** | **1.1** |
| **Females** | | | | | | |
| Agricultural and biological sciences | 1.5 | 2.9 | 0.1 | 0.3 | - | 0.1 |
| Arts and science | 1.6 | 1.2 | - | - | - | - |
| Education | 4.8 | 7.2 | 0.8 | 1.2 | 0.1 | 0.1 |
| Engineering and applied sciences | 0.4 | 1.0 | 0.1 | 0.2 | - | - |
| Fine and applied arts | 0.9 | 1.3 | 0.1 | 0.2 | - | - |
| Health professions and occupations | 2.1 | 3.2 | 0.2 | 0.6 | - | 0.1 |
| Humanities and related | 2.9 | 4.7 | 0.5 | 0.8 | - | 0.1 |
| Mathematics and physical sciences | 0.9 | 1.1 | 0.1 | 0.2 | - | 0.1 |
| Social sciences and related | 8.0 | 13.8 | 1.0 | 2.0 | 0.1 | 0.2 |
| **Total** | **23.1** | **36.4** | **2.9** | **5.4** | **0.3** | **0.7** |

1   Does not include undergraduate and graduate certificates and diplomas.
2   Typical age at graduation is 22 for Bachelor's and first professional degrees, 24 for Master's and 27 for Earned doctorates.
*Source: Centre for Education Statistics, Statistics Canada.*

TABLE 4.13    NUMBER OF DIPLOMAS AND DEGREES GRANTED, BY LEVEL OF EDUCATION, CANADA AND JURISDICTIONS, 1991 TO 1997

| Level | Canada | Nfld. | P.E.I. | N.S. | N.B. | Que.[1] | Ont. | Man. | Sask. | Alta. | B.C.[2] | Y.T. | N.W.T. |
|---|---|---|---|---|---|---|---|---|---|---|---|---|---|
| **Community college diplomas** | | | | | | | | | | | | | |
| 1991 | 83,824 | 969 | 519 | 1,041 | 1,031 | 39,694 | 24,814 | 1,729 | 1,315 | 7,460 | 5,146 | 33 | 73 |
| 1992 | 85,949 | 1,064 | 495 | 1,034 | 1,256 | 40,394 | 25,662 | 1,520 | 1,403 | 7,705 | 5,143 | 26 | 247 |
| 1993 | 92,515 | 1,268 | 433 | 1,336 | 1,241 | 42,933 | 29,234 | 1,691 | 1,422 | 7,304 | 5,457 | 26 | 170 |
| 1994 | 95,296 | 1,293 | 486 | 1,388 | 1,324 | 43,221 | 30,306 | 1,669 | 1,555 | 7,634 | 6,183 | 29 | 208 |
| 1995 | 97,195 | 1,364 | 655 | 1,895 | 1,469 | 40,891 | 33,326 | 1,376 | 1,545 | 8,094 | 6,418 | 54 | 108 |
| 1996 | 104,202 | 1,796 | 692 | 3,692 | 1,287 | 39,998 | 38,372 | 1,496 | 1,431 | 8,212 | 6,995 | 40 | 191 |
| 1997 | .. | .. | .. | .. | .. | .. | .. | .. | .. | .. | .. | .. | .. |
| **University level diplomas and certificates** | | | | | | | | | | | | | |
| 1991 | 24,023 | 96 | 52 | 703 | 316 | 18,469 | 1,909 | 271 | 1,011 | 418 | 778 | ... | ... |
| 1992 | 25,744 | 274 | 37 | 703 | 347 | 19,742 | 1,797 | 231 | 1,231 | 413 | 969 | ... | ... |
| 1993 | 26,670 | 292 | 47 | 716 | 371 | 20,453 | 1,814 | 239 | 1,296 | 376 | 1,066 | ... | ... |
| 1994 | 26,982 | 406 | 64 | 830 | 401 | 20,740 | 1,702 | 267 | 1,032 | 324 | 1,216 | ... | ... |
| 1995 | 25,986 | 413 | 79 | 723 | 369 | 20,059 | 1,644 | 280 | 896 | 429 | 1,094 | ... | ... |
| 1996 | 24,641 | 426 | 59 | 745 | 421 | 18,683 | 1,587 | 284 | 888 | 326 | 1,222 | ... | ... |
| 1997 | 22,862 | 473 | 51 | 734 | 349 | 17,089 | 1,539 | 225 | 836 | 302 | 1,264 | ... | ... |
| **Bachelor's and first professional degrees** | | | | | | | | | | | | | |
| 1991 | 114,820 | 2,249 | 405 | 5,275 | 2,901 | 27,246 | 49,620 | 4,980 | 4,117 | 9,274 | 8,753 | ... | ... |
| 1992 | 120,745 | 2,128 | 452 | 5,786 | 3,008 | 28,163 | 52,220 | 4,975 | 4,252 | 9,467 | 10,294 | ... | ... |
| 1993 | 123,202 | 2,263 | 438 | 5,998 | 3,157 | 28,917 | 52,892 | 5,061 | 4,425 | 9,441 | 10,610 | ... | ... |
| 1994 | 126,538 | 2,350 | 498 | 6,150 | 3,208 | 29,668 | 54,318 | 5,375 | 3,894 | 10,047 | 11,030 | ... | ... |
| 1995 | 127,331 | 2,207 | 503 | 6,025 | 3,339 | 29,362 | 55,160 | 5,353 | 4,273 | 9,967 | 11,142 | ... | ... |
| 1996 | 127,989 | 2,208 | 459 | 5,923 | 3,542 | 29,812 | 55,670 | 5,084 | 4,245 | 10,188 | 10,858 | ... | ... |
| 1997 | 125,729 | 2,174 | 514 | 5,982 | 3,518 | 28,783 | 53,987 | 5,000 | 3,926 | 10,544 | 11,301 | ... | ... |
| **Master's degrees** | | | | | | | | | | | | | |
| 1991 | 18,033 | 202 | 5 | 890 | 325 | 5,298 | 7,685 | 458 | 370 | 1,290 | 1,510 | ... | ... |
| 1992 | 19,435 | 207 | 9 | 1,033 | 364 | 5,787 | 8,182 | 538 | 453 | 1,283 | 1,579 | ... | ... |
| 1993 | 20,818 | 260 | 14 | 1,017 | 385 | 6,081 | 8,688 | 553 | 411 | 1,453 | 1,956 | ... | ... |
| 1994 | 21,292 | 221 | 11 | 1,051 | 361 | 6,474 | 8,704 | 523 | 417 | 1,511 | 2,019 | ... | ... |
| 1995 | 21,356 | 248 | 3 | 1,053 | 402 | 6,422 | 8,552 | 582 | 517 | 1,502 | 2,075 | ... | ... |
| 1996 | 21,558 | 243 | 10 | 979 | 416 | 6,668 | 8,800 | 562 | 480 | 1,339 | 2,061 | ... | ... |
| 1997 | 21,254 | 272 | 6 | 989 | 408 | 6,576 | 8,458 | 556 | 472 | 1,442 | 2,075 | ... | ... |
| **Earned doctorates** | | | | | | | | | | | | | |
| 1991 | 2,947 | 27 | ... | 79 | 17 | 792 | 1,259 | 79 | 69 | 319 | 306 | ... | ... |
| 1992 | 3,136 | 24 | ... | 69 | 29 | 895 | 1,348 | 86 | 71 | 314 | 300 | ... | ... |
| 1993 | 3,356 | 30 | ... | 77 | 31 | 884 | 1,410 | 104 | 84 | 368 | 368 | ... | ... |
| 1994 | 3,552 | 31 | ... | 72 | 35 | 971 | 1,465 | 120 | 73 | 398 | 387 | ... | ... |
| 1995 | 3,716 | 28 | ... | 86 | 38 | 1,015 | 1,506 | 100 | 97 | 373 | 473 | ... | ... |
| 1996 | 3,928 | 30 | ... | 81 | 49 | 1,093 | 1,606 | 102 | 103 | 388 | 476 | ... | ... |
| 1997 | 3,996 | 32 | ... | 81 | 38 | 1,143 | 1,579 | 113 | 103 | 430 | 477 | ... | ... |

1   College data include completions of career-technical and university transfer programs.
2   Postsecondary degrees granted by university colleges have not been captured historically and are therefore not reflected in these data. However these degrees will be captured in the near future by Statistics Canada through the Enhanced Student Information System (ESIS), scheduled for implementation at the national level beginning in the year 2000.

*Source: Centre for Education Statistics, Statistics Canada. Source for 1996 Quebec CEGEP diploma data is:* Statistiques de l'éducation - Enseignement primaire, secondaire, collégial et universitaire, *Ministère de l'éducation, Gouvernement du Québec.*

TABLE 4.14  NUMBER OF UNIVERSITY DEGREES GRANTED[1], BY GENDER AND FIELD OF STUDY, CANADA AND PROVINCES, 1987

| 1987 | Canada | Nfld. | P.E.I. | N.S. | N.B. | Que. | Ont. | Man. | Sask. | Alta. | B.C. |
|---|---|---|---|---|---|---|---|---|---|---|---|
| **Both sexes** | 140,666 | 2,618 | 358 | 6,269 | 3,314 | 43,098 | 54,229 | 5,668 | 5,261 | 10,149 | 9,702 |
| **Physical, natural and applied sciences** | 29,293 | 416 | 67 | 1,578 | 924 | 7,844 | 11,316 | 1,353 | 1,229 | 2,435 | 2,131 |
| Agricultural and biological sciences | 7,934 | 120 | 27 | 550 | 209 | 1,802 | 2,819 | 476 | 504 | 711 | 716 |
| Engineering and applied sciences | 11,344 | 116 | 25 | 565 | 455 | 3,310 | 4,551 | 359 | 317 | 953 | 693 |
| Mathematics and physical sciences | 10,015 | 180 | 15 | 463 | 260 | 2,732 | 3,946 | 518 | 408 | 771 | 722 |
| **Humanities and social sciences** | 81,247 | 1,816 | 216 | 3,381 | 1,754 | 21,423 | 34,431 | 3,570 | 3,009 | 5,678 | 5,969 |
| Education | 22,883 | 1,165 | 66 | 787 | 740 | 6,413 | 7,298 | 959 | 1,301 | 2,459 | 1,695 |
| Fine and applied arts | 3,980 | 13 | 6 | 177 | 44 | 1,460 | 1,383 | 188 | 95 | 273 | 341 |
| Arts and science | 7,056 | ... | 4 | 286 | 87 | 754 | 5,232 | 323 | 7 | 97 | 266 |
| Humanities and related | 15,628 | 325 | 43 | 639 | 284 | 4,810 | 6,675 | 493 | 482 | 746 | 1,131 |
| Social sciences balance | 31,700 | 313 | 97 | 1,492 | 599 | 7,986 | 13,843 | 1,607 | 1,124 | 2,103 | 2,536 |
| **Commerce, management and administration** | 20,042 | 164 | 75 | 832 | 467 | 9,650 | 5,792 | 369 | 753 | 991 | 949 |
| **Health professions and occupations** | 10,084 | 222 | ... | 478 | 169 | 4,181 | 2,690 | 376 | 270 | 1,045 | 653 |
| **Males** | 66,754 | 1,205 | 163 | 3,005 | 1,604 | 19,781 | 25,823 | 2,870 | 2,554 | 4,965 | 4,784 |
| **Physical, natural and applied sciences** | 20,972 | 314 | 41 | 1,065 | 701 | 5,544 | 8,111 | 953 | 867 | 1,815 | 1,561 |
| Agricultural and biological sciences | 3,722 | 68 | 10 | 229 | 98 | 792 | 1,300 | 224 | 269 | 359 | 373 |
| Engineering and applied sciences | 9,994 | 107 | 22 | 490 | 409 | 2,854 | 4,025 | 329 | 293 | 848 | 617 |
| Mathematics and physical sciences | 7,256 | 139 | 9 | 346 | 194 | 1,898 | 2,786 | 400 | 305 | 608 | 571 |
| **Humanities and social sciences** | 31,377 | 730 | 77 | 1,334 | 640 | 7,755 | 13,467 | 1,536 | 1,195 | 2,243 | 2,400 |
| Education | 7,247 | 442 | 14 | 284 | 245 | 1,951 | 2,318 | 287 | 398 | 783 | 525 |
| Fine and applied arts |  | 6 | 2 | 76 | 15 | 511 | 485 | 56 | 36 | 109 | 114 |
| Arts and science | 3,029 | ... | - | 114 | 30 | 287 | 2,249 | 203 | 4 | 37 | 105 |
| Humanities and related | 5,885 | 124 | 23 | 226 | 112 | 1,736 | 2,475 | 212 | 264 | 285 | 428 |
| Social sciences balance | 13,806 | 158 | 38 | 634 | 238 | 3,270 | 5,940 | 778 | 493 | 1,029 | 1,228 |
| **Commerce, management and administration** | 11,405 | 101 | 45 | 490 | 255 | 5,268 | 3,425 | 222 | 393 | 593 | 613 |
| **Health professions and occupations** | 3,000 | 60 | ... | 116 | 8 | 1,214 | 820 | 159 | 99 | 314 | 210 |
| **Females** | 73,912 | 1,413 | 195 | 3,264 | 1,710 | 23,317 | 28,406 | 2,798 | 2,707 | 5,184 | 4,918 |
| **Physical, natural and applied sciences** | 8,321 | 102 | 26 | 513 | 223 | 2,300 | 3,205 | 400 | 362 | 620 | 570 |
| Agricultural and biological sciences | 4,212 | 52 | 17 | 321 | 111 | 1,010 | 1,519 | 252 | 235 | 352 | 343 |
| Engineering and applied sciences | 1,350 | 9 | 3 | 75 | 46 | 456 | 526 | 30 | 24 | 105 | 76 |
| Mathematics and physical sciences | 2,759 | 41 | 6 | 117 | 66 | 834 | 1,160 | 118 | 103 | 163 | 151 |
| **Humanities and social sciences** | 49,870 | 1,086 | 139 | 2,047 | 1,114 | 13,668 | 20,964 | 2,034 | 1,814 | 3,435 | 3,569 |
| Education | 15,636 | 723 | 52 | 503 | 495 | 4,462 | 4,980 | 672 | 903 | 1,676 | 1,170 |
| Fine and applied arts | 2,570 | 7 | 4 | 101 | 29 | 949 | 898 | 132 | 59 | 164 | 227 |
| Arts and science | 4,027 | ... | 4 | 172 | 57 | 467 | 2,983 | 120 | 3 | 60 | 161 |
| Humanities and related | 9,743 | 201 | 20 | 413 | 172 | 3,074 | 4,200 | 281 | 218 | 461 | 703 |
| Social sciences balance | 17,894 | 155 | 59 | 858 | 361 | 4,716 | 7,903 | 829 | 631 | 1,074 | 1,308 |
| **Commerce, management and administration** | 8,637 | 63 | 30 | 342 | 212 | 4,382 | 2,367 | 147 | 360 | 398 | 336 |
| **Health professions and occupations** | 7,084 | 162 | ... | 362 | 161 | 2,967 | 1,870 | 217 | 171 | 731 | 443 |

1  University degrees include university certificates and diplomas.
*Source: Centre for Education Statistics, Statistics Canada.*

TABLE 4.15  NUMBER OF UNIVERSITY DEGREES GRANTED[1], BY GENDER AND FIELD OF STUDY, CANADA AND PROVINCES, 1997

| 1997 | Canada | Nfld. | P.E.I. | N.S. | N.B. | Que. | Ont. | Man. | Sask. | Alta. | B.C. |
|---|---|---|---|---|---|---|---|---|---|---|---|
| **Both sexes** | **173,841** | **2,951** | **571** | **7,786** | **4,313** | **53,591** | **65,563** | **5,894** | **5,337** | **12,718** | **15,117** |
| **Physical, natural and applied sciences** | **34,352** | **625** | **171** | **2,023** | **942** | **8,777** | **13,620** | **1,280** | **1,147** | **2,681** | **3,086** |
| Agricultural and biological sciences | 11,811 | 267 | 135 | 821 | 275 | 2,223 | 4,699 | 605 | 548 | 1,030 | 1,208 |
| Engineering and applied sciences | 12,798 | 164 | 13 | 680 | 474 | 3,834 | 4,908 | 356 | 343 | 994 | 1,032 |
| Mathematics and physical sciences | 9,743 | 194 | 23 | 522 | 193 | 2,720 | 4,013 | 319 | 256 | 657 | 846 |
| **Humanities and social sciences** | **101,938** | **1,764** | **283** | **4,113** | **2,497** | **28,592** | **41,394** | **3,656** | **3,076** | **6,948** | **9,615** |
| Education | 27,808 | 496 | 51 | 1,014 | 929 | 8,602 | 9,265 | 1,209 | 1,124 | 2,690 | 2,428 |
| Fine and applied arts | 5,215 | 40 | 9 | 232 | 54 | 1,690 | 2,088 | 193 | 122 | 388 | 399 |
| Arts and science | 5,529 | 29 | 1 | 217 | 58 | 2,131 | 1,428 | 286 | 10 | 372 | 997 |
| Humanities and related | 21,380 | 363 | 79 | 836 | 496 | 6,370 | 9,109 | 463 | 502 | 1,029 | 2,133 |
| Social sciences balance | 42,006 | 836 | 143 | 1,814 | 960 | 9,799 | 19,504 | 1,505 | 1,318 | 2,469 | 3,658 |
| **Commerce, management and administration** | **24,582** | **370** | **91** | **1,132** | **618** | **11,236** | **6,892** | **454** | **806** | **1,546** | **1,437** |
| **Health professions and occupations** | **12,969** | **192** | **26** | **518** | **256** | **4,986** | **3,657** | **504** | **308** | **1,543** | **979** |
| **Males** | **73,078** | **1,256** | **204** | **3,288** | **1,811** | **21,549** | **28,198** | **2,554** | **2,324** | **5,442** | **6,452** |
| **Physical, natural and applied sciences** | **21,699** | **392** | **77** | **1,161** | **631** | **5,778** | **8,537** | **738** | **746** | **1,713** | **1,926** |
| Agricultural and biological sciences | 4,807 | 119 | 51 | 309 | 107 | 854 | 1,947 | 225 | 262 | 448 | 485 |
| Engineering and applied sciences | 10,141 | 141 | 8 | 515 | 382 | 3,033 | 3,869 | 287 | 280 | 798 | 828 |
| Mathematics and physical sciences | 6,751 | 132 | 18 | 337 | 142 | 1,891 | 2,721 | 226 | 204 | 467 | 613 |
| **Humanities and social sciences** | **35,160** | **634** | **87** | **1,406** | **809** | **9,058** | **14,602** | **1,365** | **1,138** | **2,534** | **3,527** |
| Education | 8,039 | 174 | 9 | 315 | 294 | 2,094 | 2,753 | 357 | 366 | 885 | 792 |
| Fine and applied arts | 1,711 | 19 | 3 | 91 | 13 | 541 | 671 | 67 | 43 | 140 | 123 |
| Arts and science | 1,738 | 12 | - | 62 | 22 | 557 | 541 | 138 | 5 | 110 | 291 |
| Humanities and related | 8,039 | 132 | 35 | 296 | 188 | 2,269 | 3,351 | 193 | 240 | 432 | 903 |
| Social sciences balance | 15,633 | 297 | 40 | 642 | 292 | 3,597 | 7,286 | 610 | 484 | 967 | 1,418 |
| **Commerce, management and administration** | **12,775** | **176** | **40** | **589** | **336** | **5,386** | **4,024** | **280** | **351** | **844** | **749** |
| **Health professions and occupations** | **3,444** | **54** | **-** | **132** | **35** | **1,327** | **1,035** | **171** | **89** | **351** | **250** |
| **Females** | **100,763** | **1,695** | **367** | **4,498** | **2,502** | **32,042** | **37,365** | **3,340** | **3,013** | **7,276** | **8,665** |
| **Physical, natural and applied sciences** | **12,653** | **233** | **94** | **862** | **311** | **2,999** | **5,083** | **542** | **401** | **968** | **1,160** |
| Agricultural and biological sciences | 7,004 | 148 | 84 | 512 | 168 | 1,369 | 2,752 | 380 | 286 | 582 | 723 |
| Engineering and applied sciences | 2,657 | 23 | 5 | 165 | 92 | 801 | 1,039 | 69 | 63 | 196 | 204 |
| Mathematics and physical sciences | 2,992 | 62 | 5 | 185 | 51 | 829 | 1,292 | 93 | 52 | 190 | 233 |
| **Humanities and social sciences** | **66,778** | **1,130** | **196** | **2,707** | **1,688** | **19,534** | **26,792** | **2,291** | **1,938** | **4,414** | **6,088** |
| Education | 19,769 | 322 | 42 | 699 | 635 | 6,508 | 6,512 | 852 | 758 | 1,805 | 1,636 |
| Fine and applied arts | 3,504 | 21 | 6 | 141 | 41 | 1,149 | 1,417 | 126 | 79 | 248 | 276 |
| Arts and science | 3,791 | 17 | 1 | 155 | 36 | 1,574 | 887 | 148 | 5 | 262 | 706 |
| Humanities and related | 13,341 | 231 | 44 | 540 | 308 | 4,101 | 5,758 | 270 | 262 | 597 | 1,230 |
| Social sciences balance | 26,373 | 539 | 103 | 1,172 | 668 | 6,202 | 12,218 | 895 | 834 | 1,502 | 2,240 |
| **Commerce, management and administration** | **11,807** | **194** | **51** | **543** | **282** | **5,850** | **2,868** | **174** | **455** | **702** | **688** |
| **Health professions and occupations** | **9,525** | **138** | **26** | **386** | **221** | **3,659** | **2,622** | **333** | **219** | **1,192** | **729** |

1  University degrees include university certificates and diplomas.
*Source: Centre for Education Statistics, Statistics Canada.*

CHAPTER 4 TABLES

TABLE 4.16  DISTRIBUTION OF THE ABORIGINAL[1] AND NON-ABORIGINAL POPULATIONS AGED 20 TO 29, BY HIGHEST LEVEL OF EDUCATION ATTAINED, 1986 AND 1996

|  | Less than high school[2] % | High school diploma[3] % | College/ trade[4] % | University[5] % |
|---|---|---|---|---|
| **1986** | | | | |
| Aboriginal population | 60 | 24 | 15 | 2 |
| Non-Aboriginal population | 27 | 34 | 28 | 12 |
| **1996** | | | | |
| Aboriginal population | 45 | 32 | 20 | 4 |
| Non-Aboriginal population | 17 | 36 | 28 | 19 |

1  Aboriginal population refers to those persons who reported identifying with at least one Aboriginal group, I.e., North American Indian, Métis or Inuit (Eskimo) and/or who reported being a Treaty Indian or a Registered Indian as defined by the *Indian Act of Canada* and/or who were members of an Indian Band or First Nation.
2  Includes individuals having at least some pre-elementary, elementary or secondary education.
3  Includes high school graduates and individuals who have some postsecondary education (not completed).
4  Includes graduates of college and trade-vocational programs.
5  Includes individuals with a university degree or certificate.
*Source: 1986 and 1996 Census, Statistics Canada.*

TABLE 4.17  DISTRIBUTION OF THE ABORIGINAL POPULATION[1] AGED 25 TO 29, BY HIGHEST LEVEL OF EDUCATION ATTAINED, CANADA AND JURISDICTIONS, 1996

|  | Total population | Less than high school[2] Count | % | High school diploma[3] Count | % | College/ Trade[4] Count | % | University[5] Count | % |
|---|---|---|---|---|---|---|---|---|---|
| **Canada** | 135,890 | 55,835 | 41 | 38,775 | 29 | 34,595 | 25 | 6,685 | 5 |
| Newfoundland and Labrador | 2,715 | 720 | 26 | 580 | 21 | 1,175 | 43 | 225 | 8 |
| Prince Edward Island | 155 | -- | -- | 25 | 16 | 100 | 65 | -- | -- |
| Nova Scotia | 2,290 | 650 | 28 | 710 | 31 | 725 | 32 | 205 | 9 |
| New Brunswick | 1,915 | 435 | 23 | 590 | 31 | 715 | 37 | 150 | 8 |
| Quebec | 12,140 | 6,020 | 50 | 2,875 | 24 | 2,605 | 21 | 625 | 5 |
| Ontario | 24,310 | 8,340 | 34 | 7,445 | 31 | 7,025 | 29 | 1,515 | 6 |
| Manitoba | 21,350 | 10,885 | 51 | 5,335 | 25 | 4,490 | 21 | 640 | 3 |
| Saskatchewan | 17,745 | 8,065 | 45 | 5,025 | 28 | 3,700 | 21 | 965 | 5 |
| Alberta | 22,010 | 8,485 | 39 | 6,950 | 32 | 5,585 | 25 | 1,000 | 5 |
| British Columbia | 23,195 | 8,640 | 37 | 7,210 | 31 | 6,160 | 27 | 1,170 | 5 |
| Yukon | 1,135 | 295 | 26 | 270 | 24 | 485 | 43 | 65 | 6 |
| Northwest Territories | 6,930 | 3,275 | 47 | 1,700 | 25 | 1,855 | 27 | 80 | 1 |

1  Aboriginal population refers to those persons who reported identifying with at least one Aboriginal group, i.e., North American Indian, Métis or Inuit (Eskimo) and/or who reported being a Treaty Indian or a Registered Indian as defined by the *Indian Act of Canada* and/or who were members of an Indian Band or First Nation.
2  Includes individuals having at least some pre-elementary, elementary or secondary education.
3  Includes high school graduates and individuals who have some postsecondary education (not completed).
4  Includes graduates of college and trade-vocational programs.
5  Includes individuals with a university degree or certificate.
*Source: 1996 Census, Statistics Canada.*

EDUCATION INDICATORS IN CANADA

TABLE 4.18  DISTRIBUTION OF THE ABORIGINAL POPULATION[1] AGED 25 TO 54, BY HIGHEST LEVEL OF EDUCATION ATTAINED, CANADA AND JURISDICTIONS, 1996

|  | Total population | Less than high school[2] Count | % | High school diploma[3] Count | % | College/ Trade[4] Count | % | University[5] Count | % |
|---|---|---|---|---|---|---|---|---|---|
| Canada | 617,745 | 260,815 | 42 | 140,830 | 23 | 176,630 | 29 | 39,450 | 6 |
| Newfoundland and Labrador | 11,610 | 4,505 | 39 | 1,855 | 16 | 4,645 | 40 | 590 | 5 |
| Prince Edward Island | 815 | 310 | 38 | 90 | 11 | 255 | 31 | 75 | 9 |
| Nova Scotia | 9,915 | 3,050 | 31 | 2,270 | 23 | 3,535 | 36 | 1,030 | 10 |
| New Brunswick | 8,105 | 2,250 | 28 | 2,140 | 26 | 2,905 | 36 | 790 | 10 |
| Quebec | 58,930 | 27,845 | 47 | 12,825 | 22 | 13,895 | 24 | 4,350 | 7 |
| Ontario | 119,435 | 44,570 | 37 | 29,615 | 25 | 36,750 | 31 | 8,495 | 7 |
| Manitoba | 93,640 | 48,160 | 51 | 18,375 | 20 | 21,700 | 23 | 5,355 | 6 |
| Saskatchewan | 73,080 | 33,170 | 45 | 15,380 | 21 | 18,125 | 25 | 6,410 | 9 |
| Alberta | 93,380 | 37,035 | 40 | 22,960 | 25 | 28,490 | 31 | 4,855 | 5 |
| British Columbia | 116,165 | 45,415 | 39 | 28,885 | 25 | 35,470 | 31 | 6,365 | 5 |
| Yukon | 5,460 | 1,610 | 29 | 1,180 | 22 | 2,275 | 42 | 340 | 6 |
| Northwest Territories | 27,170 | 12,770 | 47 | 5,050 | 19 | 8,570 | 32 | 735 | 3 |

1  Aboriginal population refers to those persons who reported identifying with at least one Aboriginal group, I.e., North American Indian, Métis or Inuit (Eskimo) and/or who reported being a Treaty Indian or a Registered Indian as defined by the *Indian Act of Canada* and/or who were members of an Indian Band or First Nation.
2  Includes individuals having at least some pre-elementary, elementary or secondary education.
3  Includes high school graduates and individuals who have some postsecondary education (not completed).
4  Includes graduates of college and trade-vocational programs.
5  Includes individuals with a university degree or certificate.

*Source: 1996 Census, Statistics Canada.*

TABLE 4.19  DISTRIBUTION THE NON-ABORIGINAL POPULATION AGED 25 TO 29, BY HIGHEST LEVEL OF EDUCATION ATTAINED, CANADA AND JURISDICTIONS, 1996

|  | Total population | Less than high school[1] Count | % | High school diploma[2] Count | % | College/ Trade[3] Count | % | University[4] Count | % |
|---|---|---|---|---|---|---|---|---|---|
| Canada | 3,909,695 | 660,620 | 17 | 1,067,550 | 27 | 1,236,835 | 32 | 944,690 | 24 |
| Newfoundland and Labrador | 78,030 | 19,150 | 25 | 16,100 | 21 | 28,800 | 37 | 13,985 | 18 |
| Prince Edward Island | 17,485 | 4,240 | 24 | 3,885 | 22 | 6,005 | 34 | 3,355 | 19 |
| Nova Scotia | 121,170 | 23,540 | 19 | 27,160 | 22 | 43,010 | 35 | 27,455 | 23 |
| New Brunswick | 100,180 | 19,205 | 19 | 29,295 | 29 | 32,205 | 32 | 19,480 | 19 |
| Quebec | 946,575 | 170,505 | 18 | 220,990 | 23 | 326,050 | 34 | 229,030 | 24 |
| Ontario | 1,515,560 | 227,585 | 15 | 442,215 | 29 | 447,810 | 30 | 397,940 | 26 |
| Manitoba | 128,680 | 25,365 | 20 | 37,935 | 29 | 36,355 | 28 | 29,010 | 23 |
| Saskatchewan | 102,175 | 20,510 | 20 | 26,605 | 26 | 33,660 | 33 | 21,410 | 21 |
| Alberta | 374,235 | 68,540 | 18 | 106,160 | 28 | 121,195 | 32 | 78,355 | 21 |
| British Columbia | 516,890 | 80,910 | 16 | 154,945 | 30 | 158,770 | 31 | 122,260 | 24 |
| Yukon | 3,715 | 560 | 15 | 970 | 26 | 1,185 | 32 | 975 | 26 |
| Northwest Territories | 4,990 | 475 | 9 | 1,260 | 25 | 1,790 | 36 | 1,460 | 29 |

1  Includes individuals having at least some pre-elementary, elementary or secondary education.
2  Includes high school graduates and individuals who have some postsecondary education (not completed).
3  Includes graduates of college and trade-vocational programs.
4  Includes individuals with a university degree or certificate.

*Source: 1996 Census, Statistics Canada.*

## CHAPTER 4 TABLES

TABLE 4.20  DISTRIBUTION OF THE NON-ABORIGINAL POPULATION AGED 25 TO 54, BY HIGHEST LEVEL OF EDUCATION ATTAINED, CANADA AND JURISDICTIONS, 1996

|  | Total population | Less than high school[1] Count | % | High school diploma[2] Count | % | College/ Trade[3] Count | % | University[4] Count | % |
|---|---|---|---|---|---|---|---|---|---|
| **Canada** | 25,426,900 | 5,703,795 | 22 | 6,525,855 | 26 | 7,854,650 | 31 | 5,342,570 | 21 |
| Newfoundland and Labrador | 487,100 | 167,285 | 34 | 81,500 | 17 | 173,050 | 36 | 65,245 | 13 |
| Prince Edward Island | 112,980 | 34,770 | 31 | 22,795 | 20 | 37,225 | 33 | 18,210 | 16 |
| Nova Scotia | 800,415 | 214,170 | 27 | 154,065 | 19 | 280,275 | 35 | 151,885 | 19 |
| New Brunswick | 652,120 | 187,865 | 29 | 165,755 | 25 | 196,860 | 30 | 101,640 | 16 |
| Quebec | 6,527,405 | 1,585,215 | 24 | 1,775,590 | 27 | 1,835,680 | 28 | 1,330,905 | 20 |
| Ontario | 9,575,575 | 1,970,320 | 21 | 2,501,205 | 26 | 2,938,870 | 31 | 2,165,185 | 23 |
| Manitoba | 846,860 | 218,375 | 26 | 204,400 | 24 | 253,135 | 30 | 170,950 | 20 |
| Saskatchewan | 710,590 | 188,180 | 26 | 165,980 | 23 | 223,430 | 31 | 133,010 | 19 |
| Alberta | 2,370,330 | 501,625 | 21 | 579,600 | 24 | 806,785 | 34 | 482,310 | 20 |
| British Columbia | 3,288,005 | 628,235 | 19 | 863,225 | 26 | 1,088,105 | 33 | 708,430 | 22 |
| Yukon | 26,435 | 4,225 | 16 | 5,595 | 21 | 10,265 | 39 | 6,335 | 24 |
| Northwest Territories | 29,100 | 3,525 | 12 | 6,090 | 21 | 10,975 | 38 | 8,475 | 29 |

1 Includes individuals having at least some pre-elementary, elementary or secondary education.
2 Includes high school graduates and individuals who have some postsecondary education (not completed).
3 Includes graduates of college and trade-vocational programs.
4 Includes individuals with a university degree or certificate.
*Source: 1996 Census, Statistics Canada.*

TABLE 4.21  DISTRIBUTION OF THE POPULATION AGED 15 YEARS AND OLDER, BY MOTHER TONGUE, CANADA AND JURISDICTIONS, 1996

|  | Total Count | English Count | % | French Count | % | Other[1] Count | % | Combinations[2] Count | % |
|---|---|---|---|---|---|---|---|---|---|
| **Canada** | 22,628,925 | 12,954,115 | 57 | 5,389,710 | 24 | 3,986,010 | 18 | 299,090 | 1 |
| Nfld. | 437,345 | 430,435 | 98 | 2,035 | 1 | 4,355 | 1 | 520 | - |
| P.E.I. | 103,750 | 96,645 | 93 | 4,920 | 5 | 1,870 | 2 | 315 | - |
| N.S. | 719,970 | 664,400 | 92 | 31,375 | 4 | 21,050 | 3 | 3,145 | - |
| N.B. | 585,025 | 373,390 | 64 | 197,595 | 34 | 9,365 | 2 | 4,675 | 1 |
| Que. | 5,673,465 | 465,020 | 8 | 4,583,560 | 81 | 551,765 | 10 | 73,120 | 1 |
| Ont. | 8,429,215 | 5,891,280 | 70 | 411,030 | 5 | 1,999,990 | 24 | 126,915 | 2 |
| Man. | 855,880 | 604,695 | 71 | 41,805 | 5 | 194,785 | 23 | 14,595 | 2 |
| Sask. | 748,135 | 605,975 | 81 | 17,840 | 2 | 112,880 | 15 | 11,440 | 2 |
| Alta. | 2,055,020 | 1,611,525 | 78 | 47,955 | 2 | 369,740 | 18 | 25,800 | 1 |
| B.C. | 2,954,705 | 2,167,750 | 73 | 49,425 | 2 | 699,875 | 24 | 37,655 | 1 |
| Y.T. | 23,265 | 19,500 | 84 | 955 | 4 | 2,515 | 11 | 295 | 1 |
| N.W.T. | 43,150 | 23,500 | 55 | 1,220 | 3 | 17,815 | 41 | 615 | 1 |

1 The "other" category includes individuals whose first language is neither English nor French (including those whose first language is an Aboriginal language).
2 The "combinations" category includes any of the following linguistic combinations; English and French; English and other; French and other; English, French and other.
*Source: 1996 Census, Statistics Canada.*

# CHAPTER 5 TABLES

## Chapter 5 Tables

**TABLE 5.1** EMPLOYMENT RATE OF THE 25 TO 54 AGE GROUP BY EDUCATIONAL ATTAINMENT AND GENDER, CANADA AND PROVINCES, 1990 AND 1998

|  | Both sexes |  |  |  |  | Males |  |  |  |  | Females |  |  |  |  |
|---|---|---|---|---|---|---|---|---|---|---|---|---|---|---|---|
| 1990 | Total | Less than high school | High school graduate | College and trade graduate | University graduate | Total | Less than high school | High school graduate | College and trade graduate | University graduate | Total | Less than high school | High school graduate | College and trade graduate | University graduate |
| **Canada** | 78 | 65 | 79 | 84 | 88 | 87 | 77 | 88 | 90 | 93 | 70 | 53 | 71 | 78 | 83 |
| Nfld. | 63 | 43 | 65 | 76 | 89 | 72 | 54 | 77 | 80 | 94 | 54 | 33 | 54 | 72 | 82 |
| P.E.I. | 73 | 61 | 75 | 82 | 88 | 80 | 71 | 81 | 86 | 95 | 67 | 49 | 70 | 78 | 81 |
| N.S. | 74 | 60 | 75 | 79 | 88 | 83 | 72 | 88 | 85 | 94 | 65 | 47 | 64 | 73 | 82 |
| N.B. | 70 | 52 | 74 | 80 | 89 | 78 | 62 | 85 | 86 | 95 | 61 | 40 | 64 | 73 | 84 |
| Que. | 74 | 60 | 75 | 82 | 87 | 83 | 73 | 85 | 87 | 91 | 65 | 47 | 67 | 76 | 83 |
| Ont. | 82 | 71 | 82 | 87 | 89 | 90 | 83 | 90 | 92 | 94 | 74 | 60 | 75 | 81 | 84 |
| Man. | 81 | 72 | 81 | 88 | 89 | 89 | 82 | 89 | 93 | 94 | 74 | 60 | 74 | 83 | 83 |
| Sask. | 81 | 72 | 83 | 86 | 89 | 89 | 82 | 90 | 92 | 93 | 74 | 59 | 75 | 81 | 84 |
| Alta. | 81 | 70 | 80 | 87 | 88 | 89 | 81 | 90 | 92 | 94 | 73 | 58 | 72 | 81 | 80 |
| B.C. | 79 | 66 | 78 | 84 | 87 | 88 | 78 | 89 | 91 | 92 | 70 | 53 | 69 | 76 | 82 |
| **1998** |  |  |  |  |  |  |  |  |  |  |  |  |  |  |  |
| **Canada** | 78 | 61 | 77 | 83 | 87 | 85 | 72 | 85 | 88 | 90 | 72 | 50 | 70 | 78 | 83 |
| Nfld. | 61 | 39 | 58 | 71 | 83 | 66 | 46 | 67 | 73 | 86 | 56 | 32 | 50 | 70 | 79 |
| P.E.I. | 74 | 60 | 71 | 79 | 89 | 77 | 66 | 77 | 81 | 91 | 71 | 50 | 67 | 77 | 88 |
| N.S. | 73 | 56 | 72 | 77 | 85 | 80 | 65 | 83 | 83 | 89 | 66 | 44 | 63 | 72 | 81 |
| N.B. | 71 | 49 | 72 | 79 | 86 | 77 | 57 | 81 | 82 | 89 | 66 | 40 | 65 | 75 | 84 |
| Que. | 75 | 57 | 73 | 80 | 86 | 82 | 68 | 81 | 86 | 89 | 68 | 46 | 65 | 75 | 83 |
| Ont. | 80 | 65 | 78 | 85 | 88 | 87 | 76 | 86 | 91 | 91 | 74 | 53 | 71 | 80 | 84 |
| Man. | 83 | 70 | 83 | 88 | 89 | 89 | 81 | 90 | 91 | 94 | 77 | 56 | 77 | 84 | 84 |
| Sask. | 83 | 68 | 84 | 87 | 89 | 88 | 77 | 90 | 91 | 92 | 78 | 54 | 78 | 83 | 85 |
| Alta. | 84 | 72 | 83 | 86 | 88 | 90 | 83 | 90 | 92 | 93 | 77 | 58 | 77 | 81 | 83 |
| B.C. | 77 | 59 | 75 | 83 | 84 | 83 | 68 | 82 | 87 | 88 | 72 | 49 | 69 | 79 | 80 |

*Source: Labour Force Survey, Statistics Canada.*

**TABLE 5.2** EMPLOYMENT RATES OF THE 25 TO 29 AGE GROUP BY EDUCATIONAL ATTAINMENT AND GENDER, CANADA AND PROVINCES, 1990 AND 1998

|  | Both sexes |  |  |  |  | Males |  |  |  |  | Females |  |  |  |  |
|---|---|---|---|---|---|---|---|---|---|---|---|---|---|---|---|
| 1990 | Total | Less than high school | High school graduate | College and trade graduate | University graduate | Total | Less than high school | High school graduate | College and trade graduate | University graduate | Total | Less than high school | High school graduate | College and trade graduate | University graduate |
| **Canada** | 78 | 62 | 78 | 85 | 87 | 84 | 73 | 85 | 88 | 88 | 72 | 49 | 71 | 81 | 85 |
| Nfld. | 63 | 39 | 61 | 74 | 88 | 68 | 47 | 69 | 77 | 90 | 58 | 30 | 53 | 72 | 85 |
| P.E.I. | 69 | 52 | 71 | 81 | 81 | 74 | 61 | 76 | 84 | 90 | 64 | 37 | 67 | 79 | 71 |
| N.S. | 74 | 57 | 74 | 80 | 86 | 80 | 66 | 87 | 83 | 90 | 68 | 45 | 64 | 77 | 82 |
| N.B. | 71 | 46 | 75 | 81 | 88 | 76 | 54 | 82 | 86 | 90 | 67 | 34 | 68 | 77 | 87 |
| Que. | 76 | 61 | 74 | 83 | 84 | 81 | 70 | 84 | 84 | 85 | 71 | 49 | 66 | 82 | 83 |
| Ont. | 81 | 67 | 81 | 87 | 89 | 87 | 79 | 86 | 92 | 90 | 76 | 54 | 75 | 83 | 89 |
| Man. | 79 | 66 | 80 | 88 | 85 | 85 | 80 | 84 | 90 | 86 | 73 | 50 | 75 | 86 | 84 |
| Sask. | 78 | 61 | 79 | 85 | 86 | 84 | 72 | 86 | 89 | 88 | 72 | 46 | 72 | 81 | 85 |
| Alta. | 78 | 62 | 77 | 87 | 85 | 87 | 77 | 87 | 90 | 91 | 70 | 46 | 69 | 83 | 80 |
| B.C. | 77 | 62 | 77 | 81 | 84 | 85 | 76 | 86 | 87 | 85 | 69 | 48 | 69 | 76 | 84 |
| **1998** |  |  |  |  |  |  |  |  |  |  |  |  |  |  |  |
| **Canada** | 78 | 57 | 74 | 84 | 85 | 83 | 70 | 81 | 87 | 87 | 73 | 42 | 66 | 81 | 84 |
| Nfld. | 59 | 30 | 55 | 67 | 74 | 61 | 40 | 66 | 64 | 70 | 56 | -- | 42 | 69 | 77 |
| P.E.I. | 72 | 56 | 62 | 79 | 90 | 74 | 65 | 67 | 78 | 88 | 71 | -- | 56 | 79 | 91 |
| N.S. | 76 | 59 | 71 | 79 | 86 | 81 | 69 | 80 | 85 | 85 | 71 | 43 | 61 | 74 | 87 |
| N.B. | 72 | 45 | 70 | 79 | 85 | 75 | 51 | 78 | 80 | 82 | 70 | 36 | 61 | 78 | 87 |
| Que. | 75 | 54 | 70 | 82 | 84 | 80 | 65 | 76 | 85 | 85 | 71 | 41 | 63 | 78 | 83 |
| Ont. | 80 | 61 | 75 | 86 | 87 | 86 | 76 | 83 | 90 | 89 | 75 | 42 | 67 | 82 | 85 |
| Man. | 81 | 59 | 79 | 89 | 88 | 87 | 79 | 86 | 90 | 91 | 75 | 31 | 70 | 89 | 84 |
| Sask. | 79 | 51 | 79 | 88 | 85 | 85 | 64 | 87 | 91 | 87 | 73 | 37 | 68 | 85 | 82 |
| Alta. | 83 | 70 | 82 | 86 | 87 | 89 | 86 | 89 | 91 | 89 | 76 | 53 | 74 | 81 | 84 |
| B.C. | 75 | 52 | 73 | 82 | 82 | 79 | 61 | 79 | 84 | 82 | 72 | 43 | 65 | 80 | 81 |

*Source: Labour Force Survey, Statistics Canada.*

EDUCATION INDICATORS IN CANADA

TABLE 5.3   UNEMPLOYMENT RATES OF THE 25 TO 54 AGE GROUP BY EDUCATIONAL ATTAINMENT AND GENDER, CANADA AND PROVINCES, 1990 AND 1998

|  | Both sexes ||||| Males ||||| Females |||||
|---|---|---|---|---|---|---|---|---|---|---|---|---|---|---|---|
| 1990 | Total | Less than high school | High school graduate | College and trade graduate | University graduate | Total | Less than high school | High school graduate | College and trade graduate | University graduate | Total | Less than high school | High school graduate | College and trade graduate | University graduate |
| Canada | 7 | 12 | 7 | 6 | 4 | 7 | 11 | 7 | 6 | 4 | 7 | 12 | 7 | 6 | 4 |
| Nfld. | 15 | 26 | 14 | 11 | 4 | 14 | 25 | 11 | 11 | -- | 16 | 26 | 17 | 12 | -- |
| P.E.I. | 14 | 22 | 15 | 9 | 5 | 13 | 20 | 13 | 9 | -- | 16 | 27 | 16 | 9 | 8 |
| N.S. | 9 | 14 | 9 | 8 | 5 | 9 | 14 | 7 | 9 | 4 | 10 | 15 | 12 | 8 | 6 |
| N.B. | 11 | 18 | 9 | 8 | 4 | 10 | 17 | 8 | 8 | 3 | 11 | 19 | 10 | 9 | 5 |
| Que. | 9 | 14 | 9 | 8 | 5 | 9 | 13 | 9 | 8 | 5 | 10 | 14 | 10 | 7 | 6 |
| Ont. | 6 | 9 | 6 | 5 | 3 | 5 | 8 | 6 | 5 | 3 | 6 | 10 | 5 | 5 | 3 |
| Man. | 6 | 9 | 6 | 5 | 4 | 6 | 9 | 6 | 5 | 3 | 6 | 9 | 6 | 5 | 5 |
| Sask. | 6 | 10 | 5 | 5 | 3 | 6 | 10 | 5 | 5 | 3 | 6 | 9 | 6 | 5 | 4 |
| Alta. | 6 | 11 | 6 | 5 | 3 | 6 | 10 | 6 | 5 | 3 | 7 | 11 | 7 | 6 | 4 |
| B.C. | 7 | 13 | 7 | 6 | 4 | 7 | 13 | 7 | 6 | 4 | 8 | 12 | 8 | 7 | 4 |

| 1998 |||||||||||||||
| Canada | 7 | 13 | 7 | 6 | 4 | 7 | 13 | 7 | 7 | 4 | 7 | 13 | 8 | 6 | 4 |
| Nfld. | 16 | 27 | 18 | 15 | 5 | 17 | 28 | 17 | 17 | 5 | 15 | 25 | 19 | 12 | 5 |
| P.E.I. | 13 | 22 | 15 | 11 | 4 | 13 | 20 | 14 | 11 | 5 | 13 | 26 | 17 | 10 | 4 |
| N.S. | 9 | 15 | 8 | 9 | 5 | 9 | 15 | 8 | 9 | 5 | 9 | 15 | 9 | 8 | 5 |
| N.B. | 11 | 21 | 10 | 9 | 5 | 12 | 22 | 10 | 11 | 4 | 10 | 18 | 11 | 8 | 5 |
| Que. | 9 | 15 | 10 | 8 | 5 | 9 | 16 | 10 | 8 | 5 | 9 | 15 | 10 | 8 | 5 |
| Ont. | 6 | 10 | 7 | 5 | 4 | 6 | 9 | 6 | 5 | 4 | 6 | 11 | 7 | 5 | 4 |
| Man. | 5 | 8 | 5 | 4 | 3 | 5 | 7 | 4 | 4 | 3 | 5 | 9 | 5 | 4 | 3 |
| Sask. | 5 | 10 | 5 | 4 | 3 | 5 | 10 | 5 | 5 | 2 | 5 | 9 | 5 | 4 | 4 |
| Alta. | 5 | 8 | 5 | 5 | 3 | 5 | 8 | 4 | 5 | 2 | 5 | 9 | 5 | 5 | 4 |
| B.C. | 8 | 16 | 8 | 7 | 5 | 8 | 15 | 9 | 8 | 5 | 7 | 16 | 7 | 6 | 5 |

*Source:* Labour Force Survey, Statistics Canada.


TABLE 5.4   UNEMPLOYMENT RATES OF THE 25 TO 29 AGE GROUP BY EDUCATIONAL ATTAINMENT AND GENDER, CANADA AND PROVINCES, 1990 AND 1998

|  | Both sexes ||||| Males ||||| Females |||||
|---|---|---|---|---|---|---|---|---|---|---|---|---|---|---|---|
| 1990 | Total | Less than high school | High school graduate | College and trade graduate | University graduate | Total | Less than high school | High school graduate | College and trade graduate | University graduate | Total | Less than high school | High school graduate | College and trade graduate | University graduate |
| Canada | 9 | 17 | 9 | 8 | 5 | 10 | 17 | 9 | 8 | 5 | 9 | 18 | 9 | 7 | 4 |
| Nfld. | 17 | 31 | 19 | 14 | -- | 17 | 29 | 18 | 14 | -- | 18 | 34 | 20 | 14 | -- |
| P.E.I. | 21 | 35 | 20 | 10 | -- | 19 | 31 | 17 | -- | -- | 22 | 44 | 22 | -- | -- |
| N.S. | 12 | 22 | 12 | 11 | 6 | 13 | 23 | 9 | 12 | -- | 12 | 19 | 16 | 9 | -- |
| N.B. | 13 | 28 | 11 | 10 | -- | 14 | 27 | 11 | 10 | -- | 12 | 29 | 11 | 9 | -- |
| Que. | 11 | 18 | 11 | 9 | 7 | 12 | 18 | 10 | 11 | 8 | 10 | 18 | 12 | 7 | 7 |
| Ont. | 7 | 14 | 8 | 6 | 3 | 8 | 14 | 8 | 5 | 3 | 7 | 15 | 6 | 7 | 2 |
| Man. | 8 | 13 | 8 | 6 | 6 | 8 | 11 | 8 | 7 | -- | 8 | 16 | 7 | 6 | -- |
| Sask. | 9 | 18 | 8 | 7 | 5 | 10 | 17 | 8 | 8 | -- | 8 | 19 | 7 | 6 | -- |
| Alta. | 8 | 17 | 8 | 6 | 4 | 8 | 16 | 7 | 7 | -- | 8 | 18 | 9 | 5 | -- |
| B.C. | 10 | 18 | 8 | 9 | 7 | 9 | 17 | 7 | 9 | -- | 10 | 20 | 9 | 9 | -- |

| 1998 |||||||||||||||
| Canada | 9 | 18 | 10 | 7 | 5 | 9 | 18 | 10 | 8 | 5 | 8 | 20 | 10 | 7 | 5 |
| Nfld. | 19 | 38 | 19 | 20 | -- | 22 | 36 | 16 | 25 | -- | 16 | -- | 23 | 15 | -- |
| P.E.I. | 16 | 30 | 22 | 13 | -- | 16 | 26 | 20 | 14 | -- | 15 | -- | 23 | -- | -- |
| N.S. | 10 | 21 | 12 | 9 | 4 | 11 | 22 | 12 | 10 | -- | 9 | -- | 11 | 9 | -- |
| N.B. | 13 | 32 | 14 | 11 | 7 | 15 | 34 | 13 | 14 | -- | 11 | -- | 15 | 9 | -- |
| Que. | 10 | 21 | 14 | 8 | 6 | 11 | 22 | 14 | 8 | 6 | 9 | 17 | 14 | 8 | 6 |
| Ont. | 7 | 15 | 9 | 6 | 4 | 7 | 12 | 9 | 6 | 4 | 7 | 21 | 10 | 6 | 4 |
| Man. | 6 | 14 | 6 | 4 | 3 | 6 | 11 | 6 | -- | -- | 5 | -- | 7 | -- | -- |
| Sask. | 7 | 22 | 7 | 5 | -- | 7 | 20 | 7 | -- | -- | 7 | 25 | 8 | -- | -- |
| Alta. | 6 | 10 | 6 | 6 | 4 | 6 | -- | 6 | 5 | -- | 6 | -- | -- | 6 | -- |
| B.C. | 11 | 26 | 11 | 9 | 7 | 13 | 26 | 13 | 12 | 8 | 8 | 26 | 10 | 5 | 6 |

*Source:* Labour Force Survey, Statistics Canada.

CHAPTER 5 TABLES

TABLE 5.5  INVOLUNTARY PART-TIME WORKERS AS A PERCENTAGE OF THE LABOUR FORCE, BY EDUCATIONAL ATTAINMENT AND SELECTED AGE GROUPS, CANADA, 1976 TO 1996

|      | 15-24 age group ||||  25-34 age group ||||  35-54 age group ||||
| Year | Total | High school completion or less | College or trade graduate | University graduate | Total | High school completion or less | College or trade graduate | University graduate | Total | High school completion or less | College or trade graduate | University graduate |
|---|---|---|---|---|---|---|---|---|---|---|---|---|
| 1976 | 2  | 2  | 1  | 1  | 1  | 1 | 1  | 1  | 1 | 1  | 1 | -  |
| 1977 | 3  | 3  | 2  | 2  | 1  | 1 | 1  | 1  | 1 | 1  | 1 | 1  |
| 1978 | 3  | 4  | 2  | 3  | 1  | 1 | 1  | 1  | 1 | 1  | 1 | 1  |
| 1979 | 4  | 4  | 2  | 3  | 1  | 2 | 2  | 1  | 1 | 1  | 1 | 1  |
| 1980 | 4  | 4  | 3  | 3  | 1  | 2 | 1  | 1  | 1 | 2  | 1 | 1  |
| 1981 | 4  | 5  | 3  | 3  | 2  | 2 | 2  | 1  | 1 | 2  | 2 | 1  |
| 1982 | 6  | 6  | 5  | 4  | 2  | 2 | 2  | 2  | 2 | 2  | 2 | 1  |
| 1983 | 7  | 7  | 7  | 6  | 3  | 3 | 3  | 2  | 3 | 3  | 3 | 2  |
| 1984 | 8  | 8  | 7  | 6  | 3  | 3 | 3  | 3  | 3 | 3  | 3 | 2  |
| 1985 | 7  | 8  | 7  | 5  | 3  | 4 | 3  | 3  | 3 | 3  | 3 | 2  |
| 1986 | 7  | 7  | 6  | 6  | 3  | 4 | 3  | 3  | 3 | 3  | 3 | 2  |
| 1987 | 6  | 7  | 5  | 5  | 3  | 3 | 3  | 2  | 3 | 3  | 3 | 2  |
| 1988 | 6  | 6  | 5  | 4  | 3  | 3 | 3  | 2  | 3 | 3  | 3 | 2  |
| 1989 | 5  | 5  | 4  | 4  | 3  | 3 | 2  | 2  | 3 | 3  | 3 | 1  |
| 1990 | 5  | 6  | 4  | 3  | 3  | 3 | 3  | 2  | 3 | 3  | 3 | 2  |
| 1991 | 7  | 7  | 6  | 6  | 4  | 4 | 3  | 3  | 3 | 4  | 3 | 2  |
| 1992 | 9  | 9  | 8  | 8  | 4  | 5 | 5  | 3  | 4 | 4  | 4 | 2  |
| 1993 | 10 | 10 | 9  | 9  | 5  | 6 | 5  | 4  | 4 | 5  | 4 | 3  |
| 1994 | 10 | 10 | 9  | 8  | 5  | 5 | 5  | 4  | 4 | 5  | 4 | 3  |
| 1995 | 10 | 10 | 10 | 9  | 5  | 5 | 4  | 4  | 4 | 5  | 5 | 3  |
| 1996 | 10 | 10 | 9  | 8  | 4  | 5 | 4  | 4  | 4 | 4  | 4 | 3  |

*Source:* Labour Force Survey, Statistics Canada.

TABLE 5.6  UNEMPLOYMENT RATE, BY EDUCATIONAL ATTAINMENT AND SELECTED AGE GROUPS, CANADA, 1976 TO 1996

|      | 15-24 age group ||||  25-34 age group ||||  35-54 age group ||||
| Year | Total | High school completion or less | College or trade graduate | University graduate | Total | High school completion or less | College or trade graduate | University graduate | Total | High school completion or less | College or trade graduate | University graduate |
|---|---|---|---|---|---|---|---|---|---|---|---|---|
| 1976 | 13 | 13 | 8  | 7  | 6  | 7  | 5  | 4 | 5 | 5  | 4 | 2 |
| 1977 | 14 | 15 | 9  | 8  | 7  | 8  | 5  | 4 | 5 | 6  | 4 | 2 |
| 1978 | 14 | 15 | 9  | 8  | 7  | 9  | 6  | 4 | 6 | 6  | 4 | 2 |
| 1979 | 13 | 14 | 9  | 7  | 7  | 8  | 5  | 4 | 5 | 5  | 3 | 2 |
| 1980 | 13 | 14 | 9  | 7  | 7  | 8  | 5  | 4 | 5 | 6  | 3 | 2 |
| 1981 | 13 | 14 | 8  | 7  | 7  | 8  | 5  | 4 | 5 | 6  | 3 | 2 |
| 1982 | 19 | 20 | 12 | 10 | 10 | 12 | 8  | 6 | 8 | 9  | 5 | 3 |
| 1983 | 20 | 21 | 14 | 10 | 12 | 14 | 9  | 6 | 8 | 9  | 7 | 3 |
| 1984 | 18 | 19 | 12 | 10 | 12 | 14 | 9  | 6 | 8 | 9  | 6 | 4 |
| 1985 | 16 | 17 | 10 | 10 | 11 | 13 | 8  | 6 | 8 | 9  | 6 | 4 |
| 1986 | 15 | 16 | 10 | 9  | 10 | 12 | 7  | 6 | 7 | 8  | 5 | 3 |
| 1987 | 14 | 15 | 8  | 8  | 9  | 11 | 6  | 5 | 7 | 8  | 5 | 3 |
| 1988 | 12 | 13 | 7  | 7  | 8  | 10 | 6  | 4 | 6 | 7  | 4 | 3 |
| 1989 | 11 | 12 | 7  | 6  | 8  | 10 | 5  | 4 | 6 | 7  | 5 | 3 |
| 1990 | 13 | 14 | 9  | 7  | 9  | 11 | 7  | 4 | 6 | 8  | 5 | 3 |
| 1991 | 16 | 18 | 12 | 8  | 11 | 14 | 9  | 6 | 8 | 10 | 7 | 4 |
| 1992 | 18 | 20 | 12 | 10 | 12 | 15 | 10 | 7 | 9 | 11 | 8 | 4 |
| 1993 | 18 | 19 | 13 | 11 | 12 | 15 | 10 | 6 | 9 | 11 | 8 | 5 |
| 1994 | 17 | 18 | 12 | 10 | 11 | 14 | 9  | 6 | 8 | 10 | 8 | 5 |
| 1995 | 16 | 17 | 11 | 9  | 10 | 13 | 8  | 5 | 8 | 9  | 7 | 4 |
| 1996 | 16 | 18 | 12 | 9  | 10 | 13 | 8  | 6 | 8 | 10 | 7 | 5 |

*Source:* Labour Force Survey, Statistics Canada.

TABLE 5.7  LEVEL AND CHANGE IN PART-TIME EMPLOYMENT AND INVOLUNTARY PART-TIME EMPLOYMENT AS A PERCENTAGE OF THE LABOUR FORCE, CANADA, 1976, 1986, AND 1996

|  | Part-time employment | | Involuntary part-time employment | |
|---|---|---|---|---|
|  | Rate (%) | Change | Rate (%) | Change |
| **15 to 24 age group** | | | | |
| 1976 | 18.4 | - | 2.4 | - |
| 1986 | 27.8 | 9.4 | 7.1 | 4.7 |
| 1996 | 38.2 | 10.4 | 9.5 | 2.4 |
| **25 to 34 age group** | | | | |
| 1976 | 7.5 | - | 0.8 | - |
| 1986 | 10.4 | 2.9 | 3.4 | 2.6 |
| 1996 | 12.0 | 1.6 | 4.3 | 0.9 |
| **35 to 54 age group** | | | | |
| 1976 | 8.8 | - | 0.8 | - |
| 1986 | 11.2 | 2.3 | 3.0 | 2.2 |
| 1996 | 12.0 | 0.9 | 4.0 | 1.1 |

Source: Labour Force Survey, Statistics Canada

TABLE 5.8  PERCENTAGE OF 1986 AND 1995 UNIVERSITY GRADUATES WORKING FULL TIME, TWO YEARS AFTER GRADUATION, BY GENDER AND FIELD OF STUDY, CANADA

| | 1986 graduates | | | 1995 graduates | | |
|---|---|---|---|---|---|---|
| Field of study | Both sexes | Males | Females | Both sexes | Males | Females |
| **Total (all fields)** | **75** | **78** | **71** | **67** | **73** | **64** |
| **Physical, natural and applied sciences** | **75** | **77** | **69** | **70** | **74** | **61** |
| Agriculture and biological sciences | 59 | 61 | 57 | 56 | 60 | 54 |
| Engineering and applied sciences | 82 | 82 | 82 | 81 | 82 | 76 |
| Mathematics and physical sciences | 78 | 78 | 78 | 70 | 72 | 66 |
| **Humanities and social sciences** | **70** | **74** | **68** | **61** | **66** | **59** |
| Education | 78 | 87 | 74 | 68 | 74 | 66 |
| Fine and applied arts | 59 | 64 | 57 | 49 | 59 | 45 |
| General arts and science | 68 | 73 | 63 | 58 | 60 | 56 |
| Humanities | 65 | 64 | 66 | 56 | 65 | 52 |
| Social sciences | 70 | 72 | 68 | 61 | 63 | 60 |
| **Commerce, management and administration** | **88** | **90** | **85** | **85** | **87** | **84** |
| **Health professions** | **77** | **80** | **77** | **72** | **73** | **72** |

Source: 1988 and 1997 National Graduates Surveys, Statistics Canada.

CHAPTER 5 TABLES

TABLE 5.9  PERCENTAGE OF 1986 AND 1995 GRADUATES WORKING FULL TIME, TWO YEARS AFTER GRADUATION, BY LEVEL OF EDUCATION AND PROVINCE OF STUDY

|  | 1986 graduates ||| 1995 graduates |||
|---|---|---|---|---|---|---|
| Province | Trade-vocational | College | University | Trade-vocational | College | University |
| **Canada** | **69** | **82** | **75** | **66** | **70** | **67** |
| Newfoundland and Labrador | 58 | 81 | 71 | 58 | 75 | 61 |
| Prince Edward Island | 69 | 82 | 66 | 75 | 68 | 61 |
| Nova Scotia | 70 | 78 | 72 | 65 | 66 | 67 |
| New Brunswick | 67 | 81 | 71 | 67 | 73 | 70 |
| Quebec | 63 | 77 | 72 | 66 | 67 | 66 |
| Ontario | 74 | 85 | 79 | 63 | 71 | 67 |
| Manitoba | 78 | 82 | 71 | 73 | 74 | 70 |
| Saskatchewan | 79 | 80 | 76 | 80 | 75 | 72 |
| Alberta | 66 | 80 | 72 | 76 | 77 | 72 |
| British Columbia | 69 | 78 | 69 | 68 | 63 | 67 |

*Source: 1988 and 1997 National Graduates Surveys, Statistics Canada.*

TABLE 5.10  LABOUR FORCE PARTICIPATION RATES OF 1986 AND 1995 GRADUATES, TWO YEARS AFTER GRADUATION, BY LEVEL OF EDUCATION AND PROVINCE OF STUDY

|  | 1986 Graduates ||| 1995 Graduates |||
|---|---|---|---|---|---|---|
| Province | Trade-Vocational | College | University | Trade-Vocational | College | University |
| **Canada** | **91** | **91** | **85** | **93** | **94** | **91** |
| Newfoundland and Labrador | 90 | 94 | 84 | 92 | 95 | 89 |
| Prince Edward Island | 94 | 95 | 77 | 96 | 94 | 90 |
| Nova Scotia | 91 | 91 | 81 | 93 | 94 | 89 |
| New Brunswick | 94 | 94 | 80 | 96 | 96 | 91 |
| Quebec | 91 | 89 | 87 | 92 | 92 | 91 |
| Ontario | 93 | 93 | 83 | 93 | 94 | 90 |
| Manitoba | 94 | 96 | 83 | 96 | 97 | 90 |
| Saskatchewan | 93 | 93 | 89 | 96 | 96 | 92 |
| Alberta | 85 | 91 | 86 | 94 | 95 | 92 |
| British Columbia | 90 | 91 | 84 | 94 | 92 | 90 |

*Source: 1988 and 1997 National Graduates Surveys, Statistics Canada.*

TABLE 5.11  UNEMPLOYMENT RATE OF 1986 AND 1995 GRADUATES, TWO YEARS AFTER GRADUATION, BY LEVEL OF EDUCATION AND PROVINCE OF STUDY

|  | 1986 graduates ||| 1995 graduates |||
|---|---|---|---|---|---|---|
| Province | Trade-vocational | College | University | Trade-vocational | College | University |
| **Canada** | **17** | **8** | **9** | **15** | **9** | **9** |
| Newfoundland and Labrador | 31 | 12 | 14 | 27 | 13 | 15 |
| Prince Edward Island | 20 | 11 | 17 | 15 | 19 | 19 |
| Nova Scotia | 18 | 9 | 12 | 17 | 15 | 13 |
| New Brunswick | 25 | 13 | 13 | 18 | 13 | 12 |
| Quebec | 24 | 10 | 10 | 16 | 10 | 8 |
| Ontario | 11 | 6 | 7 | 15 | 10 | 9 |
| Manitoba | 12 | 6 | 11 | 10 | 5 | 7 |
| Saskatchewan | 12 | 9 | 10 | 6 | 5 | 6 |
| Alberta | 20 | 10 | 12 | 9 | 5 | 7 |
| British Columbia | 14 | 8 | 11 | 13 | 9 | 8 |

*Source: 1988 and 1997 National Graduates Surveys, Statistics Canada*

TABLE 5.12  MEDIAN EARNINGS OF 1986 AND 1995 GRADUATES WORKING FULL TIME, TWO YEARS AFTER GRADUATION, BY LEVEL OF EDUCATION AND PROVINCE OF STUDY (IN CONSTANT 1997 $000's)

|  | 1986 graduates ||| 1995 graduates |||
|---|---|---|---|---|---|---|
| Province | Trade-vocational | College | University | Trade-vocational | College | University |
| **Canada** | **24** | **29** | **36** | **23** | **26** | **34** |
| Newfoundland and Labrador | 22 | 30 | 38 | 22 | 29 | 33 |
| Prince Edward Island | 24 | 23 | 29 | 21 | 23 | 25 |
| Nova Scotia | 21 | 31 | 32 | 19 | 22 | 30 |
| New Brunswick | 22 | 26 | 32 | 21 | 23 | 29 |
| Quebec | 24 | 25 | 36 | 23 | 24 | 34 |
| Ontario | 25 | 29 | 36 | 27 | 26 | 34 |
| Manitoba | 25 | 26 | 33 | 22 | 24 | 30 |
| Saskatchewan | 22 | 29 | 34 | 23 | 26 | 32 |
| Alberta | 25 | 26 | 33 | 24 | 25 | 32 |
| British Columbia | 24 | 31 | 34 | 27 | 29 | 37 |

Note: As a result of a change in the wording of the income question, comparisons of the earnings of 1995 and 1986 graduates should be made with caution.
Source: 1988 and 1997 National Graduates Surveys, Statistics Canada.

TABLE 5.13  MEDIAN EARNINGS OF 1986 AND 1995 UNIVERSITY GRADUATES WORKING FULL TIME, BY GENDER AND FIELD OF STUDY, TWO YEARS AFTER GRADUATION, CANADA (IN CONSTANT 1997 $000's)

|  | 1986 graduates ||| 1995 graduates |||
|---|---|---|---|---|---|---|
| Field of study | Both sexes | Males | Females | Both sexes | Males | Females |
| **All Fields** | **36** | **38** | **33** | **34** | **35** | **32** |
| **Physical, natural and applied sciences** | **38** | **38** | **32** | **37** | **39** | **33** |
| Agriculture and biological sciences | 30 | 32 | 28 | 28 | 30 | 27 |
| Engineering and applied sciences | 39 | 39 | 38 | 40 | 40 | 40 |
| Mathematics and physical sciences | 38 | 38 | 34 | 38 | 39 | 36 |
| **Humanities and social sciences** | **34** | **37** | **33** | **32** | **32** | **30** |
| Education | 38 | 43 | 38 | 35 | 35 | 34 |
| Fine and applied arts | 30 | 32 | 29 | 25 | 26 | 25 |
| General arts and science | 33 | 36 | 33 | 30 | 32 | 30 |
| Humanities | 33 | 34 | 32 | 28 | 29 | 27 |
| Social sciences | 33 | 34 | 33 | 30 | 31 | 29 |
| **Commerce, management and administration** | **38** | **42** | **34** | **34** | **36** | **32** |
| **Health professions** | **41** | **49** | **39** | **42** | **42** | **42** |

Note: As a result of a change in the wording of the income question, comparisons of the earnings of 1995 and 1986 graduates should be made with caution.
Source: 1988 and 1997 National Graduates Surveys, Statistics Canada.

TABLE 5.14   PERCENTAGE OF 1986 AND 1995 GRADUATES WORKING FULL TIME TWO YEARS AFTER GRADUATION WHO ARE IN A JOB CLOSELY RELATED TO THEIR EDUCATION, BY PROVINCE OF STUDY AND LEVEL OF EDUCATION

|  | 1986 graduates ||| 1995 graduates |||
|---|---|---|---|---|---|---|
| Province | Trade-vocational | College | University | Trade-vocational | College | University |
| **Canada** | **63** | **63** | **48** | **58** | **56** | **53** |
| Newfoundland and Labrador | 48 | 74 | 56 | 50 | 63 | 53 |
| Prince Edward Island | 76 | 70 | 40 | 58 | 58 | 37 |
| Nova Scotia | 57 | 82 | 52 | 43 | 55 | 48 |
| New Brunswick | 65 | 69 | 56 | 57 | 55 | 52 |
| Quebec | 65 | 64 | 54 | 61 | 61 | 65 |
| Ontario | 65 | 61 | 42 | 54 | 51 | 44 |
| Manitoba | 71 | 70 | 44 | 53 | 62 | 49 |
| Saskatchewan | 64 | 66 | 53 | 61 | 66 | 56 |
| Alberta | 64 | 63 | 50 | 54 | 59 | 54 |
| British Columbia | 64 | 61 | 44 | 55 | 59 | 51 |

Note: Comparisons between 1986 and 1995 should be made with caution as a result of changes in the measurement of the relationship between education and job.

*Source: 1988 and 1997 National Graduates Surveys, Statistics Canada.*


TABLE 5.15   PERCENTAGE OF 1986 AND 1995 UNIVERSITY GRADUATES WORKING FULL TIME TWO YEARS AFTER GRADUATION WHO ARE IN A JOB CLOSELY RELATED TO THEIR EDUCATION, BY GENDER AND FIELD OF STUDY, CANADA

|  | Percentage of university graduates ||||||
|---|---|---|---|---|---|---|
|  | 1986 graduates ||| 1995 graduates |||
| Field of study | Both sexes | Males | Females | Both sexes | Males | Females |
| **Total (all fields) %** | **44** | **44** | **44** | **50** | **48** | **51** |
| **Physical, natural and applied sciences** | 50 | 51 | 48 | 50 | 51 | 48 |
| Agriculture and biological sciences | 35 | 33 | 37 | 35 | 32 | 37 |
| Engineering and applied sciences | 54 | 53 | 56 | 55 | 54 | 58 |
| Mathematics and physical sciences | 52 | 52 | 53 | 55 | 55 | 56 |
| **Humanities and social sciences** | 39 | 38 | 40 | 44 | 40 | 46 |
| Education | 62 | 57 | 64 | 68 | 65 | 70 |
| Fine and applied arts | 32 | 36 | 29 | 21 | 20 | 22 |
| General arts and science | 33 | 33 | 33 | 40 | 35 | 43 |
| Humanities | 32 | 34 | 30 | 27 | 22 | 30 |
| Social sciences | 30 | 28 | 30 | 33 | 31 | 35 |
| **Commerce, management and administration** | 45 | 45 | 44 | 56 | 56 | 56 |
| **Health professions** | 69 | 71 | 69 | 72 | 71 | 72 |

Note: Comparisons between 1986 and 1995 should be made with caution as a result of changes in the measurement of the relationship between education and job.

*Source: 1988 and 1997 National Graduates Surveys, Statistics Canada.*

# EDUCATION INDICATORS IN CANADA

**TABLE 5.16  MIGRATION CHARACTERISTICS OF 1986 GRADUATES IN THE PERIOD BEFORE ENROLLING AND TWO YEARS AFTER GRADUATION, CANADA AND JURISDICTIONS**

| | Number of graduates | | | | | | | Migration rates (%) | | | | | | |
|---|---|---|---|---|---|---|---|---|---|---|---|---|---|---|
| | | Migration to study | | | Migration after graduation | | | Migration to study[2] | | | Migration after graduation[3] | | | Overall[4] |
| Education level and jurisdiction | Residence one year before enrolling | Out | In | Residence at graduation | Out | In | Residence two years after graduation | Out | In | Net | Out | In | Net | Net |
| **Trade-vocational[1]** | | | | | | | | | | | | | | |
| Canada | 40,012 | 925 | 925 | 40,012 | 1,790 | 1,790 | 40,012 | 2 | 2 | - | 4 | 4 | - | - |
| Newfoundland and Labrador | 2,517 | -- | 58** | 2,542 | 294 | -- | 2,273 | -- | 2 | -- | 12 | -- | -- | -10 |
| Prince Edward Island | 200 | -- | 41 | 235 | 53 | 31* | 214 | -- | 21 | -- | 23 | 13 | -9 | 7 |
| Nova Scotia | 3,093 | 81* | 79* | 3,092 | 333 | 100* | 2,858 | 3 | 3 | -- | 11 | 3 | -8 | -8 |
| New Brunswick | 1,846 | -- | 63** | 1,867 | 191 | 82* | 1,758 | -- | 3 | -- | 10 | 4 | -6 | -5 |
| Quebec | 7,692 | 168* | -- | 7,562 | -- | 171* | 7,693 | 2 | -- | -- | -- | 2 | -- | -- |
| Ontario | 10,224 | 138* | 247* | 10,334 | 165* | 708 | 10,877 | 1 | 2 | 1 | 2 | 7 | 5 | 6 |
| Manitoba | 2,237 | 57* | 92* | 2,272 | 151 | 75* | 2,196 | 3 | 4 | 2 | 7 | 3 | -3 | -2 |
| Saskatchewan | 1,479 | 71* | -- | 1,431 | 140 | 79 | 1,371 | 5 | -- | -- | 10 | 6 | -4 | -7 |
| Alberta | 2,451 | 225 | 67* | 2,293 | 116* | 322 | 2,499 | 9 | 3 | -6 | 5 | 14 | 9 | 2 |
| British Columbia | 8,104 | -- | 204* | 8,247 | 279* | 119** | 8,088 | -- | 3 | -- | 3 | 1 | -2 | -- |
| Territories | 126 | -- | -- | 137 | -- | -- | 184 | -- | -- | -- | -- | -- | -- | 46 |
| **College** | | | | | | | | | | | | | | |
| Canada | 62,685 | 2,126 | 2,126 | 62,685 | 2,943 | 2,943 | 62,685 | 3 | 3 | - | 5 | 5 | - | - |
| Newfoundland and Labrador | 792 | 77 | -- | 737 | 120 | 52 | 669 | 10 | -- | -- | 16 | 7 | -9 | -16 |
| Prince Edward Island | 290 | -- | 166 | 435 | 192 | -- | 268 | -- | 57 | -- | 44 | -- | -- | -8 |
| Nova Scotia | 971 | 150 | 60 | 882 | 198 | 211 | 895 | 15 | 6 | -9 | 22 | 24 | 1 | -8 |
| New Brunswick | 1,010 | 149 | 61 | 922 | 169 | 157 | 910 | 15 | 6 | -9 | 18 | 17 | -1 | -10 |
| Quebec | 15,469 | -- | -- | 15,090 | -- | -- | 15,290 | -- | -- | -- | -- | -- | -- | -1 |
| Ontario | 28,653 | -- | 761 | 29,319 | 641 | 663 | 29,342 | -- | 3 | -- | 2 | 2 | -- | 2 |
| Manitoba | 1,461 | 3 | 63 | 1,334 | 113 | 266 | 1,487 | -- | 4 | 4 | 8 | 20 | 11 | 2 |
| Saskatchewan | 1,462 | -- | -- | 1,184 | 229 | 278 | 1,233 | -- | -- | -- | 19 | 23 | 4 | -16 |
| Alberta | 7,586 | 295 | 699 | 7,990 | 801 | 325 | 7,514 | 4 | 9 | 5 | 10 | 4 | -6 | -1 |
| British Columbia | 4,792 | 344 | 205 | 4,653 | 270 | 467 | 4,850 | 7 | 4 | -3 | 6 | 10 | 4 | 1 |
| Territories | 136 | -- | -- | 139 | -- | -- | 228 | -- | -- | -- | -- | -- | -- | 68 |
| **University** | | | | | | | | | | | | | | |
| Canada | 118,959 | 9,608 | 9,608 | 118,959 | 11,510 | 11,510 | 118,959 | 8 | 8 | - | 10 | 10 | - | - |
| Newfoundland and Labrador | 2,097 | 301 | 118 | 1,915 | 263 | 348 | 1,999 | 14 | 6 | -9 | 14 | 18 | 4 | -5 |
| Prince Edward Island | 510 | 227 | -- | 318 | 109 | 262 | 471 | 45 | -- | -- | 34 | 82 | 48 | -8 |
| Nova Scotia | 4,385 | 469 | 1,193 | 5,108 | 1,759 | 611 | 3,961 | 11 | 27 | 17 | 34 | 12 | -22 | -10 |
| New Brunswick | 2,942 | 807 | 551 | 2,686 | 957 | 532 | 2,261 | 27 | 19 | -9 | 36 | 20 | -16 | -23 |
| Quebec | 38,276 | 2,001 | 1,286 | 37,561 | 1,749 | 1,784 | 37,596 | 5 | 3 | -2 | 5 | 5 | -- | -2 |
| Ontario | 43,962 | 1,844 | 3,767 | 45,886 | 2,852 | 3,966 | 47,001 | 4 | 9 | 4 | 6 | 9 | 2 | 7 |
| Manitoba | 4,813 | 578 | 554 | 4,789 | 823 | 489 | 4,456 | 12 | 12 | - | 17 | 10 | -7 | -7 |
| Saskatchewan | 4,369 | 478 | 420 | 4,310 | 926 | 451 | 3,835 | 11 | 10 | -1 | 21 | 10 | -11 | -12 |
| Alberta | 9,371 | 1,562 | 825 | 8,634 | 1,104 | 1,479 | 9,008 | 17 | 9 | -8 | 13 | 17 | 4 | -4 |
| British Columbia | 8,112 | 1,221 | 858 | 7,750 | 968 | 1,391 | 8,172 | 15 | 11 | -4 | 12 | 18 | 5 | 1 |
| Territories | -- | -- | -- | -- | -- | 199 | 199 | -- | -- | -- | -- | -- | -- | -- |

1 Trade-vocational graduates exclude apprenticeship graduates.

2 The rate of out (in) migration to study is defined as the number of graduates who left (entered) a jurisdiction to pursue studies, as a percentage of the number of graduates by jurisdiction of residence prior to enrolment. Used as a measure of "student mobility".

3 The rate of out (in) migration after graduation is defined as the number of graduates who left (entered) a jurisdiction two years after graduation, as a percentage of the number of graduates of the jurisdiction. Used as a measure of "graduate mobility".

4 Net overall migration is defined as the difference between the number of graduates per jurisdiction based on residence two years after graduation versus residence one year before enrolment, as a percentage of the number of graduates per jurisdiction based on residence one year before enrolment.

\* Estimate has a coefficient of variation between 16% and 24% and as such is not as reliable as other values.

\*\* Estimate has a coefficient of variation between 25% and 33% and as such is much less reliable than other values.

*Source: 1988 National Graduates Survey, Statistics Canada.*

## CHAPTER 5 TABLES

**TABLE 5.17** MIGRATION CHARACTERISTICS OF 1995 GRADUATES IN THE PERIOD BEFORE ENROLLING AND TWO YEARS AFTER GRADUATION, CANADA AND JURISDICTIONS

| | Number of graduates | | | | | | | Migration rates (%) | | | | | | |
|---|---|---|---|---|---|---|---|---|---|---|---|---|---|---|
| | | Migration to study | | | Migration after graduation | | | Migration to study[2] | | | Migration after graduation[3] | | | Overall[4] |
| Education level and jurisdiction | Residence one year before enrolling | Out | In | Residence at graduation | Out | In | Residence two years after graduation | Out | In | Net | Out | In | Net | Net |
| **Trade-vocational[1]** | | | | | | | | | | | | | | |
| Canada | 58,674 | 1,075 | 1,075 | 58,674 | 1,077 | 1,076 | 58,674 | 2 | 2 | - | 2 | 2 | - | - |
| Newfoundland and Labrador | 2,233 | -- | -- | 2,268 | 333 | -- | 1,953 | -- | -- | -- | 15 | -- | -- | -13 |
| Prince Edward Island | 415 | -- | 99 | 497 | 59 | -- | 444 | -- | 24 | -- | 12 | -- | -- | 7 |
| Nova Scotia | 2,964 | 96 | -- | 2,940 | 143 | 76 | 2,873 | 3 | -- | -- | 5 | 3 | -2 | -3 |
| New Brunswick | 1,716 | 77 | -- | 1,867 | 64 | -- | 1,645 | -- | -- | -- | 3 | -- | -- | -4 |
| Quebec | 31,265 | -- | -- | 31,230 | -- | -- | 31,175 | -- | -- | -- | -- | -- | -- | -- |
| Ontario | 7,759 | 170** | 206 | 7,795 | -- | 212 | 7,952 | 2 | 3 | - | -- | 3 | -- | 2 |
| Manitoba | 894 | -- | -- | 899 | -- | -- | 900 | -- | -- | -- | -- | -- | -- | 1 |
| Saskatchewan | 1,807 | 122 | -- | 1,737 | 67 | 118 | 1,788 | 7 | -- | -- | 4 | 7 | 3 | -1 |
| Alberta | 2,168 | 196 | 168 | 2,140 | 131 | 356 | 2,365 | 9 | 8 | -1 | 6 | 17 | 11 | 9 |
| British Columbia | 7,219 | 147* | 190 | 7,262 | -- | 151 | 7,333 | -- | 3 | -- | -- | 2 | -- | 2 |
| Territories | 234 | -- | -- | 230 | -- | -- | 246 | -- | -- | -- | -- | -- | -- | 5 |
| **College** | | | | | | | | | | | | | | |
| Canada | 81,425 | 3,079 | 3,079 | 81,425 | 2,175 | 2,176 | 81,425 | 4 | 4 | - | 3 | 3 | - | - |
| Newfoundland and Labrador | 832 | 122 | -- | 720 | 149 | -- | 634 | 15 | -- | -- | 21 | -- | -- | -24 |
| Prince Edward Island | 349 | -- | 120 | 440 | 46 | -- | 419 | -- | 34 | -- | 10 | -- | -- | 20 |
| Nova Scotia | 1,799 | 325 | 144 | 1,617 | 166 | 201 | 1,652 | 18 | 8 | -10 | 10 | 12 | 2 | -8 |
| New Brunswick | 1,446 | 191 | -- | 1,289 | 77 | -- | 1,252 | 13 | -- | -- | 6 | -- | -- | -13 |
| Quebec | 17,367 | 851 | -- | 16,555 | -- | -- | 16,570 | -- | -- | -- | -- | -- | -- | -5 |
| Ontario | 36,889 | 258** | 1,448 | 38,079 | 768 | -- | 37,520 | -- | 4 | -- | 2 | -- | -- | 2 |
| Manitoba | 2,670 | 3 | 77 | 2,543 | 139 | -- | 2,491 | -- | 3 | 3 | 5 | -- | -- | -7 |
| Saskatchewan | 1,995 | -- | -- | 1,483 | 94 | 416 | 1,805 | -- | -- | -- | 6 | 28 | 22 | -10 |
| Alberta | 8,773 | 288 | 804 | 9,289 | 503 | 429 | 9,216 | 3 | 9 | 6 | 5 | 5 | -1 | 5 |
| British Columbia | 9,051 | 186 | 347 | 9,212 | -- | 535 | 9,626 | 2 | 4 | 2 | -- | 6 | -- | 6 |
| Territories | 254 | -- | -- | 198 | -- | -- | -- | -- | -- | -- | -- | -- | -- | -- |
| **University** | | | | | | | | | | | | | | |
| Canada | 153,461 | 12,735 | 12,735 | 153,463 | 6,374 | 6,374 | 153,462 | 8 | 8 | - | 4 | 4 | - | - |
| Newfoundland and Labrador | 2,784 | 671 | 161 | 2,274 | 384 | 384 | 2,274 | 24 | 6 | -18 | 17 | 17 | -- | -18 |
| Prince Edward Island | 799 | 387 | 101 | 514 | 78 | -- | 518 | 48 | -- | -- | 15 | -- | -- | -35 |
| Nova Scotia | 5,377 | 745 | 1,864 | 6,496 | 1,151 | 264 | 5,609 | 14 | 35 | 21 | 18 | 4 | -14 | 4 |
| New Brunswick | 3,959 | 961 | 754 | 3,752 | 493 | 255 | 3,514 | 24 | 19 | -5 | 13 | 7 | -6 | -11 |
| Quebec | 48,358 | 2,001 | 2,119 | 48,476 | 865* | 338** | 47,949 | 4 | 4 | - | 2 | 1 | -1 | -1 |
| Ontario | 57,207 | 3,157 | 4,050 | 58,100 | 1,455 | 1,709 | 58,354 | 6 | 7 | 2 | 3 | 3 | - | 2 |
| Manitoba | 5,467 | 529 | 573 | 5,511 | 535 | 127 | 5,103 | 10 | 10 | 1 | 10 | 2 | -7 | -7 |
| Saskatchewan | 5,248 | 688 | 560 | 5,120 | 457 | 461 | 5,123 | 13 | 11 | -2 | 9 | 9 | - | -2 |
| Alberta | 11,482 | 1,695 | 1,190 | 10,978 | 608 | 1,262 | 11,632 | 15 | 10 | -4 | 6 | 11 | 6 | 1 |
| British Columbia | 12,510 | 1,631 | 1,363 | 12,242 | 350 | 1,272 | 13,164 | 13 | 11 | -2 | 3 | 10 | 8 | 5 |
| Territories | 270 | 270 | -- | -- | -- | 221 | 221 | -- | -- | -- | -- | -- | -- | -- |

1 Trade-vocational graduates exclude apprenticeship graduates.
2 The rate of out (in) migration to study is defined as the number of graduates who left (entered) a jurisdiction to pursue studies, as a percentage of the number of graduates by jurisdiction of residence prior to enrolment. Used as a measure of "student mobility".
3 The rate of out (in) migration after graduation is defined as the number of graduates who left (entered) a jurisdiction two years after graduation, as a percentage of the number of graduates of the jurisdiction. Used as a measure of "graduate mobility".
4 Net overall migration is defined as the difference between the number of graduates per jurisdiction based on residence two years after graduation versus residence one year before enrolment, as a percentage of the number of graduates per jurisdiction based on residence one year before enrolment.
* Estimate has a coefficient of variation between 16% and 24% and as such is not as reliable as other values.
** Estimate has a coefficient of variation between 25% and 33% and as such is much less reliable than other values.
*Source: 1997 National Graduates Survey, Statistics Canada.*

# Committees and Organisations

# COMMITTEES AND ORGANISATIONS

This report was jointly produced by Statistics Canada and the Council of Ministers of Education, Canada (CMEC), in partnership with the departments and ministries of the provinces and territories with responsibility for education and training. Interjurisdictional committees that have played a key role in the development of this publication are the Canadian Education Statistics Council (CESC), the Strategic Management Committee of the CESC, and the Working Group on Quality Improvement of the Core Education Statistics Program. A number of experts have also contributed to the development of this work through their participation in the Pan-Canadian Education Indicators Program Expert Group. The following is a list of committees and organisations that have played a key role in shaping, developing and producing this publication, as well as their membership. Staff of CMEC and Statistics Canada that have a played a direct role in the production of the report are also listed. The funding contributed to this project by Human Resources Development Canada is also gratefully acknowledged.

## CANADIAN EDUCATION STATISTICS COUNCIL (CESC)

| | |
|---|---|
| Florence Delaney | (Newfoundland and Labrador) |
| Elaine Noonan | (Prince Edward Island) |
| Doug Nauss | (Nova Scotia) |
| Dennis Cochrane | (New Brunswick) |
| Raymond Daigle | (Nouveau-Brunswick) |
| Pauline Champoux-Lesage | (Québec) |
| Robert Christie | (Ontario) |
| Suzanne Herbert | (Ontario) |
| Benjamin Levin | (Manitoba) |
| Craig Dotson | (Saskatchewan) |
| Neil Yeates | (Saskatchewan) |
| Maria David-Evans | (Alberta) |
| Gerry Armstrong | (British Columbia) |
| Charles Ungerleider | (British Columbia) (Co-chair) |
| Wolf Riedl | (Yukon) |
| Mark Cleveland | (Northwest Territories) |
| Ivan Fellegi | (Statistics Canada) (Co-chair) |

## CANADIAN EDUCATION STATISTICS COUNCIL (CESC)
## STRATEGIC MANAGEMENT COMMITTEE (SMC)

| | |
|---|---|
| Gerald Galway | (Newfoundland and Labrador) |
| Kenneth Gunn | (Prince Edward Island) |
| Wayne Doggett | (Nova Scotia) |
| Judy Wagner | (New Brunswick) |
| Renée R. Davis | (Maritime Provinces Higher Education Commission) |
| Robert Maheu | (Québec) |
| Ruth Abbott | (Ontario) |
| Aryeh Gitterman | (Ontario) |
| B. James MacKay | (Ontario) |
| Judith Wright | (Ontario) |
| C. Jean Britton | (Manitoba) |
| Jan Gray | (Saskatchewan) |
| Gillian McCreary | (Saskatchewan) |
| Lois Hawkins | (Alberta) |
| Betty Notar | (British Columbia) |
| Wolf Riedl | (Yukon) |
| Dan Daniels | (Northwest Territories) |
| Paul Cappon | (Council of Ministers of Education, Canada) (Chair) |
| Scott Murray | (Statistics Canada) |
| Mike Sheridan | (Statistics Canada) |

## WORKING GROUP ON QUALITY IMPROVEMENT OF THE
## CORE EDUCATION STATISTICS PROGRAM

| | |
|---|---|
| Charlotte Strong | (Newfoundland and Labrador) |
| Blair Weeks | (Prince Edward Island) |
| Ted Vaughan | (Nova Scotia) |
| Larry Gagnon | (New Brunswick) |
| Renée R. Davis | (Maritime Provinces Higher Education Commission) |
| Luc Beauchesne | (Québec) |
| Freda Ghandour | (Ontario) |
| Ross Hamilton | (Ontario) |
| Monica Paabo | (Ontario) |
| Raghubar Sharma | (Ontario) |
| C. Jean Britton | (Manitoba) |
| Deborah Johnson | (Saskatchewan) |
| Donna Krawetz | (Saskatchewan) |
| Jan Runnells | (Saskatchewan) |
| Sandy Bellan | (Alberta) |
| Nelly McEwen | (Alberta) |
| Wayne Hoyle | (British Columbia) |
| Eulala Mills-Diment | (British Columbia) |
| Wolf Riedl | (Yukon) |
| Robert Slaven | (Northwest Territories) |

## Pan-Canadian Education Indicators Program Expert Group

| | |
|---|---|
| Valerie Clements | (Human Resources Development Canada) |
| Wayne Doggett | (Nova Scotia) |
| Rick Jones | (Ontario) |
| Robert Maheu | (Québec) |
| W.H. Bill Smith | (New Brunswick) |

## Project Team*

| | |
|---|---|
| Danielle Baum | (Statistics Canada) |
| Rita Ceolin | (Council of Ministers of Education, Canada) |
| Heather Croner | (Statistics Canada) |
| Christine de Boer | (Council of Ministers of Education, Canada) |
| Doug Drew | (Statistics Canada) |
| Jocelyne Garland | (Statistics Canada) |
| Douglas Hodgkinson | (Council of Ministers of Education, Canada) |
| Doug Lynd | (Statistics Canada) |
| Ralph MacDonald | (Statistics Canada) |
| Valancy Maydan | (Statistics Canada) |
| José Pessoa | (Statistics Canada) |
| Sandra Ramsbottom | (Statistics Canada) |
| Amanda Spencer | (Council of Ministers of Education, Canada) |
| Brenda Villeneuve | (Statistics Canada) |

\* Note of appreciation to staff of the Centre for Education Statistics at Statistics Canada for their efforts in production and analysis of the indicators, and to the staff of Communications Division, Dissemination Division and Translation Services at Statistics Canada. Appreciation is also extended to the staff of the Secretariat of the Council of Ministers of Education, Canada for their contribution to the production of this publication.

## COMMENTS AND SUGGESTIONS

Your comments and suggestions on *Education Indicators in Canada: Report of the Pan-Canadian Education Indicators Program 1999* are welcome. Please let us know what you have found useful about the report, and what we might improve for the next publication.

### SEND YOUR COMMENTS TO:

**Doug Drew**
Assistant Director
Centre for Education Statistics
Statistics Canada
17th Floor, R.H. Coats Building
Tunney's Pasture
Ottawa, Ontario K1A 0T6
Doug.drew@statcan.ca

**Douglas Hodgkinson**
Coordinator, Research and Statistics Unit
Council of Ministers of Education, Canada
95 St. Clair Ave. West, Suite 1106
Toronto, Ontario M4V 1N6
rstats@cmec.ca